I0763107

ANNE DANGAR

ACKNOWLEDGEMENT OF COUNTRY

The National Gallery of Australia respectfully acknowledges that we are on the Country of the Ngunnawal and Ngambri peoples of the Kamberri/Canberra region. We recognise their continuing connections to Country and culture, and we pay our respects to their Elders, past and present.

We respectfully acknowledge all Traditional Custodians throughout Australia whose art we care for and to whose lands National Gallery exhibitions and staff travel.

WARNING

Aboriginal and Torres Strait Islander people are respectfully advised that this publication may contain images and words of, and references to, people who have passed away. Where possible, permission has been sought to include this material.

ABORIGINAL AND TORRES STRAIT ISLANDER PLACENAMES

The National Gallery of Australia recognises Aboriginal and Torres Strait Islander cultural heritage by including First Nations placenames in the publication. The placenames are current at the time of print but may change over time.

ANNE DANGAR

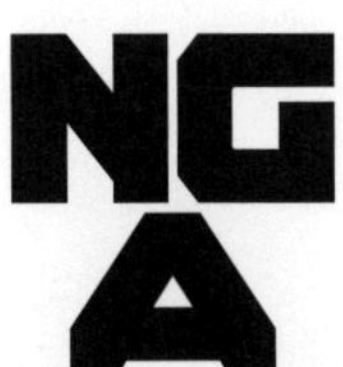

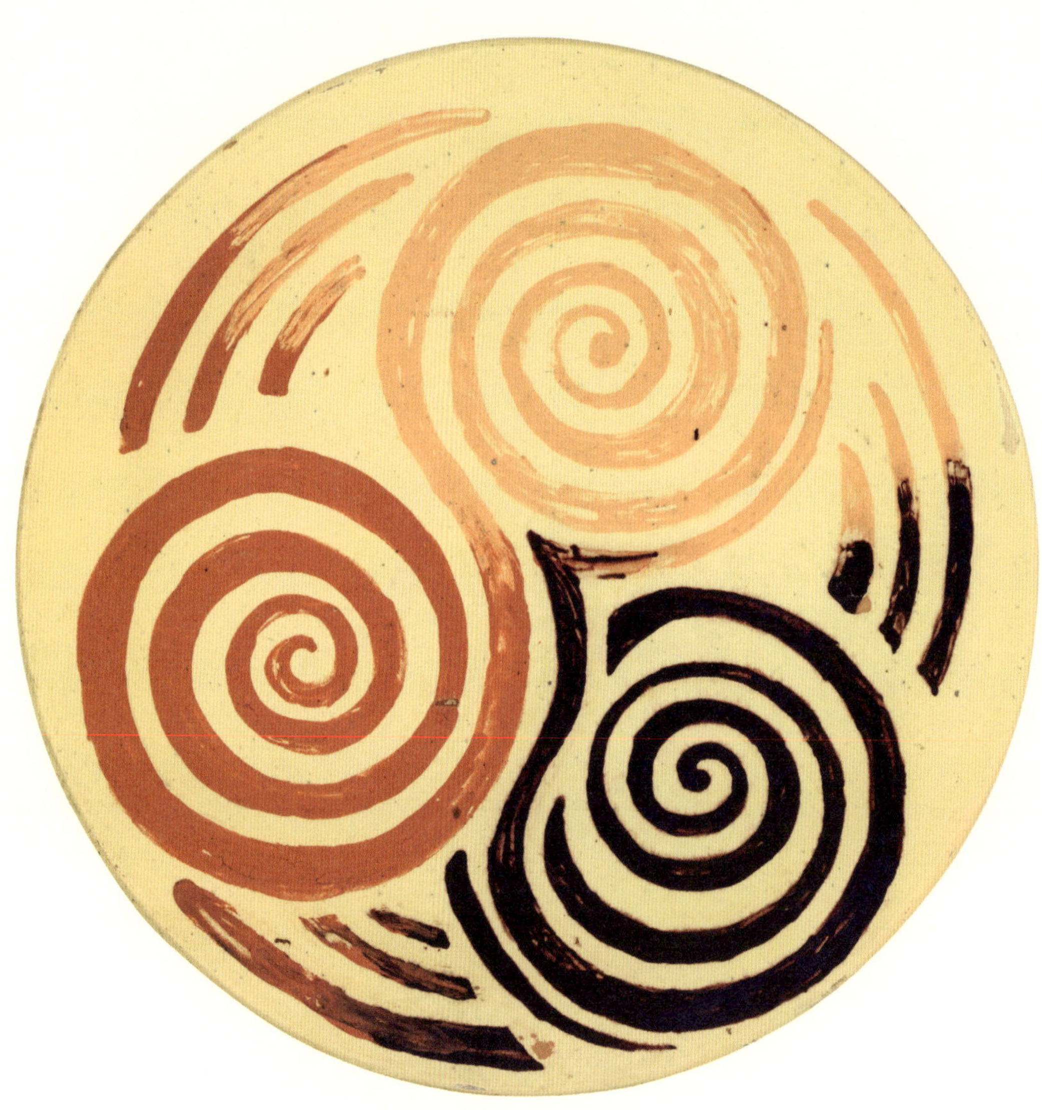

cat 68 Plate with spirals 1948–50

LENDERS

This publication and associated exhibition have been made possible with the generous support of the following institutions and private lenders:

INSTITUTIONS

Art Gallery of New South Wales, Gadigal Nura/Sydney
Art Gallery of South Australia, Tarntanya/Adelaide
Macleay River Historical Society, Thunggutti/Dunghutti Country/Kempsey, NSW
Musée des beaux-arts de Lyon, France
National Gallery of Victoria, Naarm/Narrm/Melbourne
Powerhouse Museum, Gadigal Nura/Sydney
Queensland Art Gallery | Gallery of Modern Art, Meeanjin/Brisbane

PRIVATE LENDERS

Colin Beutel and Conal Coad
Margaret Cargill
Pamela Collins
Dangar family
JJ Glassock and family
Mary Ralston and Jane Hathaway
and those lenders who wish to remain anonymous

PUBLICATION PARTNERS

Gordon Darling Foundation
Sid and Fiona Myer Family Foundation

PUBLICATION SUPPORTERS

Geoff Hassall OAM and Virginia Milson

Contents

14

58

130

II CONNECTION 1930–1936

III LEGACY 1937–1951

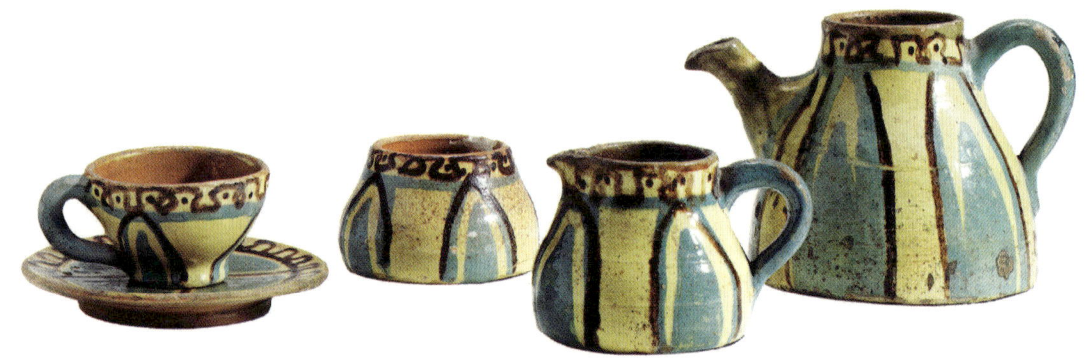

cat 59 Moroccan-style tea set 1940–48

Foreword

The National Gallery of Australia is proud to present this exhibition and publication on Australian artist Anne Dangar (1885–1951). Forming part of the National Gallery's Know My Name project, an initiative that celebrates the diversity and creativity of women artists, it celebrates the life and art of one of Australia's most dedicated modern artists.

Dangar was one of the leading Australian artists in the first half of the twentieth century and among the few to engage with and contribute to European modernism. In 1930 she travelled to Moly-Sabata in southern France, an artist colony established by the painter Albert Gleizes. Remaining there until her death in 1951, she developed a lifelong commitment to Cubism and worked as a potter, decorating her works with bold designs. Over the two decades she spent in France, Dangar exhibited alongside European cubists as their artistic peer, and through her correspondence and teaching she also influenced the development of pure abstraction in Sydney, positioning her among Australia's most significant modernists.

A major exhibition of Dangar's work in Australia is important. In recent years, her contemporaries—including Dorrit Black, Grace Cossington Smith, Grace Crowley and Margaret Preston—have all been the subject of art museum retrospectives. It is well and truly time for Dangar's work to receive the same acclaim and attention.

This exhibition is the first major survey of Dangar's work to be held in this country and follows the first exhibition of her work in Australia in 2001, also held at the National Gallery. Drawing upon public and private collections in Australia and internationally, *Anne Dangar* is the most comprehensive display of the artist's work ever mounted and encompasses more than 130 ceramics, paintings, textiles and works on paper, extensive archival material from the National Gallery Research Library and Archives, and works of art by artists in her circle. We are profoundly grateful to all the private and institutional lenders to this exhibition for making their treasured works available, particularly the major lender, the Art Gallery of New South Wales.

This project would not have been possible without the Sid and Fiona Myer Family Foundation and the Gordon Darling Foundation, whose financial support enabled exhibition curator Rebecca Edwards to undertake invaluable field research during 2022 and 2023. Through their generosity, she was able to uncover never-before-seen works of art and archival material in France and Australia that have formed the backbone of this project. We acknowledge both her comprehensive research and commitment in bringing this exhibition together.

This accompanying publication provides a lasting record of this exhibition and important new research. With essays by Rebecca Edwards, ADS Donaldson, Angela Goddard, Anne O'Hehir, Elena Taylor and the late Peter Brooke, it offers a rich account of Dangar's practice, building on previous scholarship to expand our knowledge of her vital contribution to modern art.

We wish to acknowledge the Sid and Fiona Myer Family Foundation for their support of this publication. Special thanks also to Geoff Hassall OAM and Virginia Milson.

We hope all readers and viewers, whether returning to Dangar's work or encountering it for the first time, will delight in, and be inspired by, the life and art of Anne Dangar.

RYAN STOKES AO, COUNCIL CHAIR, NATIONAL GALLERY OF AUSTRALIA
DR NICK MITZEVICH, DIRECTOR, NATIONAL GALLERY OF AUSTRALIA

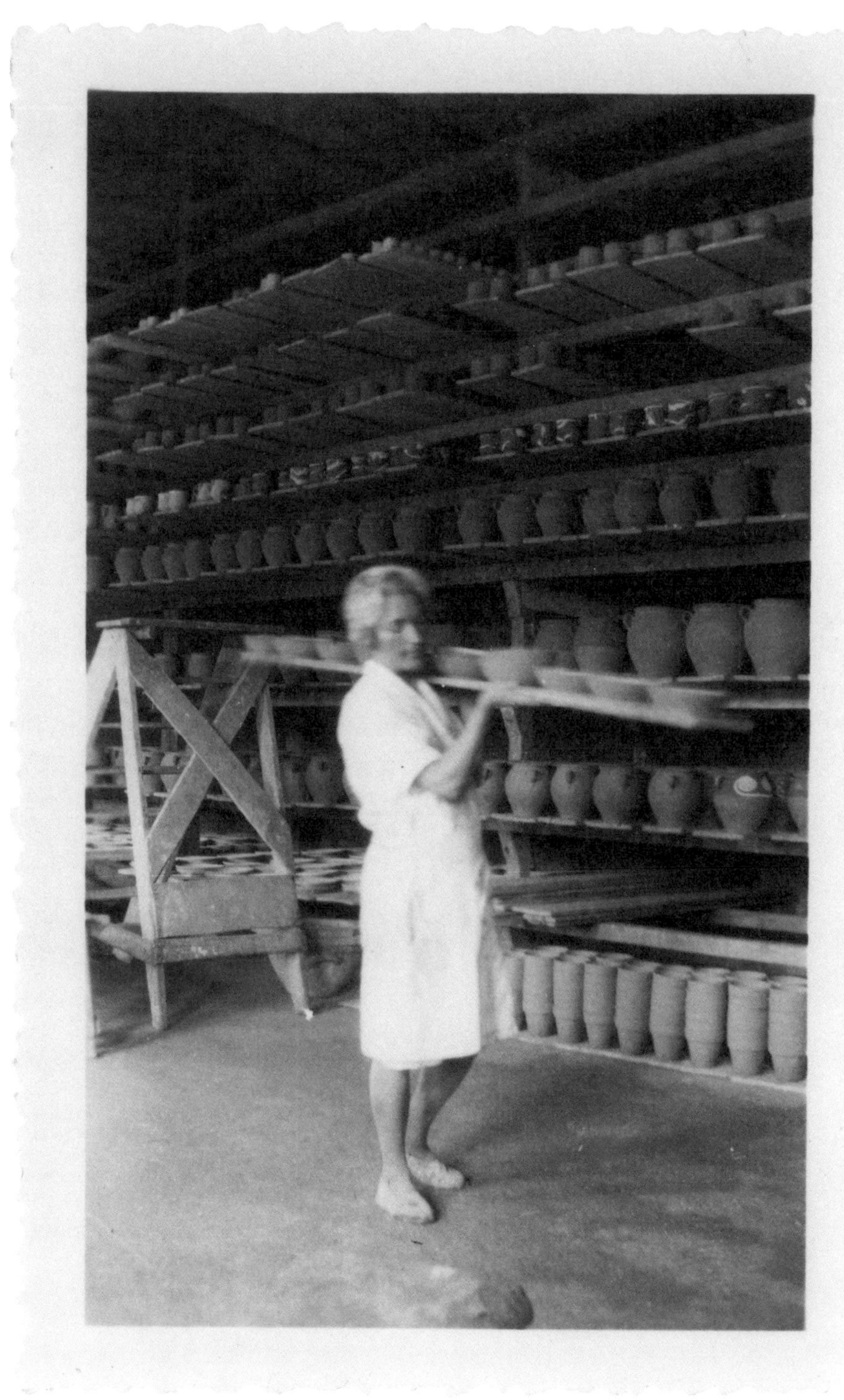

fig 1 Anne Dangar at the Clovis Nicolas pottery in Saint-Désirat, the Ardèche, June 1931

Introduction

I wonder when Sydney will deign to give you and me orders? Perhaps in 100 years they'll pay fabulous prices for us darling and we'll smile down upon 'em from above![1]

– Anne Dangar to Grace Crowley, 1951

For almost a century, Anne Dangar has occupied a unique position in art history as one of Australia's most important, yet underacknowledged modern artists. In 1930, she joined the artist community Moly-Sabata, established in Sablons, France, by the cubist painter Albert Gleizes. Living there for the next two decades, she dedicated herself to Cubism, developing a distinct practice that synthesised traditional French pottery with abstract decoration informed by cubist principles. She is among a very small number of Australian artists to ever form part of the European avant-garde in the twentieth century, and the only to meaningfully contribute to Cubism in France, her work represented there in major international exhibitions, surveys and collections. During her lifetime, Dangar was also a dedicated advocate and promoter of modern art in Australia, the first to teach and arguably to exhibit cubist art in the country, and directly influenced the development of abstraction in Sydney from the 1930s onwards.

Despite this impressive legacy, Dangar remains better known and celebrated in her adopted home of France than in Australia. As a woman, modernist, expatriate and potter, her practice did not conform to the masculine, nationalistic accounts of art that were being written mid-century, and by the time of her death in 1951 she had all but disappeared from narratives of Australian art.[2] Her work started to come back into view in the 1970s, after curators, art historians and gallerists including Daniel Thomas, Bruce Adams and Jim Alexander, seeking to recuperate histories of modernism in Australia, approached octogenarian artist Grace Crowley, to recount her life and career.[3] Slowly, the figure of Dangar—Crowley's former partner and closest friend—began to emerge, and her story and legacy were gradually revealed. Thomas and Alexander subsequently worked with Crowley to make the first acquisitions of Dangar's cubist ceramics for Australian public collections, sourced from friends who had treasured them for decades. With encouragement, Crowley bequeathed much of the remainder of her personal collection to state institutions and, following her death in 1979, her papers, chiefly comprising letters from Dangar written between 1927 and 1951, were transferred to the Mitchell Library in Sydney.[4]

Bruce Adams was one of Dangar's most ardent early champions during these years. He initially contacted Crowley during the 1970s as part of his research into her partner, the painter Ralph Balson, eventually undertaking foundational research in France that would result in the first comprehensive account of Dangar's life and career.[5] This was followed by the publication of Dangar's letters to Crowley by Helen Topliss, who also curated the first exhibition in Australia of her work, held at the National Gallery of Australia in 2001.[6] Holdings of her ceramics in Australian collections have continued to grow through the efforts of David Butcher, an Australian art historian based in France.[7] Some of the most significant examples of Dangar's cubist output are now housed in public collections across the country, including in the Art Gallery of New South Wales and the National Gallery of Australia.

Alongside the consolidation of her biography and art through collection and scholarship, the narrow rubric of Australian art history has also expanded, providing space for Dangar's unique practice and position. Feminist art-historical projects, ongoing since the 1970s, have placed renewed focus on the creative practices of women, particularly in the domain of craft.[8] More recently, art historians have also begun to reassess the role of expatriate Australian artists within national narratives, and figures such as Dangar, who participated in modernism within an international context, feature prominently.[9]

Building upon this impetus, this publication and the retrospective exhibition it accompanies—the first to be held in this country—celebrate the life and art of Anne Dangar through previously unknown, unexhibited or unpublished works, new scholarship and perspectives on her practice. The project draws upon a range of rarely accessed archival material, including an extensive collection of Dangar's sketchbooks, drawings, ceramic designs, teaching notes and materials, which was acquired by the National Gallery in 2012. The Centre Georges Pompidou, Paris, also holds two tranches of letters written by Dangar to Gleizes and his wife Juliette Roche, one set deposited in 1986 and a second, comprising more than 250 letters found in the cellar of Moly-Sabata, in early 2022.[10] Alongside further material held in the Grace Crowley archives at the Art Gallery of New South Wales, State Library of New South Wales, and other public and private archives across Australia and France, this newly discovered material forms the core of this project.

This publication provides a detailed account of Dangar's art and life, divided into three distinct chapters. The first examines her beginnings in Kempsey, her life as an art student in Sydney, and her experience of Paris, a formative period during which she established the sustaining through-lines of her practice (1885–1929). The second focuses on Dangar's first years in regional Sablons, when she became absorbed in pottery and Gleizes's cubist theories and became part of the agrarian lifestyle at Moly-Sabata, eventually emerging as the community's galvanising force and an advocate of modern art (1930–1936). The third chapter surveys the final stage of her life, difficult years disrupted by the turmoil of the Second World War, but during which she consolidated her international reputation as a potter and a cubist (1937–1951).

These chapters are accompanied by essays by curators, artists and art historians, focusing on key aspects of Dangar's life, networks and legacy. Curator Elena Taylor carefully examines the almost three years Dangar and Crowley spent in Paris, studying under André Lhote and encountering the work of Albert Gleizes—a significant episode in Australian modernism—to which she brings new insight and scholarship. Angela Goddard expands our understanding of modern artistic networks during the 1920s and 1930s, in an essay examining the life and art of one of Dangar's students in Sydney and France, the overlooked figure of Queensland-born artist Estelle Creed. Alongside, Anne O'Hehir brings a queer perspective to networks of Australian modernism in the twentieth century, contextualising and exploring the lesbian relationship between Dangar and Crowley prior to 1930, and its influence on Australian art.

Finally, the late Peter Brooke and ADS Donaldson assess Dangar's posthumous legacy, concentrating on the Rhône Valley and Australia respectively. Drawing on his personal experience, Brooke explores her influence as a cubist potter in France through the continued tradition of *terre vernissée* (low-fired earthenware pottery) and a lineage connecting Dangar to his friend potter Geneviève Dalban (née de Cissey), who oversaw the Moly-Sabata pottery during the 1950s. Donaldson concludes by exploring Dangar's reputation following her death. His account traces the efforts of Crowley and Australian painter Mary Webb to have Dangar's work recognised in the country of her birth, and more recent efforts by art historians and curators to accumulatively make visible her life and art.

These essays are followed by a comprehensive exhibition history detailing Dangar's extensive participation in artistic networks in her own lifetime and following her death, many documented for the first time, as well as a selected bibliography featuring Dangar's writings. The ongoing interest in Dangar's work demonstrated by this material underscores her increasing prominence in French and Australian art histories in the later twentieth- and twenty-first centuries as a cubist, potter, Australian modernist and woman artist.

By privileging Dangar's voice and excavating her life, process and practice through primary material, this publication and exhibition of Dangar's work seek to definitively claim her position at the centre of Australian modernism, rather than at the periphery. While she is among many women artists of the twentieth century who have gained recognition in recent years—more than 70 years after her death and almost 100 years since she resolved to devote herself to Cubism—she stands alone as one of the most unwaveringly dedicated, impactful and truly modern Australian artists of the twentieth century.

REBECCA EDWARDS, CURATOR, AUSTRALIAN ART, NATIONAL GALLERY OF AUSTRALIA

I

FOUNDATION

1885–1929

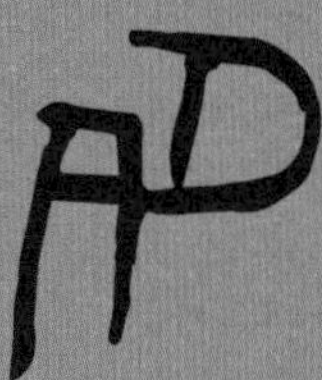

1885[1]

Anne (Annie) Garvin Dangar is born on 1 December on Thunggutti/Dunghutti Country in Kempsey, New South Wales, Australia, the fifth child of Otho Orde and Elizabeth (née Garvin) Dangar.

1891

Is living with her family in River Street on Thunggutti/Dunghutti Country in Kempsey by this time. Prior to this, the family lived in the post office at Belgrave Street and at the Commercial Emporium, Smith Street, established by Otho Orde Dangar.

1892

Following her grandfather's death, inherits coastal land at South West Rocks on Kuring-gai Country. This remains in her possession until her death in 1951. Undertakes art classes in Kempsey with either Ms Marian or Ms Adelaide Gabriel.

1904

Wins prizes for flower arrangement at the Kempsey Methodist Flower Show.

1904–05

Undertakes art classes with Horace Moore-Jones on Eora Country in Sydney at the age of 19.

1906–07

Oversees the 'sweet stall' as part of the Kempsey Presbyterian branch of the Young People's Mission Band bazaar in the Smith Street schoolroom (1906) and the Good Templars Hall (1907).

1909

Takes part in a parlour play in the Kempsey Musical Society concert. Repeats concert in September. Wins a prize for flower arranging at the Kempsey Methodist Flower Show. Arranges a tableau with three children as part of a concert and tea meeting held in the nearby locality of Warneton.

1910

Her parents purchase land in Gabriel Avenue, Thunggutti/Dunghutti Country/Kempsey, and build a large house named 'Shaweetah' (now 8 Gabriel Avenue).

1911

Spends five months studying on Eora Country in Sydney, possibly with Julian Ashton at the Sydney Art School. Upon her return to Thunggutti/Dunghutti Country/Kempsey in May, she offers art classes in outdoor sketching, still life, copy painting, drawing and stencilling, as well as a special class for children. She likely conducts these classes from her studio at Shaweetah.

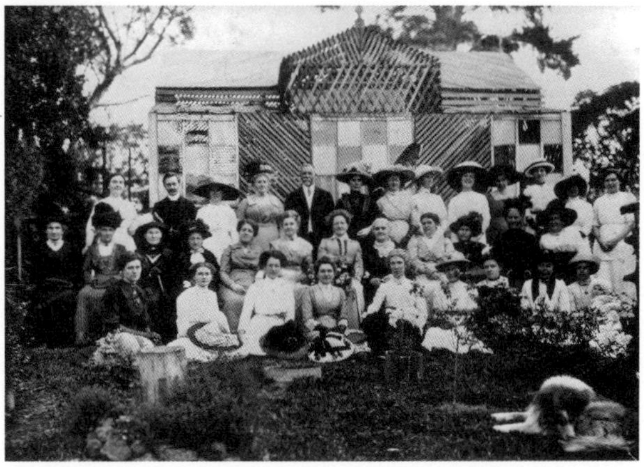

fig 2 Farewell to Mr and Mrs John Bryson, in Elizabeth Dangar's garden (Anne Dangar far right, back row), 1912

1914–17

Continues to study at the Sydney Art School with Julian Ashton from 1914 to 1920, supporting herself by working in a chocolate factory. Gets a job in the map department of the publishers and booksellers Angus & Robertson in George Street, Gadigal Nura/Sydney, and transfers to the evening school.

Meets Grace Crowley in late 1914 at a sketching camp conducted by Julian Ashton at Gerringong on Tharawal Country, a coastal town south of Eora Country/Sydney. Crowley becomes her partner and lifelong friend. In Sydney, shares lodgings with Crowley, Dorrit Black and Bell Walker in Derawun/Potts Point and then at 'Craigielea', a large boarding house on Cammeraygal Country/Neutral Bay.

In June the First World War commences. All exhibitions at the Sydney Art School cease until the end of the war in 1918.

1912

Holds an exhibition of her own and her students' work at Kempsey Good Templars Hall. By this time has commenced studying at the Sydney Art School, overseen by Julian Ashton.

1913

Judges the 'Drawings and Paintings' section of the Macleay Show.

1918

Crowley becomes Julian Ashton's assistant teacher and later head teacher. Remains working at the school until 1923.

1919

Her sister Zillah dies on 10 September from complications following the amputation of her leg.

1920

Becomes assistant teacher to Julian Ashton, with Crowley as head teacher. Is responsible for running the school—alongside Crowley—as Ashton is frequently ill. By this time is living with Crowley at Grange Cottage, Rosa Gully, near Móring/Moring/Diamond Bay (now Vaucluse). Otho Orde and Elizabeth Dangar retire to Eora Country/Sydney.

1921

Exhibits work, as Crowley also does, in the exhibition *Paintings in oil and water colours and drawings in black and white by eleven Australian women* at Anthony Horderns' Fine Art Gallery, Gadigal Nura/Sydney, alongside Karna Birmingham, Dorrit Black, Viola Macmillan Brown, Myra Cocks, Alice Creswick, Olive Crane, Marion Ferrier, Georgina Hughes and Bell Walker.

1923

Otho Orde Dangar dies on 25 September.

1924

Helps form the Younger Group of Australian Artists. Continues to teach alongside Henry Gibbons when Crowley leaves Ashton's school.

SEPTEMBER

Elizabeth Dangar dies on 14 September.

OCTOBER

Roland Wakelin returns from two years overseas and delivers a lecture at the Sydney Art School on Cézanne. Dangar is greatly impressed by Cézanne's theories of pictorial construction. Resolves to save her income to travel to Europe and study modern art.

Takes a group of art students, including Lucy Andreas, Ruth Ainsworth and Mrs Proud, to Gamilaroi Country/ Castlereagh, New South Wales, for a two-week sketching trip. They stay at an old house called 'The Oaks' and spend days sketching outdoors in the morning with free time in the afternoons.

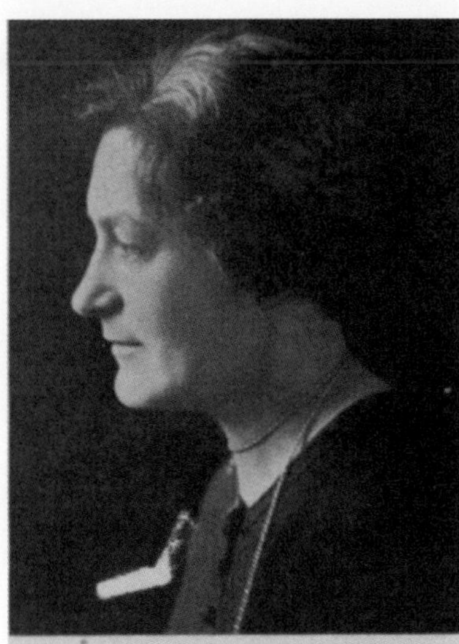

[*Judith Fletcher, Photo.*

Anne Dangar is not only a student of Julian Ashton, she is now one of the Master's assistants at the Sydney Art School in the Queen Victoria Markets. Her work was a notable feature of the Exhibition of eleven Women Painters.

fig 3 Portrait of Anne Dangar in *The Home: An Australian Quarterly*, 1 December 1921

1925

Becomes a regular contributor to the Sydney Art School student journal *Undergrowth*, first published under the editorship of Nancy Hall and Dore Hawthorne.

DECEMBER

With Crowley, takes a sketching class to Kuring-gai Country/Wagstaffe Point, New South Wales. Students of the Sydney Art School hold a farewell party on 12 December in the Mosman garden of artist Livingstone Hopkins before she departs overseas with Crowley.

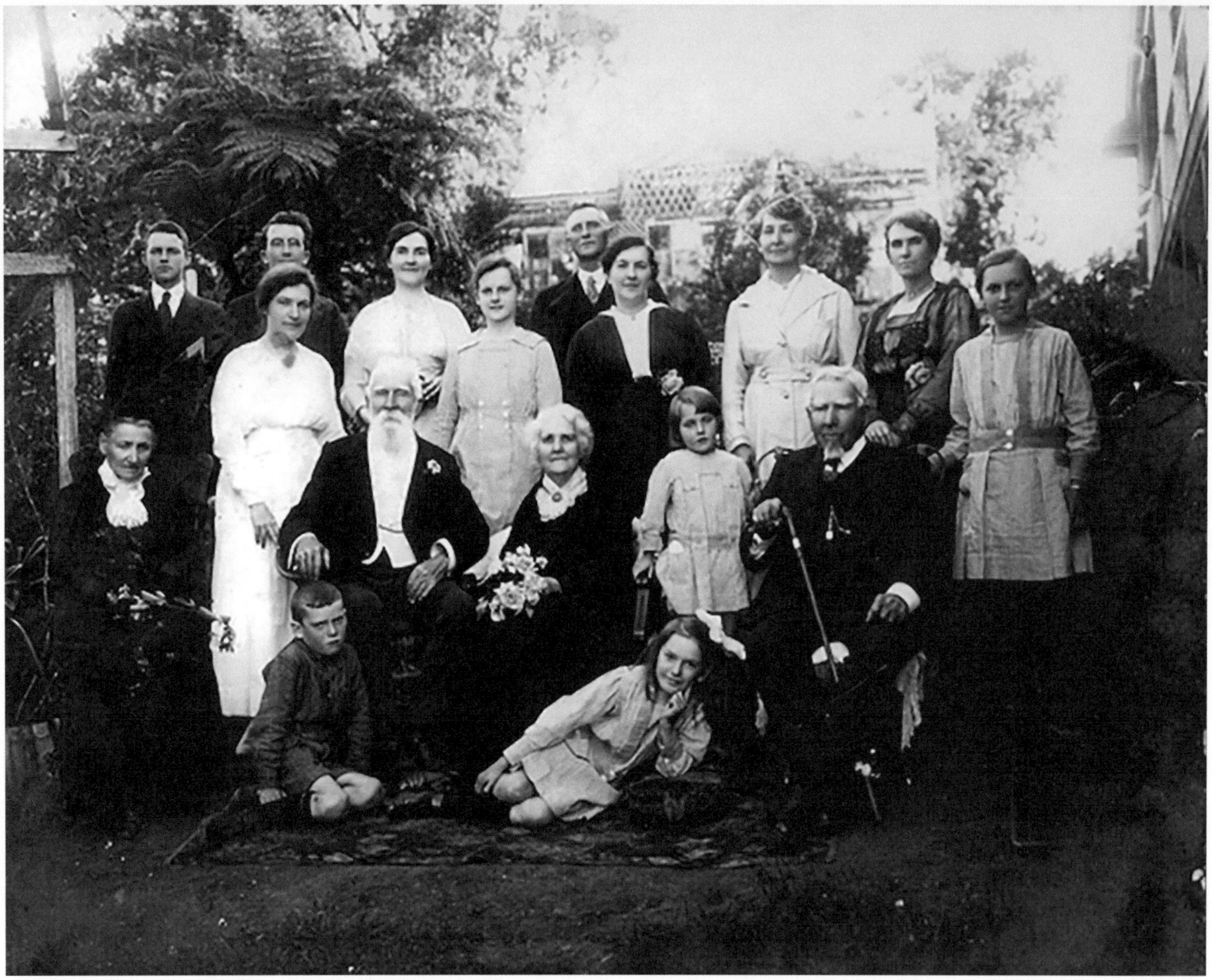

fig 4 Otho Orde and Elizabeth Dangar's golden wedding anniversary (Anne Dangar second row from back, second from left), 1918

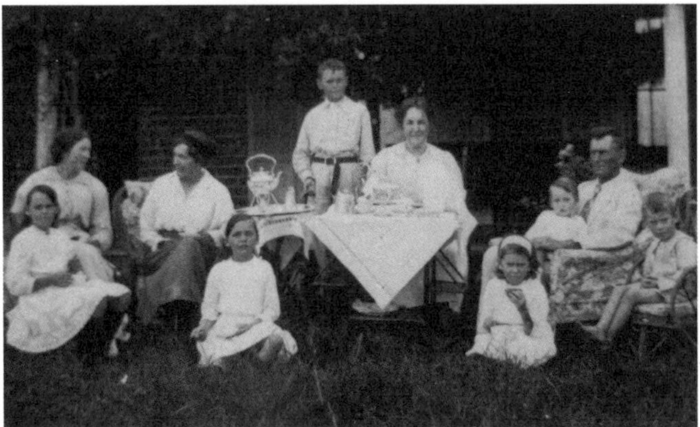

fig 5 The Singleton family at Mondrook (Anne Dangar back, far left), 1917

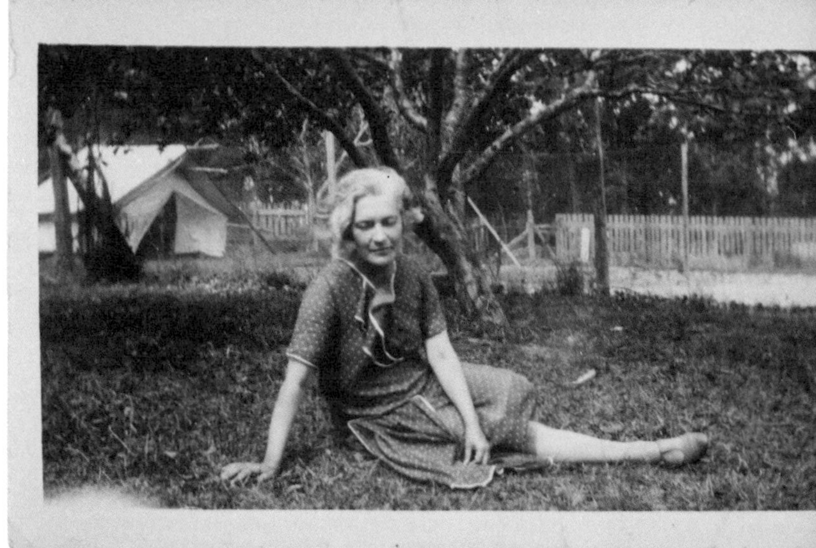

fig 6 Anne Dangar, c 1925

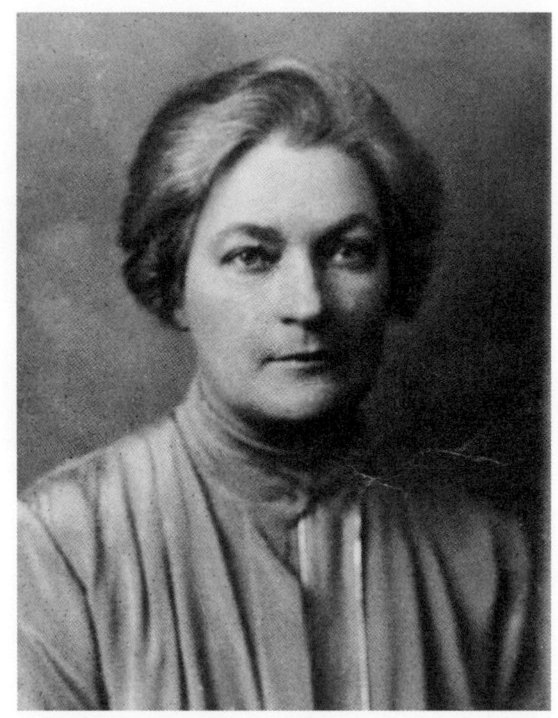

fig 7 Passport photograph of Anne Dangar, 1926

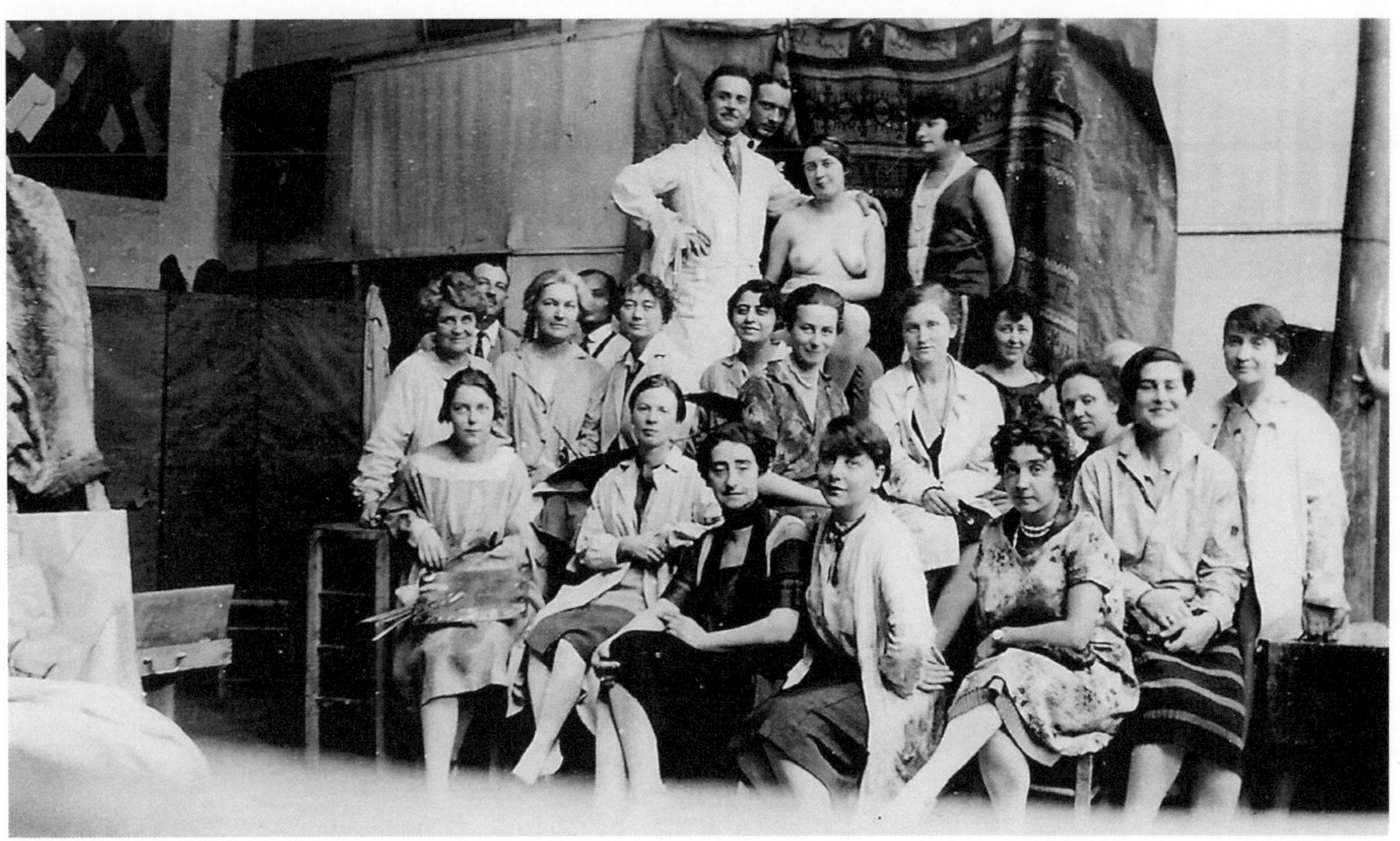

fig 8 Académie Lhote, Paris (Anne Dangar standing, second from left; Grace Crowley seated, second from left; André Lhote standing with hand on hip), 1927–28

1926

JANUARY

With Crowley, departs Eora Country/Sydney on 17 January upon the steamer *Ville de Strasbourg.*

MARCH–APRIL

Arrives in Marseille in mid March. Travels with Crowley for approximately a month, staying with friends near Aubagne, and visiting Saint-Tropez, Tournon, Avignon and Arles. Visits Aix-en-Provence to see the studio of Cézanne before arriving in Paris. Initially stays at a hotel, before moving to a *pension* owned by Madame Fonterne, Latin Quarter, boulevard Saint-Michel. Fonterne becomes a valued friend.

MAY–JUNE

With Crowley, attends the *atelier libre* at Colarossi, La Grande Chaumière and Académie Julian. Crowley sees the work of Louis Roger (professor at the École des beaux-arts) at the Spring Salon of the Société des artistes français and they arrange to take private lessons with him in his studio. Plans to move into the studio occupied by Australian painter Hilda Rix Nicholas in October following her return to Australia.

JULY–AUGUST

With Crowley, visits Brittany over summer, staying at an eleventh-century guesthouse and painting outdoors. Visits Pont-Aven, Le Pouldu and Quimper. Sees traditional stoneware being made by hand and decides to learn more about the medium.

SEPTEMBER

Returns to Paris, staying at a *pension.* Visited by Australian artist Myra Cocks and is unwell during much of her visit.

OCTOBER–DECEMBER

Instead of moving into Rix Nicholas's studio, secures a space, with Crowley, in the Villa Leone studio complex, recently built in a small, dead-end street in Montrouge—Atelier 25, 16 bis rue Bardinet. They live in their shared studio. Continues studying with Roger but soon becomes frustrated. Begins taking lessons in porcelain painting with Mademoiselle Ne in Paris and, in late 1926 or early 1927, undertakes lessons in wheel-thrown pottery with Henri Bernier, a French potter in Viroflay. Meets young potter Sue Alexandre, who becomes a close friend. Spends Christmas in the studio with Crowley.

1927

JANUARY

Enters the Académie André Lhote at 18 rue d'Odessa, Montparnasse, overseen by cubist painter André Lhote, continuing with Roger for a period. Becomes seriously ill and undergoes an unknown operation. While recovering over six weeks, Crowley paints her portrait (location unknown). Dangar is unable to continue with wheel-thrown pottery but continues porcelain painting. Spends two weeks of her convalescence in Aubagne.

MARCH–APRIL

Recommences classes with Lhote. Crowley continues with Roger but leaves him by the end of April after commencing with Lhote that month.

MAY–JUNE

With Crowley, joins Viva Blackwell and her sister, who are visiting Paris, to tour the battlefields of the First World War.

JULY–AUGUST

Travels to London with Crowley. Visits Rah Fizelle and Douglas Dundas, former Sydney Art School students. Views Cézanne's work in person at the Tate Gallery and undertakes further lessons in pottery at an unknown location. Leaves London by the end of August and, with Crowley, travels to the south of France, possibly via the Netherlands and Belgium.

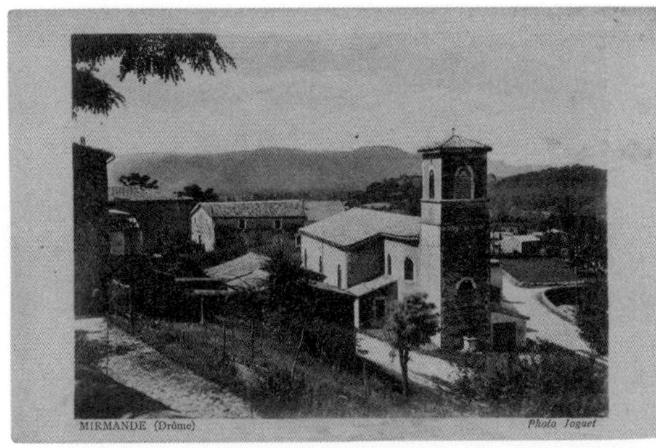

fig 9 Postcard of Mirmande (the Drôme), date unknown

1928

JANUARY–APRIL

Decides to return to Australia due to limited finances. Makes plans with Crowley to visit Italy before her departure. Ashton advises that she can have her old job back in Eora Country/Sydney. With Crowley, continues to study with Lhote and transcribes a lecture on Cubism, which is published in *Undergrowth* in the March–April issue.

MAY–JUNE

Sees three large paintings by Albert Gleizes at the 1928 Salon des Tuileries, held in the Palais de bois, porte Maillot, which affect her deeply. Acquires a copy of Gleizes's publication *La peinture et ses lois* 1923 (*Painting and its laws*). Alongside Crowley, receives a certificate from Lhote of good progress.

Attends lecture by Amédée Ozenfant in Paris with Crowley during the first half of the year. Her lecture notes form the basis of a subsequent essay, 'To-day', which is published in *Undergrowth* in the January–February 1929 issue.

SEPTEMBER

Attends Lhote's summer school sketching class in the town of Mirmande in the Drôme, north of Avignon. There is no room in the guesthouse, so she and Crowley stay outside the village.

OCTOBER–DECEMBER

Returns to Paris and continues studying with Lhote. Fizelle and Dundas visit Paris.

NOVEMBER

Stays with Bernier and his family in Viroflay and gains further skills in pottery.

DECEMBER

Returns to her studio in Paris from Viroflay. In late 1927 or early 1928 is offered a position making pottery in Paris (possibly with Primavera) but is unable to accept. Dorrit Black arrives in Paris from London. Dangar has Christmas with Black, Crowley, and Edith and Norman Lloyd in the Lloyds' studio.

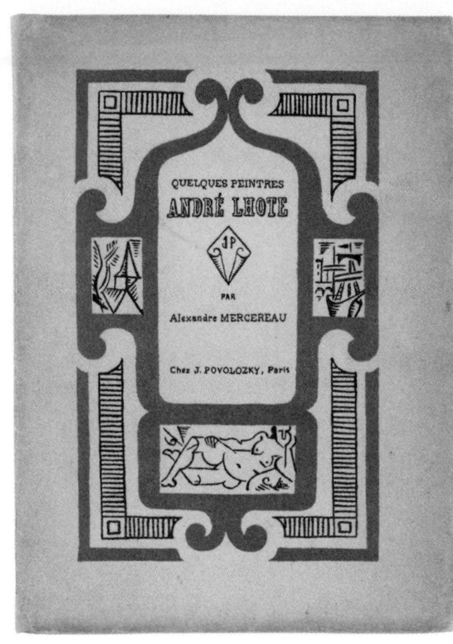

fig 10 Alexandre Mercereau, *Quelques peintres: André Lhote*, 1921 (owned by Anne Dangar)

JULY

With Crowley, travels to Mirmande in advance of Lhote's summer school and spends two weeks there staying with shopkeeper Madame Rouvier. Advertises her return to Australia and a January sketching class in *Undergrowth* (July–August issue).

AUGUST–SEPTEMBER

Joins Lhote's summer school in Mirmande, staying in the accommodation of Gabriel Simian with Crowley. They are joined by Dorrit Black and Isabel Huntley from 10 August. In early September travels south with Crowley and Huntley to Marseille, then to Italy, visiting Genoa, Milan, Venice, Florence, Assisi and Rome.

OCTOBER–DECEMBER

Departs Naples on 18 October and arrives in Eora Country/Sydney on 3 December.

1929

JANUARY–JUNE

Takes a group of 25 art students, including Estelle Creed, Nancy Hall, Florence Taylor, Guenn Fitzgerald, Jessie Digby, Valerie Lazarus, Lucy Andreas, Gwen Ridley, Ella Walker, Mrs Green, Mrs Gibson and Mildred Raymond to Wamberal on Kuring-gai Country on the Central Coast of New South Wales for several weeks. Obtains a studio at 12 Bridge Street, Gadigal Nura/Sydney, and recommences teaching at Julian Ashton's school. Continues creating pottery. Becomes deeply despondent about the lack of interest in modernism in Sydney and asks Crowley to find more information on Albert Gleizes.

JULY–AUGUST

Advertises classes in design in her Bridge Street studio in *Undergrowth* (July–August issue) and begins teaching Cubism in Sydney. Crowley and Black take several lessons with Gleizes in Paris before Black returns to Australia.

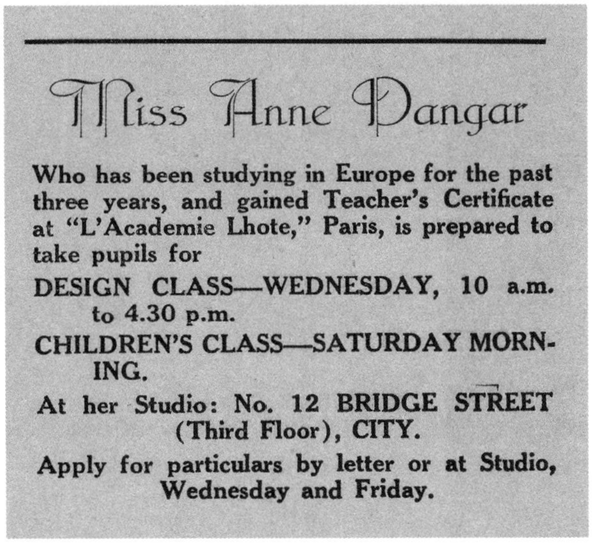

Miss Anne Dangar

Who has been studying in Europe for the past three years, and gained Teacher's Certificate at "L'Academie Lhote," Paris, is prepared to take pupils for

DESIGN CLASS—WEDNESDAY, 10 a.m. to 4.30 p.m.

CHILDREN'S CLASS—SATURDAY MORNING.

At her Studio: No. 12 BRIDGE STREET (Third Floor), CITY.

Apply for particulars by letter or at Studio, Wednesday and Friday.

fig 11 Advertisement for Anne Dangar's art instruction in *Undergrowth: A Magazine of Youth and Ideals*, July–August 1929

SEPTEMBER

Delivers a lecture, 'Modern art and craft work', to the Society of Arts and Crafts at the Blue Tea Room, Rowe Street, Gadigal Nura/Sydney.

OCTOBER

Crowley visits Gleizes's studio in Serrières and his artist community Moly-Sabata in Sablons for three weeks, where she works with Robert Pouyaud and Albert Gleizes. Through Crowley, Dangar receives an invitation from Gleizes to join Moly-Sabata. Accepts via telegram on 13 October.

DECEMBER

Following correspondence with Gleizes, decides to produce pottery at Moly-Sabata. Crowley leaves Marseille for Eora Country/Sydney via Colombo.

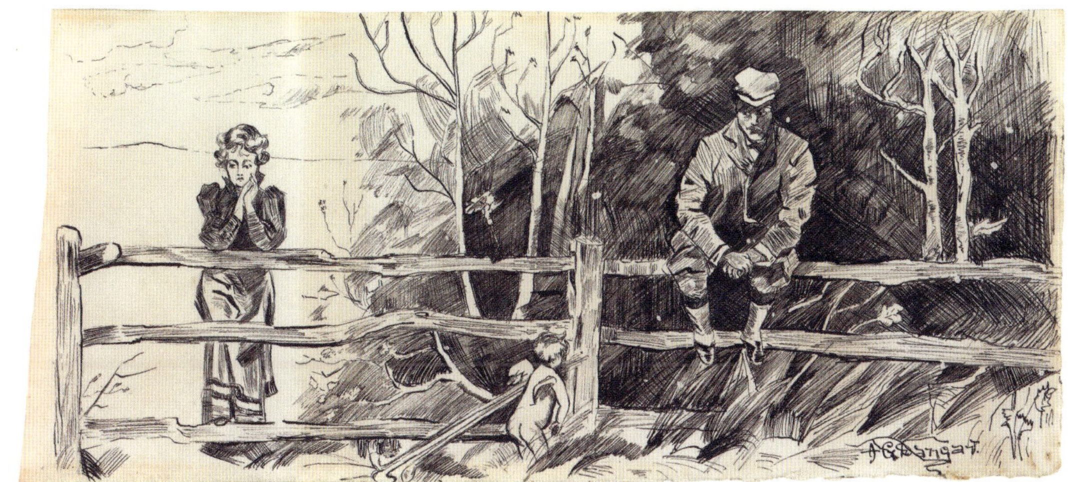

cat 72 *Golf is not the only game on earth* after an illustration by Charles Dana Gibson 1911–12

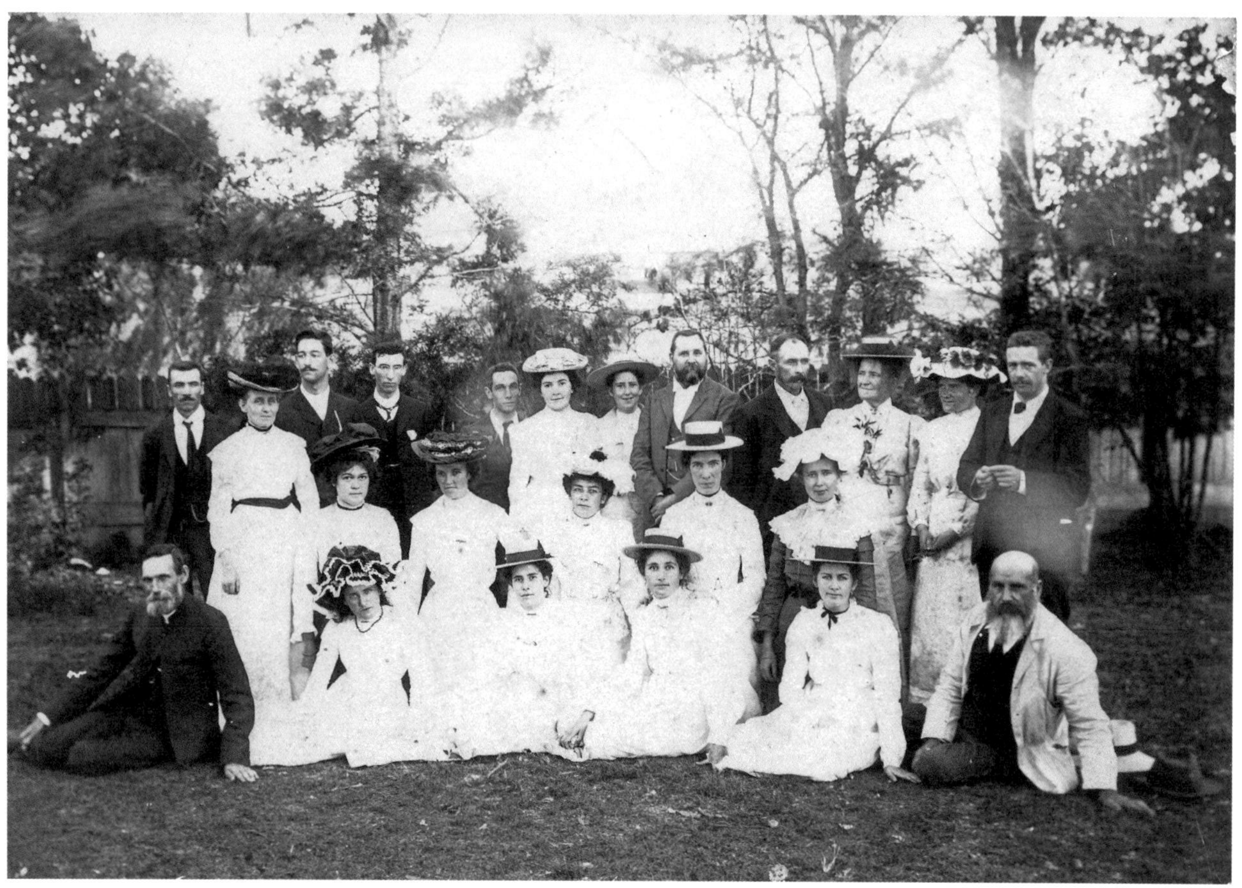

fig 12 Presbyterian church members at a picnic (Anne Dangar back row, fifth from left), early 1900s

I

REBECCA EDWARDS

The earliest known photograph (fig 12) of Anne Dangar was taken around 1900 in Kempsey, a small town in regional New South Wales where she spent the first decades of her life.[1] Looking youthful and bright-eyed, Dangar wears a straw hat and fashionable high-necked tea dress, happily participating in the conventional social activities expected of a young woman during the Edwardian period. Coming of age in regional Australia at the turn of the century, her future seemed predictable: polite, acceptable work—perhaps teaching—before marriage, children, possibly life on the land as a farmer's wife. But this was a path she would determinedly resist. Instead, Dangar charted a unique course in pursuit of modern art, both as a woman and an artist, becoming one of Australia's most important modernists. She would never marry, nor have children, and her only known relationship would be with another woman, Grace Crowley, a partnership kept so private it is almost impossible to trace today.[2]

The most exceptional feature of Dangar's story is her decision to move to France in 1930 to join the artist colony established by cubist painter Albert Gleizes in Sablons, where she would remain for the rest of her life, directly engaged with the cubist movement and members of the avant-garde in Europe. Writing decades after her death, Benedictine monk Dom Angelico Surchamp observed that Dangar was so associated with Moly-Sabata that it was impossible to imagine her outside of this context.[3] Indeed, the contribution to modern art and culture she made while living in France is the core of her story. Yet Dangar was 44 years old when she arrived in Sablons and had already established the major throughlines of a practice—teaching, pottery and Cubism—that would define the rest of a life lived in the dedicated pursuit of art.

Anne Garvin Dangar was born on 1 December 1885 in Kempsey, more than 400 kilometres north of Sydney. Known locally as Annie, she was the youngest of five children born to Otho Orde and Elizabeth (née Garvin) Dangar, her siblings being Pauline, known as Birdie (1870–1876), Otho Orde Hastings (1874–1954), Ruby (1878–1956) and Zillah, known as Queenie (1882–1919). Her father was a prominent figure in the community, working as a postmaster, auctioneer, estate agent, as alderman for the first Kempsey Borough Council in 1886 and as the member for Macleay in the Parliament of New South Wales from 1889 to 1893.[4] He squandered his family's fortune through error and mismanagement on multiple occasions, declaring insolvency or bankruptcy in 1884, 1893 and 1895.[5] Dangar's mother Elizabeth was the daughter of Irish immigrants, and although Dangar was born in regional Australia she felt a deep connection to her Celtic roots, regularly describing herself as a 'wild Irishwoman' in later years.[6]

Few details are known of Dangar's early life. She was educated in Kempsey and was active in its social life. Alongside her sister Zillah, she was closely involved in the local church group and regularly entered flower arrangement competitions in agricultural shows, often winning first place.[7] From a young age, she undertook drawing lessons from sisters Marian and Adelaide Gabriel, who also gave her elder siblings lessons in music.[8] Despite her father's financial misfortunes, these were relatively untroubled years. Dangar remained nostalgic about her youth in Kempsey, recalling the 'particular light, colour and scents of Australia', and mounting a horse and riding 'with [her] brother at dawn in the dew laden "bush" with its intoxicating perfume of gum leaves and ti-tree'.[9]

Around 1904, at the age of 19, Dangar moved to Sydney, where she studied under the Aotearoa New Zealand painter Horace Moore-Jones.[10] While Moore-Jones had little enduring influence on her art, she found the experience liberating. As she later recalled, 'for the 1st time ... I [felt] satisfied and FREE! Yes free to do what I like.'[11] Dangar spent the following years pursuing her artistic education, living between her parents' home and Sydney. By 1911, she was advertising her services as an art teacher in Kempsey, promoting herself as having studied under 'some of Sydney's best masters' and offering lessons in 'Out-Door Sketching, Still Life, Copy Painting, Drawing and Stencilling'.[12] She also ran art classes for children, with the *Macleay Chronicle* reporting that 'all her old and many new pupils [were] entering' her classes.[13]

Over the following years, Dangar coordinated at least two exhibitions of her own and her students' work in Kempsey, first in 1912 at the Kempsey Good Templars Hall, and again in 1915 when she established a 'local gallery' at 'Shaweetah', the Dangars' grand home in Kempsey.[14] She displayed watercolours, oil paintings (including one of her dog Dake), and so-called 'black-and-white work'—lively ink drawings copied from engraved illustrations by figures such as Charles Dana Gibson.[15] Dangar's sketch (cat 72) of a quarrelling couple and *putti* in the landscape is likely to have been included in the 1912 exhibition and was copied directly from Gibson's illustration 'Golf is not the only game on earth' from his publication *Pictures of people* from 1896.[16] In 1915 the *Macleay Argus* reported of Dangar's 'district views, landscape and seascape ... really fine paintings and sketches of South West Rocks and Crescent Head', as well as 'sketches of Sydney Harbour beauty spots'.[17] Her painting of Trial Bay 1912–15 (cat 69), a well-observed view of South West Rocks where her family owned land, is one of the rare oils to survive from this period, and reflects the conventional yet competent style she had developed by the mid 1910s.

By the time of the 1915 exhibition, Dangar was living in Sydney and attending the Sydney Art School, overseen by British-born artist Julian Ashton. She became his student as early as (and possibly before) 1912, with the *Macleay Argus* proudly reporting that year on her return from several months studying with Ashton and 'other leading Sydney artists'.[18] Painter and china painter Mildred Lovett and landscapist Elioth Gruner were among the other teachers, having joined Ashton as assistants by 1910 and 1914 respectively. Ashton had established his reputation in Australia in the 1880s through painting *en plein air* and opened his own art school in Sydney in 1890. His classes emphasised rigorous draughtsmanship, drawing upon the teaching format of Parisian ateliers with students instructed to copy plaster casts of classical sculptures before advancing to life drawing from models. These more traditional classes were coupled with lessons in landscape painting with a focus on painting *en plein air*, and with regular sketching excursions into the bush and an annual summer camp.

Dangar joined Ashton's sketching camp at the beach town of Gerringong, New South Wales, in 1914, where she met fellow student and artist Grace Crowley. Crowley was also from regional New South Wales, raised on her family's farm 'Glen Riddle' in Barraba, and had commenced studying with Ashton in her late teens, eventually becoming his preferred student.[19] Dangar and Crowley's initial meeting gave no indication that a friendship was likely: Dangar thought Crowley 'looked as though she wouldn't say BOO to a goose', while Crowley remembered being bemused by the sight of Dangar hiding her money away every evening in her shoes.[20] Yet, despite this curious beginning, Crowley, known as 'Smudge' to her friends, became Dangar's closest and most enduring friend, confidante and, for several years, lover. Their personal and professional lives were soon intertwined: they shared lodgings with fellow students Dorrit Black and Bell Walker, before moving together into a cottage in Vaucluse. In 1918, Crowley took over Gruner's teaching position when he enlisted in the First World War, and from 1920 Dangar began to work closely with her as an assistant, since the aging Ashton was regularly ill. Dangar's previous

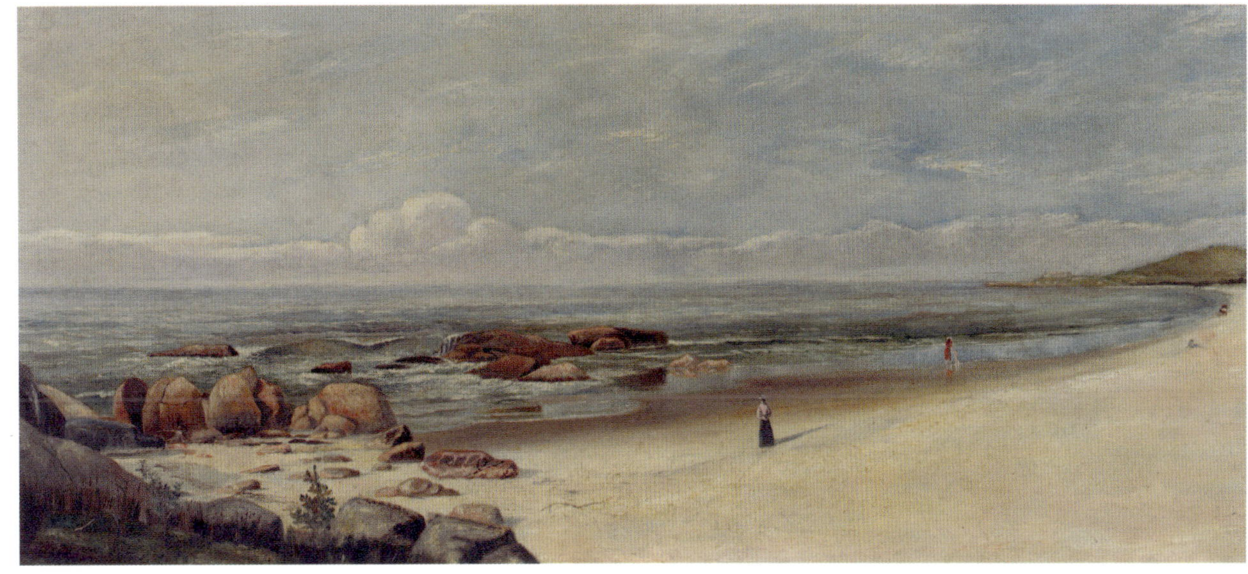

cat 69 Trial Bay landscape 1912–15

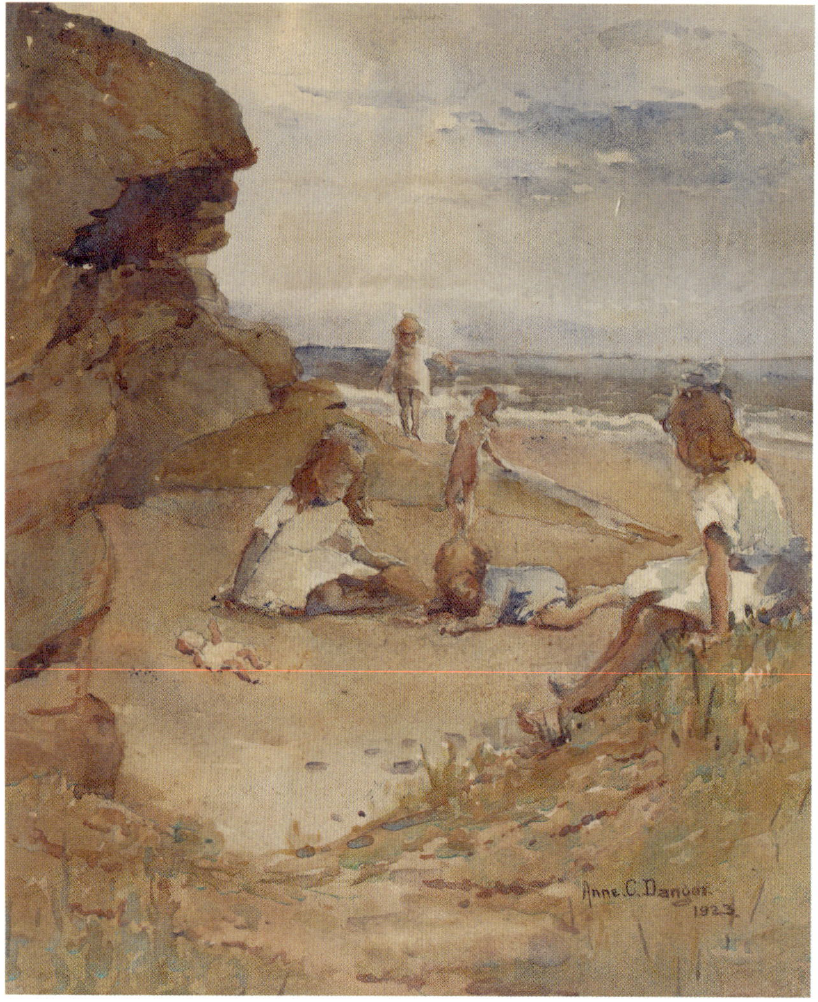

cat 74 Beach at Henley 1923

experience teaching in Kempsey prepared her well for this work and Ashton, himself a skilled teacher, had passed on much of his knowledge. Crowley and Dangar effectively ran the entire Sydney Art School in his absence, Dangar proving popular with her students, who said she possessed 'the magic of sympathy, and the eye that sees the one good part of the picture before it sees anything else'.[21]

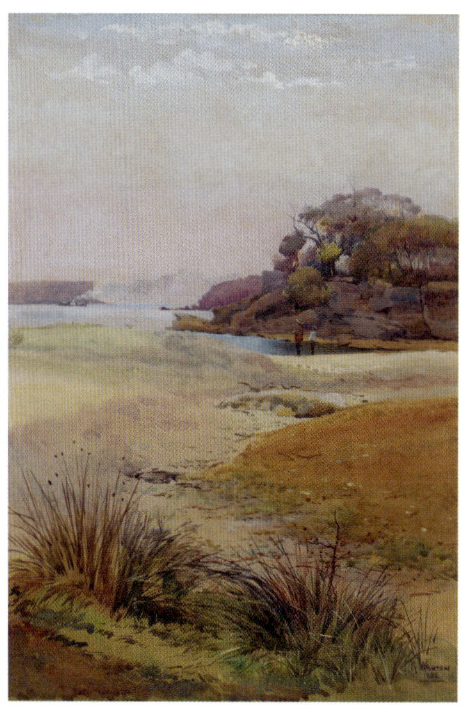

fig 13 Julian Ashton, *View of the North Head, Sydney Harbour* 1888

Crowley ceased teaching in mid 1923 to focus on painting full-time, hoping to win the NSW Society of Artists travelling scholarship. To her dismay and Ashton's fury, she lost to the more modern work of Roy de Maistre and fled to Melbourne to undertake further study, leaving Dangar as second-in-command.[22] While the highly skilled Crowley was Ashton's favourite, he greatly depended on and trusted Dangar. She later recalled how he requested she repair his paintings for him when his eyesight began to fail and, on several occasions, she oversaw sketching excursions on his behalf.[23] Quietly and without fuss, Dangar became a prominent figure in Sydney's younger art world and in early 1926 Ashton himself acknowledged that, because of his poor health, she had come to virtually run the school.[24]

Few traces of Dangar's artistic output from this period exist. Sadly, much of the work she produced in the 1910s and 1920s was lost in 1930, when a fire destroyed the home of her sister Ruby and brother-in-law Andrew Singleton.[25] Nonetheless, a sense of her practice can be gained through her few surviving works, and in the years after the First World War she actively exhibited her work in Sydney, firmly positioning herself alongside a cohort of younger artists connected to the Sydney Art School. Watercolours created around 1923 depicting her young nieces and nephews show both her assimilation of Ashton's approach at this time and a discernible lack of engagement with modern art. Her watercolour of the beach at Henley (cat 74) was likely executed *en plein air*, with pigment applied rapidly in broad sweeps and overlaid with staccato surface marks. The youthful figures lack individual detail, and Dangar instead captures the playful poses of the children.

As well as emulating Ashton's technical methods, other works of this period, now known only through exhibition catalogues and reviews, demonstrate that Dangar did not stray far from his prescribed subjects. Titles such as *A bush kitchen*, *The old barn*, *At Watson's Bay* and *Early morning, Berrima*, appearing in the exhibition *Eleven Australian women* in June 1921,[26] reflect the scenic landscapes and historical and sentimental subjects generally favoured by Ashton, and to which Crowley was also drawn at this time. Three years later, in 1924, Dangar was a founder of the 'Younger Group of Australian Artists', and showed work with Crowley in the group's first and second exhibitions.[27] Notably, however, neither artist was technically young—Dangar was 38 and Crowley in her mid 30s—and, as reviewers of the exhibition observed, the work exhibited was hardly youthful, appearing no different to the paintings of Sydney's older generation of artists, notably Ashton, who opened their inaugural exhibition.[28]

Roland Wakelin's return to Sydney in late 1924, after two years working abroad, signalled a significant moment of revelation and galvanised Dangar's burgeoning interest in modernism in Europe. It also coincided with the death of her parents, heralding a period of freedom and autonomy. By this time, the Sydney art world was on the cusp of transformation. Modern art was beginning to be promoted in the pages of the *Home* and *Art in Australia* magazines and displayed within the Society of Artists' annual exhibitions. Grosvenor Galleries and Macquarie Galleries, both opened in recent years, also began to feature increasingly modern work in exhibitions by artists such as Wakelin, Margaret Preston, Thea Proctor, Roy de Maistre and Grace Cossington Smith.[29]

Delivering a lecture at the Sydney Art School in October 1924, Wakelin spoke of the influence of Paul Cézanne in Europe and discussed his theories of pictorial construction. He asserted that

> the supreme influence on modern art, not so much in England as on the Continent, is Cézanne ... Monet, the founder of impressionism, being preoccupied in getting beautiful effects of light, his works were often lacking in form ... Cézanne aimed at giving design a sounder basis.[30]

Cézanne's emphasis on compositional design was a radical alternative to the focus on draughtsmanship and the painterly effect of working directly *en plein air* that had prevailed in the works of Dangar and her circle. Indeed, as Crowley later acknowledged, despite the solid, academic nature of Ashton's teaching, he 'did not teach composition'.[31]

This encounter with Cézanne's work was a pivotal experience for Dangar. As she recalled: 'Cézanne ... converted me to what was called "modern art" ... It was he who made me see with a frightening violence the lack of construction in everything I had learnt from my impressionist masters, in everything I taught to my students.'[32] Assuming the role of enlightened conduit, Dangar soon sought to influence those around her, encouraging her students to visit Wakelin's exhibition and incorporating Cézanne's ideas in her classes at the Sydney Art School.[33] Neither Crowley nor Ashton shared her enthusiasm, with Ashton reportedly uttering 'Anne and her damned old Cézanne!' when she raised the topic.[34] Indeed, she stood almost alone as one of the very few artists in her cohort to respond to modernism strongly during this period. Perhaps the experience of discovering Cézanne's paintings hinted at the same joyous liberation she felt when first undertaking lessons with Moore-Jones, freedom that resonated more broadly with her desire to live without the patriarchal expectations of conservative society. Regardless, this event established a pattern of almost devout dedication to understanding and sharing modern art with others that would characterise the rest of her career.

Throughout 1925, Dangar saved her earnings so she could go 'to Europe to study "modern art" in the manner of Cézanne', planning to return and impart her knowledge to others.[35] Crowley aspired to visit London and study at the Slade School of Art, but Dangar was single-mindedly focused on Paris, and following a farewell party held by the students of the Sydney Art School, they both departed for the port city of Marseille in January 1926, beginning a journey that would have an irrevocable impact on both their lives and artistic practices.[36]

Arriving in France in March, Dangar insisted they travel to Aix-en-Provence to visit Cézanne's studio before journeying to Paris, an experience she recounted with elation in an essay published in Sydney Art School student club journal *Undergrowth: A Magazine of Youth and Ideals* later that year:

> The great front window claimed our attention and made us gasp in rapture ... The rich valley with its farmlands, behind this the mountains. In their rhythmic contours I saw Cézanne again, or perhaps I should say, Cézanne taught me to see his mountains.[37]

Undergrowth (1924–30) had been established by former Sydney Art School students Dore Hawthorne and Nancy Hall and was initially conceived as a forum for ideas, eventually becoming a valuable platform for modern art in Sydney. A key feature of its contents was the publication of letters from Australians in Europe giving accounts of their travels and studies. For several decades, expatriates had played an influential role in communicating artistic ideas from Europe to Australia, and during the 1920s they circulated information on developments in modern art in London and in Paris, the established centre of the avant-garde. Like expatriates before them, Dangar and Crowley sent regular updates on their travels to their friends in Sydney. These were shared in *Undergrowth* and gave insight into their time abroad.

Once in Paris, Dangar and Crowley explored options for different studios and academies, briefly attending the *atelier libre* of the Académie Colarossi before approaching the portrait painter Louis Roger for private lessons after seeing his work on display in the Spring Salon. Dangar was quickly frustrated by his teachings, writing in early 1927 that 'he ignores design, and this hurts me like knives sticking in me. He doesn't know it ... design is to me the most precious power in art.'[38]

Soon after, she joined the Académie André Lhote in Montparnasse, established by cubist painter André Lhote. Although she conformed to his particular manner of pictorial construction for only a few years, Lhote's teaching gave Dangar access to a new way of considering composition and design and swiftly affirmed her enthusiasm for modernism. Drawing together an appreciation for great classical painters of the past with an intellectual interest in geometry and mathematics, Lhote taught his students to adopt an invisible grid dictated by the ratios of the golden mean. He insisted they carefully arrange figures observed from life within this framework, unifying the composition through tonal gradation and faceted planes to merge separate forms across the foreground, middle-ground and background, a technique used by Cézanne known as *passage*.

Within a few months, Dangar was joined at the Académie Lhote by Crowley, whose works of this period give great insight into both students' experience of his methods (cats 138 & 139). The pair attended his classes diligently over the following two years, as well as his summer school in Mirmande in the Drôme, first in 1927 and again in 1928 when they were joined by their friends Dorrit Black and Isabel Huntley.[39] Lhote's lessons were transformative for Dangar, Crowley and Black, exemplified in their different depictions of the hilltop town of Mirmande (cat 70), with pyramidal arrangements of fractured tonal planes that were radical departures from the direct and polite views of Sydney and its surrounds they had been producing only two years earlier.

As well as Cubism, Dangar concurrently discovered an aptitude for pottery, identifying it as a way to generate an income alongside an artistic career and foreshadowing the future direction of her practice.[40] During the summer of 1926, prior to commencing with Lhote, she and Crowley travelled to Brittany, where they visited Quimper, a town well known since the 1700s for its faience—tin-glazed ceramics featuring handpainted designs (often rustic Breton figures) on a white background. As Crowley later recounted, Dangar was already 'mad on pots', having collected ceramics when they were living in Sydney and regularly coming home 'with some huge pot or plate on her lap grinning from ear to ear in triumph like a happy school-kid'.[41] Yet as Dangar later wrote, her encounter with these French ceramics inspired her to attempt creating pottery herself: 'what a Heaven-sent thought came to me at Quimper when I felt I must learn pottery!'[42] Dangar subsequently pursued lessons in wheel-throwing

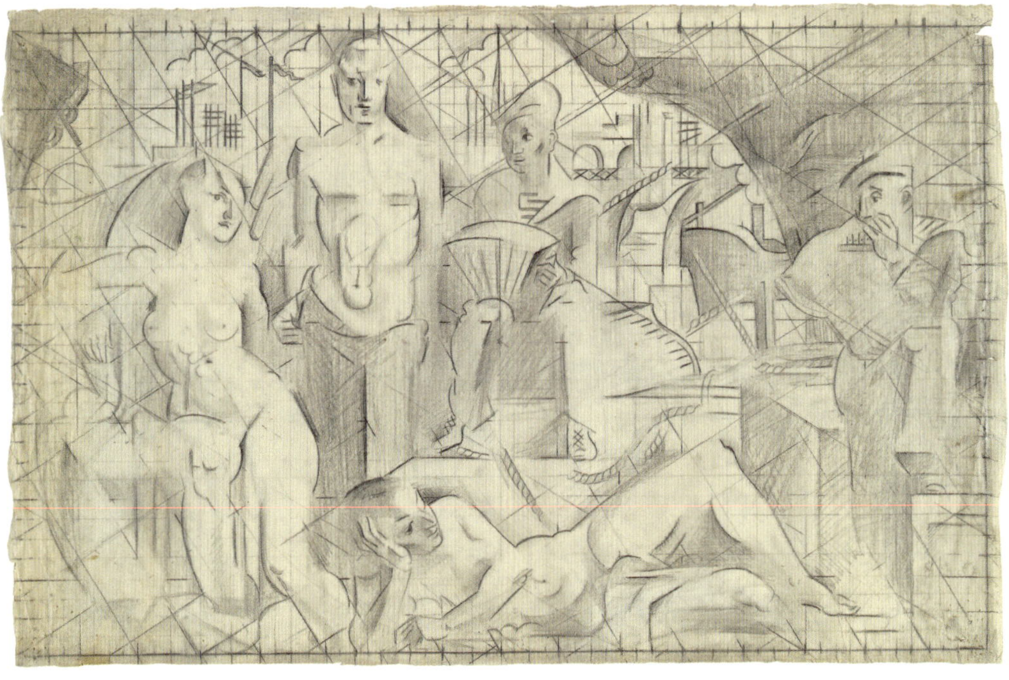

cat 138 Grace Crowley, Study for *Sailors and models* 1928–29

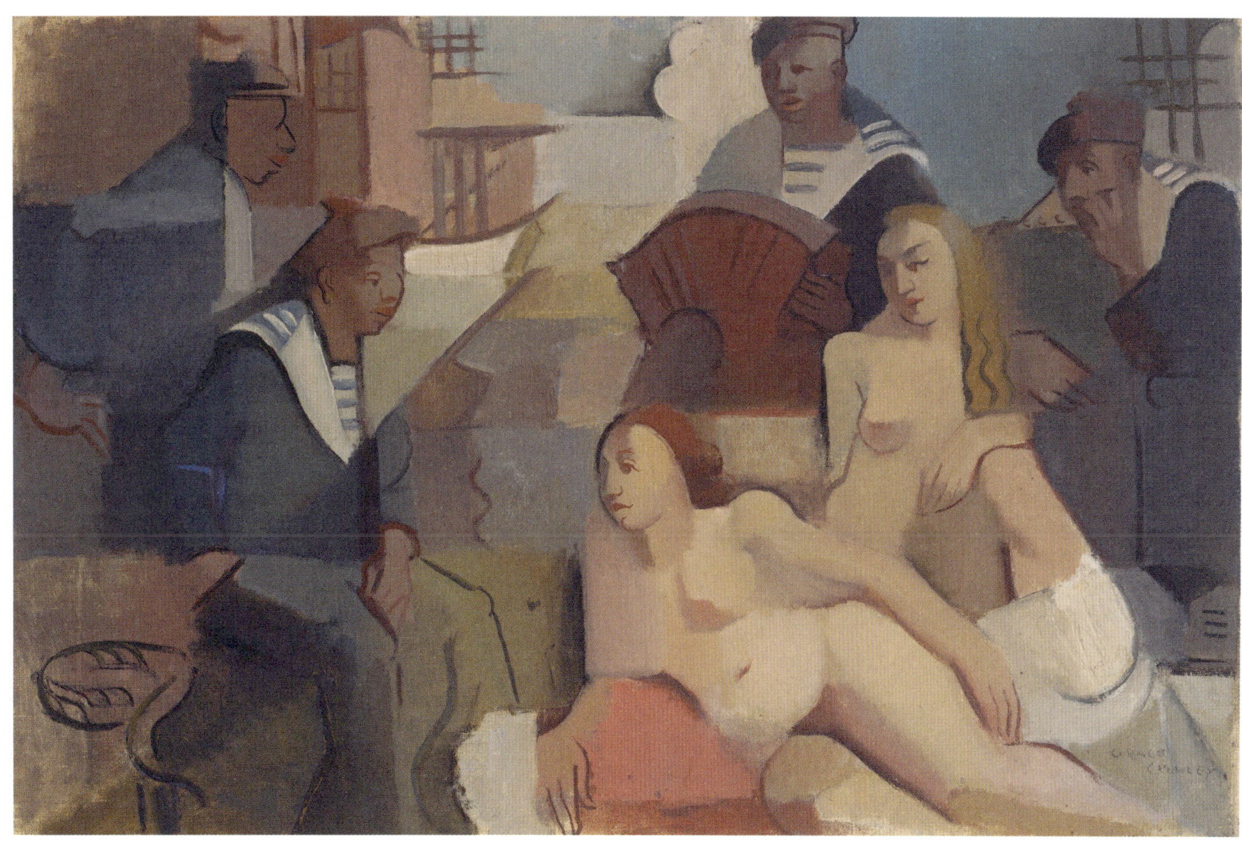

cat 139 Grace Crowley, *Sailors and models* 1928–29

with Henri Bernier, a French potter based in Viroflay, near the porcelain manufacturing centre Sèvres in the south-western suburbs of Paris, and, as she also noted, took some further lessons in London during a trip with Crowley in the summer of 1927.[43] Crowley was impressed by Dangar's endeavours, writing enthusiastically for *Undergrowth* that year, 'I do hope she will be able to keep on with her pottery. I am sure she would do it well. Her hands are made for moulding pots as M. Bernier says.'[44]

While Dangar did not like Bernier's pottery style, she greatly admired his methods, and towards the end of 1927 stayed with him and his family in Viroflay, where she embraced his lessons with great energy.[45] Writing to Dorrit Black she proclaimed that she was

> doing pottery all the time now—8.30 AM to 6.30 PM but it's the only way to learn and by Feb I will know the job very thoroughly. I work at the wheel two hours a day—the rest of the time I help M. Bernier in whatever he is doing so I get practical knowledge of the whole business.[46]

During this same period, Dangar also undertook classes in porcelain painting, with a 'very excellent little teacher' named Mademoiselle Ne.[47] This was an activity with which she was already familiar, having decorated small porcelain objects such as trinket boxes with floral motifs while teaching in Kempsey.[48] By comparison, her sketchbook from Paris contains bold, modern gouache designs, vibrant bands of stylised decoration influenced by the geometric patterns of Art Deco, and flowers and scrolls from traditional pottery simplified into repeated graphic forms (cat 75). This work complemented her lessons with Lhote and continued to impress upon her the importance of compositional design, which was intrinsic to both the modern painting taught by Lhote and ceramic decoration. As she commented, 'to learn to paint on china one had to learn design and my teacher believes in making you design anything and everything!'[49] Her subsequent ceramic decorations show great ingenuity in this respect, responding to the three-dimensional form of the pottery as much as the surface itself. A delicate teacup and saucer painted between 1926 and 1929 feature sail-like segments that fan outwards, dynamically circling around the porcelain form (cat 2). Modern design and pottery can also be seen unified in a plate decorated during this same period, with the figure mapped to an invisible angular grid in the style of Lhote but surrounded by patterns drawn from the visual lexicon of porcelain painting—flowers, bees and wiggling lines, arranged in repeated, regular segments (cat 3).

With her skills and design sensibility developing, Dangar was approached to undertake work for Primavera, the successful design firm operated by the Parisian department store Printemps.[50] Primavera had been established in 1912, and by the late 1920s was widely known for its fashionable

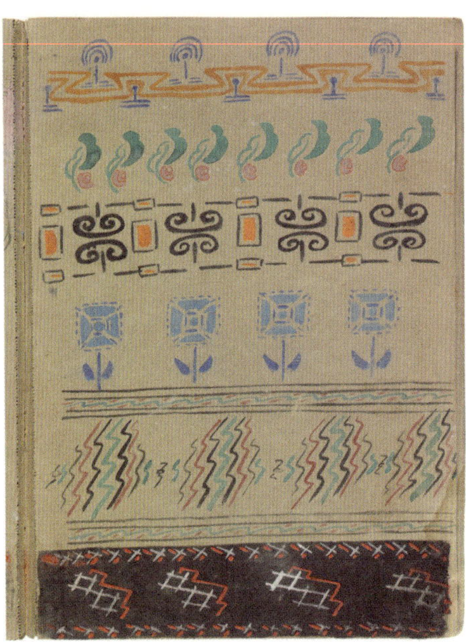

cat 75 Repeat designs for porcelain painting 1926–28 in Sketchbook 1926–32

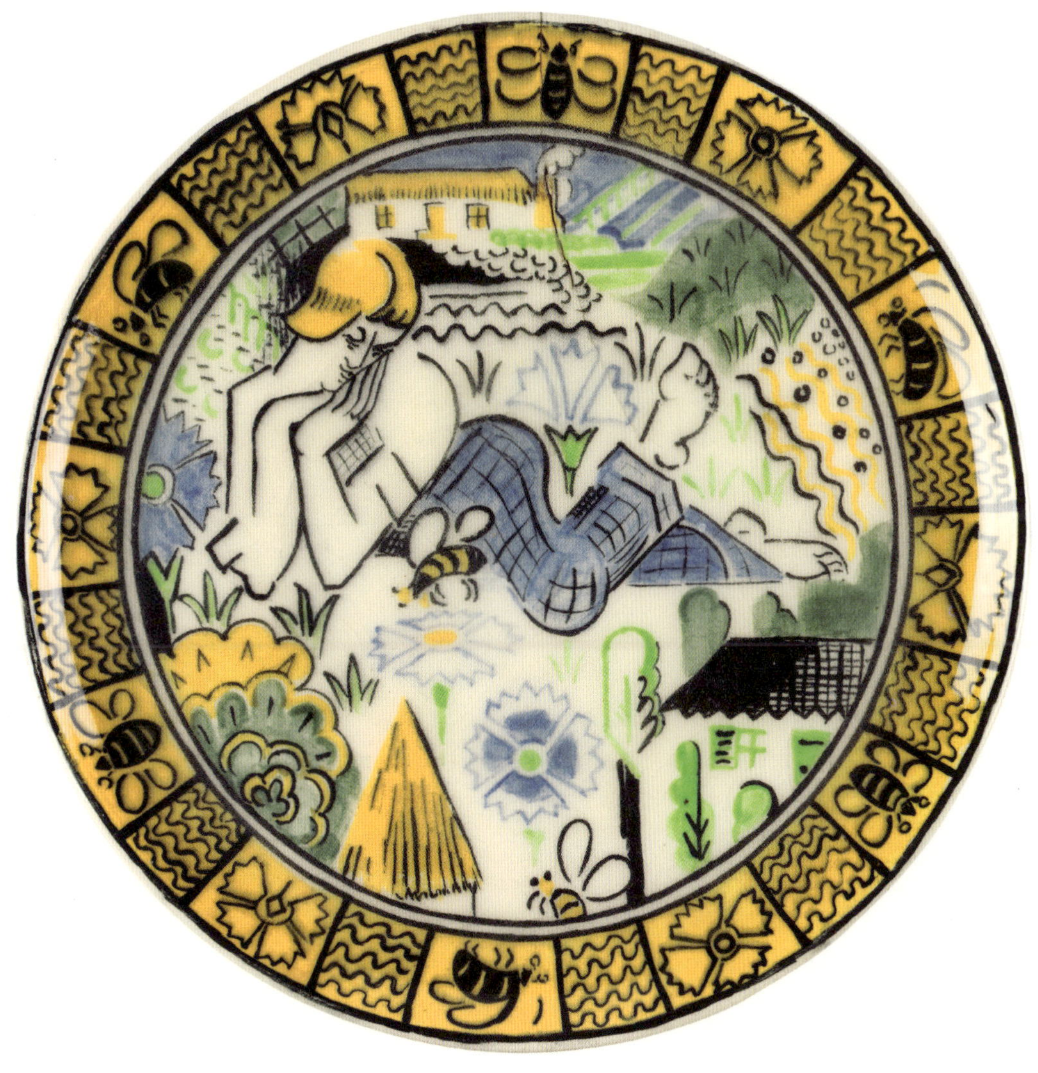

cat 3 *Illustration to a poem by James Stephens* plate 1926–29

Art Deco designs. The firm reached its zenith at this time, purchasing a ceramics factory and employing a range of subcontractors to create and decorate objects.[51] It is not known for certain whether Dangar ever formally worked for Primavera, but she did not create objects for them on the wheel using Bernier's techniques, later recalling her promise to 'never use any of his secrets to make money in France' and that he would not 'free me from that promise when I was offered a position in Paris'—likely Primavera.[52] It is possible she was employed to paint factory porcelain to other artists' designs; however, as these objects were not signed, no examples indisputably by Dangar have been discovered.

While Dangar's limited finances forced her return to Sydney in December 1928, her time in France had been a major period of transition. In Lhote's studio, she finally came face to face with modernism and found an inroad to Cubism. She also discovered pottery, both the process of its creation upon the wheel and its exterior decoration. The central role played by compositional design in Lhote's teaching found resonance in the regimented systems of repeated pattern, colour and shapes circling a hand-thrown teacup or vase. For Dangar, modernism and pottery became inextricably linked.

Reluctantly, but with ambitions to share all she had learnt about modern art in France, Dangar resumed teaching for Ashton in 1929. Earlier, *Undergrowth* had excitedly announced her return to Sydney, advertising classes in landscape painting by her to be held in the countryside in the new year.[53] While promoted as being held through the Sydney Art School, Dangar formulated her own lessons, 'a series of vivid and interesting lectures, illustrated with reproductions of the works of European masters', likely derived from her experience at the Académie Lhote.[54] In January she led a group of art students, most of whom were connected with the Sydney Art School, 'in devious painting adventures' in Wamberal, New South Wales, close to Terrigal.[55] Although the trip was cut short due to bushfires, it was seen overall as 'an unmitigated success'.[56] Students came and went, working as much as they pleased, and came together to receive criticism from Dangar, who one described as 'vivid, thorough and instructive'.[57]

Concurrently, she published a manifesto-like essay, 'To-day', in the January–February issue of *Undergrowth*, in which she advocated for the 'fundamental need' of art in twentieth-century society to 'satisfy the need of to-day' and the 'need which makes us appreciate the art of other days'.[58] This text was adapted from a lecture she likely attended in 1928 by French cubist and purist painter Amédée Ozenfant. While Ozenfant's emphasis on mechanical beauty was inconsistent with her later work, the essay openly declared Dangar's allegiance to modern art, to 'the laws of composition' and the 'exquisite conceptions of rhythm, form and colour [that] give the modern mind a satisfaction'.[59]

Despite this promising homecoming, Dangar soon realised that Ashton remained ardently opposed to modernism. He had promised that she could teach 'as she wanted to teach'; however, it became clear that Cubism and modern art had no place at the Sydney Art School.[60] She even experienced opposition from some of her students, later warning Dorrit Black to 'expect NOTHING from the students of Sydney. I thought they were hungry and isolated and that they would be eager for what I had to give and all they said was "you know Miss Dangar we take what you say with a grain of salt".'[61]

By winter of 1929, she advertised her own art classes in her studio at 12 Bridge Street, offering a design class all day on Wednesdays and one for children on Saturday mornings. She boasted no affiliation with the Sydney Art School, but instead proudly stated that she had '[studied] in Europe for the past three years' and that she had gained a 'Teacher's Certificate at "L'Académie Lhote"'.[62]

Soon after, she began teaching her students Cubism, effectively establishing the first modern art school in Australia. This radical endeavour precedes by several years efforts made by Black and Crowley in the early 1930s, which have previously been acknowledged as the beginnings of modern art education in Australia.[63] Viewed alongside her lectures to students on Cézanne in 1925 and letters, essays

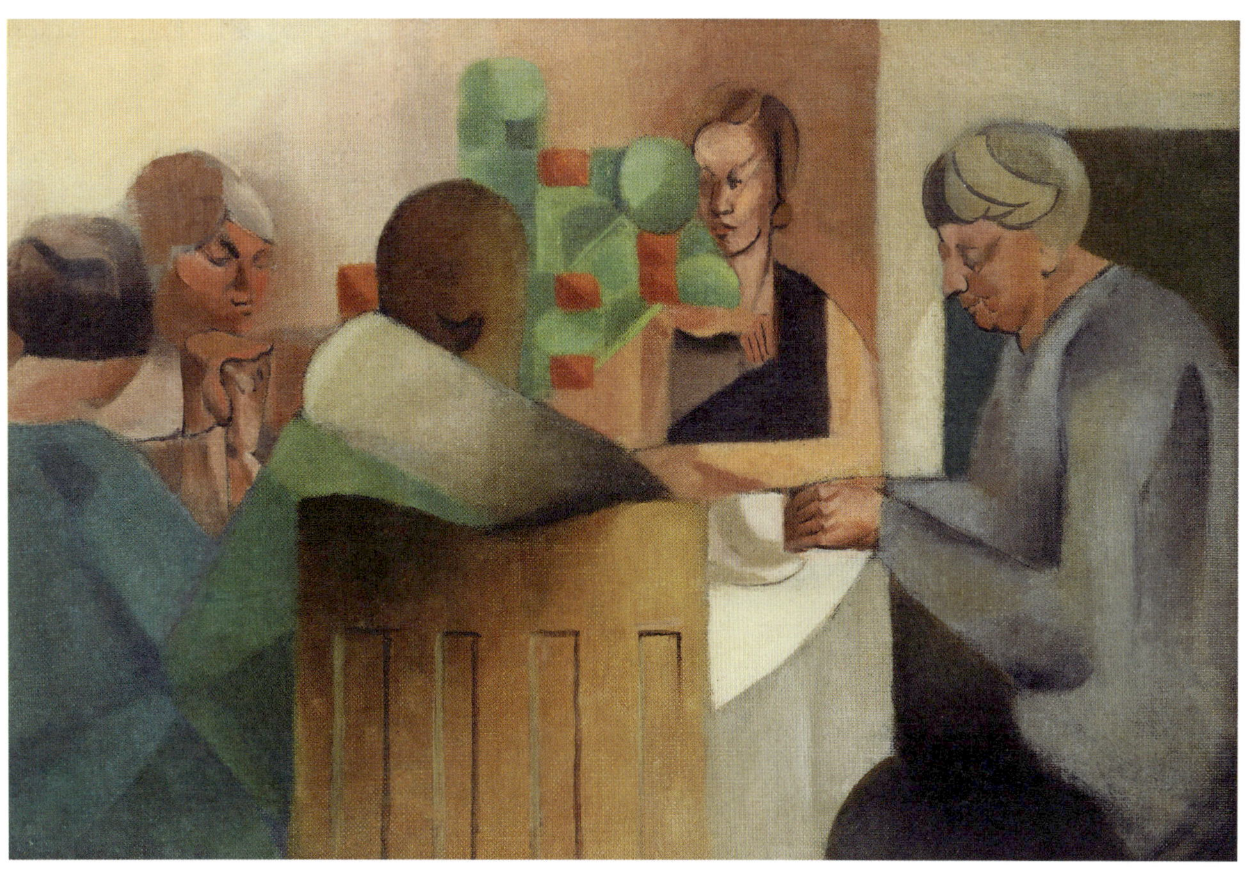

cat 150 Dore Hawthorne, *Some of Grace Crowley's Port Macquarie class* 1930

and bold manifestos published in *Undergrowth* throughout the years that followed, these significant efforts to advance modernism in Sydney situate Dangar alongside the most influential women artists of the 1920s, Margaret Preston and Thea Proctor, who are widely acknowledged for their central role in the development of modern art in Australia.[64]

Within six months, Dangar had 23 pupils (for the most part friends and former students) to whom she taught the principles of Cubism she had learnt at Lhote's academy.[65] Among them was *Undergrowth* co-editor Dore Hawthorne, who translated her teachings into a sophisticated cubist composition of 1930 (cat 150), which depicts the first sketching trip Crowley led following her return to Australia. It is clear Dangar lucidly explained Lhote's methods—Hawthorne's figures and furniture are sharply aligned along invisible angles corresponding to his mathematical framework, and united through passages of graduating tone.[66] Similarly, Estelle (known as Stella) Creed, who also joined Dangar's Wamberal trip in early 1929, created several advanced cubist compositions under Dangar's instruction. Among her most impressive is a still-life painting composed of harmonious greens, golds and pale yellows, her subjects fractured into an assortment of angular planes filtered through a cubist grid (cat 134). Creed sourced elements for her composition from Dangar's studio, most notably the elegant jug decorated with blue and white, which is also featured in an accomplished Lhote-inflected cubist still life painted by Dangar that same year (cat 71) as a wedding present for her niece Annette Singleton.

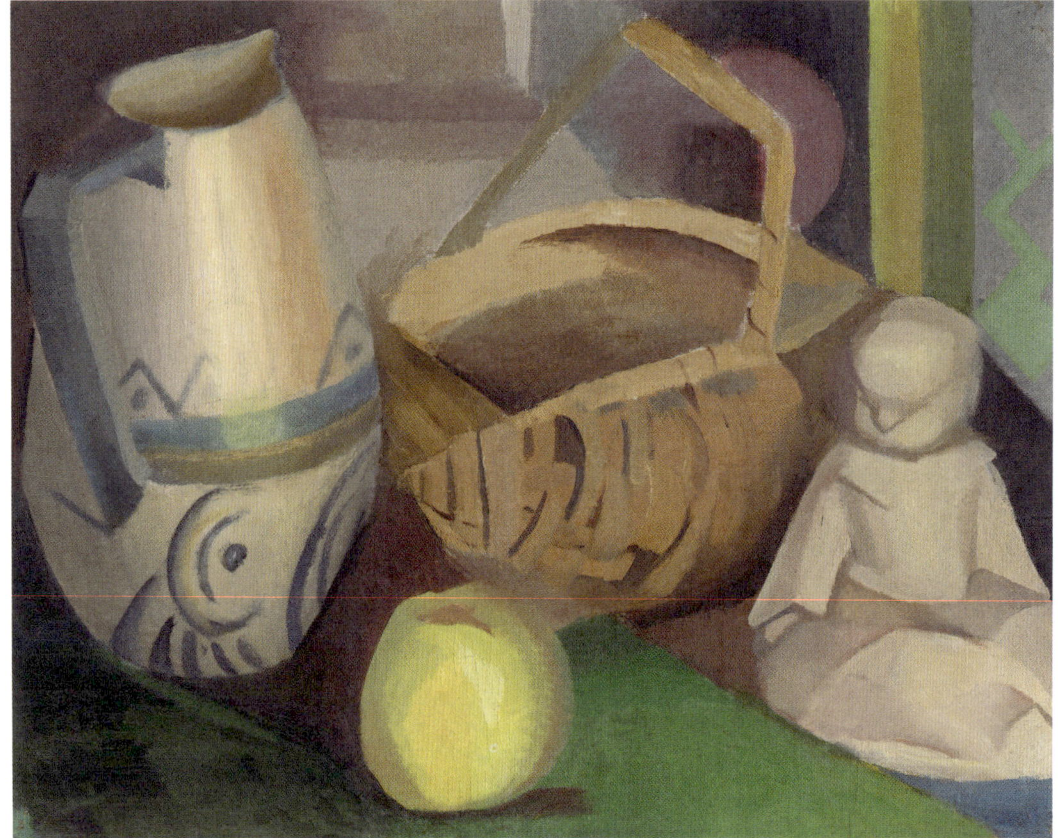

cat 134 Estelle Creed, Still life with jug 1929

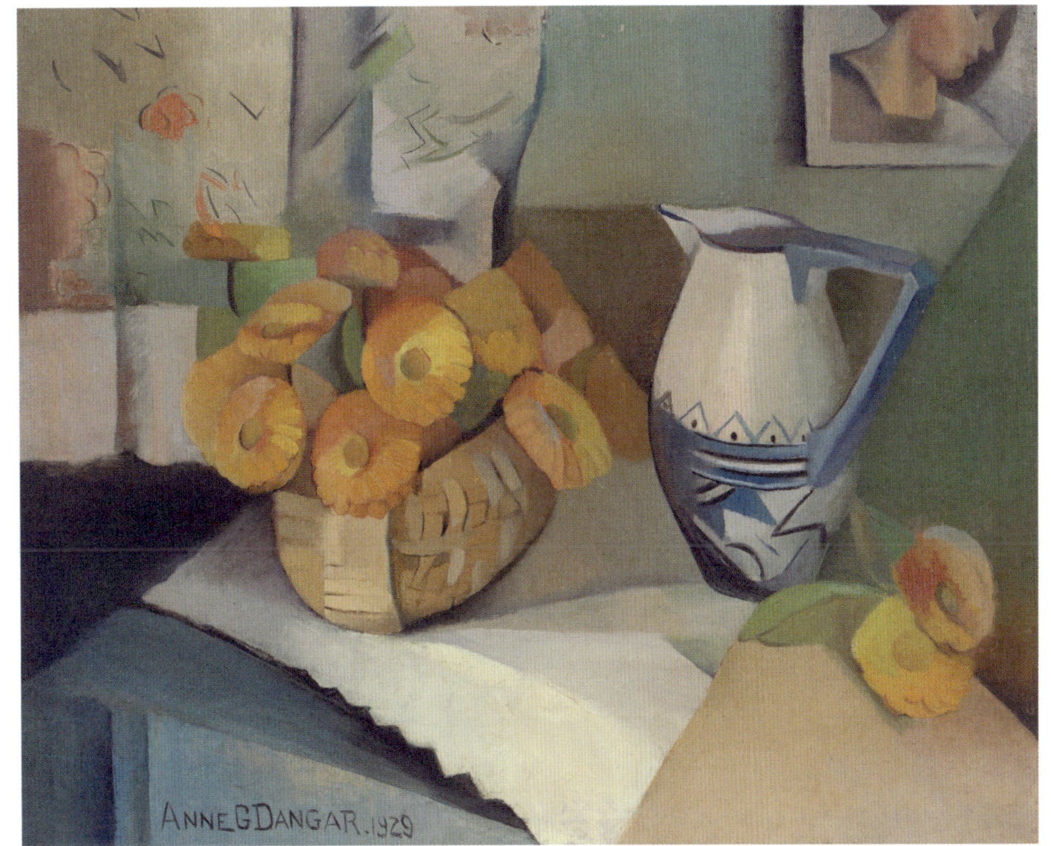

cat 71 Still life 1929

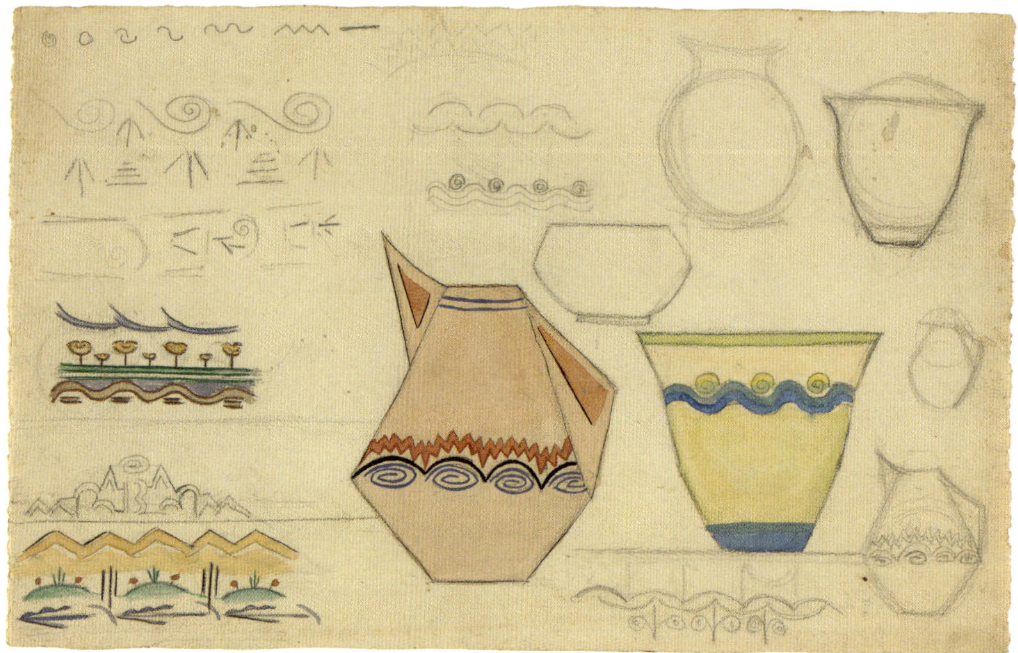

cat 133 Estelle Creed, Designs for ceramics and decoration 1929

This jug was likely a porcelain blank handpainted by Dangar in Paris or upon her return to Sydney. She later recalled that much of her 'Paris Pottery' had been smashed on its journey home.[67] The angular, geometric patterning of the jug's surface resembles the Art Deco style popular at Primavera and corresponds closely with examples of her handpainted porcelain from the late 1920s. In France, Dangar had resolved to begin her own pottery in Sydney, expressing her desire to Crowley's mother, affectionately called 'Mother bird', in February 1927: 'if only I can stay here for long enough to really understand the whole job I think I will be alright when I get back'.[68] She was particularly inspired by functional ware and the idea of creating simple but artistically designed objects for use in the home, similar to those she would have seen at Primavera and produced by regional potters. As she wrote to Mrs Crowley,

> it is the everyday, common china I love over here—the drawing room things are exquisite too but lots of women in Sydney are dabbling at those. But the casseroles, washing up dishes, kitchen jugs, breakfast sets, everyday teapots! Oh they are <u>shocking</u> in Australia. We take refuge in pure white because the colours and patterns are so hideous … I want to learn just how to make these common things.[69]

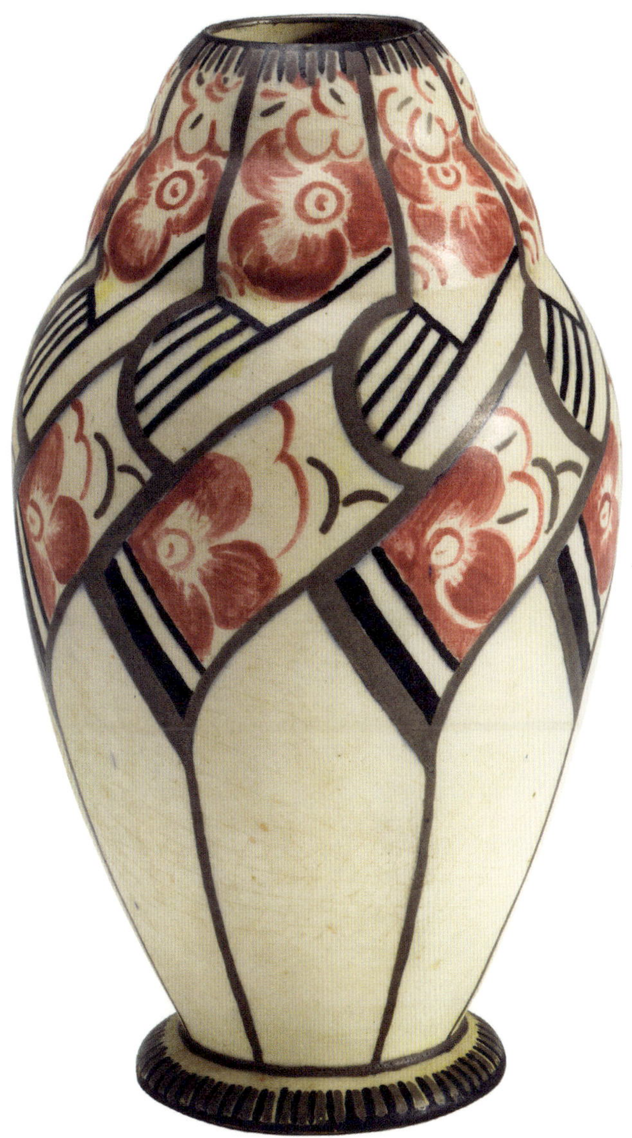

cat 1 Vase 1926–29

Margaret Preston, who created and decorated pottery with Gladys Reynell in the mid 1910s, made similar remarks on the state of the craft in Sydney, commenting in 1930 that there were few potters working there and the 'tendency is to lean too much towards the commercial type of work'.[70]

While these aspirations did not come to fruition, Dangar certainly attempted to generate interest in pottery and the way it could be integrated with modernism. In September, she delivered a lecture on 'Modern art and craft work' at the Society of Arts and Crafts, and gave some of her students tuition in pottery and decoration.[71] A drawing by Creed from 1929 (cat 133) features the forms of several designs for vessels alongside decorative designs which draw on the same vocabulary of geometric patterns and floral motifs seen in Dangar's Paris sketchbook and upon her own painted pieces (cat 1). Dangar continued decorating blanks and may even have continued to pursue wheel-throwing, for her student Karna Birmingham later recalled, 'Pottery was the obvious thing for her—I remember how she used to throw herself on her drawings with a sort of ferocity, her hands working as if she were moulding the figures in the air.'[72]

Although Dangar's modern approach to painting and enthusiasm for Cubism were received positively by her circle of like-minded artist-friends, she was soon deeply despondent with what she perceived as the conservative and commercial art world of Sydney, a shock after her 'three pure vision years' with Lhote in Paris.[73] She and Ashton remained respectful friends; however, she could see that he 'was too old to have sympathy for modern art' and 'for that reason I couldn't stay with him—nor give lessons in the same city as him', a realisation that placed her in an untenable position.[74]

In letters 'full of misery', she lamented her situation to Crowley (who remained in Paris) and implored her to send 'ANYTHING' ever written by the cubist artist Albert Gleizes. Dangar had encountered Gleizes's work during her final months in Paris in 1928, when she saw his 'astonishing' religious canvases on display at the Salon des Tuileries.[75] From the late 1910s, Gleizes had developed a highly theorised approach to painting and wrote several foundational texts explaining his ideas. Among these was *La peinture et ses lois* 1923 (*Painting and its laws*), which Dangar purchased soon after seeing his work in Paris and regularly reread when she was in Sydney. While drawn to his concepts, especially the way he connected the planar qualities of Cubism to the flattened perspective of pre-Renaissance Christian art, she was bewildered by his writing and lacked the wider context for his aesthetic and spiritual ideas to engage with them fully.[76] Nonetheless, the experience of viewing his paintings was unforgettable and remained a sustaining force in the stifling artistic environment of Sydney.

To aid Dangar, Crowley bought a number of books and eventually approached Gleizes himself for lessons; he was amused by her story and invited her to join him at his home in Paris, where he guided her and Black through some of his principles.[77] Hearing Crowley was to travel to Italy for the summer, he invited her to visit his artist community Moly-Sabata in Sablons, a short distance across the river from the studio he and his wife Juliette Roche shared in the town of Serrières. Arriving by October, Crowley spent time working with Gleizes's follower, artist Robert Pouyaud, later joined by the cubist painter himself. She made several abstract exercises in gouache following his pictorial system over this period, as well as elaborate pencil drawings (cat 144) in which she analysed the formal construction of his major painting *Le Couronnement de la Vierge* 1927 (*Coronation of the Virgin*, fig 15), which she saw displayed in his studio. During the course of their time together, Crowley also discussed her friend Dangar and her situation in Australia, reading her latest unhappy letter aloud, and asked Gleizes and Roche whether it would be possible for Dangar to earn a living at Moly-Sabata. According to Crowley, Gleizes responded 'elle est [déjà] ici' (she's here already) and advised her to cable Dangar, inviting her to join the Moly-Sabata community.[78]

Despite knowing Gleizes only through his work and his writing, Dangar accepted without question and after a short telegram exchange her future took form.[79] Having heard about her aptitude and interest in pottery, Gleizes himself wrote to Dangar in late 1929 asking if she would be willing to continue the craft at Moly-Sabata, a prospect that reinforced her confidence in her decision: 'there is nothing I would love so much!'[80] In her later years, Dangar attributed this invitation to divine intervention, recounting in a letter to Gleizes her memory of finishing classes at the Sydney Art School for the day and entering George Street, where

> slowly your paintings came down like a blind before my eyes—the noises and the world no longer exist for me—I looked at these curves, these rhythmic lines as I had looked at them at the Salon des Tuileries and then I became aware of the crowd and the buzz of the high street. From the bottom of my heart this prayer was torn 'Oh God let Albert Gleizes take me from here and bring me to you!' It was Thursday. Saturday at noon I received your telegram.[81]

By January 1930, Dangar had dismantled and vacated her Bridge Street studio, storing her 'handmade pottery and other valuable objects' with friends and packing trunks with books and sketchbooks to accompany her to Moly-Sabata.[82] Crowley returned to Australia, days before Dangar left for France.[83] She acknowledged that Dangar's departure would result in their 'life-long separation', while also knowing this was Dangar's only future, writing, 'she must live, she must be happy, she must have work for her energetic mind'.[84] Only four short months after receiving Gleizes's invitation, Dangar farewelled Sydney on 5 February 1930 and departed for Marseille aboard the *Commissaire Ramel*, from where she would continue on to Sablons and Moly-Sabata, resolutely beginning a new life in which modern art and craft would be at the centre.

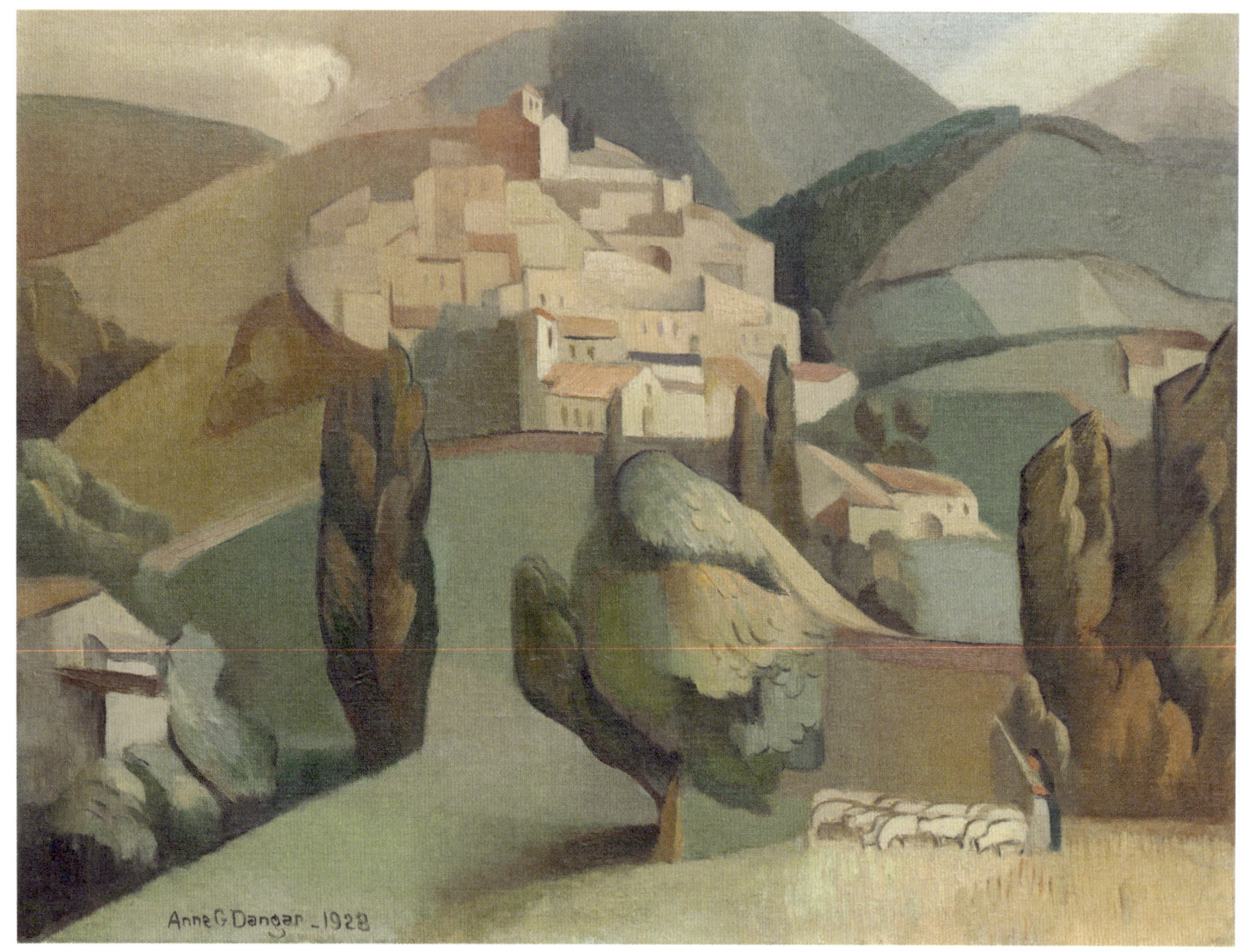

cat 70 *Mirmande, La Drôme* 1928

Together and apart: Anne Dangar, Grace Crowley and modern Paris

ELENA TAYLOR

In 1934 Dangar wrote that her two-and-a-half years in Paris from 1926 to 1928 were the 'happiest of my life'.[1] This period was a watershed, marking the divide between Dangar's first forty years in Australia and her last two decades at Moly-Sabata. Her experiences in Paris were critical to Dangar's future artistic and personal development, yet comparatively little art-historical attention has been given to these years.

Much of what we know about Dangar's time in Paris comes from Grace Crowley:

> I seem to be talking a lot about myself and this written effort is supposed to be all about Anne Dangar. And so it is ... but we shared all the same experiences, shared the same studio ... Travelled together, went to the same schools ... so I can't very well separate myself from Anne in telling her story whilst we were still abroad.[2]

Crowley's account, given late in her life, emphasised the commonality of their experiences; however, upon closer examination a more nuanced picture emerges, with important and ultimately telling differences between the experiences of the two artists. What then did Dangar see and do in France between 1926 and 1928? And how did these experiences change her, and how were they different from Crowley's?

By 1924 Dangar had made up her mind to go to Paris to learn about modern art and she subsequently convinced Crowley to go with her. At a time when modern art was publicly condemned by leaders of the art establishment in Sydney, Dangar had already committed herself to modernism, at least the limited version she knew. Her insistence upon Paris was unusual for the interwar years, with the majority of Australian artists (including friends such as Myra Cox, Florence Mofflin and Douglas Dundas) preferring to head for London, and to its more conservative art schools. Study at the Slade School in London was also Crowley's original plan, and, by her own admission, she was 'afraid' of modern art.[3] Dangar intended to return to Australia, at her farewell party informing her former students that she was going to Europe to learn more in order to be able to teach more.[4]

Was an additional attraction that Paris offered greater opportunity for women to live a more liberated life than was possible in London, further away from familial expectations and outside of social conventions? The artistic quarters of Montmartre and Montparnasse were known to be tolerant of unconventional lifestyles, and queer Australian women artists such as Bessie Davidson and Agnes Goodsir had made Paris their home in the early twentieth century.

Dangar and Crowley disembarked at Marseille in mid March 1926, staying for almost a month with friends Monsieur Pébeyre and Monsieur C, in their country house in Aubagne, only a short distance from Marseille.[5] From there, Dangar and Crowley made numerous excursions with their hosts, including a visit to Cézanne's studio in Aix-en-Provence.

By the end of April, the pair had arrived in Paris and were staying in a *pension* opposite the Luxembourg Gardens. Two pressing questions faced them—where to live and where to study. Almost immediately they made the rounds of the well-known art schools, including the Académie Julian and the Académie Colarossi, both established in the nineteenth century, and the long-running Académie de la Grande Chaumière. These privately run schools did not have any entry requirements and attracted large numbers of foreign students, who did not need to know French and could join classes as they pleased.

Dangar and Crowley were shocked at the low standard of the students' work, but feeling they needed to start working joined the *atelier libre* at Colarossi's, where they drew from the model but without tuition. In Crowley's view, the students' work at this school was 'the stuffiest, weakest effort in the way of drawing and painting that it had ever been my misfortune to witness'.[6]

They instead decided to try to find an artist who could give them private tuition, and with this in mind visited the salon of the Société des artistes français (SAF), the oldest and most conservative of the huge annual salons in Paris. Crowley's aim was to find a teacher who could improve her 'finish' in portraiture, and while she considered the majority of works to be 'extraordinarily bad', she had liked a portrait by Louis Roger, a conventional academic painter who also taught at the École des beaux-arts.[7] Crowley contacted Roger and soon after, in late May, Dangar and Crowley began private lessons in his studio.

Dangar and Crowley had also visited the slightly more progressive salon of the Société nationale des beaux-arts (SNBA), which that year had exhibited works by 11 Australian artists.[8] Most notable among these were the three drawings and five paintings by recently elected *sociétaire* Hilda Rix Nicholas, including *Une Australienne* 1926 (National Gallery of Australia). Born in 1884, Rix Nicholas was an almost exact contemporary of Dangar and had lived and studied in France before the First World War. During the 1920s she was one of the most highly regarded women artists in Australia, and it is possible that she was known to Dangar and Crowley through connections in Sydney, where she had held a well-received solo exhibition in 1923. In a letter back to Australia, Crowley reported excitedly that they had arranged to take over Rix Nicholas's large studio at 84 rue d'Assas, which they had already seen twice, but for reasons unknown this was to fall through.[9] Rix Nicholas and Dangar would certainly have had artistic differences, and when interviewed on her return to Australia, Rix Nicholas described modern art as 'decadent' and that 'Australian students … would have no excuse in taking up the ultra-modern movement'.[10]

Studios in Paris were hard to come by at that time and it took weeks of searching before Dangar and Crowley were able to secure an unfurnished one-room studio in the Villa Leone complex, a recently completed, purpose-built *cité d'artistes* at 16 bis rue Bardinet, just south of Montparnasse, although as it required some work, they were not able to move in until later in October. This small *impasse* (blocked-off street) was accessible via a high archway off rue Bardinet and was lined with one- and two-storey studios. Dangar and Crowley rented Atelier 25, which remained their address throughout their time in Paris. Later Dangar wrote, 'One studio has done in Paris for dressing, cooking, painting, everything for two …'.[11]

Dangar and Crowley spent their first European summer in Brittany, where they visited the well-known artists' haunts of Le Pouldu and Pont-Aven, and where they also painted landscapes *en plein air*, following their Sydney Art School training.[12] It was in Quimper that Dangar saw traditional pottery being made, and first considered it as a means to make a living. Unlike Crowley, who was from a well-off family who supported her financially, the independent Dangar had to earn her own money. She had 'scrimped and saved' for two years to go to France, and money was an ever-present concern when she lived there, as she often mentioned in her correspondence and notebooks.[13]

On returning to Paris after their summer holiday, Dangar began taking lessons in pottery manufacture from Henri Bernier at his pottery in Viroflay, a small village near Versailles and only a short train trip from Paris. She also began lessons in porcelain decoration with a Mademoiselle Ne, of whom nothing further is known. It was around this time that Dangar ceased taking lessons with Roger, writing that while Crowley was continuing and had made progress with him, 'I can only go ahead when I feel my master is leading me up the path which I have already started on …'.[14]

—

Dangar's path was towards modern art, and in the first weeks of 1927 she enrolled at the Académie André Lhote, founded by André Lhote in 1925, and one of only two schools in Paris which offered the opportunity to study with an artist who taught a modernist approach to painting.[15] However, Dangar was there only briefly before she became seriously ill (she later reported having not felt well since Brittany). On 17 January Dangar underwent a major operation, which required four weeks of recovery in hospital followed by two weeks of recuperation with her friends near Aubagne. Returning with Crowley to Paris at the start of March, Dangar immediately resumed her classes with Lhote, although she was not yet strong enough to begin her pottery lessons again.

Within a few weeks, Dangar was joined at the Académie Lhote by Crowley, who by this stage was 'fed up to the teeth' with Roger.[16] Crowley's response to Lhote's teaching was immediate, and as Bruce Adams has observed,[17] unintentionally resembled that of a sexual awakening:

> To my amazement his teaching was only the confirmation of the WANT I had been feeling so long without knowing exactly what the want was ...
>
> I feel rather dazed, but very happy, bewilderingly happy, and am continually confronted with the amazing fact that 'it doesn't hurt,' that I've not had to do a single thing I didn't want to do.[18]

Dangar's response to Lhote had been more restrained: 'It is a very serious school, and he is a good and sympathetic teacher.'[19]

Born in Bordeaux in 1885, the same year as Dangar, Lhote had been an early cubist, an exhibitor in the 1911 Salon des indépendants, known as the 'cubist salon', and a member of the Section d'or group of cubists that included Jacques Villon, Robert Delaunay, Fernand Léger and Albert Gleizes. As with others in the 1920s, Lhote sought to distance his work from Cubism and instead his work was part of the *rappel à l'ordre* (return to order) within French art of the period, which saw a renewed interest in classicism and an attempt to align modernity with tradition.

Lhote was an experienced teacher who had taught at various Paris atelier schools since 1916. At the Académie he taught students to simplify forms into geometric solids such as spheres, cubes, cones and cylinders and lines into straights and curves; and to structure compositions according to a mathematically derived armature. His teaching included frequent analysis of works by earlier artists, such as Vermeer, Ingres and Seurat. Above all, Lhote taught with reference to Cézanne, which must have particularly resonated with Dangar. Lhote's popularity with students was largely due to his accessible and coherent approach to a modernism based upon such laws and principles, though these could lead to a formulaic approach. American student Emlen Etting, who studied with Lhote from 1928 to 1931, observed that 'a lot of students invariably copied his style, but he never encouraged anyone to paint as he did. He only wanted students to learn traditional fundamentals.'[20]

The wider impact of Lhote's modernist teaching cannot be overstated, and it is thought that over two thousand artists studied at the Académie Lhote over the six decades of its existence.[21] The majority of these were foreigners, with Americans making up the greatest number, along with large cohorts of Scandinavians and other Europeans, as well as painters from South America, Turkey, Egypt, Asia and Australasia. Numerous of these students, just like Crowley and Dorrit Black in Australia and John Weeks in Aotearoa New Zealand, became pioneering modernists and influential teachers when they returned to their home countries, and Lhote is recognised as a key figure in the development of global modernisms.[22]

Crowley later recalled the internationalism of the class: 'Every country in Europe seemed to be represented there—only one Eng.—preponderance Americans (whom I loved) very few French much to Lhote's regret.'[23] In a photograph of the class, probably taken in 1927, Lhote is standing at the rear with his arm across the shoulders of the model (fig 8). Dangar is standing second from the left. To her right is American Jane Gallatin Powers, behind her the Argentine painter Héctor Basaldúa, and in front of her Crowley sits with legs crossed. The first Australian known to have studied with Lhote was Mary Cockburn Mercer, around 1922; Dangar and Crowley were soon followed by a wave of others, and by 1930 one artist reported that among Australians 'the most popular French teacher of the day is [André] Lhote'.[24]

Located near the gare Montparnasse at 18 rue d'Odessa, the Académie Lhote was entered via an outside staircase in the passage du Départ. The large studio used for teaching had a high ceiling with a skylight and the walls hung with Lhote's paintings as well as reproductions of works by Cézanne and others that he would refer to in his classes. At the beginning of the week, Lhote would set the pose for the model, returning on Fridays to give criticisms of students' work that the entire class would follow. Throughout the term there would be weeks devoted to multi-figure compositions, as well as to still life and portraiture. Lessons were conducted in French, with students translating Lhote's comments for each other.

Dangar and Crowley soon fell into a comfortable routine, Crowley recalling:

> Later when we became acquainted with other students and were more sophisticated, Le Quartier Latin seemed especially to be our home ... The Carrefour Vavin is the heart of the Latin Quarter. The three cafes, Le Dôme, La Rotonde and [La] Coupole are clustered near it and our daily activities were centred between La Rue d'Odessa where we worked and La Grande Chaumière where there was a shop which sold artist materials ... The little restaurant La Corbeille was found close to the Dôme in the [Rue] Delambre. One could get an excellent meal there and Anne and I and other students frequented it every evening.[25]

While the artist colony of Montparnasse was thoroughly international, it was the Americans, who arrived in Paris in ever-increasing numbers due to a favourable exchange rate in the 1920s, that formed by far the largest group. Most Americans and British spoke only English, and very few formed close ties with French artists or those of other nationalities. And while Dangar and Crowley had made efforts to learn French, taking Berlitz classes on their arrival, for the most part their friendships in Paris were also with other English speakers, including their friends from Sydney—Dorrit Black, and Norman and Edith Lloyd. Dangar and Crowley did not have any contact with the Australian artists of an older generation, such as Kathleen O'Connor and Bessie Davidson, who had been living in Paris since before the First World War.[26]

Although Dangar and Crowley's social interactions were mostly within the Anglosphere, Lhote encouraged his students to keep up to date with the latest art then being shown in Paris. Etting recalled:

> Lhote had been an art critic for ten years at the prestigious *Nouvelle Revue Française* ... so he was fully aware of everything that was going on, and this also kept us on our toes. In pairs or small groups we would inspect all the exhibitions from the rue de la Boétie to the Left Bank, and pay visits to the Orangerie, the old Luxembourg, the various salons. Students spent hours discussing all the latest trends at café tables spread out on the sidewalk.[27]

Encouraged by Dangar, Crowley's artistic horizons were expanding, and she wrote back to Australia of the exhibitions she had seen:

> Paris is full of rotten shows of pseudo-modern work, but my word, you come across the real stuff now and then—modern, mind you, the sincerity and force of which makes you sit up and think. We saw a ripping modern exhibition of Dutch work once which really was a revelation.[28]

With few exhibitions of modern Dutch art held in Paris at this time, this could only have been Piet Mondrian's one-day exhibition of twenty recent paintings held at the American University Women's Club on 12 March 1927, organised by De Klomp (The Clog), a new association of Dutch painters living in Paris.[29]

Throughout 1927 and 1928 it is Crowley's rapidly evolving response or 'conversion' to modern art that is documented in their letters home. This was not the case for Dangar, whose letters instead reveal her widening knowledge of modern art and increasing sophistication. While she was in Sydney, Dangar's knowledge of modern art had been limited, but following a visit to the Tate Gallery in mid 1927 she is able to comment insightfully upon Degas's composition and Modigliani's use of colour to build form, and to compare the Gauguins in the Tate with those in the French national collection.[30]

—

During the 1927 summer break, Dangar and Crowley visited London for several weeks, although by this stage Crowley had completely given up her original intention to study at the Slade. In London they met up with Norman and Edith Lloyd, and Douglas Dundas and Rah Fizelle. They then travelled back to France where in September they joined André Lhote's newly established summer school in the small village of Mirmande, near Valence in the south of France.[31] The previous year, while travelling through the region, Lhote had come across the semi-abandoned hilltop village of Mirmande and considered it an ideal place to hold summer classes, with a focus on landscape painting.

This visit to Mirmande by Dangar and Crowley in 1927 has not previously been known; however, a contemporaneous letter from Crowley and the discovery of her painting *Le tour* 1927 (*The tower*, private collection),[32] a Mirmande subject, confirm that she and Dangar did indeed take part in what was Lhote's first summer school at Mirmande.[33] Their account of Lhote's teaching, 'To the landscape class', must date from this trip, and was published in *Undergrowth* in 1927.[34]

On returning to Paris at the start of the autumn term, Dangar and Crowley continued their studies with Lhote. However, from at least November to February, Dangar focused her energies on working at the pottery with Bernier, writing to Black from Viroflay that 'I am doing pottery all the time now … by Feb I will know the job very thoroughly … I help M. Bernier in whatever he is doing.'[35] For some of this time Dangar also stayed with Bernier and his wife while Crowley remained in Paris studying with Lhote.

At the end of 1927 Dangar and Crowley were joined at Lhote's by Dorrit Black and thus the friendship between the three artists that had begun in Sydney when they attended Julian Ashton's school continued into their studies at the Académie Lhote. They made plans to celebrate an 'Australian Christmas' together with Norman and Edith Lloyd, who had also recently moved to Paris. However, as the new year rolled in, Dangar would have been keenly aware that 1928 would be her last year in France, knowing that she would be returning to Australia after the European summer, although Crowley was to stay on in Paris for another year.

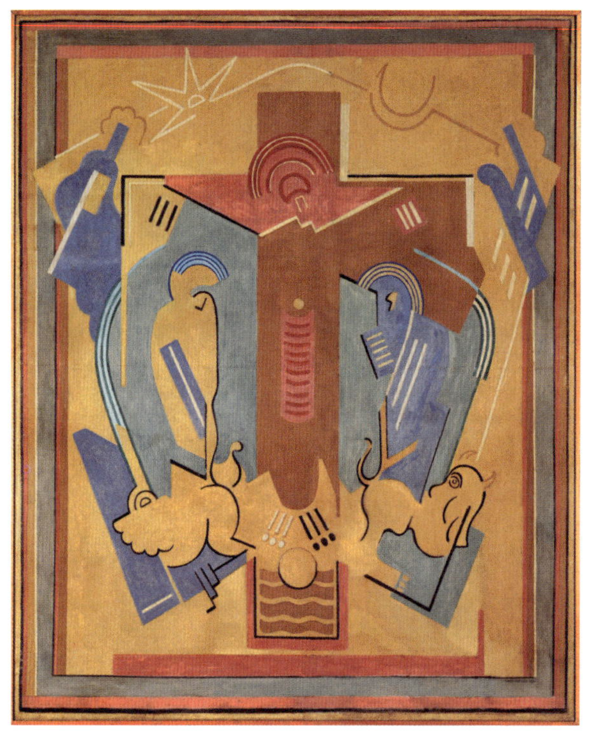

fig 14 Albert Gleizes, *La Crucifixion* (*The Crucifixion*) 1927

Dangar had also realised that Lhote was not the master to lead her on the path towards modern art, writing to Black in late November 1927, that 'I do not like his productions, but I respect his teaching.'[36] She had not found in Europe what she had hoped to find, and her time was running out. It was in this frame of mind that in May or June 1928, she and Crowley visited the Salon des Tuileries, founded only four years earlier as a breakaway from the SNBA to be more welcoming of modern art and younger artists. Opening on 4 May, it included almost three thousand works by an astonishing range of artists—from establishment stalwarts René-Xavier Prinet and Lucien Simon to Henri Matisse, Maurice de Vlaminck, Mondrian, Natalia Goncharova, Mikhail Larionov and Suzanne Duchamp with Alberto Giacometti's sculpture *Femme cuillère* 1926–27 (*Spoon woman*, Museum of Modern Art, New York) and Constantin Brâncuși's bronze *Bird in space* 1927 (National Gallery of Art, Washington, DC) also on display.

Among this abundance, it was a painting by Albert Gleizes that was to leave an indelible impression upon Dangar.[37] *La Crucifixion* 1927 (*The Crucifixion*, fig 14) is one of three large paintings—with *Descente de croix* 1927 (*Descent from the Cross*, Skissernas Museum, Lund) and *Le Couronnement de la Vierge* 1927 (*Coronation of the Virgin*, fig 15)—by Gleizes, working closely with his follower the Irish artist Mainie Jellett, made as studies for murals for the church of Sainte-Blanche in Serrières in the Ardèche.

Gleizes was a leading figure in French avant-garde art, both as an artist and a theoretician. He had been central to the early development of Cubism, having founded in 1912 the Section d'or group and published in the same year an important account of the movement, *Du 'cubisme'* (*On Cubism*), with Jean Metzinger. Following the First World War, Gleizes developed a new conceptual basis for his work, expressed in his treatise *La peinture et ses lois* 1923 (*Painting and its laws*), which art historian Peter Brooke has argued is closely related to his earlier conversion to belief in God.[38] The three paintings for the church at Serrières were Gleizes's most ambitious work of this period, and his first use of explicitly religious themes.[39]

Dangar later described her response to Gleizes's work at the Salon des Tuileries as a spiritual experience:

> After having looked at hundreds of canvases in this exhibition, I reached the depths of the wooden building and found myself in a little room with three large astounding pictures. In front of these canvases I was filled with a perfect satisfaction, with an internal joy that the Hindus call 'intellectual beatitude' and describe as a 'savorous taste'. It was the same peace for the heart that I feel in front of a mediaeval cathedral or the wall-paintings of the same period.[40]

Wanting to know more about Gleizes, Dangar purchased a copy of *La peinture et ses lois* and attempted unsuccessfully to contact Gleizes before her and Crowley's departure from Paris on 10 July for Lhote's summer school in Mirmande.[41]

—

Dangar and Crowley arrived in Mirmande a fortnight before the class was due to start in August. They lodged in the home of Gabriel Simian, alongside their friends from the Académie Lhote, the Americans Jane Gallatin Powers and Emily Shotwell Goeller and the Frenchwoman Suzanne Camin (Camin-Bermann), whose sister Simone would later become the second Madame André Lhote. They were soon joined by Dorrit Black and Isabel Huntley, who stayed in other accommodation. It was a communal and sociable experience; as Black then described, they were 'a party of twenty who have meals together at the hotel & scattered about in sundry rooms through the village ... They are a very nice lot.'[42]

While Dangar had already decided that her path forward was not through Lhote, she nevertheless applied herself diligently to recording his teaching. Her notebook contains transcriptions of Lhote's corrections of other students' works; his discussions of artists, including Seurat, Matisse and Vermeer; and she notes in particular his dictum 'when in doubt think of Cézanne', with a view to giving this advice to her own students back in Sydney.[43]

Dangar's bucolic *Mirmande, La Drôme* 1928 (cat 70) is the only known surviving painting of her two-and-a-half years in France. Depicting the village from the plain below and framed by mountains, *Mirmande, La Drôme* is the epitome of the synthesising cubist approach taught by Lhote. Idealised, generalised, geometrically constructed and tonally restricted, it demonstrates Dangar's full understanding of Lhote's principles of painting.[44]

The previous year in Mirmande, Lhote had instructed his students to 'Work with your intellect more and let your eyes have a holiday' and had given them instruction on how to compose or 'construct' their landscapes upon a geometric scaffold based upon the ratio of the golden rectangle (1:1.618).[45] In Dangar's 1928 notebook there are several diagrams of some of the possible divisions of a golden rectangle (cat 76) and we can see in her *Mirmande, La Drôme* that she has carefully positioned all of the major elements (trees, village, curve of hills) according to vertical, horizontal, diagonal and curved lines created through the division of the canvas according to this proportion.

These weeks in Mirmande must have been bittersweet for Dangar, who knew that she was soon to return to Australia alone. In late September the four Australians left Mirmande, heading south, with Black continuing to Malta, while Dangar, Crowley and Huntley travelled through Italy, arriving in Rome on 15 October. Dangar and Crowley continued to Naples, where the two friends farewelled each other.[46]

—

Crowley remained in Italy for over a month before returning to Paris in late December. At the start of 1929 Crowley was back painting (with Black) at the Académie Lhote, and she later considered 1929 to be her 'best painting year abroad',[47] one in which she had completed major works such as her *Portrait of Lucie Beynis* 1929 (Art Gallery of New South Wales). Important recognition came when in February two of her paintings were hung alongside Lhote's in the first Salon d'art français indépendant (where they were reviewed positively), which brought Crowley an invitation to exhibit at the prestigious Galerie Bernheim-Jeune.[48]

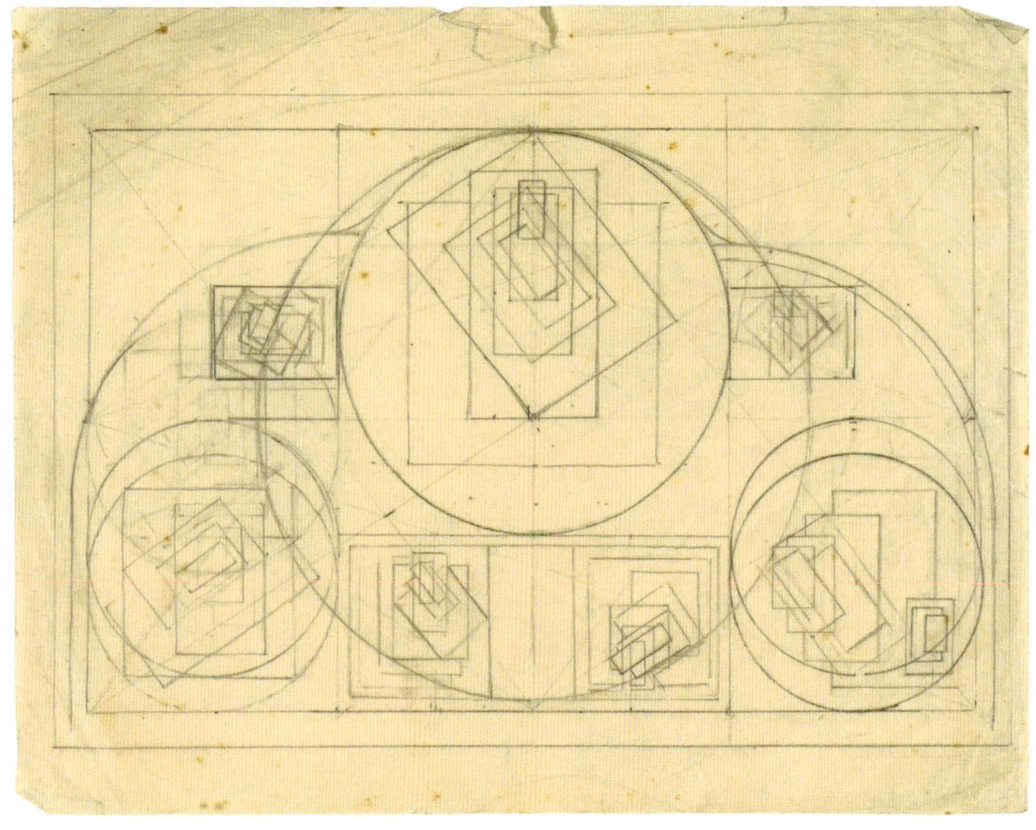

cat 144 Grace Crowley, Cubist composition, study for a mural decoration by Albert Gleizes 1929

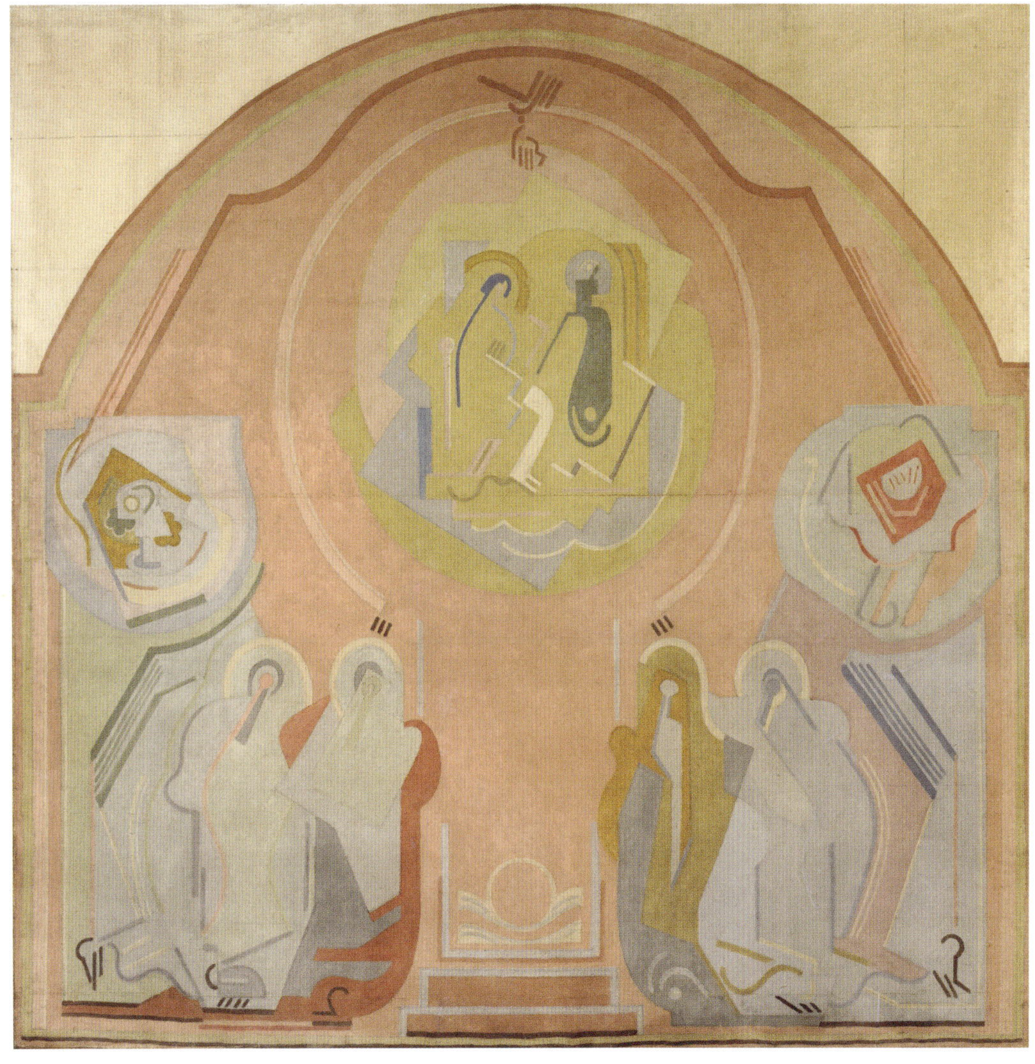

fig 15 Albert Gleizes, *Le Couronnement de la Vierge* (*Coronation of the Virgin*) 1927

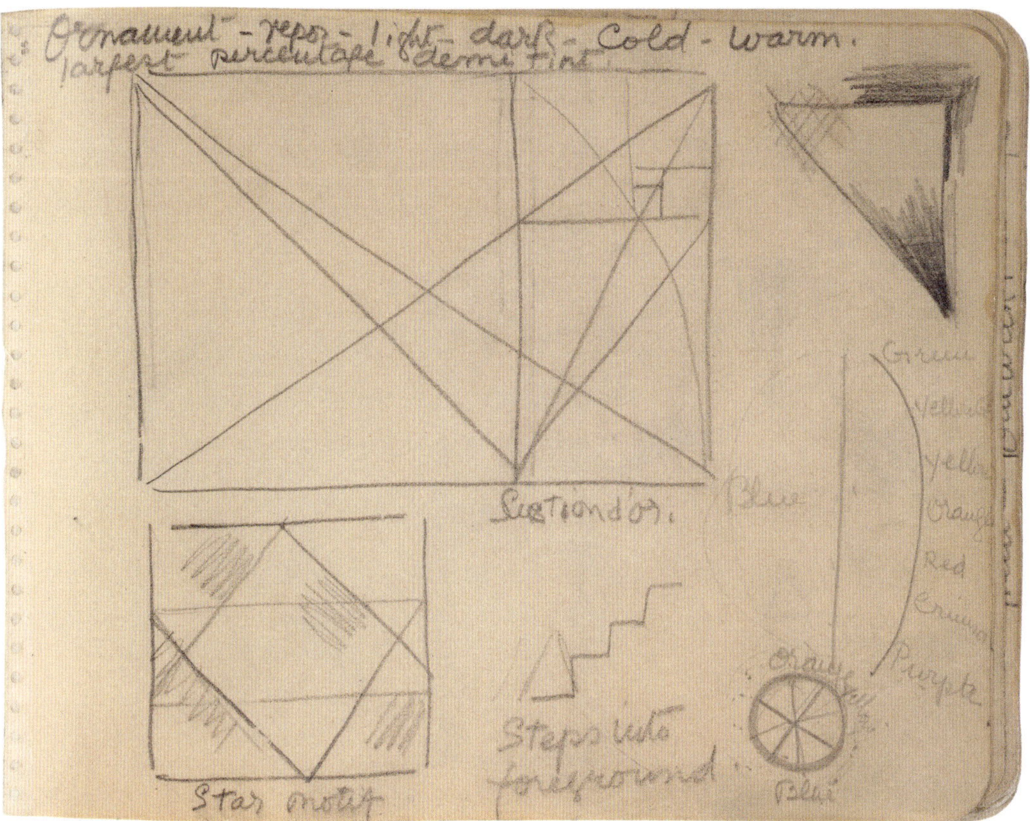

cat 76 Compositional diagrams using the *section d'or* (golden mean) in Notebook 1927–29

In Sydney, 1929 was anything but a good year for Dangar. The previous two-and-a-half years in Paris had set her even further apart from the isolationist Sydney art world. Acutely unhappy, she frequently recalled her spiritual response to Gleizes's painting in the Tuileries, 'the composition of the paintings did not remain clearly in my memory, but … the long lines which had evoked in me a Divine music were constantly in my thoughts'.[49]

> I suddenly got a deep desire to draw nearer to God—Sydney—Mr Ashton—the commercial outlook on Art … shocked me … and my whole thought was a prayer to be rescued from that dreadful throng I found myself amongst. *La Peinture et ses lois*, although so hard to understand, was to me the one confirmation of my belief in Art being God's Creative Spirit, therefore my hopes clung to the name of Albert Gleizes.[50]

Dangar asked Crowley to send her as much material about Gleizes as she could find, and on her own initiative Crowley contacted Gleizes directly. Her intention was to take lessons with him, which she could then transmit back to Dangar. While Gleizes did not take students as such, he responded to Crowley's letter with an invitation for her and Black to visit him in his Paris studio. Over two or three sessions in June, Gleizes demonstrated his approach, with Crowley and Black completing several exercises in gouache under his tutelage. Crowley was then invited to visit his recently founded experimental artistic community at Moly-Sabata in Sablons. Arriving at the start of October, Crowley stayed for approximately three weeks, taking lessons with Robert Pouyaud and again with Gleizes. Most importantly of all, she also asked Gleizes whether Dangar could come to work there, to which he famously replied, 'elle est [déjà] ici' (she's here already).[51] Crowley, on the other hand, had no interest in joining Gleizes's utopian project, nor did her experience with him bring about any immediate change in her work.[52] In Sydney, Dangar received Crowley's telegram informing her of Gleizes's invitation as an 'answer to a prayer'. Later she described her reaction: 'distinctly I heard the command: "Go—Albert Gleizes will help you find God."'[53]

After three-and-a-half years away, Crowley returned to Sydney in early 1930, only a few short days before Dangar's departure back to France. Unbeknown to either of them, this was to be the last time they would see each other. While Dangar and Crowley were united in recalling their years together in France as the happiest of their lives, from that time on, the lives and artistic paths of the two friends diverged forever.[54]

Lhote's teaching had provided Crowley with an approach to modern art that was to become the basis of her own artistic development and teaching for the next decade. For Dangar, already in advance of Crowley in her interest and understanding of modernism, Lhote was a false start. Instead, it was her brief encounter with the spirituality of Gleizes's conceptually rich work at the Salon des Tuileries that was her true new beginning, propelling her away from Australia and back to France—to the long years at Moly-Sabata, to her late religious conversion to Catholicism, and to her place in the history of French art as Cubism's great artist–potter.

II

CONNECTION

1930–1936

MSD

1930[1]

JANUARY–FEBRUARY

Vacates Bridge Street studio and stores belongings with friends and family. Moves in with Crowley's family at 'Glen Riddle' on Kamilaroi/Gomeroi Country near Barraba, New South Wales. Crowley returns to Australia in time to see Dangar before she departs Eora Country/ Sydney on 5 February, accompanied by Estelle Creed and another unidentified student.

MARCH

Arrives in Marseille on 19 March. Meets François Manevy and Robert Pouyaud at the Saint-Rambert-d'Albon train station and travels to Moly-Sabata on 21 March. Is accompanied by Pouyaud to Gleizes's studio in Serrières for the first time. Receives commission from Gleizes to create pochoirs—multi-layered prints using zinc stencils—and is paid in advance. Completes first set of 25 pochoirs within a week but never completes entire commission.

MAY–JULY

Decides to establish a pottery and develop an artisanal craft centre at Moly-Sabata. Pouyaud announces he is leaving Moly-Sabata. Dangar sends Crowley a pochoir by Pouyaud after Gleizes and sends Basil Burdett, director of Macquarie Galleries, a suite of pochoirs after Gleizes. Through Pouyaud's introduction, begins working with Clovis Nicolas at the potteries in Saint-Désirat.

Sydney artist Florence Turner Blake (also known as Florence Dash, Florence Greaves and Florence Mofflin) visits Moly-Sabata from London. She stays for several weeks and receives lessons with Robert Pouyaud. Dangar sends a set of gouache studies to Crowley and advises she return completed exercises for correction. Sends Crowley lessons in colour theory in relation to translation and rotation.

Musicians César and Mido Geoffray, from Lyon, visit Moly-Sabata for a month.

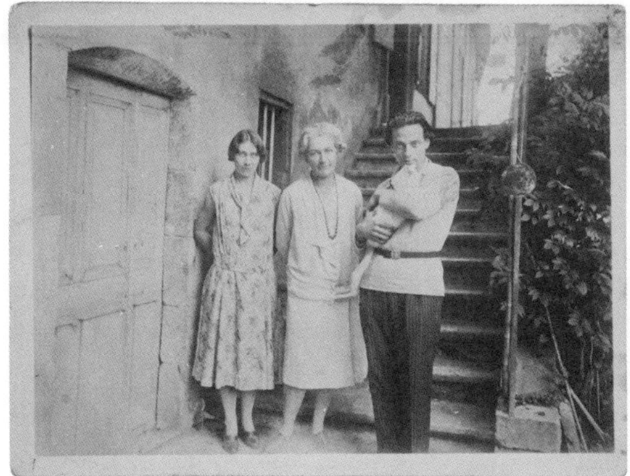

fig 16 Cécile Pouyaud, Anne Dangar and Robert Pouyaud at Moly-Sabata, 1930

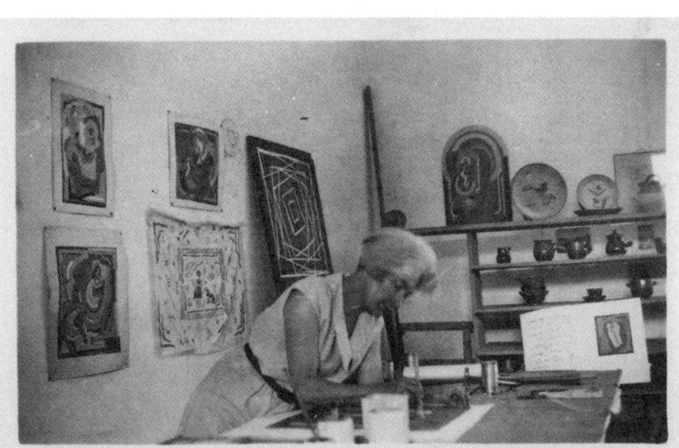

fig 17 Anne Dangar creating pochoirs at Moly-Sabata, c 1931

SEPTEMBER–OCTOBER

A fire destroys the home of her sister Ruby and brother-in-law Andrew Singleton in Mondrook on Biripi Country, and its contents. Much of her work and correspondence is destroyed.

NOVEMBER

Manevy, Pouyaud and Pouyaud's wife Cécile leave Moly-Sabata on 1 November, leaving Dangar alone at Moly-Sabata.

DECEMBER

Estelle Creed arrives at Moly-Sabata to study with Gleizes for several weeks.

1931

JANUARY–FEBRUARY

Undertakes lessons with Gleizes and is worried he does not like her or her work. Her relationship with Creed deteriorates. Evie Hone and Mainie Jellett visit Moly-Sabata late January. André Grelin moves to Moly-Sabata with his wife and two children. Dangar's relationship with Grelin sours quickly as he does little to contribute to communal duties.

Receives first pottery commission—jugs and butter saucers from the Schaeffers, who run the Hôtel Schaeffer in Serrières. Asks Creed to move to the nearby hotel, as tensions with her escalate. Creed is eventually hospitalised and returns to Australia.

MARCH

Completes seven compositions, which she feels are gaudy. Gleizes had forbidden her from using greys and asked her instead to harmonise pure colours. Visits the pottery with Hone and Jellett. Hone buys Moly-Sabata 200 francs worth of dining ware and the pair compliment Dangar's ceramics. Jellett and Hone return to Ireland. The Gleizeses depart Serrières, not planning to return until Easter.

APRIL–MAY

Continues to work at the pottery. Grelin departs Moly-Sabata. César and Mido Geoffray leave Lyon to live at Moly-Sabata with their daughter Gilka. Their former servant Lucie Deveyle wishes to accompany them and join the community. Deveyle becomes Dangar's close companion.

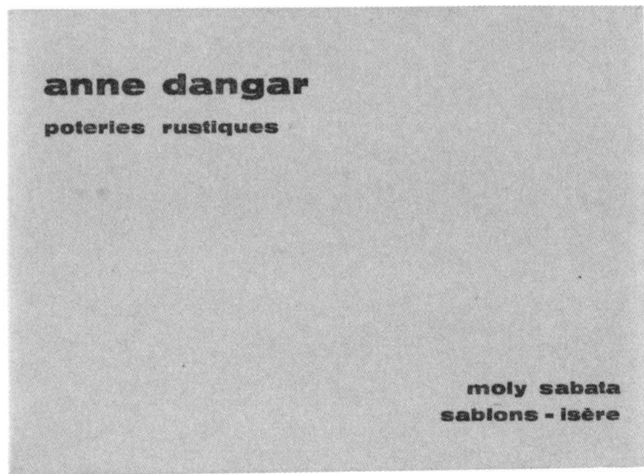

fig 18 Anne Dangar's business card, 1930s–40s

OCTOBER

Decides she would like to introduce weaving to the community. Writes to Crowley about her moving to Moly-Sabata. Crowley wants only to paint and not to follow the strict rules of the community, so writes that she would like to live in a house together in Sablons. Following tensions with Gleizes and his wife Juliette Roche, Dangar's plans for Crowley to join her do not eventuate. Dangar holds her first exhibition at Moly-Sabata, which is a great success. Sells many pieces to locals from Sablons and Serrières, as well as to a Monsieur and Madame Béchetoille from Annonay, a Turkish artist from Lhote's Mirmande group, and Americans from Montparnasse. Contemplates returning to Australia and setting up a pottery near Ruby's home in Mondrook on Biripi Country but decides against the idea.

1932

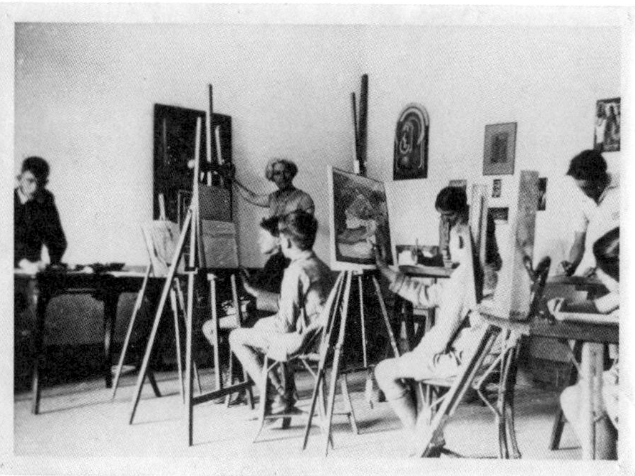

fig 19 Anne Dangar and students at Moly-Sabata, c 1931

JANUARY–FEBRUARY

Works with Gleizes three mornings a week for two months. Considers returning to Australia and working at the Frensham School in Mittagong on Tharawal/ Dharawal Country, New South Wales, but is advised by its headmistress Winifred West that she will not be able to start a pottery. Begins offering art classes for local children. Struggles to find time for painting and is busy at the pottery. Crowley sends money, the first of many similar gifts she makes over the next 20 years.

MARCH

Makes her first ceramics independently at the potteries in Saint-Désirat. The Gleizeses are present for the opening of the kiln. Hone and Jellett visit again.

OCTOBER

Michel Seuphor arrives on 1 October and stays at Moly-Sabata for several weeks. Tensions develop between Dangar and the Gleizeses. Dangar expresses her displeasure about the previous six weeks of hardship and receives a harsh response from Roche. Contemplates using the last of her money to return to Australia. Attends the wedding of Mademoiselle Rattier (later Steinbach) at Château Peyraud. Madame Steinbach becomes a close friend and supporter.

MAY

Arranges to send pottery to store-owner Margaret Jaye in Sydney. Sue Alexandre, friend and fellow potter, stays at Moly-Sabata.

JULY

Begins working at Poterie Bert in Roussillon with Henri Bert and potter Jean-Marie Paquaud. Allows Crowley to buy her a bicycle to make the 14-kilometre round trip journey to the pottery easier; however, it is cumbersome and she does not use it. The shipment of pottery for Margaret Jaye arrives in Eora Country/Sydney and much is broken. Jaye puts in another order regardless.

AUGUST–SEPTEMBER

Alexandre visits Moly-Sabata for at least a fortnight. She pays someone to come and attend to household duties so Dangar can teach her. Together they visit Saint-Vallier, Ponsa and Saint-Uze, visiting regional potteries including those specialising in *grès* (stoneware). Dangar becomes interested in teaching children craft and encourages Crowley to incorporate craft in her teaching in Australia. Decides Jaye's prices are too high and sends pottery to Crowley instead, to sell from her studio.

NOVEMBER

Exhibits pottery at Musée d'Annonay. The museum acquires several pieces. Receives commissions from prominent Annonay families: the Montgolfiers and the Béchetoilles. Julian Ashton writes to advise he is holding an exhibition of past and present students' work and she wishes to submit *Mirmande, La Drôme* 1928 and some pottery. There is no evidence these works were included; likely they were too modern for Ashton. Begins to receive commissions and payment for pottery from friends in Australia. Provides classes in decoration to the girls of Sablons.

DECEMBER

Exhibits work and the work of her students in the Tournon-sur-Rhône regional craft exhibition. Wins a prize and the exposure results in more commissions. Visits the potteries at Saint-Vallier and Saint-Uze in the Drôme.

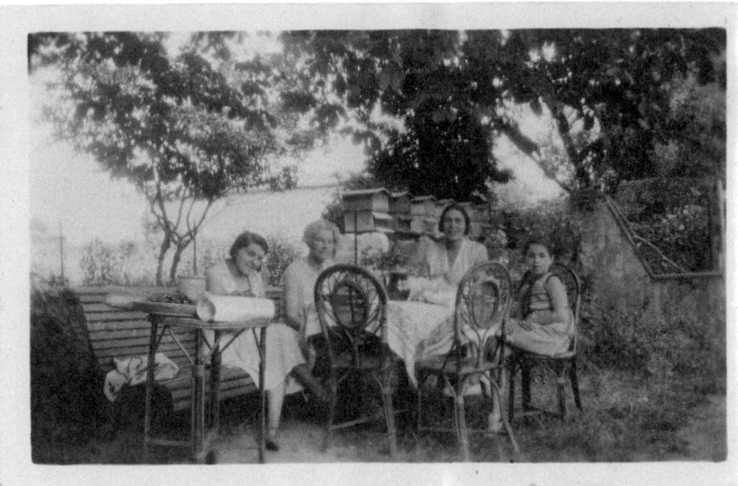

fig 20 Lucie Deveyle, Anne Dangar, Mido and Gilka Geoffray at Moly-Sabata, 1930s

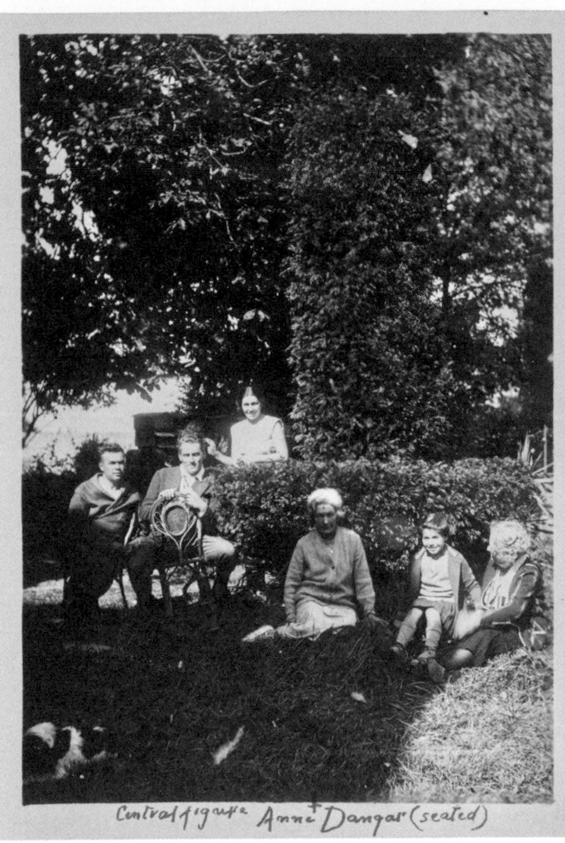

fig 21 César Geoffray, René Corniot, Mido Geoffray, Anne Dangar, Gilka Geoffray and Madame Geoffray-Mandy in the gardens at Moly-Sabata, 1931

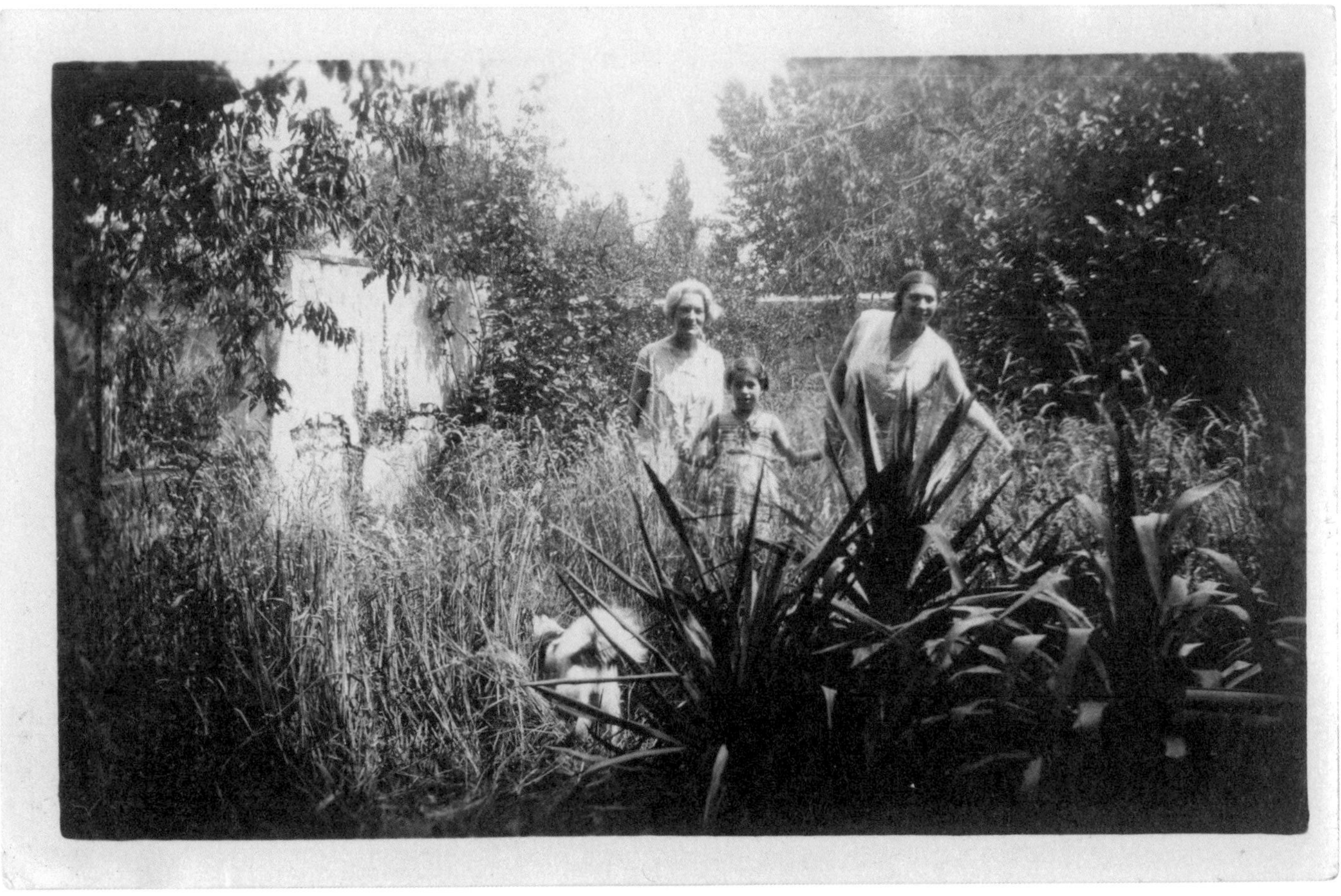

fig 22 Anne Dangar, Gilka and Mido Geoffray at Moly-Sabata, 1931

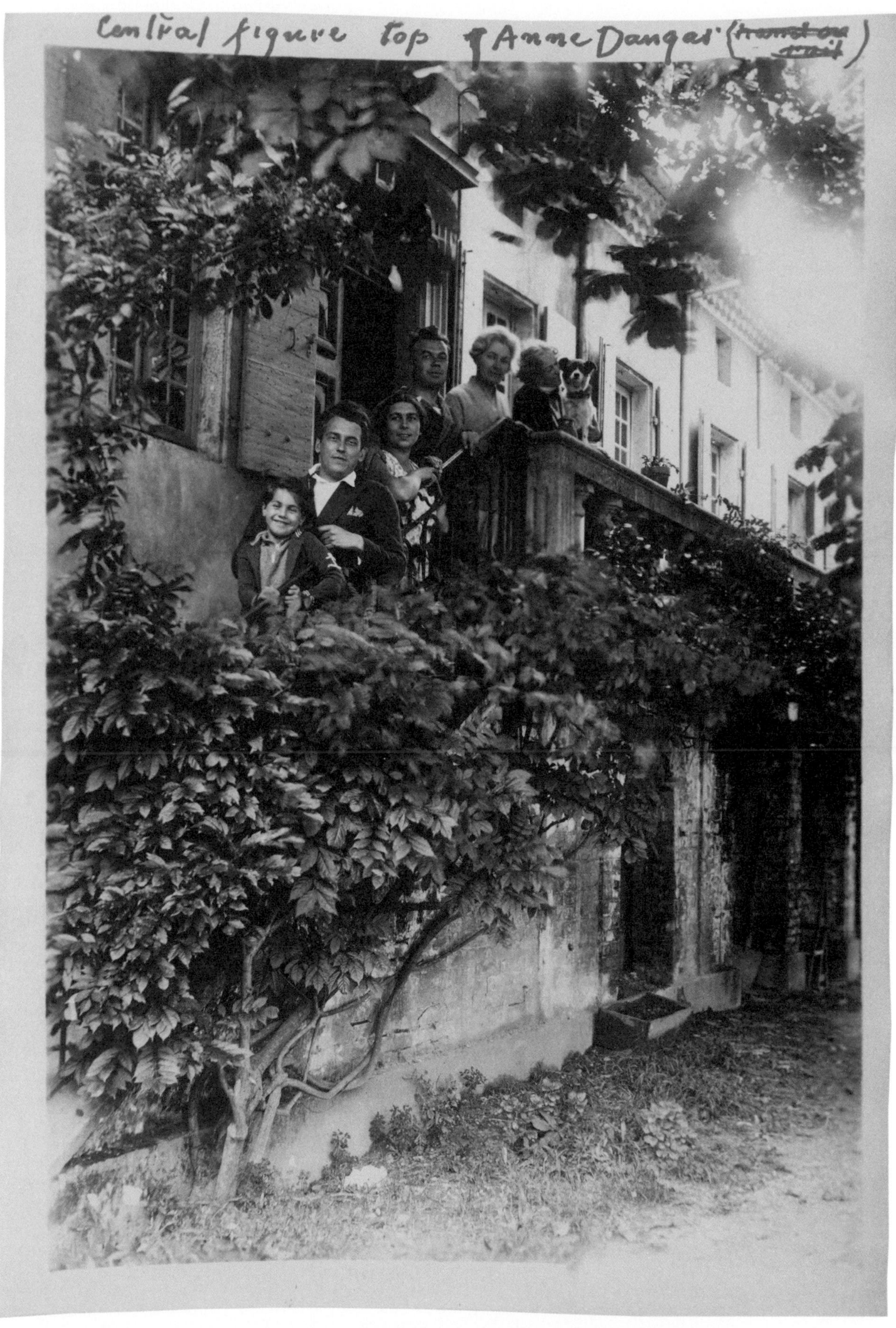

fig 23 Gilka Geoffray, René Corniot, Mido and César Geoffray, Anne Dangar and Madame Geoffray-Mandy on the stairs at Moly-Sabata, 1931

1933

JANUARY–FEBUARY

Works in Gleizes's studio and decorates plates. Their relationship improves. Sends Crowley an essay and diagrams by Pouyaud as well as François Forichon's book on colour *La couleur: ses manifestations, son rôle dans les arts, ses harmonies: manuel du coloriste* 1916 (*Colour: its manifestation, role in art, harmonies: colour manual*).

MARCH

Tells Crowley that she is happy to hear of Crowley's developing relationship with Rah Fizelle. Her relationship with Roche deteriorates. After witnessing Roche pull a sword out of her cane to reprimand a dog, claims she is not safe and asks Crowley to look out for any work whatsoever in Australia. Crowley writes to Roche asking her to be kinder. Painter Jacques Plasse and his wife Bilou Le Caisne move to Moly-Sabata with their two children and set up a weaving workshop.

MAY

Asks Gleizes whether she should begin signing her pottery pieces 'MSD', to represent herself and the Moly-Sabata community. Crowley proposes an exhibition of Dangar's work in Eora Country/Sydney.

JULY–AUGUST

Attends the Annonay fete and sells 200 francs' worth of work in half an hour. Gleizes sends Dangar copies of *Abstraction & Creation*, *Art & Science* and *Sud Magazine*. Becomes interested in the Oxford Movement of the 1830s after Hone sends her articles around the time of its centenary. She is drawn to the movement's focus on early Christian traditions of faith which she identifies as allied with Gleizes's work and philosophies.

1934

JANUARY–FEBRUARY

A shipment of pottery arrives in Eora Country/Sydney and is sold and dispersed among Crowley and her friends.

With the Geoffrays spending time working in Lyon, Deveyle moves into Dangar's part of the house. Overseen by the potter Anjaleras, Dangar begins working at the pottery at Cliousclat near Mirmande, where she produces large plates.

MARCH

Is invited by Gleizes to join the Abstraction-Création collective. Dorrit Black and her mother visit Moly-Sabata and stay in the area for several days, also visiting Gleizes in Serrières.

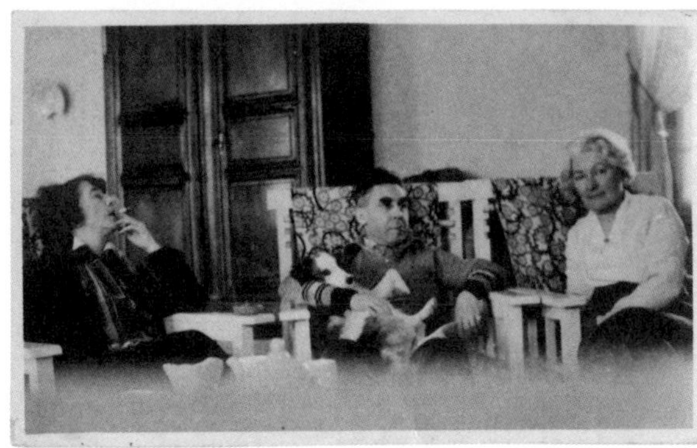

fig 24 Juliette Roche, Albert Gleizes and Anne Dangar, 1930s–40s

MAY–JUNE

Receives first commission for a plaque of the Virgin and Child from the Geoffrays. Translates two lectures by Gleizes from French to English for him to deliver at the Slade School in London. They are attended by Ruth Ainsworth, Dorrit Black and Mainie Jellett.

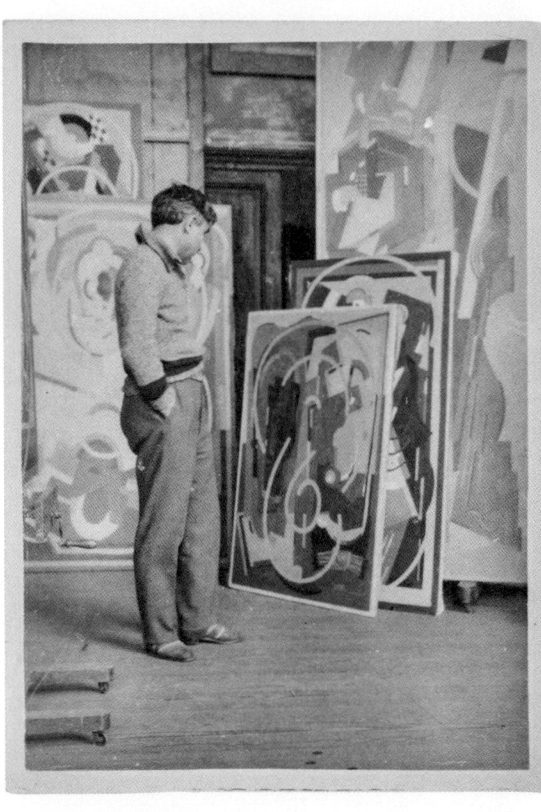

fig 25 Albert Gleizes in his studio, c 1934

1935

MARCH

Jacques Plasse and Bilou Le Caisne leave Moly-Sabata, taking their looms.

APRIL

Ailsa Lee Brown and family visit, spending Good Friday (21 April) at Moly-Sabata.

MAY

Receives a commission for a dinner service from the doctor who accompanied Estelle Creed to Australia. Attends tea at the Lyon home of the British Consul Mr Bullock, to celebrate King George's Silver Jubilee.

JULY

Dangar's pottery consignment arrives in Eora Country/Sydney. A quarter of the pottery is broken. Dangar's friend John Pye visits Moly-Sabata, staying nearby.

AUGUST

Has been producing pochoirs and is slowly paying off debt to Gleizes. Undertakes a four-day sketching trip in Thorrenc, a town three kilometres from Saint-Désirat. Visits Cliousclat and Mirmande, travelling via Nice with Pye.

OCTOBER

Contemplates returning to Australia and establishing a pottery outside Eora Country/Sydney.

NOVEMBER–DECEMBER

Jules Pignault, an old potter from Saint-Désirat, dies. Dangar sends the first of five lessons to Crowley and her students with the instruction that they return their exercises by mail for Gleizes to review and make comment on.

AUGUST–SEPTEMBER

Ruth Ainsworth visits Moly-Sabata and stays for several weeks. She learns pottery and in exchange brings a small loom and teaches Deveyle to weave. With Ainsworth, Dangar undertakes a walking tour to Mount Pilat and surrounds in September. They undertake a road trip with Maurice Grimaud to Saint-André (near Nîmes), returning via Montélimar and Mirmande.

OCTOBER

An exhibition of work from Moly-Sabata is held at Marcel Michaud's gallery Stylclair in Lyon. From late 1935 until the end of her life, exhibits regularly with Michaud, first at Stylclair, and from 1938 at Folklore. Sends more pottery to Crowley in Eora Country/Sydney. Is asked by Michaud to create a tiled tabletop—her first. He provides the table and sources industrial tiles from Monsieur Boissonnet of Saint-Vallier.

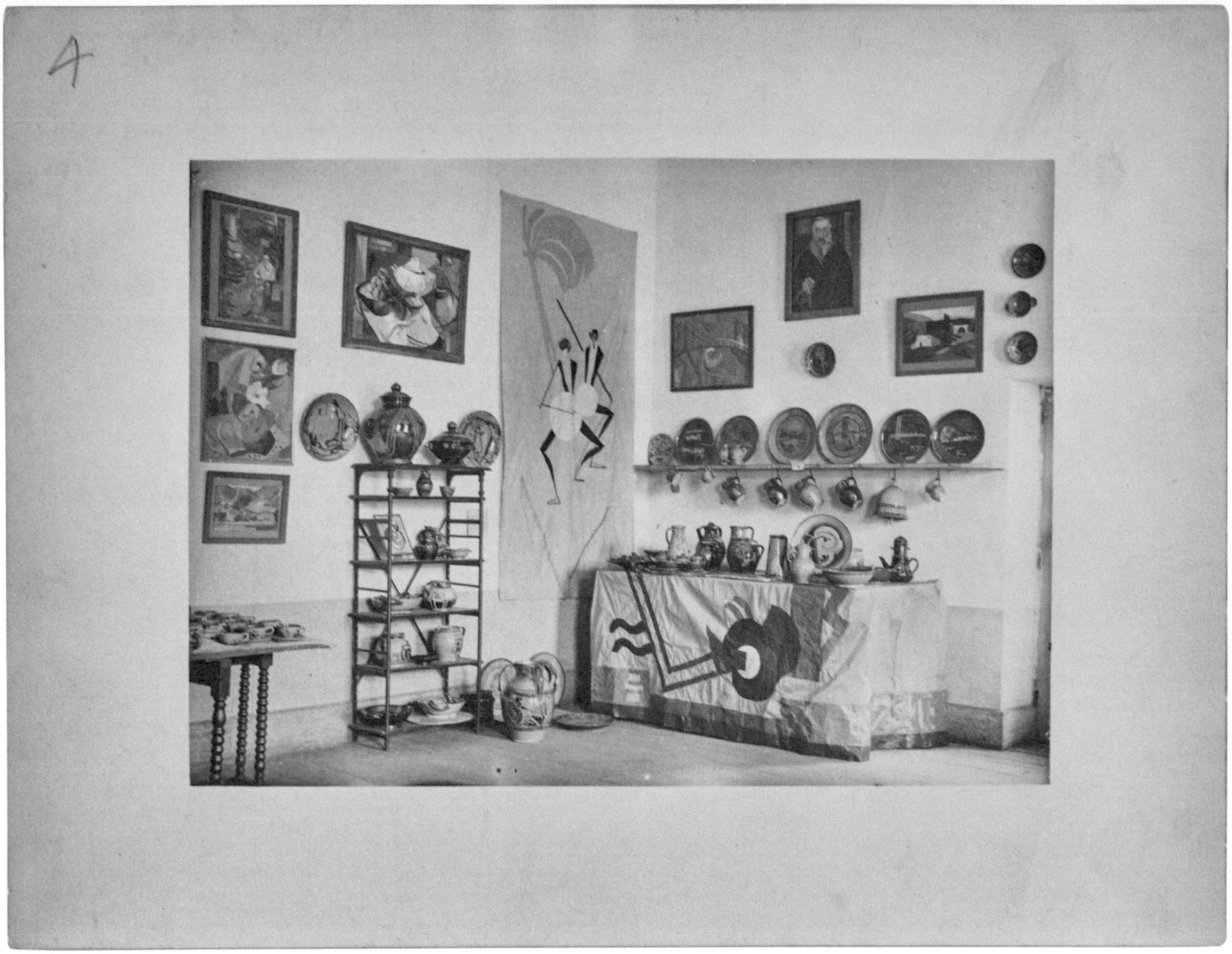

fig 26 Installation view featuring ceramics by Anne Dangar, textiles by Juliette Roche and paintings by the Moly-Sabata community, annual exhibition at Moly-Sabata, 1934

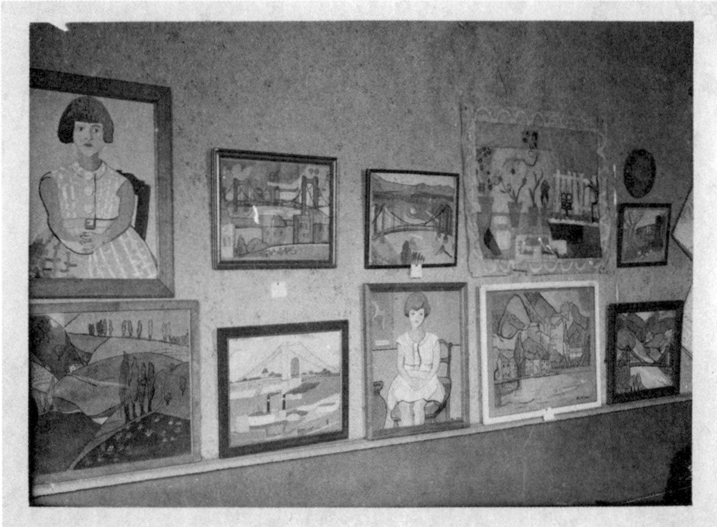

fig 27 Paintings by Anne Dangar's students on display at the annual Moly-Sabata exhibition, c 1934

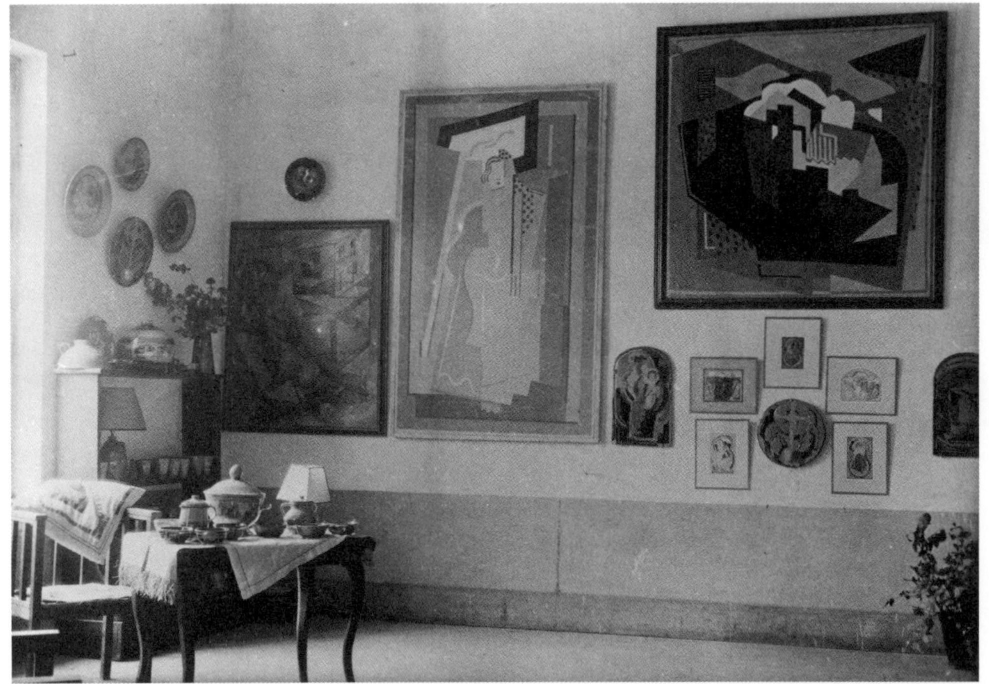

fig 28 Installation view featuring ceramics by Anne Dangar and paintings by Albert Gleizes, annual exhibition at Moly-Sabata, 1934

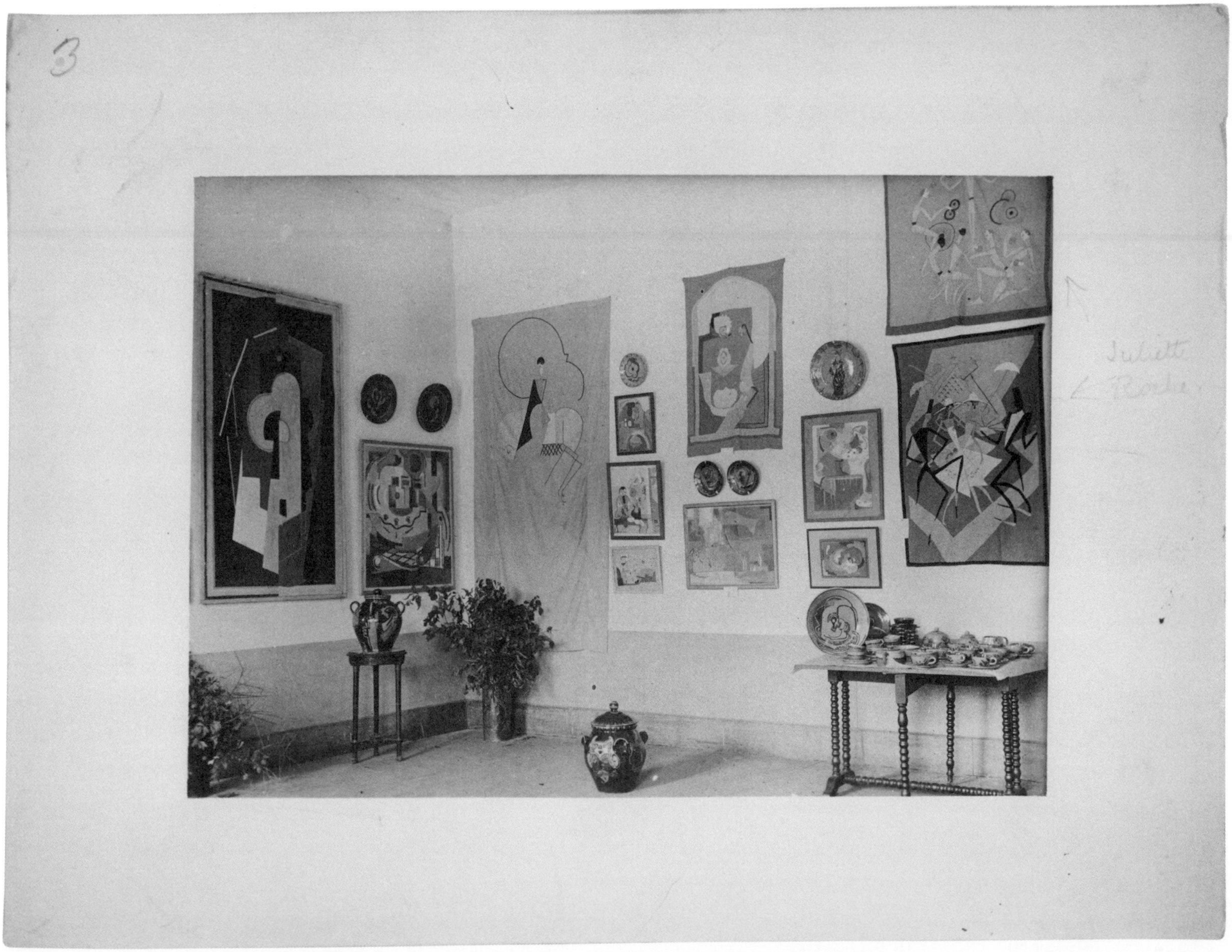

fig 29 Installation view featuring ceramics by Anne Dangar, textiles by Juliette Roche and paintings by Albert Gleizes, annual exhibition at Moly-Sabata, 1934

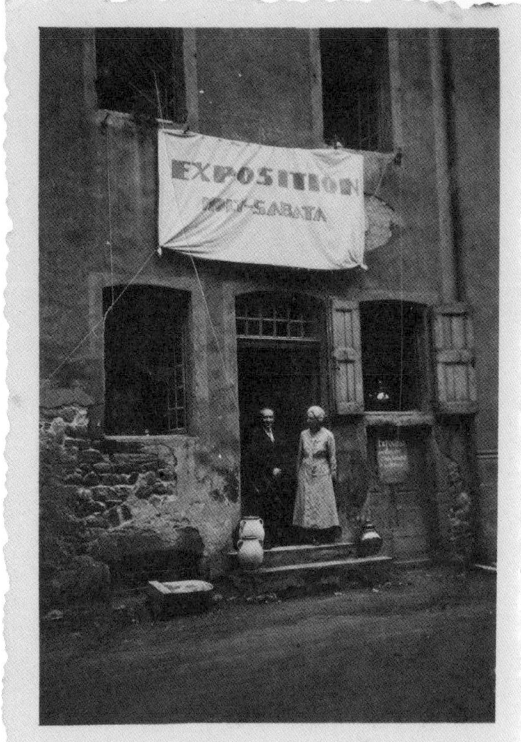

fig 30 Annual exhibition of Moly-Sabata, quai Jules-Roche, Serrières, 15–25 August 1935

SEPTEMBER

With Sue Alexandre, undertakes a walking trip in the Haute-Loire. Travels to Grenoble with John Pye and explores the mountains.

OCTOBER

Winsome 'Winty' Hall, the sister of her friend and former student Nancy Hall, visits Moly-Sabata.

NOVEMBER

Gains new pupil, Monsieur Raibaud of Pélussin, who becomes a close friend.

1936

APRIL

Visits pottery at Saint-Uze and works with the potter Monsieur Delaunay.

MAY–JUNE

Attends a lecture by Gleizes at Annonay. Crowley cancels plans to visit as she must pay additional taxes and no longer has sufficient funds for passage. Dangar argues with Roche and contemplates leaving Moly-Sabata in three years. Relationship with Gleizes improves. They spend time together while Roche visits Paris, travelling to the Cliousclat pottery and Mirmande for the day, where they meet with Marguerite Lhote, André Lhote's wife. Gleizes invites her to spend Pentecost (31 May) with them in Sablons.

AUGUST

Dangar's pottery arrives in Eora Country/Sydney and there is an issue processing it in customs until Julian Ashton intervenes. All pieces are purchased by Dangar's friends and supporters.

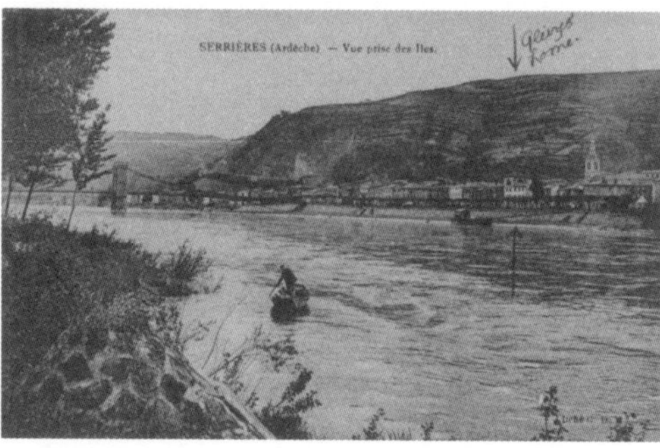

fig 31 Postcard of Serrières sent to Dorrit Black, inscribed by Anne Dangar, c1930

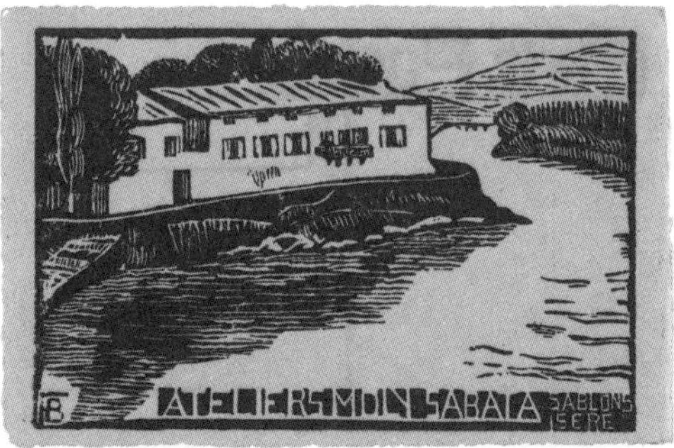

fig 32 Francine Bensa, *Ateliers Moly Sabata Sablons Isère* 1937

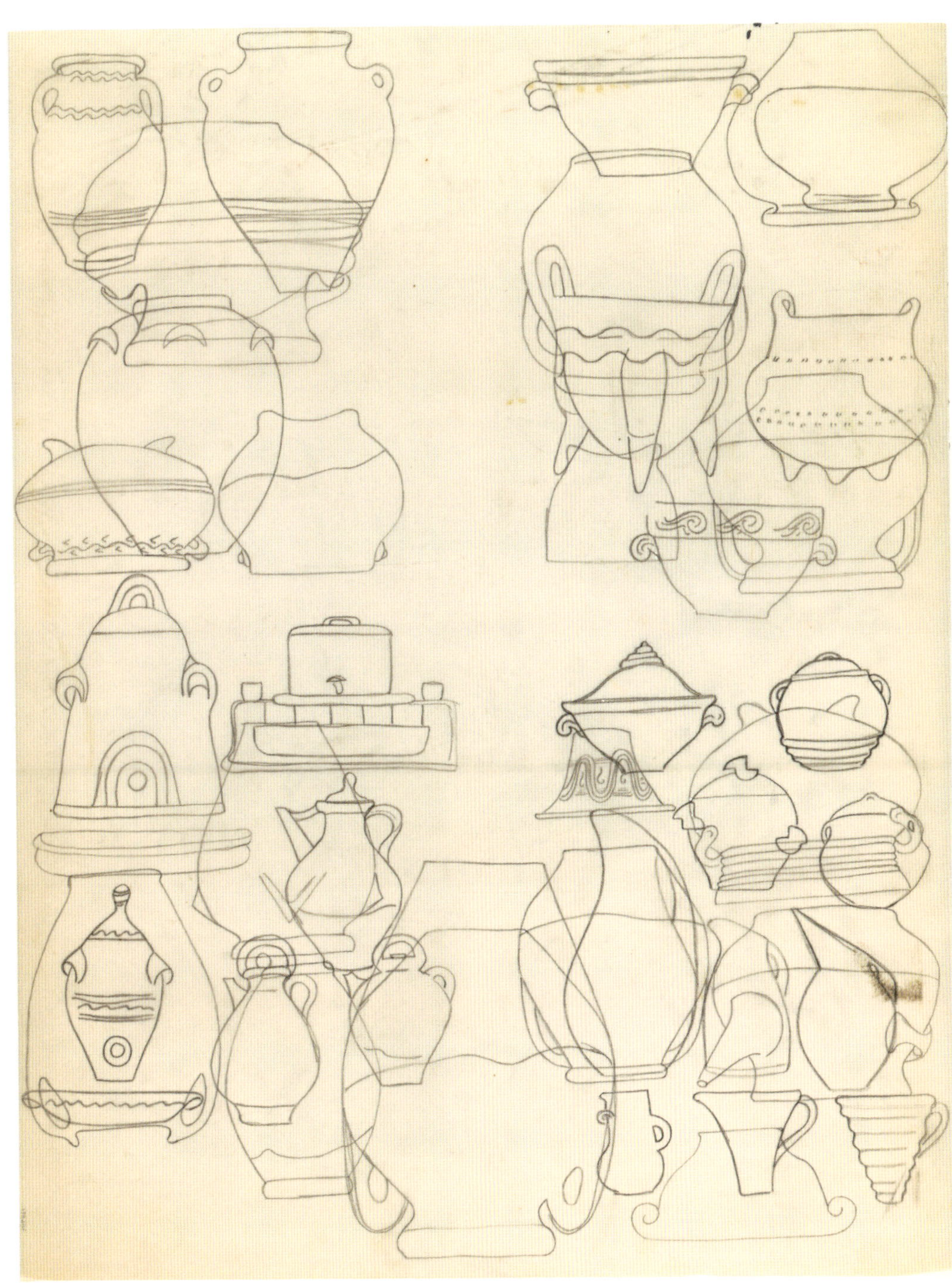

cat 88 Designs of ceramic forms 1930s

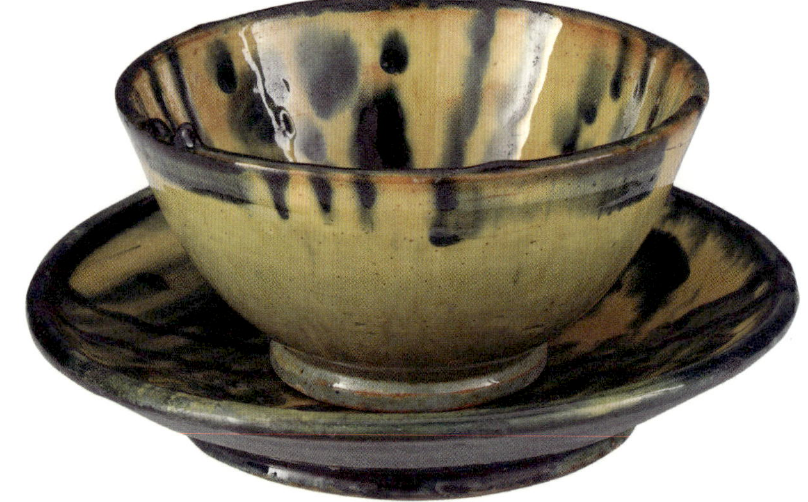

cat 5 Bowl and saucer 1930–32

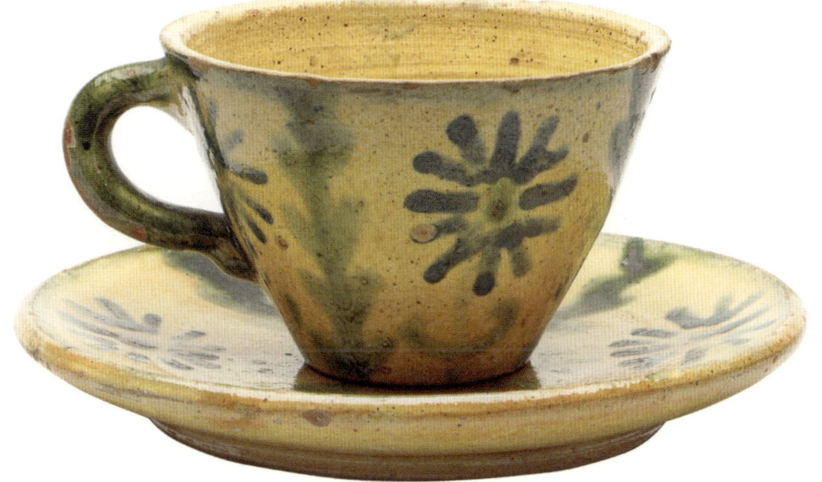

cat 6 Cup and saucer 1930–32

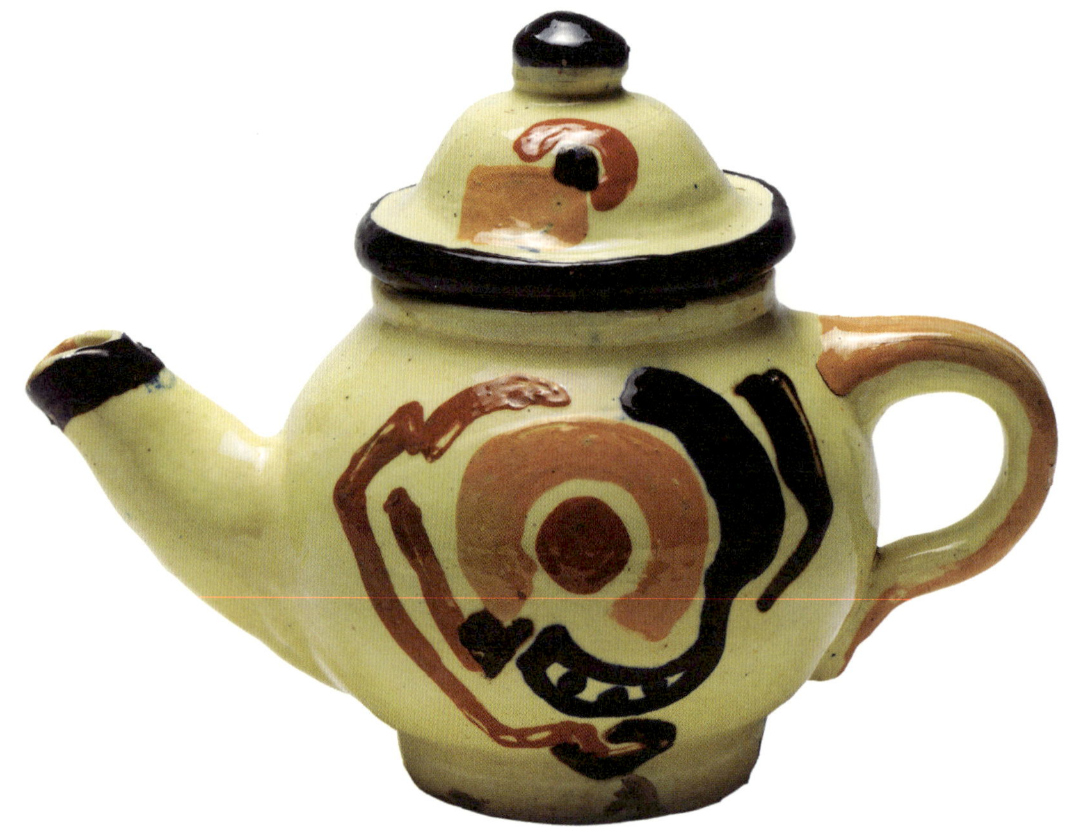

cat 14 Teapot 1932–33

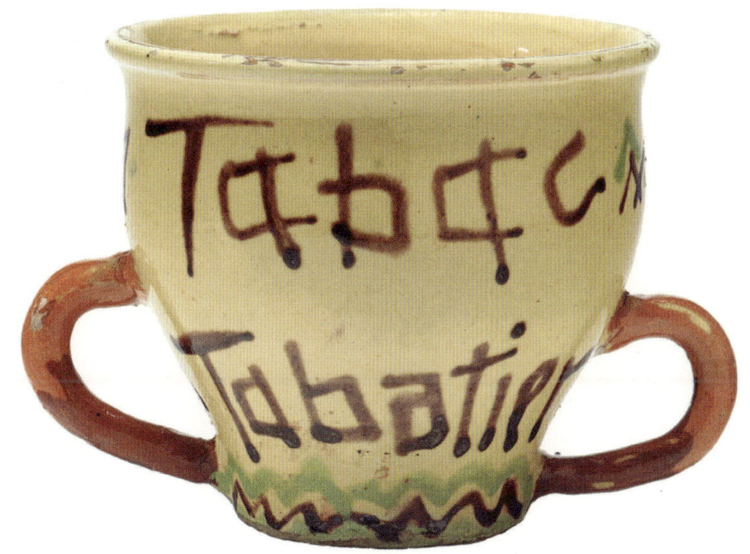

cat 15 Tobacco jar 1932–33

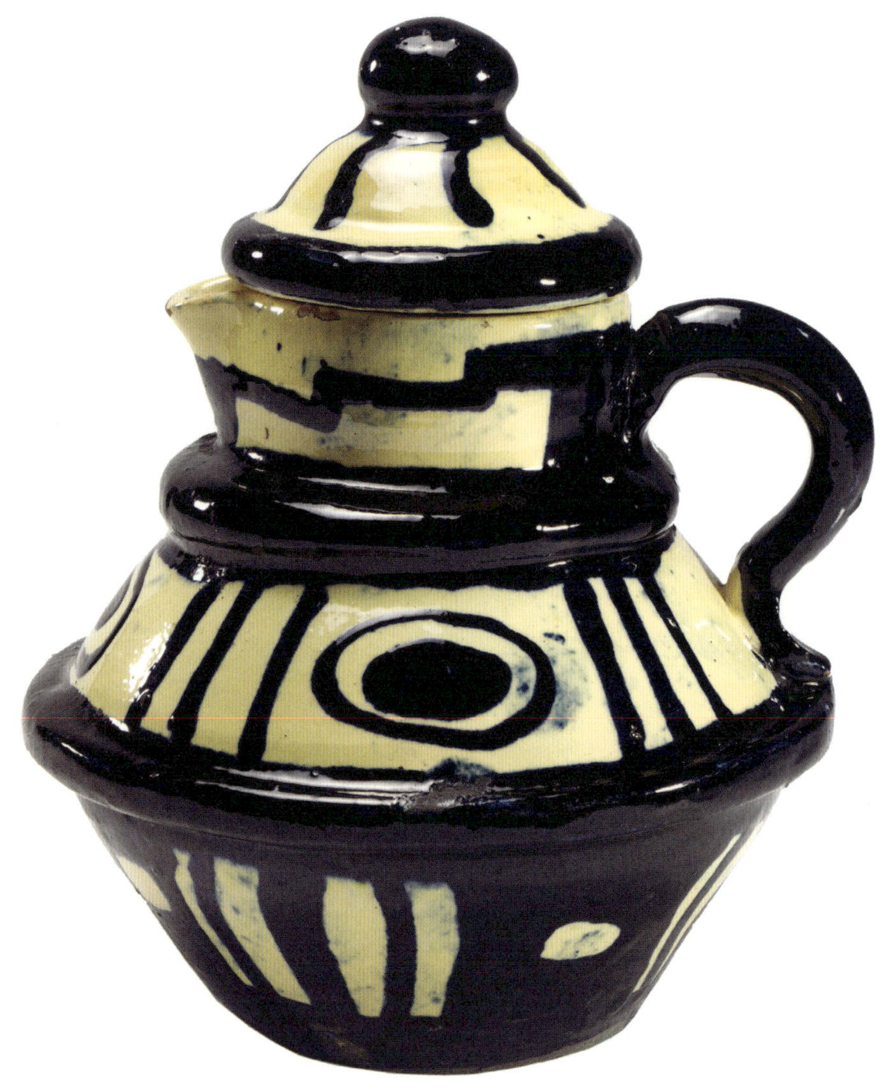

cat 17 Coffee pot with lid 1932–33

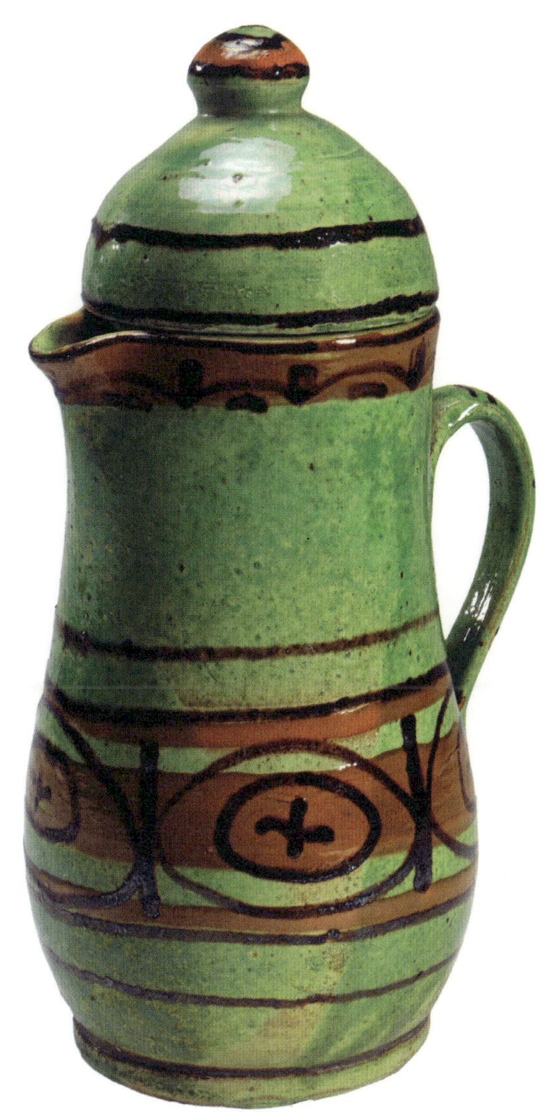

cat 8 Coffee pot with lid 1931–33

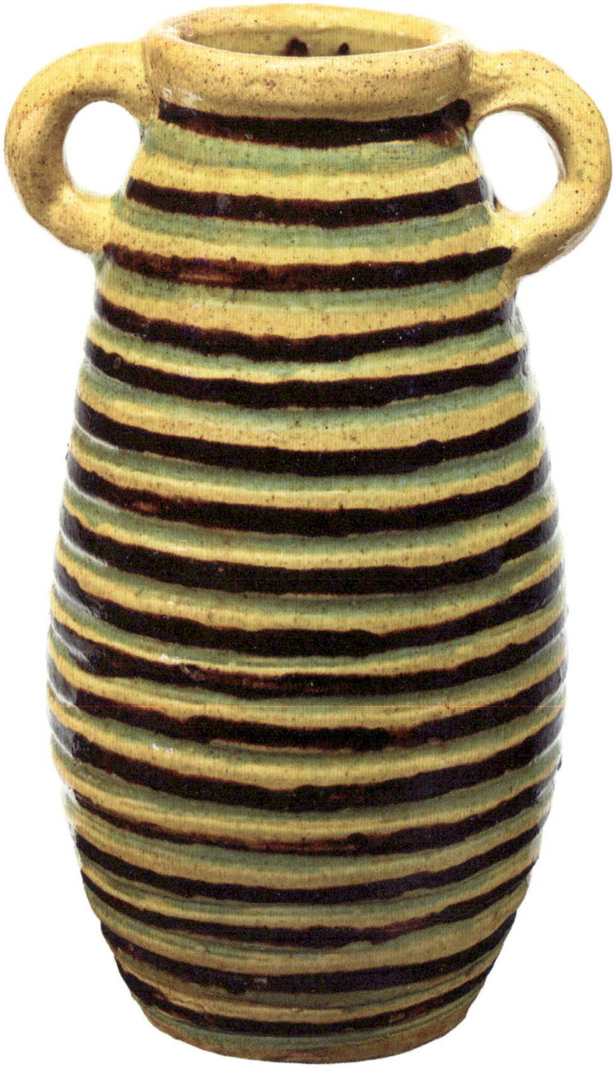

cat 31 Vase 1933–46

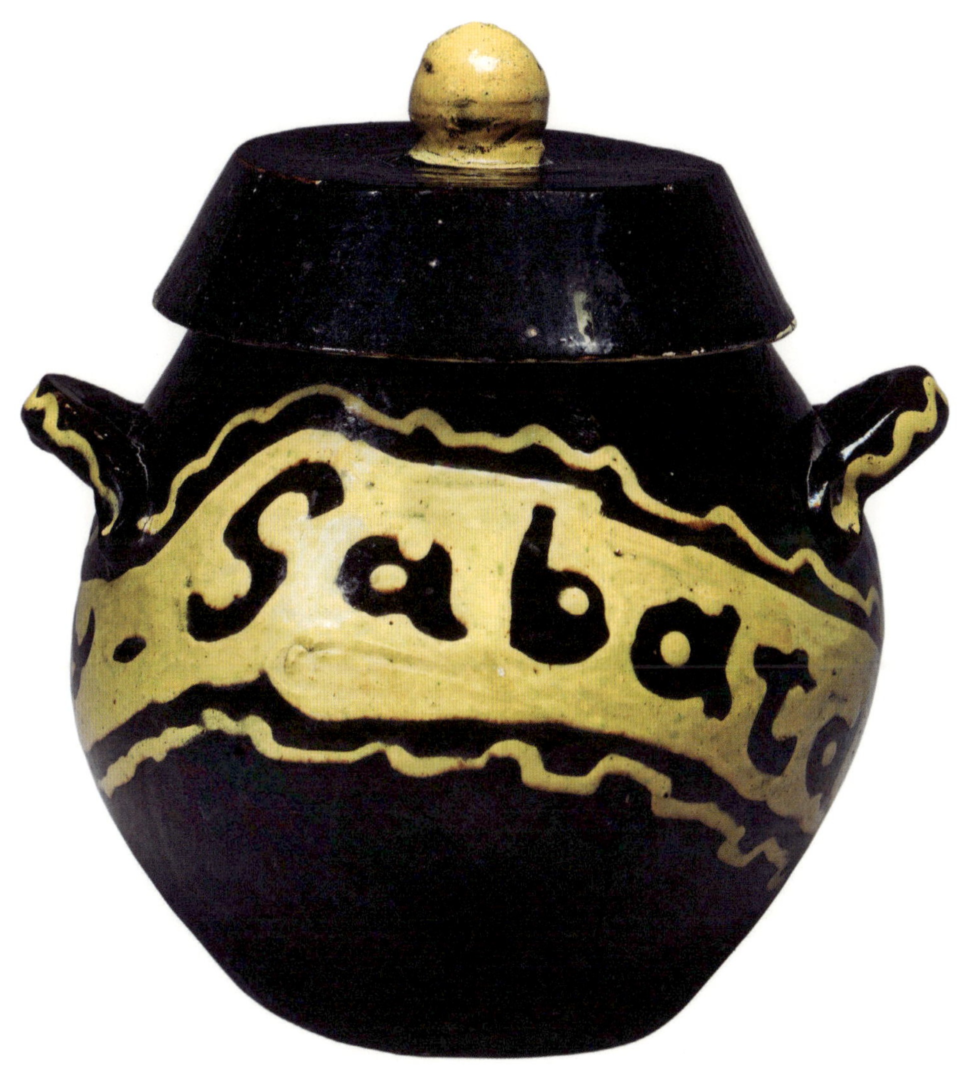

cat 7 Moly-Sabata honey pot with lid 1931–33

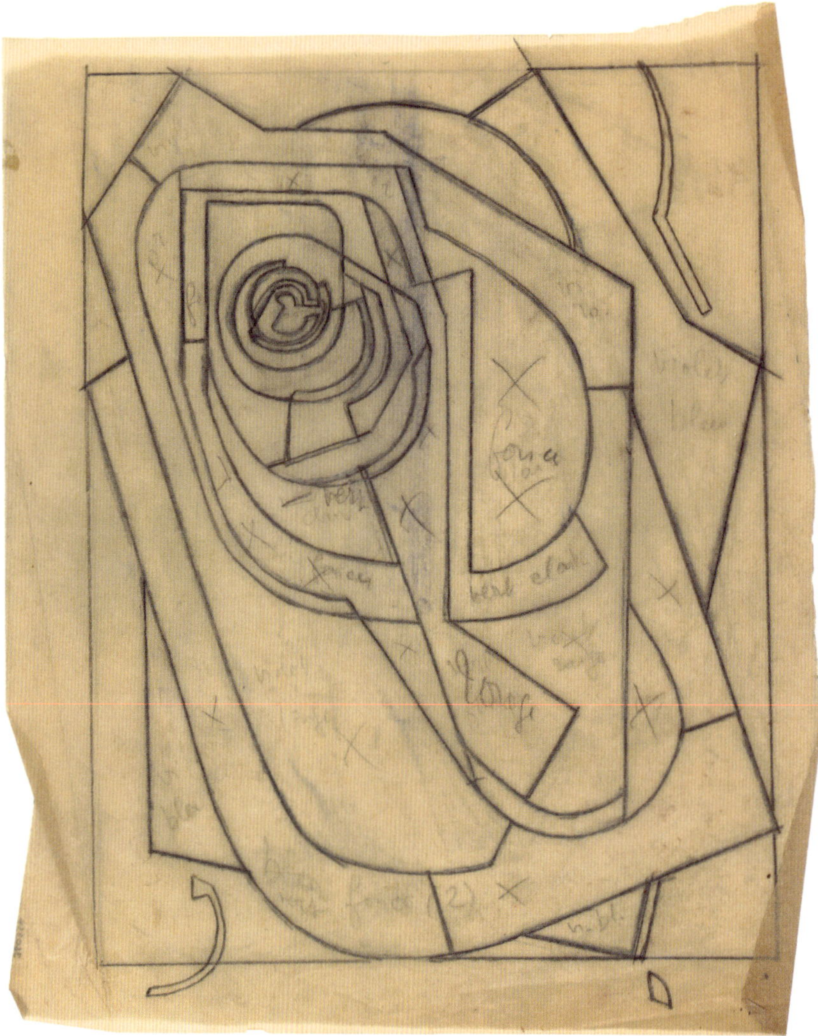

cat 79 Design for cubist composition with colour notes 1930s

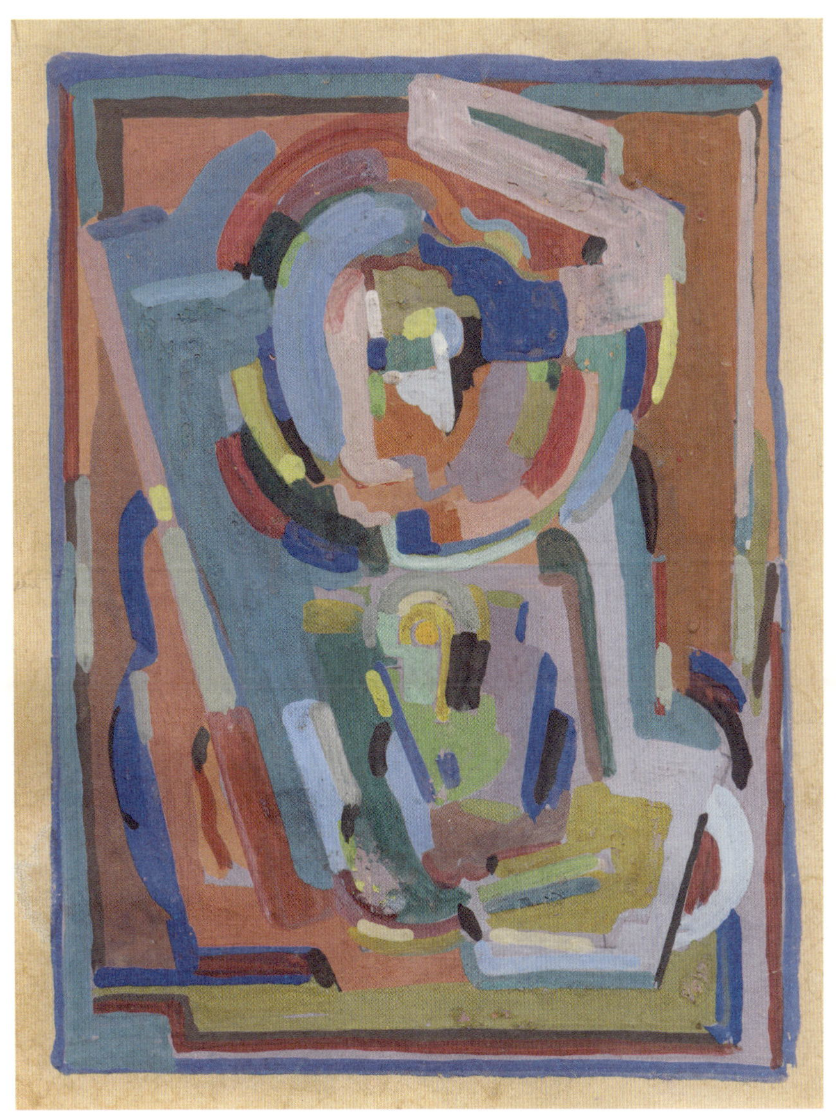

cat 90 Cubist composition 1931–33

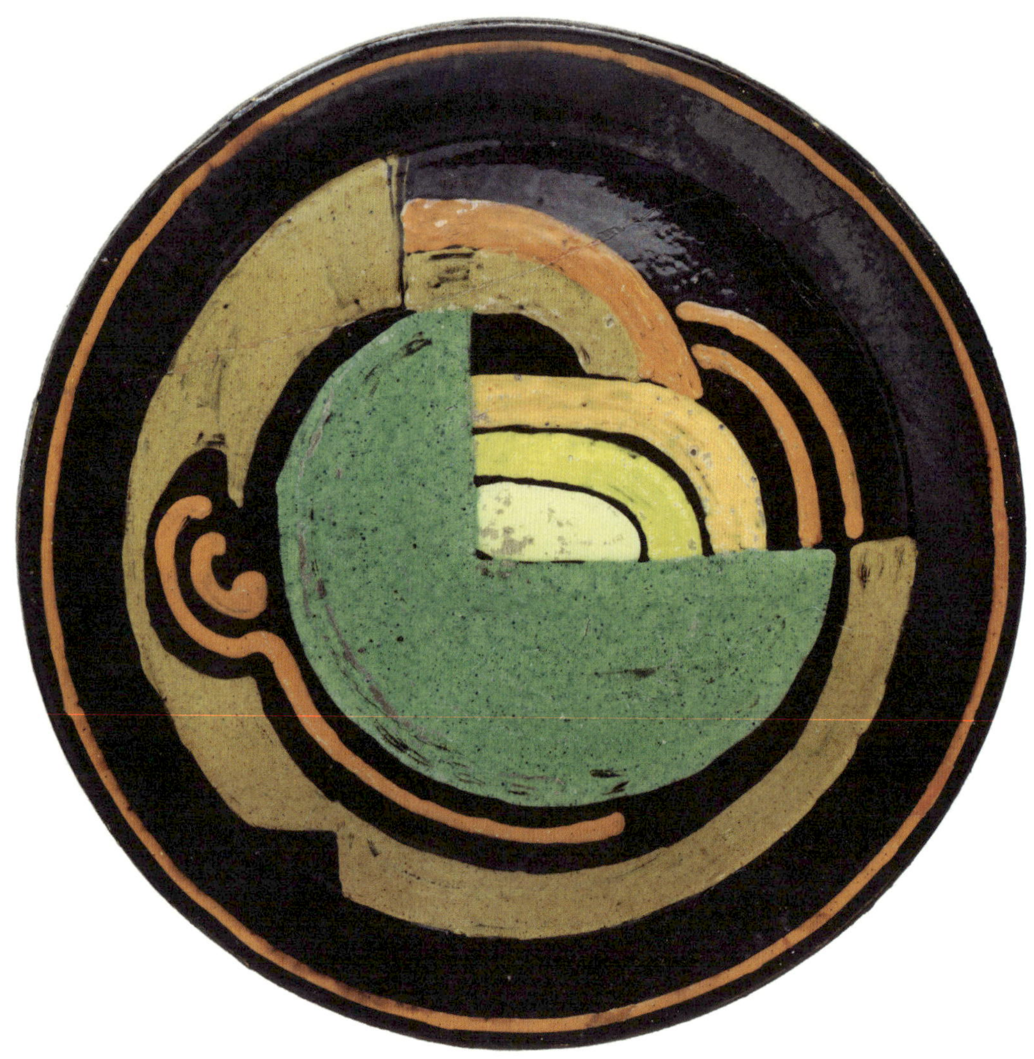

cat 16 Plate with cubist design 1932–33

II

REBECCA EDWARDS

Anne Dangar arrived at Moly-Sabata, Gleizes's artist community in Sablons, on 21 March 1930, almost two months after leaving Sydney. Located south of Lyon in the French department of Isère, Sablons is a small town situated on a river island, bordered in all directions by the Rhône, which branches out into two distributaries at its southern end and merges again in the north. To the west in the Ardèche, nestled in the hill-slope and only a short distance across the bridge, is the larger town of Serrières, where Gleizes and his wife Juliette Roche lived part-time and had a studio. The Drôme lies directly to the south, a large region encompassing Mirmande that stretches almost all the way to Avignon.

Built in the eighteenth century, Moly-Sabata is located directly on the banks of the Rhône on the Sablons side, offering spectacular views of the water and Serrières landscape. Its name supposedly derives from the French term *sabots mouillés*, meaning 'wet clogs', referring to the flooding that residents regularly experience.[1] With its quaint, pale-pink exterior and green shutters, rambling gardens and picturesque aspect, 'Moly', as it is affectionately known, appeared to Dangar and many others who passed through its gates to be a 'dream'.[2] Even so, life at Moly-Sabata was often intensely difficult. Over the following years, Dangar would establish a life and her reputation as a cubist potter within its gates, dedicating herself to the artistic and cultural community it represented.

When Dangar arrived the centrepiece of Moly-Sabata was Gleizes, a man she had never met and had corresponded with only briefly but quickly accepted as her artistic and spiritual master. Gleizes was one of the earliest exponents of Cubism and among several avant-garde artists who had exhibited cubist paintings for the first time at the Salon des indépendants in 1911. The following year he helped form the Section d'or, a collective of cubist painters with a shared interest in aesthetic theories drawn from mathematics and vitalist philosophy, and co-authored with Jean Metzinger the first major account of the movement to provide a theoretical basis for their formal experimentation, *Du 'cubisme'* (*On Cubism*).[3] Gleizes retained an intellectual approach to art throughout his life, writing several significant texts, including *La peinture et ses lois* 1923 (*Painting and its laws*), which Dangar had purchased in Paris in 1928.[4]

In 1918 while in New York escaping the unrest of the First World War, Gleizes experienced a religious awakening, leading him away from a purely objective cubist approach and towards the quasi-religious paintings he began producing in the late 1920s.[5] Dissatisfied with art devoid of spiritual meaning, he began to develop a rhythmic art that aspired to harmony with the universe and natural world. He returned to the basic elements of painting that he had identified in pre-Renaissance art and ancient Celtic and pre-Columbian cultures—shape, line, colour and tone—and compositional arrangements centred around what he described as the horizontal and vertical 'translation' and 'rotation' of planar forms.

Summarising these ideas, he wrote that 'to paint is to give life to a flat surface; to give life to a flat surface is to endow it with rhythm'.[6] According to Gleizes, this had been mastered by artists such as Cimabue in the thirteenth century, and in future paintings he translated their well-known compositions into semi-abstract arrangements using his own principles that reinforced his lineage from religious art of the past.[7] *Femme au gant noir* 1920 (*Woman with black glove*, cat 148) is an early attempt to synthesise these formal principles. Gleizes fragmented his figure into planes of flat and patterned colour that overlap and shift away from one another through simple movements of translation—up, down, left and right—and rotation. This circular motion is reinforced by the arched doorway forming the background, a format common to religious centre- and altarpieces that also anticipates the composition of Gleizes's more complex future paintings.

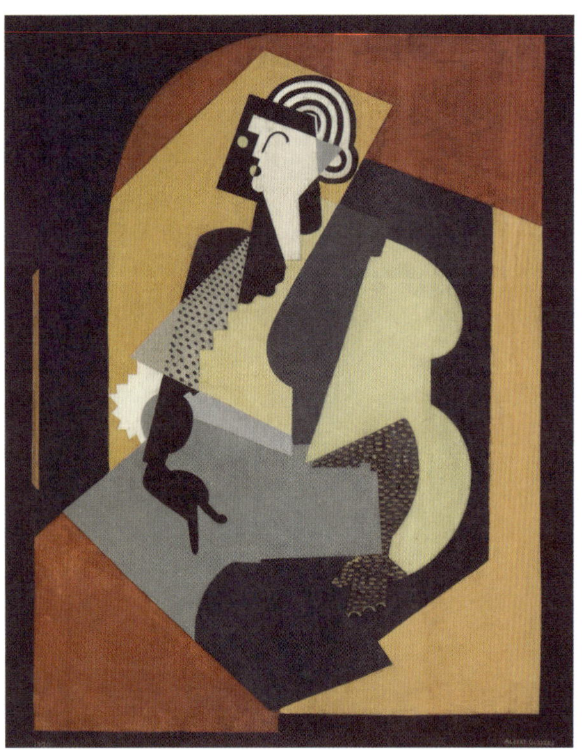

cat 148 Albert Gleizes, *Femme au gant noir* (*Woman with black glove*) 1920

While cubists had broken with the idea of perspective and the distinction between space and object, an innovation Gleizes identified in acts of translation, he sought to extend this idea further by representing the truly abstract concept of time, something realised only in mind and memory. This he identified in rotary movement, which he saw as collapsing past, present and future into one plane. Dangar explained this simply in 1934: 'Time's movement is circular—dawn, noon, night, spring, summer, autumn, winter, the regular recurrence of tides, the Moon's monthly visitation, life itself with its toothless, helpless baby stage, developing to youth, manhood, and returning to toothlessness and helplessness.'[8]

As Gleizes's religious conviction developed, he became drawn to the motif of the spiral, which symbolised the cyclical nature of time and the representational world's relationship with a greater spiritual force. This energy remained unseen and constant at the centre of the spiral while all matter revolved around it. In time, Gleizes began to identify this form throughout the symmetries and patterns found in nature, ancient cultures and religious imagery, a coincidence that reinforced its significance. These ideas formed the basis of *La forme et l'histoire* 1932 (*Form and history*), his most ambitious book, in which he traced the manifestation of the spiral across an array of seemingly disparate cultural, chronological and material contexts.[9]

Gleizes's ideas attracted a small circle of adherents, who followed his aesthetic principles in the 1920s. They included Irish artists Mainie Jellett and Evie Hone who, like Crowley and Dangar, encountered Gleizes after studying at the Académie Lhote, as well as Robert Pouyaud, then a young artist in Paris.[10] In 1927 Gleizes established Moly-Sabata, with the idea of providing a space for his followers and other artists and artisans to focus on their work free from the city and commercial pressures. Pouyaud was the first to become a resident, with Jellett and Hone briefly joining and staying with Gleizes in Serrières later that year.[11] Gleizes had already experienced similar endeavours, having been involved in 1906 in the short-lived Abbaye de Créteil, an artistic and literary group founded on similar communal and anti-commercial ideals.[12] Parallels can also be made with the Bauhaus School in Germany, which Gleizes was involved with from the mid 1920s; he likely modelled aspects of Moly-Sabata on its focus on craft, collaborative ethos and workshop system.[13]

Unlike the state-funded Bauhaus, however, with its focus on standardised, industrial production, Moly-Sabata was a rustic, self-sufficient venture.[14] Residents were expected to work collectively to grow their own food, contribute to chores, and generate income through communal artistic and craft work such as the creation of pochoirs—multi-layered prints using zinc stencils—of Gleizes's paintings that were sold as editions through publisher Jacques Povolozky, an associate from the Abbaye de Créteil. This arrangement also corresponded with Gleizes's belief in the ideals of the *retour à la terre*, an agrarian movement that emerged in France following the First World War and emphasised the decentralisation of cities, repopulation of towns and regions, and overall return to the perceived simplicity of peasant culture. French earth, having been physically torn apart by bombardment and trench warfare, became a potent symbol of French nationalism in the interwar period, and redolent with aspirations for recovery and prosperity. This agrarian ideology reinforced Gleizes's own aesthetic and spiritual theories: the patterns of the spiral were mirrored in the rhythms of self-subsistence, with the annual preparation of soil, sowing, tending to and harvesting of crops occurring in harmony with the seasons.[15]

Arriving in 1930, Dangar was shocked by the labour expected of her, having assumed she would spend her time studying with Gleizes and creating artistic work, rather than toiling in the garden and stencilling pochoirs. Nevertheless, driven by her desire to impress Gleizes and understand his ideas, she resolutely adapted to the rigorous rhythms of daily life, taking ownership of a small plot of garden, learning the process of creating pochoirs, and studying with Pouyaud and later Gleizes himself. She was particularly drawn to his spiritual teachings, an aspect of his work that would have appealed to her broadly Protestant upbringing, and soon began to equate her experience at Moly-Sabata with that of a nun in a religious community. As she wrote to Crowley, 'Oh I am so happy ... you have put me in the shelter of a convent.'[16]

Within two months of her arrival, Dangar wrote to Gleizes about obtaining a simple wheel and constructing a furnace to commence her pottery, and of her wish to establish a workshop encompassing other crafts.[17] 'All ... night I planned and built air castles—our little pottery grew and grew ... we started other industries, basket-making, rush-mats and chairs and stools—we even knocked down a wall between two small rooms because our big loom for carpet and rug weaving needed space and light.'[18] These dreams were short-lived. The following day, Pouyaud announced he and his wife were leaving the community, putting an end to her immediate plans. In truth, Dangar had arrived during a difficult period, with Pouyaud growing increasingly frustrated with the lifestyle, the limited income gained from time-consuming pochoirs, and ongoing difficulties with fellow residents. By the end of 1930, he had left the community, leaving Dangar on her own at Moly-Sabata less than a year after she had arrived.

With Pouyaud's departure, it was not yet feasible for Dangar to build a pottery—she had neither money nor resources. But knowing she had studied pottery in Paris and hoping to provide her with a way of generating income other than the production of pochoirs, Pouyaud sought to connect her with potteries in the region.[19] By June 1930 he had introduced her to Clovis Nicolas, from a pottery at Saint-Désirat, nine kilometres south of Moly-Sabata, across the river in the Ardèche, and Dangar began working there regularly alongside senior potter Jules Pignault.[20] Not permitted to employ the methods she learnt from Bernier in the late 1920s, Dangar embraced their instruction wholeheartedly and by September the potters were 'pleased with [her] progress', even if she was 'disgusted by [her] slowness'.[21]

Entering the masculine space of the Saint-Désirat pottery as a woman was difficult and, having come to the medium later in life, Dangar had not completed the full seven-year potter's apprenticeship. Her relations with Pignault were initially tense; she found him 'coarse and disgusting' and called him the 'old drunken potter'.[22] Certainly, as a woman in her late forties with limited French and vastly different world experience and social background to the peasant potters she encountered, Dangar was a curious anomaly in this context and likely an easy target. In time, however, Pignault and the other potters became impressed by her resolve. Dangar later credited him with being 'the best potter [she had] ever known' and that she owed him 'all [she knew] regarding real pottery'.[23]

In mid 1932, Dangar began working alongside Henri Bert and potter Jean-Marie Paquaud at Poterie Bert, north of Moly-Sabata in an industrial area outside of the town of Roussillon. The local region was known for *terre vernissée* ('glazed earth'), a traditional form of earthenware employing terracotta clay that was sourced from local claypits, fired at low temperatures in a wood fire and decorated using a slip trailer named a *barolet*, a clay vessel with duck-quill nib, to trace vibrant slip and lead-sulphate glaze decorations on the clay surface.

Although closer than Saint-Désirat, Roussillon was still a seven-kilometre journey which, without any other form of transport, Dangar made on foot, occasionally relying on friends to drive her or staying overnight. In 1932 Crowley purchased a bicycle for Dangar; however, it was too heavy for her to manage and she continued to make the daily trek on foot.[24] At Roussillon, she encountered similar issues to those she had faced with the male potters at Saint-Désirat. She found Paquaud, only a young man when she arrived, particularly vexing for his apparent laziness and unreliability. Even so, she came to depend upon him over the 20 years she spent working at Roussillon, and while she became skilled at producing small objects, she relied on his strength and experience to turn many of her larger and more complex forms.[25]

Pottery was soon a great distraction from other artistic work and creating pochoirs—Dangar never fulfilled Gleizes's order of stencils—and in September 1931 she reported that while she had made over '400 articles of pottery, decorated over 700 and grown lots of vegetables', 'painting always [seemed] just a week or so beyond my reach'.[26] She initially began creating simple, utilitarian wares aimed at a local market—chunky, solid vessels with basic patterns based on designs traditional to the region. She brought her sketchbook from Paris, which featured delicate bands of porcelain decoration, but soon learnt it was difficult to replicate such fine details with the nib of the *barolet*. Her earliest ceramics of 1930–32 show glaze broadly applied and bleeding across the surface (cat 5), but as she gained more control, her marks became more direct, nimble and fluid. She developed more figurative designs as her skills advanced, depicting well-known local landmarks such as the suspension bridge in Serrières or hot air balloons, long associated with the region through the Montgolfier brothers of nearby Annonay (fig 33).[27]

Gaining confidence in her work, in 1932 Dangar featured her pottery in an exhibition at Moly-Sabata, the first of regular annual exhibitions she would convene featuring her and the artistic community's work. At the end of the same year she was invited to participate in two major regional exhibitions showcasing local craft, the first at the Musée d'Annonay, which acquired ten pieces of her work, and the second in the town of Tournon-sur-Rhône, at the *Exposition régionale artisanale de Tournon*, where she was awarded a gold medal and 200 francs.[28] Major commissions in Annonay from the prominent Béchetoille and Montgolfier families swiftly followed.

With her profile growing and seeing a sustainable future in her pottery, in May 1933 Dangar wrote to Gleizes asking whether she could begin to sign her pottery 'MSD', referring both to the ideals of the collective of Moly-Sabata [MS] and herself [D].[29] All subsequent works are signed in this way. It is, however, difficult to date Dangar's work precisely or definitively. While she documented her finished pieces in a stock book (cat 89), few are dated, and she regularly repeated forms and stylistic and iconographic attributes upon request, using at-scale tracing paper templates for popular patterns.[30]

By this time, Dangar's decorative lexicon merged an eclectic range of regional and modernist sources that would form the basis of her pottery throughout most of her career. Her ceramics incorporated stylised bands of repeated geometric Art Deco patterns, adapted from porcelain painting, the traditional motifs of Isère and the Ardèche and, as her understanding of Gleizes's theories solidified, the cubist motifs and compositions associated with his pochoirs and paintings. With little time to paint, she viewed the pottery surface as an alternative support to canvas or board and described her pots as 'pictures—they need as much thought and knowledge to compose …'[31]

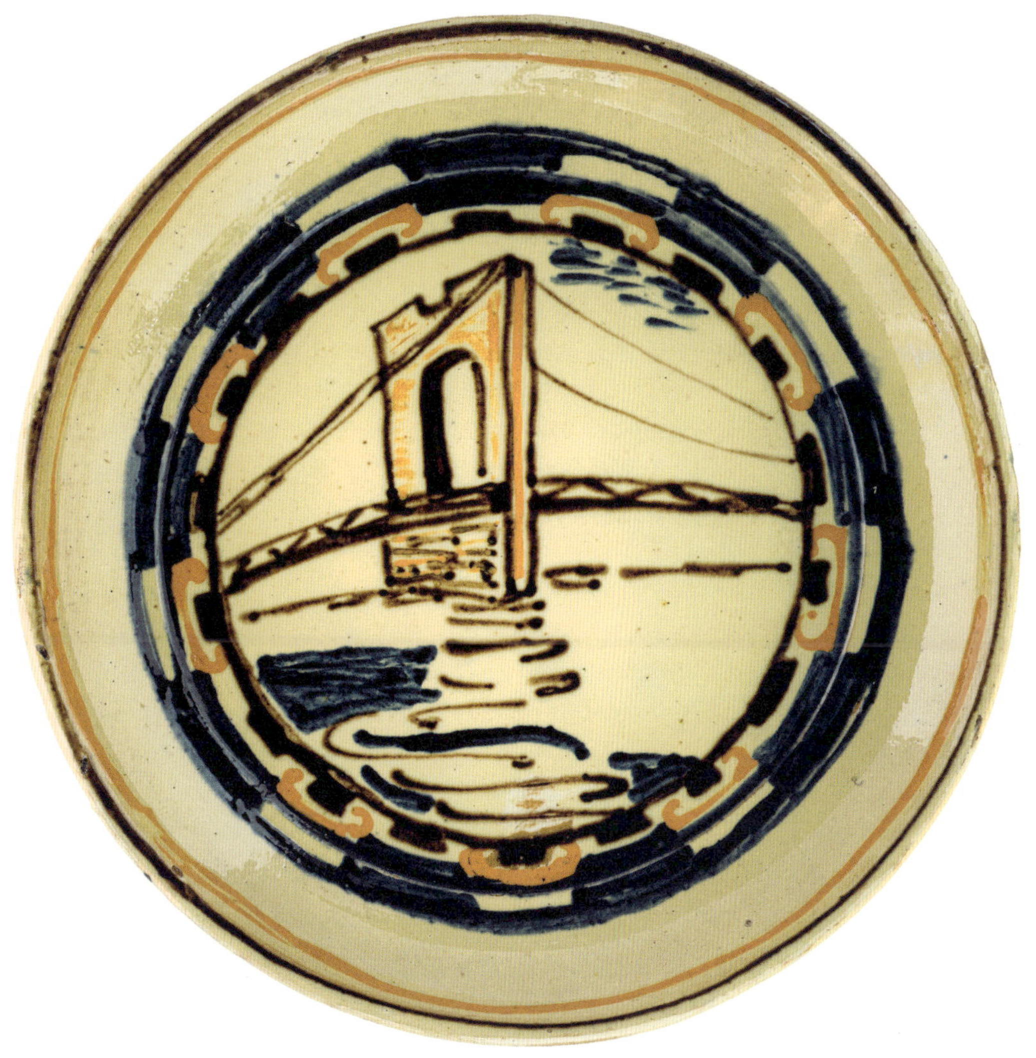

fig 33 Plate depicting Serrières bridge 1930–34

Dangar had been ambitious to combine Cubism and pottery since she first received Gleizes's invitation to join Moly-Sabata in 1929, and she already understood the integral role played by design in modern painting and decoration. As she wrote to Juliette Roche, 'I long to understand Monsieur Gleizes's work, I feel its deep beauty and realise his method a very wonderful means of expression in painting, pottery and in life.'[32] The circular forms of pottery—plates, bowls, tubular candlesticks and wide-bellied vessels such as vases and tureens—were ideal supports for small, cubist compositions underpinned by Gleizes's principles of translation and rotation. Rotary movement was echoed in the intrinsically spherical forms of some of Dangar's pieces and their three-dimensional nature meant they were to be viewed in the round. Some of Dangar's most effective abstract designs feature simple circular and semicircular motifs that follow the contours of the entire pottery form, arranged in expanded movements that place the viewer in perpetual orbit with the object (cat 34).

The process of throwing and turning pots also complemented Gleizes's ideas, with the rhythms of the potter's wheel mirroring the rotary movements he associated with time. The almost meditative state reached when the potter's body, centred ball of clay and spinning wheel are in synchronous movement seemed analogous to the spiritual exaltation Gleizes sought in his painting. Dangar later acknowledged that her efforts in pottery brought her to understand Cubism, writing to Gleizes that 'the very act of making pots taught me to understand your lessons. A little honey pot with its two handles and a lid can possess all the fundamental necessities of a huge cubist composition.'[33] She drew on Pignault's early pottery lessons in particular, writing to Crowley that 'he made me understand pottery & much about the true meaning of Cubism, for what is Cubism but "le mouvement de la forme [comprise]"?' (the movement of understood form).[34]

As Dangar discovered, Gleizes's cubist ideas and traditional peasant pottery represented the perfect marriage of motif and medium, as his principles, connected to a lineage of ancient spiritual cultures were 'far older than … 400 year old pottery'.[35] The symbolism of the spiral, with a spiritual force at its centre, made particular sense to her, and many examples of her work, created throughout her career, feature configurations of spiral forms, interlocked and woven together or joined at the tail. Prior to Pouyaud's departure, she observed him creating detailed, linear drawings for Gleizes's *La forme et l'histoire* that presented the spiral within different chronological and cultural contexts. The design of her large-bellied pot (cat 46) draws direct inspiration from Etruscan pottery illustrated in the book's pages (fig 34), seen both in the trio of spirals in relief and in the vessel's form itself, with handles positioned close to the opening. Similarly, the radiating central motif in the sophisticated decoration of a mid 1930s plate (cat 45) seems inspired by the engraved stones of the Cairn of Gavrinis, a neolithic tomb on an island off the coast of Brittany, also illustrated by Pouyaud. These spiral motifs also resonated with Dangar's deep connection to ancient Celtic decoration. She brought with her to Moly-Sabata a book on illuminated Celtic manuscripts and was sent additional material by Hone in Ireland, and regularly drew on this influence in her pottery, incorporating stylised Celtic knots as woven borders and ornament as well as serpents, animals central to Celtic folklore, in interlocking arabesque arrangements (cat 38).[36]

In 1934, Dangar developed a relationship with the Anjaleras Pottery in Cliousclat in the Drôme. She admired the careful firing of the Cliousclat potters that allowed her to create large presentation pieces suitable for display. Among the first of these was the decorative plaque *La Vierge et l'enfant Jésu* (*Virgin and Child*, cat 44).[37] In a letter to Crowley describing her approach, Dangar wrote that she tried 'not to be influenced by the Renaissance "prettiest women possible idea" (making a woman an idol) but [to] use the images in a purely symbolic way'.[38] Reduced to simple planes incised with decorative spiral details, the two figures tesselate into the broader cubist composition, reminiscent of Gleizes-influenced gouaches Dangar produced during her first years at Moly-Sabata (cat 92).

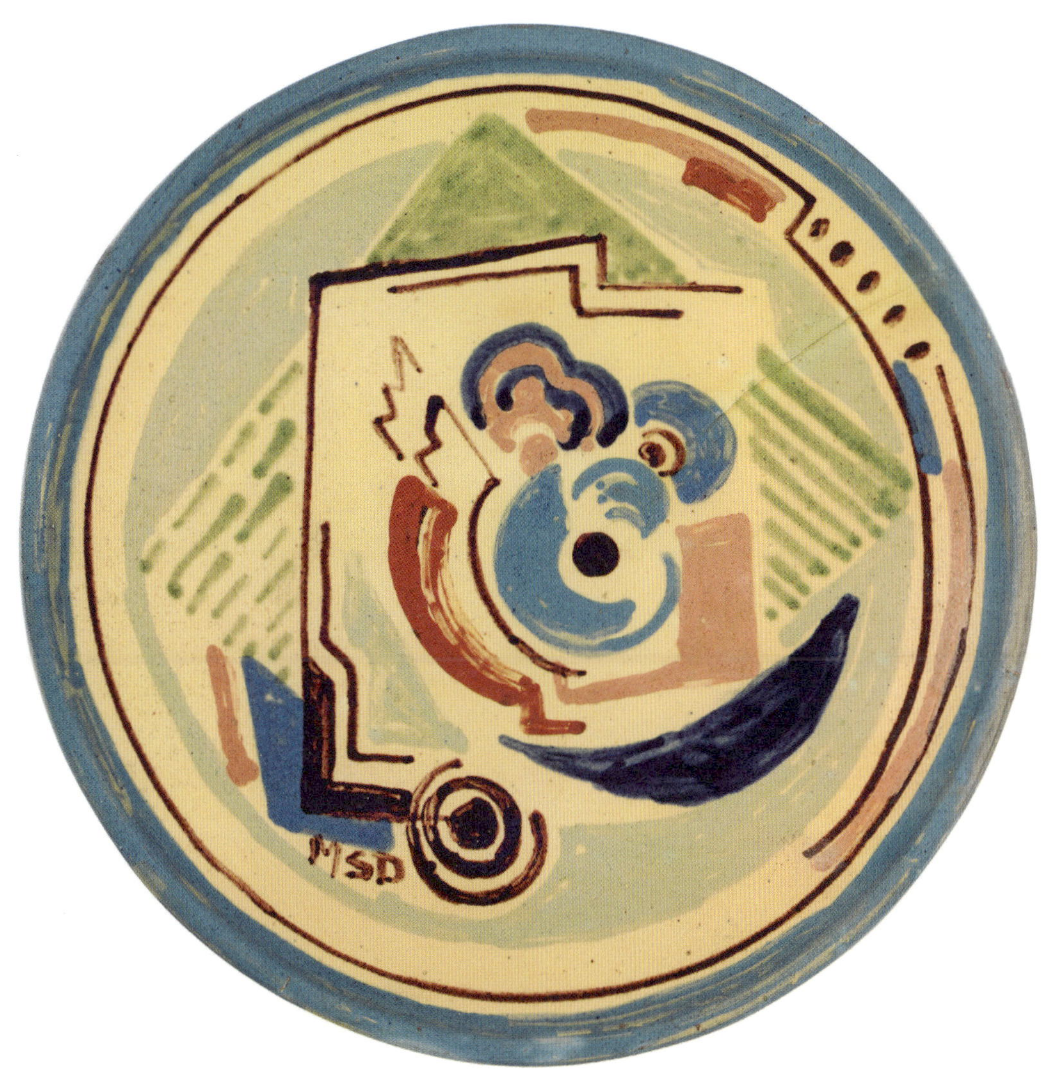

cat 34 Cubist plaque 1933–50

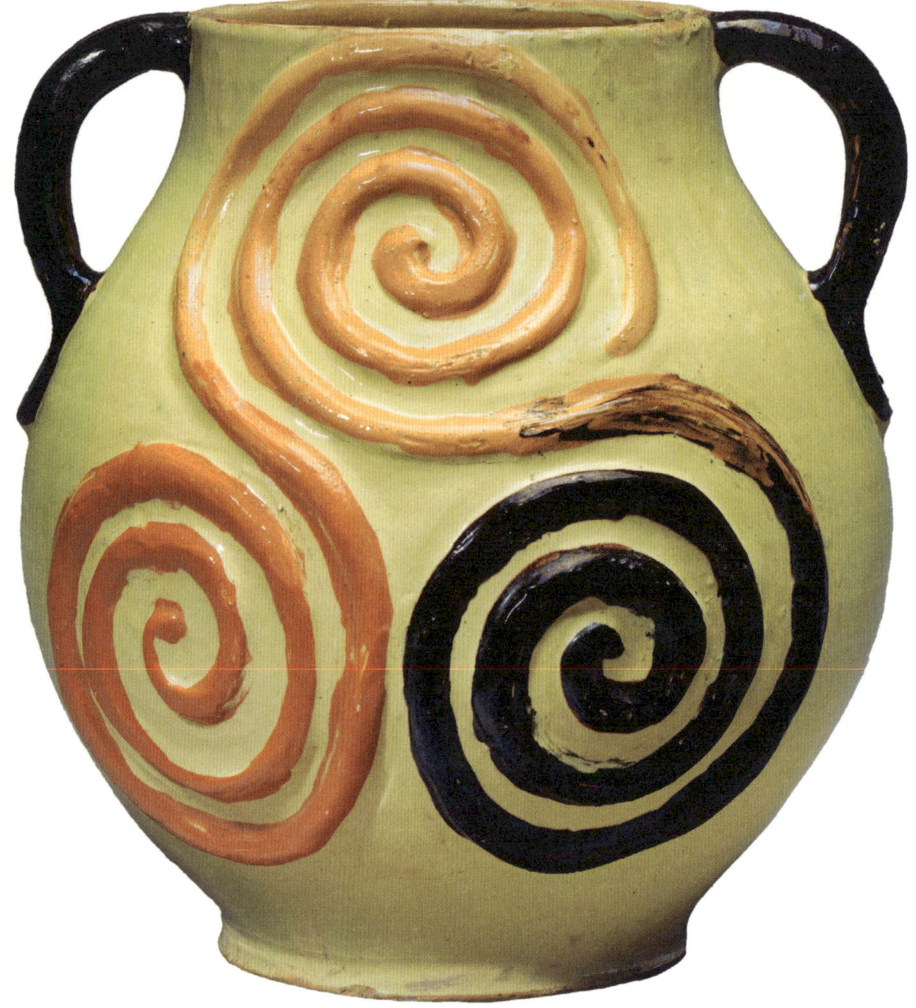

cat 46 Pot with spiral decoration 1934–50

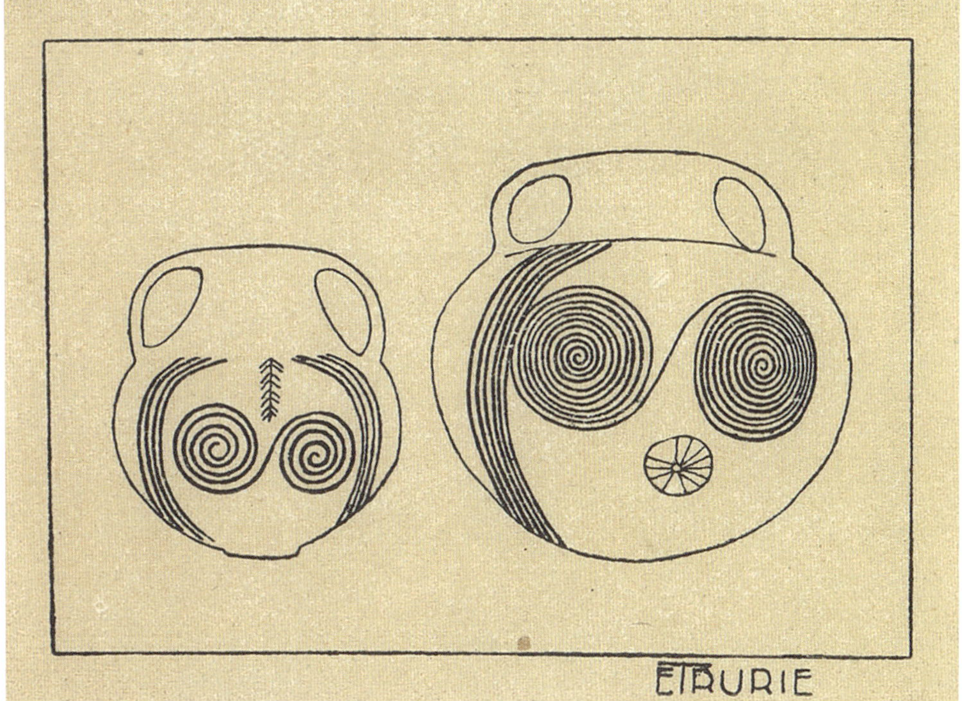

fig 34 Robert Pouyaud, *Poteries d'Etrurie* in Albert Gleizes, *La forme et l'histoire*, 1932

Over the following two decades Dangar collaborated with the potters at Cliousclat almost exclusively on her major cubist works for exhibition, working with the potters at Roussillon on more rustic functional ware produced at high volume for general sale. The Cliousclat pottery also neighboured the town of Mirmande, which she remembered fondly since attending Lhote's summer school, and over the following years she stayed there whenever she worked at Cliousclat, which enabled her to remain in contact with the artist community associated with Lhote. Around this time, she also began working with the industrial pottery at Saint-Vallier, owned by a man named Boissonnet who used local sandstone to manufacture tiles. Dangar began collaborating with the potters there, decorating tiles to serve as mural panels and to adorn tabletops and fireplaces. From the mid 1930s, this larger-scale 'artistic ware' began to occupy more of her time and by the end of 1935 her market expanded when she began exhibiting and selling large decorative plates, vessels and tiled tables at Marcel Michaud's gallery Stylclair in Lyon, and later at Folklore. Michaud was among the few gallerists with whom Dangar had a sustained working relationship, as her distaste for commercial wares and commercialisation developed in Sydney continued alongside her agrarian, peasant values in France.[39]

Impressed by the expanded production of her work, Gleizes began to commission Dangar to produce pottery decorated with his designs for inclusion in his exhibitions, which she signed 'MSGD'—'Moly-Sabata, Gleizes, Dangar'. Although Dangar's earliest pieces after Gleizes were rarely attributed to her publicly, they were not, as David Butcher notes, simply copies of his work, but collaborative

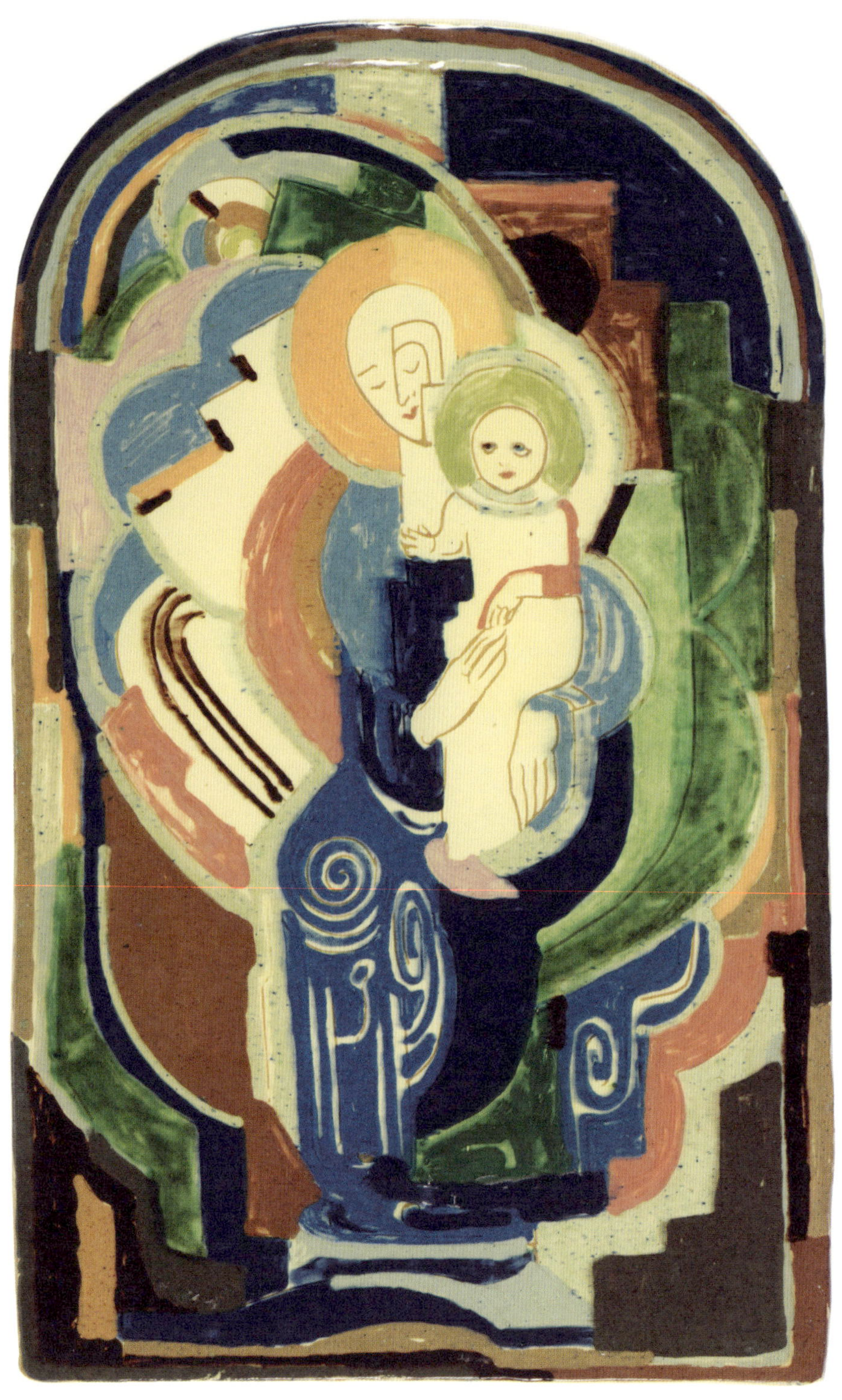

cat 44 *La Vierge et l'enfant Jésu* (*Virgin and Child*) 1934

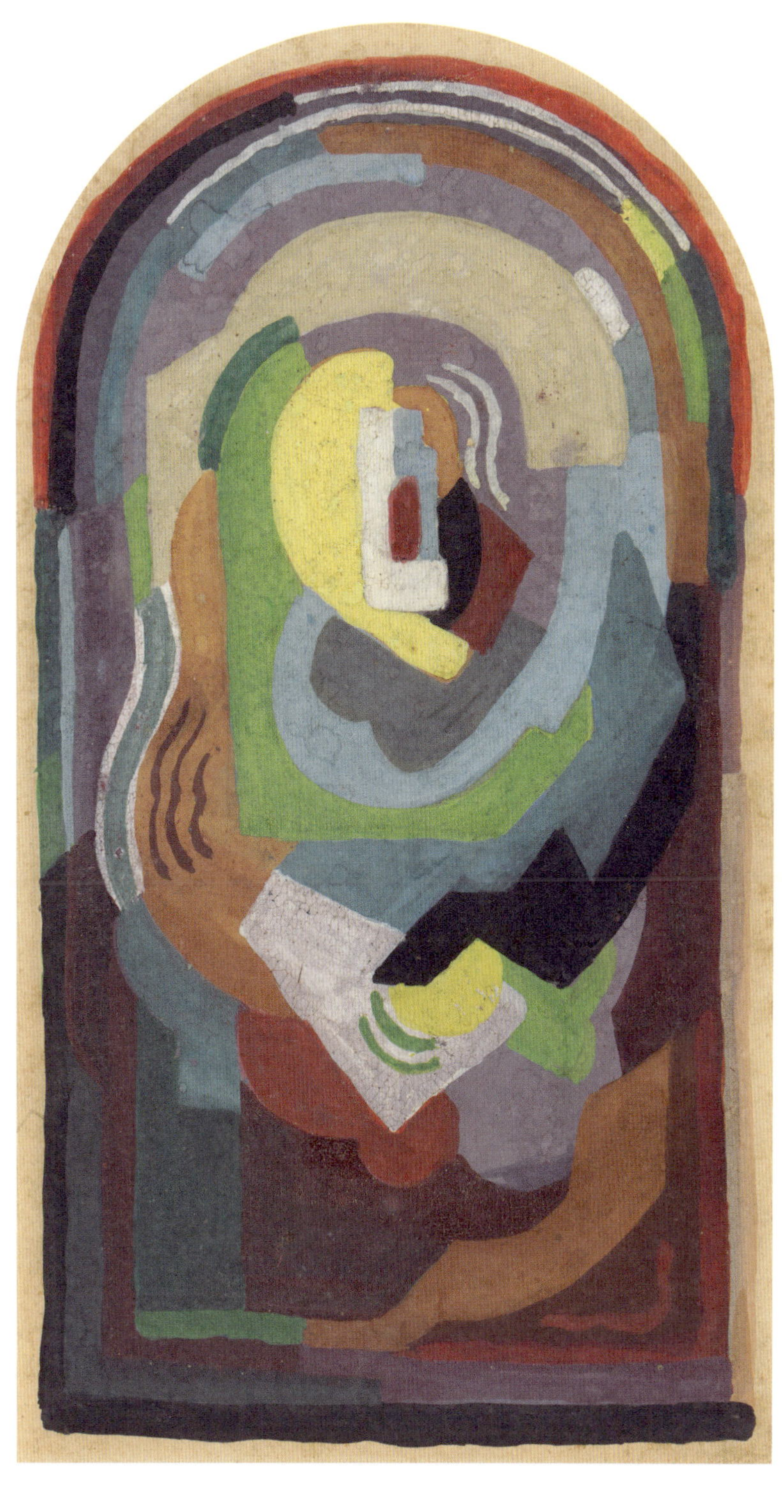

cat 92 Cubist composition, 1931–33

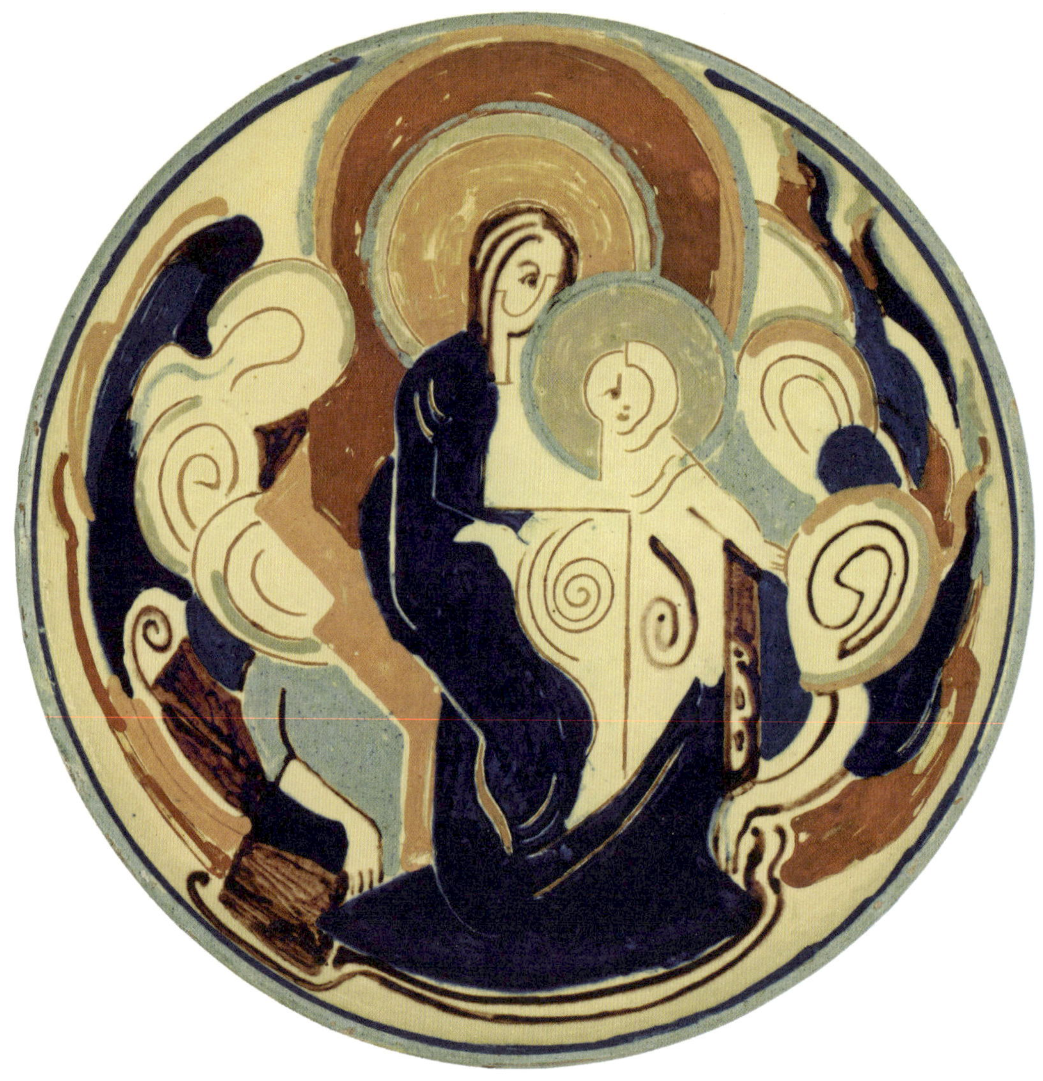

cat 113 after Albert Gleizes, *La Vierge et l'Enfant en majesté entourés de six anges* (*Virgin and Child in majesty surrounded by six angels*) after Cimabue 1936–37

'interpretations', with Dangar given liberty to modify colour and composition for the new format.[40] Their most well-known collaborations were produced from around 1936 onwards and depict the Virgin and Child (cat 113), a swirling, centrifugal image adapted directly from Cimabue's late thirteenth-century tempera painting *La Vierge et l'Enfant en majesté entourés de six anges* (*Virgin and Child in majesty surrounded by six angels*, fig 35). This was a popular composition and Dangar repeated it well into the next decade. In the late 1930s she also created three plates derived from Gleizes's unrealised mural designs for the auditorium of the Conservatoire national des arts et métiers, Paris, *Les quatre personnages légendaires du ciel* 1936–37 (*Four legendary figures of the sky*). Each represented a different individual, Aladdin (cat 115), Icarus (cat 116) or Sinbad; while Gleizes had intended to include a fourth legend, Leonardo da Vinci, Dangar refused, faulting him for replacing the rhythm of Romanesque art with perspective.[41]

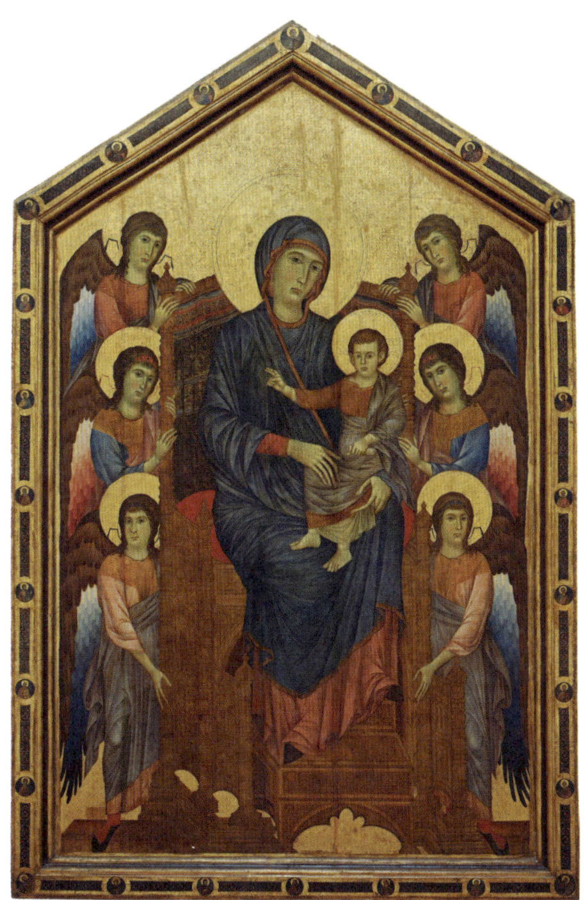

fig 35 Cimabue (Cenni di Pepe), *La Vierge et l'Enfant en majesté entourés de six anges (maestà)* (*Virgin and Child in majesty surrounded by six angels*) 1275–1300

—

As Dangar's pottery reputation grew, the Moly-Sabata community also began to gain momentum. In May 1931, Dangar was joined at Moly-Sabata by composer and musician César Geoffray, his wife Mido, daughter Gilka and eventually a son, Luc. Geoffray was familiar with Gleizes and Moly-Sabata, having visited in 1929 and collaborated with Pouyaud on the illustrated musical score *Suite de sons et de couleurs pour piano* 1931 (*Sequence of sounds and colours for piano*), which included three original gouache designs by Pouyaud following Gleizes's principles (cat 153).[42] As part of the annual fete and exhibition, he coordinated concerts featuring theatrical and musical productions as well as children's choirs, with Dangar sometimes enlisted to create paper costumes and backdrops.[43] While Dangar was regularly irritated by Geoffray, feeling he did not contribute to the daily chores at Moly-Sabata, she enjoyed spending time with Mido and Gilka, and found particular support in the friendship of their former maid Lucie Deveyle, who accompanied them to the community. Up until her arrival, Dangar had overseen all the activities associated with life at Moly-Sabata while attempting to generate an income and advance her pottery. Deveyle's reliable presence was a great relief to her and the pair became close companions.[44]

By early 1932, Dangar had begun holding weekly 90-minute lessons for children between the ages of 7 and 13.[45] With her previous experience, teaching was a logical way for her to supplement her income and she provided lessons in drawing and painting as well as practical skills in decoration, teaching basic motifs and patterns drawn from Adolfo Best Maugard's *A method for creative design* 1926, which she may also have used in her pottery decoration.[46] She gained great pleasure from her young charges and was often charmed by their work: an enamelled tabletop (cat 124) she sent to Crowley in Sydney in 1937 was based on a student's drawing of a woman and child.[47]

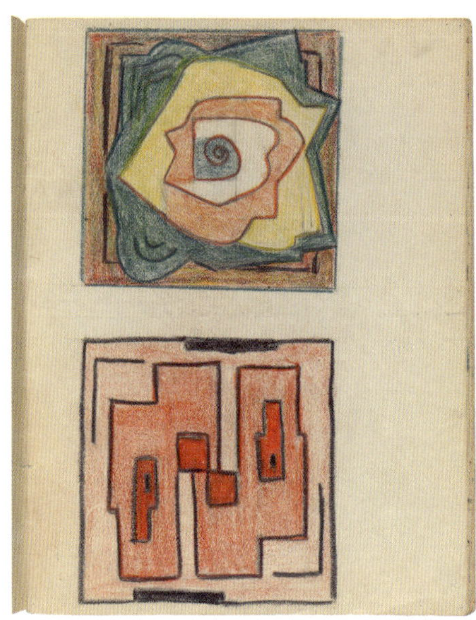

cat 155 Ninette Doz, Exercises in translation in Student workbook 1940s

Dangar also taught her students a simplified version of Cubism. Their exercise books show diagrammatic guides for Gleizes's principles of translation and rotation and the students experimented with these ideas through simple exercises, shifting brightly coloured geometric shapes up, down, left and right and, in more complex compositions, spinning them on the spot at the central point.[48] The workbook of student Ninette Doz, the Geoffrays' niece, shows her rapid development under Dangar's instruction through her use of organic, irregular shapes that gently spiral around the composition (cat 155).

In 1933 Dangar, Deveyle and the Geoffrays were joined by Jacques Plasse, his wife Bilou Le Caisne and their two children. They remained less than two years, but introduced weaving to the community, setting up a workshop, sourcing second-hand looms, and teaching themselves the technique. Upon their departure in early 1935, Dangar engaged Ruth Ainsworth, a friend from Sydney staying in London, to visit and teach Deveyle to weave. Deveyle was a diligent student and became a fine weaver, later buying her own loom.[49] With these developments, Dangar's initial visions of a grand craft centre were alive again, and through its growing artistic community, Moly-Sabata gained renown in the region.[50] During the 1930s, the endeavour was profiled in several French journals, accompanied by photographs showing the house, grounds and workshops and featuring annual exhibitions comprising a rich array of art and craft wares assembled by Dangar—her utilitarian and artistic ceramics, weavings by Jacques Plasse and Bilou Le Caisne and later Deveyle, students' paintings, drawings and ceramic *crèches* (nativity scenes), as well as appliqué textiles by Roche and paintings and works on paper by Gleizes, Pouyaud and other artists from the cubist circle.[51] In 1934, the literary magazine *Hebdo* profiled the community, including a photograph of Dangar shaping a small pot at the wheel at Poterie Bert.[52]

Ainsworth was not the only Australian to visit Moly-Sabata. In Dangar's first year, she was joined by former students Estelle Creed and Florence Turner Blake, in 1934 by Dorrit Black, and in 1936 by her friend Winsome 'Winty' Hall, the sister of *Undergrowth* founder Nancy Hall. Several of these visitors returned to Australia with examples of Dangar's and the community's work.[53] She also played host to several individuals invited by Gleizes, most notably the Belgian artist, writer and critic Michel Seuphor, who arrived in late 1932 and stayed for several weeks. At this time, Seuphor was a central figure in the European avant-garde, having recently founded Cercle et carré, an artistic group dedicated to abstraction that included Wassily Kandinsky, Le Corbusier and Piet Mondrian, his mentor and collaborator. Seuphor would later become an influential advocate and historian of abstract art, authoring important texts in French including *L'art abstrait: ses origins, ses premiers maîtres* 1949 (*Abstract art: its origins, its first masters*) and *Dictionnaire de la peinture abstraite, précédé d'une histoire de la peinture abstraite* 1957 (*Dictionary of abstract painting, with a history of abstract painting*).

Dangar was impressed by his ideas and enthusiastically worked alongside him during his stay. At the same time, however, she grew frustrated when he offered no help with household chores and expected to share her supplies, furiously recounting to Crowley that 'he sits in the sun & makes poems & writes philosophies while I plant onions & lettuces enough for four people ... My coal warms him ... My garden feeds him.'[54] Seuphor's memories of Dangar were similarly critical, and he recalled she was 'a very severe and unpleasant woman' who 'suspected me of having all the faults of men. Then, little by little, she was appeased and took me as a cook's assistant ... I shared her poor small portion, which most often consisted only of a tasteless rice dish.'[55]

Seuphor was one of several visitors to Moly-Sabata with whom Dangar had similar issues. While she had turbulent relationships with her peers—she remained wary and critical of Juliette Roche, for example, feeling she exercised too much control over Gleizes and Moly-Sabata—these conflicts were generally with young men.[56] Certainly Dangar was not always gracious and could be overly principled, stubborn and harsh. But she had worked hard to avoid the traditional hierarchies imposed by patriarchal society. As a woman over the age of 40 who had sacrificed all aspects of her previous life, including her relationship with Crowley, she quickly became frustrated by the uninvited dependence of these young men. She had very little to share, her financial existence was precarious, and she worked hard to survive. As she described to Gleizes and Roche in 1937, her daily routine was long and arduous:

> I plunge into the [Rhône] at 5am—make my coffee and start forth on my six mile walk to the pottery at 6.30. I get back at nine at night, make my bed and tumble into it. In summer I boil eggs or potatoes on a little spirit lamp, eat raw vegetable and fruit.[57]

Gleizes offered Dangar little support with these conflicts, and she was galled by the way he chastised her for her treatment of his visitors. In 1938, for instance, she wrote to him angrily,

> you think me so hard ... I know I'm hard on boys and men ... who pretend such superior intelligence & do not understand the simple laws of the 10 Commandments. I believe it is necessary to ... [force] decency and deference for women if it doesn't belong naturally, by showing that all intercourse with decent people is cut off ...[58]

Despite his 'tremendous ideals', Gleizes was in no way 'practical'.[59] While he happily promoted Moly-Sabata widely—notably delivering a lecture at the Bauhaus in 1932 and publishing an essay in *Sud Magazine* in the same year that described the merits of the *retour à la terre* community—he was, as Adams notes, 'aloof' to the challenging realities of life.[60] In letters to Crowley and Gleizes, Dangar regularly recounted the constant state of disrepair of the building and her anxieties associated with poverty and fractious relationships between residents. By contrast, Gleizes and Roche lived in great comfort through her inheritance, dividing their year between several residences, including their home in Serrières, an apartment in Paris and a farm, 'Les Méjades', in Saint-Rémy-de-Provence. Although Gleizes was the initiator and artistic and spiritual master of Moly-Sabata, by the mid 1930s he was rarely present, and the community functioned through the efforts of Dangar, who promoted his ideas through teaching and pottery, and who coordinated all aspects of practical and cultural life.[61] As Ainsworth observed during her six-week visit in 1935, 'he was away ... she was really the support of the place as far as the idea was concerned'.[62]

—

Although Dangar focused much of her energy during the 1930s on Moly-Sabata and her pottery, thoughts of her friends in Australia were ever-present. She wrote to Crowley regularly, and throughout the decade actively kept her cognisant of developments in art in Europe, as Crowley, in turn, informed Dangar of events in Sydney. She also sought to assist Crowley and Black in their efforts to advance modern art by sending publications, exhibition catalogues and notes summarising Gleizes's theories. In 1930, within months of her arrival in Sablons, Dangar sent Crowley pochoirs created by Pouyaud after Gleizes, as well as instructions on how to achieve their powdery, matte surface.[63] A few weeks later, she sent a set of gouache studies and diagrams, again by Pouyaud, advising Crowley to keep them and do exercises to send back for correction (cat 152).[64]

In 1932 Crowley left the Modern Art Centre, where she had been teaching alongside its director Black, and launched her own school with Rah Fizelle, which became a key meeting place for artists and individuals interested in modern art, including Ralph Balson and Frank and Margel Hinder.[65] By 1934 Dangar had begun sending lessons for Crowley's students, including Mary Alice Evatt and Eileen Berndt, which summarised Gleizes's theories into a series of talks. She addressed her lectures directly to her 'students' in her own voice, opening the first by writing it was a 'delightful privilege to have the chance of talking ... about things we used to talk [about] together, to ignore distance ... and just settle down to study as if I were in the same studio'.[66] Midway through the following year, Dangar sent through five lessons which distinguished non-objective from representational art, and stepped the students through the ideas and process of translation and rotation.

Alongside these lessons, between 1932 and 1938 Dangar also sent several consignments of pottery and other works to Sydney to be shared among her friends and family, thereby providing applied examples of the aesthetic theories she was describing. Indeed, as Mary Alice Evatt later described, the lessons Dangar sent worked in tandem with her pottery:

> She ... continued to tell of the abstract work of Albert Gleizes and of the tapestries and pottery made at Moly-Sabata. This was a great help to students here and helped bring Sydney and the little group ... into the stream of creative work being done in Europe.[67]

Sadly, as Dangar's correspondence records, many early consignments arrived broken and had to be glued together but, as Evatt remarked, this allowed them to study her forms and designs closely: 'we all helped and this truly made you feel shapes were important'.[68]

As well as serving instructive purposes, Dangar earned some income through the work she sent to Australia. She initially sold her pots through Margaret Jaye's store in Sydney, but by September 1932 grew frustrated with the amount Jaye charged and asked Crowley to sell them for 'honest prices' on her behalf.[69] Crowley did so, and even displayed Dangar's ceramics in small exhibitions in her studio, where they were viewed by the wider artistic community in Sydney. In 1937 Dangar received news of one such event—arguably the earliest exhibition of cubist art in Australia—reporting to Gleizes there was a 'magnificent exhibition on view in Grace's studio. Am now awaiting 16 letters about it, perhaps more.'[70] Soon after, she was contacted by an architect in Sydney who had viewed her pottery and was interested in commissioning her to create tiled wall murals for buildings, 'great flat shapes in lovely colours'.[71]

Many of Dangar's friends and former students acquired examples of her pottery in this way, but she also sent specific pieces as gifts to friends and family, as payment for the loan of money, as well as on commission. For example, in 1937, via Crowley, she sent her cousin Effie (known as Fairy) Mills

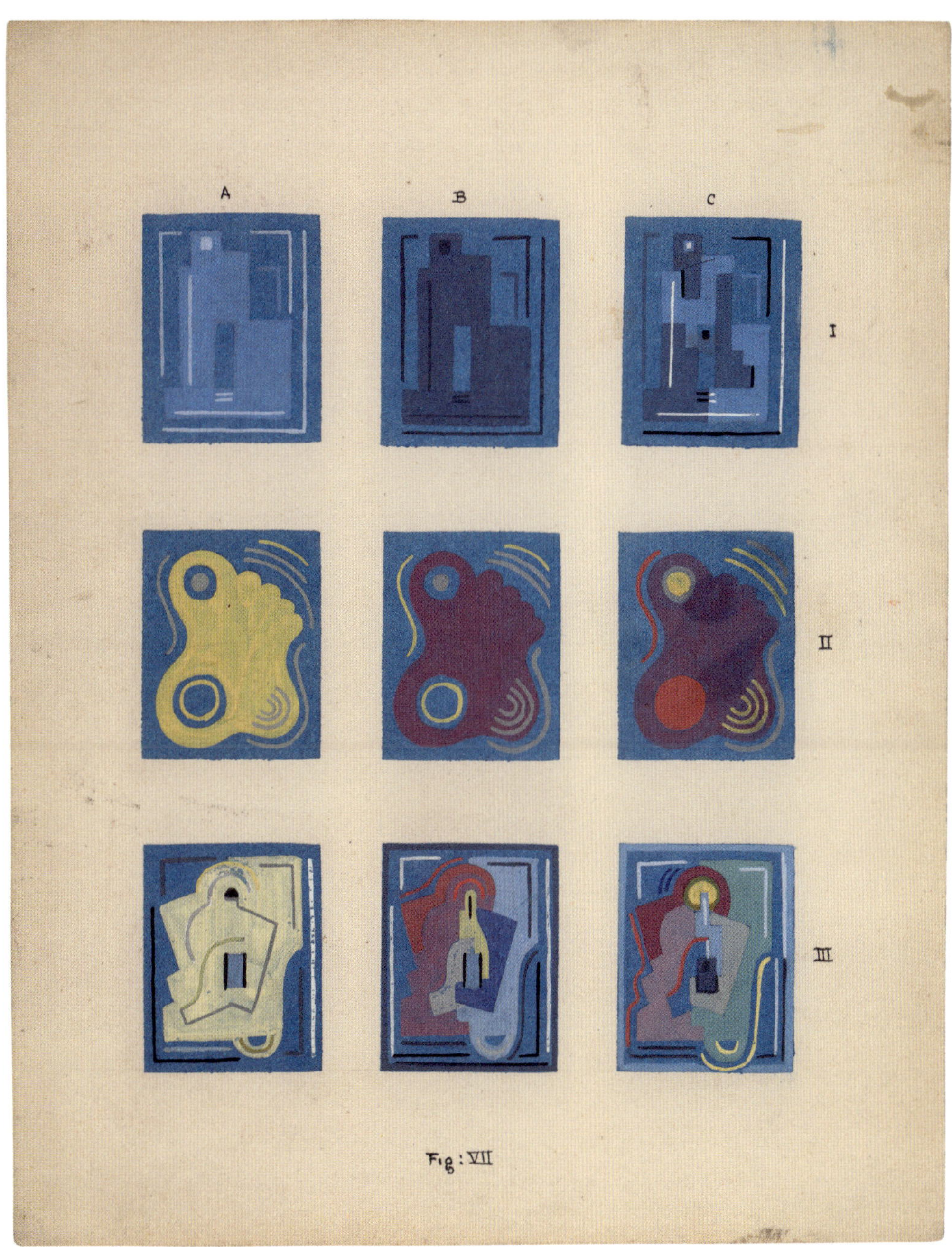

cat 152 Robert Pouyaud, Diagrams illustrating pochoir technique and Gleizes's principles of translation and rotation 1930

100

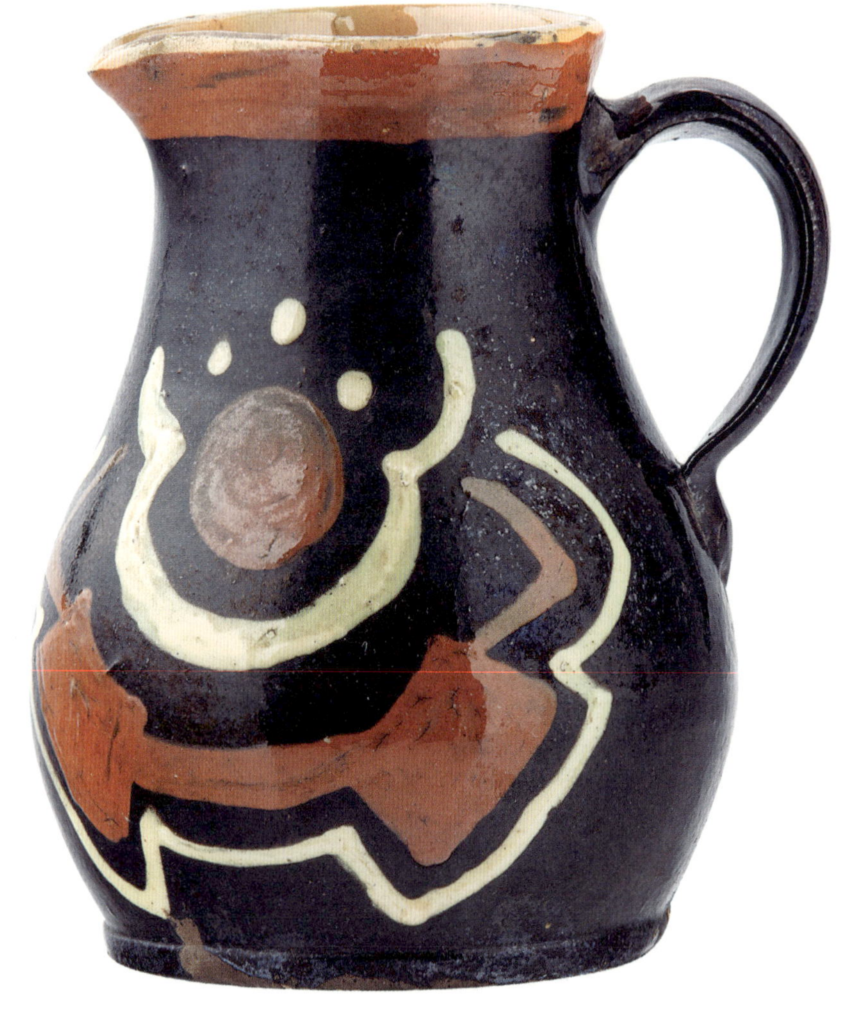

cat 11 Jug 1931–33

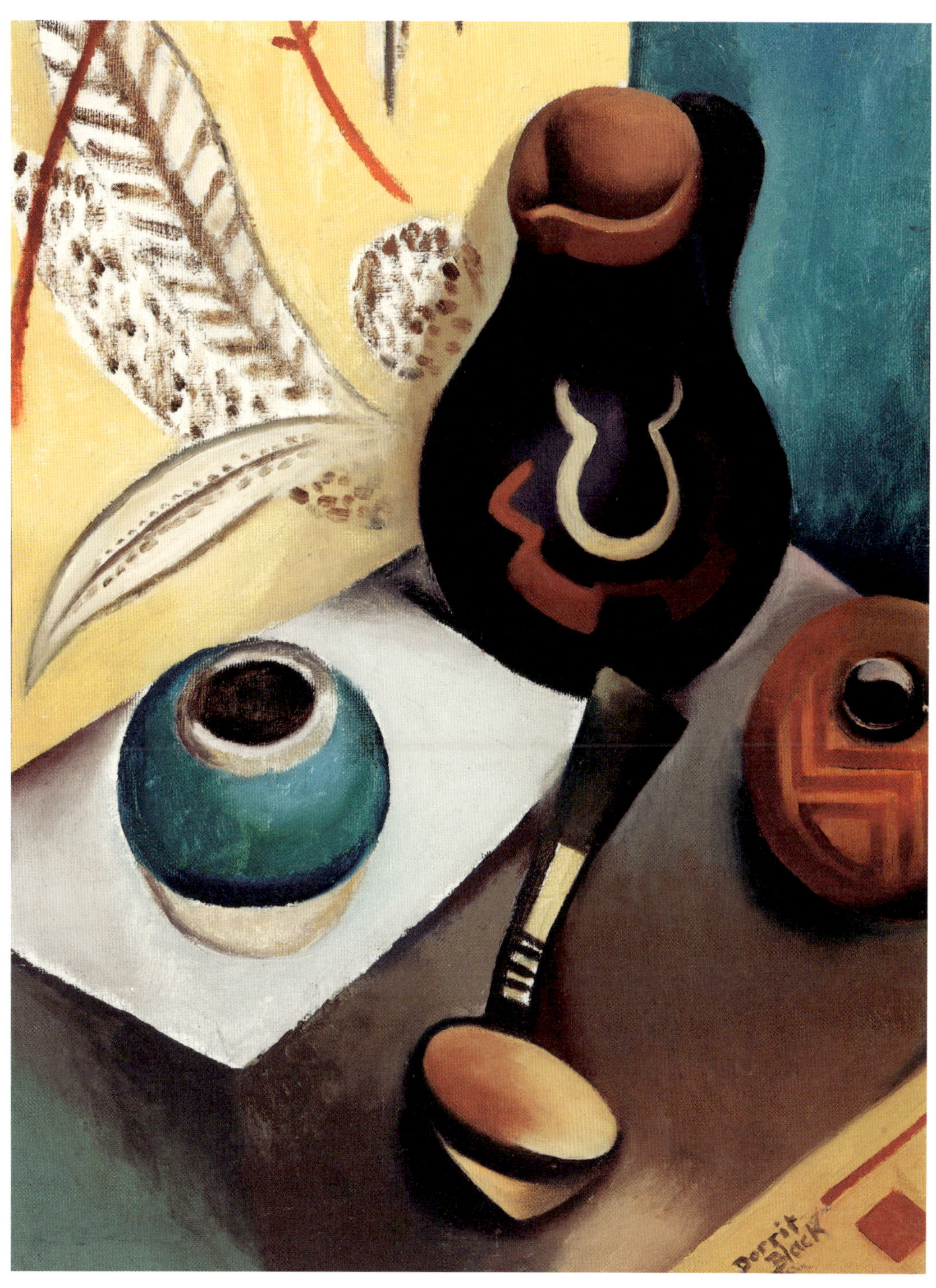

cat 131 Dorrit Black, *Still life with jug and ladle* c 1935

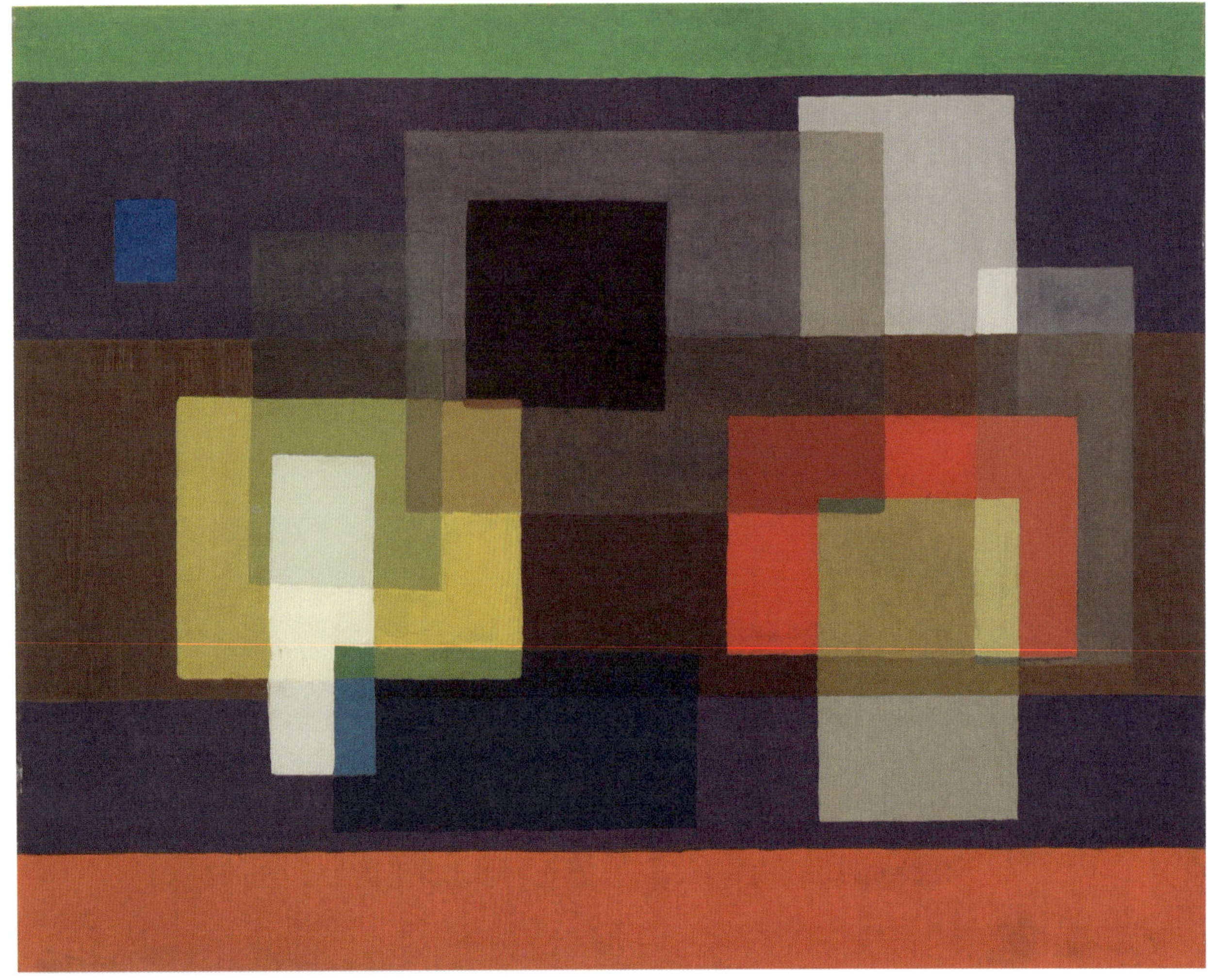

cat 129 Ralph Balson, *Constructive painting* 1951

decorated tiles to be assembled as a tiled tabletop (cat 56) and a group of beer mugs monogrammed 'RF' for Rah Fizelle (cats 53–55). Evatt and her husband HV 'Doc' Evatt (federal attorney-general and External Affairs minister—later president of the UN General Assembly) were well-known advocates of modern art, and particularly supportive of her work, paying her 1000 francs in 1938 for a commission of ceramics valued at far less by Dangar, as well as textiles executed by Deveyle.[72] Despite his dislike for modern art, even Julian Ashton showed support, using his influence as a well-known, senior Sydney figure to release one of Dangar's consignments from customs when there was an issue with import in 1936.[73]

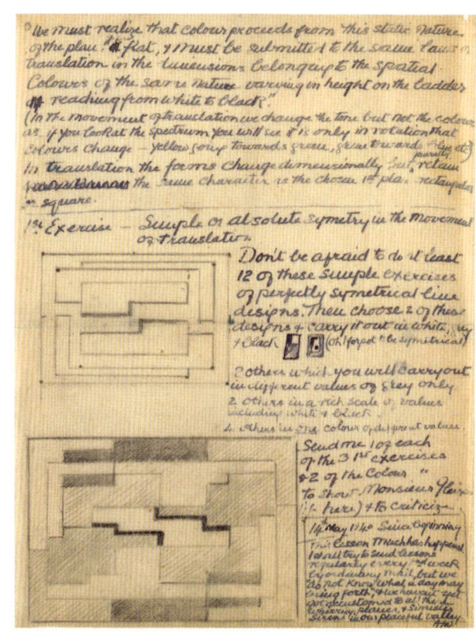

cat 105 Drawing and translation of *La forme et l'histoire* by Albert Gleizes 1940

By the close of the decade, Dangar's cubist designs were owned and used by numerous artists, writers and advocates associated with modern art in Sydney, including Crowley and the Evatts, Rah Fizelle, Nancy Hall, Ruth Ainsworth, Eileen Berndt, Bill Cantwell and Dorrit Black who featured some pieces (cat 11) in her still lifes of the period (cat 131). Many of these works are now held in public collections.[74] Although some pieces were decorated simply, others boasted complex cubist forms, original designs underpinned by Dangar's sophisticated understanding of Gleizes's ideas. A jug owned by Fizelle dated to this period is a key example, decorated on its exterior with semi-circular arrangements of black, brown and cream that display the principles of translation and rotation in three dimensions (cat 25).

Importantly, Dangar's correspondence and lessons would have a significant impact on her friends, and helped to set Crowley and Balson on their path towards abstraction. As Crowley later described, it was a difficult journey in the stifling environment of Sydney: 'we find the path of an abstract painter an exceedingly difficult one ... Balson and I are the only two painters I am aware of who think seriously about abstract painting here at all.'[75] By the late 1930s, Crowley and Balson were experimenting with abstraction, and around 1940 producing their first geometric paintings.[76] These early works owe much to the example of Gleizes and the geometric diagrams illustrating translational movement outlined in Dangar's teaching notes during this period (cat 105), and examples of this 'translation–rotation' can be seen in their subsequent abstract paintings (cat 129).[77] Balson's solo exhibition at Anthony Horderns' Fine Art Gallery in 1941 was the first exhibition dedicated solely to abstract art in Australia, and Crowley exhibited her first abstract paintings the following year.[78] These exhibitions now represent defining moments in the history of Australian abstraction and both artists continued to develop an inventive and refined abstract practice in the years that followed. Painted almost a decade later, Crowley's finely calibrated *Painting* 1951 (cat 146) is among the most sophisticated abstract paintings of her oeuvre, if not twentieth-century abstract painting in Australia.

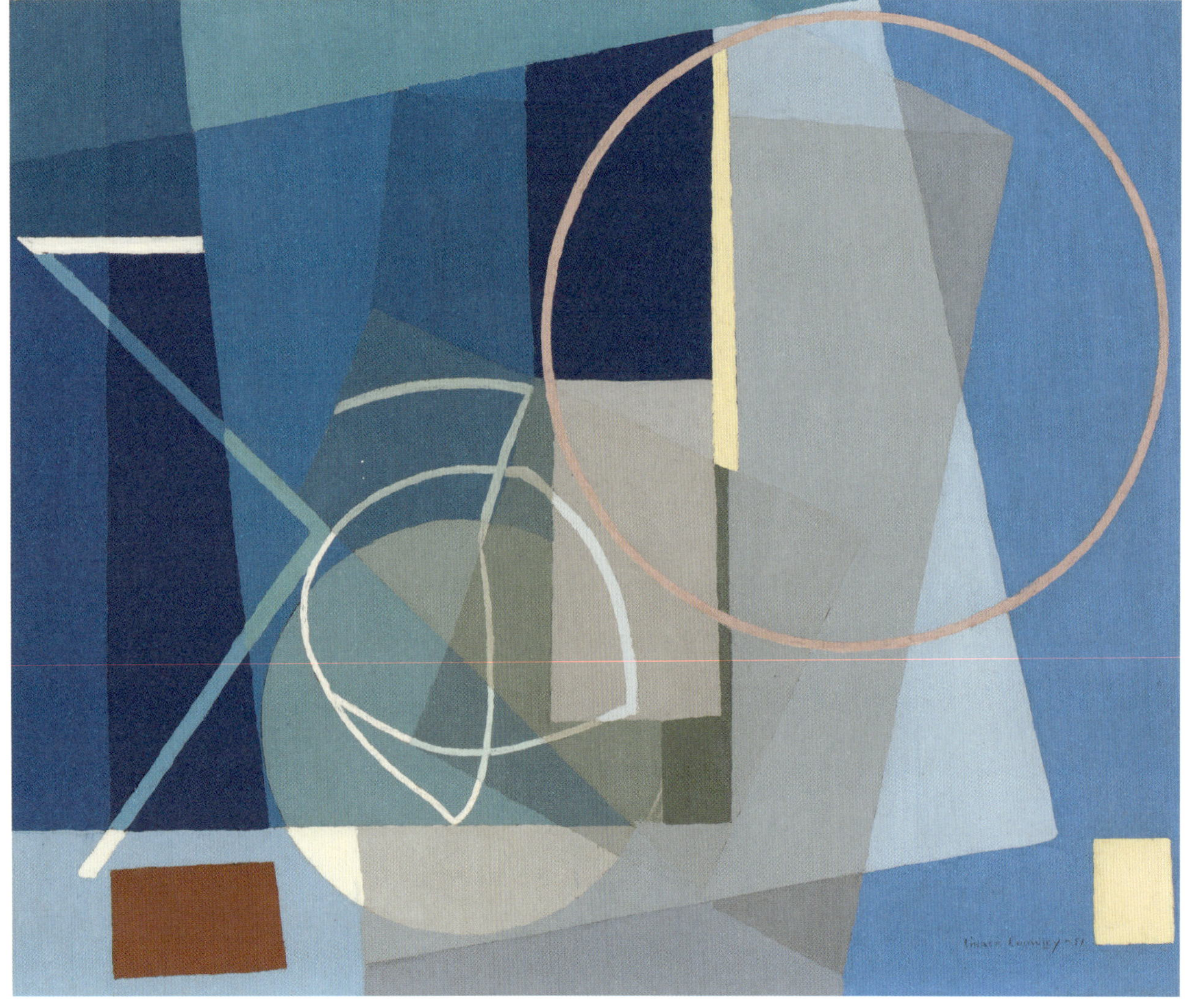

cat 146 Grace Crowley, *Painting* 1951

At the beginning of 1937 these developments in Australian art still lay in the future and, likewise, Dangar's greatest successes as an artist in France were yet to be realised. Even so, since arriving in Sablons seven years earlier, her life had radically transformed. Despite arduous circumstances, she had established herself at Moly-Sabata and within the region as one of Gleizes's most ardent followers, working hard to absorb his theories and meet the craft focus of the community and the *retour à la terre* ideals upon which it was founded. Artistically she had also advanced, developing her skills and reputation as a potter swiftly, and transitioning away almost entirely from her polite, *en plein air* practice. No longer simply a painter on canvas or board, by the final years of the 1930s she was first and foremost a potter, thinking and painting in three dimensions, and on the threshold of a new chapter in her career when her position as a cubist in France would be recognised and consolidated.

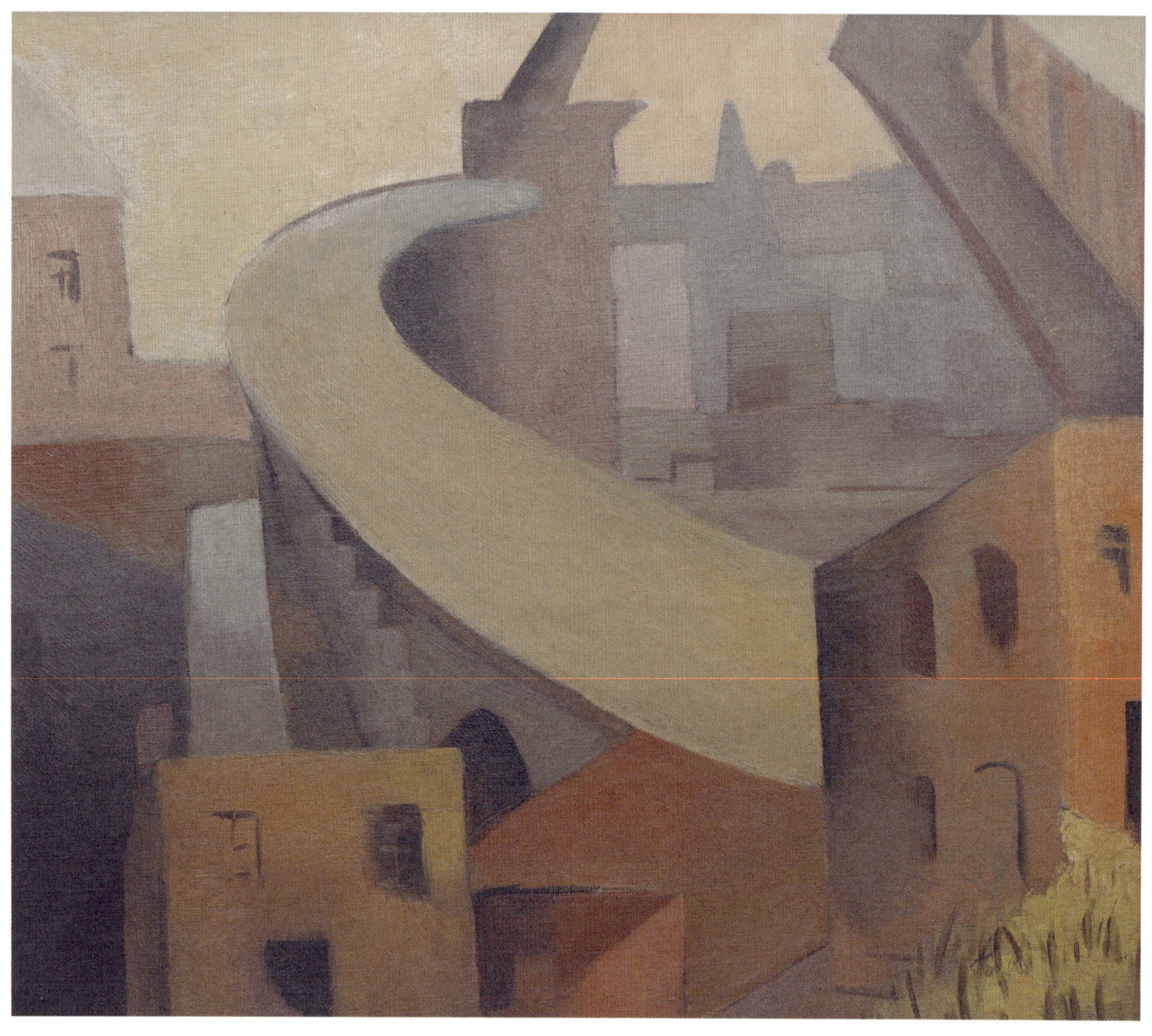

fig 36 Estelle Creed, Sydney Harbour Bridge under construction 1929

Journeys through Australian and French modernism: Anne Dangar and Stella Creed

ANGELA GODDARD

The story of forgotten modernist Stella Creed spans a journey from a pastoral station near Rockhampton to the French avant-garde of the 1920s and 1930s. Many of Creed's numerous paintings, drawings and letters, including several from Anne Dangar, have only recently been located.[1] Her rediscovery is particularly significant in that it expands on the story of the introduction of modernism in Australia and extends the links between Australian and French art of this period.

Creed's artistic endeavours place her in an environment of profound innovation as a student under three figureheads: Anne Dangar, André Lhote and Albert Gleizes. The tutelage of Anne Dangar, key figure in the development of modernism in Australia, underpinned Creed's artistic endeavours. Under the mentorship of Lhote at his Académie in Paris, Creed found herself immersed in a world that challenged artistic norms and fostered a bold and experimental approach to her work. Her time at Moly-Sabata with Gleizes further propelled Creed's work into visionary abstraction. Despite the brevity of her guidance under these mentors, Creed's artistic legacy resonates as a testament to her embrace of diverse influences and teachings in a remarkably advanced body of work that defied the conventions of her time.

Born on 1 March 1904, Estelle Avalon Creed, known as Stella, was raised in a pastoral family in Rockhampton, Queensland. The eldest of five children, she demonstrated an early interest in art, winning prizes at school. Upon graduating from Maryborough Girls Grammar School in 1921, she moved to Sydney, enrolling at Julian Ashton's Sydney Art School from 1922.[2] Grace Crowley was head teacher and Dangar was on the teaching staff at this time, but both departed for France in 1926, where Dangar, Crowley and later Dorrit Black spent time studying with Lhote.

Dangar reluctantly returned to Australia in October 1928 due to her financial situation,[3] resuming her job teaching at Julian Ashton's, while Crowley and Black went on to visit Albert Gleizes at his home in Paris. While disillusioned to be back in Australia (writing to Crowley and Black about her misery) Dangar began teaching a modernist approach to painting.[4] Her influence began to appear in Creed's works after a sketching and painting camp at Wamberal in January 1929 that was reported in the student magazine *Undergrowth*.[5] While the importance of Dorrit Black's Modern Art Centre from 1931 and the Crowley–Fizelle School from 1932 are well documented, Dangar's teaching in Sydney in 1929 is not. In mid 1929 she advertised her lessons in *Undergrowth*, mentioning her teacher's certificate from Lhote.[6] Based on the style of her paintings, Creed is the first student to be identified as one of Dangar's school. She produced Australian scenes in a cubist style inspired by Lhote through Dangar, and in 1929, student and teacher painted the same distinctive jug and basket in still life (cats 134 & 71). Though Dangar's work is larger and more resolved, clearly signed and dated 1929, Creed's smaller studies nevertheless establish that she was one of the first artists to take up Cubism in Australia and reveal her teacher Dangar as the first of the modernist teachers to introduce the techniques of this advanced art movement to Sydney.

One of Creed's most accomplished works is a scene of the Sydney Harbour Bridge under construction in 1929 (fig 36). A compact composition of sweeping arcs and heavy buttresses, this work predates Dorrit Black's *The bridge* 1930 (Art Gallery of South Australia), which, until recently, has been claimed as 'the first Australian cubist landscape'.[7] With the bridge clearly at an earlier point of construction in Creed's painting, this achievement can now be claimed for her, a discovery that modifies our understanding of Cubism in Australia. The legacy of Cubism in this country moves beyond the great achievements of Picasso and Braque in the early years of the twentieth century. Antipodean and global art histories grant prominence to Cubism's later disseminators, including Lhote and Gleizes, due to their role in informing broader modernisms across the world through their students. In Australia, they became the key figures in the teaching and reception of artistic modernism. Such a revision of Cubism's development is central to the business of art history, where we art historians are always looking for something new or details that more accurately reflect the dissemination of ideas, often moving beyond the well-documented major figures to neglected ones and thus expanding the relational networks.

Crowley soon found a solution to Dangar's distress at being back in Australia, and in October 1929 passed on Gleizes's invitation to Dangar to join his artist colony Moly-Sabata in Sablons, a village in south-eastern France.[8] Dangar and Creed must have been close by then, and perhaps Dangar was also encouraged to bring a paying student, because Creed accompanied her in the same cabin on the *Commissaire Ramel*, leaving for France on 5 February 1930.[9] After the ship arrived in Marseille, Dangar made her way to Moly-Sabata, while Creed continued on to Paris, with some helpful tips from Dangar in her notebook to purchase *Un livre d'arrondissements* (a little square red book with maps of Paris, trams, buses, etc) and a *carte d'identité*, and a reminder to ask Lhote about obtaining a discounted museum pass.[10] Creed was fluent in French, writing to her family, 'I feel I don't want to talk read or write English', and by 2 May 1930 had become a student of Lhote's, one of a very small number of Australian artists to study with the French artist.[11] She spent a term at the Académie André Lhote, then attended his summer school, before joining Dangar in Sablons.

Several works in the Creed family archives are classic examples of Lhote's teachings: abstracted female figures in interiors, several clothed in three-quarter poses, as well as several full-length sitting or lounging nudes. Creed's untitled painting of a reclining nude (fig 37) is a typical example of a Lhote student's work and has several correspondences with the more complex and refined painting by Crowley, *Sailors and models* 1928–29 (cat 139), and associated studies from the National Gallery's collection, with their diagonal planes and analytical, schematic character. An attentive and diligent student, Creed took several pages of notes on the 'Theory of "clair-obscure"', or modelling with light and dark.[12]

In April 1930, Dangar encouraged Creed to come to Moly-Sabata, and spoke of the charismatic Gleizes in glowing terms:

> Monsieur Gleizes the dearest kindest soul in the world. He just goes about doing good the who[le] time bless him. Madame is altogether charming & brilliant etc but Albert Gleizes is more saint than man … he talks about God as naturally as about Art for he cannot separate the two.[13]

Again, in mid 1930, Dangar asked Creed to join her as quickly as possible, writing: 'hurry up & go along & all your troubles will turn to bliss. Life is very sweet, very full, very simple.'[14] Dangar's letters to Crowley also mention her unerring admiration for Gleizes, describing Moly-Sabata as 'A house of love & hope & peace & kindness!'[15] Creed, however, chose to go to Lhote's summer camp at Mirmande in September 1930, where she produced numerous watercolours of rural townscapes and a couple of larger oils, though regrettably no long-range views of the pyramidal medieval hilltop village such as those Dangar, Crowley and Black had produced during and after their trip together two years earlier. Around 80 kilometres north at Moly-Sabata, Dangar was obliged to participate in the religious and social activities underpinning Gleizes's community, and to provide income. Apart from the 19-year

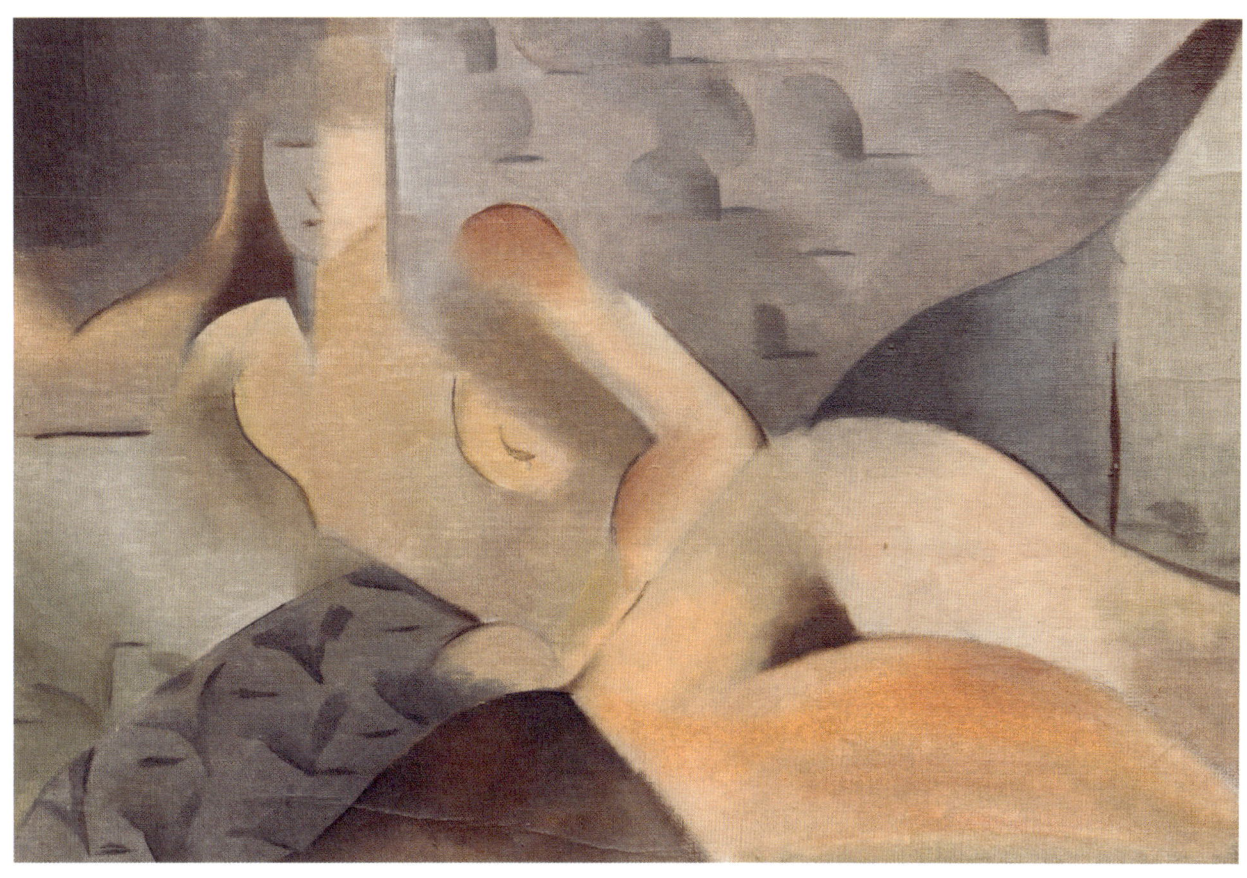

fig 37 Estelle Creed, Reclining nude 1929

age difference between the women, there was also a substantial gap in their finances. In contrast to Dangar's perpetually straitened circumstances, Creed and her four siblings had inherited in partnership the substantial Queensland property Prior Park, after Creed's mother Clara had died in 1926 and her father Tom in 1927, ensuring her financial security.[16]

Creed finally arrived at Moly-Sabata in December 1930 as a paying student, making her one of a handful of Australian artists who studied with Albert Gleizes, deeply influential not only on Dangar, but also on Crowley and Black.

At Moly-Sabata Creed was again a studious and attentive student—her archives contain pages of notes and many preparatory geometric sketches using zinc stencils for the gouache pochoirs (cat 136) that were painted en masse by community members to generate income. Several examples demonstrate Gleizes's theory of translation–rotation or are based on the image of the Madonna and Child, an important motif for Gleizes and his followers. Elena Taylor has observed that Creed's gouaches join just a handful of small studies by Crowley and Black in the post-cubist, highly abstracted style of Gleizes, in step with contemporary painting in France and among the most advanced works by any Australian artist at this time.[17]

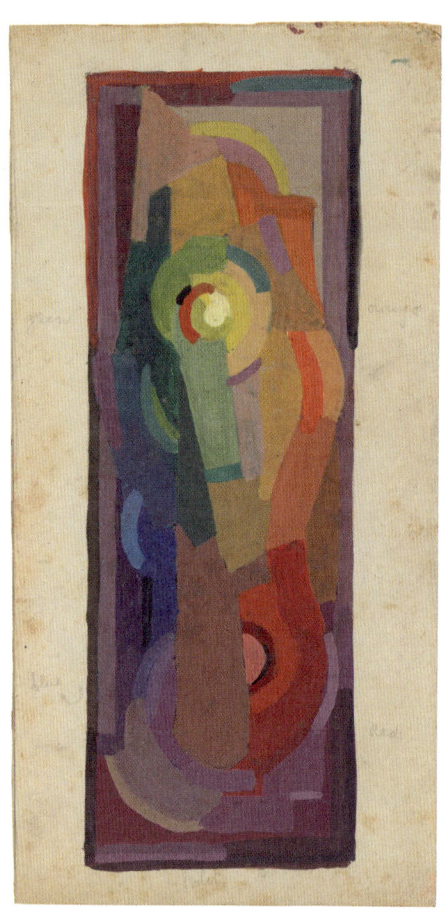

cat 136 Estelle Creed, Cubist exercise using Gleizes's principles 1930–31

However, discord had developed between Creed and Dangar. Soon after Creed's arrival, Dangar reported to Crowley that 'Miss Creed is a wretch [and] never gives me credit for having taught her a thing & pretends she never heard things I told her at Wamberal a week after I landed.'[18] And in a letter of 10 February 1931, Dangar's resentment of Creed erupted:

> I've just told Miss Creed I want her to go to the Hotel. I'm sick to death of her. Sulks & rudeness when for 25 francs per day I have to run a first-class hotel for her. She has got so rude (she always was rude over food) that if I asked her would she have more of a dish she wouldn't bother to say a word, would just grunt upwards or downwards. Her empty self-indulgent existence is altogether out of keeping with Moly's principles, & the strain of having to live publicly her life & yet following my own in snatches when I had a moment to myself has made me do neither well ... She has a despicable way of pretending to Gleizes I taught her nothing.[19]

It was later in this same letter to Crowley, perhaps added to over several days, that Dangar wrote as if Creed had already departed:

> And this wretched Miss Creed (fancy her never asking me to call her by her name, I think she considers herself vastly superior to me) is taking all my thoughts. I'll have to do *pochoirs* now to keep myself, but I can do twenty-five in one fortnight in the hours I gave to waiting on her & still go to Monsieur Gleizes every day. In fact I'll have more time than when she was here & earn enough to keep me fed.[20]

Though Dangar's letters never mention that Creed had experienced a nervous breakdown, it must have happened around the time of this letter, almost exactly a year after her arrival in France. Creed was sent to the psychiatric clinic Saint-Just, in Lyon, and by March 1931 was on a ship home, travelling with a French doctor paid to accompany her.[21]

Creed disembarked in Melbourne on 19 May 1931 and returned north to Prior Park to recuperate. Dangar wrote to her three times again that year, her letters friendly and reassuring, with no sign of the earlier resentment and discord, yet their correspondence does not appear to continue beyond November 1931. We don't know if Creed replied, as Dangar's personal effects and correspondence don't survive.

As far as is known, Creed's work was never included in a public exhibition, even with the student groups from Julian Ashton's Sydney Art School, nor was her work sold, and none of her works from this period are signed with a concurrent signature.[22] Until now, art historians have come across her name but not pursued her story. Bruce Adams mentioned Creed just once in his 2004 Dangar biography *Rustic Cubism*, incorrectly noting her as being from Sydney.[23] Dangar mentioned Creed several times in her letters to Grace Crowley, as documented in Helen Topliss's anthology published in 2000. But Topliss erroneously described Creed as Jewish, and uncovered no further details, apart from recounting that Creed was 'dealt with in a particularly savage fashion' by Dangar in her letters.[24]

Upon her return to Australia, Creed would have found very little appreciation for the cubist-inflected abstraction of either Lhote or Gleizes, even if she had sought out a local artistic circle. In Queensland in the 1930s, neither Vida Lahey, Daphne Mayo, Kenneth Macqueen nor the designer Douglas Annand ever approached the avant-garde work by Creed. Despite the encouragement we see in Dangar's later letters, it seems that Creed's nervous breakdown triggered a decisive break, and she largely abandoned art-making once she returned to Queensland. She then lived a quiet single life, staying close to her large family, and died in her nineties in Toowoomba in 1997.

Stella Creed's career as an artist, despite being short, was made extraordinary due to her intrepid travels—from central Queensland to Sydney, then to Paris and rural France—to follow her ambitions to explore and learn from cutting-edge artists, a journey that demonstrates the close links between Australian and French modernism in the 1920s and 1930s through the key intermediary Anne Dangar. In addition, the realities of cultural and class differences, social expectations and prejudices were all influential on Creed's experiences. Despite the interruption to her artistic trajectory in 1931 in a still-early stage of development, and ultimately its abandonment, Creed can rightly be described as the most modern artist produced by Queensland in the 1920s, and one of the most advanced Australian artists working at this time. This is a minor narrative in the story of modernism across the world, but one that shifts slightly our axis of understanding the reception of modern art in Australia.

The unearthing of Creed's archive of surviving works, numbering around 40 paintings, 60 watercolours and gouaches, and many more pencil sketches and sketchbooks, as well as several letters from Dangar, is instructive in showing how expatriate Australian artists, especially women, were taught and influenced by modernist artists in Europe in the late 1920s. We have these works to remind us not only of Stella Creed's extraordinary life story, but to prompt us to consider what might have been if her circumstances and support networks had been more favourable.

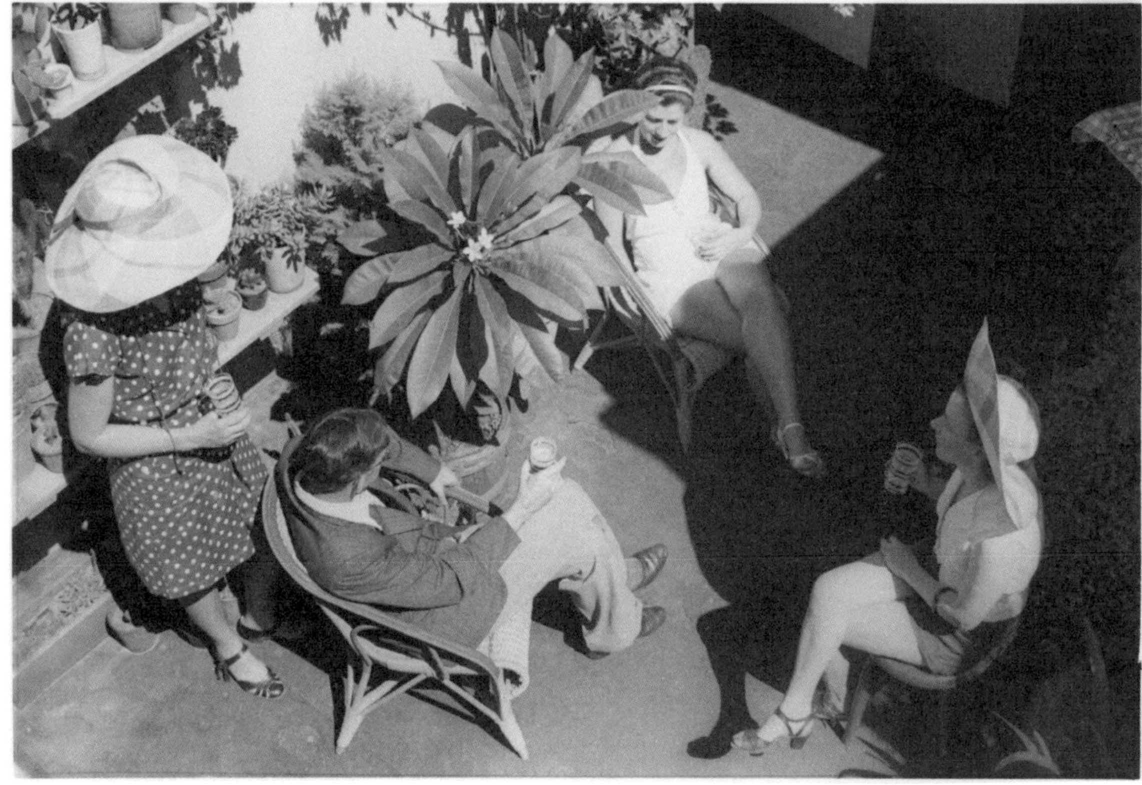

fig 38 Grace Crowley (far right) with Rah Fizelle (centre) and friends in Crowley's roof garden, 227 George St, Sydney, c 1935

'My only home is your heart': the relationship between Anne Dangar and Grace Crowley

ANNE O'HEHIR

The oral historian Hazel de Berg went in search of Grace Crowley in 1966, to ask the Australian painter about her work and partnership with the artist Ralph Balson. Reading de Berg's notes from their interactions, I get a sense of Crowley. She is hard to pin down: 'She refused,' de Berg recalls, 'in fact she half-refused—then half agreed—we wrote endless letters—talked endlessly on the phone.'[1] They had arranged to meet at Crowley's home in Mittagong, but de Berg arrived to find it empty. De Berg is moved; affected by Crowley, she senses something in the self-effacement. 'I shall never forget the desolation of the first time I came here—the mist and rain and the note on the door saying Grace Crowley was out.' The interview itself, when it finally happens, is illuminating. After Crowley has spoken formally of Balson, the tape is left running, and conversation turns to her friend Anne Dangar. Suddenly, Crowley seems to come to life, she becomes animated and full of stories. De Berg worried later about the recording, not sure that Crowley knew she was being recorded, uncomfortable about the idea of 'catching people unawares with a mike'. She planned to erase it but she couldn't: it's too good. It remains.

It is only in the last ten years that art historians and curators have overtly stated that Dangar and Crowley were a couple from the time they met at the end of 1914 to their separation in 1930, and that they maintained a loving bond right up to Dangar's death in 1951.[2] Why does this matter? It matters for queer histories and the endeavour to build ever-richer genealogies. On top of that, queerness is a disruptor of habitual ways of thinking, a position that pushes back against heteronormative power structures, especially when—for women in Dangar's time—not to do so meant time and energy that could be devoted to creative work was often given over to running a household and raising children. As Eve Kosofsky Sedgwick famously articulated, 'queer refers to the open mesh of possibilities, gaps, overlaps, dissonances and resonances, lapses and excesses of meaning'.[3]

The place of lesbians in the history of modernism has been the focus of recent studies, with the importance of their contribution now firmly established and recognised. Some of this research has focused on the 'women of the Left Bank', a group of women in Paris during the early twentieth century.[4] These include Sylvia Beach, the owner of the bookshop and lending library Shakespeare and Company, who published, in the face of almost insurmountable difficulties, James Joyce's *Ulysses* in 1922, when no one else would; the American-born writer Gertrude Stein, who offered crucial early support to Pablo Picasso, Georges Braque, Henri Matisse and Juan Gris; and the English writer and patron Bryher (Annie Winifred Ellerman), an important figure in early experimental cinema and the force behind *Close Up*, the first international journal devoted to film.[5] Critical to the significance of these women is their queerness, and the central role their partners played in their lives: Sylvia Beach and fellow bookshop owner Adrienne Monnier, Gertrude Stein and Alice B Toklas, Bryher and H.D. (the American-born poet Hilda Doolittle). These women's rejection of heteronormative conventions both signalled and allowed for a commitment to new, modernist ways of thinking, seeing and living.

Dangar and Crowley are a part of this queer history of modernism. Their story played out variously in France and Australia. They were part of a group of Australian women artists whose lives during the early twentieth century deviated from the conventional lines of gender and sexuality expected of their generation, including Agnes Goodsir, Bessie Gibson, Anne Alison Greene, Margaret Preston, Bessie Davidson, Mary Cockburn Mercer, Janet Cumbrae Stewart and Kathleen O'Connor, all of whom also made their way to Paris in the early decades of the twentieth century.

Crowley and Dangar met at the end of 1914 when they were both studying under Julian Ashton at the Sydney Art School. Dangar had just turned 29, while Crowley was five years her junior. From the beginning, their personal and artistic lives were intertwined. They were soon living together, initially with fellow art school students Bell Walker and Dorrit Black in Potts Point and then in 'Craigielea' at Neutral Bay, before renting a cottage together near Diamond Bay (now Vaucluse) by 1920.[6] They also taught together, Crowley joining the teaching staff at Ashton's school following the departure of Elioth Gruner in 1918, and Dangar becoming co-assistant teacher in 1920; both came to effectively run the school together with Ashton experiencing bouts of illness.

In 1925 Dangar characterised their initial meeting, at a sketching camp in the coastal town of Gerringong, New South Wales, as being 'the happiest memory of our lives'.[7] Many years later, fellow student Nancy Hall spoke of the women as a couple, recalling that while the more 'forthright' Dangar appeared to call the shots, it was the 'diminutive' Crowley 'who exercised the controlling influence over the relationship'; indeed, Crowley had money, being supported by a wealthier family than Dangar, and did not need to make her own way in the world as Dangar did. And then Hall concludes, as told by historian Bruce Adams, that 'both women sublimated their other desires for art'.[8]

While Crowley had wished to study at the Slade School of Fine Art in London,[9] in 1926 she set off with Dangar to Paris to further her studies. During the mid 1920s, Paris was an important cultural centre, attracting writers, performers and artists from around the world. It was also known for its liberal views on sexuality and personal freedom and as the epicentre of radical lesbian culture—as writers including Diana Souhami have detailed, Paris was 'the sapphic centre of the Western world'.[10] Crowley and Dangar chose to situate themselves in this city and took instruction at the Académie André Lhote on rue d'Odessa in Montparnasse, around the corner from the most famous of the lesbian bars, Le Monocle on boulevard Edgar Quinet.

Crowley wrote to her friends in Sydney that she and Dangar were studying at an institution that was 'serious, hard-working and sincere',[11] and that they were committed and ambitious, determined to make the most of their opportunities. Regardless of whether they engaged with the queer community, they were living in a place where it was large and visible (if you knew where to look), and where lifestyles beyond heteronormativity were accepted and celebrated. They were among a large population of women, as historian Jennifer Shaw has written, 'who came to Paris to be taken seriously in art and literature and to live as they pleased'.[12] They were a long way from Sydney. Escaping the familial and social expectations of conformity and leaving home was part of the queer experience then, as it still is today.[13] It was to Paris, for instance, that the English writer Vita Sackville-West and her lover, the socialite and author Violet Keppel, escaped in the midst of their affair in the late 1910s, Sackville-West cross-dressing as a soldier, Julian, and the two women dancing in the lesbian bars. 'I shall never forget,' Sackville-West later recounted, 'the evenings when we walked back slowly to our flat through the streets of Paris. I, personally, had never felt so free in my life.'[14]

But despite the apparent freedom parts of the city offered, many of the avant-garde women who gravitated toward Paris during the 1910s and 1920s were discreet in navigating same-sex relationships in the public sphere. The non-binary writer, actor and photographer Claude Cahun lived with her partner, artist Marcel Moore, under the convenient guise that, as well as lovers, they were stepsisters. Gertrude

Stein was famously guarded. As the composer Virgil Thomson commented, there were two things you never asked Stein—about her being a lesbian and about what her writing meant.[15] Similarly, when interviewed at the very end of her life, Sylvia Beach referred to Adrienne Monnier, with whom she had had a relationship for 36 years, as her 'friend'.[16]

Dangar and Crowley grew up in a time of shifting yet highly ambivalent attitudes to lesbianism, when pioneering sexologists such as Richard von Krafft-Ebing and Havelock Ellis, and the psychoanalyst Sigmund Freud, were producing problematic accounts of lesbian and queer sexuality. The fact alone that these men acknowledged the existence of women's same-sex sexuality was progressive, radical even, but their theories reflected broader societal attitudes that considered the 'normal' object of sexual love as one's opposite sex.[17] Ellis even equated lesbianism with pathological violence and mental illness; he included in his chapter on 'sexual inversion in women' in his *Studies in the psychology of sex, volume 2* published in 1900, the story of Alice Mitchell, a 'typical invert', who cut her lover's throat. He followed this with two other accounts of murder and attempted murder by 'sexually inverted women', and then went on to state that lesbianism was a cause of suicide.[18] Many lesbians closely followed this work.[19] At the same time, they were born into the Victorian era in which many viewed romantic infatuations among girls as part of a normal progression to adulthood. As Lisa Featherstone discusses in her study of sexuality in Australia, 'Romantic Friendship is a useful tool for describing some early twentieth century relationships between women, for it undercuts the duality between heterosexual/lesbian that was only emerging as a strong polarity in this period.'[20]

In the face of social and cultural pressures, men and women defied norms, despite, in the case of lesbians, being depicted in popular culture and literature as, if not 'evil or morbid', then as 'simply weird'.[21] Women, in particular, were able to maintain hidden relationships, with asexuality assumed once they stepped away from heteronormativity. As late as the early 1970s, psychologist Charlotte Wolff asserted, 'it is not homosexuality but homoaffectionality which is at the centre and the very essence of women's love for each other … The sex act is always secondary with them.'[22]

Indeed, Dangar and Crowley's relationship has invariably been couched in terms of friendship, with descriptors such as 'longtime friend', 'dearest friend', 'close friend', 'friend and fellow teacher' and 'artistic co-adventurer' lining accounts of their time together, and their relationship characterised as one of 'regard and affection'.[23] The artists themselves used the ambivalent language of romantic friendship. A documentary made about Crowley in 1975 shows her walking through her first survey exhibition at the Art Gallery of New South Wales.[24] Elderly and frail, her hair back in a bun and wearing dark glasses, she comes across a display case. 'This is a plate of Anne Dangar's,' she says, staring at it, 'I went … abroad with her in 1926.' Another small pause. 'She was my *best* friend. She was a *tremendous* personality.'

But while their love was not openly discussed, a story has come down through the Dangar family that, in a quiet way, acknowledges the truth of their relationship. Dangar's niece recounted the two women attending the 1923 Artists' Ball in Sydney, Dangar dressed as a cavalier and 'courting', as historian Bruce Adams paraphrases it, 'Crowley's coquettish princess', in 'their parodies of conventional gender roles'.[25] Even though in Australia at the time, according to historian Lisa Featherstone, 'cross-dressing may not have always been associated with lesbian desire, and slippage between cross-dressing mannish appearance and lesbianism was common',[26] Dangar and Crowley were able to push the boundaries of gendered norms through discretion and ambiguity.

In 1930 Dangar left Sydney for the second time, after having returned there alone in late 1928 after her money ran out. She was deeply unhappy, yearning for the freedom of Europe, and chafing against what she perceived to be an art establishment conservative and resistant to the exciting new modern ideas

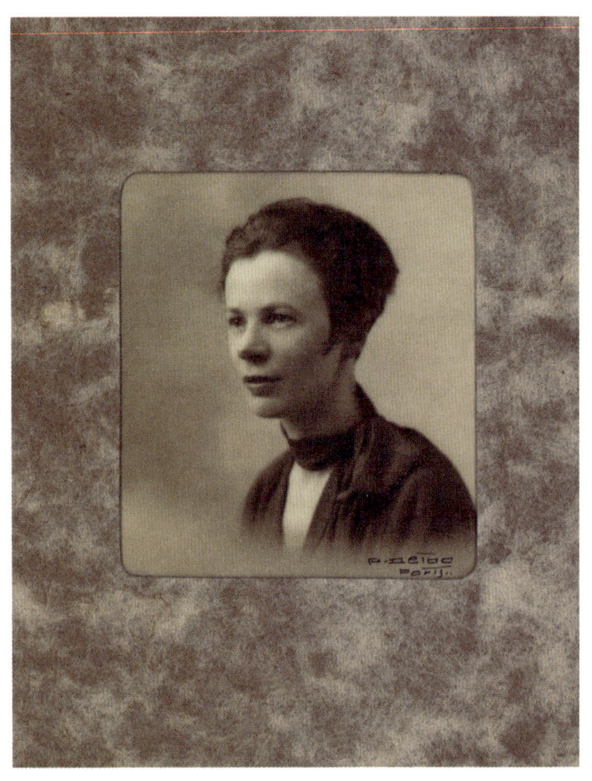

fig 39 Portrait of Grace Crowley, c 1927

she had discovered in France, in those years that she later described as the happiest in her life.[27] Though there was often talk in her letters to Crowley of a return to Australia,[28] Dangar settled in France, permanently as it turned out, at Moly-Sabata in Sablons on the Rhône, established only three years before as a utopian artist community by the French cubist painter Albert Gleizes.

Over more than 20 years, the couple maintained their intimacy through letters they wrote back and forth until Dangar's death in 1951.[29] Upon hearing this news, Crowley saw to it that her letters to Dangar were destroyed, writing to Gleizes, 'Anne told me only a few months ago that she kept every letter I ever wrote. Would you kindly see that all those letters are burned.'[30] Dangar's side of the correspondence survives to this day, kept private by Crowley for many decades, until she donated them to the Mitchell Library, Sydney—redacted and with pages removed. She made available these precious letters but under her own terms.

The letters Dangar sent to Crowley provide invaluable insight into her life in Sablons as well as her growing understanding of Cubism as she actively sought to keep Crowley abreast of developments in France. She took notes of what she was learning of Gleizes's theories of colour and form, expressly to pass onto Crowley,[31] advocating in her letters for Gleizes's method over Lhote's, noting for example that Lhote spoke in a similar vein but 'he didn't show how to do it!'[32] After only a couple of months of being back in France, Dangar sent Crowley a long letter with detailed instructions about how colours and planes play off one another and how to mix colours.[33] She also sent pochoirs by Robert Pouyaud, who was instructing Dangar in Gleizes's concepts and working method, for Crowley to work off, advising her to 'keep them three months & do exercises & send the exercises to him & he'll be really happy to correct & advise' and noting that 'then I'll feel I have been able to do a little thing for you'.[34]

By 1934 Crowley had gathered around herself a group of fellow travellers—artists including Rah Fizelle (with whom she had formed a school in 1932), Frank Hinder, Margel Hinder and Ralph Balson—with whom she shared Dangar's notes and instructions in regular meetings at her studio. In the mid 1930s, Dangar sent a series of five lectures for Crowley to share with students, distinguishing pure abstraction and articulating Gleizes's theories of translation and rotation of form, as well as a lecture on colour. These teachings were a vital piece in the puzzle—for Dangar's associates and friends but most particularly and impactfully for Crowley and Balson—as they moved toward pure abstraction in the 1930s. Crowley made her first abstractions in the early 1940s, exhibited her first abstract works in 1942, and was working purely in abstraction by 1947. Balson's paintings, in which the influence of Gleizes's theories is easily discernible, were exhibited at Anthony Horderns' Fine Art Gallery in 1941, signalling publicly the arrival of abstraction in Australia. This narrative has become an important chapter in Australian art history.

Crowley may have been a long way away physically, but Dangar was able to keep their collaborative artistic adventure alive in a way that collapsed distance. The letters are a tender demonstration of Dangar and Crowley's continuing intimacy and deep emotional bond. Many of them begin with terms of endearment: 'My precious', 'Sweetheart!', 'My dearest one', 'Treasure', 'Chérie', 'My Smudge darling', 'My poor, precious Smudge', 'My dearest little mate', 'My darling my best friend'.[35] Letters also contain revealing disclosures: 'Darling I talk so much about myself & yet I dream of you nearly every night … I go to sleep & dream she is smiling with her pretty little teeth & gives me a quick little teasing kiss!'[36] They include instructions to 'take care of your precious precious self for you are my one & only'.[37] Dangar writes to Crowley of how the arrival of letters leaves her deliriously happy: 'I kissed & kissed the envelope with a thumping bumping heart,' she writes, 'when I found it in the letter box!';[38] a lack of letters leaves her feeling despondent.[39] A longing for Crowley leads to outbursts: 'I can't understand why oh why my mate can't come to me. I call & call all the while. God keep my Darling safe & give her strength to stand the awful life in Australia until she can come.'[40]

The letters were a safe space for Dangar to gossip and vent her frustrations over circumstances and people she encountered at Sablons, where life was difficult. When she was interviewed by artist James Gleeson in 1978, Crowley commented that Dangar had 'had a very hard time in the beginning. In fact, I think she had a hard time all the time.'[41] In her letters to Crowley, Dangar could continue to affirm her love, as the period they spent apart grew longer and longer. 'I just ache & yearn to see you & hear you, feel your touch again', she wrote in March 1933, 'No I don't mind if you have made another friend as long as you keep my place also in your warm noble heart! Oh Smudge what a gift love is!'[42] At times, Dangar describes their separation in heartbreaking terms: 'All the time I trust you & many times a day I offer up a little thanksgiving,' Dangar writes, 'but I'm only a broken detached fragment without any hold on anybody & my only home is your heart.'[43] In another letter, Dangar wrote of a discussion which she had had with the Gleizeses, in which she had explained to them, 'how lonely I would always be without you, how I'd never feel settled until we were together, that nowhere could be my home without you', with a down-the-side sign-off, 'you are in my every thought & your trust in me is my strength'.[44] Most explicitly, in a letter recounting her dream of building a life together with Crowley in France, Dangar wrote to Gleizes and Juliette Roche of her desire that Crowley should join her at the artistic colony 'as my wife'.[45]

On Dangar's birthday on 1 December 1932, she wrote to Crowley of the longevity of their deep love:

> Darling I am so very very thankful you are happy & have found your real self again in your work. I too am working & losing myself again in my work which is our only way of finding our real selves … Smudgie your work is the reflection of your mind—that noble beautiful mind I have loved each year for ~~twentyone~~ nineteen years more & more & more. I admire you for that tenacity which prevents you from throwing all your training to the winds & going after new (false?) gods.[46]

In this letter, as in so many others, Dangar compounds their commitment to a shared love with a commitment to being true to their identities as modern artists. She draws a clear thread between that love, their respective practices, and their 'real' selves. Indeed, Dangar makes very clear that the act of making art was for her deeply bound to identity and underpinned with passion and love (both bodily and psychic) as indeed it may have been for Crowley: it was, Dangar believed, 'always from the secret places of her heart' that Crowley painted, revealing 'the beauty of the real Smudge'.[47] Surfacing Dangar and Crowley's status as a couple serves to open and enrich our understanding of the origins of abstraction in Australian art, and of the course of modernism in Australia more generally. Anne Dangar and Grace Crowley. By bringing their names together we acknowledge the vital role their intimate relationship and remarkable letters played in both determining the course of their lives and in shaping the artistic landscape.

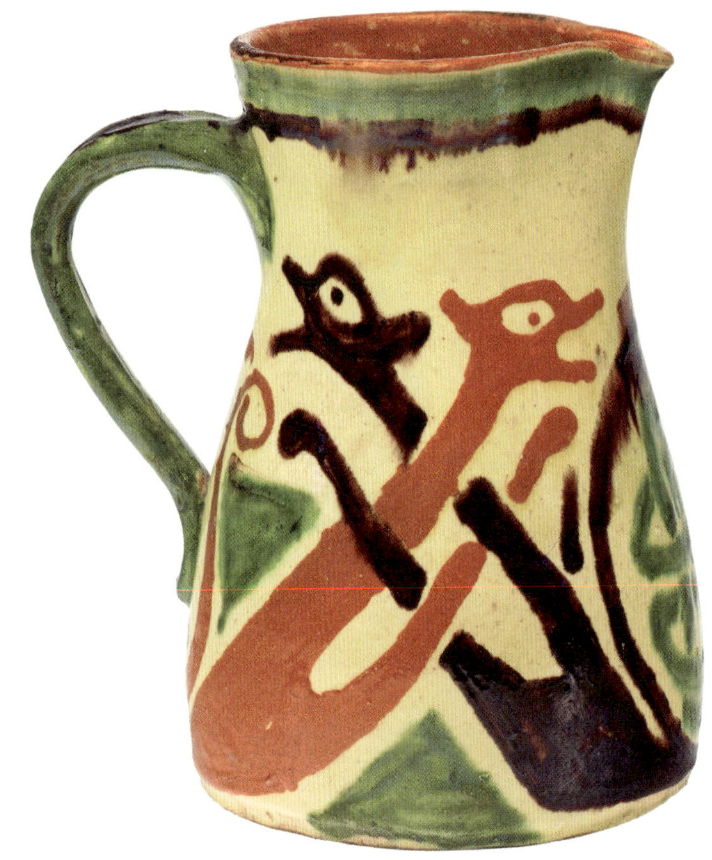

cat 38 Jug with Celtic serpent design 1933–50

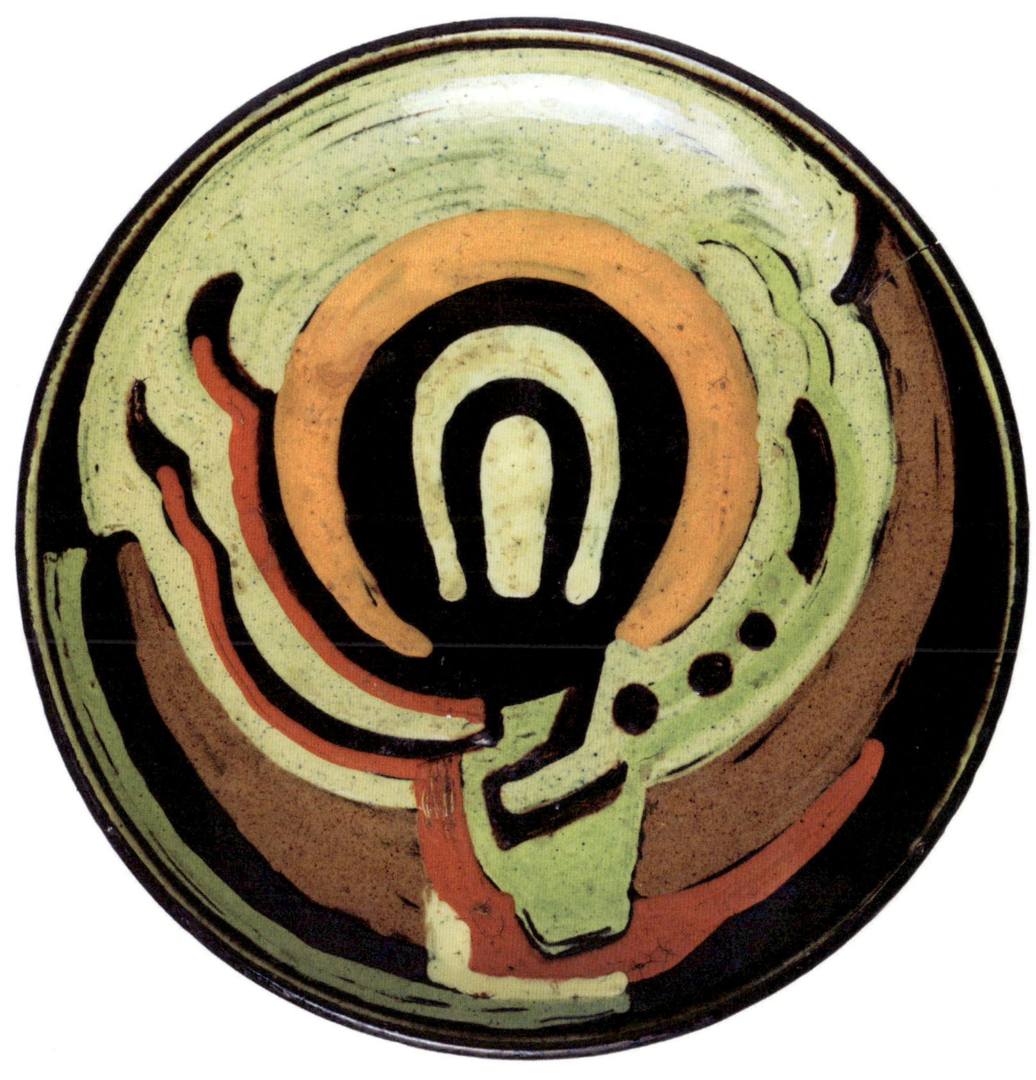

cat 45 Plate 1934–35

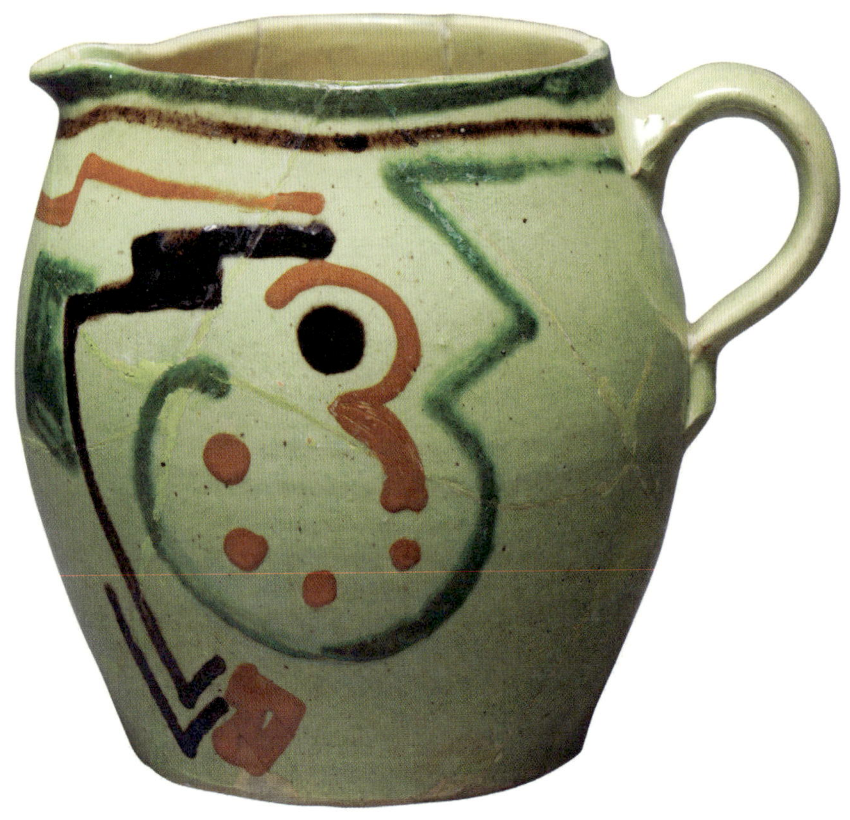

cat 20 Jug 1933–38

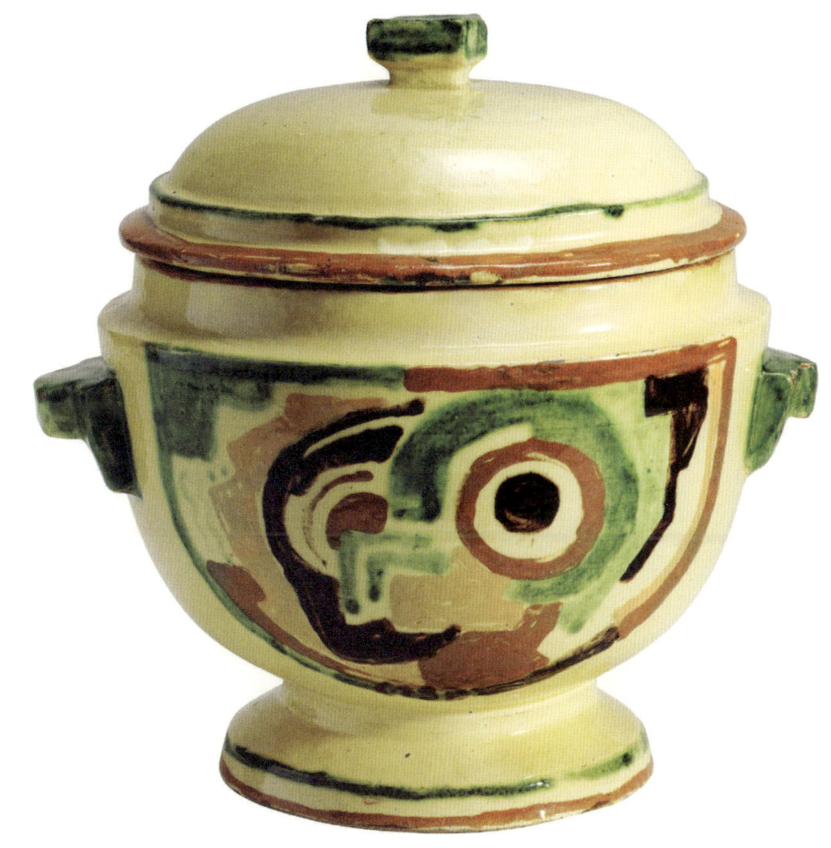

cat 21 Soup tureen with cubist design 1933–38

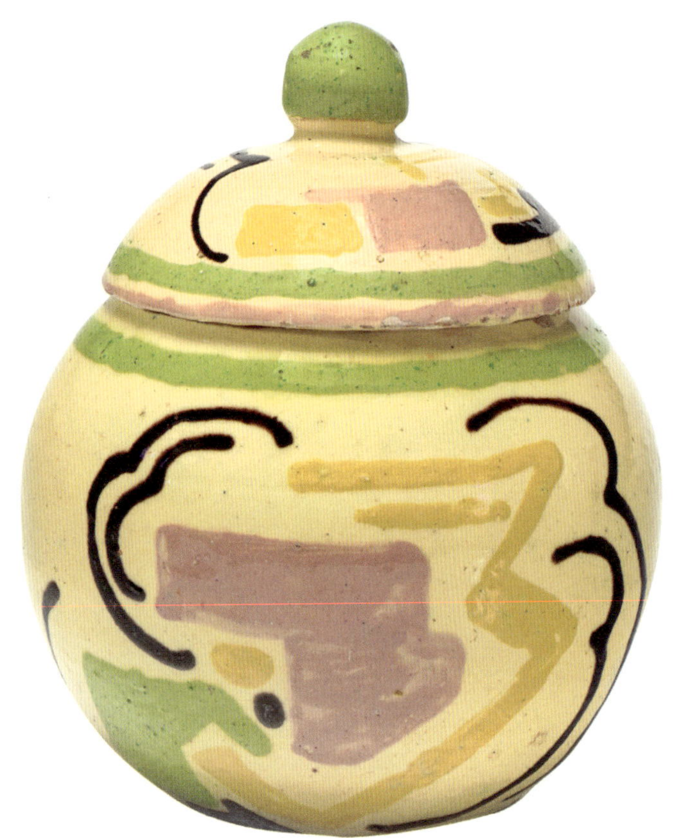

cat 35 Jar with cubist design 1933–50

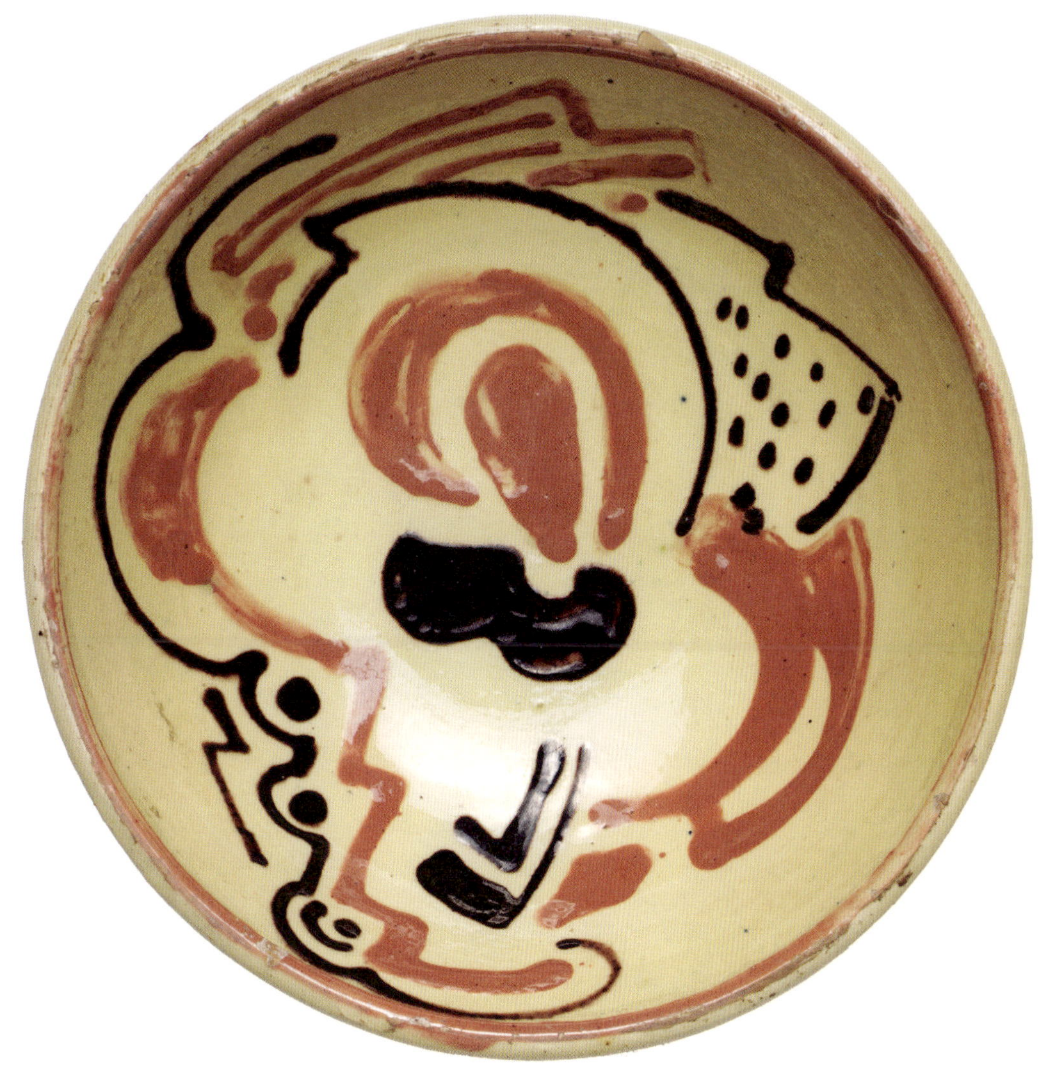

cat 12 Bowl 1931–33

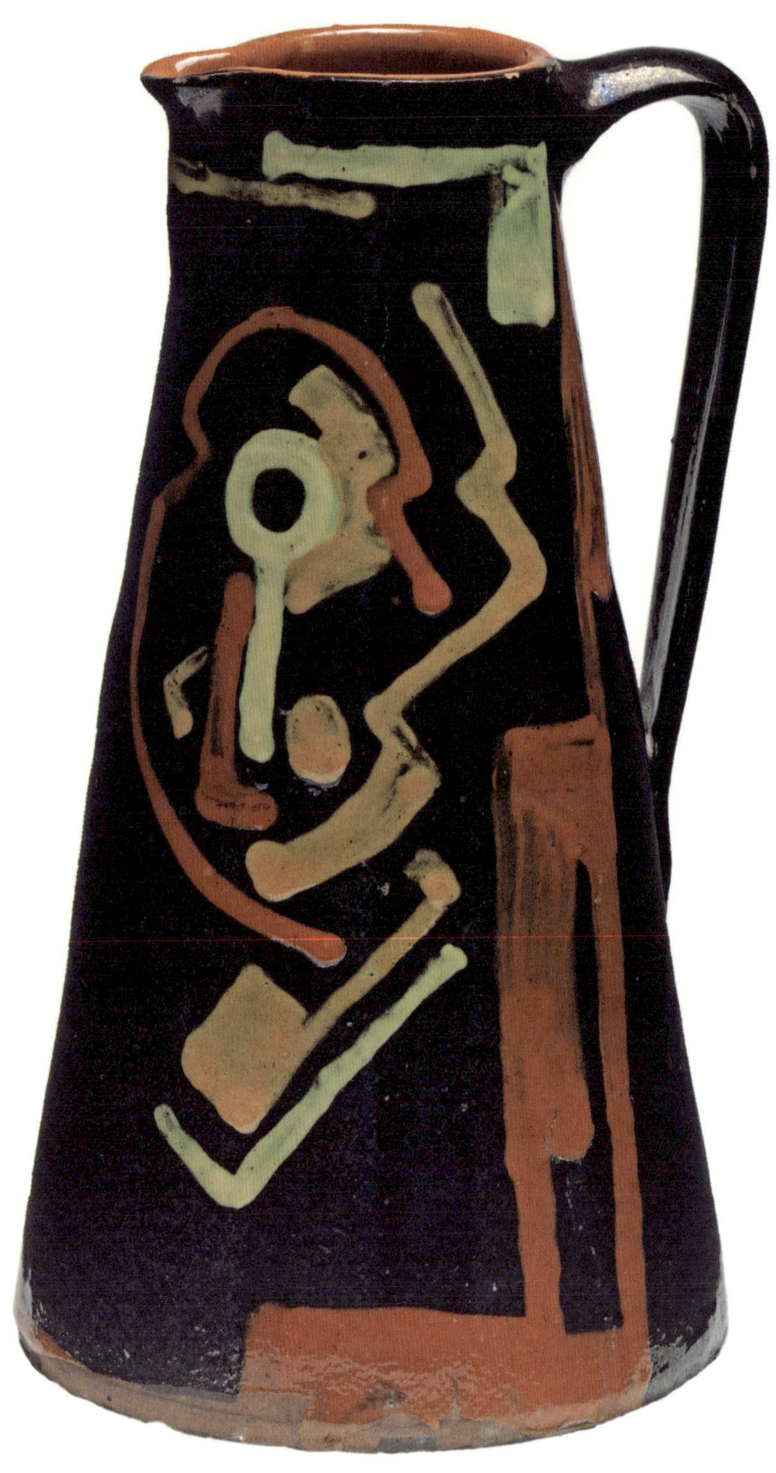

cat 24 Jug 1933–38

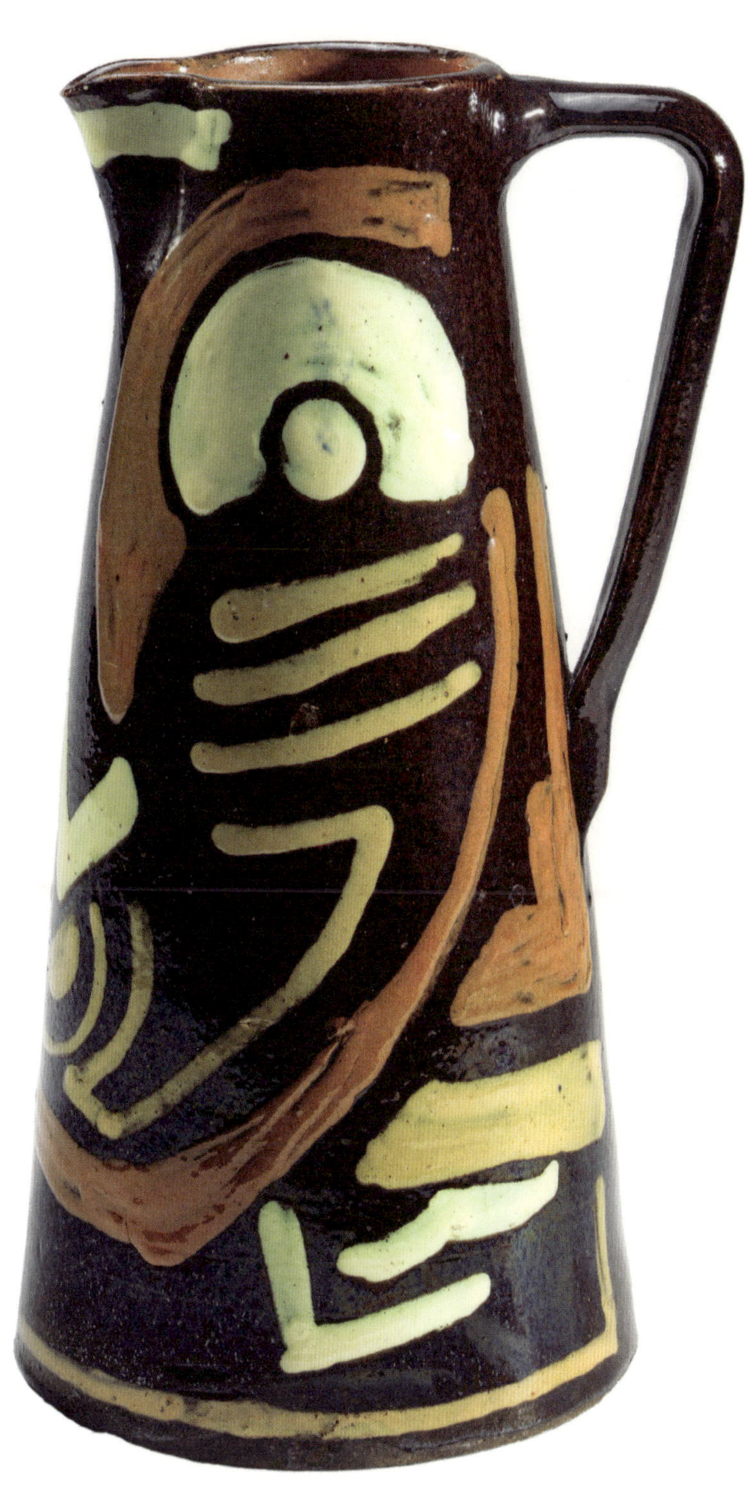

cat **25** Jug 1933–38

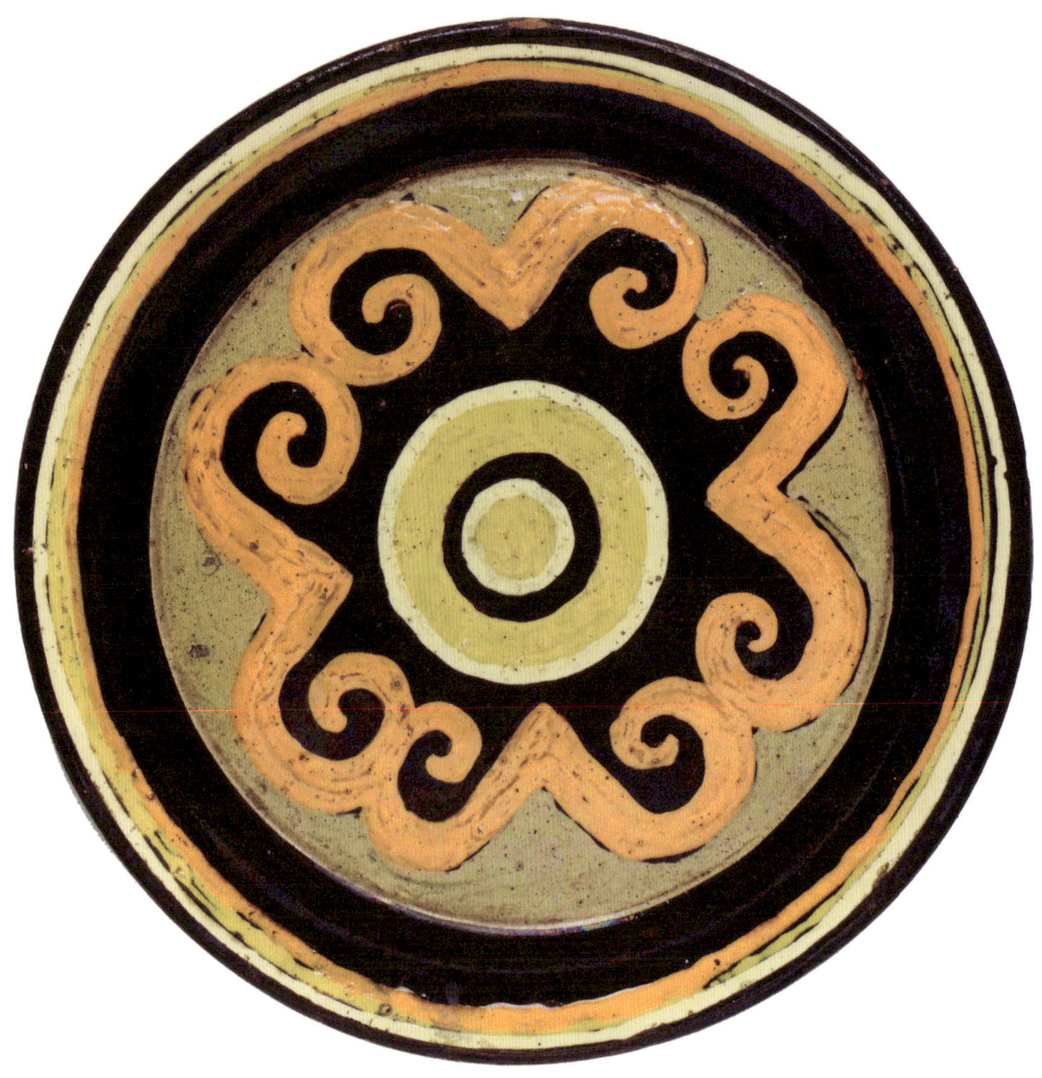

cat 30 Plate 1933–38

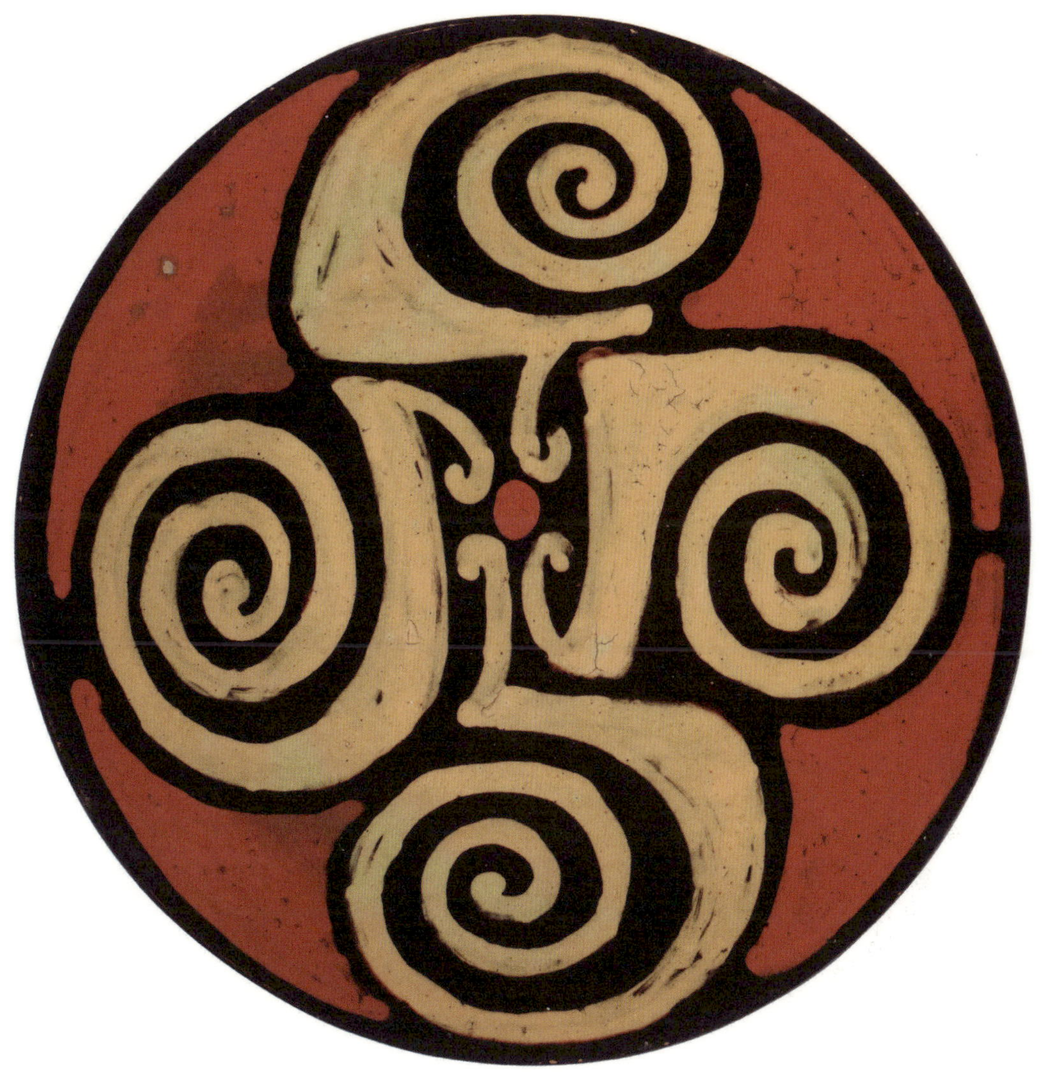

cat 40 Plate with spiral design 1933–50

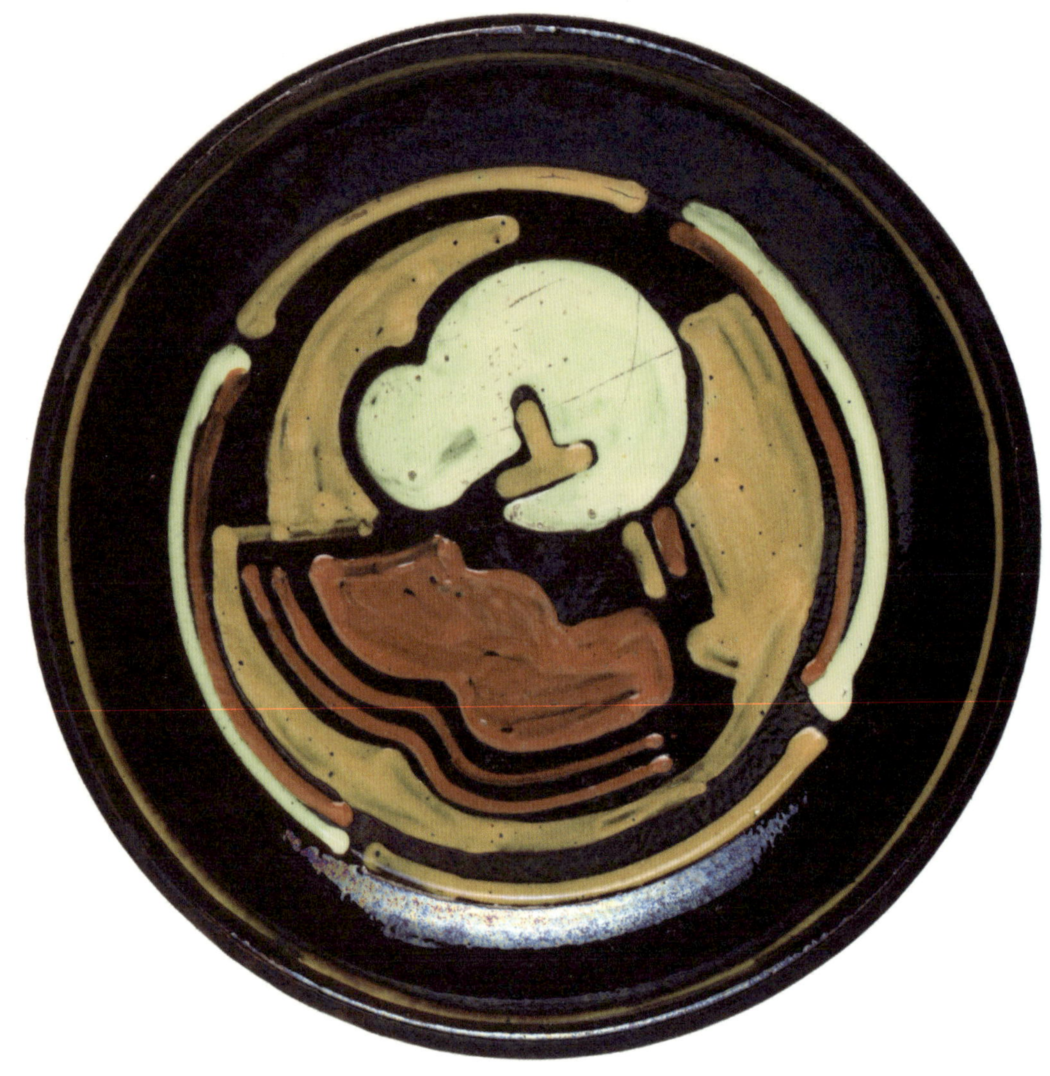

cat 27 Plate with cubist design 1933–38

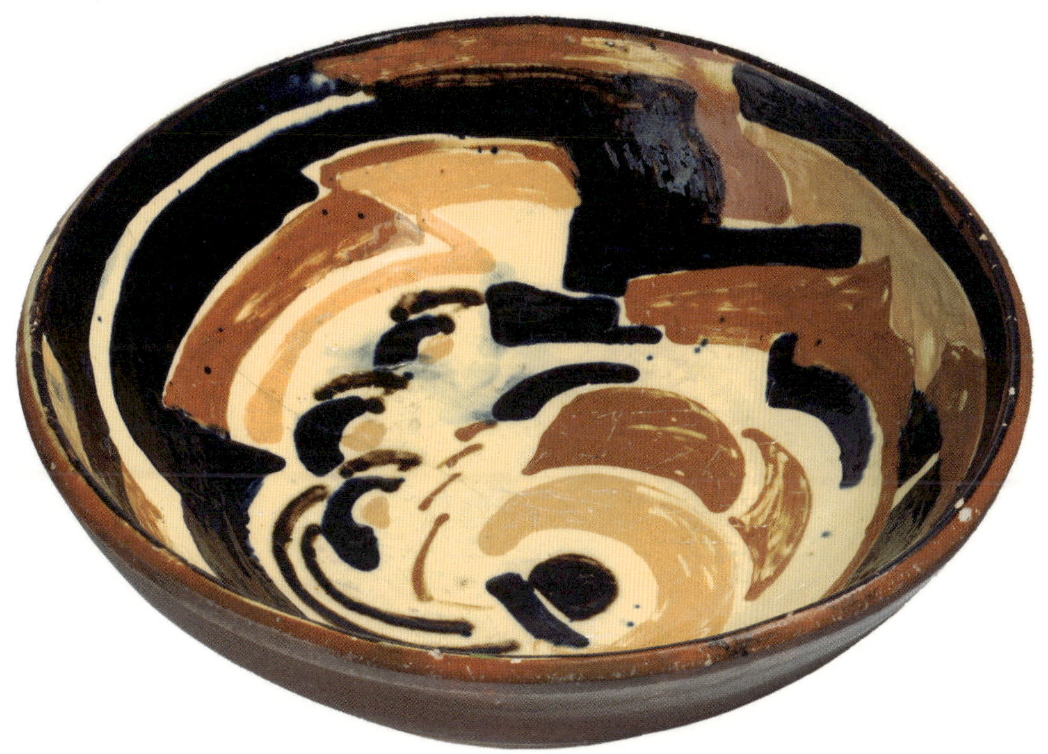

cat 22 Bowl with cubist design 1933–38

III

LEGACY

1937–1951

1937[1]

MARCH

Becomes angry when Paquaud copies her ceramic forms and decoration and sells the works at a church fete at Roussillon.

APRIL

Sends a consignment of pottery to Crowley in Eora Country/Sydney. Crowley holds an exhibition in her studio. Dangar is contacted by a Sydney architect who is interested in commissioning her to create tiled wall murals for buildings (these commissions do not eventuate due to the war).

MAY–JUNE

Exhibits pottery in the Exposition internationale des arts et techniques dans la vie moderne, Paris, and in an associated exhibition. Receives a gold medal and 500 francs prize for her pottery.

JULY

Sends two cases of pottery to Eora Country/Sydney, including tiles for a table for Crowley, tiles for relatives, and mugs for Fizelle.

OCTOBER

Travels to Paris to visit the Exposition internationale, staying with Sue Alexandre. Is joined by her cousin Effie 'Fairy' Mills, who is visiting from Australia.

NOVEMBER

Fairy offers to lend money to build a kiln at Moly-Sabata. Roche opposes the idea. Dangar is commissioned to create pottery and advise on renovations to the Hôtel Schaeffer restaurant in Serrières. Enlists Grenoble designer Jacques Martin to assist.

1938

JANUARY

Spends the year debating whether to return to Australia or whether to remain and build a pottery at Moly-Sabata. Is asked to send sketches and samples to Sydney for a possible outdoor commission (this does not eventuate due to the war).

FEBRUARY–MARCH

Meets painters Robert and Sonia Delaunay. Receives commission from the Delaunays for three plates.

APRIL

The Hôtel Schaeffer reopens.

MAY

Exhibits alongside Paul Beyer, Marcel Duchamp, Claude Stahly and artists from the Témoignage group at the Galerie Matières et Formes, Paris.

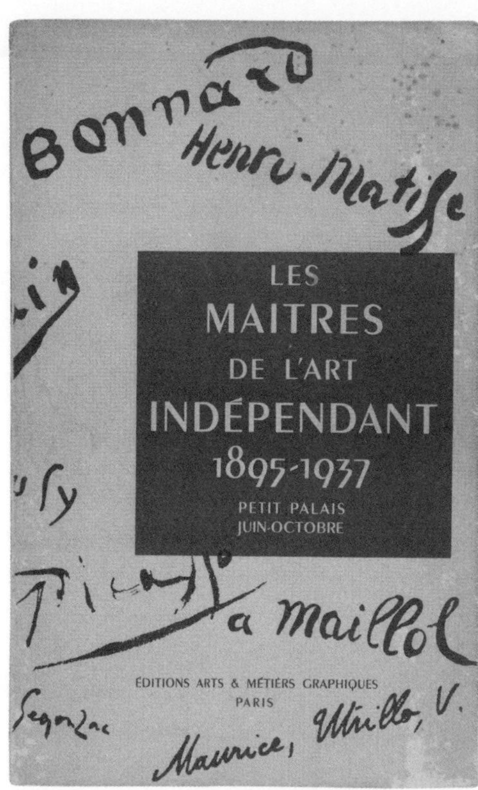

fig 40 *Les maîtres de l'art indépendant, 1895–1937*, catalogue for exhibition in which Anne Dangar's work was displayed, 1937

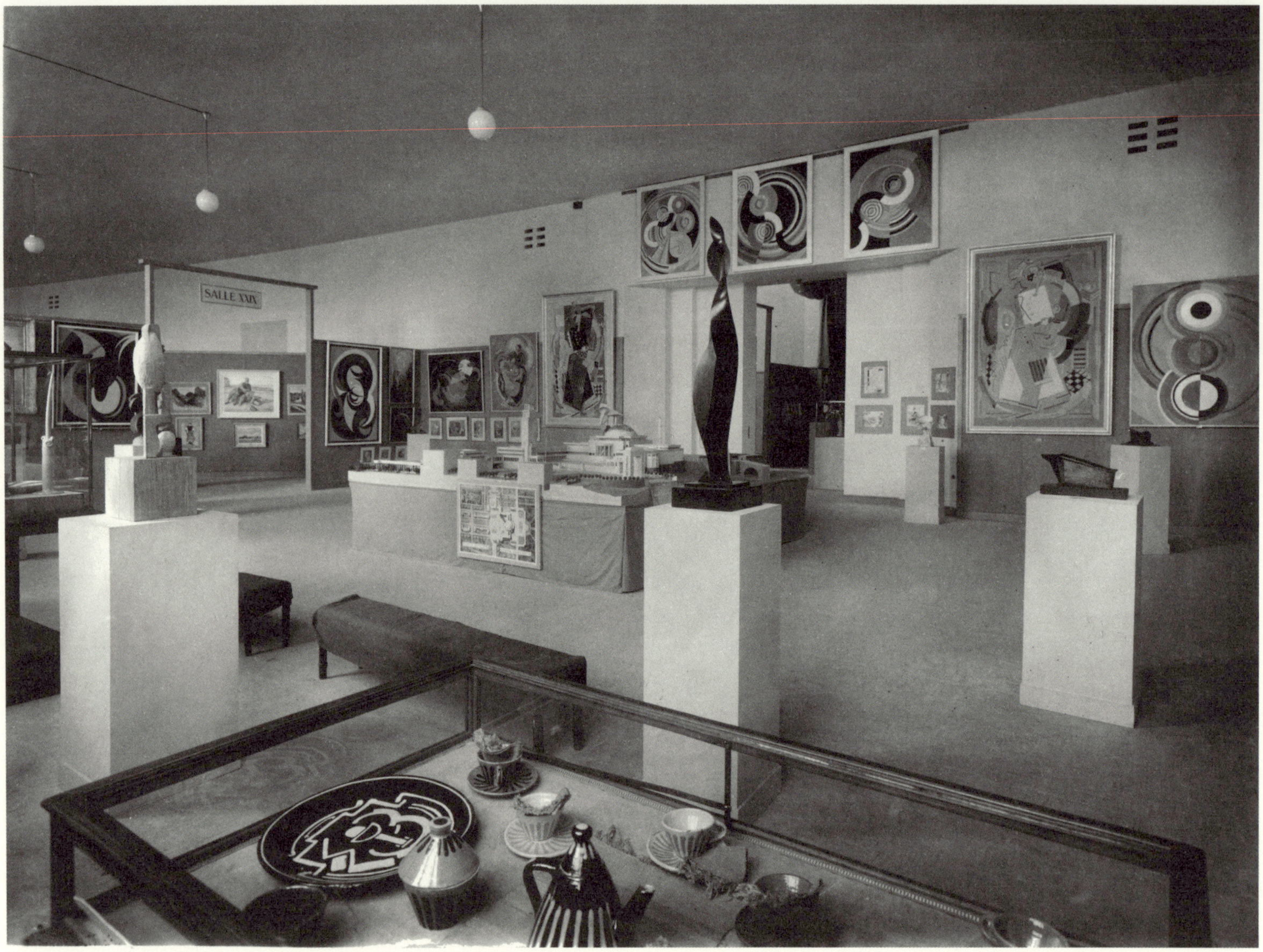

fig 41 *Aspect actuel du cubisme chez quelques aînés et quelques jeunes*, Salon d'automne, 1938, featuring ceramics and gouaches by Anne Dangar, and paintings by Robert Delaunay and Albert Gleizes

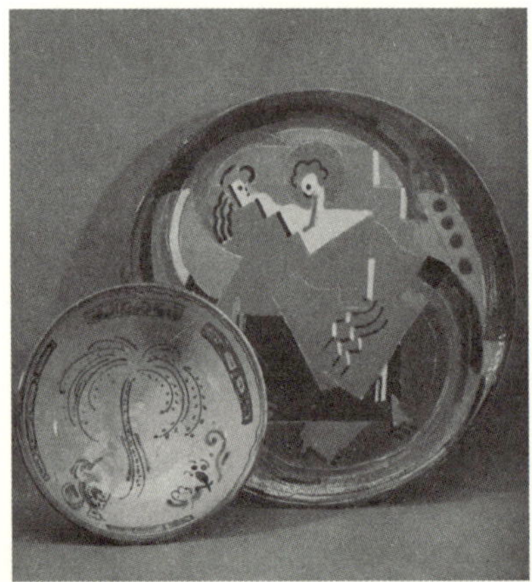

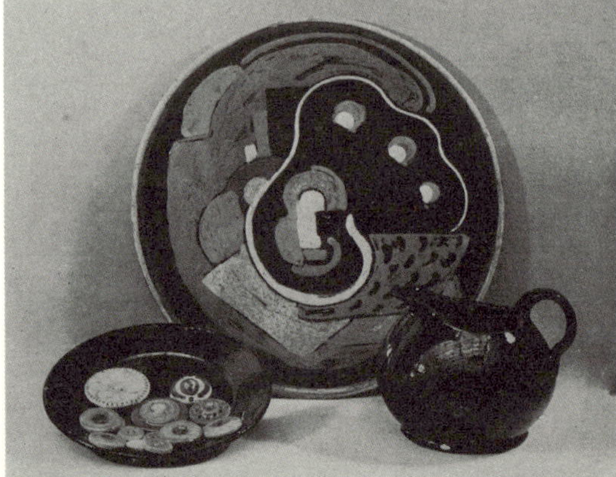

figs 42–43 Anne Dangar's ceramics, including *Mère et enfant* (*Mother and child*) 1935–37 in Maximilien Gauthier, 'Moly-Sabata', *Art et Décoration*, September–October 1938

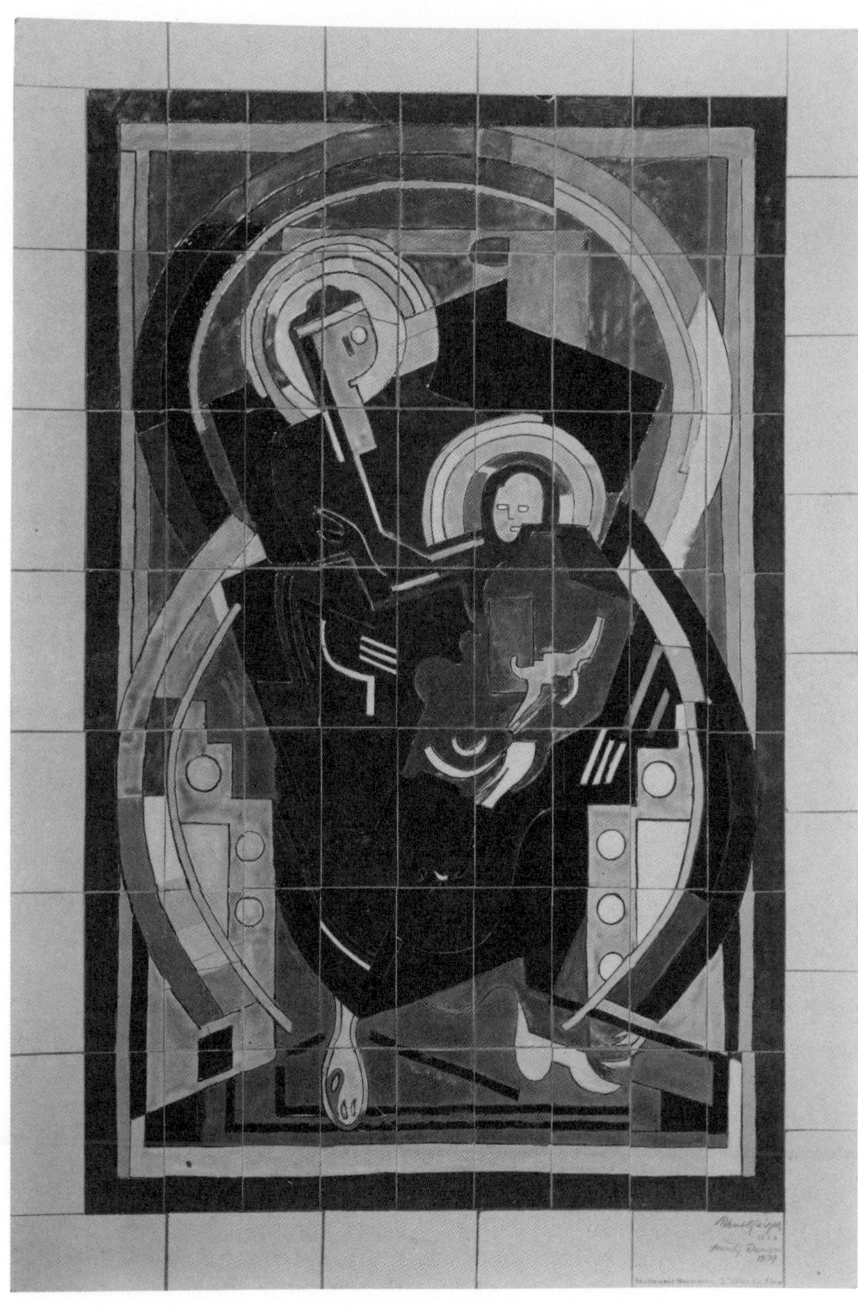

fig 44 Photograph of Anne Dangar's tiled panel 'after Albert Gleizes' displayed in the Exposition internationale des arts et techniques dans la vie moderne, Paris, 1937

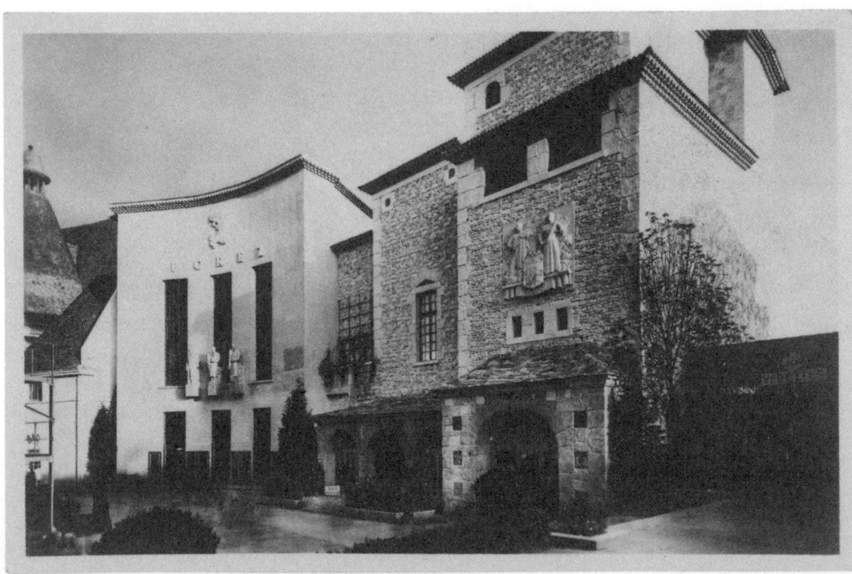

fig 45 The Forez-Vivarais pavilion in the Centre Regional at the Exposition internationale, Paris, 1937

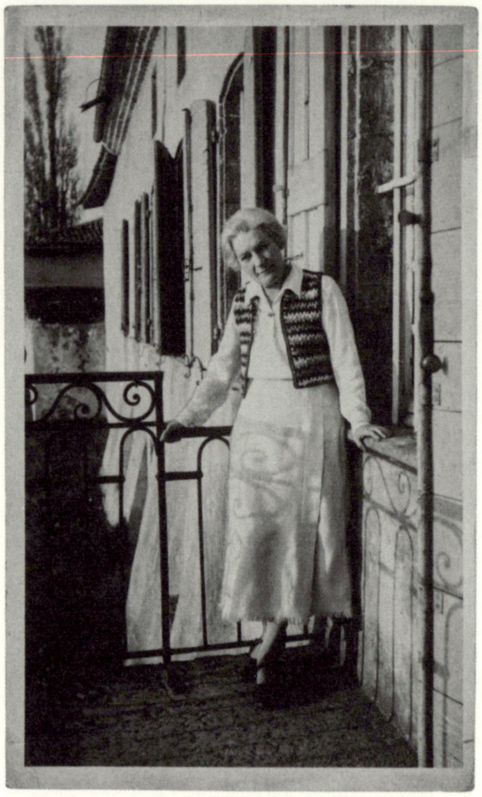

fig 46 Anne Dangar on the balcony at Moly-Sabata, 1940s

1939

FEBRUARY

Works at Cliousclat for three weeks, staying in Mirmande and creating 30 large dishes with cubist motifs.

MARCH

Receives an invitation from Madame Noguès, the wife of the resident-general of Morocco, to come to Fez and share her expertise with local potters.

APRIL

Visits Cliousclat to create three plates commissioned by French museums and decorates 42 others.

JULY

Works at Cliousclat in the summer, staying in Mirmande.

AUGUST

Meets Gleizes's student Jean Chevalier and gives him lessons in Cubism.

NOVEMBER–DECEMBER

Sends pottery commission for HV 'Doc' Evatt and Mary Alice Evatt to Eora Country/Sydney. Includes a tapestry by Deveyle. Has little money for coal or shoes during a cold winter.

MAY–JUNE

Departs for Morocco with Sue Alexandre, travelling through Casablanca and Rabat before arriving in Fez. Is based at the Ateliers des beaux-arts. Works in Bab Ftouh (potters' quarters) on the outskirts of the medina. Becomes frustrated with Noguès, who wants her to teach the potters French methods and designs. Meets Jacques Berque, the director of Les corporations d'artisans and the French director of Artistic Affairs in Algeria, who oversees the activity of the artists.

JULY

Proposes an exhibition of the potters' work and there is great excitement among the potters.

SEPTEMBER–DECEMBER

Debates returning to Australia following the outbreak of the Second World War. Returns to Moly-Sabata in December following orders from Gleizes. Crowley writes, requesting further artistic instruction from Gleizes. He agrees to provide lessons over correspondence. Dangar sends initial lessons in early 1940, before the war makes this impossible.

1940

JANUARY–APRIL

Gleizes departs Serrières for Saint-Rémy-de-Provence. Dangar decides to pursue building a pottery again, and asks Gleizes to sign an agreement giving her tenure for 20 years. Robert Pouyaud and Louis Raibaud visit.

JUNE–JULY

Paris is occupied by German soldiers and power is transferred to Philippe Pétain and the Vichy government, who adopt a position of collaboration with Germany. Sablons is subject to aerial bombing and violent battles occur in the nearby Rhône Valley. Residents take shelter in the cellars of Moly-Sabata. Sablons and Serrières are occupied by German soldiers. Officers occupy Gleizes's house in Serrières for two weeks. Dangar, as an Australian citizen, is not permitted to work in France. Loses income due to decreased sales of her pottery and is the subject of nasty commentary from locals in Sablons who have adopted an anti-British stance.

AUGUST

The British consul in Lyon advises Dangar's repatriation but Gleizes dissuades her.

SEPTEMBER

Begins to disagree with Gleizes over her defence of Britain and its people during the war. Builds a Berber kiln for the children. A buyer from the Galeries Lafayette, Paris, visits and buys all available pottery, putting in an order for Christmas.

OCTOBER

As a foreigner, requires a *carte de circulation* for identification and travel within France, but it does not guarantee *sauf-conduit* (safe passage). Is unable to work. The kiln at Roussillon collapses, the Cliousclat pottery is unable to fire and she cannot travel to Saint-Uze. Photographer Marius Cochard visits and documents the children's classes.

NOVEMBER–DECEMBER

Receives a *carte de circulation* that is valid for only three months. Visits Gleizes at Les Méjades in Saint-Rémy-de-Provence to assist with painting three large panels, before travelling to Cliousclat and Mirmande.

1941

FEBRUARY–MAY

Contracts mumps. With Lucie Deveyle, moves contents of Gleizes's studio to Moly-Sabata. As she is unable to travel freely or work, her friends assist with prohibited trips to the potteries. Supplies are limited and many of the nearby potteries are unable to operate due to a lack of supplies and potters. Henri Bert talks of closing the pottery at Roussillon and Paquaud is forced to work at a Nazi-operated Polish sawmill.

JUNE

Contemplates asking the Vichy government for money to build a kiln at Moly-Sabata. Resolves to return to Australia eventually, but wants to ensure Moly-Sabata is able to grow and continue without her.

JULY

Jean Chevalier and his wife visit Moly-Sabata.

DECEMBER

Visits Cliousclat and Mirmande. Is reproached by Gleizes for not training someone to take her place.

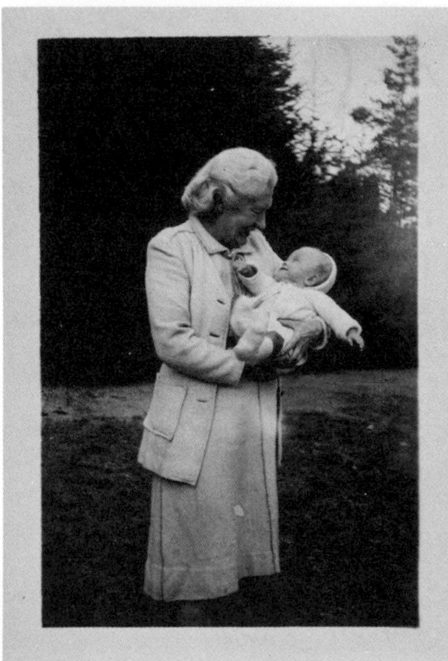

fig 47 Anne Dangar and baby at Moly-Sabata, 1940s

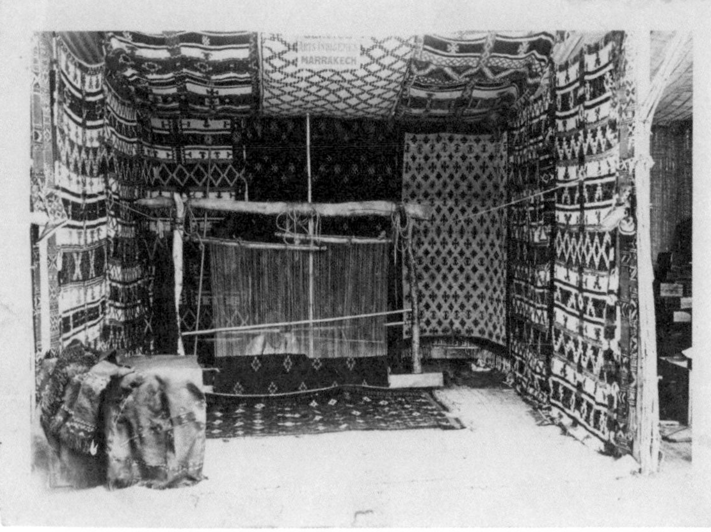

fig 48 Arts indigènes Marrakech, 1939

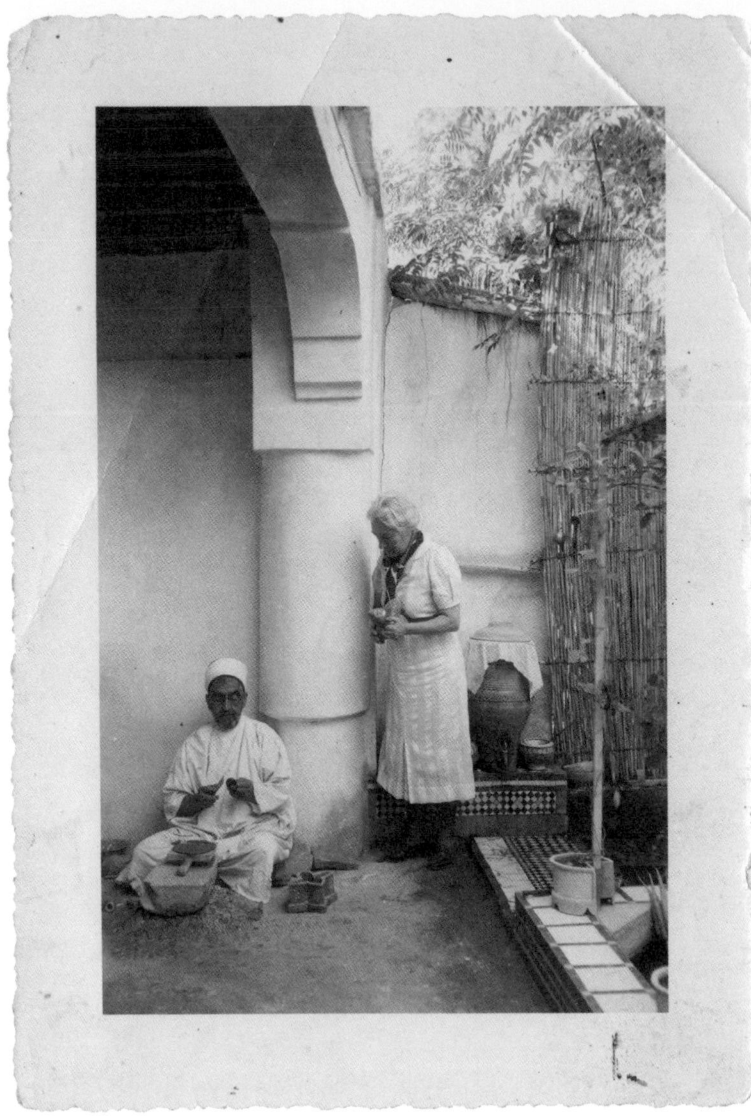

fig 49 Sidi Hassan Ben-Cherif and Anne Dangar, Fez, 1939

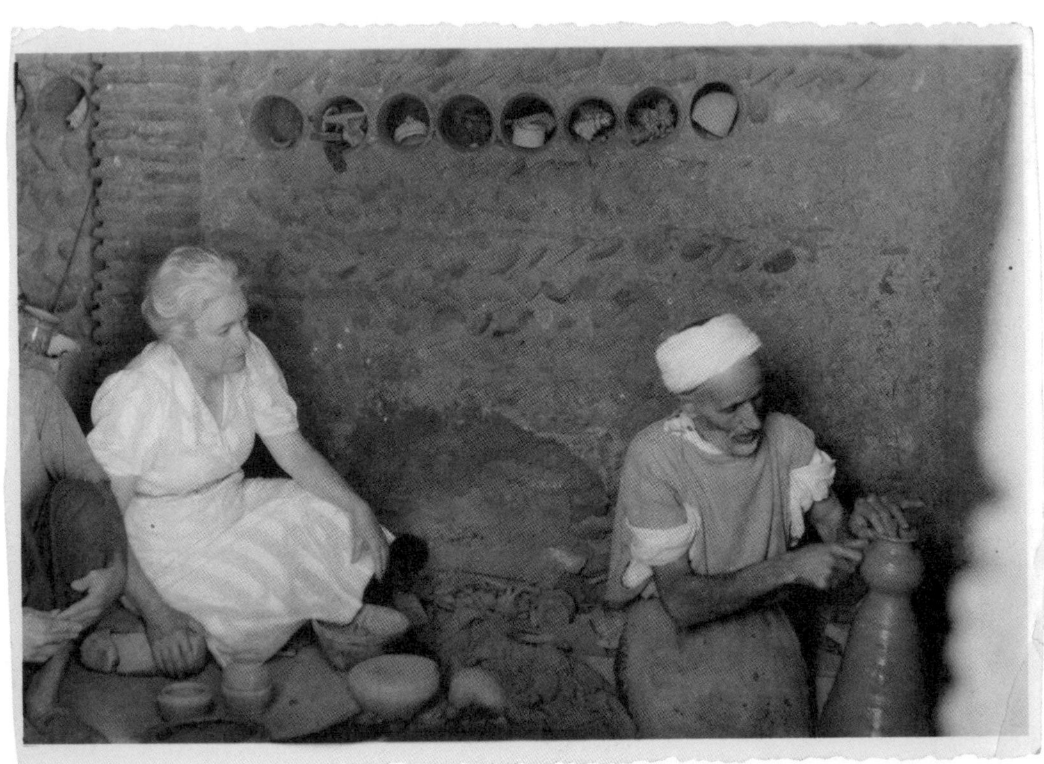

fig 50 Anne Dangar and potter, Fez, 1939

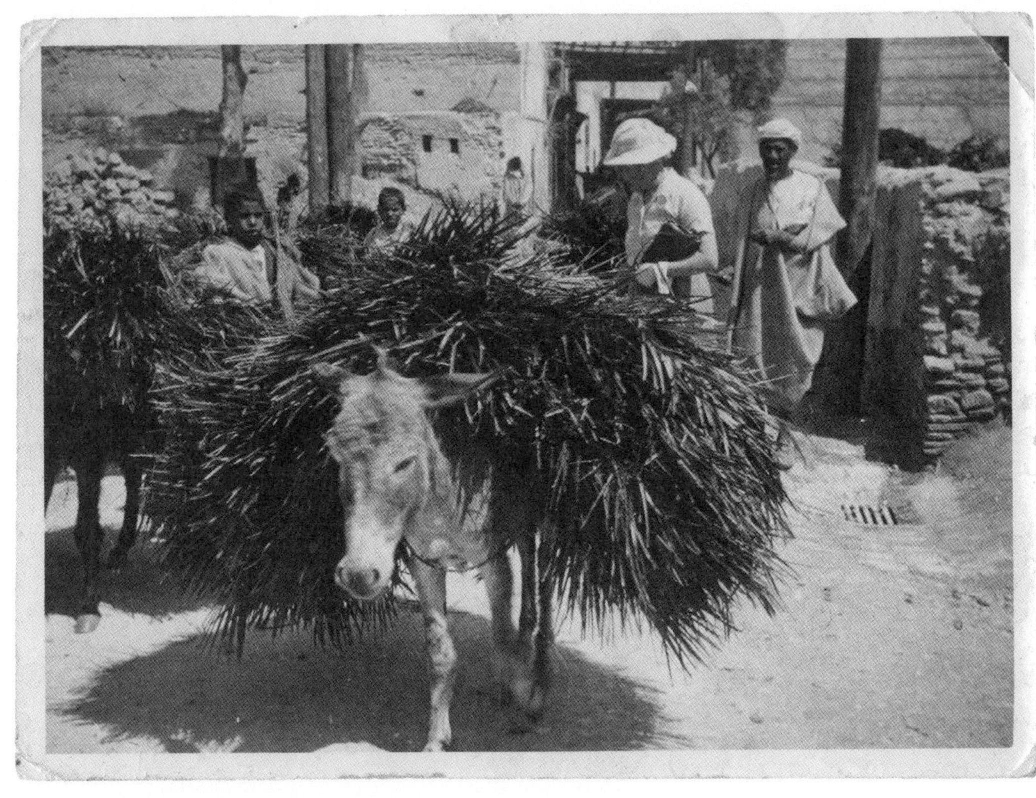

fig 51 Anne Dangar in Fez, 1939

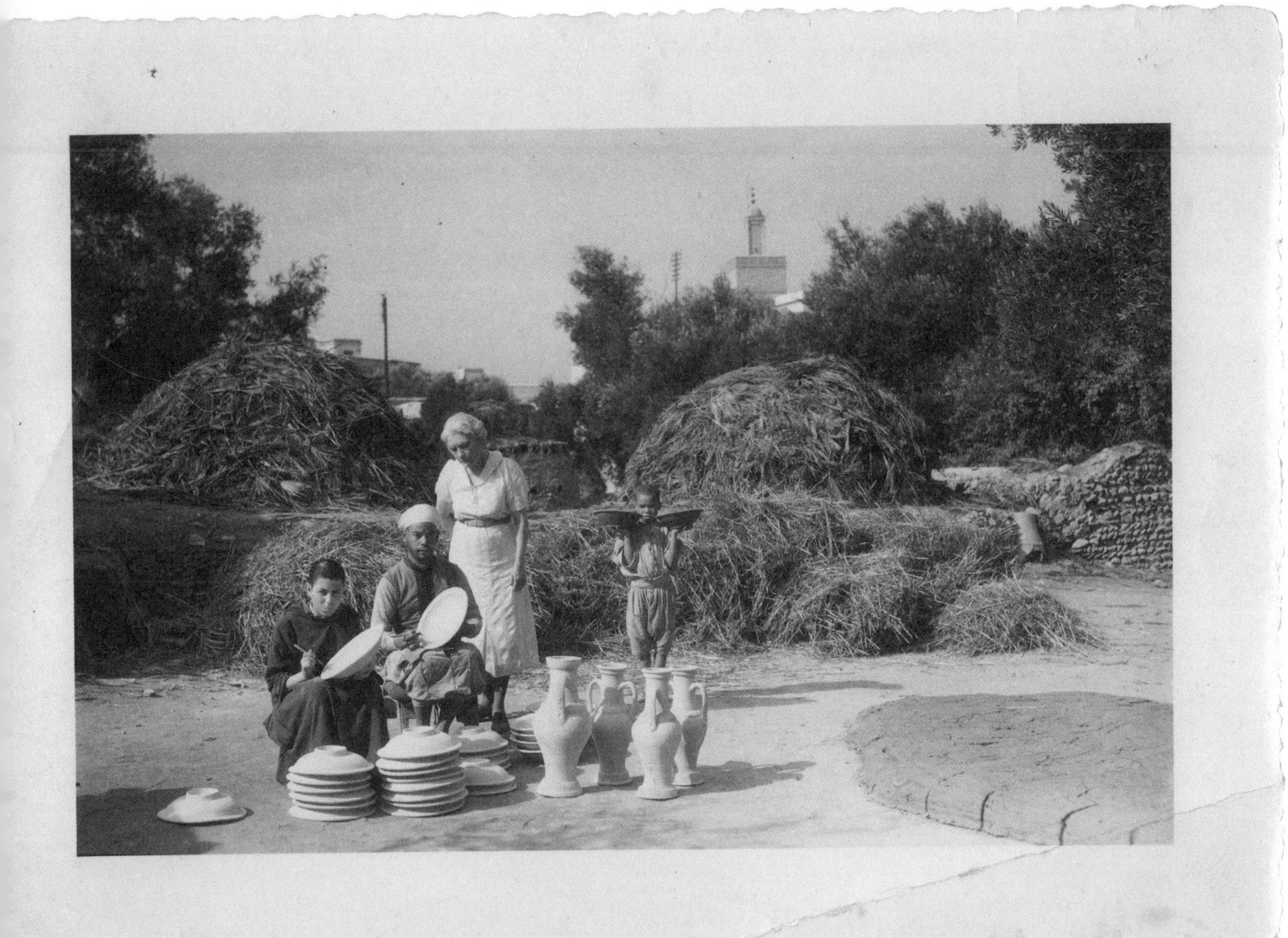

fig 52 Anne Dangar and potters, Fez, 1939

1942

JANUARY

Gleizes visits and convinces her to stay at Moly-Sabata. Dangar is invited by Jeune France, an arm of the Vichy government, to teach pottery at the Centre artisanal de poterie et arts plastiques in Mâcon. The potter Étienne Noël, from Dieulefit, asks to meet her.

FEBRUARY–MARCH

Works at the Centre artisanal at Mâcon for six weeks. Dislikes the director and his approach to running the curriculum. Meets young potter Jacqueline Bouvet (later Lerat). Returns to Sablons in March.

APRIL

Jacqueline Bouvet visits Moly-Sabata. Jeune France ceases to exist.

JUNE

The Geoffrays leave Moly-Sabata permanently.

AUGUST–SEPTEMBER

Refuses evacuation to the Spanish border as proposed by the British consul in Lyon. Staff from the American Embassy visit Moly-Sabata and purchase work by Dangar and Deveyle.

DECEMBER

The curator from the Musée de Valence acquires her pottery for the museum.

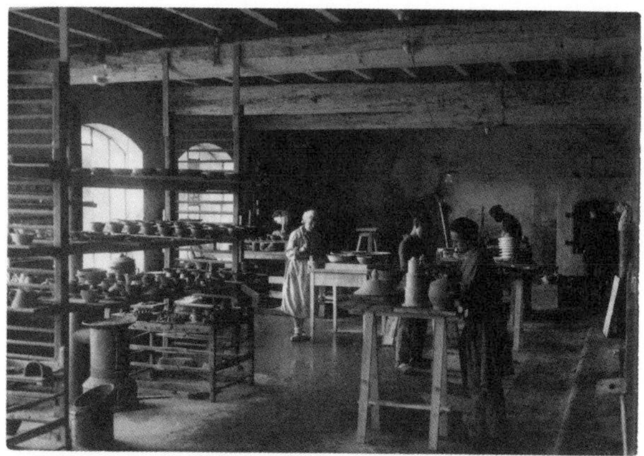

fig 53 Anne Dangar with pottery apprentices at the Centre artisanal de poterie et arts plastiques de Mâcon, 1942

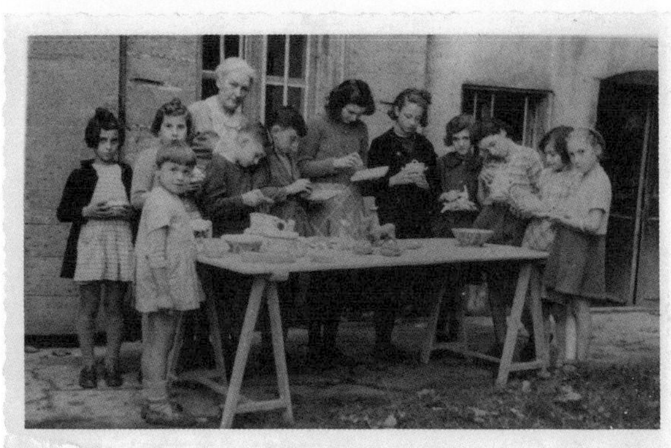

fig 54 Anne Dangar and students at Moly-Sabata, c 1942

1943

MARCH–MAY

Sent to an internment camp in Grenoble for five days (2–6 March), likely because of her foreign national status. Suffers from a nervous condition in the following months. With Deveyle, attempts to make bags and belts from scraps for sale. Creates ceramic buttons and pendants in Madame Steinbach's small kiln.

SEPTEMBER

Falls down the stairs, severely injuring her ankle. Travels to Annonay for radiography and requires a passport to cross the bridge out of Sablons. Unable to walk for a month.

Asked to participate in the exhibition project *Les colonies françaises* with the local schoolteacher Monsieur Coste, and the children of Sablons. Works with pupils to create paintings of imaginary scenes of the French colonies chosen by the Department of Education.

OCTOBER

René Pascal, a young potter friend from Montpellier, visits to help finish firing Dangar's pottery while her ankle is injured.

NOVEMBER

Her ankle improves and she is permitted to go to the pottery but cannot use the wheel. Makes designs and decorates works that don't need turning. Completes many drawings and begins painting again.

1944

APRIL

Gleizes asks why she has not written. Dangar responds angrily about his lack of support and blames him for convincing her to remain at Moly-Sabata during the war.

JULY

Moly-Sabata is requisitioned for refugees from Nice, and three people move into the apartment previously occupied by the Geoffrays. Dangar has no supplies for teaching.

AUGUST–SEPTEMBER

The Allies approach Arles and the electricity at Moly-Sabata is cut off. German soldiers occupy the bridge connecting Serrières and Sablons. Residents take refuge at Moly-Sabata. The Serrières bridge is bombed. Gleizes and Roche's house at Serrières is requisitioned for an infirmary. Befriends an American soldier and talks to him about Cubism, Picasso and Gleizes, encouraging him to visit Moly-Sabata.

NOVEMBER–DECEMBER

The region surrounding Moly-Sabata and Sablons is liberated.

Visits Lyon for the first time in over three years and offers her services as an interpreter to the British Consulate.

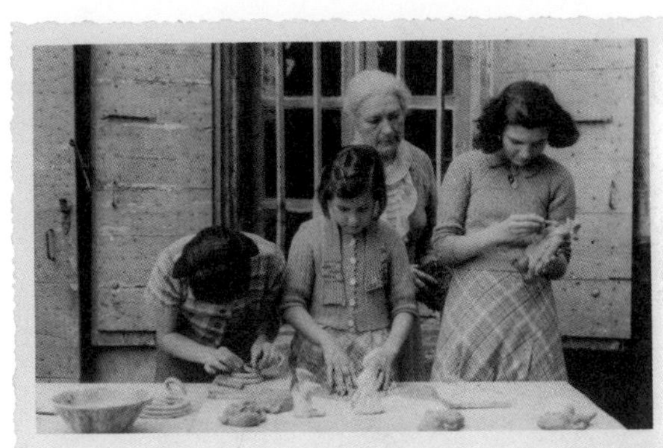

fig 55 Anne Dangar and students at Moly-Sabata, c 1942

1945

MARCH

Geoffrey Dangar, a flight lieutenant in the Royal Air Force based in Italy and Dangar's nephew, visits Moly-Sabata.

APRIL–MAY

Germany surrenders to the Allies on 7 May. Dangar sees Gleizes for the first time in three years. Spends two weeks at Les Méjades painting and drawing with him. Stays with the Grimaud family in Saint-André-de-Cruzières, returning to Moly-Sabata via Mirmande. Visits old friends, Czech-born Joseph Husek and his Tunisian–French wife Blanche Husek, while in Mirmande. Mary Alice Evatt warns that it is unsafe to travel until the war with Japan is over and the troops are home. Also advises that materials to construct a pottery will be scarce in Australia.

JULY

Visits Lyon and plans to repatriate after Christmas so she can hold a final exhibition at Folklore and farewell France. Travels to La Borne pottery in Bourges to work with Jacqueline Lerat (née Bouvet).

SEPTEMBER

Japan surrenders to the Allies and the Second World War comes to an end.

Restages the student exhibition *Les colonies françaises* at Moly-Sabata.

NOVEMBER

Asks sister Ruby to write to her friend, former politician Sir Earle Page, and later to the prime minister Ben Chifley, to ask whether she can return to Australia with her potter's wheel, books and other necessities free of charge. Ruby receives a formal reply, Chifley advising that he will consider her request.

1946

FEBRUARY

Travels to south-west France with Sue Alexandre, visiting Saint-Jean-de-Luz, Bayonne, and the abbey of Saint-Savin. Travels to Limoges and attempts enamelling in the workshop of artist Georges Magadoux.

MARCH–MAY

Returns to Moly-Sabata and teaches pottery at the Péage-de-Roussillon artisanal centre. Exhausted from illnesses, stops teaching after only a few weeks. Contracts diphtheria and is treated for heart trouble. The cost of treatment delays her plans to return to Australia. Gallerist Marcel Michaud spends Easter at Moly-Sabata. He opens Galerie M.A.I. (Meubles, Architectures, Installations) in Paris and buys 29 of Dangar's large plates for the opening exhibition. Dangar is commissioned by the Schaeffers to design murals for the Hôtel Schaeffer, which she creates with their daughter Yvette.

NOVEMBER

Robin Ironside, assistant keeper at the Tate Gallery, London, visits France and gives a lecture on the 'Modern Movement in Art in London' in Vienne. He visits Moly-Sabata. Dangar finds him delightful but too interested in Surrealism. He buys a plate for his private collection.

DECEMBER

Decides against leaving Moly-Sabata as she has spent too much time away from Australia. Attends Gilka Geoffray's wedding on 21 December.

AUGUST

Decides to stay in France one more year. Invited by Gleizes to exhibit in the first Salon des réalités nouvelles—an exhibition of abstract paintings. Has no work but pays the membership fee, planning to contribute the following year. Gleizes invites Crowley and Balson to exhibit; however, shipping strikes mean this does not eventuate.

OCTOBER

Spends several days at Les Méjades with Gleizes and Roche. Becomes interested in the writing of historian and curator Ananda Coomaraswamy, who, like Gleizes, believed in the spiritual power of symbols, analysing and comparing their use across cultures and time. Dangar recommences teaching after stopping due to scarce materials. Friends send pencils, erasers, etc.

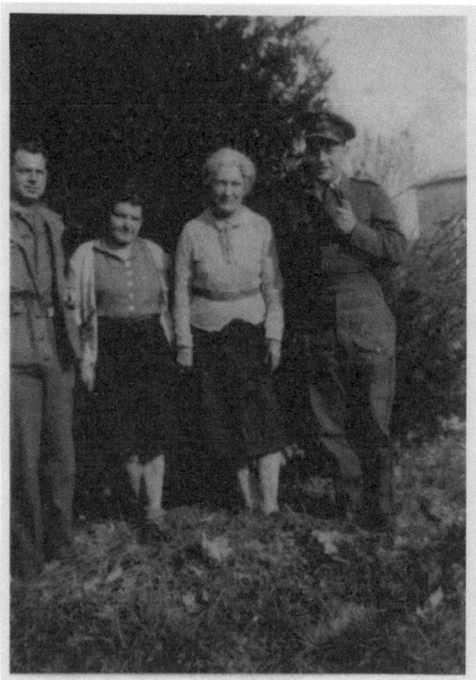

fig 56 Unidentified man, Lucie Deveyle, Anne Dangar and Geoffrey Dangar at Moly-Sabata, 23 February 1945

1947

JANUARY

Makes plans to construct a pottery at Moly-Sabata, saving money and accumulating materials. Crowley writes to Dangar about Joan Miró, Piet Mondrian and Naum Gabo, but Dangar dismisses their work in favour of Gleizes.

FEBRUARY

Receives approval from the mayor to construct a kiln at Moly-Sabata. Marquetry artisans Monsieur and Madame Lardon move to Sablons and give her lessons.

APRIL

Completes the *salle des fêtes* panels and commences the cinema panels for the Hôtel Schaeffer. Poterie Bert begins copying her designs and selling them at a shop in Le Péage-de-Roussillon.

MAY

Visits Gleizes at Les Méjades to see Evie Hone, who is visiting from Ireland.

JUNE

Receives the first order for liturgical objects for the chapel of the abbey of La Pierre-qui-Vire in Saint-Léger-Vauban. Has trouble with her knee and is advised by the doctor that her heart is dilated.

JULY–OCTOBER

The kiln at Moly-Sabata is completed in July and the first firing is held in August with the help of local potters. Paquaud installs the wheel. Moly-Sabata is too far from the electrical transformer so it is wood fired. The first few firings are unsuccessful.

Meets Dom Angelico Surchamp, a young monk from the abbey of La Pierre-qui-Vire and student of Gleizes. They become correspondents and develop a friendship. Thinks more about Catholicism, influenced by Gleizes and Surchamp. Former student Jean-Marcel Héraut-Dumas visits. He is now the secretary of the Beaux-arts at Lyon and requests lessons in translation and rotation.

NOVEMBER–DECEMBER

Receives a donation of 1000 francs from the abbey of La Pierre-qui-Vire, which she invests in varnishes.

1948

JANUARY–FEBRUARY

Is asked by Gleizes for 30 ceramic works for an exhibition in Paris in April. Initially refuses but undertakes the work, staying for a week at Les Méjades to copy his gouaches for translation. Jacques Martin is made director of a gallery in Algeria and orders works from Dangar and Deveyle. Surchamp publishes her essay 'Spirituality of the potter' in issue 17 of *Témoignages*, published by Cahiers de la Pierre-qui-Vire. A specialist examines the kiln.

MARCH

Works in excess of 15 hours per day in order to have enough work for Gleizes's exhibition. Successfully fires pieces for the abbey of La Pierre-qui-Vire.

APRIL

With the help of Deveyle, creates and decorates Gleizes's pieces and sends them to Paris for exhibition. They are poorly received by the gallery owner but the city of Paris collection (later Musée d'art moderne de Paris) acquires a piece.

JUNE

Travels to Avignon to see an exhibition that features Deveyle's and Yvette Schaeffer's work as well as her own. Following the death of an old Roussillon potter, Monsieur Henri, is asked by the potters to decorate a vase for his grave and is deeply touched.

Completes the final mural panels for the Hôtel Schaeffer. Painters Paul Régny and Andrée Le Coultre visit Moly-Sabata. Dangar and Deveyle attend the summer congress of painters organised by Gleizes at Les Méjades.

SEPTEMBER–OCTOBER

Pablo Picasso begins decorating ceramics and many people compare his work with Dangar's.

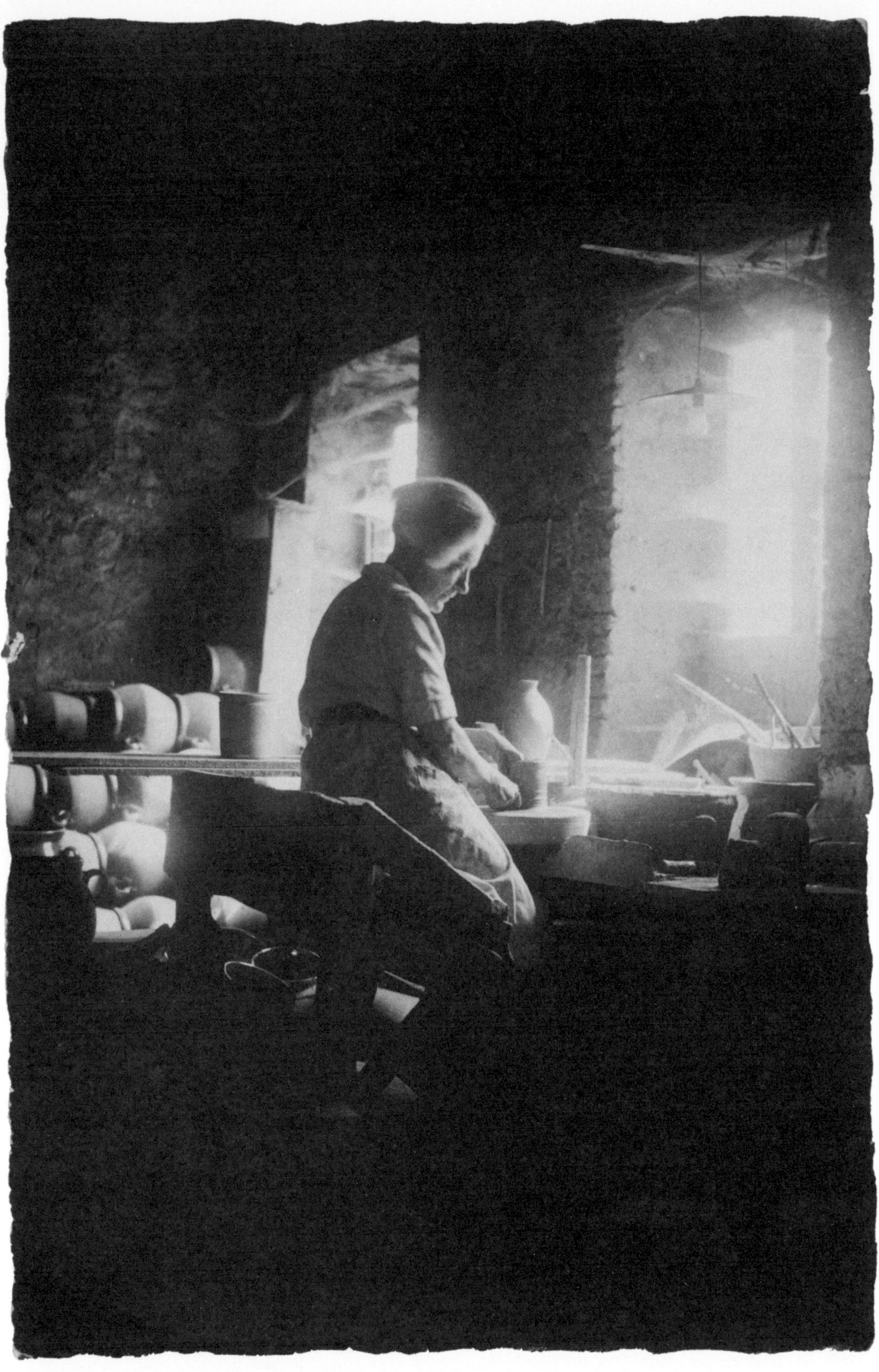

fig 57 Anne Dangar at work in the pottery, Roussillon, 1940s

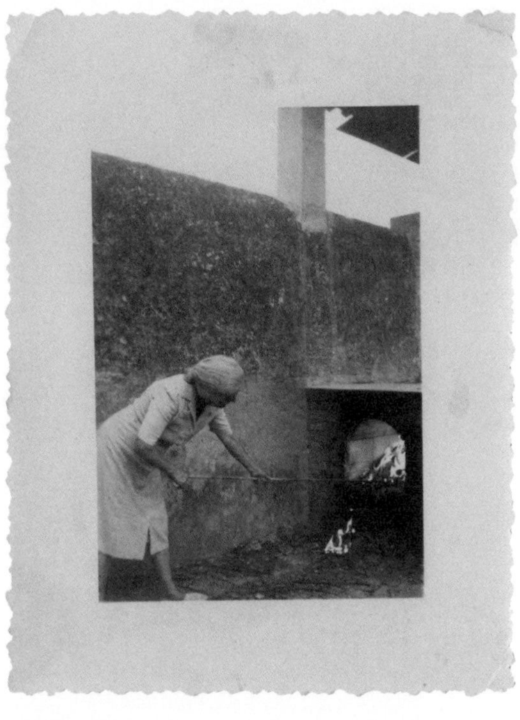

fig 58 First firing in the kiln at Moly-Sabata, August 1947

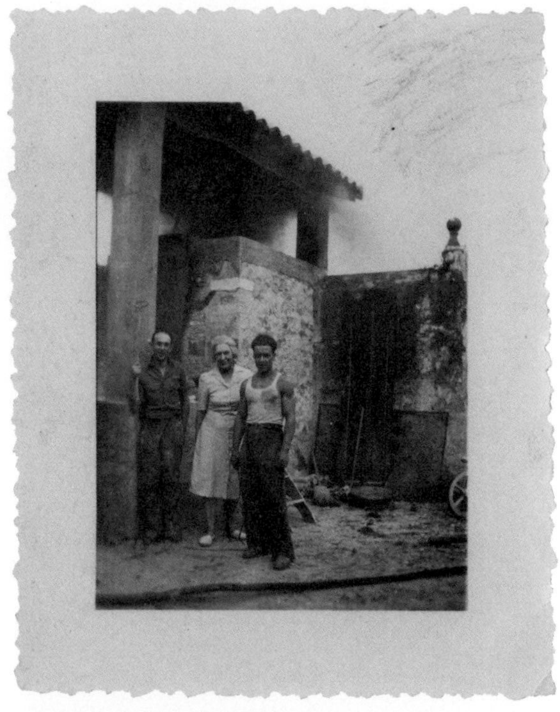

fig 59 Jean-Marie Paquaud, Anne Dangar and unknown potter at Moly-Sabata, August 1947

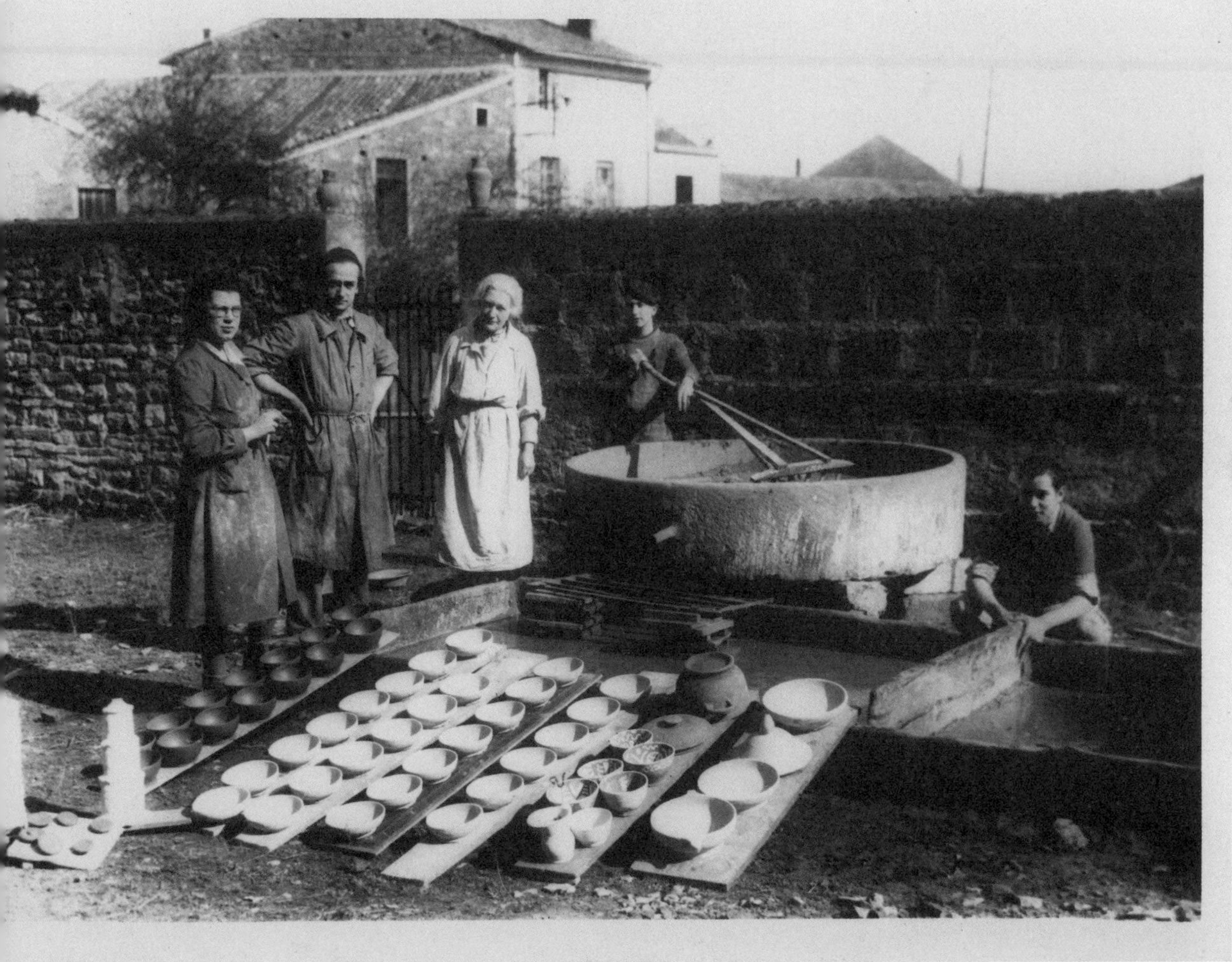

fig 60 Jacqueline Bouvet (later Lerat), Anne Dangar (centre) and pottery apprentices at the Centre artisanal de poterie et arts plastiques de Mâcon, 1942

fig 61 Anne Dangar (right) at wedding in Saulce-sur-Rhône, July 1950

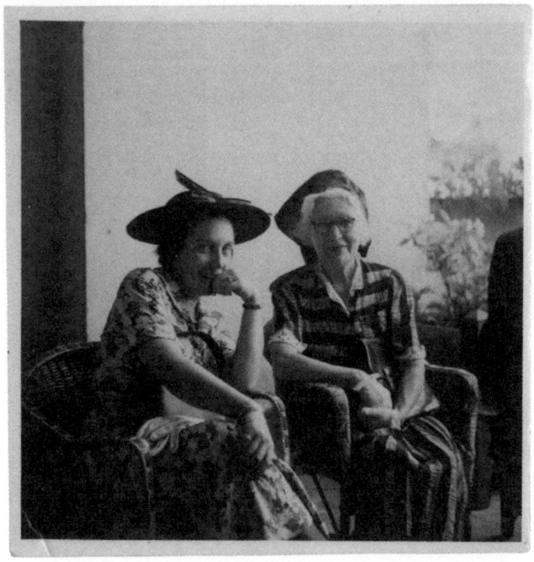

1949

JANUARY

Visits Sue Alexandre in Bayonne and makes jewellery in her electric kiln.

APRIL–JUNE

Visits Grenoble to undertake research on the Dauphiné region for an upcoming exhibition. Jean-Claude Libert visits Moly-Sabata.

AUGUST

Conducts a three-week summer school at Moly-Sabata for adult students, including Maryse Doz (niece of the Geoffrays); Mademoiselle Crouzet; former students Hélène Boiron and Jean-Marcel Herault; and Geneviève de Cissey, who later becomes a potter in the manner of Dangar. Visits Cliousclat and Mirmande and views an exhibition of Lhote's paintings, which also includes works by many friends from the area. John Pye visits Moly-Sabata.

NOVEMBER–DECEMBER

A museum in Saint-Étienne buys a small plate for its collection. Receives a commission from Gaetano Ballardini at the Museo internazionale delle ceramiche in Faenza, Italy.

Surchamp encourages her to respond. Visits Toulon, Avignon and Saint-Étienne to view her exhibition at Style gallery. Gleizes asks her to read his new manuscript, *L'homme devenu peintre* (*Man becomes painter*). Jean-Claude Libert visits Moly-Sabata. Dangar asks Gleizes for money for repairs to Moly-Sabata—four beams in the *grande salle* give way and the floor is extremely dangerous.

SEPTEMBER–OCTOBER

Visits Saint-Rémy-de-Provence and participates in the creation of a new group of Gleizes's followers: Pouyaud, Jean Chevalier, Dom Angelico Surchamp, René-Maria Burlet and Paul Régny.

NOVEMBER–DECEMBER

Presents a lecture on pottery at René-Maria Burlet's studio at his Académie du Minotaure in Lyon. Attends the opening of the Christmas exhibition at Folklore. This is her last exhibition with Michaud. Laments that she and Deveyle have not sold work, but that all the Picasso plates, which are not signed, have sold and are more expensive.

1950

FEBRUARY

Travels to Strasbourg with the Schaeffers. Works on several commissions including works for La Pierre-qui-Vire. The doctor is concerned about her ocular circulation.

MARCH–APRIL

21 March marks 20 years since moving to Moly-Sabata. Has the best firing in her kiln since it was constructed.

APRIL–MAY

Visits Gleizes at Les Méjades and spends two weeks resting.

JULY

Jean-Claude Libert decides to move to Moly-Sabata and work in the pottery. Dangar feels she has spent many years working to build her pottery and work in peace, while many young potters now wish to work there. Meets Russian painter Marie Vassilieff, who visits Moly-Sabata. Attends Roger Grimaud's wedding in Saulce, visiting nearby Cliousclat and Mirmande.

AUGUST

Gleizes visits the kiln at Moly-Sabata for the first time. The director of the Musée des beaux-arts de Strasbourg visits and buys one of Deveyle's textiles. Dangar slips and falls while cleaning, fracturing her arm and two ribs.

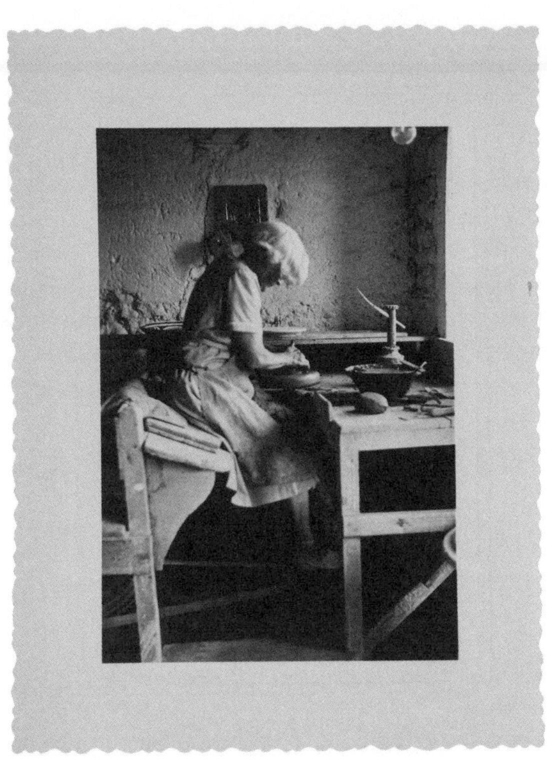

fig 62 Anne Dangar at her pottery wheel in her studio at Moly-Sabata, July 1950

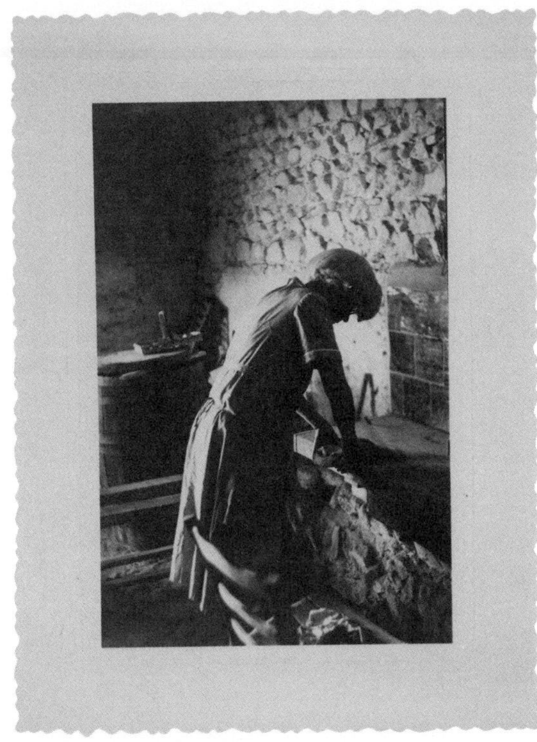

fig 63 Anne Dangar wedging clay in her studio at Moly-Sabata, July 1950

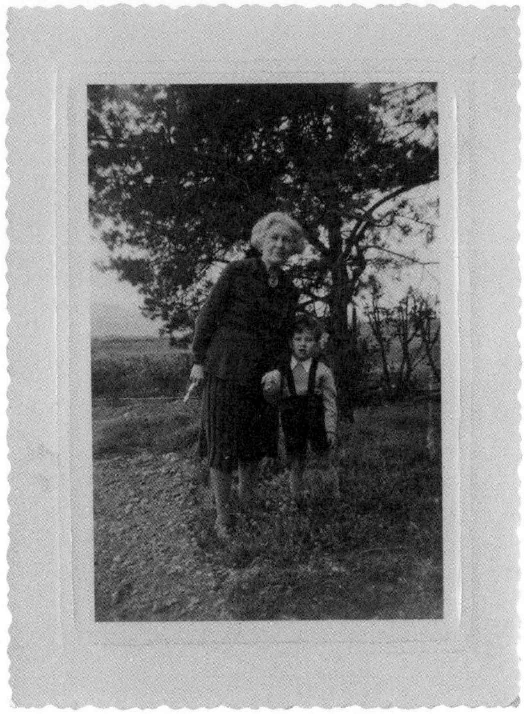

fig 64 Anne Dangar and her godson Daniel Steinbach at Moly-Sabata, March 1951

1951

JANUARY–FEBRUARY

Collapses on the street in Serrières and is hospitalised. Is forced to rest completely, with no visitors, reading or drawing. Receives doctor's permission to visit Poterie Bert to complete the decoration of several large pieces.

MARCH–APRIL

Converts to Catholicism on 3 March 1951 and is baptised. Receives doctor's permission to do three or four hours work a day at the pottery. Madame Steinbach drives her each day and Paquaud helps with physical labour. The curator from a museum in Saint-Étienne visits Moly-Sabata.

MAY–JULY

Paquaud continues to assist by turning pots for her to decorate. Dangar finds his ceramic forms uninteresting so offers him a large drawing with several different designs to show his clients. Creates designs for liturgical robes for Deveyle to weave for the Sablons church.

AUGUST–SEPTEMBER

Suffers from a stroke. Dies several weeks later on 4 September. A large funeral is held and she is interred in the cemetery of Serrières on 6 September in the Roche family vault. At the end of September, Paquaud, Deveyle and Yvette Schaeffer decorate her unfinished pieces.

SEPTEMBER–OCTOBER

Remains in a plaster cast for most of September. Crowley sends Dangar a copy of *Australian Aboriginal decorative art* by Frederick D McCarthy, featuring a foreword by Professor AP Elkin, and she is greatly impressed.

NOVEMBER–DECEMBER

Her arm improves and she begins to turn pots again. The people of Sablons and local potters assist. Knowing she has little money, many buy pieces from her. Her family and Crowley send money so she can buy wood and coal over the Christmas period.

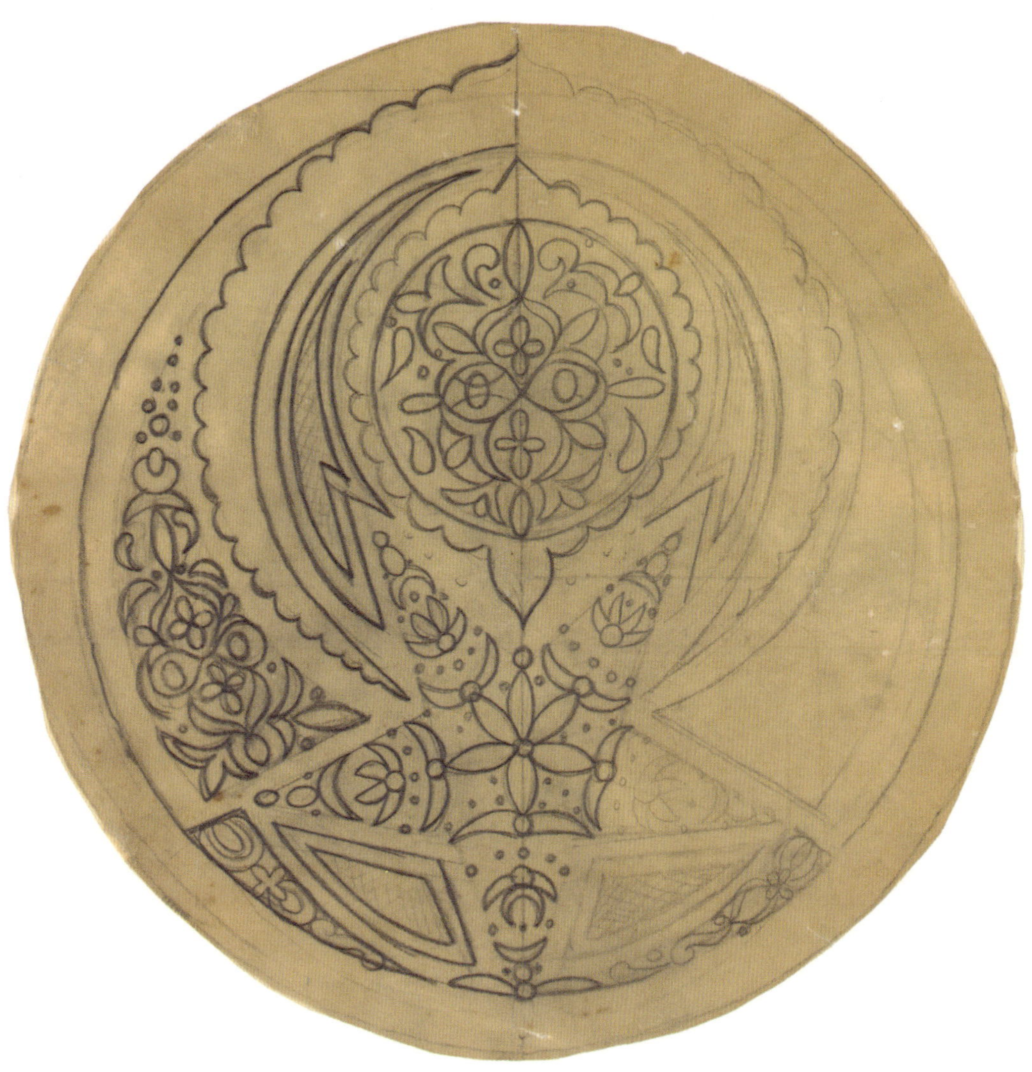

cat 104 Design for plate with Moroccan-inspired design 1940–48

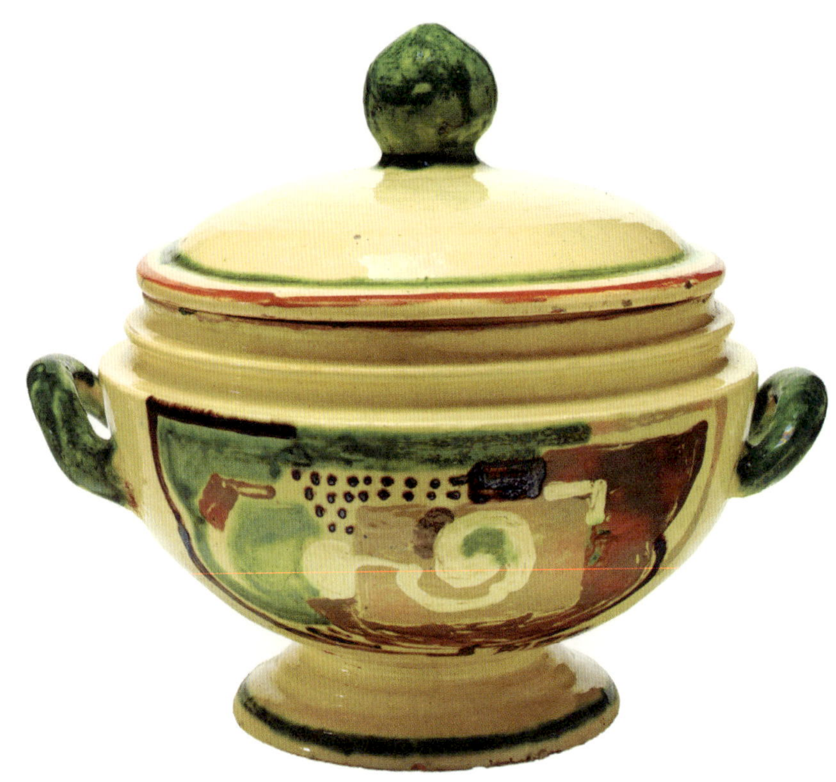

cat 48 Soup tureen with cubist design 1936–37

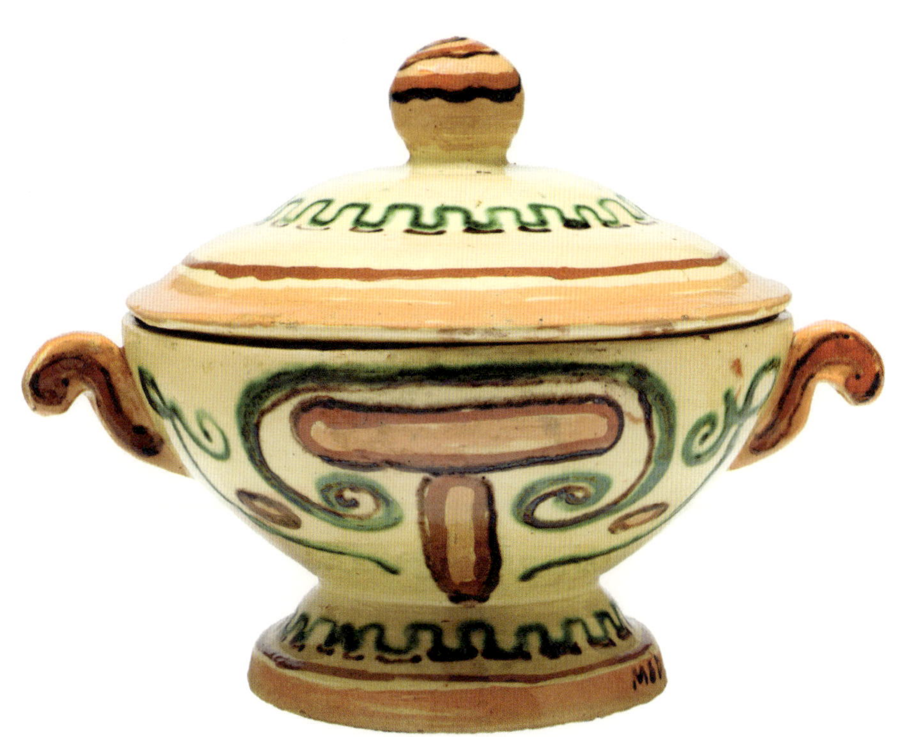

cat 52 Soup tureen with geometric designs 1936–38

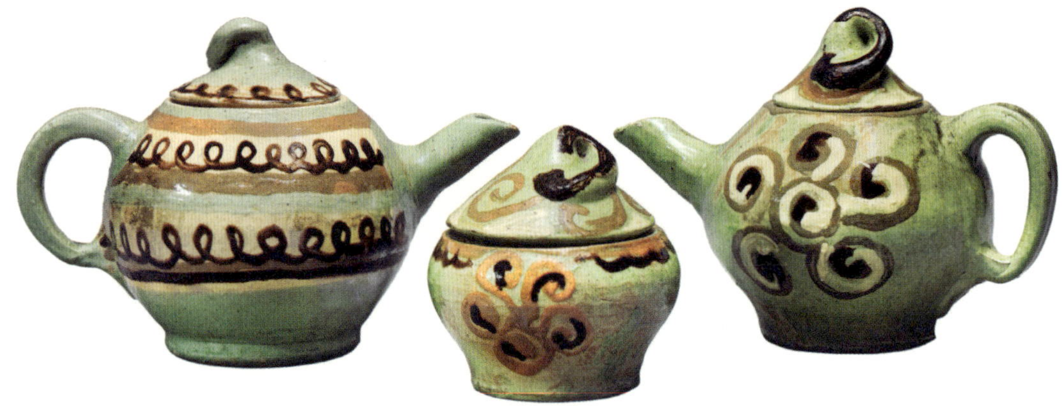

cat 58 Moroccan-style tea set 1940–48

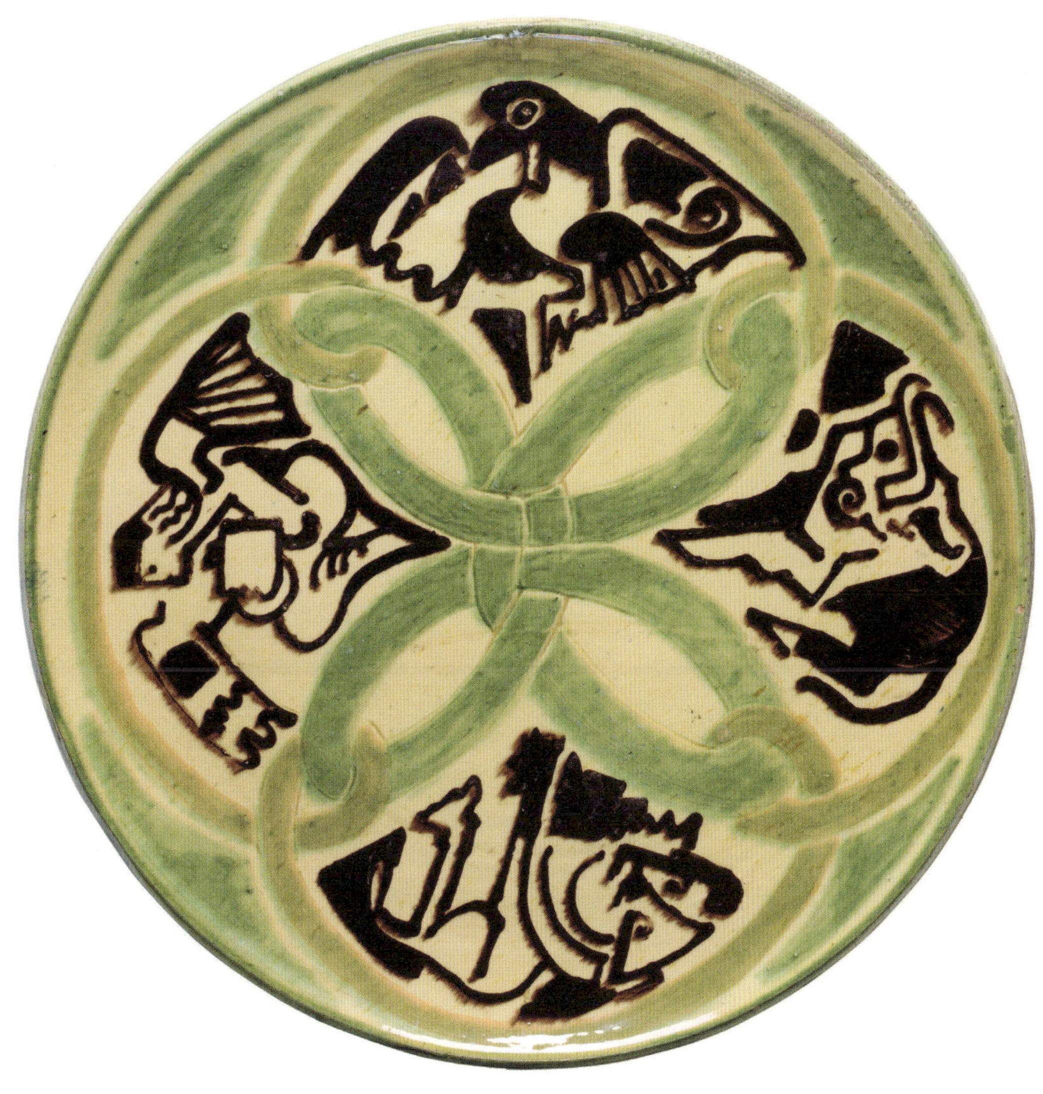

cat 67 Plate with Celtic motifs and figures representing the four beasts from Revelation 4 1948–49

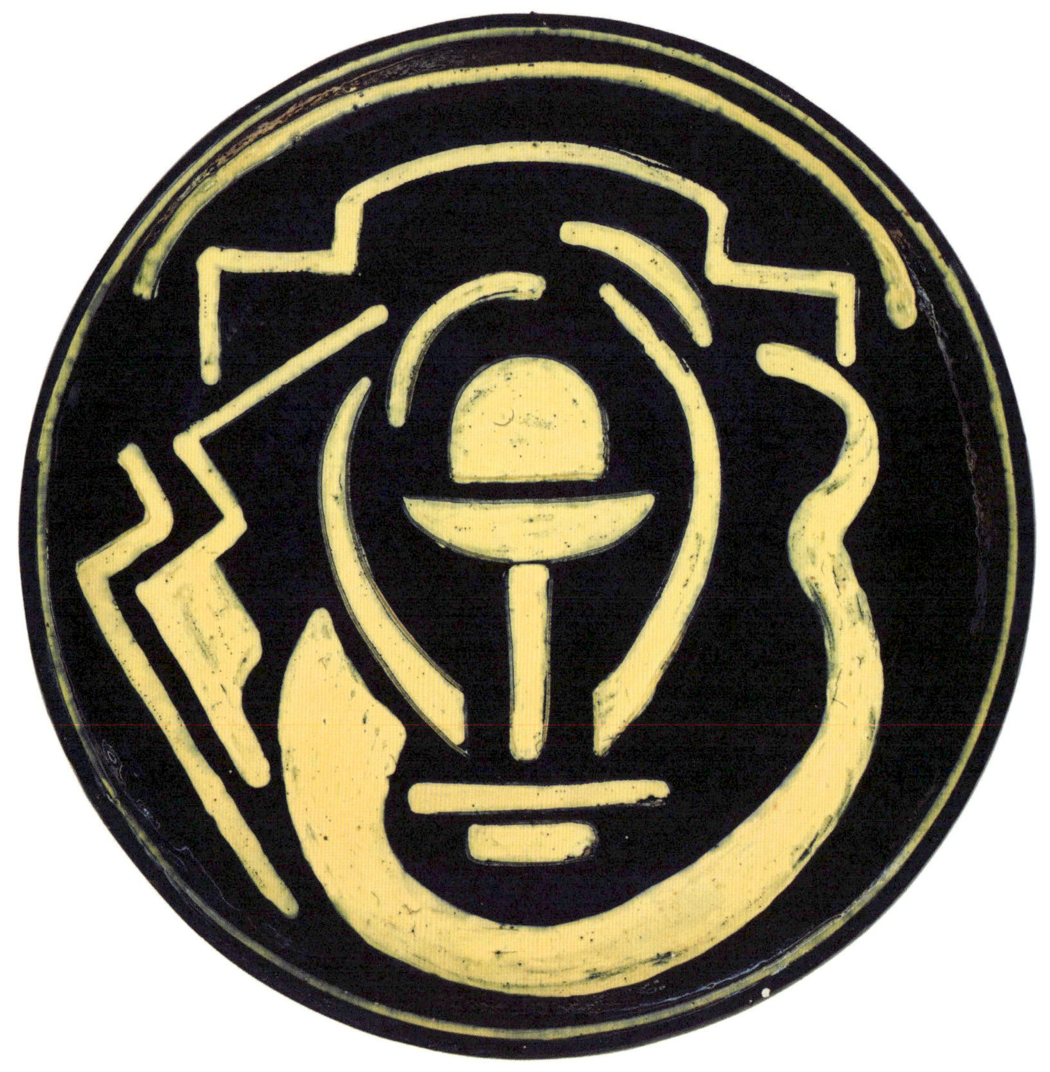

cat 49 Plate with cubist design 1936–38

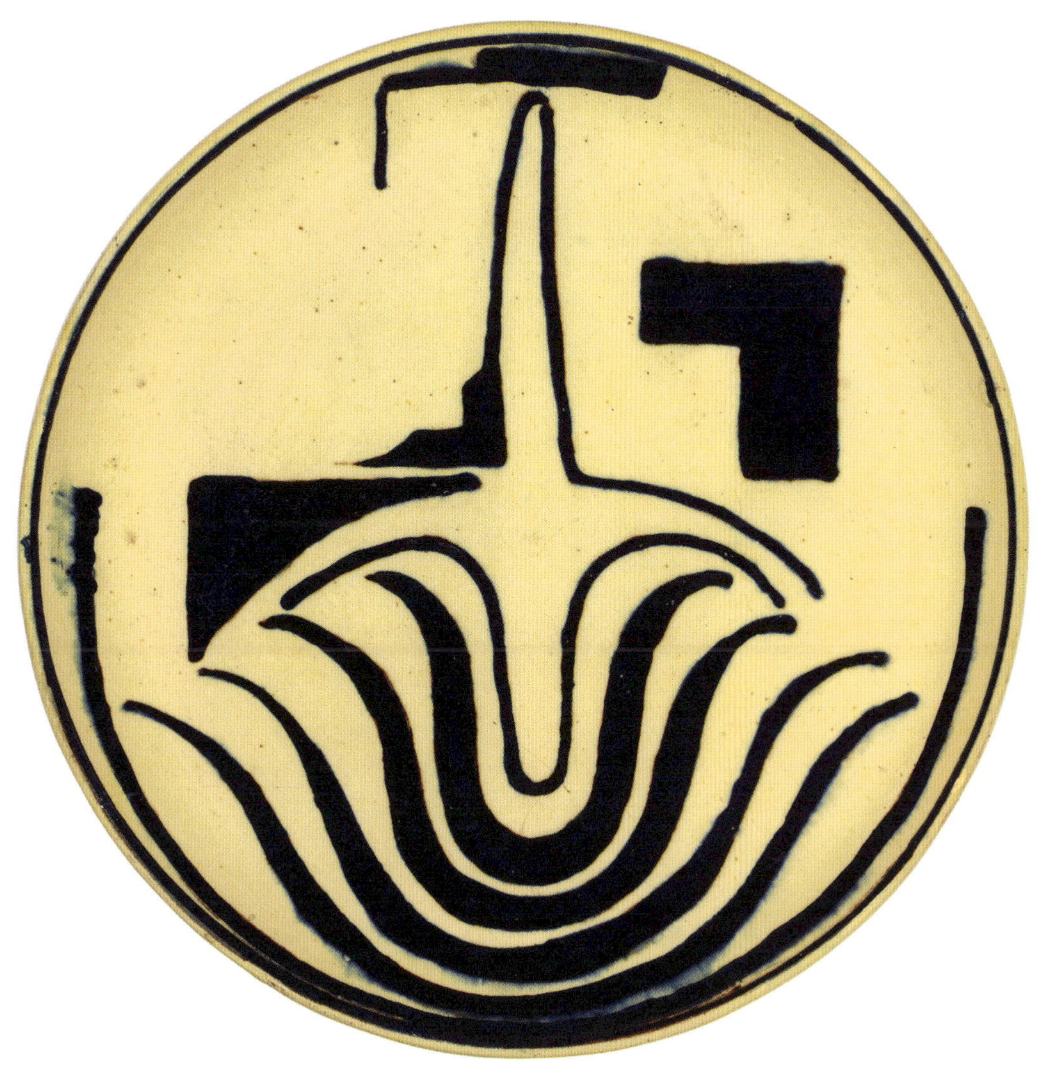

cat 50 Plate with cruciform design 1936–38

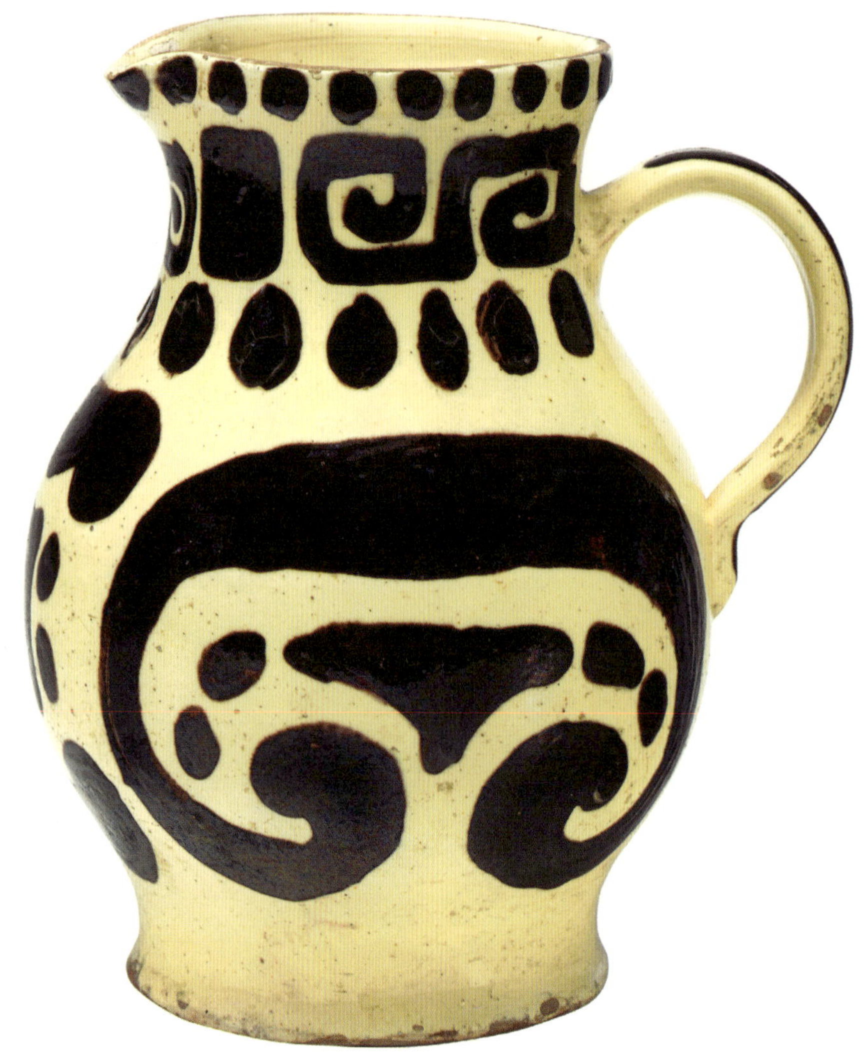

cat 41 Water jug 1933–50

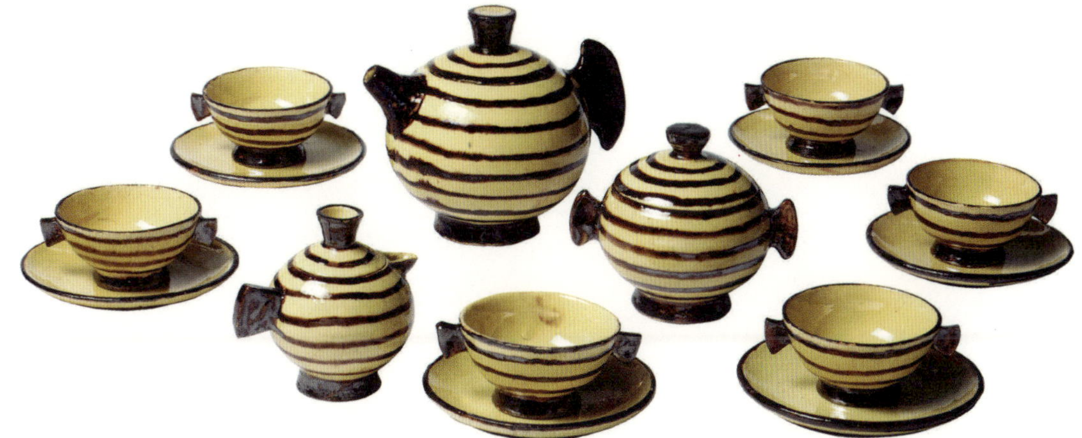

cat 63 Tea service 1945–50

158

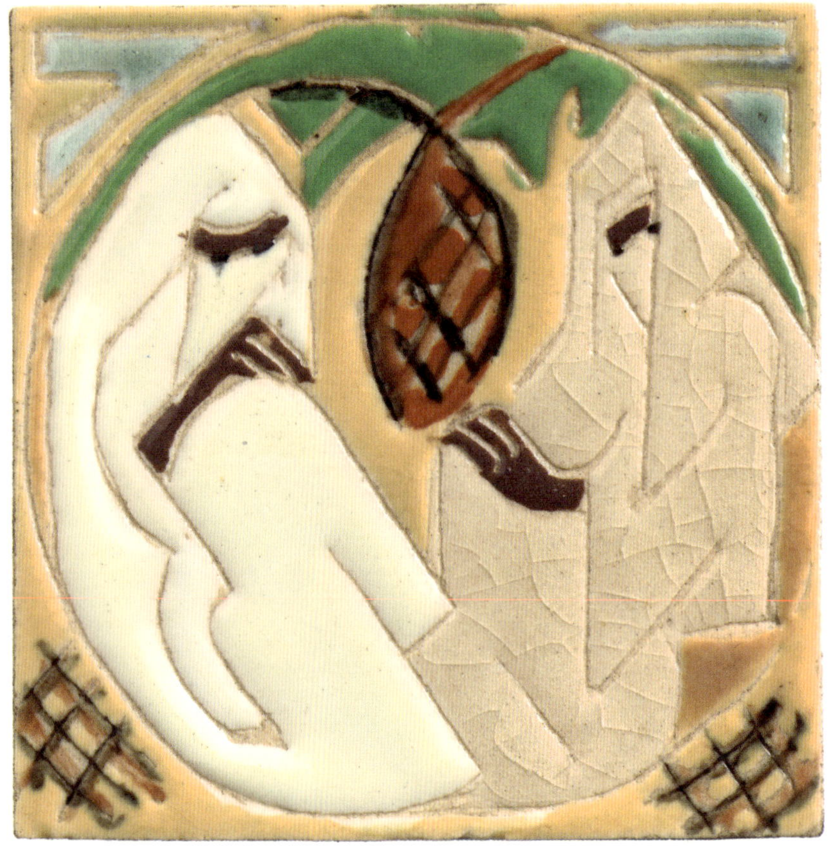

cat 62 Two Moroccans 1943–45

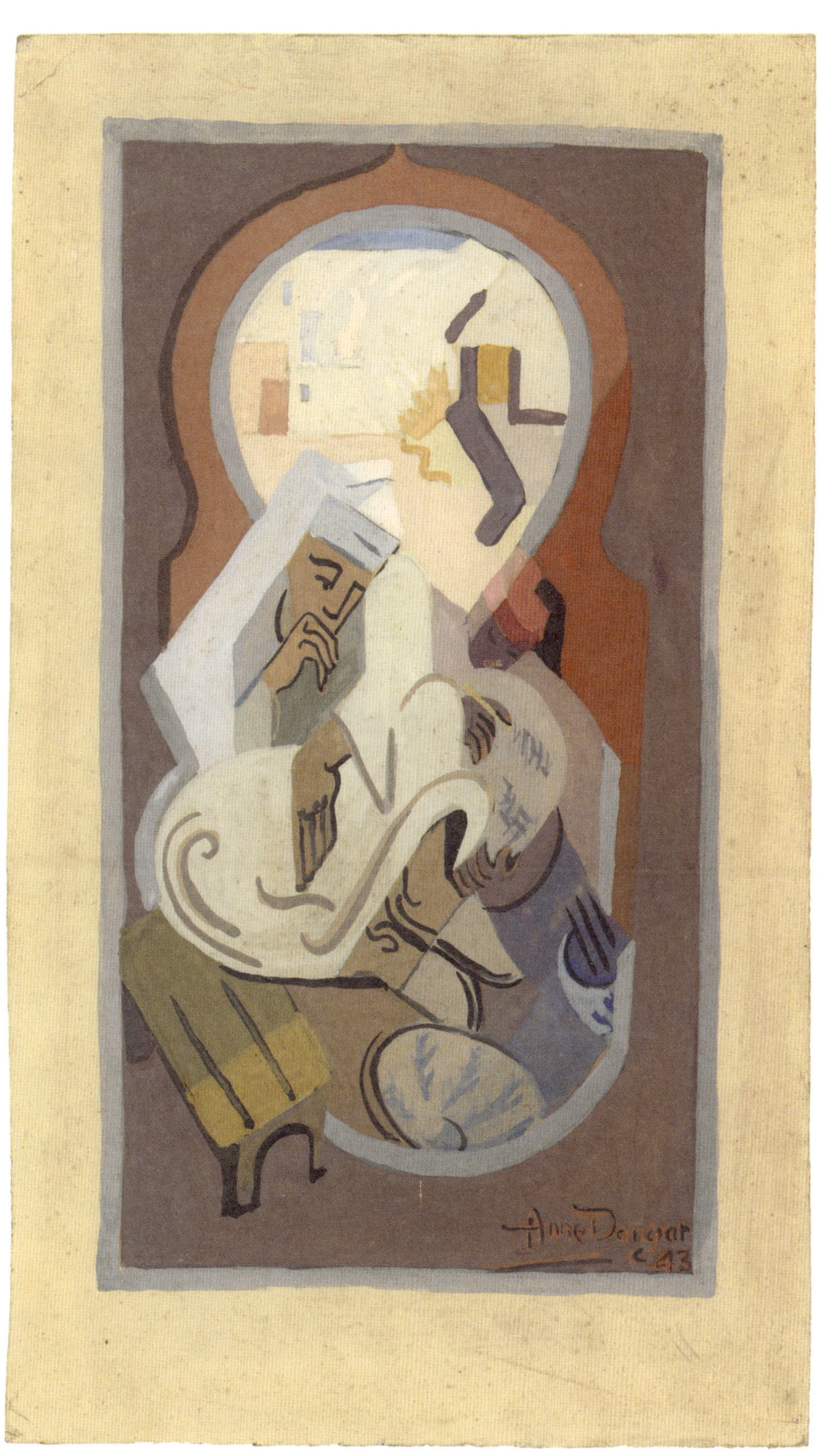

cat 107 Moroccan figure in doorway 1943

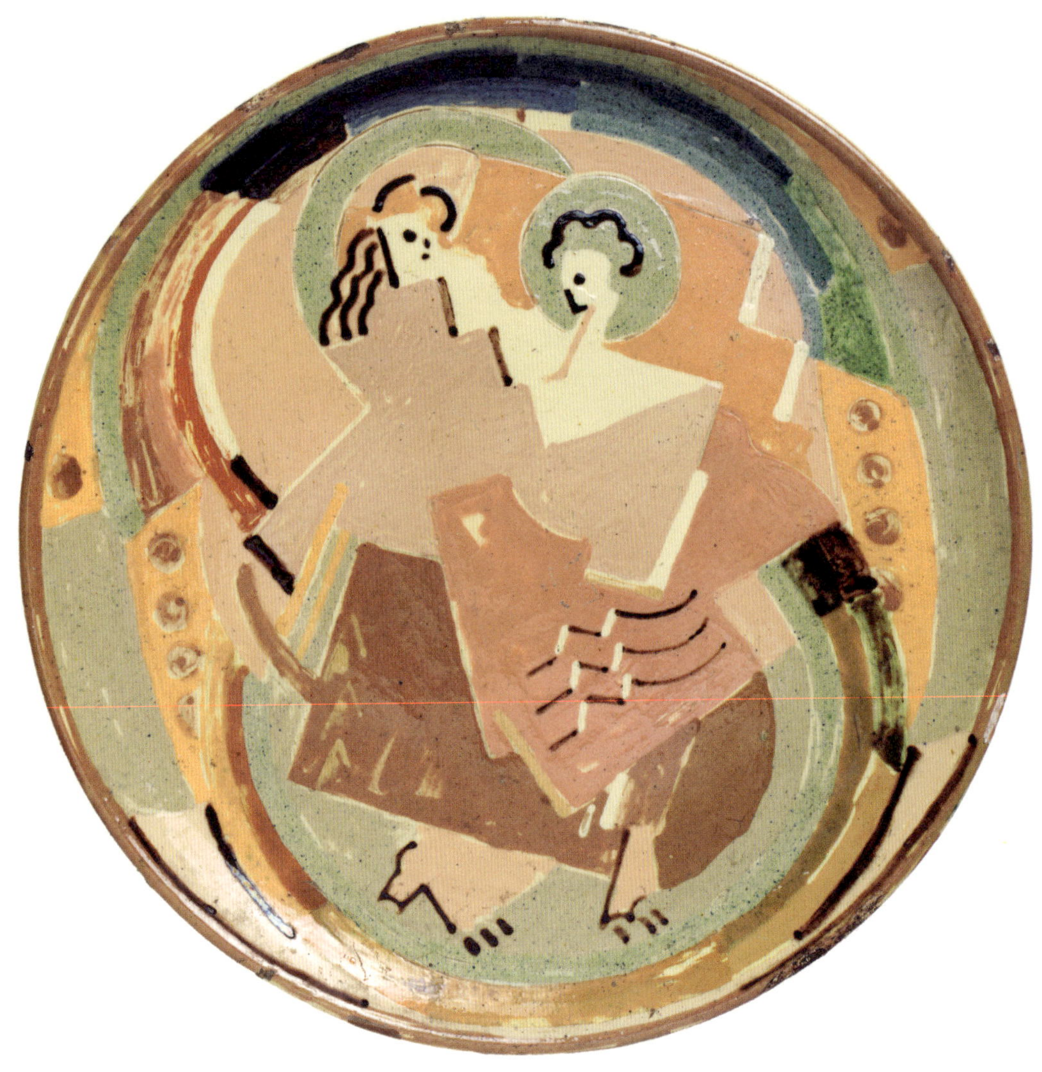

cat 112 after Albert Gleizes, *Mère et enfant* (*Mother and child*) 1935–37

REBECCA EDWARDS

After several years at Moly-Sabata, Dangar was the most dedicated of Gleizes's followers, embedding his aesthetic and spiritual principles into her art and life. Through a combination of her own reticence and limited means, however, she remained at the periphery of his wider artistic circle. In 1934, he 'insisted' she join the art society Abstraction-Création, a group of artists led by Auguste Herbin that included Gleizes, Piet Mondrian, Wassily Kandinksy and the Australian JW Power that was dedicated to promoting abstract art in Europe. Dangar paid her membership but did not contribute any work to their exhibitions between 1934 and 1936, exhibiting her work regionally instead.[1]

By the end of the decade, these circumstances shifted, and through several major exhibition opportunities, Dangar's work was elevated from a regional to an international context. While she had little interest in commercial success, she greatly valued the recognition of her peers. This exposure heralded a period of critical acclaim that gave her renewed confidence in her work and secured her position as a cubist alongside some of France's most acclaimed modern artists.

In 1937 Dangar was included in the Exposition internationale des arts et techniques dans la vie moderne, a major world fair event held in Paris, where she was represented across multiple locations, including the pavilion of the Union des artistes modernes (UAM). There she was credited as a collaborator with Gleizes on a tiled panel she created after his design.[2] Dangar's ceramics were also displayed in the Regional Pavilion for the provinces of Forez-Vivarais (an ancient demarcation of the region surrounding the Ardèche) in a display showcasing the wares of Moly-Sabata.[3] Her pottery was exhibited alongside work by Deveyle, her students and other members of the community, with the centrepiece being a major appliqué textile themed around the history of the Rhône region designed by Dangar and her students, with assistance from Deveyle and local Sablonnais women (cat 127). The display was well-received; Dangar won a gold medal and 500 francs for her pottery and a *diplôme d'honneur* for her education program, and Moly-Sabata was awarded a further 4000 francs.[4]

Most important was the display of her work in the curated exhibition *Les maîtres de l'art indépendant, 1895–1937* (*Masters of independent art, 1895–1937*), arranged by the Petit Palais as part of the Exposition internationale, which showcased artists associated with the French School over the previous four decades.[5] She was represented by several works after Gleizes's designs, a tiled panel depicting the Virgin and Child (fig 44) and four plates likely of the same subject.[6] Writing to Crowley earlier that year, she had expressed her excitement that Gleizes had given her 'carte blanche' with the panel design, providing her with a 10-inch gouache to enlarge, adapt and recolour as she wished.[7]

The inclusion of Dangar's cubist pottery in the exhibition's distinctly French spaces was a rare achievement for an Australian artist and reflected her growing reputation in France. Significantly, her works bore no relationship to those presented in the Australian Pavilion, and after viewing this display Dangar was appalled by its parochialism, writing to Crowley, 'Australia is a blot on the hemisphere! I nearly wept when I entered … Poor Gruner I once admired him! Margaret Preston got a prize for her jammed full pot of Australian flowers.'[8] Now moving in radically different artistic circles that included Gleizes, Pouyaud, Hone and Jellett, Dangar's already modern outlook had utterly transformed since she had left Sydney. In the months after the Exposition internationale, she met artists Sonia and Robert Delaunay, both influential exponents of abstraction who subsequently commissioned examples of her ceramics for their personal collection.[9] Robert Delaunay had been part of the same avant-garde circles

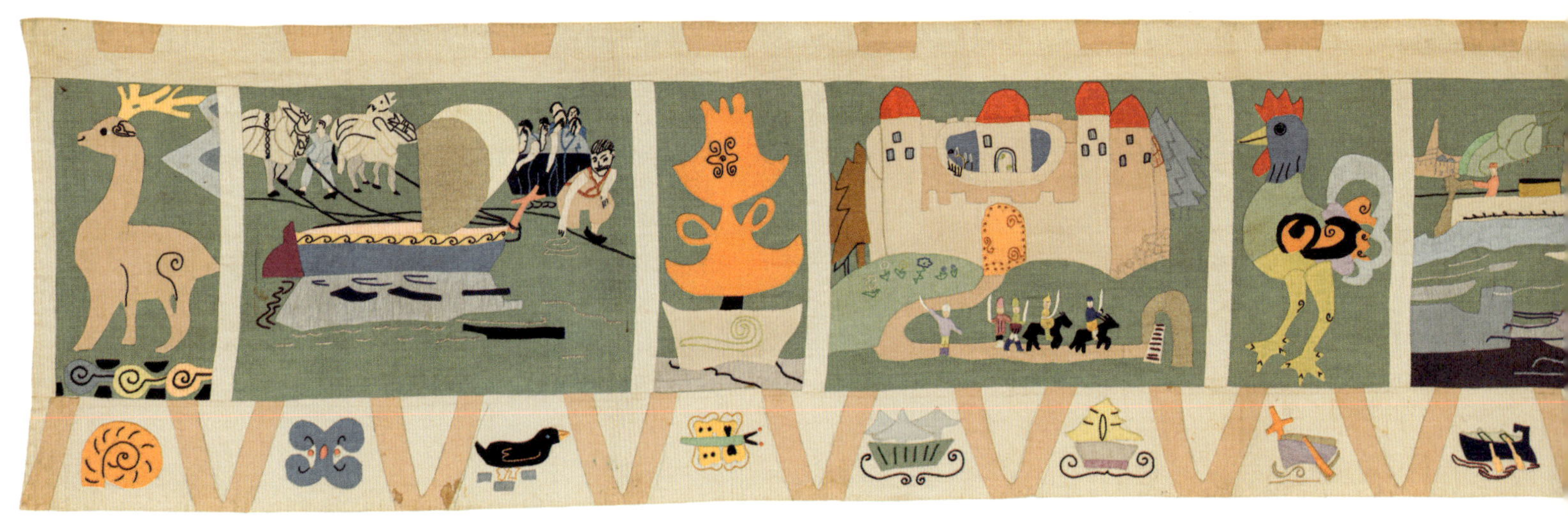

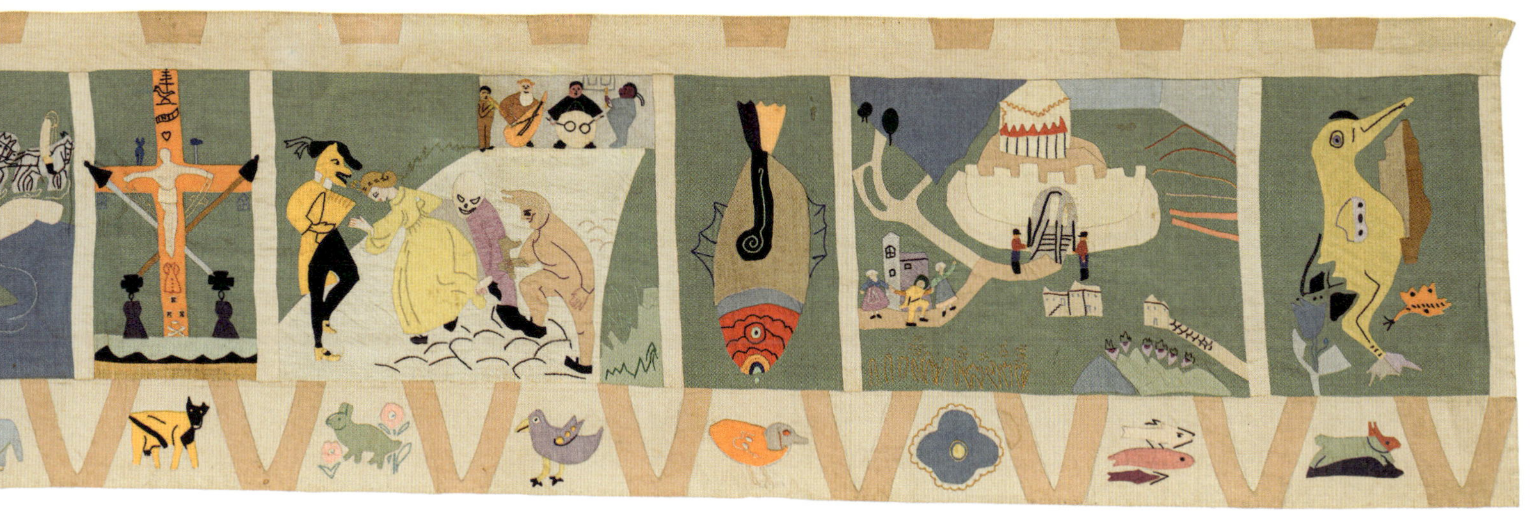

as Gleizes in the 1910s and Dangar warmed to him quickly, 'he gripped my hand & said … Gleizes has always spoken about you … I thought you were a fairy tale, but now I see that what he said was true.'[10]

Following the success of Moly-Sabata at the Exposition internationale, Dangar and the community's work was included in the exhibition *32e groupe des artistes de ce temps* (*32nd group of artists of today*), held at the Petit Palais in 1938. The display brought together the works she had shown across different pavilions the year before, reuniting her with Gleizes, the Delaunays and other influential figures of the French avant-garde, including Auguste Herbin, Georges Valmier and Jean Metzinger.[11] An extensively illustrated article focused on Dangar's pottery published in *Art et Décoration* showcased her work further. Included among the numerous reproductions were her tiled panel of the Virgin and Child, rustic pottery and cubist presentation pieces, including *Mère et enfant* 1935–37 (*Mother and child*, cat 112), and *Figure en gloire* (*Figure in glory*) after Gleizes's earlier paintings, as well as other abstract designs of her own invention (figs 42 & 43).[12] The Petit Palais retained two pale green vegetable dishes for its collection.

The year concluded with Dangar's inclusion in the Salon d'automne, the progressive alternative to the official Paris Salon, where she was featured in a section coordinated by Gleizes that traced the evolution of Cubism to abstraction, *Aspect actuel du cubisme chez quelques aînés et quelques jeunes* (*The current appearance of Cubism among older and younger artists*). This was the first and only time her work would be presented at the Salon and an event that publicly affirmed her participation in the cubist movement in France.

Earlier in 1938 she had complained that she no longer wanted to copy Gleizes's designs and had found little time for her own practice.[13] A photograph of the installation reveals she presented several examples of original work—ceramics in showcases as well as gouache abstracts hung alongside major paintings by Gleizes and Delaunay around the doorway.[14] Although smaller in scale, her vibrant *Gouache* 1936 (cat 102) matches their formal complexity, the trio of overlapping circular shapes spiralling upwards. Among the ceramics was an angular coffee-set and plate featuring a graphic black-and-white abstract design deviating from Gleizes's model. Reporting in *Beaux-Arts*, Renée Moutard-Uldry reviewed Dangar's ceramics positively, noting they were 'robust, rustic and gay … The colour, themes and shapes are of true originality; there is in these pots, these cups, these figurines a true vitality, a peasant characteristic that feels neither intellectual fantasy nor false naivety.'[15] Moly-Sabata again attracted attention and was awarded a silver medal and 500 francs for the communal display.[16] According to Dangar she was also nominated as a life associate of the Salon; however, that year no one was elected. She was not perturbed, noting to Crowley that Robert Delaunay had also not been elected.[17]

This exposure and success eventuated the following year in an invitation from the French government to travel to Morocco and work alongside local potters as a craft adviser. This unusual opportunity came from Suzanne Noguès, the wife of Resident-General Charles Noguès, who wanted to establish an artisanal training scheme in Fez. Dangar, on the back of her and Moly-Sabata's success at the exhibitions, was an obvious candidate for such a role.[18] Granted a six-month residency and a stipend—the most guaranteed income offered to her since arriving in France—she excitedly accepted, arriving at the Ateliers des beaux-arts in Fez in May.[19] Over the next six months, Dangar supervised around 100 potters and their assistants, all working around Bab Ftouh, the potters' quarters on the outskirts of the old city.[20]

Reports undertaken by the French colonial government in the late 1930s indicated that the Moroccan craft industry was in a state of crisis, though ironically it had declined substantially since the beginning of the French Protectorate in 1912.[21] Dangar herself arrived with little knowledge of Morocco or its culture, naively anticipating a rudimentary craft industry. But she was enraptured by what she encountered. The pottery created at Bab Ftouh was fascinating to her, all formed manually without mechanical

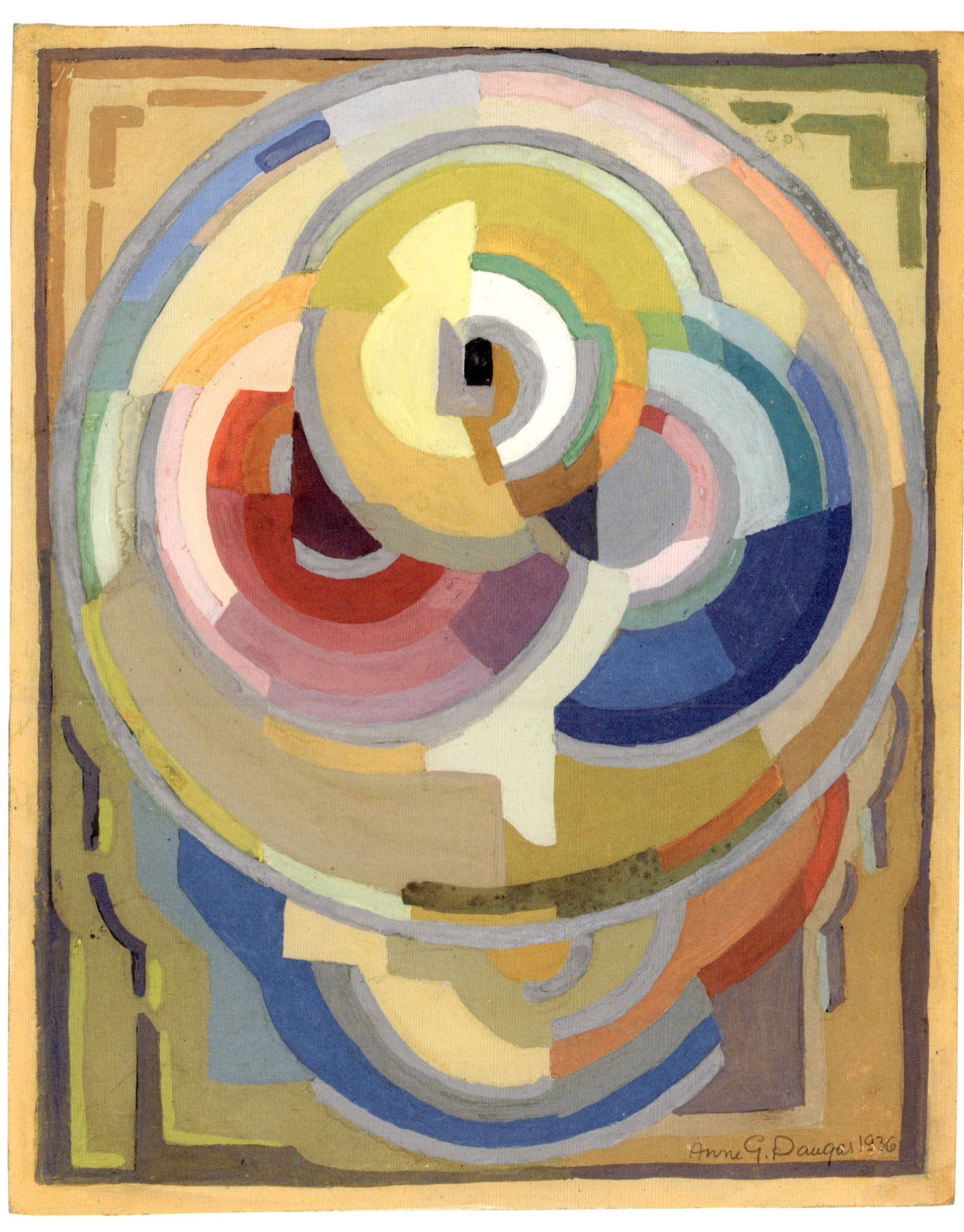

cat 102 *Gouache* 1936

previous spread: **cat 127** Anne Dangar, Lucie Deveyle, Marguerite Haché, Madame Chananaille and the children of Sablons, History of the Rhône wall hanging 1936–37

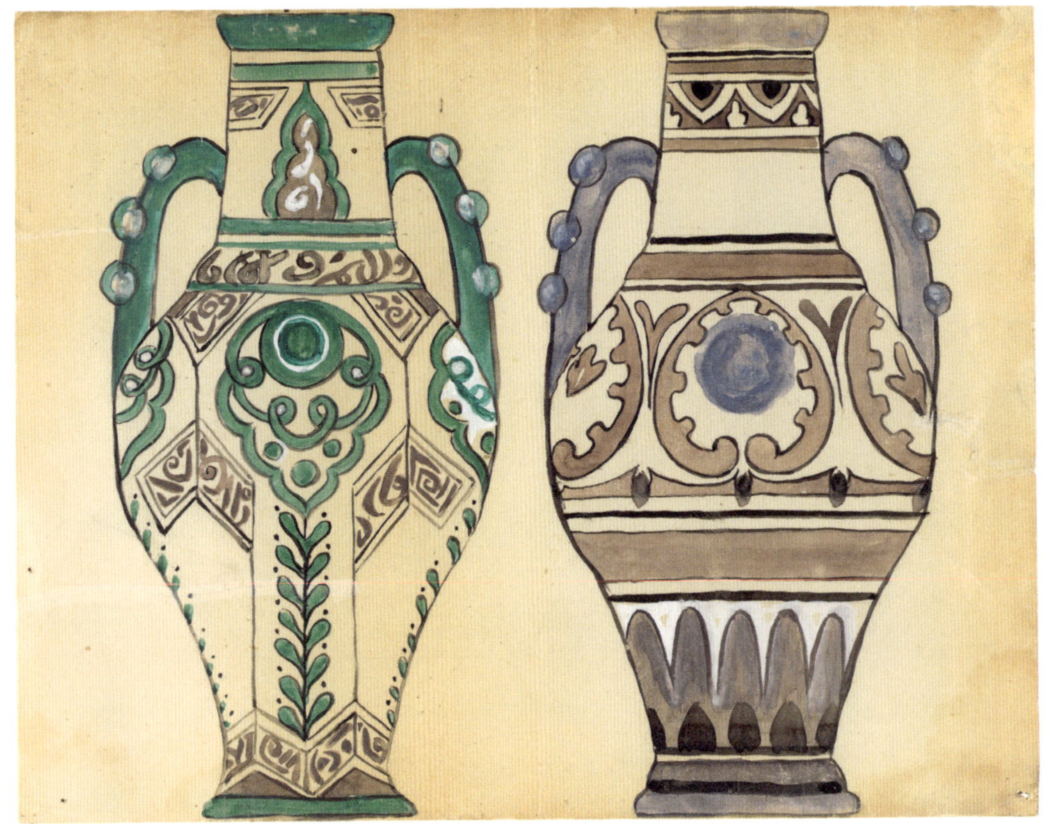

cat 103 Drawings of Moroccan vases 1939

intervention, and decorated with interlaced 'ruminating designs' branching into various points like a star. She was particularly interested in the process of decoration, which commenced at the centre and expanded outwards, in movements mirroring the path of the spiral.[22] Moroccan ornament and decoration also reinforced her belief in Gleizes's spiritual and artistic teachings. Writing to him, she described exteriors and ceiling decorations she had seen that incorporated her favourite Celtic symbols from manuscripts, a legacy of the city's Christian past, enthusing that her experience was 'proof positive of your teaching ... the composition was such a lesson! ... only a Gleizes student could unwind and enter in, and be caught up by those great enveloping circles'.[23]

Endeavouring to record 'every conceivable article for French homes upon the basis of their traditions', Dangar made drawings of Moroccan forms and fine pieces on display at the Musée des beaux-arts in Fez, including watercolours of jewel-green and purple long-necked vases (cat 103).[24] She did not create any Moroccan-inspired pottery until her return to France, when she crafted pieces that combined the conical silhouettes of tagines and traditional tea sets with looping linear decoration reminiscent of the 'ruminating designs' she had seen (cats 58–61). She also undertook lessons in Arabic, compiling a notebook of useful vocabulary, proudly recounting to Gleizes that she had made many potter friends.[25] Photographs show her observing potters at work and examining their wares, a quiet yet incongruous presence in a white dress.

With her stipend, Dangar travelled to Marrakesh, using her official colonial position to enter closed workshops to observe the operations of other artisanal industries, experiences she described in letters to Deveyle illustrated with quick pen drawings of weavers at work and textile designs.[26] She was especially interested in the processes of the Berber potters of the Atlas Mountains, who employed ancient techniques to fire clay in an open flame, and she later emulated this process to fire her students' work at Moly-Sabata.[27] She befriended many of the children at the pottery, offering them drawing classes, and was so impressed by their youthful skill on the potter's wheel that she resolved to teach pottery to the children at Moly-Sabata, declaring that 'here they start at about seven years old and are most useful'.[28]

Even though, as Bruce Adams notes, Dangar's appreciation of Moroccan design was colonialist in its perspective—filtered through her cubist lens and resonating particularly because it affirmed Gleizes's existing ideas—she was concerned by the paternalistic tenor of the artisanal scheme she was involved in.[29] She became frustrated with Noguès, who insisted she teach the potters French methods and designs, emulating the commercial style of Primavera for exportation to France, rather than traditional Moroccan forms and decoration.[30] Dangar resolved she 'would have to refuse to go on with this work. It was nothing else but killing the artisans to make them copy French pots.'[31] Seeking to elevate the potters' practice and enable them to 'create things they ... never dreamt they could make', she swiftly developed plans to establish a permanent space in the old city where they could 'present works with taste and put human interest into the presentation, instead of the cold, shop way' and gained the support of Noguès and Jacques Berque, who worked with the French administration.[32]

These ambitious plans never eventuated and Dangar's time in Morocco came to an unexpected end when Adolf Hitler oversaw Germany's invasion of Poland, signalling the outbreak of the Second World War. Her situation in Morocco quickly changed. Without French citizenship, she was not permitted to teach, and her position was given to the wife of one of the French officers.[33] Following telegram instructions from Gleizes, Dangar returned to Sablons in December believing conflict would soon end and she could return. The situation deteriorated rapidly and barely six months later in June 1940, the Nazis invaded Paris and power was transferred to Philippe Pétain and the Vichy government, who fast adopted a position of collaboration with Germany. In the following weeks, the war arrived at Moly-Sabata; over

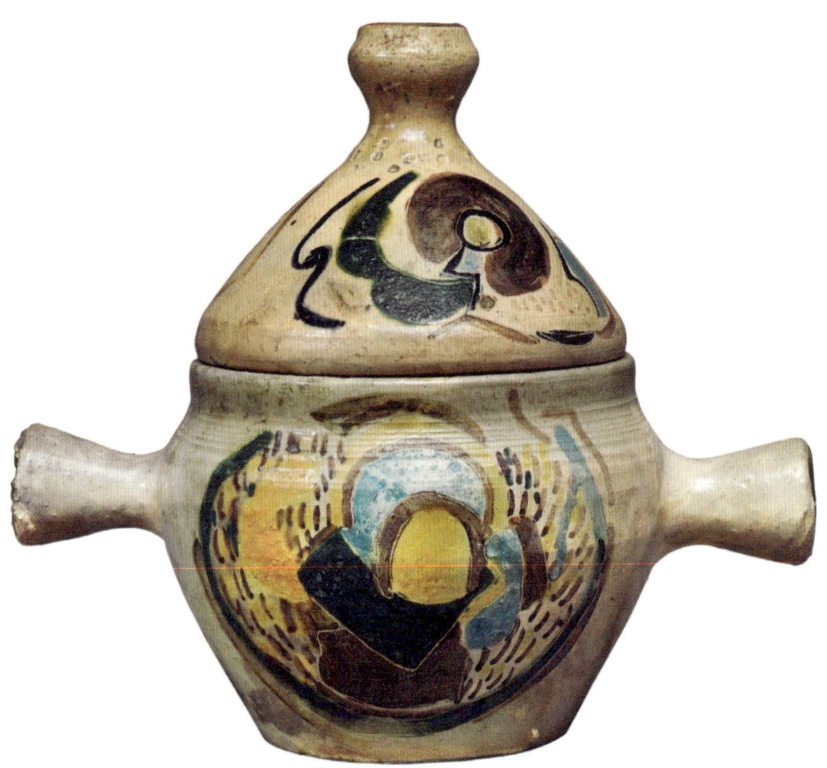

cat 61 Couscoussier 1940–48

several days, violent battles occurred in the Rhône Valley, and Sablons and Serrières were occupied by German troops.[34] Gleizes avoided this situation, having moved to Les Méjades in early 1940.

Despite experiencing pressure from friends and family to return home to Australia ever since she had arrived in France, Dangar had continually delayed her plans as opportunities arose. War in Europe was a different proposition, and she felt keenly her situation as a foreign national. Writing to Gleizes and Roche from Fez, she expressed her trepidation about returning to Moly-Sabata: 'Do you think Sablons will treat me as "une [étrangère]"? Do you think I shall be forbidden to try and earn a few francs to keep me, if I return?'[35]

As anti-British sentiment grew in the region under Vichy command, Dangar's experience in Sablons became difficult. Supplies were limited, and her income was drastically affected as she made fewer sales and lost students. For periods she was labelled as *une étrangère*, as she had predicted, and was not granted a work permit or *carte de circulation* allowing her to travel to and work at the potteries.[36] She relied on a small circle of sympathetic French friends to assist by secreting her to the potteries to work, and generated a small income through making clay buttons (figs 65–67) and pendants in a friend's kiln.[37] Among the few substantial works she created during this period was a decorative plate (fig 68) she designed in 1940 after Pouyaud was mobilised, depicting him within a circular cubist composition as Saint Francis of Assisi, hands raised in a pacifying gesture and surrounded by animals.[38]

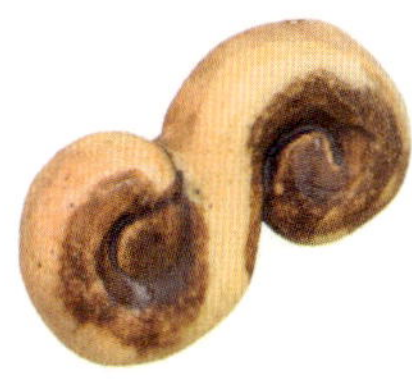

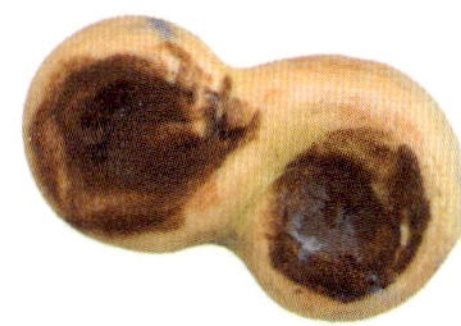

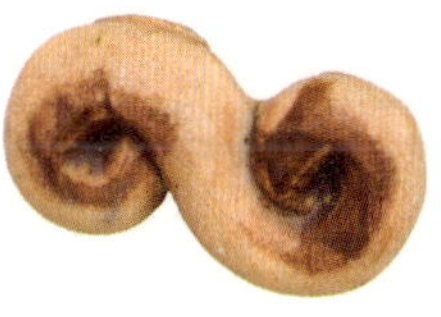

figs 65–67 Buttons 1943–45

After the first tumultuous months of war, Dangar contemplated the idea of returning to Australia, fearful for her situation and missing friends and family, with whom she increasingly had little contact. Eventually her isolation became unbearable and in December 1941 she wrote to Gleizes informing him of her decision to return to Australia. 'I need my friends … but I shall carry on my work and if you would like me to call my pottery or school or whatever I shall be able to build up "Moly-Sabata" I shall be happy to do so.'[39] He subsequently made a rare trip to Sablons to remind her of her dedication to the community, undoubtedly motivated by his own interests as Moly-Sabata would cease to exist without her efforts. Barely a fortnight later, any plans to repatriate had vanished and she wrote to him: 'It was lovely to see you again, to find you were still interested in Moly. I feel buoyed up to go on making a bigger effort than ever.'[40] Dangar remained in France for the duration of the war.

Gleizes occupies an ambiguous position in histories of wartime France. The ideals of the *retour à la terre* and regionalism that emerged as part of postwar reconstruction in the 1920s gained potency in the lead-up to the Second World War. As Romy Golan has outlined, the opposition to industry,

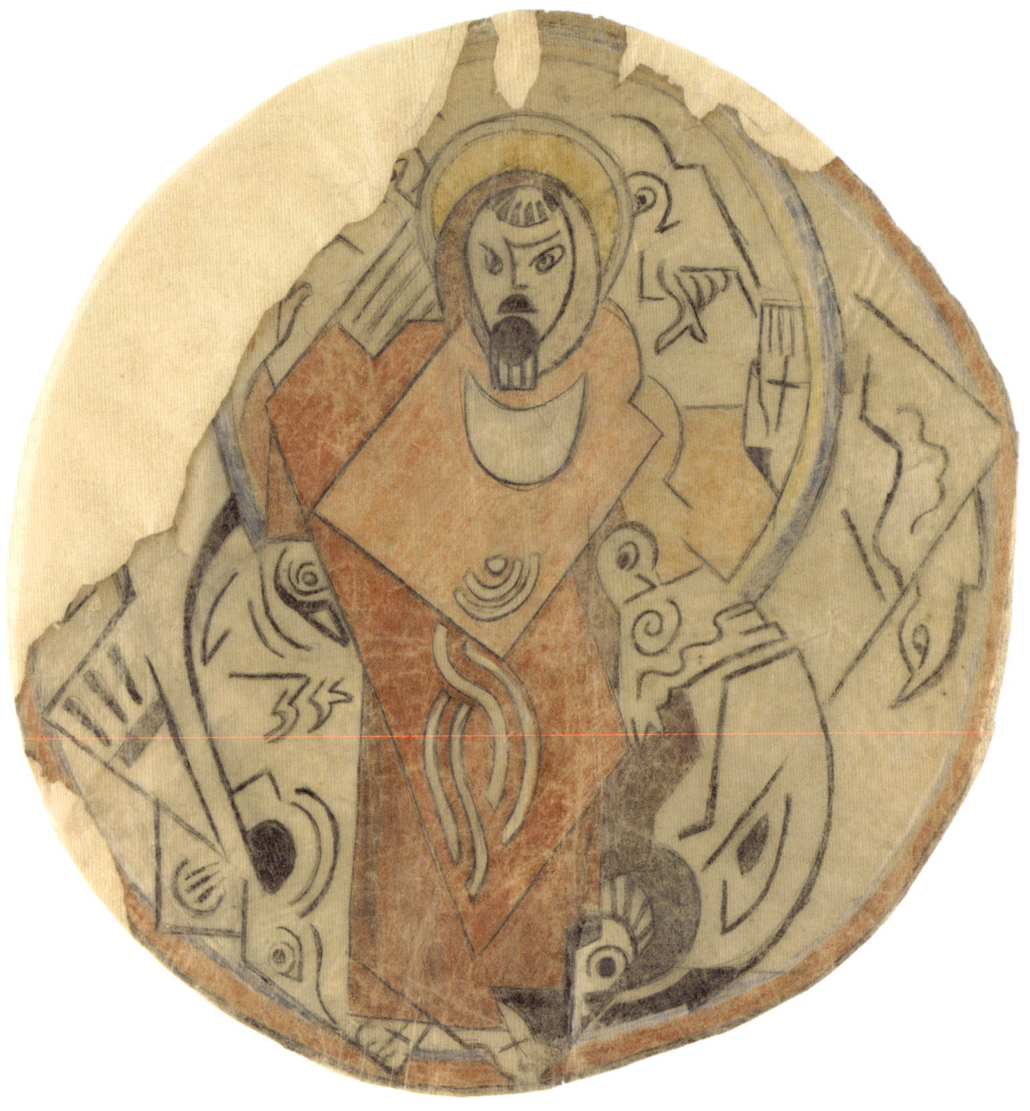

cat 106 Preparatory drawing for plate depicting Robert Pouyaud as Saint Francis of Assisi 1940

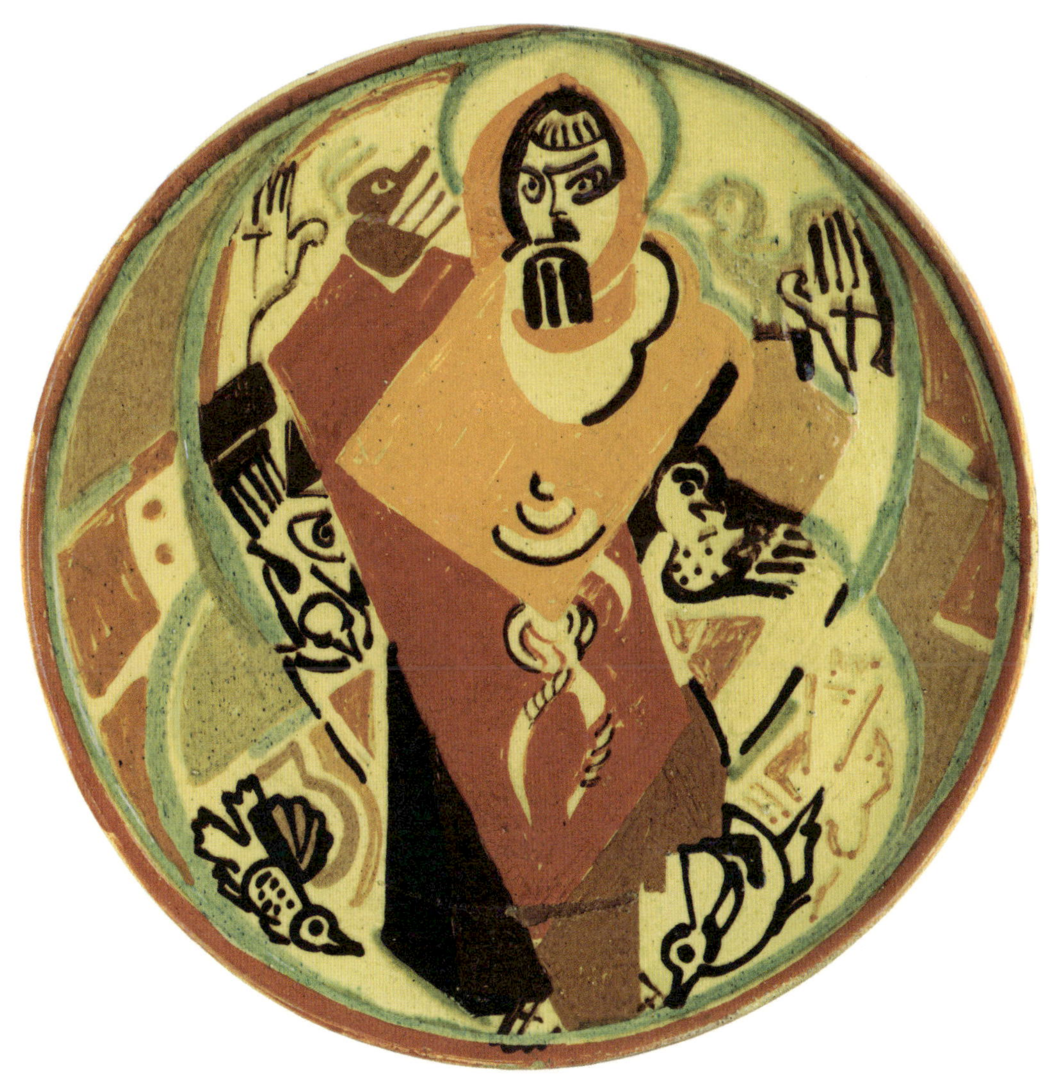

fig 68 Saint Francis of Assisi 1940

mechanisation and urbanisation associated with the movement formed a pillar of the values of the Vichy regime and the rhetoric of Nazi Germany.[41] These ideals had always been the foundation of Gleizes's conception of Moly-Sabata and corresponded closely with those he developed in his artistic and spiritual theories.

Gleizes's active promotion of himself and the community in these terms in the lead-up to and during the war has been discussed by several scholars, his actions interpreted as either strategic self-preservation or disturbing evidence of deliberate collaboration and his Nazi sympathies.[42] During the 1930s he was a contributor to the journal *Régénération*, which promoted the policies of Hitler's new administration; in an unpublished essay of the same period, he criticised the French government for ending its dialogue with Hitler.[43] He expressed his approval of Nazi youth camp initiatives where forgotten values of manual labour were learnt, much as they were at Moly-Sabata, and sought direct assistance from the Vichy government to establish his own youth program at Les Méjades in 1940, citing Moly-Sabata's as proof of his success.[44] Indeed, he arranged to have Dangar's art classes photographed around this time, as propaganda to promote the community and garner Vichy support.[45] In 1943 he was invited to participate in a Congrès de folklore in Nice, delivering a lecture where he promoted Moly-Sabata as a model of Vichy's new youth camps, *chantiers*, and called for the *retour à la terre*, quoting directly from Pétain and reinforcing the importance of regional craft: 'the soil cannot lie to man any more than the objects he has crafted with his own hands'.[46]

Gleizes's political allegiance notwithstanding, Dangar's letters to him reveal he was open in his hatred of Britain. As an Australian, her national loyalty as a British subject was staunchly apparent, though initially complicated by her investment in *retour à la terre*. Along with many people, she naively saw the war as a tragic inevitability and result of overindustrialisation that would end swiftly, paving the way for a new era. At times, she even parroted some of Gleizes's antisemitism.[47] But as the realities of the war became tangible, her position shifted. Gleizes's ideological stance wounded her personally and she attempted to reason with him, writing in late August 1940 that 'not one soldier in a thousand is fighting to save industry, capitalism & money, & yet he is fighting of his own free will ... to save the inexplicable something they love more than life ... the British Empire ... please try to believe we are not only bad'.[48] Dangar received a fierce response and rarely broached the topic again.[49]

Aside from her resistance to Gleizes's Anglophobia, given her vulnerable status Dangar was outwardly apolitical and cooperative for much of the war. In 1942 she was approached by Jeune France, an arm of the Vichy government's Department for Education and Youth, to teach pottery at the Centre artisanal de poterie et arts plastiques de Mâcon.[50] The centre was one of many established under Vichy auspices that sought to decentralise cultural activity and encourage distinct regional identities through folk and vernacular traditions. She enthusiastically agreed, hoping her personal situation would improve and that 'Vichy [would] not prevent [her] from working here after'.[51]

After four weeks at Mâcon, Dangar decided not to continue, openly recounting 'the affair was too Vichy Government' in a letter to Crowley in 1944.[52] By this time, her stance had shifted dramatically; in March the prior year she had been forced to spend five days with other foreign and British subjects in an internment camp in Grenoble, likely due to her status as a foreign national. She later dismissed the experience, writing to her brother Hastings that 'they were the funniest five days and nights of my life, but they could have ended in Germany very easily, and I wouldn't find it very funny to be there still'.[53] But the internment had a marked impact, and several easily avoided accidents only a few months after her return—slipping on the stairs and breaking her leg as well as burning herself severely—indicate her fragile mental state.

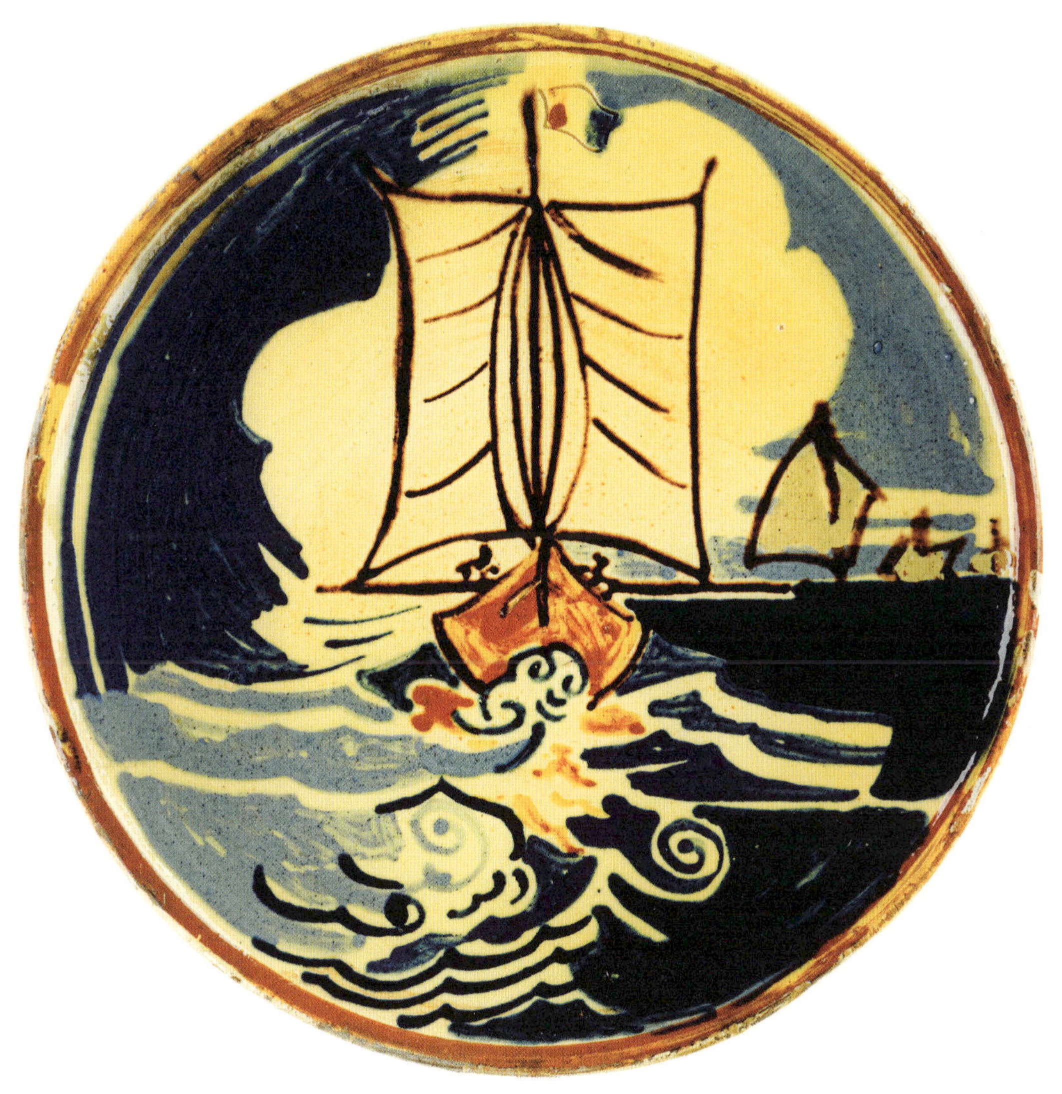

fig 69 The landing 1944

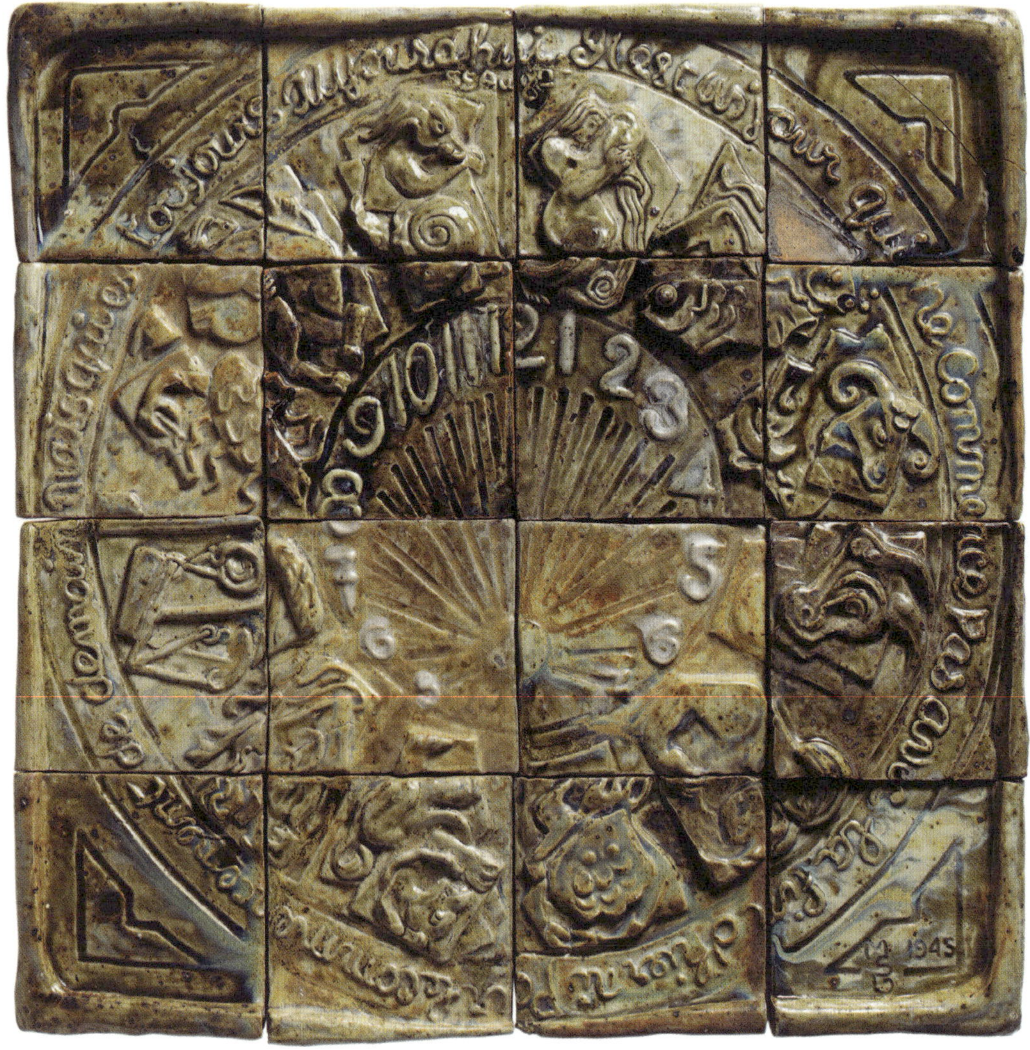

cat 125 Anne Dangar and Jacqueline Lerat, Sundial 1945

In the months after her internment, Dangar began incorporating Moroccan imagery into her work, creating a series of drawings, gouaches (cat 107) and enamelled tiles (cat 62) depicting robed figures and potters.[54] Seemingly inspired by her experience in Fez several years earlier, they were instead covert declarations of her political stance.[55] In late 1942 French North Africa was successfully invaded by British and American military forces. As a French protectorate, Morocco had been aligned with Vichy, but changed its allegiance after this event—an important turning point in the Second World War. Imagery associated with unoccupied Morocco came to symbolise the Resistance, and these small images became quiet but potent demonstrations of Dangar's support of the Allies.[56] The figures in these works, depicted as single, angular forms rather than as a collection of independent planes, appear to rely on Lhote's teaching, a discernible shift away from Gleizes's approach that may reflect Dangar's frustration with him.

Dangar's most overt declaration of her politics exists in a plate created the following year (fig 69), decorated with an atypically figurative image of a ship and inscribed '6/6/44' on the base, the date Allied forces invaded Normandy from the sea, an operation marking the beginning of a campaign to liberate the north-west of Europe.[57] She created this piece for her close friends the Steinbachs, who actively supported the Resistance and aided her during the war—Madame Steinbach often drove her to the pottery illegally and sent her sons to Dangar's art classes.

By the final months of war, Dangar was utterly exhausted. She had had no regular contact with friends and family and felt abandoned by Gleizes, who had convinced her to remain in France despite her status but left her in Sablons alone while he openly denigrated Britain and cooperated with the Vichy government. Over the course of the conflict, she did not see him in person for three years. As she wrote,

> I cannot pretend … your indifference to this 'stranger within your gate' has not hurt me … Tell me Monsieur Gleizes what would you feel if you were in a foreign country during war time and asked by friends to remain, even when offered a free passage home and every help by your country. Would you not feel hurt if you had to suffer hunger and [a lack of] necessary nourishing food during four years? … You alone are responsible for this mouth which is one too many for France to nourish.[58]

The liberation of France precipitated by the Normandy landings came as a great relief. With safe passage in France, Dangar embarked on trips in the region, visiting old friends and other potteries. In 1945 she travelled to La Borne, a pottery in Bourges operated by the potter Jacqueline Lerat and her husband Jacques, both of whom would become central figures in postwar ceramics in France.[59] Dangar had met 21-year-old Lerat (née Bouvet) as an apprentice potter at the Centre artisanal in Mâcon during the war, and they corresponded regularly following her return to Sablons, with Dangar providing advice on how to navigate male-dominated pottery workshops: 'don't let the potters ignore you because you're a woman … I know the men do not want to take women seriously in pottery but insist that you have more than the necessary qualities for a potter than two men.'[60]

Over the fortnight she spent with Lerat, Dangar produced her most singular work, a multi-panelled sundial with the signs of the zodiac and the times of day spiralling from the centre (cat 125). She departed from the vibrant cubist works for which she was now well regarded, and used the hand-building methods and unpredictable salt glazes traditional to the Bourges region to create *grès au sel* (salt-glazed stoneware). Although not stylistically cubist, with animated figures representing each of the zodiac signs, this imagery was a tangible link between her cubist philosophies and the natural world. Astrology's associations with the celestial movements of the Sun, Moon and planets, underscored

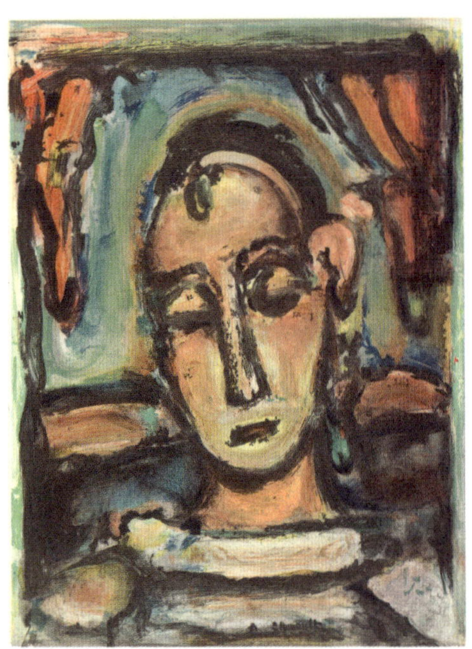

fig 70 Georges Rouault, *Tête de jeune fille* 1939 in *Verve*, July–October 1939

by the function of the sundial to determine the time, mirrored her belief in rotation and the spiral as spiritual motifs. The composition was completed by the incorporation of a quote on time describing the eternal nature of the present by Saint Augustine, a phrase that repeats itself in circular perpetuity around the edge of the dial.[61]

This is one of several works Dangar created in the immediate postwar period in which she departed from Gleizes's methods and influence. In June 1945, she viewed paintings by Georges Rouault in a prewar copy of *Verve* magazine (fig 70), noting she 'should get more of this vigorous plastic construction into my big plate designs'.[62] Subsequent ceramics after Gleizes's watercolour *L'Adoration des Mages* 1945–46 (*Adoration of the Magi*, cat 118) combine elements of both artists' work, with the frenzied and painterly cubist composition of Gleizes gaining structure through the application of black line as outline and skeleton, an effect used in Rouault's paintings to stabilise his own gestural marks.

By the closing months of the war, Dangar had resolved to return to Australia, acknowledging that she was too 'old to continue here'.[63] For the two years following, she negotiated the timing and details of her repatriation, at one point attempting to convince Australian authorities to transport her pottery wheel and personal items 'free of charge', so she could immediately establish a workshop in Australia.[64] In the meantime, Dangar returned to the routines of her life in Sablons before wartime. Her children's art classes had continued during the war, and she triumphantly restaged an exhibition in September 1945 at Moly-Sabata of their paintings on the theme of 'Les colonies françaises', originally coordinated with the local school in 1943.[65]

In 1946 the owners of the Hôtel Schaeffer in Serrières commissioned Dangar to create a cycle of mural schemes for their *salle des fêtes* and cinema. Again, Dangar departed from Gleizes's principles, adopting a folkloric approach inflected by the Lhote-inspired angularity of her Moroccan figures. The Schaeffers were already generous supporters, having commissioned her to decorate and advise on renovations to the hotel in the late 1930s with Grenoble designer and friend Jacques Martin. She had taught the Schaeffers' daughter Yvette from childhood, and Yvette worked closely with Dangar on the design (cat 109) and execution of the murals in situ between 1946 and 1948 (fig 71). The pair developed imagery centred around regional folklore, depicting traditional dances and incorporating musical notation with lyrics in the local vernacular.[66] Dangar found the murals too representational and was amused that some Serrières locals found them 'too cubist!', but felt they served their purpose when many danced at their unveiling.[67]

Although the Australian press advertised her return, Dangar's plans for repatriation ended in 1947 when she received approval from Gleizes and local authorities to build a kiln and pottery at Moly-Sabata, something she had imagined since 1930.[68] She had delayed her return repeatedly in

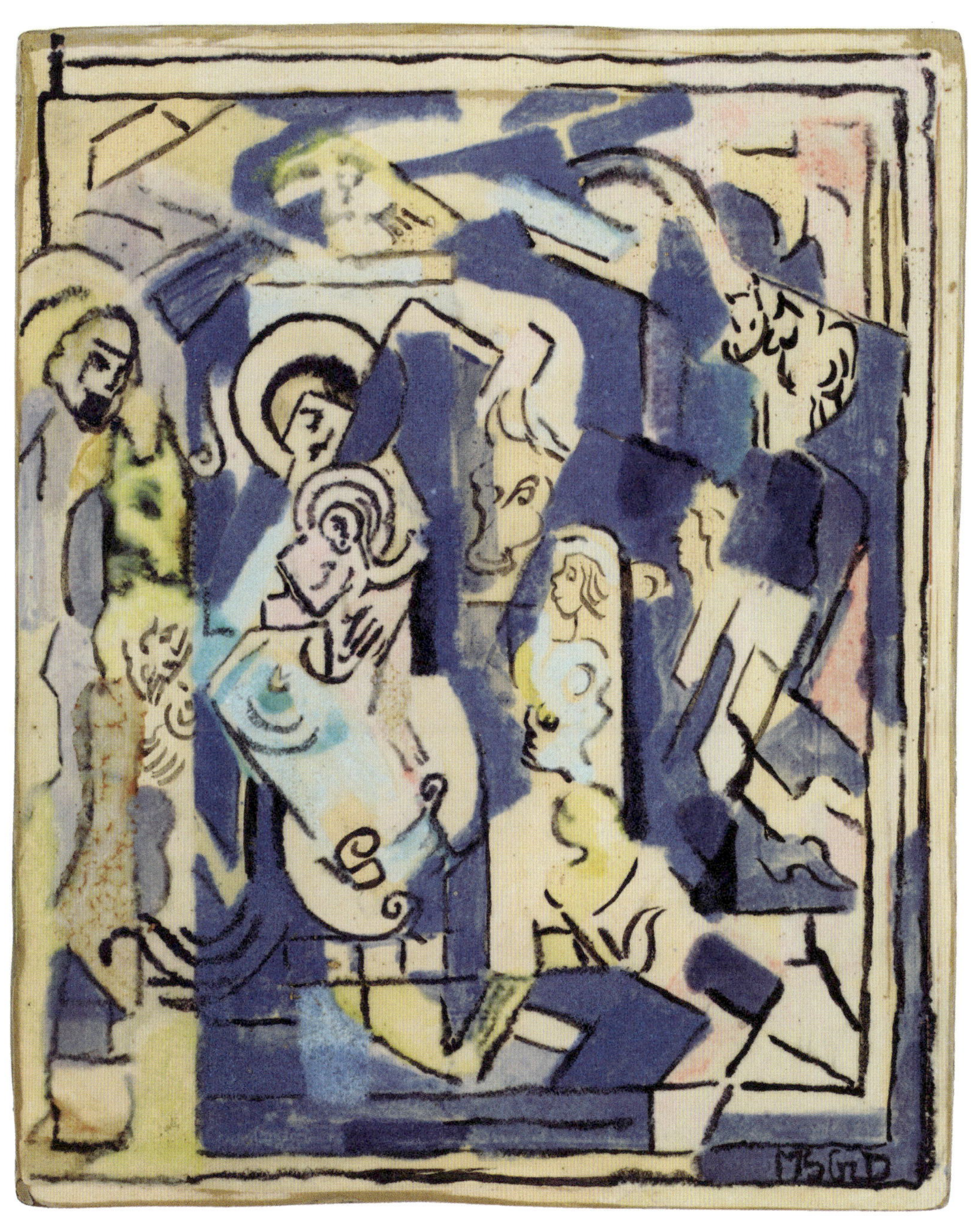

cat 118 after Albert Gleizes, *L'Adoration des Mages* (*Adoration of the Magi*) 1945–46

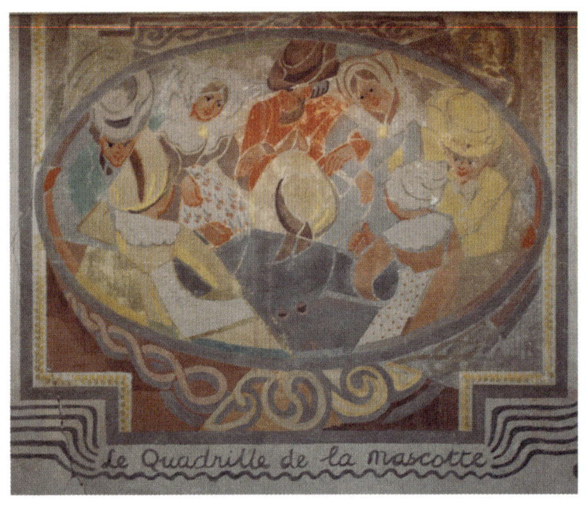

fig 71 Mural in the *salle des fêtes* 1947, Hôtel Schaeffer

previous years, citing her commitment to the Schaeffer murals and limited finances, but had always been torn between Sydney and Sablons, stating in 1946, 'I have become a part of France and France a part of me. I shall regret having left, but to stay is suicide.'[69]

Over several weeks, the kiln was constructed alongside the entrance gate to Moly-Sabata, and an outbuilding converted into a studio with a wheel and workbench. On 26 August 1947, Dangar proudly announced the completion of the pottery to Gleizes and Roche with delight, 'The painful long long birth is over—I'm sure no mother ever suffered more in giving birth to a child.'[70] Dangar was devastated after the first firing was unsuccessful when smoke was trapped in the kiln, staining all of the pots black, but through successive attempts and modifications suggested by Bert and others over the following months, she began to turn and fire works at Moly-Sabata. Paquaud and potters from the region regularly assisted and she was touched by their changed attitude towards her since their first meeting, writing to Gleizes that 'when I worked with them they always made me feel an outsider, now that I have left there they make me one of them and I am happy about it'.[71]

Among the major pieces she wished to fire in her new kiln were liturgical objects (cat 111) for the chapel of the abbey La Pierre-qui-Vire, in Saint-Léger-Vauban, one of several commissions she received through young Benedictine monk Dom Angelico Surchamp in the late 1940s. Dangar met Surchamp in 1947 after he undertook lessons with Gleizes and stayed for several weeks at Moly-Sabata.[72] He formed a friendship with Dangar and Deveyle, becoming a great confidant and supporter. In the final years of her life, Dangar corresponded with him frequently and he encouraged her to undertake high-profile commissions of her original work despite her arduous living circumstances, notably for the Museo internazionale delle ceramiche in Faenza, Italy, which acquired a plate in 1951.[73]

By 1948, Dangar's health was deteriorating. While only in her early sixties, years of physical labour and malnourishment had left her exhausted and she began experiencing vision problems and heart issues. Nonetheless she remained dedicated to her work, creating pottery with the assistance of Paquaud, who turned large forms for her to decorate. She gleefully described cubist artist Pablo Picasso's recent ceramics in a letter to Crowley later that year, 'Picasso from being Gleizes's rival has become mine!! What fun! … I have received many letters comparing my little pots born in love to these tortured powerful last efforts of the Spanish art hero.'[74] In 1948, at Gleizes's request, she undertook an order of more than 20 plates after his design for his solo exhibition at the Galerie des Garets in Paris, one of which was acquired by the Petit Palais, and she contributed to the Salon d'automne in Lyon during the same year and in those following.[75] She also continued her art classes, and in 1949 oversaw a cubist summer school for adult students. Over three weeks, she guided pupils through Gleizes's principles of translation and towards the end, 'the joy of rotation'.[76] Among her students was 22-year-old Geneviève de Cissey (later Dalban), who was greatly inspired by her experience at Moly-Sabata and continued to correspond with Dangar over the ensuing years, much as Lerat did.[77]

In August 1950, Dangar slipped while cleaning, fracturing her arm and two ribs.[78] Only a few months later, in early 1951, she collapsed and fell unconscious in Serrières, and was later instructed by her doctor that she must rest and refrain from all activity including drawing and reading.[79] As she relayed to Surchamp, this experience convinced her to convert to Roman Catholicism, the dominant religion in the area.[80] Raised loosely Protestant, Dangar developed a generalised appreciation of Christianity, which was further amplified by Gleizes's identification of universally applied symbols and sacred motifs.[81] During the 1940s, her faith increasingly became intertwined with the spiritual basis of her work, something which was of no interest to Crowley, who explicitly forbade Dangar from mentioning religion in connection with painting in their correspondence.[82] Dangar saw her conversion both as the final step in her informal naturalisation in France alongside Gleizes, an ardent Catholic, and many of his followers, and, more practically, as assurance that she would receive an appropriate burial upon her death. She 'did not want to be buried like a dog' and there had been no Anglican priest in Lyon or Grenoble since before the war.[83] On 3 March 1951 Dangar was baptised by the local priest with Gleizes as her godfather.[84]

Although Dangar had lost confidence in Gleizes during the war, she remained a devoted adherent to his aesthetic and spiritual philosophies throughout her life, writing to Crowley, 'perhaps I'm very narrow to feel no need of another master, I can't help it'.[85] She was open in her dislike of painters such as Mondrian and Miró, dismissing their abstraction for what she perceived as a lack of significance and spirituality.[86] In late 1950, her belief in Gleizes's philosophies was reaffirmed when Crowley sent her a copy of *Australian Aboriginal decorative art* 1948 (fig 72), then recently published by the Australian Museum in Sydney.[87] Within its pages she discovered spiral-like motifs used on engraved sacred stones and scar tree carvings created by First Nations peoples in Australia and excitedly drew annotated copies in pencil to send to Pouyaud and Surchamp (fig 73).[88] She was profoundly affected by their formal resonance with her own aesthetic philosophies and their continuous use in ceremonial contexts over millennia in Australia, the country she had left—repelled by its narrow view of art—more than 20 years ago.[89] While she always remained connected to her friends and family, the artistic and spiritual tether to her home offered by these cultural designs, previously unknown to her though practised over generations, validated her commitment to her chosen cubist path in France, even as *une étrangère*.

In the following months, Dangar received permission from her doctor to visit Roussillon and finish the decoration of several large pieces, which would be among the last she ever produced. She was weak, and, even when aided by Deveyle and Paquaud, decorating was a 'terrible effort'.[90] But these works are among the most sophisticated of her career, complex and even transcendental cubist designs applied to the pottery form that reflect her dedicated transformation over the previous two decades. Dangar became particularly attached to a large pot (fig 74), and despite her very limited means, refused to sell it, proclaiming that it was 'magnificent … I sense that I will never have the strength to give birth to another like it.'[91]

—

Anne Dangar died barely six months later, on 4 September 1951, after suffering from a stroke that left her partially paralysed weeks earlier.[92] Deveyle, Paquaud and Yvette Schaeffer worked together to complete her final commissions, among them teacups and saucers Dangar had decorated but not fired as part of a tea service (cat 126). Spanning her life and death, and fired months apart under different conditions, the glazed surfaces of these pieces vary greatly, with those overseen by Dangar finished in deep cream and

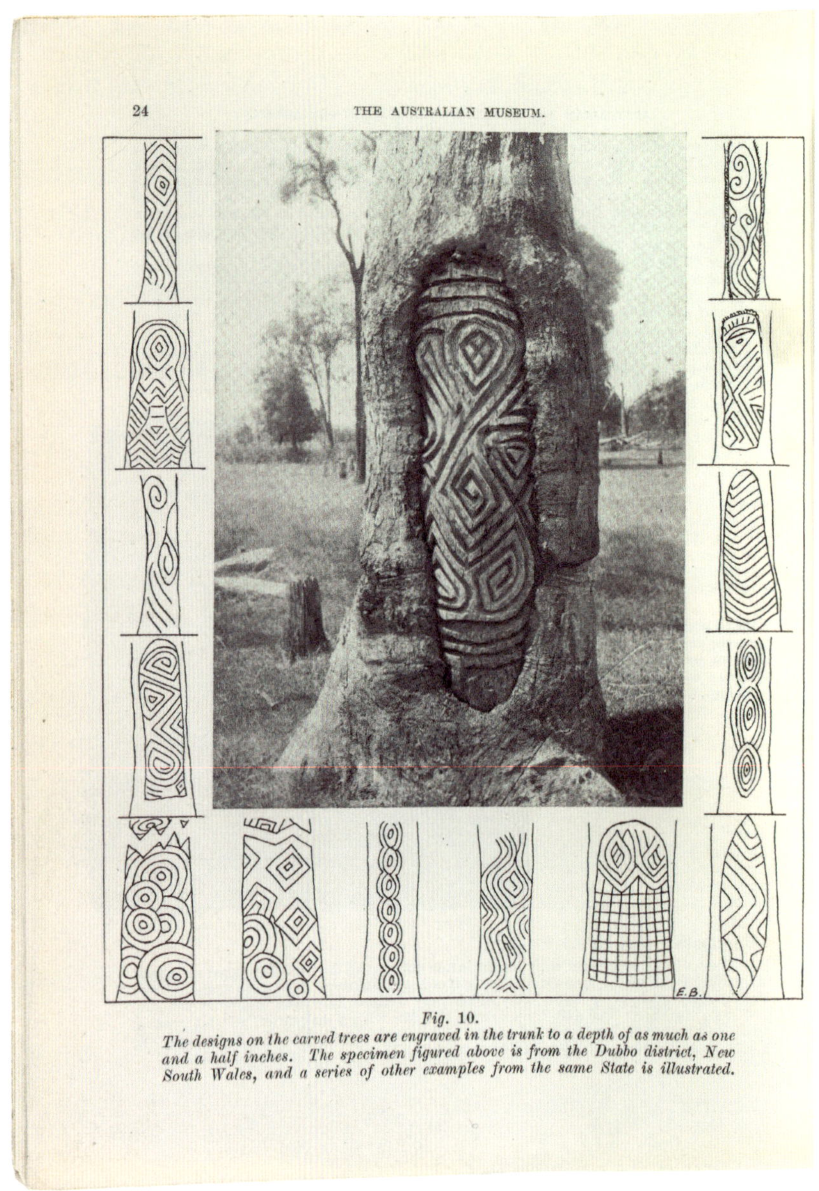
24 THE AUSTRALIAN MUSEUM.

Fig. 10.

The designs on the carved trees are engraved in the trunk to a depth of as much as one and a half inches. The specimen figured above is from the Dubbo district, New South Wales, and a series of other examples from the same State is illustrated.

fig 72 Carved trees in Frederick D McCarthy, *Australian Aboriginal decorative art*, 1948

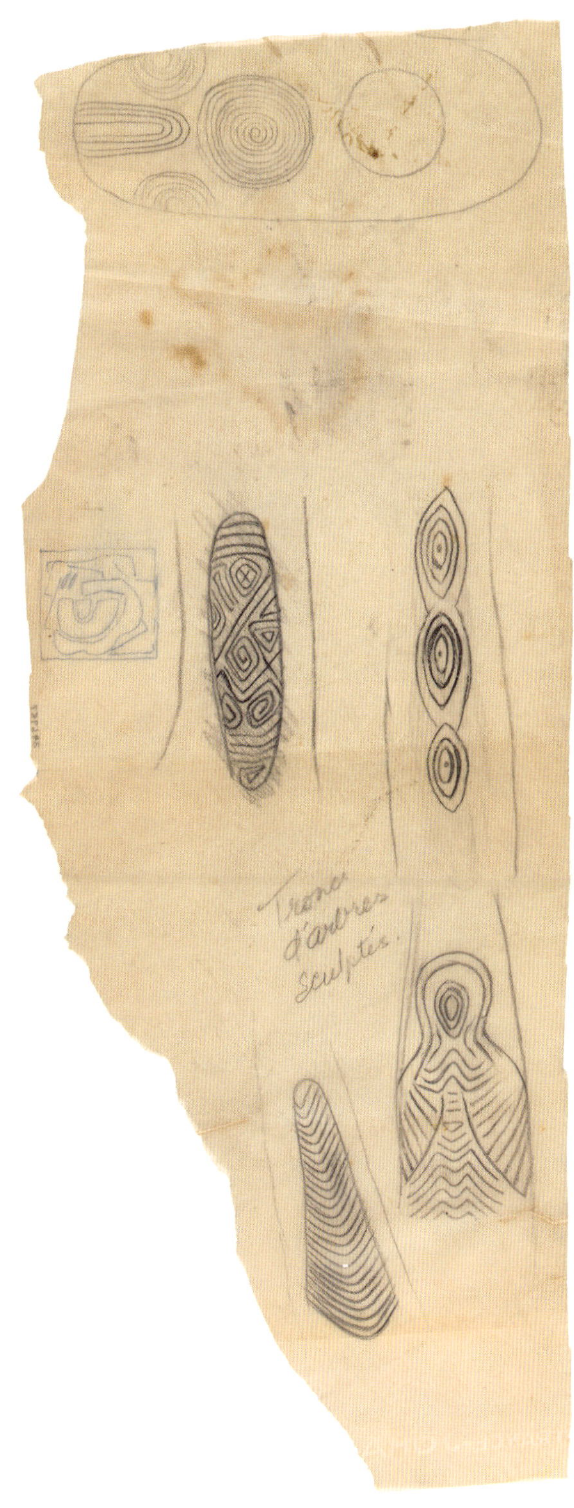

fig 73 First Nations scar tree designs copied from *Australian Aboriginal decorative art* 1950

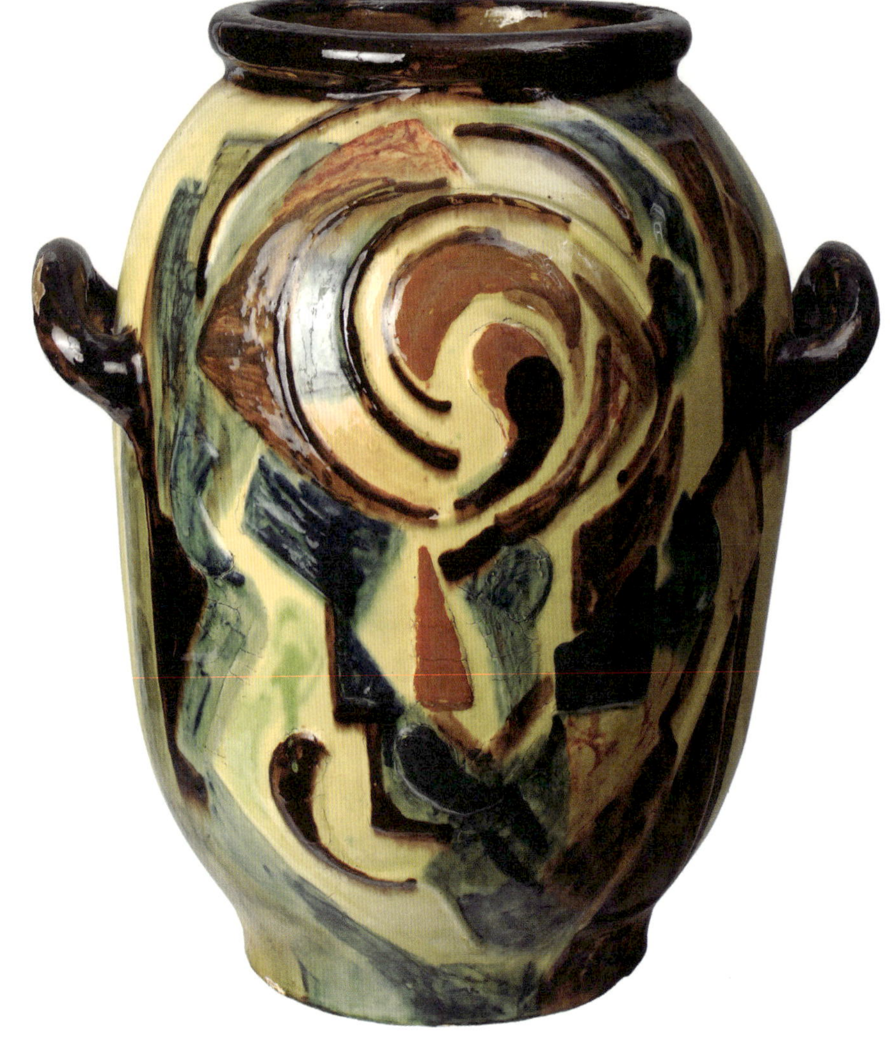

fig 74 Pot 1950–51

blue, and those lovingly completed posthumously by her friends emerging from the kiln in contrasting hues of lemon and pale teal.

At her funeral, Lyon-based modern art critic and writer René Deroudille pronounced that Dangar was 'the greatest potter in France' and she was interred in the Roche family vault in the Serrières cemetery, her tomb providing a view of Moly-Sabata across the river.[93] Despite his sporadic ambivalence, Gleizes confessed to Crowley that Dangar was 'the soul of Moly-Sabata' and, indeed, the community continued for only a few years without her energy.[94]

Although abandoned in the 1960s, Moly-Sabata has since been transformed into an artist residency, with Dangar's longed-for kiln and workshop hosting contemporary artists from around the world, inspired by her life and legacy. She is now firmly entrenched in French histories of Cubism and ceramics, having featured in numerous exhibitions on both subjects, beginning in 1953 with the inclusion of her pottery posthumously in the survey exhibition *Du cubisme aux arts traditionnels* held in Paris and travelling throughout France.[95]

Dangar's quiet and gradual passing in Sablons seems ill-fitting for a figure who lived her life with such determination. Her death went unnoticed by the press in Australia, but was deeply felt by her friends and family, notably Crowley, who worked tirelessly to bring her practice to wider recognition. These efforts have come to fruition only in recent decades, as Dangar's legacy has slowly been excavated from the archive.[96]

Today Dangar is among a small number of Australian artists who can be said to have truly responded to the call of modern art. Engaging directly with the European avant-garde and working alongside its members as their peer, she developed a sustained and substantial cubist practice, an achievement matched by few others. Additionally, as an advocate and teacher, she exerted an irrevocable influence upon modern art in Australia, and actively encouraged the development of pure abstraction. Although she did not live to see her work recognised in her country of birth, almost a century after encountering modern art for the first time, Anne Dangar stands among the most significant figures in Australian modernism and alone as Australia's only cubist potter.

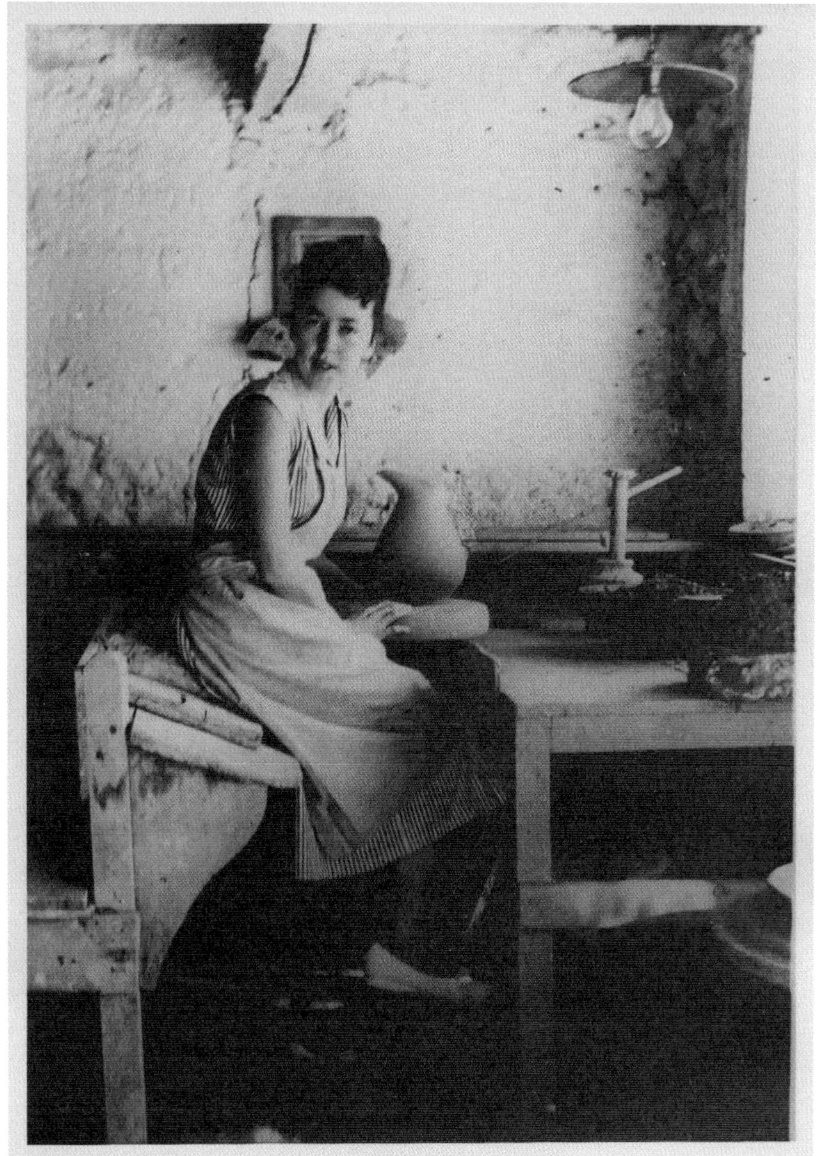

fig 75 Geneviève de Cissey-Dalban in Anne Dangar's pottery at Moly-Sabata, c 1956

After Anne Dangar:
Geneviève Dalban and the amis d'Albert Gleizes

PETER BROOKE

It is rather sad in the context of this publication to have to say that the form of pottery practised by Anne Dangar—*terre vernissée*, the 'glazed earth' traditional to the Rhône region—is now illegal. The problem is the combination of a lead-based glaze—the *alquifoux*—and a wood-fired kiln. Through holes at the top of the kiln, lead-laden smoke is released into the atmosphere. Nowadays most potters using the *terre vernissée* technique will use gas- or electricity-fired kilns, which will provide a much more controlled and predictable result. The advantage of the wood-fired kiln, for those who love it, is precisely its unpredictability. The colours alter following the movement of the fire playing round the pottery. This is most obvious in the iron-oxide reds and oranges. According to the play of the fire, the colours can vary from a luminous orange to a light or dark brown, sometimes a brown illuminated with splashes of orange.[1]

There is an irony in the situation since Albert Gleizes had established Moly-Sabata as a 'centre for detoxification' from the moral, psychological and physical harms done by a 'machinist' (technologically driven) society. Robert Pouyaud, the first person to become a resident at Moly, had worked using spray-paints in a mannequin factory which, according to Gleizes's account, had affected his health.[2] Many of the people living in Serrières and Sablons, the area where Moly-Sabata was situated, worked in the great Rhône-Poulenc chemical works which dominated—and still dominate—the region. These were the people who sent their children to Anne Dangar's drawing and craft classes, and indeed a number of the trade unionists working at Rhône-Poulenc took an interest in her work, notably André Moulin, a CFDT (Confédération française démocratique du travail) organiser who took up an interest in the manufacture of traditional dyes used by his son Bernard to make tapestries following Gleizes's principles of 'translation–rotation'.

It occurs to me that I must have witnessed some of the last firings integrating the traditional method to have taken place in the Rhône Valley. I had the privilege of living for some ten years with Geneviève Dalban and her family—husband Charles, son Paul-Louis and daughter Aguilberte. Geneviève de Cissey—she was not yet married—had attended a course organised by Dangar in 1949 to teach Gleizes's principles. It was a difficult experience for Dangar since in the middle of it she received the manuscript of Gleizes's *L'homme devenu peintre* (*Man becomes painter*) which proposed a thoroughgoing revision of the principles of translation–rotation as they were taught in *La peinture et ses lois* 1923 (*Painting and its laws*), the basis of her own work until that time and of the teaching she had planned for the course.[3] But Geneviève had been totally captivated, and in the course of an exchange of letters with Dangar she made the decision to devote the rest of her life to the promotion of the idea. That was why I had gone to stay and work with her. She was the person who had best mastered Gleizes's philosophy and *mode opératoire* (way of working) and was most determined to pass it on to future generations.

Geneviève had lived for a time at Moly-Sabata. After Anne Dangar died in 1951, her place had been taken by Jean-Claude and Yvette Libert. Jean-Claude was a painter, at the time heavily influenced by Gleizes. At Moly he also devoted himself to pottery. When the couple left in 1956, Geneviève de Cissey took over, living with Dangar's own close friend and collaborator, the weaver Lucie Deveyle. Geneviève had hardly known Gleizes, and despite her correspondence with Dangar she had not had much opportunity to work with her. She always insisted that it was Lucie Deveyle, a woman from a working-class background who had first arrived at Moly as maidservant to the musician César Geoffray and his family, who had taught her most of what she knew.

Or at least what she knew regarding Gleizes and his method. Like Dangar herself, Geneviève had undergone an apprenticeship in the Roussillon-based pottery Les Chals (formerly Poterie Bert), under the direction of Jean-Marie Paquaud. This despite the fact that she had already undergone a course in ceramics at the École nationale des beaux-arts in Dijon. But Les Chals was a working pottery, still producing tableware used by the local population, and that was where the *terre vernissée* could best be mastered—even though Geneviève, coming from a devoutly Catholic, semi-aristocratic family (an ancestor, General Ernest Courtot de Cissey, had been active in the suppression of the Paris Commune), had the same initial difficulties as Dangar had with the apparently coarse manners of the communist potters of Les Chals. But, also like Dangar, she soon developed an immense respect for them. To quote Geneviève:

> That was Paquaud's pottery. As the wheels turned there were silences, wonderful silences, some loose rustling of the transmission belt, a little noise from the pedal, all following the rhythm of the leg pushing the pedal, the rhythm of breath which would vary with the size of the pot and so with the effort put into it, following the rhythm of the beating of the heart, rhythm of the building up of the pot in full harmony and identity with the person producing it, that is to say, the man, body and spirit, breath and will.
>
> A spontaneity always renewed, never routine; and Paquaud knew it, the pottery was never burdened with silences that were too long, he kept us alert with jokes, not sufficiently coherent to distract our minds but enough to keep us awake—*'Marguerite, elle sait faire les frites'*—and sometimes he told us about his childhood and youth, his apprenticeship as a potter, his 'tour de France' [part of the process of becoming a master potter], everything in him spoke of a territory much loved. All his tricks, all his jokes—'I was a bit of a naughty boy' he would finish by saying, still laughing over this happy life—brought serenity and warmth to the space of the pottery.[4]

Geneviève de Cissey continued living at Moly-Sabata after the death of Lucie Deveyle in 1956, but grew to feel that her position there was untenable. She was living alone in the large property and needed help, but Madame Gleizes (Gleizes himself had died in 1953) was having great difficulty finding anyone suitable and her ideas as to who might be suitable were not necessarily going to be the same as Geneviève's. She left early in 1958. Soon afterwards, in 1960, she married Charles Dalban and settled in Ampuis, some 20 kilometres north of Sablons, an area well known for its local wine, Côte-Rôtie. There she established a pottery workspace with several wheels, and had a succession of young people who came to study with her, either pottery or, like myself, the principles of Gleizes's painting, teaching that she offered free of charge, though those who were living there, as I was, were invited to contribute what they could to living expenses. She had a wood-fired kiln built along the lines of the kiln at Moly.

The firings were an impressive affair. The pottery, which we had seen beautifully decorated by Geneviève and by Aguilberte, was now coated in the uniform grey of the lead-based *alquifoux*—in mourning, as Geneviève would say. The installation in the kiln was itself a work of architecture, ensuring enough room for the fire to pass round each piece, and planned according to what pieces should be placed at the bottom where the heat was most intense. Then, when the kiln was full, the entrance was bricked up—a scene rather reminiscent of Edgar Allen Poe's *Cask of amontillado* 1846. The actual firing

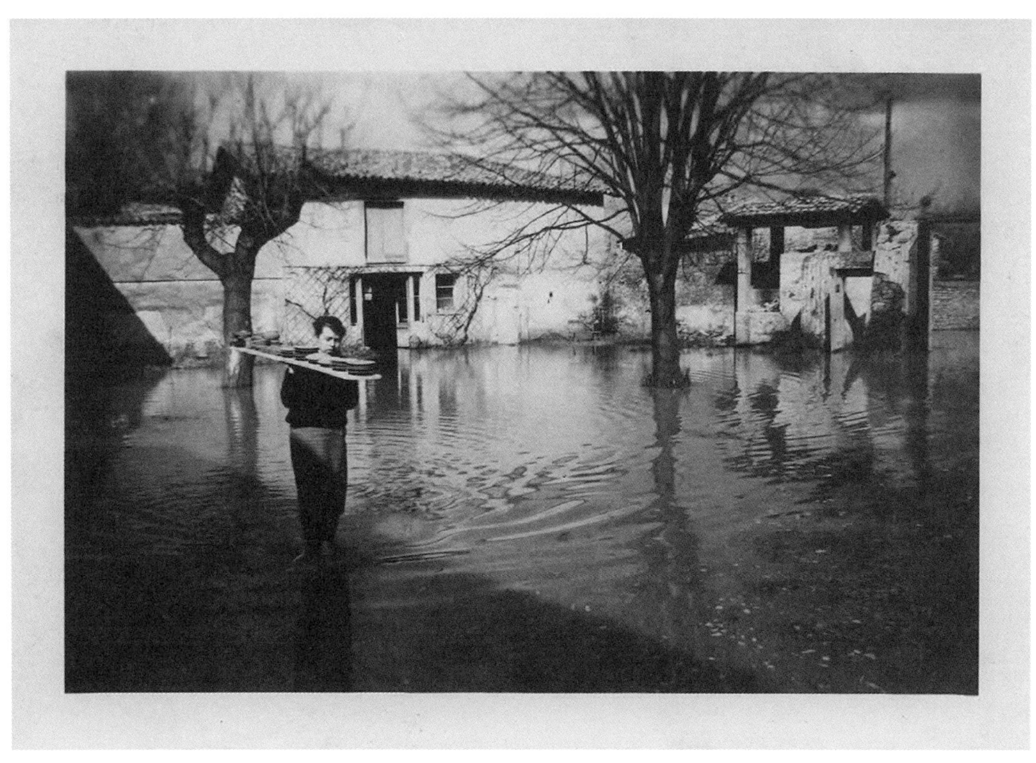

fig 76 Geneviève de Cissey-Dalban crossing the courtyard of Moly-Sabata during a flood of the Rhône, 1955 or 1957

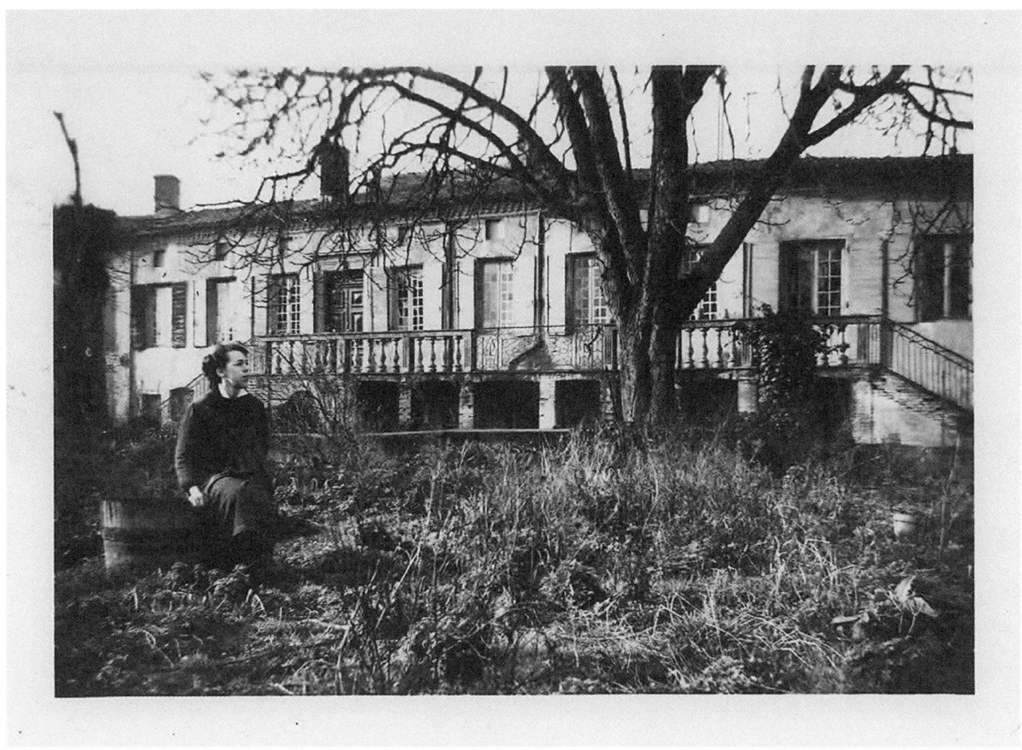

fig 77 Geneviève de Cissey-Dalban in the garden of Moly-Sabata, c1955

would take a whole day, as a team kept the fire going, throwing huge quantities of wood, including whole tree trunks, into the bottom segment of the kiln. And let us not forget the clouds of black smoke that billowed out into the atmosphere. That added to the drama! The decision as to when to stop was a delicate matter and sometimes Geneviève would consult with other potters. Then it was left for several days to cool down. The opening of the kiln was a festive occasion, with friends and family gathered round. The pottery that had entered clad in grey now appeared in radiant, luminous colours. Each piece was taken out and commented on, passing from hand to hand. Sometimes there was a little disappointment that a section had not been fired sufficiently, with maybe a matte surface and a little of the grey glaze remaining; sometimes a delicate design had been almost completely obliterated because the heat was too intense. But for the most part it was just cries of delight at the beauty that was being revealed. I know well that I shall never experience anything like it ever again.

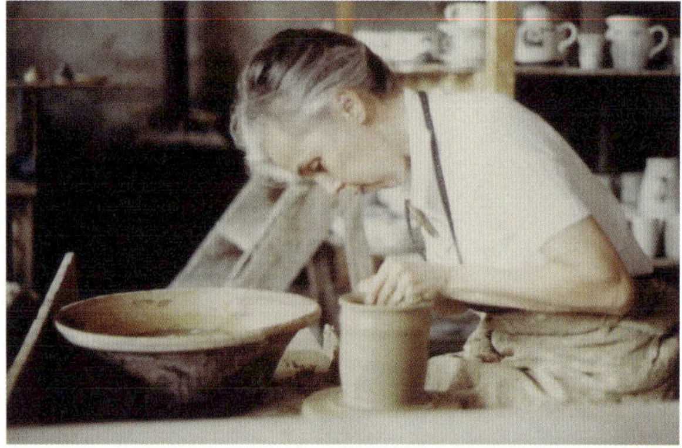

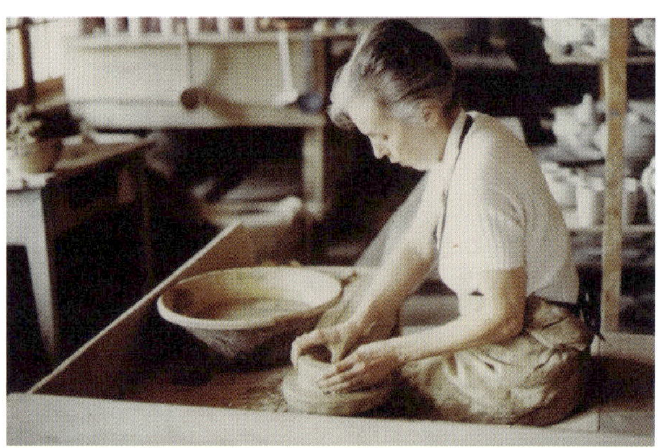

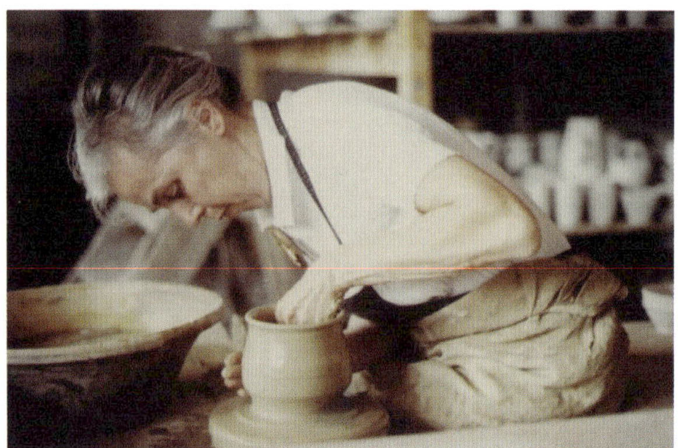

figs 78–80 Geneviève de Cissey-Dalban in her pottery at Ampuis, 1978

The house had a large barn attached to it which was converted into an exhibition space. In addition to the most recently fired pottery, this housed large paintings by Gleizes and his circle, most notably Pouyaud, but there were also tapestries by Bernard Moulin and Jacqueline Dürrbach (who made the tapestry of Picasso's *Guernica* that used to hang in the UN Security Council room). The Gleizes paintings were lent by supportive friends: the collector and historian André Dubois (whose collection is now housed in the Musée des beaux-arts in Lyon); and the publisher Henri Viaud, whose Éditions Présence, in addition to publishing writings by Gleizes, pioneered the publication of not-quite-mainstream religious writers—Henry Corbin, specialist in Iranian sophiology; Henri Le Saux, Benedictine monk who lived as intensely as possible the Hindu religious experience; and Archimandrite Sophrony, whose life of Saint Silouan, first published in translation by Viaud, is now recognised as a major classic of twentieth-century Orthodox Christian literature.

Geneviève had what could be regarded as an advantage or as a disadvantage in relation to Dangar in that, given the work of her husband Charles Dalban, she was under less pressure to sell her work. It was an advantage because she was free to do what she really wanted, which was to explore the possibilities offered by Gleizes's principles in depth. Yet at the same time she felt that in comparison with Dangar her own work was rather stiff and *scolaire*, or didactic. She felt that she lacked Dangar's lightness of touch. By contrast, I was constantly amazed at the variety and freedom Geneviève achieved in her work, even as it never strayed very far from the basic *mode opératoire*. She also regretted that she was, necessarily, participating in the transition from artisan to artist, of pottery from an everyday service to a local community to an art form. The same process was occurring at Les Chals, which continued under Paquaud's successor Jean-Jacques Dubernard, himself a very fine potter, but it was no longer the great collective family venture with a massive production of other times. It was, unavoidably, turning into a tourist attraction. It is today overseen by new owners, not themselves potters but very keen to restore at least the buildings and to invite potters to come and make use of it. Not what it was, but as good as possible under the circumstances.[5]

Ampuis had become the centre for the Association des amis d'Albert Gleizes. On Geneviève's urging I became its secretary and produced a *Courrier* for the Association as well as various pamphlets with texts by Gleizes and associates. There was an annual reunion attended by, for example: Henri Viaud and André Dubois; Walter Firpo, the poet–painter who had introduced me to the Gleizes adventure; Henri Giriat, the writer and specialist in traditional religious philosophy who had worked as a farmhand in Gleizes's estate in Provence during the war; and the painters Paul Régny and Daniel Gloria (himself also a mosaicist) who had been part of the group based in Lyon which had gathered around Gleizes. There was also usually a representative of the Communauté de Pomeyrol, a Protestant religious order whose founder, Sister Antoinette Butte, greatly admired Gleizes; and the ebullient Claude Revol, who followed André Moulin's role as a representative of the CFDT at Rhône-Poulenc.

The Association as I knew it had been revived by Geneviève and Henri Giriat after a long somnolence. It had originally been founded after Gleizes's death in 1954, but the *amis* were a quarrelsome bunch. The Lyon-based painter Jean Chevalier, closely working with Gleizes during and after the war and to all appearances his obvious successor, had been the first president but had developed a manner of painting far removed from the original principles—though he himself saw a logical continuity— and he and Geneviève could not work together. René Dürrbach, sculptor and painter, perhaps best known for the powerful stained-glass windows he designed for churches in Charleville-Mézières and in Épenoy, had stopped coming after Geneviève had invited a friend of Charles Dalban to give a talk on the importance of the human hand. Unfortunately, he had framed his talk in the context of Darwin's theory of evolution, of which Dürrbach disapproved. Dom Angelico Surchamp, close friend of Dangar's and founder of the remarkable *Zodiaque* series of photographic studies of Romanesque art, had refused from early on to have anything to do with the Gleizes circle. While retaining his loyalty to what he had learnt from Gleizes personally, he objected to the enthusiasm many of the circle had for the traditionalist philosophy of René Guénon.[6]

Guénon's thought had been introduced into the circle, and to Gleizes himself, early on, about 1930, by Pouyaud. Gleizes's circle—and to some extent Gleizes himself—were pulled apart by the rival attractions of the Catholic Church and the 'esoteric' philosophy of Guénon—the search for a teaching that, it was thought, lay hidden beneath the forms of the major world religions. The result had been two rival periodicals—Surchamp's Catholic-oriented *Zodiaque* and the 'traditionalist' Guénon-oriented *L'Atelier de la Rose*. Geneviève Dalban, like Anne Dangar, leading up to and following her conversion, was very much on the Catholic side of the dispute but Pouyaud, who had died before I arrived, was still very supportive of her and of what he hoped would be the revival of Moly-Sabata at Ampuis.

In my time, perhaps the most prominent 'Guénonian' was Henri Giriat, who had worked closely with René Dürrbach on the symbolic schema used for his windows. The evocation of different religious traditions in Giriat's proposals brings to mind the symbolic references used in the music of

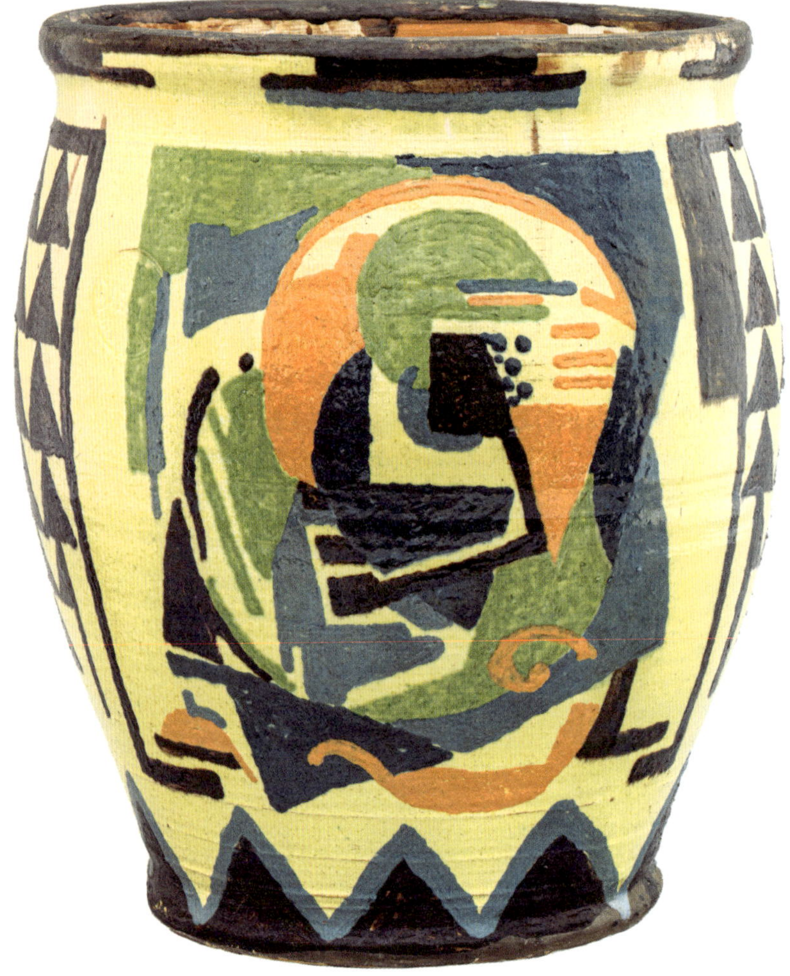

fig 81 Geneviève de Cissey-Dalban and Aguilberte Dalban, Pot with cubist designs (recto) 1995–98

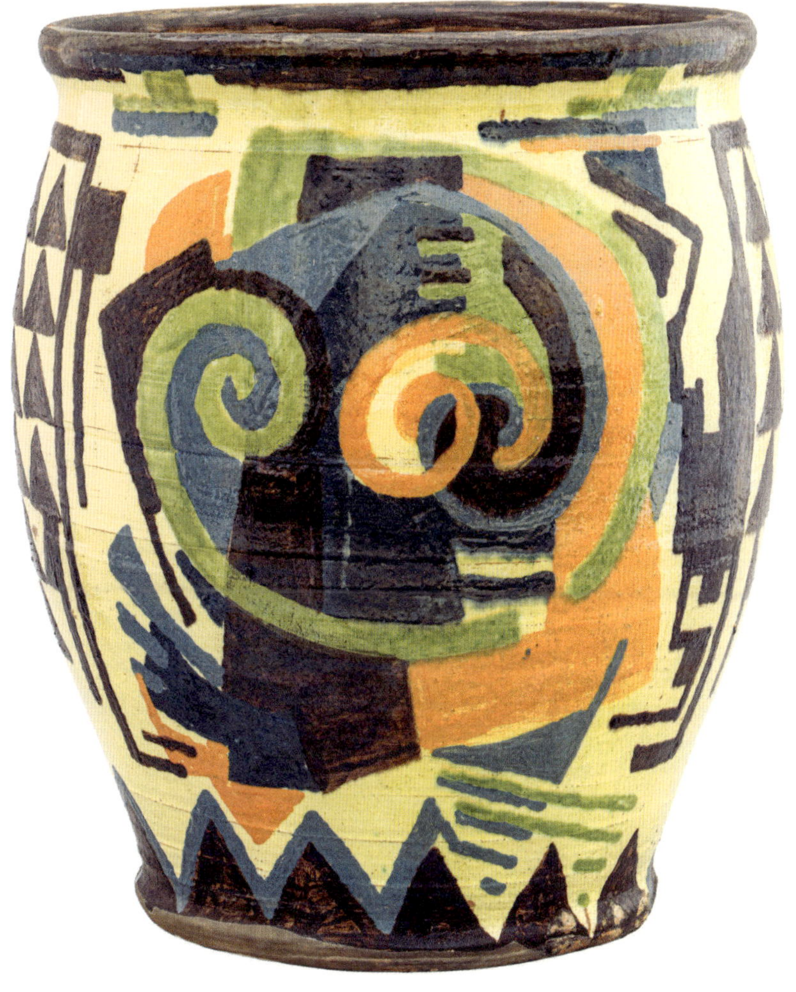

fig 82 Geneviève de Cissey-Dalban and Aguilberte Dalban, Pot with cubist designs (verso) 1995–98

Olivier Messiaen. It was perhaps Giriat, with his open-minded generosity of spirit who, more than Geneviève, held the whole project together. The Association lived in a state of some tension with the Fondation Albert Gleizes, established to manage the estate of Madame Gleizes, which administered a large collection of paintings, the copyright of Gleizes's writings and the properties at Moly-Sabata, Les Méjades and Cavalaire. Giriat, in addition to being active in the Association, was on the organising committee of the Fondation. He played a very important part in helping Anne Varichon prepare the Fondation's catalogue raisonné of Gleizes's work. He organised a beautiful Gleizes exhibition in conjunction with the Van Gogh Museum in Saint-Rémy-de-Provence, an exhibition which, more than any other I have seen, breathed the spirit of Gleizes. He was, so to speak, the representative on the Fondation of the moral and philosophical side of Gleizes's legacy, as opposed to the straightforward art-historical side.

He was also a frequent contributor to the literature I was producing on behalf of the Association. Given the age of those who had been closest to Gleizes, this often took the form, as Giriat remarked, of a 'necrology', a series of obituaries, most of them taking place in 1989, beginning with the death of the air force officer Captain Montatême, a frequent visitor to Moly during the war, rigorist Guénonian turned rigorist traditional Catholic. His obituary was written by Paul Régny. This was followed by the death of Charles Dalban, a terrible loss to Ampuis, where his scepticism and lively sense of humour did much to lighten the sometimes rather heavy atmosphere of devotion to Gleizes (their son, Paul-Louis, talked of 'les cinglés de saint Gleizes'—the crazy devotees of Saint Gleizes!). The *Courrier* published a beautiful tribute to Charles in the form of a letter from Walter Firpo. Régny wrote a dedication to his close friend Daniel Gloria, a delightfully modest soul from a working-class background who was a particular favourite of Geneviève's. Then Giriat wrote on potter and weaver René Pascal, whom he had known when he worked with Gleizes during the war and then later as one of the administrators chosen by Madame Gleizes for the Fondation. It was also Giriat who wrote the obituary for Jacqueline Dürrbach, who died in 1990. Jean-Claude Libert died in 1996 but by that time the *Courrier* had ceased publication as I had gone to live with Viaud in the Alpes-de-Haute-Provence, using his impressive archive of material relating to Gleizes to write my book. I did, however, return to Ampuis, and continued producing the little pamphlets. Giriat wrote one that was a tribute to both René and Jacqueline Dürrbach after René's death in 1999.

The last he wrote, and the last pamphlet issued by the Association, was an obituary for Geneviève Dalban, published in 2003, the year after her death at the age of 76. During the period I was with her she had lost the use of her right arm, horribly swollen almost overnight, yet she continued working to near the end of her life. She could no longer turn but in addition to continuing to decorate the pottery (turned by Aguilberte or, in the case of the larger pieces, Jean-Jacques Dubernard), she conceived a number of ambitious—in one case almost insanely ambitious—projects to be realised in decorated tiles, most successfully a large reproduction of Gleizes's painting *Terre et ciel* 1935 (*Earth and sky*, Musée des beaux-arts de Lyon). I was set to making the tiles, as someone who would never have been trusted with a wheel (in all honesty I never showed an inclination in that direction). The insanely ambitious project was to reproduce in pottery tiles—to scale—Gleizes's cubist-era painting *Le dépiquage des moissons* 1912 (*Harvest threshing*, National Museum of Western Art, Tokyo), the largest of all paintings produced by artists defined as 'cubist' prior to the war (269 × 353 centimetres). Using her left hand for the drawing and holding the long strips of wood that served as rulers down with the dead weight of her right arm, she got as far as making a full-scale reproduction on tracing paper. Much more than a 'copy', it was a deep study of the construction, a work of dedication and love that seemed to me almost more than human.

In devoting this essay mainly to Geneviève Dalban, and to her project in Ampuis, her effort to keep alive the impetus created by Gleizes, I do not feel I have been unfaithful to the spirit of Anne Dangar. It really was a case of a torch being passed from one hand to the other, as if, through Geneviève Dalban, Anne Dangar was able to continue her work. To quote the obituary by Henri Giriat:

> Through Anne Dangar she would assimilate the different aspects of the thought of Albert Gleizes, pictural, human, communitarian, knowing that their unity was assured by a religious vision of the world. One could never find the slightest disagreement between Geneviève and Miss Dangar. Anne Dangar, so severe with regard to intellectual pretentiousness and worldly prejudice, found in Geneviève de Cissey the apprentice and, soon, the friend who would accept the teaching with the most attentive submission: a slow process of maturing in acquiring the principles of painting based on the flat surface, and a progressive mastery of the techniques of traditional pottery.[7]

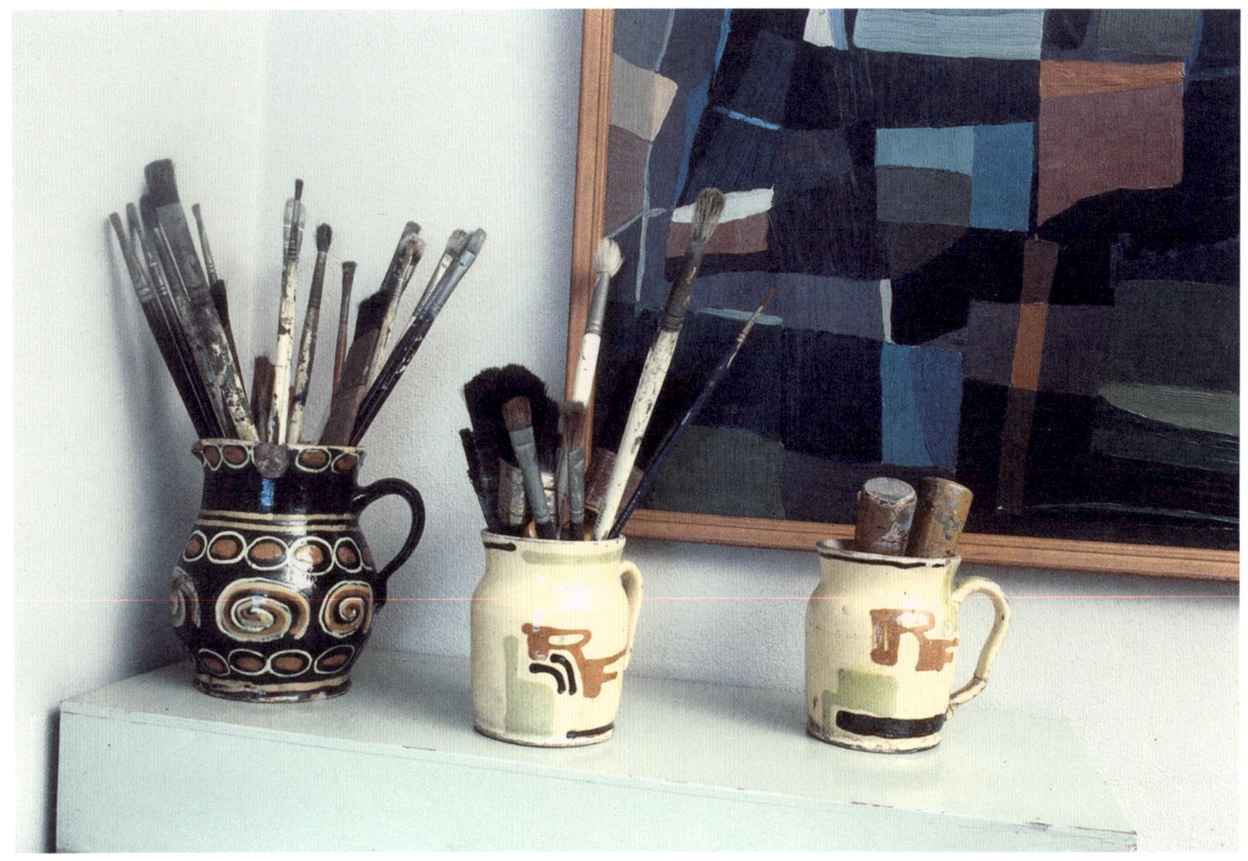

fig 83 The interior of Grace Crowley's flat in Manly, 1979

‘The beautiful day is over ...’: on the afterlife of Anne Dangar

ADS DONALDSON

In Australia, Anne Dangar is now being rediscovered. We might even say she has been rehabilitated. In France, on the other hand, she has been revered for decades. At her burial in the cemetery at Serrières in 1951, the French art critic René Deroudille declared, ‘We are attending the funeral of a potter, the greatest potter in France.’[1] Dangar had worked hard for more than two decades in difficult circumstances at the small artists’ commune Moly-Sabata, under the often-indifferent eye of its founder, the first-generation cubist painter Albert Gleizes. Despite this, Dangar had shown her ceramics all over France with success and seen her work collected by important museums. She had survived the war, too, despite a brief internment; but now, at the age of 65 and as a recent convert to Catholicism, she was being farewelled by the community to whom she had meant the most.

In the years after her death, Dangar would have a street named after her and, eventually, one infants school and then another. Today there are young French adults who have studied at the École élémentaire Anne Dangar and the École maternelle Anne Dangar in Sablons in Isère. The rue Anne Dangar leads to the entrance of Moly-Sabata, where today it is possible to visit her rooms, her kiln and her garden inside the small complex that rests on the banks of the Rhône. Recognised and remembered by the Sablonnais, for whom she was ‘La Miss’, her name has been inscribed into the geography of the town that she gave herself to for more than 20 years. As the American art historian Daniel Robbins has noted, ‘the relatively long life of Moly-Sabata was due more to the strength of her commitment than to the general workability of such a semi-agrarian scheme’, the one imagined by Gleizes.[2] In his memorial essay ‘The beautiful day is over ...’, Gleizes calls Dangar his ‘spiritual daughter!’ and it was at Moly-Sabata that she eventually had her own kiln and where she taught art to generations of children and adults, and became a much-loved and respected figure.[3]

Yet in Australia last century, Dangar was nearly invisible. She has become known to us this century chiefly because her close friend Grace Crowley preserved her letters. In the immediate aftermath of Dangar’s death, too, Crowley did all she could to ensure her colleague would not be forgotten. Perhaps because Dangar’s chosen medium was clay, or perhaps because she was an expatriate, she remained outside Australia’s cultural narratives until the publication of Bruce Adams’s careful and comprehensive monograph *Rustic Cubism: Anne Dangar and the art colony at Moly-Sabata*, published in 2004, which followed Helen Topliss’s book *Earth, fire, water, air: Anne Dangar’s letters to Grace Crowley, 1930–1951*, published in 2000, and the show *Anne Dangar at Moly-Sabata: tradition and innovation* at the National Gallery of Australia in 2001.[4] It is these books and this small exhibition that mark the return of Dangar to the country of her birth. Nearly unknown in the twentieth century, today Dangar is recognised as one of our finest artist–potters, and a pivotal figure in the development of both Australian and French modernism.

—

From Sydney, just ten days after Dangar's funeral, Crowley commenced a more than five-year-long process of untangling Dangar's affairs in France. She began by writing to Gleizes (whom she had met in 1929), letting him know that 'the first news of Anne's death received by me arrived yesterday through a friend of ours in Paris who enclosed a clipping concerning Anne from the journal "Arts" published 7/9/51. This notice appears to have been inserted by yourself.'[5] That friend was likely the Sydney artist Mary Webb, who had been living in Paris since 1949, and an important, though little-known, correspondence now grew between the two artists as Webb replaced Dangar as Crowley's chief conduit and confidante for events in France.

Uppermost in Crowley's mind was to ensure Dangar's life and work would be recognised, that 'she should', as she wrote to Gleizes,

> be represented in her own country by some of her best pieces to remind Australians—if tardily—that Anne Dangar was one of the few fine artists that this country has produced ... And if our National Art Gallery secured some pieces we would thus erect some permanent tribute to her memory.[6]

To this end she first contacted her friend on the ground and, in concert, these two women, Crowley and Webb, set about the task of finding examples of Dangar's work that could be gifted to a museum in Australia. Although they would eventually be thwarted, the task they set themselves—the 'quest', as they called it—was important to them both and stands as testament to the mutual concerns and respect artists have for each other in the face of institutional uninterest.[7]

Webb, who was represented in Paris by the renowned Galerie Colette Allendy (where, indeed, she had met Gleizes, who also showed there), first began looking for suitable work in the private galleries of Paris but met with little success. By chance, however, on a summer break in 1952, Webb did happen to catch what must have been Dangar's first posthumous showing. In Vézelay, she reported to Crowley, she had seen 'an exhibition of Sacred Art (in the Gothic rooms adjoining the Basilica) & included in this exhibition was some pottery of Anne Dangar (very lovely) and some paintings by Gleizes'.[8] This was perhaps a memorial exhibition for Dangar and was likely organised by her friend Robert Pouyaud, the painter who had met Dangar at the station on her arrival at Moly-Sabata and had taught her how to produce Gleizes's pochoirs, but who now lived at Asnières-sous-Bois, just 10 kilometres from Vézelay.

In the autumn of 1953, Webb made her first trip to Moly-Sabata, where she established her own relationship with Dangar's close friend, the weaver Lucie Deveyle. 'Lucie,' she wrote to Crowley, 'was pleased to see me & I went each day to visit her & enjoy a good talk & a cup of tea in the garden. We got along very well together & I enjoyed very much my little holiday at Serrières.'[9] Back in Paris, Webb continued her search for Dangar's pottery. In her letters to Crowley, she began to express her frustration in what would become a theme in her correspondence.

> Mme Gleizes should send something on her own account & I'm sure she must have some important pieces in her own possession but what can you do when she's so difficult, so aloof & indifferent. She did say something vague about asking some of her friends if they would 'sell' anything & said she would get in touch with me when she came to Paris (last October) but I never heard a word from her.[10]

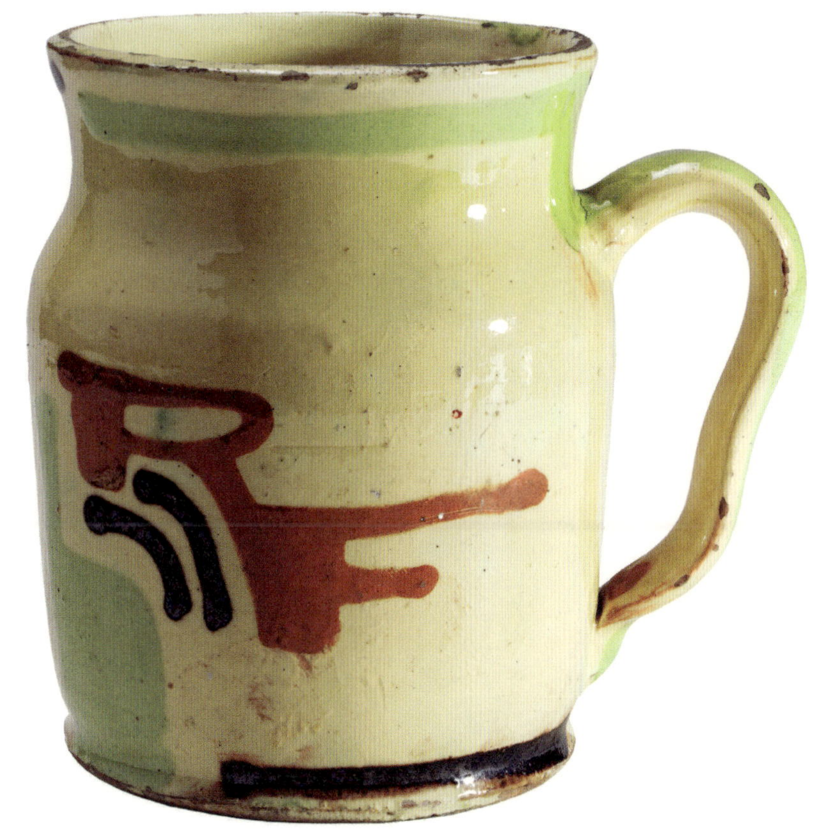

cat 53 Beer mug for Rah Fizelle 1937

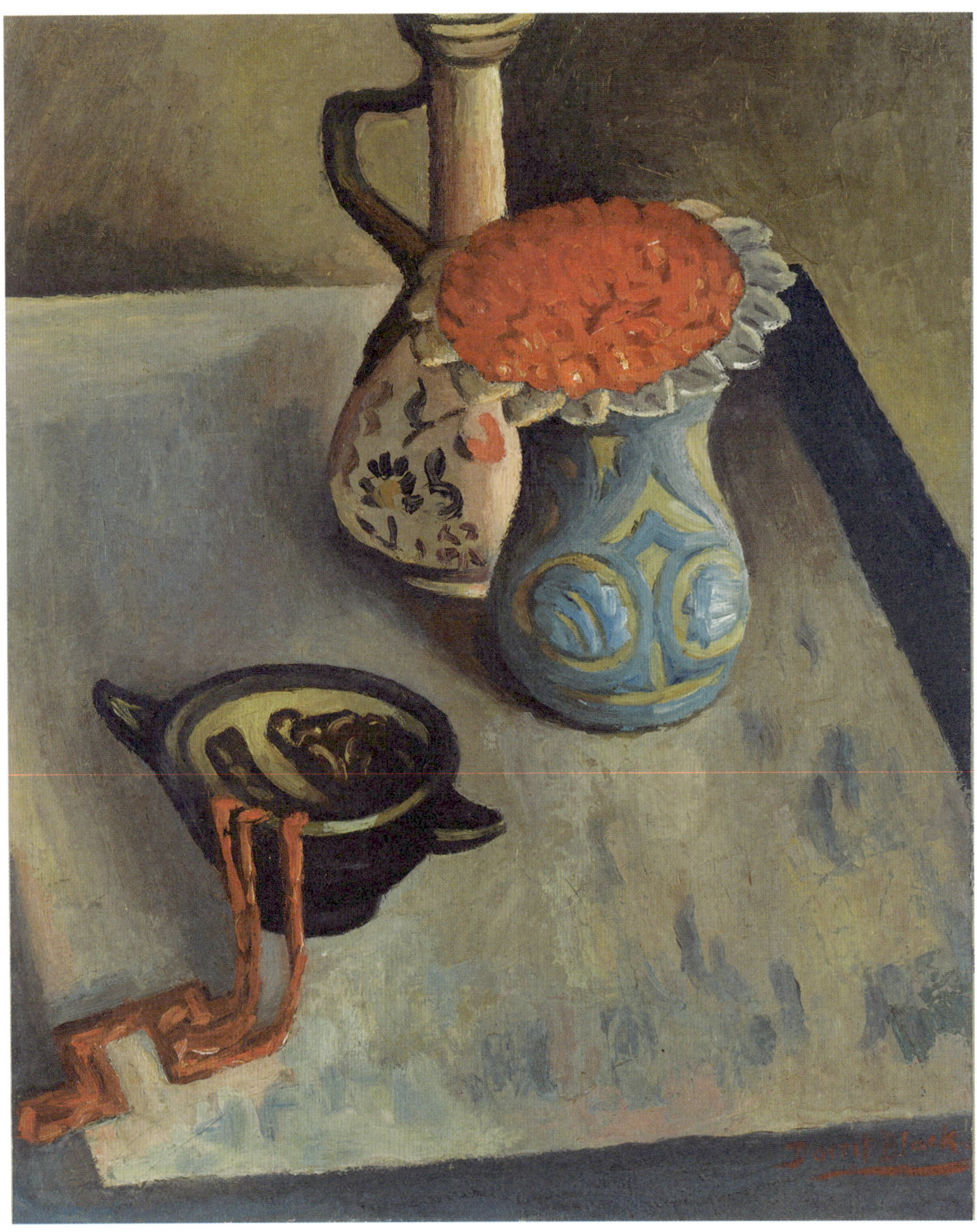

cat 132 Dorrit Black, *The posy* 1945

A month later, she reports that she hadn't 'asked Mme. Gleizes to sell anything, for I think as you do, that she should have given something & sent it out at her own expense & she should have done this long ago, & at least have answered your letters'.[11]

Then, by good fortune, in early 1954, Webb found what she thought might be a suitable piece. She had received a letter from Suzanne Seuphor, wife of the eminent art historian, writer and artist Michel Seuphor, who told her that her brother Jacques Plasse, who had been a resident at Moly-Sabata in the early 1930s, owned a plate and a *soupière* (soup tureen) by Dangar and might be willing to sell one of them. She let Crowley know, too, that both Seuphors 'evidently knew Anne D. personally and thought highly of both herself & her work',[12] confirming the view of Dangar and Michel Seuphor's relationship evident in Dangar's letters from 20 years earlier. In the meantime, Webb had made

> a swift visit again to the Museum of Modern Art [Musée national d'art moderne, Paris] to refresh my memory of the plates that are there (gift of Gleizes). I don't know what period, they're simply labelled, Anne Dangar, [céramiques d'après] des compositions de A. Gleizes, don de A. Gleizes. They are of course very lovely & I should think probably amongst her most recent.[13]

This was all news that must have pleased Crowley.

Less than a month later, however, the quest was shut down. After more than two years' searching, Webb wrote that she 'was very sorry to hear that the Gallery has refused so abruptly even to receive as a gift some pottery of Anne Dangar'.[14] Crowley had been the recipient of a three-sentence letter from the director of the Art Gallery of New South Wales:

> The trustees at their meeting of the 26th February, had before them your letter of the 17th. I regret to tell you that they could not agree to your suggestion in regard to the acquisition of a work by the late Anne Dangar. I thank you for your attention in bringing this matter to our notice.[15]

This refusal of Crowley's proposed gift reflects the power of the trustees, whose patriarchal conservatism enabled and then oversaw the exclusion of Dangar from her hometown gallery. It was a wilful blindness that typified Australia's troubled institutional engagement with modernism in the twentieth century. Both Crowley and Webb must have been devastated that their efforts had been for nothing. Prophetically, Webb writes that 'it just means patience & waiting' and expressed the 'hope that one day you will have the pleasure of seeing the work of Anne Dangar represented in her own country'.[16]

Artists and friends in France, meanwhile, were still determined to build a legacy for Dangar. In the middle of 1954, Deveyle informs Webb that Dangar would be featured in a forthcoming issue of Dom Angelico Surchamp's cultural journal *Zodiaque*.[17] This, Webb writes,

> will be another document for you to add to the documentation you already have on Anne Dangar, and maybe you could get an article published in Australia on her life & work, & perhaps it would bring the historians there (& possibly the museums, art galleries) to a realisation of her value as an artiste-potter, and as an Australian artist a record of her work could also be in the historical archives of Australia. In any case it's interesting for the public to know of the work of some of their artists whether at home or abroad.[18]

By this time Webb and Deveyle's friendship had developed and Webb, bringing our attention to a remarkable object, writes to Crowley that 'I love always the big scarf I bought from her which has in it some of the wool you sent her.'[19] Two years later she calls it 'treasure'.[20] This must have been a particularly sentimental piece of Webb's wardrobe, bringing together as it did the threads of the lives of Webb, Crowley, Dangar and Deveyle. While it is a scarf that speaks of the story of artistic interactions between Australia and France in the mid twentieth century, it was also an intimate object, part of Webb's everyday life and a permanent reminder of the relationships closest to her.

Eventually, in 1969, two plates and a mug by Dangar were acquired by the Art Gallery of New South Wales, the first of her works to enter any public collection in Australia. Later, ceramics owned by Crowley (cat 26) held pride of place in the central vitrine in her survey exhibition at the Art Gallery in 1975, probably the first occasion Dangar's work had been on public display in Australia since the mid 1930s. A year later, Crowley reflected on how shabbily her friend had been treated by the Art Gallery:

> The world of art lost Anne Dangar when she died in 1951. Immediately after her death we, a relative of Anne's (now deceased), a friend of mine in Paris (now deceased), Michel Seuphor, a friend of Anne's (still alive) and a celebrated writer on art, attempted to get examples of Anne's pottery out for the Sydney Art Gallery. We offered to buy the work and present it to the Gallery. The Art Gallery of Sydney refused to accept it! Now in 1976 the same gallery is breaking its neck to secure some of Anne's work.[21]

—

While efforts to gain recognition for Dangar's work in Australia were foundering, her reputation in France had been rising since the mid 1950s. In the spring of 1953, her work was part of the first important exhibition following her death, *Du cubisme aux arts traditionnels*, which opened in Paris at the École des beaux-arts before touring France. It was a survey of Gleizes and his followers, most with connections to Moly-Sabata, and opened just two months before Gleizes's own passing.[22] Then, in the winter of 1955, Webb reports to Crowley of a new display in the Musée national d'art moderne:

> I noticed they have now placed Anne Dangar's pottery in one of the most important rooms on the ground floor, one of the rooms devoted to masters of the modern movement, & in which figures Gleizes, Villon etc & the pottery of Anne D. is in a glass case all to itself, & in fact the only pottery in that room, so it is extremely well & prominently displayed. So that is comforting isn't it.[23]

Fortuitously, Crowley had the opportunity in 1960 to see Dangar's works on display for herself at the Musée national d'art moderne. Accompanied by Ralph Balson in that year, she was able to make her first journey back to France since she had left in 1929. Sadly, though, Webb, who had been talking about the trip in her letters, had passed away just over a year before they arrived. Nevertheless, Crowley was able to meet Michel and Suzanne Seuphor and thank them for all they had done for her, and for Webb.[24] It must have been especially bittersweet, then, that at the Musée national d'art moderne, in a vitrine placed in the centre of a room hung with paintings by Albert Gleizes and Robert Delaunay, Crowley came across four plates by Anne Dangar.[25]

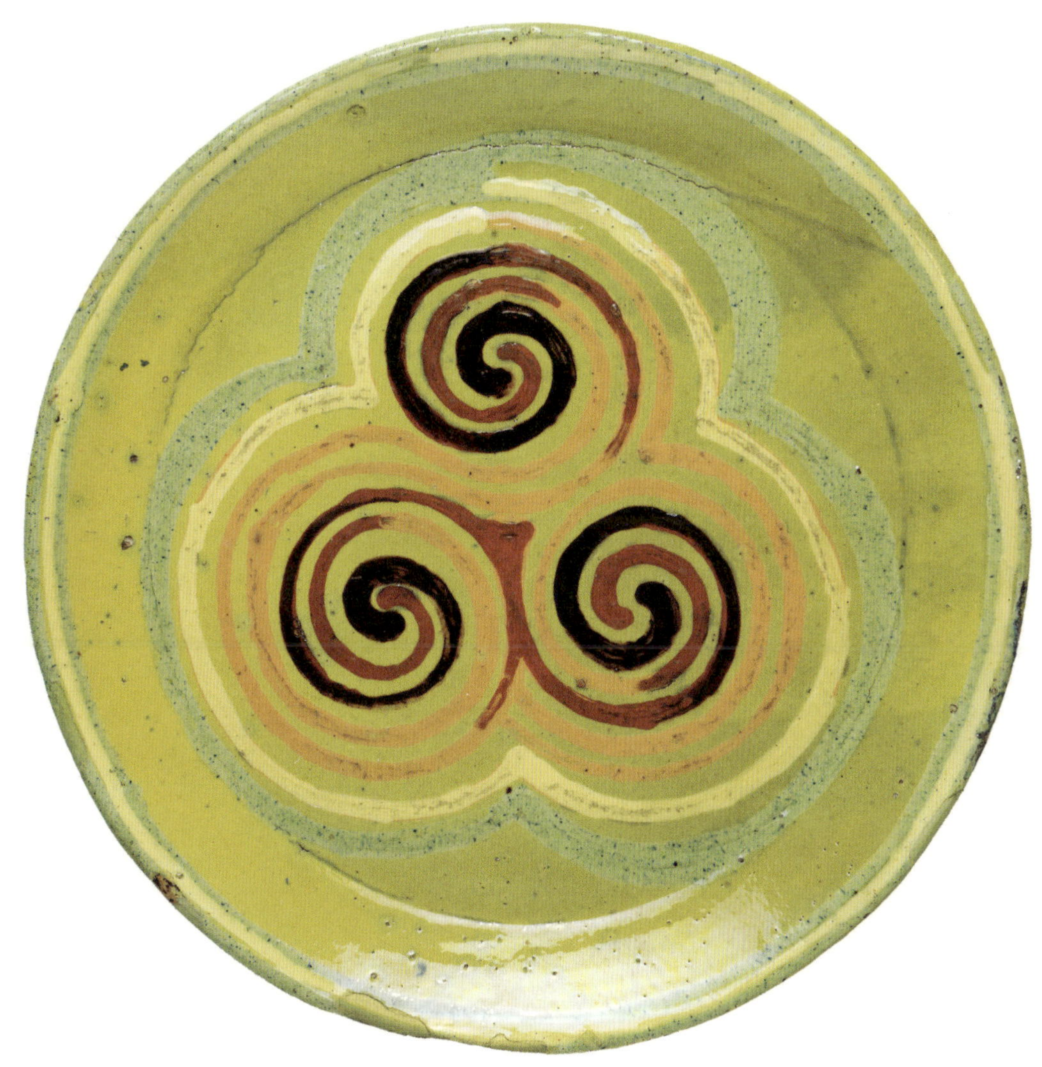

cat 26 Plate 1933–38

—

The same year as Crowley made her return to Paris, it was possible, too, to see Dangar's work in Tokyo, when it was included in the exhibition *École de Paris: art décoratif* at the National Museum of Western Art. From this time on, through the exhibitions in which her work figured, we can follow Dangar's incorporation into the history of both Cubism and French decorative arts, in France and around the world. To mention just a few: in 1964 in New York, Gleizes's small painting *Étude dédiée à Anne Dangar* 1944 (*Study dedicated to Anne Dangar*) and inscribed 'pour ma chère élève Anne Dangar Saint-Rémy-de-Provence Avril 1945 Les Méjades Albert Gleizes' was on view in the retrospective *Albert Gleizes* at the Guggenheim Museum, lent to the exhibition by Juliette Roche; Dangar's pottery was included in *L'art de la poterie en France de Rodin à Dufy*, held at the Musée national de céramique, Sèvres, in 1971; and, notably, her ceramics were part of the landmark exhibition *Paris-Paris: créations en France, 1937–1957*, held in 1981 at the then recently opened Centre Georges Pompidou in Paris. This was the same year she was identified as one of '*Les précurseurs*' in the catalogue for *Céramique française contemporaine: sources et courants* held at the Musée des arts décoratifs in Paris. Since then, she has featured in no fewer than nine surveys of ceramics in France and been the subject of at least four exhibitions devoted solely to her work.[26]

Anne Dangar, then, has been considered part of the international avant-garde, part of the art history of France and part of the art and social history of the region around Lyon and of Sablons-Serrières in particular. Indeed, it is even possible to speak of an École Dangar. Following her death in 1951, the painter and potter-to-be Jean-Claude Libert stepped onto Dangar's wheel and fired up her hard-won kiln but following the floods of 1955 he and his young family moved to Villeneuve-lès-Avignon, where they set up their own pottery workshop. In the same year, Geneviève de Cissey moved to Moly-Sabata. She had been a student of Dangar in 1949 and produced pottery beside Deveyle until the latter's death in 1956, continuing there alone until the beginning of 1958 when she moved to Ampuis, 27 kilometres up the river. There she continued her work as a potter, firing her glazed earthenware in a kiln bedecked with traditional motifs inspired by Dangar. And it was de Cissey, too, who effectively founded the Association des amis d'Albert Gleizes, when in 1954 she started asking friends to meet annually in Ampuis on the last Sunday of each June. Three decades later, following the death of Gleizes's widow Juliette Roche, the Fondation Albert Gleizes was formalised and today Moly-Sabata is both an exhibition space and a *résidence d'artiste*.

In some ways, the greatest testament to Dangar was the exhibition *Anne Dangar—Geneviève de Cissey—Aguilberte Dalban* held at Moly-Sabata in 2012. This exhibition brought together works by the avant-garde ceramicist Anne Dangar; her student and the potter who last worked her wheel, Geneviève de Cissey, who had moved to her own kiln in Ampuis; and de Cissey's daughter Aguilberte Dalban, who worked her mother's kiln until the early 2000s. It was a line of potter–artists begun by Dangar in 1930 that lasted more than 70 years. Dangar, *the* potter of Cubism, has participated equally in exhibitions of Cubism, in exhibitions of French ceramics, in shows about the history of modern art in Lyon and in displays with the children she taught. The kind of painting on clay she had pioneered in the 1930s—from her secular Cubism and spiritual and religious iconography to her sensitive and lumpy abstraction—was carried on until the beginning of the twenty-first century in France, perhaps ironically ending just as she began to enter Australia's art history.

—

In Australia, for the past 70 years at least, Anne Dangar has worn a kind of cloak of invisibility, existing only in a nether-worldly afterlife with its resurrection yet to come. Her work was first seen in an Australian museum in 1975, the first ever International Women's Year, and the necessary and corrective recovery project undertaken by female art historians in the 1970s would be crucial to the return of Crowley to the narratives of Australian art history. But, just like the male creators of Australia's art-historical canon, the one which excluded women, they too had a blind spot—our expatriates—so that while Crowley now came into view, Dangar did not.

It is only this century, then, that Dangar's rehabilitation has taken place in Australia. In France her reputation was only further enhanced by David Butcher's *Anne Dangar, céramiste: le cubisme au quotidien*, published in 2016 to accompany the exhibition of the same name curated by him at the Musée de Valence art et archéologie. Butcher, an Australian–French art historian and curator, has been a crucial conduit for the acquisition of the numerous works by Dangar that have recently entered our public collections, succeeding where in the 1950s Crowley and Webb's efforts had been cut short. Now that Dangar has been put back into Australian art history, one of the things she allows us to think is how easily this recognition might not have happened. What if Crowley had not kept her letters? What if her friends had not cherished her pottery? Let Dangar stand, then, for all those artists left out of the art history of this country, and all the stories about ourselves we have yet to tell. Let her be the first of many, or, better, one of many. Let us think what it is to be 'Australian' through the life and work of Anne Dangar.

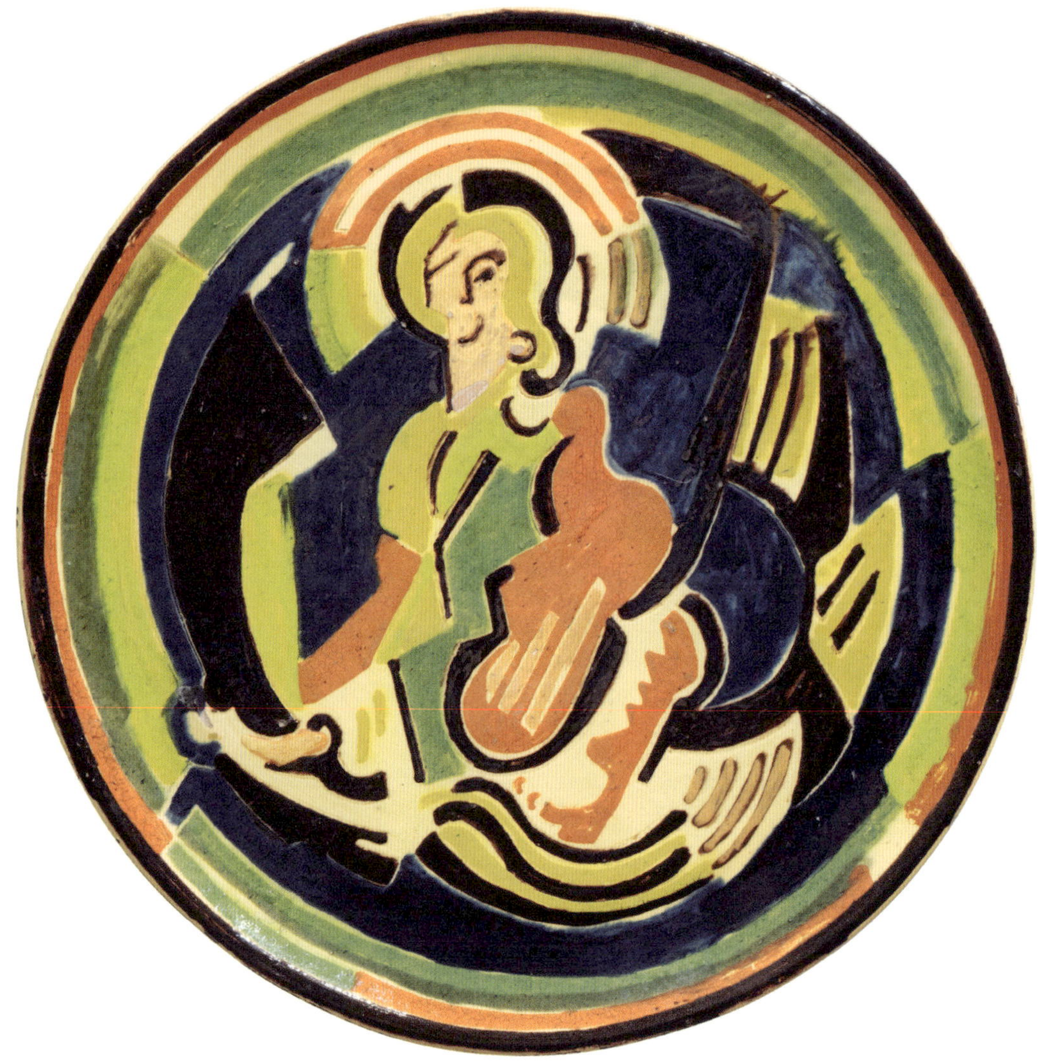

cat 121 after Albert Gleizes, *Figure en gloire* (*Figure in glory*) 1948

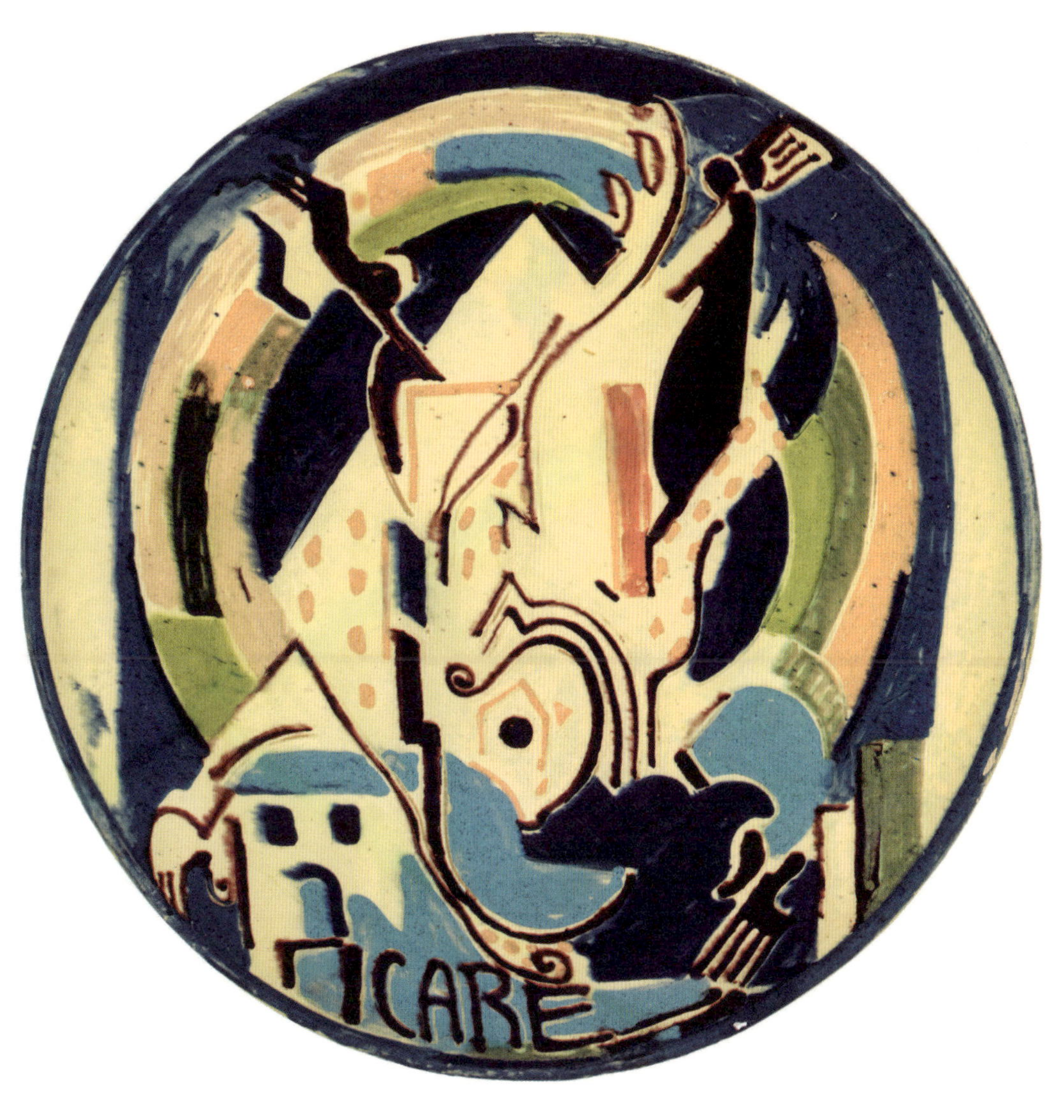

cat 116 after Albert Gleizes, *Icare* (*Icarus*) 1939

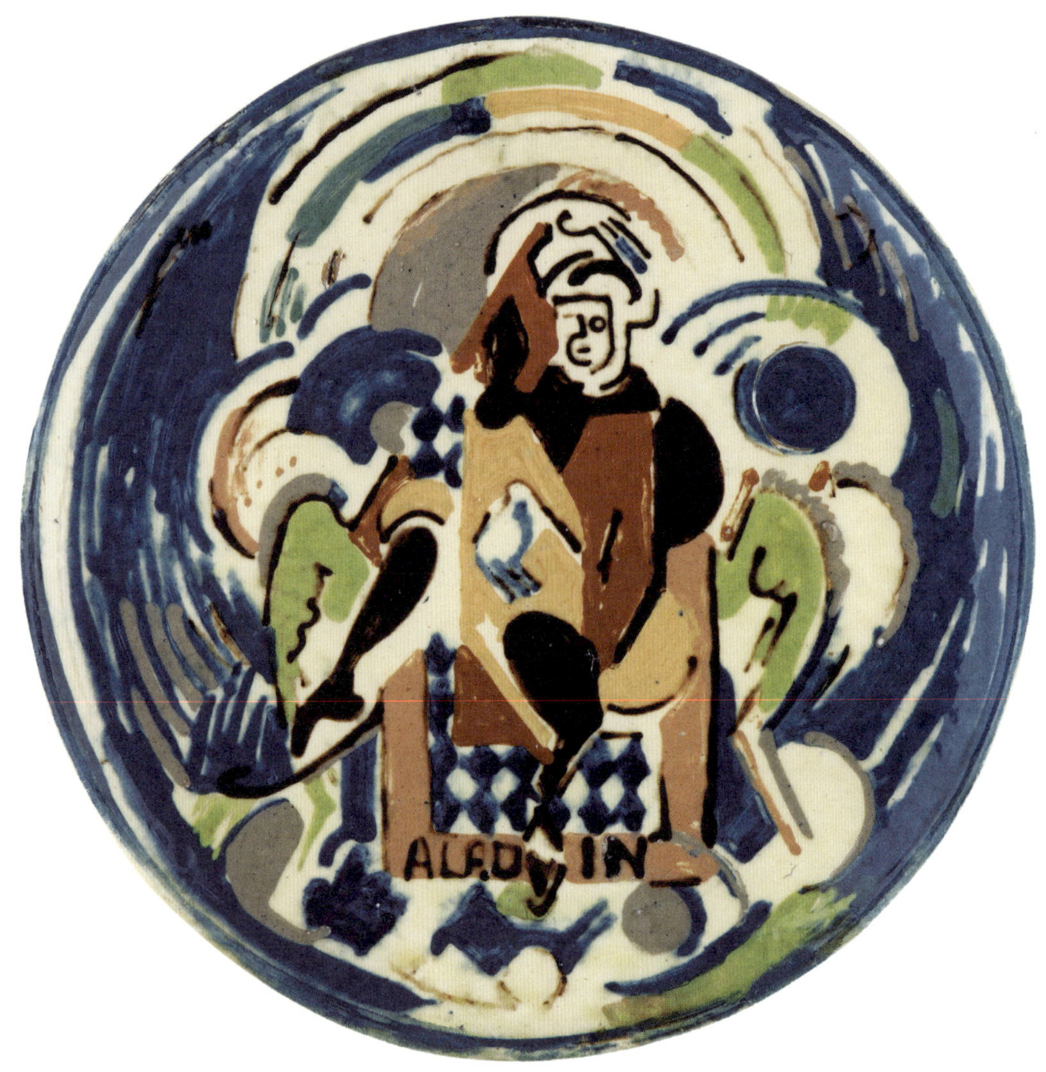

cat 115 after Albert Gleizes, *Aladin* (*Aladdin*) 1938–48

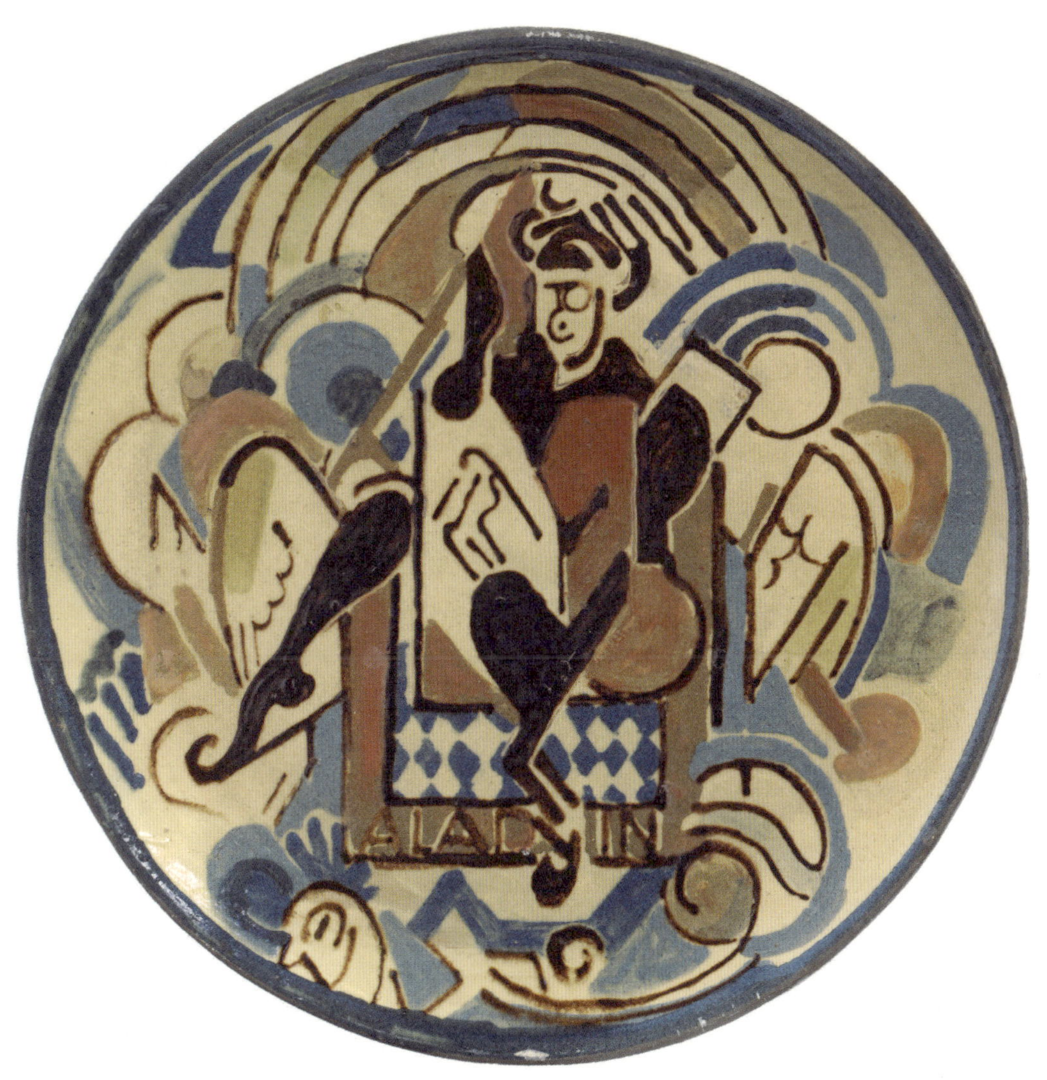

cat 120 after Albert Gleizes, *Aladín* (*Aladdin*) 1948

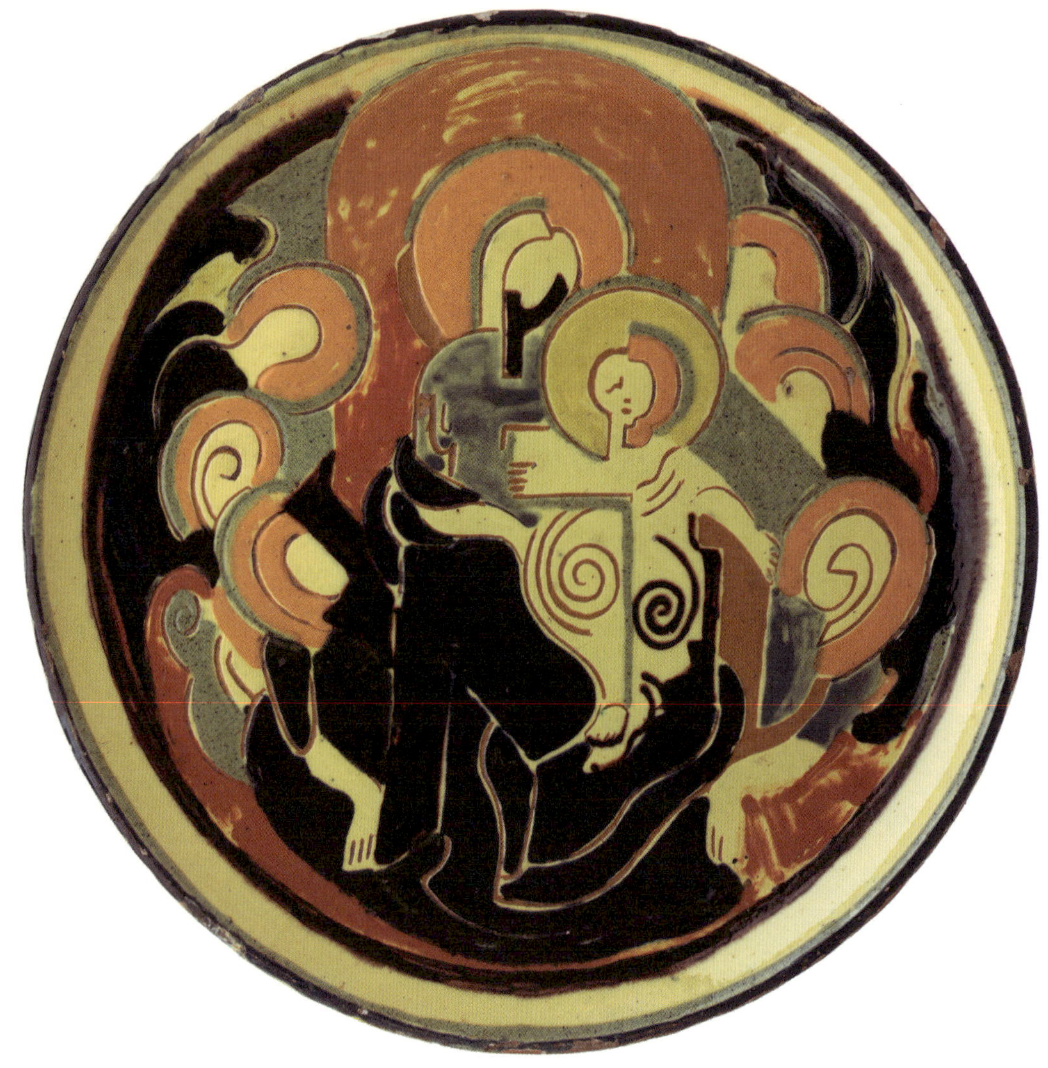

cat 122 after Albert Gleizes, *La Vierge et l'Enfant en majesté entourés de six anges* (*Virgin and Child in majesty surrounded by six angels*) after Cimabue 1948

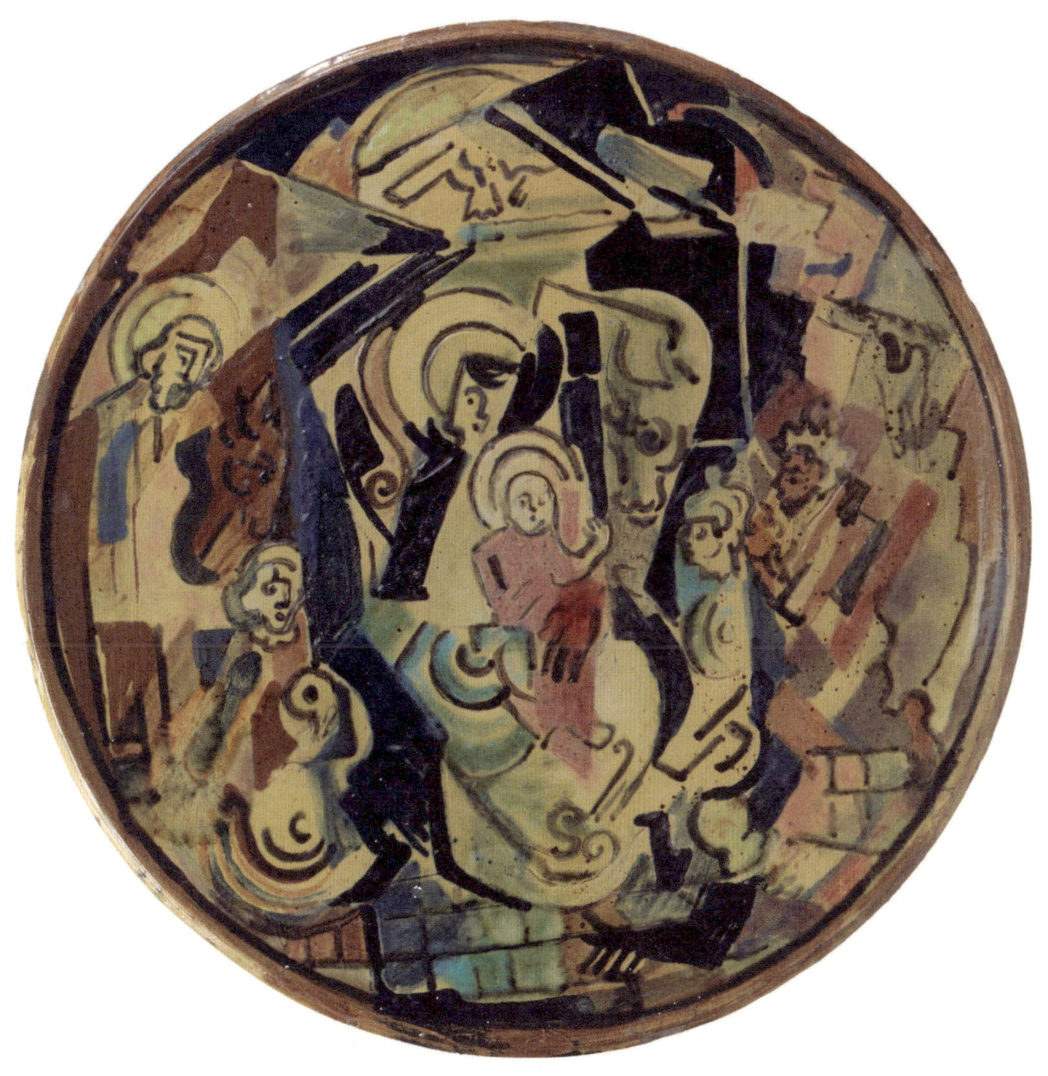

cat 117 after Albert Gleizes, *L'Adoration des Mages* (*Adoration of the Magi*) 1945–46

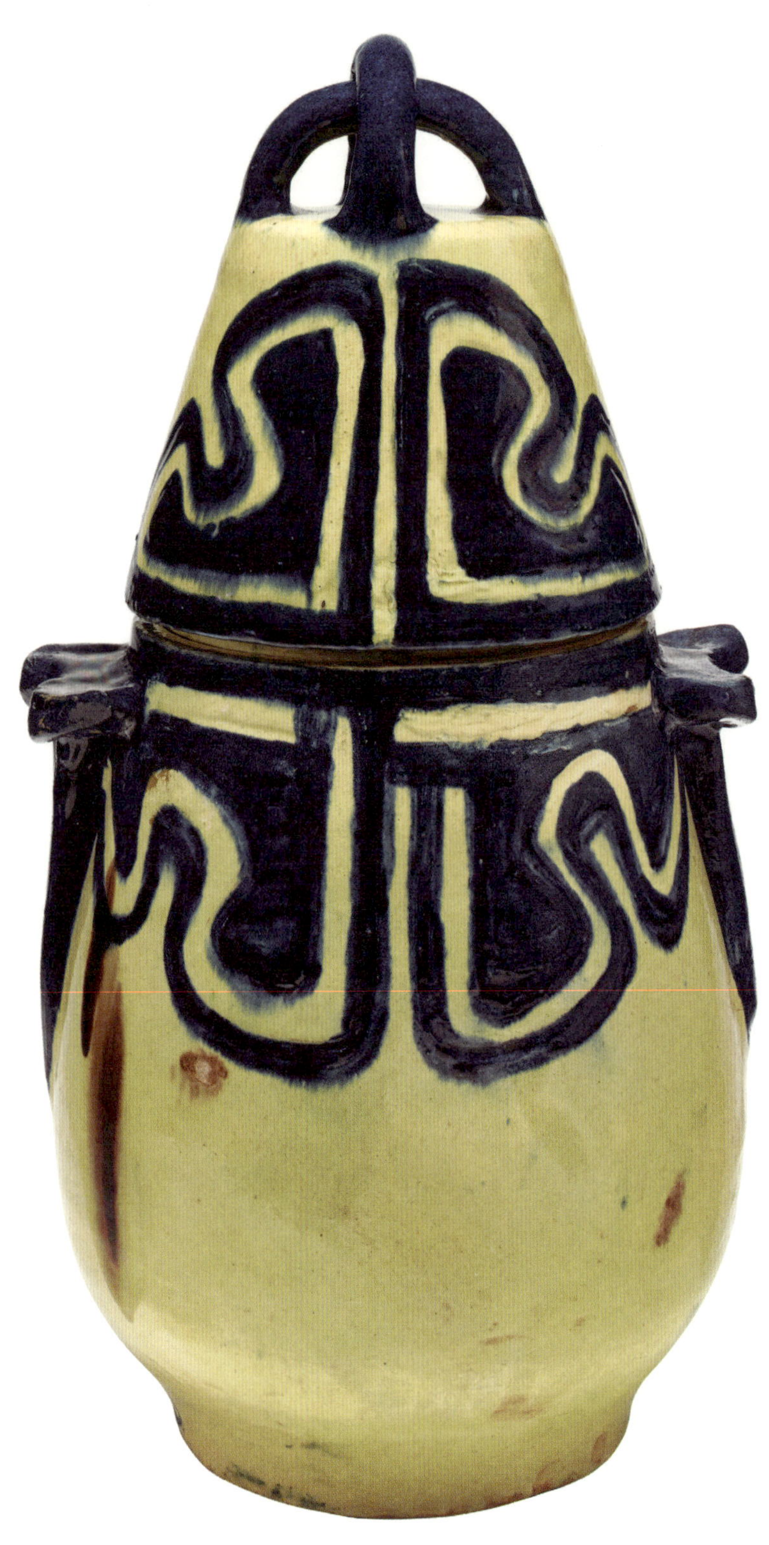

cat 64 Conical pot with lid 1947–49

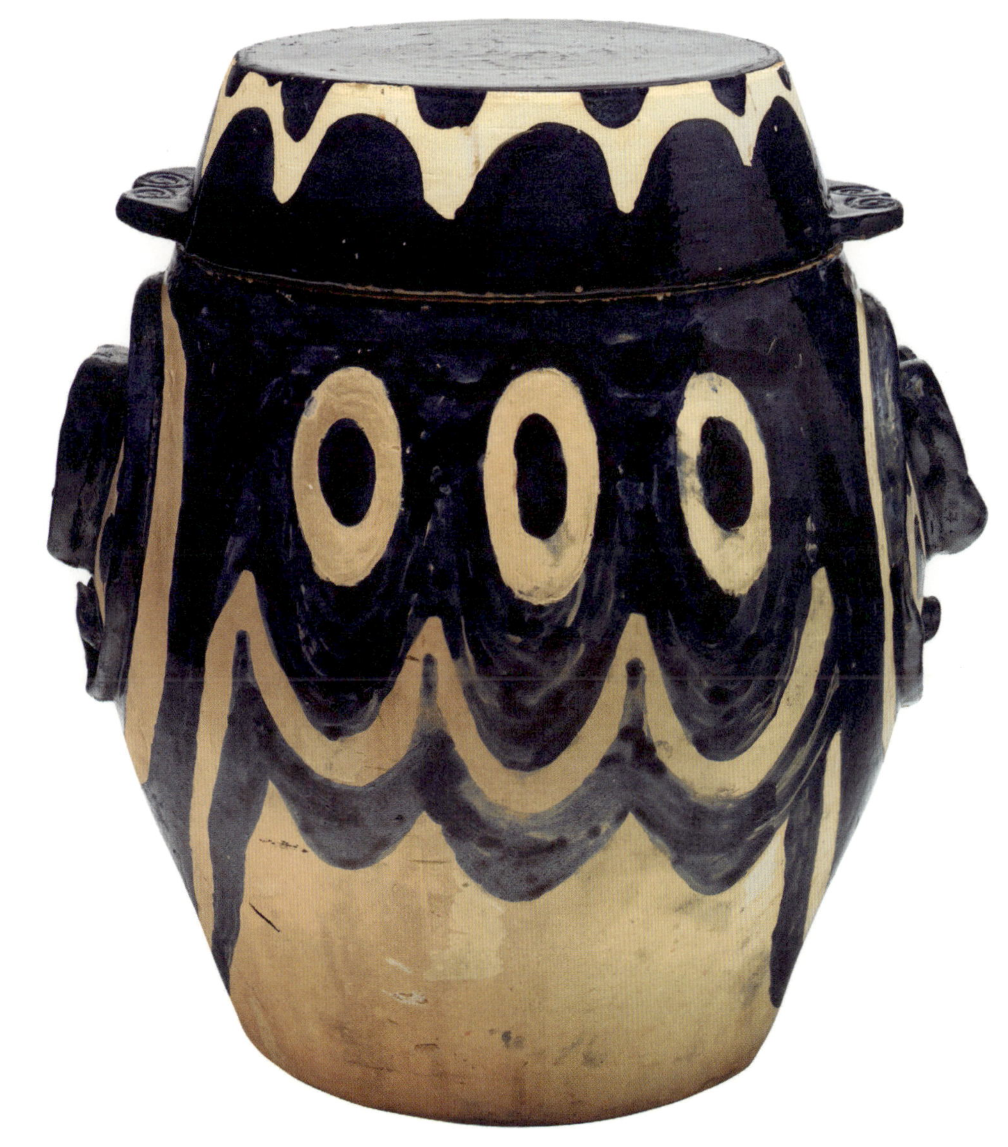

cat 65 Jar with lid 1947–49

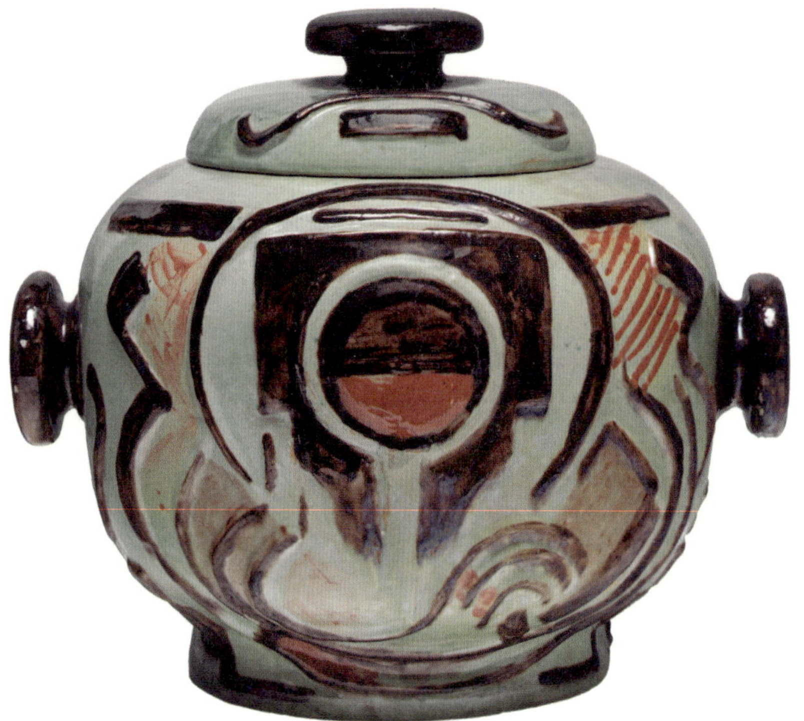

cat 119 after Albert Gleizes, Pot with lid and handles 1946–49

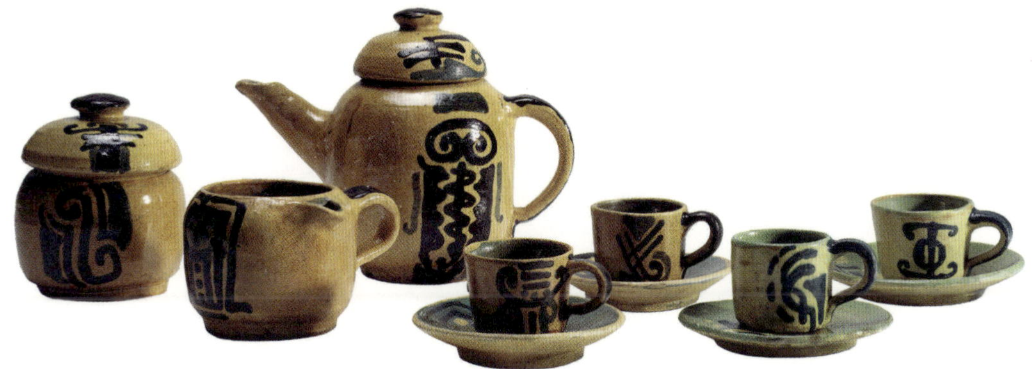

cat 126 Anne Dangar, Lucie Deveyle and Jean-Marie Paquaud, Tea service 1949–51 (detail)

Notes

First references to a source in each essay's notes are listed in full; repeated references within each essay are abbreviated. Misspellings have been corrected in some quotes. Unless otherwise noted, all translations from the French are by Rebecca Edwards.

Introduction

1 Anne Dangar, letter to Grace Crowley, 18 February 1951, Grace Crowley papers, 1927–1974, MLMSS 3252/vols 2–7, MLMSS 3252/vol 1X, State Library of New South Wales, Gadigal Nura/Sydney (hereafter Grace Crowley papers, SLNSW).

2 William Moore mentions Dangar only fleetingly in relation to her early years in Sydney, mistakenly stating she moved to France to teach with Albert 'Bleizes'. See William Moore, *The story of Australian art: from the earliest known art of the continent to the art of to-day*, Angus & Robertson, Sydney, 1934. As ADS Donaldson outlines in this publication she was absent from canonical accounts of art history, including Bernard Smith's foundational texts on Australian art, *Australian painting, 1788–1960* 1962 and *Place, taste and tradition: a study of Australian painting since 1788* 1979.

3 In the 1970s Daniel Thomas was chief curator and curator of Australian art at the Art Gallery of New South Wales, and, from 1978 to 1986, head of Australian art at the National Gallery of Australia. Bruce Adams was a postgraduate student at the University of Sydney at this time, undertaking research on artist Ralph Balson as part of his thesis, later curating the first exhibition on Balson's art. Jim Alexander was a gallerist and researcher, preparing in Melbourne to open the commercial gallery Important Women Artists, which focused on showcasing work by little-known women artists. For Alexander and Crowley's correspondence, see the Grace Crowley file in the Jim Alexander Gallery papers, MS 13705, State Library Victoria, Naarm/Narrm/Melbourne (hereafter Jim Alexander Gallery papers, SLV).

4 Bernard Smith, then Power Professor of Contemporary Art at the Power Institute of Fine Arts, University of Sydney, wrote to Crowley in the 1970s and asked to make copies of the notes on Cubism Dangar had sent her, later suggesting she donate them to the Mitchell Library, State Library of New South Wales or the National Library of Australia. See letters from Bernard Smith to Grace Crowley, 26 April 1974, 24 June 1974 and 24 August 1976, Grace Crowley archive, MS1980.1, National Art Archive, Art Gallery of New South Wales, Gadigal Nura/Sydney (hereafter Grace Crowley archive, National Art Archive, AGNSW).

5 Bruce Adams, 'The promise of the rainbow: Anne Dangar at Moly-Sabata 1930–1951', PhD thesis, University of Sydney, 1998; Bruce Adams, *Rustic Cubism: Anne Dangar and the art colony at Moly-Sabata*, University of Chicago Press, Chicago, 2004.

6 Helen Topliss (ed), *Earth, fire, water, air: Anne Dangar's letters to Grace Crowley, 1930–1951*, Allen & Unwin, St Leonards, NSW, 2000; *Anne Dangar at Moly-Sabata: tradition and innovation*, exhibition, National Gallery of Australia, Kamberri/Canberra, 13 July – 18 October 2001.

7 Butcher also curated an exhibition of Dangar's work in France (Musée de Valence art et archéologie, 16 June 2016 – 26 February 2017), which was accompanied by a major exhibition catalogue. See David Butcher, *Anne Dangar, céramiste: le cubisme au quotidien*, exh cat, Musée de Valence art et archéologie, Valence, 2016.

8 See, for example, Joan Kerr, *Heritage: the national women's art book*, Craftsman House, Roseville, NSW, 1995; Helen Topliss, *Modernism and feminism: Australian women artists 1900–1940*, Craftsman House, Roseville, NSW, 1996; and the National Gallery of Australia's more recent Know My Name initiative, realised in a program of exhibitions, events and the publication edited by Natasha Bullock, Kelli Cole, Deborah Hart and Elspeth Pitt, *Know My Name*, National Gallery of Australia, Canberra, 2020.

9 Rex Butler and ADS Donaldson, *UnAustralian art: ten essays on transnational art history*, Power Publications, Sydney, 2023, p 25. Butler and Donaldson have presented a range of papers and essays on their revisionist art-historical project 'unAustralian art' since 2007. Australian expatriates John Russell and JW Power operated within progressive circles of the European avant-garde and have been the subject of major exhibitions in the last decade, as have Australian impressionist artists living and working in France during the late nineteenth and early twentieth centuries. See also the exhibitions *John Russell: Australia's French impressionist*, Art Gallery of New South Wales, Gadigal Nura/Sydney, 21 July – 11 November 2018, curated by Wayne Tunnicliffe; *Abstraction-Création: JW Power in Europe 1921–1938*, National Library of Australia, Kamberri/Canberra, 25 July – 26 October 2014, and Heide Museum of Modern Art, Naarm/Narrm/Melbourne, 15 November 2014 – 22 March 2015, curated by Ann Stephen and ADS Donaldson; and *Australian impressionists in France*, National Gallery of Victoria, Naarm/Narrm/Melbourne, 12 June – 6 October 2013, curated by Elena Taylor.

10 My thanks to chief curator Christian Briend and archivist Anne Delebarre, Kandinsky Library, Centre Georges Pompidou, for giving me access to these letters prior to processing and cataloguing in June 2022.

Timeline 1885–1929

1 Key references for the chronologies in this publication include letters from Anne Dangar and biographical notes held across numerous archives, chiefly the following:

- Grace Crowley papers, 1927–1974, MLMSS 3252/vols 2–7, MLMSS 3252/vol 1X, State Library of New South Wales, Gadigal Nura/Sydney.
- Grace Crowley archive, MS1980.1, National Art Archive, Art Gallery of New South Wales, Gadigal Nura/Sydney.
- Papers of Anne Dangar, MS 158, National Gallery of Australia Research Library and Archives, Kamberri/Canberra.
- Fonds Albert Gleizes, MV 698–699, Kandinsky Library, Musée national d'art moderne, Centre Georges Pompidou, Paris.

These chronologies also draw on the foundational work published by Bruce Adams in his PhD thesis and publication *Rustic Cubism* 2004 and David Butcher's exhibition catalogue *Anne Dangar, céramiste: le cubisme au quotidien* 2016. I would also like to acknowledge the input of Elena Taylor to this timeline, especially in relation to the period 1926 to 1929.

I

1 I would like to thank Shaune Lakin, Elena Taylor, Alison Inglis and Leanne Santoro for their careful reading of my essays and thoughtful suggestions.

2 My thanks to the descendants of Anne Dangar for sharing their knowledge of Crowley and Dangar's relationship.

3 Dom Angelico Surchamp, in Anne Dangar, *Lettres à la Pierre-qui-Vire*, Zodiaque, Saint-Léger-Vauban, 1972, p 6.

4 Phil Lee, 'Anne Garvin Dangar and the Dangar family of Kempsey', *Macleay River Historical Society Journal*, no 234, November 2023, p 1.

5 Lee, p 3.

6 See, for example, 'Thank you for your patience & understanding with your wild Irishwoman, you always know how to tame her down.' Anne Dangar, letter to Albert Gleizes and Juliette Roche, 9 January 1942, Fonds Albert Gleizes, MV 698–699, Kandinsky Library, Musée national d'art moderne, Centre Georges Pompidou, Paris (hereafter Fonds Albert Gleizes, Kandinsky Library, Centre Georges Pompidou).

7 'Methodist flower show', *The Macleay Argus*, 27 October 1906, p 9.

8 Lee, p 4.

9 Anne Dangar, letter to Albert Gleizes, 6 September 1950, Fonds Albert Gleizes, Kandinsky Library, Centre Georges Pompidou.

10 Bruce Adams, *Rustic Cubism: Anne Dangar and the art colony at Moly-Sabata*, University of Chicago Press, Chicago, 2004, p 10.

11 Anne Dangar, letter to Grace Crowley, 28 January 1931, Grace Crowley papers, 1927–1974, MLMSS 3252/vols 2–7, MLMSS 3252/vol 1X, State Library of New South Wales, Gadigal Nura/Sydney.

12 'Notice' and 'Local and general', *The Macleay Chronicle*, 17 May 1911, p 5.

13 'Local and general', p 5.

14 'Local picture show: exhibition of paintings', *The Macleay Argus*, 28 June 1912, p 15; 'A local art gallery', *The Macleay Argus*, 17 December 1915, p 10.

15 One review made particular note of Dangar's work created after Gibson, stating, 'The black and white work by Miss Dangar (especially the copies from C. Dana Gibson) are very clever, and even if Miss Dangar had only her own work to exhibit she need not feel ashamed of submitting it to public criticism.' See 'Local picture show: exhibition of paintings', p 15.

16 See Charles Dana Gibson, *Pictures of people*, John Lane, London, & RH Russell & Son, New York, 1896.

17 'A local art gallery', p 10.

18 'Local picture show: exhibition of paintings', p 15. She may have commenced with Ashton earlier, as *The Macleay Chronicle* reported in 1911 that she had returned to her Kempsey studio following five months studying 'under some of Sydney's best masters' and was now prepared to take pupils. 'Local and general', p 5.

19 Elena Taylor, *Grace Crowley: being modern*, exh cat, National Gallery of Australia, Canberra, 2006, p 9.

20 See Grace Crowley, notes on Anne Dangar, c 1975, Grace Crowley archive, MS1980.1, National Art Archive, Art Gallery of New South Wales, Gadigal Nura/Sydney; See also Taylor, pp 9–10.

21 LR, 'Farewell in a garden', *Undergrowth*, January–February 1926, unpag.

22 Adams, p 11.

23 Anne Dangar, letter to Albert Gleizes, nd [before 1943], Fonds Albert Gleizes, Kandinsky Library, Centre Georges Pompidou.

24 LR, 'Farewell in a garden', unpag.

25 'Fire at Mondrook. Mr Singleton's home destroyed', *The Northern Champion*, 17 September 1930. See also Joyce Moncreiff (née Singleton), letter to Jim Alexander, 22 March 1977, Jim Alexander Gallery papers, MS 13705, State Library Victoria, Naarm/Narrm/Melbourne. The Singletons' home was again destroyed by fire in 1936. See 'Fire at Mondrook. Cottage and contents destroyed', *The Northern Champion*, 1 August 1936, p 4. Aside from some clothing, a sewing machine and some crockery, the house and its contents, including the work Dangar had stored there and her correspondence predating this time, were destroyed. It is possible Dangar's painted ceramics from the late 1920s were among the crockery pieces that survived.

26 *Paintings in oil and water colours and drawings in black and white by eleven Australian women*, exh cat, Anthony Horderns' Fine Art Gallery, Gadigal Nura/Sydney, 1921.

27 It is likely Dangar and Black were involved in the establishment of the group, though reviewers focused on the male members. 'The prompters were Norman Lloyd, Herbert Gallop, HC Gibbons and Adrian Feint with whom were associated Anne Dangar and Dorrit Black.' See William Moore, 'The art world: the Younger Group', *The Daily Telegraph* (Sydney), 12 July 1924, p 13.

28 'The younger artists: first exhibition', *The Daily Telegraph* (Sydney), 5 July 1924, p 15; Mary Eagle, *Australian modern painting between the wars 1914–1939*, Bay Books, Sydney, 1990, p 57.

29 Eagle, pp 55–57.

30 Roland Wakelin, quoted in William Moore, 'The art world', *The Daily Telegraph* (Sydney), 31 October 1924, p 9.

31 Grace Crowley, biographical notes, c 1975, Grace Crowley archive, National Art Archive, AGNSW. See also Taylor, p 9.

32 Anne Dangar, letter to Dom Angelico Surchamp, 10 October 1949, in Dangar, 1972, p 88.

33 Eagle, p 57; Bruce Adams, 'The promise of the rainbow: Anne Dangar at Moly-Sabata 1930–1951', PhD thesis, University of Sydney, 1998, p. 17.

34 Grace Crowley, interviewed by James Gleeson, 25 August 1978, James Gleeson Oral History Collection, MS 23, National Gallery of Australia Research Library and Archives, Kamberri/Canberra (hereafter National Gallery Research Library and Archives).

35 Dangar, letter to Dom Angelico Surchamp, 10 October 1949, in Dangar, 1972, p 88.

36 LR, 'Farewell in a garden', unpag.

37 Anne Dangar, 'The house with blue shutters', *Undergrowth*, July–August 1926, unpag.

38 Anne Dangar, letter to Mrs Henry Crowley, 28 February 1927, Grace Crowley papers, SLNSW.

39 It has previously been thought that Dangar and Crowley visited Mirmande only once in 1928; however, a letter to Marguerite Lhote, André Lhote's wife, from Crowley prior to their arrival in 1928 indicates they had also joined Lhote's summer school the previous year and were forced to stay just outside of the town as there were no rooms available. Grace Crowley, letter to Marguerite Lhote, 17 July 1928, Archives André Lhote, private collection, Paris. My thanks to Dominique Bermann Martin for providing access to these letters.

40 Crowley, interviewed by Gleeson, 25 August 1978.

41 Grace Crowley, 'Grace Crowley's student years', in Janine Burke, *Australian women artists, 1840–1940*, Greenhouse Publications, Collingwood, Vic, p 84; Crowley, biographical notes, c 1975.

42 Anne Dangar, letter to Grace Crowley, 29 November 1934, Grace Crowley papers, SLNSW.

43 Anne Dangar, letter to Juliette Roche, 26 December 1929, Fonds Albert Gleizes, Kandinsky Library, Centre Georges Pompidou.

44 Grace Crowley, 'Letters from abroad: learning in Paris', *Undergrowth*, May–June 1927, unpag.

45 'I do not like his productions but I respect his teaching. He knows the fabrication of an exquisite quality of pottery—I see nothing better in Paris or England in the actual clay but I hate his 1500 jugs in orange and black etc.' See Anne Dangar, postcard to Dorrit Black, 21 November 1927, Papers of Dorrit Black, MS 74, National Gallery Research Library and Archives.

46 Dangar, postcard to Black, 21 November 1927.

47 Grace Crowley, 'Letters from abroad', unpag.

48 My thanks to Phil Lee of the Macleay River Historical Society and Val Miles and Ruth Woodward for bringing this early work to my attention.

49 Dangar, letter to Mrs Crowley, 28 February 1927.

50 Dangar's involvement in Primavera was reported to Bruce Adams by Mido Geoffray, in an interview in 1991. See Adams, 2004, p 235, n 41.

51 Alain René-Hardy, *Primavera, 1912–1972: atelier d'art du Printemps*, Faton Editions, Quétigny, 2014, pp 333–36.

52 Dangar, letter to Roche, 26 December 1929.

53 Advertisement in *Undergrowth*, July–August 1928, unpag.

54 Advertisement in *Undergrowth*, July–August 1928, unpag.

55 Sergius [Nancy Hall], 'Summer school at Wamberal', in *Undergrowth*, January–February 1929, unpag. Among these students were Dore Hawthorne, Nancy Hall, Florence Taylor, Estelle Creed, Lucy Andreas and Gwen Ridley.

56 Sergius, 'Summer school', unpag.

57 Sergius, 'Summer school', unpag.

58 Anne Dangar, 'To-day', *Undergrowth*, January–February 1929, unpag.

59 Dangar, 'To-day', unpag. See 'Notes by Dangar from a lecture by Ozenfant', nd, Grace Crowley archive, National Art Archive, AGNSW. Crowley is known to have attended Ozenfant's lectures in 1928; Dangar's lecture notes indicate she joined her. See Crowley, interviewed by Gleeson, 25 August 1978.

60 Crowley, interviewed by Gleeson, 25 August 1978.

61 Anne Dangar, postcard to Dorrit Black, c 1930, Papers of Dorrit Black, National Gallery Research Library and Archives.

62 Advertisement in *Undergrowth*, July–August 1929, unpag.

63 Upon her return the following year, Crowley took a group of students on a trip to Port Macquarie where she gave them instruction on the golden mean, dynamic symmetry, translation and rotation, as per the teachings of Lhote and Gleizes. A year later, in March 1931, Dorrit Black began offering classes based on what she had learnt in France at her newly established Modern Art Centre in Sydney, joined by Crowley as a teacher in 1932. By the end of the same year, Black and Crowley had split acrimoniously, the latter joining forces with Rah Fizelle to launch the Crowley–Fizelle School at 215a George Street. See Tracey Lock-Weir, *Dorrit Black: unseen forces*, exh cat, Art Gallery of South Australia, Adelaide, 2014, p 66; Taylor, p 33.

64 Anne Dangar, 'By way of reply', *Undergrowth*, September–October 1928, np; See Dangar, 'To-day', unpag.

65 Anne Dangar, letter to Dom Angelico Surchamp, 15 August 1950, in Dangar, 1972, p 113.

66 Crowley also gave her students lessons in Cubism on this trip; however, it is likely Dangar had a greater influence on Hawthorne here given the sophistication of her composition—this was Crowley's first class following her return from Europe. See Lucy Andreas, Port Macquarie sketchbook, 1930, private collection.

67 Anne Dangar, letter to Grace Crowley, 15 August 1932, Grace Crowley papers, SLNSW.

68 Dangar, letter to Mrs Crowley, 28 February 1927.

69 Dangar, letter to Mrs Crowley, 28 February 1927.

70 Margaret Preston, 'Pottery as a profession', *Art in Australia*, third series, no 32, June–July 1930, unpag.

71 'Society of Arts and Crafts', *The Sydney Morning Herald*, 11 September 1929, p 8.

72 Mrs K Livingston (Karna Birmingham), letter to Grace Crowley, 30 May, nd [late 1970s], Jim Alexander papers, SLV. Dangar may have had access to pottery supplies and equipment through artist Violet Eyre (née Hodgson), a Sydney-based ceramicist who advertised classes in china painting and pottery in *Undergrowth* in early 1926 and had a kiln in her back garden in Coogee. See advertisement in *Undergrowth*, January–February 1926, unpag; and Keith Free and Megan Martin, 'Vy Eyre' in Kevin Fahy et al (eds), *Australian art pottery 1900–1950*, Casuarina Press, Sydney, 2004, p 149.

73 Anne Dangar, letter to Grace Crowley, 23 June 1932, Grace Crowley papers, SLNSW.

74 'I left him, but stayed the most sincere friends.' See Anne Dangar, letter to Jean Chevalier, 29 August 1938, Musée des beaux-arts de Lyon library archive.

75 Crowley, interviewed by Gleeson, 25 August 1978; Crowley, biographical notes, c 1975. Anne Dangar, '1ière le[ç]on, August 1949', Papers of Anne Dangar, MS 158, National Gallery Research Library and Archives. This text is in French, and Dangar used the term '[é]tonnant'.

76 Adams, 2004, p 25.

77 Crowley, interviewed by Gleeson, 25 August 1978.

78 Crowley, interviewed by Gleeson, 25 August 1978; Grace Crowley, biographical notes, c 1975.

79 Anne Dangar, telegram to Grace Crowley, 13 October 1929, private archive, quoted in Adams, 2004, p 26.

80 Dangar, letter to Roche, 26 December 1929.

81 Anne Dangar, letter to Albert Gleizes, 22 February 1951, Fonds Albert Gleizes, Kandinsky Library, Centre Georges Pompidou.

82 'Miss A. Dangar', *The Macleay Chronicle*, 1 January 1930, p 4.

83 Crowley's biographical notes written in the 1970s record that she returned to Sydney on 6 February 1930, 'just in time' to see Dangar before her departure on 11 February, dates which have been repeated in multiple secondary sources. Dangar also notes 11 February as her departure date in a letter from 1936. Crowley, biographical notes, c 1975; Anne Dangar, letter to Grace Crowley, 9 August 1936, Grace Crowley papers, SLNSW. Shipping reports show that both artists misremembered events and Crowley returned to Sydney in late January with Dangar departing 5 February. This is also corroborated by the stamp in the passport of Estelle Creed, who travelled with Dangar to France. 'Isabel Ramsay says', *Sunday Times* (Sydney), 12 January 1930, p 21; 'By Commissaire Ramel', *Daily Pictorial* (Sydney), 5 February 1930, p 13.

84 Grace Crowley, letter to Albert Gleizes, 22 October 1929, Fonds Albert Gleizes, Kandinsky Library, Centre Georges Pompidou.

Together and apart: Anne Dangar and Grace Crowley in modern Paris

1 'Les années dans votre atelier étaient le[s] plus heureuses de ma vie', Anne Dangar, letter to André Lhote, 2 October 1934, Archives André Lhote, private collection, Paris.

2 Grace Crowley, manuscript notes on Anne Dangar, nd [c 1975], Grace Crowley archive, MS1980.1, National Art Archive, Art Gallery of New South Wales, Gadigal Nura/Sydney.

3 Crowley only decided not to study at the Slade in early 1927. See Grace Crowley, 'Letters from abroad', *Undergrowth*, October–November 1927, unpag.

4 LR, 'Farewell in a garden', *Undergrowth*, January–February 1926, unpag.

5 Dangar refers to their home as Le Château Rufisque. This is most likely the Château des Creissauds in the Clos Rufisque, Aubagne, Bouches-du-Rhône.

6 Grace Crowley, 'A letter: Paris June 19th 1926', *Undergrowth*, September–October 1926, unpag.

7 Crowley, 'A letter', 1926, unpag.

8 Anne-Marie Gerard, 'The greatest voyage: Australian painters in the Paris salons 1885–1939', vol 2, PhD thesis, University of Sydney, 2014, p 198. Appendix 2 of Gerard's thesis lists all Australian exhibitors at the main Paris salons from 1885 to 1939.

9 Crowley, 'A letter', 1926, unpag.

10 'Decadent art', *The Sun* (Sydney), 28 October 1926, p 20.

11 Anne Dangar, letter to Mrs Henry Crowley, 28 February 1927, Grace Crowley papers, 1927–1974, MLMSS 3252/vols 2–7, MLMSS 3252/vol 1X, State Library of New South Wales, Gadigal Nura/Sydney.

12 No works by either artist survive from this period. Anne Dangar, 'Fantomes', *Undergrowth*, January–February 1927, unpag.

13 For example, 'Hard to get anything under 35 liras a day. Italy terribly expensive.' Anne Dangar, postcard to Dorrit Black, 15 October 1928, Papers of Dorrit Black, MS 74, National Gallery of Australia Research Library and Archives, Kamberri/Canberra.

14 Dangar, letter to Mrs Crowley, 28 February 1927.

15 The other school was the Académie moderne, where Amédée Ozenfant and Fernand Léger were teaching at the time. In 1928 Crowley attended several of Ozenfant's lectures but was not impressed with him. See Grace Crowley, interviewed by James Gleeson, 25 August 1978, transcript, p 7, James Gleeson Oral History Collection, MS 23, National Gallery Research Library and Archives.

16 Grace Crowley, biographical notes, c 1975, Grace Crowley archive, National Art Archive, AGNSW.

17 Bruce Adams, *Rustic Cubism: Anne Dangar and the art colony at Moly-Sabata*, University of Chicago Press, Chicago, 2004, p 17.

18 Crowley, 'Letters from abroad', unpag.

19 Anne Dangar, 'Letters from abroad, learning in Paris' *Undergrowth*, May–June 1927, unpag.

20 Emlen Etting and Marina Pacini, 'Studio in Paris', *Archives of American Art Journal*, vol 28, no 3, 1988, p 27.

21 Karin Sidén and Anna Meister, 'André Lhote's impact on Swedish Cubism and modernism: an important teacher-student relationship lasting five decades', in Zeynep Kuban and Simone Wille (eds), *André Lhote and his international students*, Innsbruck University Press, Innsbruck, 2020, p 104.

22 In 2017, the conference 'André Lhote and his students', at the Istanbul Technical University, Faculty of Architecture, Taksim, Turkey, examined Lhote's influence upon the development of modern art around the world.

23 Crowley, biographical notes, c 1975.

24 Arthur d'Auvergne Boxall, 'Modern art near perfection', *The Observer* (Adelaide), 11 January 1930, p 44. By 1930, other Australians who had studied with Lhote included Dorrit Black, Isabel Huntley, Douglas Dundas (very briefly), Eveline Syme, Ethel Spowers, Mildred Lovett and Florence Dash (née Taylor).

25 Grace Crowley, 'Grace Crowley's student years', in Janine Burke, *Australian women artists, 1840–1940*, Greenhouse Publications, Collingwood, Vic, 1980, p 84.

26 These included Agnes Goodsir, Bessie Gibson, Kathleen O'Connor and Bessie Davidson, and English artist Ethel Carrick, who had been married to the Australian artist E Phillips Fox.

27 Etting and Pacini, p 29.

28 Crowley, 'Letters from abroad', unpag.

29 Yve-Alain Bois et al, *Piet Mondrian 1872–1944*, exh cat, Leonardo Arte & Museum of Modern Art, New York, 1994, p 390. The American University Women's Club at 4 rue de Chevreuse, Montparnasse, would have been known to Dangar and Crowley through American fellow students at Lhote's academy. They would possibly already have known of Mondrian through his article 'Neo-plasticism', in their September 1926 copy of *Cahiers d'Art*.

30 Anne Dangar, 'By way of reply', *Undergrowth*, September–October 1928, unpag.

31 '[T]hen we return … to join Lhote's Outdoor Sketch Class at Drome (North of Avignon) in the South of France', Grace Crowley, 'Letters from abroad', 1927, unpag. 'Miss Dangar and Miss Crowley went back yesterday, and will probably be gone to the South of France for M Lhote's sketching class by the time we arrive', Douglas Dundas, 'Letters from abroad', *Undergrowth*, October–November 1927, unpag. It was previously thought that in London Dangar and Crowley had changed their minds and visited Scotland and Ireland instead.

32 *Le tour* was exhibited in the *Government House garden fete art exhibition*, Sydney, 6–7 October 1932, no 26.

33 Grace Crowley, letter to Marguerite Lhote, 17 July 1928, Archives André Lhote, private collection, Paris. That this trip was never mentioned by Crowley in any of her later accounts (all written in her 80s) may be simply an act of forgetting, or of conflating the two trips.

34 Anne Dangar or Grace Crowley, 'Jottings from a sketch book abroad. (To the landscape class)', *Undergrowth*, November–December 1927, unpag.

35 Anne Dangar, postcard to Dorrit Black, 21 November 1927 Papers of Dorrit Black, National Gallery Research Library and Archives.

36 Dangar, postcard to Black, 21 November 1927.

37 While she later wrote of seeing 'three large astounding pictures', the salon catalogue lists only one work, no 1253 *Évangiles (peinture murale)*, most certainly *La Crucifixion*, which includes four symbols of the evangelists. See Anne Dangar, '1ière le[ç]on', August 1949, Papers of Anne Dangar, MS 158, National Gallery Research Library and Archives. It is possible that Dangar made an error in this account, as she was to see the other two paintings later. On Dangar's arrival at Moly-Sabata in 1930, she wrote to Crowley, 'How wonderfully you described those two beautiful pictures for the new religion Gleizes believes in!' but did not mention that she had herself seen these paintings in the Salon des Tuileries. Anne Dangar, letter to Grace Crowley, 29 March 1930, quoted in Helen Topliss (ed), *Earth, fire, water, air: Anne Dangar's letters to Grace Crowley, 1930–1951*, Allen & Unwin Australia, 2000, p 35.

38 Peter Brooke, *Albert Gleizes: for and against the twentieth century*, Yale University Press, New Haven, CT, pp 86–88.

39 Brooke, p 159. The murals were never realised.

40 See Dangar, '1ière le[ç]on', August 1949.

41 According to Juliette Roche, the wife of Albert Gleizes, Dangar had tried to contact Gleizes. See Brooke, p 134.

42 Dorrit Black, 10 August 1928, quoted in Tracey Lock-Weir, *Dorrit Black: unseen forces*, exh cat, Art Gallery of South Australia, Adelaide, 2014, p 45.

43 See Anne Dangar, 11.1 ring-bound notebook, 60 pp, c 1928, unpag, National Art Archive, AGNSW.

44 Crowley and Black completed views from a similar vantage point, which provide an interesting comparison of how each artist has applied Lhote's teaching. For an illustrated discussion of these works, see Lock-Weir, pp 46–49.

45 Dangar or Crowley, 'Jottings', unpag.

46 It was most likely that Dangar and Crowley thought they would be reunited in Sydney, although Crowley later stated that she only reluctantly returned to Sydney in 1929 as she was recalled by her parents.

47 Crowley, biographical notes, c 1975.

48 Grace Crowley, letter to Ian North, 10 September 1974, Papers of Dorrit Black, Art Gallery of South Australia Research Library, Tarntanya/Adelaide.

49 Dangar, '1ière le[ç]on', August 1949.

50 Dangar to Crowley, 23 June 1931, quoted in Topliss, p 62.

51 Grace Crowley, quoted in Adams, p 26.

52 It was only in the late 1930s that Crowley began to experiment with aspects of Gleizes's method of 'translation–rotation' in her own work as a path to abstract art, although she never had any interest in its spiritual dimension.

53 Dangar to Crowley, 23 June 1931, quoted in Topliss, p 62.

54 'Les trois années le[s] plus heureu[ses] de [ma] vie!', Grace Crowley, letter to André Lhote, 17 April 1938, Archives André Lhote.

Timeline 1930–1936

1 See note 1 under Timeline 1885–1929, p 215.

II

1 Bruce Adams, *Rustic Cubism: Anne Dangar and the art colony at Moly-Sabata*, University of Chicago Press, Chicago, 2004, p 47.

2 Dom Angelico Surchamp, in Anne Dangar, *Lettres à la Pierre-qui-Vire*, Zodiaque, Saint-Léger-Vauban, 1972, p 7.

3 Albert Gleizes and Jean Metzinger, *Du 'cubisme'*, Eugène Figuière Éditeurs, Paris, 1912. For discussion of this text, see Mark Antliff and Patricia Leighton, *Cubism and culture*, Thames & Hudson, London, 2001, pp 18–19; David Cottington, *Cubism in the shadow of war: the avant-garde and politics in Paris 1905–1914*, Yale University Press, New Haven, CT, 1998, pp 145–47; and 'Commentary on Albert Gleizes and Jean Metzinger', in Mark Antliff and Patricia Leighten (eds), *Du 'cubisme': a cubism reader, documents and criticism, 1906–1914*, University of Chicago Press, Chicago, 2008, pp 435–37.

4 Albert Gleizes, *La peinture et ses lois: ce qui devait sortir du cubisme*, Imprimerie Croutzet & Depost, Paris, 1923; Albert Gleizes, *Tradition et cubisme: vers une conscience plastique, articles et conférences, 1912–1924*, Chez Jacques Povolozky, Paris, 1927.

5 Peter Brooke, *Albert Gleizes: for and against the twentieth century*, Yale University Press, New Haven, CT, 2001, p 63.

6 Gleizes, 1923, p 14. Translation in Brooke, p 98.

7 Brooke, p 88.

8 Anne Dangar, '1st talk. Introduction to some of the reasonings which lie behind the methods we will study together', 17 December 1934, Grace Crowley papers, 1927–1974, MLMSS 3252/vols 2–7, MLMSS 3252/vol 1X, State Library of New South Wales, Gadigal Nura/Sydney.

9 Brooke, p 150.

10 See Adams, p 42. Dangar later met Hone and Jellett in the 1930s and developed friendships and correspondences with each of them. Hone commenced studies with Gleizes in 1920, Jellett in 1921. See Bruce Arnold, *Mainie Jellett and the modern movement in Ireland*, Yale University Press, New Haven, CT, 1991, pp 44–46.

11 Arnold, pp 106–07.

12 See Brooke, pp 1–12.

13 In 1928 Gleizes's essay on Cubism—'Kubisme'—was published through the Bauhaus by László Moholy-Nagy and Walter Gropius. He was the only French contributor to this publication series. Many of Gleizes's writings were appreciated in Germany, at the Bauhaus in particular, and he gave a lecture on his ideas at the Bauhaus in 1932, prior to its closure. See Brooke, p 115; p 130. See also Adams, p 48.

14 See Adams, p 48.

15 Romy Golan, *Modernity and nostalgia: art and politics in France between the wars*, Yale University Press, New Haven, CT, 1995, pp 7–8.

16 Anne Dangar, letter to Grace Crowley, 29 March 1930, Grace Crowley papers, SLNSW.

17 Anne Dangar, letter to Albert Gleizes and Juliette Roche, 23 May 1930, Fonds Albert Gleizes, MV 698–699, Kandinsky Library, Musée national d'art moderne, Centre Georges Pompidou, Paris.

18 Dangar, letter to Gleizes and Roche, 23 May 1930.

19 Robert Pouyaud, in *Moly-Sabata*, Éditions Atelier de la Rose, Société des amis d'Albert Gleizes, Lyon, 1955, p 23, quoted in Laurence Berthon 'Céramiques d'Anne Dangar au musée des Beaux-Arts de Lyon', in *Bulletin des Musées et Monuments Lyonnais*, no 1, 1998, p 25.

20 Pignault is also referred to by Dangar as Pignot and Pignoud.

21 Anne Dangar, letter to Juliette Roche, 26 December 1929; Anne Dangar, letter to Albert Gleizes and Juliette Roche, September 1930, both in Fonds Albert Gleizes, Kandinsky Library, Centre Georges Pompidou.

22 Anne Dangar, letter to Juliette Roche, 8 April 1931, Fonds Albert Gleizes, Kandinsky Library, Centre Georges Pompidou.

23 Anne Dangar, letter to Grace Crowley, 29 November 1934, Grace Crowley papers, SLNSW.

24 Anne Dangar, letter to Grace Crowley, 26 July 1932, Grace Crowley papers, SLNSW; Adams, p 95.

25 David Butcher, *Anne Dangar, céramiste: le cubisme au quotidien*, exh cat, Musée de Valence art et archéologie, Valence, 2016, p 86.

26 Anne Dangar, letter to Albert Gleizes, 1 September 1931, Fonds Albert Gleizes, Kandinsky Library, Centre Georges Pompidou.

27 The Montgolfier brothers pioneered this novel form of aviation in the early 1780s.

28 Anne Dangar, letter to Albert Gleizes and Juliette Roche, 29 March 1931, Fonds Albert Gleizes, Kandinsky Library, Centre Georges Pompidou.

29 Anne Dangar, letter to Albert Gleizes, 9 May 1933, Fonds Albert Gleizes, Kandinsky Library, Centre Georges Pompidou.

30 Jacqueline Lerat, conversation quoted in Adams, p 159.

31 Anne Dangar, letter to Albert Gleizes, 26 December 1945, Fonds Albert Gleizes, Kandinsky Library, Centre Georges Pompidou.

32 Dangar, letter to Roche, 26 December 1929.

33 Anne Dangar, letter to Albert Gleizes, 13 January 1941, Fonds Albert Gleizes, Kandinsky Library, Centre Georges Pompidou.

34 Dangar, letter to Crowley, 29 November 1934.

35 Anne Dangar, letter to Albert Gleizes and Juliette Roche, 31 May 1932, Fonds Albert Gleizes, Kandinsky Library, Centre Georges Pompidou.

36 Robert Pouyaud, letter to Albert Gleizes, 25 March 1930, Fonds Albert Gleizes, Kandinsky Library, Centre Georges Pompidou.

37 This was commissioned by César Geoffray who, as explored later in this essay, joined the Moly-Sabata community with his family in 1931.

38 Anne Dangar, letter to Grace Crowley, 1 May 1934, Grace Crowley papers, SLNSW.

39 Marion Falaise, 'Les arts décoratifs à Lyon, 1864–1937', PhD thesis, Université de Lyon, 2021, p 323.

40 See Butcher, pp 88–90; Dangar wrote to Crowley that she was given 'carte blanche' to reinterpret Gleizes's designs. Anne Dangar, letter to Grace Crowley, jour de Pâques [Easter Sunday], 1937, Grace Crowley papers, SLNSW.

41 Butcher, p 92.

42 Gleizes initially resisted this publication as it did not carry his name. Adams, pp 47, 109.

43 Adams, p 117; Anne Dangar, letter to Albert Gleizes and Juliette Roche, 1932, Fonds Albert Gleizes, Kandinsky Library, Centre Georges Pompidou.

44 It is believed by residents of Sablons that Dangar and Deveyle had a romantic relationship, but this cannot be substantiated. Conversation with staff at Moly-Sabata, June 2022.

45 Dangar, letter to Gleizes, 1 September 1931.

46 Adolfo Best-Maugard, *A method for creative design*, AA Knopf, New York, 1926.

47 Anne Dangar, letter to Grace Crowley, 18 July 1937, Grace Crowley papers, SLNSW.

48 These exercise books are held in the Papers of Anne Dangar, MS 158, National Gallery of Australia Research Library and Archives, Kamberri/Canberra.

49 Like Dangar, Ainsworth was an art teacher at Frensham, a private school in Mittagong, New South Wales, and had been sent overseas by headmistress Winifred West to develop her knowledge of various craft practices, in particular weaving and pottery. She spent six weeks at Moly-Sabata, teaching Deveyle, as well as observing Dangar's children's art classes and work at the pottery, later returning to Australia where she recommenced her teaching and established the Sturt Workshop as part of Frensham, a craft centre which no doubt owes some of its genesis to Moly-Sabata. See Helen Maxwell, 'Ruth Ainsworth printmaker and teacher', *Australian National Gallery Association News*, nos 1–2, 1989, pp 12–14.

50 Anne Dangar, letter to Albert Gleizes and Juliette Roche, Thursday 1935, Fonds Albert Gleizes, Kandinsky Library, Centre Georges Pompidou.

51 Humphery d'Honfroi, 'Les artistes au village', *Le Magasin Pittoresque*, 1 July 1937, pp 30–31.

52 Georges Finaud, 'Moly-Sabata ou le retour à la terre des artistes', *Hebdo*, 8 June 1934, pp 8–9.

53 Anne Dangar, letters to Juliette Roche, 20 June 1930, 4 October 1936, Fonds Albert Gleizes, Kandinsky Library, Centre Georges Pompidou. See Angela Goddard, 'Estelle interrupted: Stella Creed, a lost Queensland modernist', *Queensland History Journal*, vol 24, no 11, November 2021, pp 1006–19.

54 Anne Dangar, letter to Grace Crowley, 10 November 1932, Grace Crowley papers, SLNSW.

55 Christiane Germain and Paul Haim (comps), Michel Seuphor, *Michel Seuphor: une vie à angle droit*, Éditions de la Différence, Paris, 1988, p 68.

56 See Adams, p 56. As Adams describes, early confrontations with Roche left Dangar in despair and Crowley interceded, writing to Roche in an attempt to assist her friend.

57 Anne Dangar, letter to Albert Gleizes and Juliette Roche, 11 July 1937, Fonds Albert Gleizes, Kandinsky Library, Centre Georges Pompidou.

58 Anne Dangar, letter to Albert Gleizes, 12 August 1938, Fonds Albert Gleizes, Kandinsky Library, Centre Georges Pompidou.

59 Grace Crowley, interviewed by James Gleeson, 25 August 1978, James Gleeson Oral History Collection, MS 23, National Gallery Research Library and Archives.

60 See Adams, p 48; 'Untitled lecture on Moly-Sabata delivered to Warsaw and Dessau', April 1932, quoted by Adams, p 113. Albert Gleizes, 'Moly-Sabata ou le retour des artistes au village', *Sud Magazine* (Marseille), vol 6, no 102, 1932, pp 40–41.

61 Daniel Robbins, *Albert Gleizes 1881–1953: a retrospective exhibition*, exh cat, The Solomon R Guggenheim Museum, New York, in collaboration with Musée national d'art moderne, Paris, & Museum am Ostwall, Dortmund, 1964, p 24.

62 Ruth Ainsworth, interviewed by Ian North, Sydney, April 1974, Dorrit Black Papers, MS 74, National Gallery Research Library and Archives.

63 Anne Dangar, letter to Grace Crowley, 11 May 1930, Grace Crowley papers, SLNSW.

64 Anne Dangar, letter to Grace Crowley, dated by Crowley 24 June 1930, Grace Crowley papers, SLNSW.

65 Elena Taylor, *Grace Crowley: being modern*, exh cat, National Gallery of Australia, Canberra, 2006, p 33.

66 Dangar, '1st talk', 17 December 1934.

67 Mary Alice Evatt, 'The Crowley Fizelle School', *Quarterly* (Art Gallery of New South Wales), October 1966, pp 314–15.

68 Anne Dangar, letter to Grace Crowley, 31 May 1932, Grace Crowley papers, SLNSW; Anne Dangar to Albert Gleizes, 6 July 1934, Fonds Albert Gleizes, Kandinsky Library, Centre Georges Pompidou; Evatt, p 316.

69 Anne Dangar, letter to Grace Crowley, 4 September 1932, Grace Crowley papers, SLNSW; Peter McNeil, 'Designing women: gender, modernism and interior decoration in Sydney, c 1920–1940', MA thesis, Australian National University, 1993, p 60.

70 Anne Dangar, letter to Albert Gleizes, 15 April 1937, Fonds Albert Gleizes, Kandinsky Library, Centre Georges Pompidou.

71 Although the outbreak of the Second World War meant these plans never eventuated, his interest indicates the gentle impact of these studio exhibitions. Anne Dangar, letter to Grace Crowley, 1 September 1937, Grace Crowley papers, SLNSW.

72 Anne Dangar, letters to Grace Crowley, 11 April 1938, 24 April 1938, Grace Crowley Papers, SLNSW.

73 Anne Dangar, letter to Grace Crowley, 9 August 1936, Grace Crowley papers, SLNSW.

74 Ainsworth and Black may also have acquired examples of Dangar's pottery during their visits to Moly-Sabata in 1934 and 1935 respectively.

75 Grace Crowley, letter to Albert Gleizes, 20 June 1947, Fonds Albert Gleizes, Kandinsky Library, Centre Georges Pompidou.

76 Taylor, pp 35, 41, quoting letter from Grace Crowley to Peter Pinson, 1979, Grace Crowley papers, SLNSW. As Taylor outlines, Crowley's earliest attempt at pure abstract painting in the early 1940s was discovered on the back of her *Abstract painting* 1947 (National Gallery of Australia). Featuring a centralised form shaped like an arched doorway, it recalls the religious compositions of Gleizes that she had seen, and made diagrams of, in 1929. Kim Brunoro, 'Discovering a Grace Crowley painting', *Artonview* (National Gallery), summer 2006, pp 28–29.

77 Anne Dangar, 'Teaching notes sent to Grace Crowley', nd, Grace Crowley archive, MS1980.1, National Art Archive, Art Gallery of New South Wales, Gadigal Nura/Sydney.

78 Ralph Balson exhibited abstracts in his solo exhibition at Anthony Horderns' Fine Art Gallery, Gadigal Nura/Sydney, 29 July – 9 August 1941. Crowley exhibited two abstract paintings in the Society of Artists annual exhibition, Education Department Gallery, Gadigal Nura/Sydney, 2–24 September 1942.

Journeys through Australian and French modernism: Anne Dangar and Stella Creed

1 I am grateful to Stella Creed's family for their support and encouragement and for giving me access to the Stella Creed family archives. This research was part of the Sheila Foundation's research project Into the Light: Recovering Australia's Lost Women Artists 1870–1960. Thanks also to Glenn Cooke, Elena Taylor, Conal Coad, Adam Ford and Zara Yerbury.

2 'Grammar School speech day', *Maryborough Chronicle*, 15 December 1922, p 6.

3 Elena Taylor, 'The revelation of Paris—learning cubism', essay two, *Grace Crowley: being modern*, 23 December 2006 – 6 May 2007, exhibition website, viewed 29 April 2024, https://nga.gov.au/exhibitions/grace-crowley-being-modern.

4 Helen Topliss (ed), *Earth, fire, water, air: Anne Dangar's letters to Grace Crowley, 1930–1951*, Allen & Unwin, St Leonards, NSW, 2000, p 4.

5 Sergius [Nancy Hall], 'Summer school at Wamberal', *Undergrowth*, January–February 1929, unpag.

6 Sergius, 'Summer School at Wamberal', unpag.

7 Bruce Adams and Tracey Lock, 'Missionaries of modernism: the women artists who took André Lhote's art and teachings to Australia: Dorrit Black, Grace Crowley and Anne Dangar', in Zeynep Kuban and Simone Wille (eds), *André Lhote and his international students*, Innsbruck University Press, Innsbruck, 2020, p 244.

8 Bruce Adams, *Rustic Cubism: Anne Dangar and the art colony at Moly-Sabata*, University of Chicago Press, Chicago, 2004, p 26.

9 Stella Creed, passport stamp, 5 February 1930, Stella Creed family archives; 'Everyday and everybody', *The Labor Daily* (Sydney), 5 February 1930, p 4, viewed 8 August 2021, http://nla.gov.au/nla.news-article237032167.

10 Anne Dangar, note in Stella Creed's notebook, c March 1930, Stella Creed family archives.

11 Stella Creed, postcard to Mildred Creed, 2 May 1930, Stella Creed family archives.

12 Stella Creed, handwritten notes, 5 pages, Stella Creed family archives.

13 Anne Dangar, letter to Stella Creed, 14 April 1930, Stella Creed family archives.

14 Anne Dangar, postcard to Stella Creed, mid 1930, Stella Creed family archives.

15 Anne Dangar, letter to Grace Crowley, 29 March 1930, in Topliss, p 35.

16 Creed family, Dead Farm File, Item ID ITM3479538, Queensland State Archives, Meeanjin/Brisbane.

17 Elena Taylor, email to the author, 18 October 2021.

18 Anne Dangar, letter to Grace Crowley, nd [c 1930], in Topliss, p 46.

19 Anne Dangar, letter to Grace Crowley, 10 February 1931, in Topliss, p 55. According to Dangar's letter to Creed on 10 February 1931, Stella Creed family archives, the payment was 26 francs per day.

20 Dangar, letter to Crowley, 10 February 1931.

21 Creed's passport is stamped '19/5/1931' for her return date, Stella Creed family archives. Anne Dangar wrote years later to Grace Crowley that Creed's doctor returned to Moly-Sabata and commissioned a work from her. Dangar, letter to Crowley, 17 May 1935, in Topliss, p 139.

22 Some of Creed's works were signed decades later, in the shaky script of an elderly person.

23 Adams, p 51.

24 Topliss, p 63.

'My only home is your heart': the relationship between Anne Dangar and Grace Crowley

1 Hazel de Berg, notes on interviews, 'Ralph Balson painter 1890–1964' and 'Grace Crowley painter—talking about Ralph Balson and herself', unpublished transcripts, National Gallery of Australia Research Library and Archives, Kamberri/Canberra.

2 See, for example, Peter Di Sciascio, 'Australian lesbian artists of the early twentieth century', in Yorick Smaal and Graham Willett (eds), *Out here: gay and lesbian perspectives VI*, Monash University, Clayton, Vic, 2011, p 147; Jo Darbyshire, exhibition notes for *HERE&NOW20: perfectly queer*, Lawrence Wilson Art Gallery, University of Western Australia, Boorloo/Perth, 29 August – 5 December 2020, curated by Brent Harrison, viewed 26 May 2024, https://jodarbyshire.com/exhibitions/herenow20-perfectly-queer; Beckett Rozentals, 'Grace Crowley, *Olga 2* 1928', in Ted Gott et al (eds), *Queer: stories from the NGV Collection*, National Gallery of Victoria, Melbourne, 2021, pp 448–50; and Peter McNeil, '"The first homosexuals": connecting Australian art and design to the world', Australian Academy of the Humanities, January 2024, viewed 5 February 2024, https://humanities.org.au/power-of-the-humanities/australian-queer-art-and-design-pre-1930.

3 Eve Kosofsky Sedgwick, *Tendencies*, Duke University Press, Durham, NC, 1993, pp 5, 8.

4 The literature is vast, encompassing popular histories including Shari Benstock, *Women of the Left Bank: Paris 1900–1940*, Virago, London, 1986; Tirza True Latimer, *Women together, women apart: portraits of lesbian Paris*, Rutgers University Press, New Brunswick, NJ, 2005; and Diana Souhami, *No modernism without lesbians*, Head of Zeus, London, 2020.

5 Latimer, p 35.

6 Bruce Adams, *Rustic Cubism: Anne Dangar and the art colony at Moly-Sabata*, University of Chicago Press, Chicago, 2004, p 11.

7 Anne Dangar, 'Reminiscences', *Undergrowth*, May 1925, cited in Adams, p 11.

8 Adams, p 15.

9 Grace Crowley, interviewed by James Gleeson, 25 August 1978, James Gleeson Oral History Collection, MS 23, National Gallery Research Library and Archives.

10 Souhami, p 286.

11 Grace Crowley, 'Letters from abroad: Learning in Paris', *Undergrowth*, May–June 1927, quoted in Adams, p 18.

12 Jennifer L Shaw, *Exist otherwise: the life and works of Claude Cahun*, Reaktion Books, London, 2017, p 48.

13 Queer men, of course, also took advantage of the freedom Paris afforded, by choice but also out of necessity when they couldn't stay where they were: writer Oscar Wilde and Pre-Raphaelite painter Simeon Solomon, for example, lived out their lives in exile in France after falling foul of the law in England.

14 Nigel Nicholson, *Portrait of a marriage*, Weidenfeld & Nicolson, London, 1973, p 112.

15 Souhami, p 295.

16 Sylvia Beach, interviewed in Dublin in 1962 by Niall Sheridan for 'Self-portrait: Sylvia Beach', RTÉ Ireland, 2 October 1962, viewed 26 May 2024, https://www.youtube.com/watch?v=R1Zbw39MCm4&t=9s.

17 Shaina Paige Maciejewski, 'The relationship between sexology and the lesbian identity in early 20th-century Britain', honours thesis, Spring 2016, p 12, University of New Hampshire Scholars' Repository, viewed 2 June 2024, https://scholars.unh.edu/cgi/viewcontent.cgi?article=1271&context=honors.

18 Lillian Faderman, *Surpassing the love of men: romantic friendship and love between women from the Renaissance to the present*, The Women's Press, London, 1985, p 241.

19 Claude Cahun, for example, translated Havelock Ellis into French in 1929 and she and others in her group studied Freud's writings and other texts on psychosexual subjectivity. See Latimer, pp 88–90.

20 Lisa Featherstone, *Let's talk about sex: histories of sexuality in Australia from Federation to the pill*, Cambridge Scholars Publishing, Newcastle-upon-Tyne, 2011, p 30.

21 Faderman, 1985, p 353.

22 Lillian Faderman, *Odd girls and twilight lovers: a history of lesbian life in 20th-century America*, Columbia University Press, New York, 1991, p 31. In Sébastian Lifshitz's documentary *Les invisibles*, a series of interviews is conducted with elderly gay men and lesbians living around Lyon in the south of France. Babette and Catherine's story illustrates this: as they establish a goat farm in a rural village, locals are accepting of them, assuming tragedy has befallen their husbands. *Les invisibles* 2012, dir Sébastian Lifshitz, video, 1 hr 55 mins. Produced by Eugénie Michel-Villette, Bruno Nahon and Mathilde Raczymow, Zadig Films, Rhône-Alpes Cinéma, Sylicone.

23 The sources: 'longtime friend', Adams, p 3; 'dearest friend', Helen Maxwell, 'Anne Garvin Dangar (1885–1951)', *Australian dictionary of biography*, viewed 6 June 2024, https://adb.anu.edu.au/biography/dangar-anne-garvin-9899; 'close friend', 'DANGAR, Anne', Alan McCulloch, Susan McCulloch and Emily McCulloch Childs, *The new McCulloch's encyclopedia of Australian art*, Miegunyah Press, Carlton, Vic, 2006, p 364; 'friend and fellow-teacher', Janine Burke, *Australian women artists, 1840–1940*, Greenhouse Publications, Collingwood, Vic, 1980, p 52; 'artistic co-adventurer', Clem Gorman and Therese Gorman, *Intrépide: Australian women artists in early twentieth-century France*, Monash University Publishing, Clayton, Vic, 2020, p 140; and 'regard and affection', Helen Topliss (ed), *Earth, fire, water, air: Anne Dangar's letters to Grace Crowley, 1930–1951*, Allen & Unwin, St Leonards, NSW, 2000, p 6. Similar terms were also used by the women themselves, with Crowley remembering Dangar in their Paris years as a 'good staunch courageous pal', for example, quoted in Burke, p 83.

24 *Grace Crowley* 1975, dir Esben Storm, film, 30 mins, Smart Street Films, Sydney, produced by Haydn Keenan. The film was part of the Australia Council Archival Film Program (1974–99), as a series of interviews with Australian arts identities.

25 Adams, p 15. Dangar's acceptance in the Crowley family is best illustrated by a letter written by Dangar in France dated 28 December 1927 to Crowley's mother, 'To my dearest Mother Bird', with 'much love from your eldest daughter', in which she speaks of her love for Crowley, Grace Crowley papers, 1927–1974, MLMSS 3252/vols 2–7, MLMSS 3252/vol 1X, State Library of New South Wales, Gadigal Nura/Sydney.

26 Featherstone, p 33.

27 'le[s] plus heureuses de ma vie', Anne Dangar, letter to André Lhote, 2 October 1934, Archives André Lhote, private collection, Paris.

28 'Gosh Smudgie if we had a bit of capital we should start a school at Canberra or somewhere where there is good clay & we'd make things HUM!!!', 1 August 1932, and 'I've quite decided to wait another year. It's no use going out there if I can't find anywhere to work', 28 August 1946, Anne Dangar, letters to Grace Crowley, Grace Crowley papers, SLNSW.

29 'others drift in & drift out but you are my soul mate, beside me & I am beside you & distance doesn't count', Anne Dangar, letter to Grace Crowley, 20 January 1931, Grace Crowley papers, SLNSW.

30 Grace Crowley, letter to Albert Gleizes and Juliette Roche, 16 September 1951, Fonds Albert Gleizes, MV 698–699, Kandinsky Library, Musée national d'art moderne, Centre Georges Pompidou, Paris.

31 '<u>Later</u> Last night St F [Pouyaud] took me thro' the color notes he has given me … I said, "Do you mind if I copy these for mon amie?"', Anne Dangar, letter to Grace Crowley, 24 June 1930, Grace Crowley papers, SLNSW.

32 Dangar, letter to Crowley, 24 June 1930.

33 As well as instruction, Dangar also sent words of encouragement, support and praise to Crowley. 'You have a talent for drawing such as I have never never come across in another being. You also have a great knowledge & sensibility of colour.' Anne Dangar, letter to Grace Crowley, 27 November 1950, Grace Crowley papers, SLNSW. And the letters also reveal that Crowley's now-destroyed correspondence served to keep Dangar strong too: 'How wonderful it is to have a true, trusting, believing friend always beside me—always reassuring one & giving one confidence', Dangar, letter to Crowley, 24 June 1930.

34 Dangar, letter to Crowley, 24 June 1930.

35 Anne Dangar, letters to Grace Crowley, 21 March 1932, 10 February 1931, 28 June 1939, 26 December 1934, 1 May 1934, 18 March 1951, 28 February 1946, 4 February 1940, 11 November 1948, Grace Crowley papers, SLNSW.

36 Anne Dangar, letter to Grace Crowley, 12 October 1932, Grace Crowley papers, SLNSW.

37 Anne Dangar, letter to Grace Crowley, 19 March 1933, Grace Crowley papers, SLNSW.

38 Anne Dangar, letter to Grace Crowley, 1 December 1932, Grace Crowley papers, SLNSW.

39 'No letter again—I'm terrified you have whooping cough—only one letter from you in two months', 'I can't go on without you, I just live waiting for a letter from you', Dangar, letters to Crowley, 21 March 1932, 18 March 1951.

40 Anne Dangar, letter to Grace Crowley, 17 March 1932, Grace Crowley papers, SLNSW.

41 Crowley, interviewed by Gleeson, 25 August 1978, p 8.

42 Anne Dangar, letter to Grace Crowley, 30 March 1933, Grace Crowley papers, SLNSW.

43 Dangar, letter to Crowley, 24 June 1930.

44 Dangar, letter to Crowley, 21 March 1932.

45 Anne Dangar, letter to Albert Gleizes and Juliette Roche, 5 November 1931, Fonds Albert Gleizes, Kandinsky Library, Centre Georges Pompidou.

46 Dangar, letter to Crowley, 1 December 1932.

47 Anne Dangar, letter to Grace Crowley, 4 March 1933, Grace Crowley papers, SLNSW.

Timeline 1937–1951

1 See note 1 under Timeline 1885–1929, p 215.

III

1 Anne Dangar, letter to Albert Gleizes, 22 June 1934, Fonds Albert Gleizes, MV 698–699, Kandinsky Library, Musée national d'art moderne, Centre Georges Pompidou, Paris. Anne Dangar, letter to Grace Crowley, 11 March 1934, Grace Crowley papers, 1927–1974, MLMSS 3252/vols 2–7, MLMSS 3252/vol 1X, State Library of New South Wales, Gadigal Nura/Sydney. Gleizes also extended an invitation through Dangar to Crowley to join the group. At this time, Crowley was not producing abstract art.

2 *Exposition internationale des arts et des techniques dans la vie moderne, Paris 1937, catalogue général officiel*, exh cat, book 1, 2nd edn, R Stengel, Paris, 1937. The exhibition was held from 25 May to 25 November.

3 As she noted in a letter to Gleizes, she was asked to exhibit her own work only, but she 'had no wish to exhibit unless all the work of Moly-Sabata is shown together'. Anne Dangar, letter to Albert Gleizes, 13 November 1936, Fonds Albert Gleizes, Kandinsky Library, Centre Georges Pompidou; *Exposition internationale des arts et des techniques dans la vie moderne*, 1937.

4 Bruce Adams, 'The promise of the rainbow: Anne Dangar at Moly-Sabata 1930–1951', PhD thesis, University of Sydney, 1998, p 123.

5 *Les maîtres de l'art indépendant, 1895–1937: Petit Palais, juin–octobre*, exh cat, Éditions arts et métiers graphiques, Paris, 1937.

6 Anne Dangar, letter to Grace Crowley, jour de Pâques [Easter Sunday], 1937, Grace Crowley papers, SLNSW. Dangar's work was not listed in the catalogue; however, it is likely these works were a late addition to the exhibition after the catalogue was printed and that they were originally intended for display in the UAM Pavilion. She described her work in the Petit Palais in a letter to Crowley, and ceramics 'decorated by Gleizes' in this component of the Exposition internationale were also mentioned in French reviews of his contribution to the Salon d'automne later that year. See Anne Dangar, letter to Grace Crowley, 8 November 1937, Grace Crowley papers, SLNSW; Pierre Morel, 'Le Salon d'automne', *Revue Bleue Politique et Littéraire*, 4 December 1937, p 759.

7 Dangar, letter to Crowley, jour de Pâques [Easter Sunday], 1937. The tiles were later permanently installed at Gleizes's property Les Méjades in Saint-Rémy-de-Provence.

8 Anne Dangar, letter to Grace Crowley, 8 November 1937, Grace Crowley papers, SLNSW.

9 In 1939 the Delaunays commissioned a set of Dangar's Aladdin, Sinbad and Icarus plates for their personal collection (Anne Dangar, letter to Albert Gleizes, 10 March 1939), though it later became a great source of frustration that they never paid her (Anne Dangar, letter to Albert Gleizes, 23 April 1947), Fonds Albert Gleizes, Kandinsky Library, Centre Georges Pompidou.

10 Anne Dangar, letter to Grace Crowley, 6 February 1938, Grace Crowley papers, SLNSW.

11 'Art et expositions', *Le Petit Journal*, 2 July 1938, p 5; see the exhibition's invitation card: 'Carton d'invitation de l'exposition du 32e groupe des artistes de ce temps', Petit Palais, 1938, Archives of the Petit Palais, Musée des beaux-arts de la Ville de Paris.

12 Maximilien Gauthier, 'Moly-Sabata', *Art et Décoration*, September–October 1938, pp 293–300.

13 Anne Dangar, letter to Grace Crowley, 24 July 1938, Grace Crowley papers, SLNSW.

14 Two gouaches are listed in the catalogue; however, Dangar wrote to Crowley that she exhibited three. 'I'm happy to have these 3 little gouaches shown with Evie & Mainie, Pouyaud, Herbin, Villon and Gleizes.' See Anne Dangar, letter to Grace Crowley, 6 November 1938, Grace Crowley papers, SLNSW; *Salon d'automne. Catalogue des ouvrages de peinture, sculpture, dessin … exposés au Palais de Chaillot … du 11 novembre au 18 décembre 1938*, exh cat, E Puyfourcat fils, Paris, pp 259–64.

15 Moutard-Uldry misattributed Dangar's efforts to Gleizes. See Renée Moutard-Uldry, 'L'art décoratif au Salon d'automne', *Beaux-Arts*, 25 November 1938, p 3.

16 'Au salon d'automne', *Petit Parisien*, 21 November 1938, p 10. See also Bruce Adams, *Rustic Cubism: Anne Dangar and the art colony at Moly-Sabata*, University of Chicago Press, Chicago, 2004, p 124.

17 Anne Dangar, letter to Grace Crowley, 26 March 1939, Grace Crowley papers, SLNSW.

18 Adams, 2004, p 133. She was no doubt recommended by Maurice Grimaud who worked with Noguès and whose Annonay-based family were friends and great supporters of Dangar's work.

19 Dangar lists her residence as the Ateliers des beaux-arts in her letters, but it is likely she stayed at the 'Maison des artistes', a small complex of workshops and a gallery space established by the French Commissaire résident général's Service des antiquités, beaux-arts et monuments historiques in Morocco.

20 Adams, 2004, p 135. Anne Dangar, letter to Albert Gleizes, 23 June 1939, Fonds Albert Gleizes, Kandinsky Library, Centre Georges Pompidou.

21 Orit Ouaknine-Yekutieli, 'Narrating a pending calamity: artisanal crisis in the medina of Fes, Morocco', *International Journal of Middle East Studies*, vol 47, no 1, 2015, pp 117–18.

22 Anne Dangar, letter to Albert Gleizes, 29 July 1939, Fonds Albert Gleizes, Kandinsky Library, Centre Georges Pompidou.

23 Anne Dangar, letter to Albert Gleizes, 27 May 1939, Fonds Albert Gleizes, Kandinsky Library, Centre Georges Pompidou.

24 Dangar, letter to Gleizes, 23 June 1939; Adams, 2004, p 137.

25 Anne Dangar, letter to Albert Gleizes, 20 June 1939, Fonds Albert Gleizes, Kandinsky Library, Centre Georges Pompidou; Dangar, letter to Gleizes, 27 May 1939.

26 Anne Dangar, letter to Lucie Deveyle, 25 June 1939, Papers of Anne Dangar, MS 158, National Gallery of Australia Research Library and Archives, Kamberri/Canberra.

27 Anne Dangar, letter to Lucie Deveyle, nd [1939], Fonds Albert Gleizes, Kandinsky Library, Centre Georges Pompidou; Anne Dangar, letter to Juliette Roche, 11 September 1940, Fonds Albert Gleizes, Kandinsky Library, Centre Georges Pompidou. These firings were usually unsuccessful given the damper climate in Sablons.

28 Dangar, letter to Gleizes, 23 June 1939.

29 Adams, 2004, pp 134–36.

30 Dangar, letter to Gleizes, 23 June 1939.

31 Dangar, letter to Gleizes, 27 May 1939.

32 Dangar, letter Gleizes, 20 June 1939; Dangar, letter to Gleizes, 27 May 1939.

33 Anne Dangar, letter to Albert Gleizes, 17 November 1939, Fonds Albert Gleizes, Kandinsky Library, Centre Georges Pompidou.

34 Anne Dangar, letter to Albert Gleizes and Juliette Roche, 5 July 1940, Fonds Albert Gleizes, Kandinsky Library, Centre Georges Pompidou.

35 Dangar, letter to Gleizes, 20 June 1939; Anne Dangar, letter to Albert Gleizes and Juliette Roche, 1939, Fonds Albert Gleizes, Kandinsky Library, Centre Georges Pompidou.

36 Adams, 2004, p 157.

37 Anne Dangar, letter to Albert Gleizes, 9 May 1943, Fonds Albert Gleizes, Kandinsky Library, Centre Georges Pompidou.

38 Adams, 2004, p 146. Crowley had developed this name for him when she travelled to Moly-Sabata in 1929.

39 Anne Dangar, letter to Albert Gleizes, 22 December 1941, Fonds Albert Gleizes, Kandinsky Library, Centre Georges Pompidou.

40 Anne Dangar, letter to Albert Gleizes and Juliette Roche, 9 January 1942, Fonds Albert Gleizes, Kandinsky Library, Centre Georges Pompidou.

41 Romy Golan, *Modernity and nostalgia: art and politics in France between the wars*, Yale University Press, New Haven, CT, 1995, p 87.

42 See Adams, 2004, pp 149–50; Peter Brooke, *Albert Gleizes: for and against the twentieth century*, Yale University Press, New Haven, CT, 2001, pp 195, 211. During the occupation of Serrières, it is known that several Nazi officers took up residence in Gleizes's house. According to Seuphor in later years, this was upon Gleizes's direct invitation, and his letter to the Mayor of Annonay in which he offered his home for their use was allegedly pinned to his door after liberation. Letters from Dangar to Gleizes do not provide any further insight into how the Nazis were given access to Gleizes's house, but indicate that it was left filthy, ransacked and greatly damaged following their departure. See Michel Seuphor's autobiography compiled by Christiane Germain and Paul Haim, *Michel Seuphor, une vie à angle droit*, Éditions de la Différence, Paris, 1988, p 72; Anne Dangar, letter to Albert Gleizes and Juliette Roche, 7 September 1944, Fonds Albert Gleizes, Kandinsky Library, Centre Georges Pompidou. This episode, and the Second World War more generally, is not discussed by Daniel Robbins in his text published a decade or so after Gleizes's death. See Daniel Robbins, *Albert Gleizes 1881–1953: a retrospective exhibition*, exh cat, The Solomon R Guggenheim Museum, New York, in collaboration with Musée national d'art moderne, Paris, & Museum am Ostwall, Dortmund, 1964.

43 Golan, p 103.

44 Golan, p 103; Adams, 2004, p 152.

45 Adams, 2004, p 153.

46 Golan, p 209, n 21.

47 Anne Dangar, letter to Albert Gleizes, 2 September 1939, Fonds Albert Gleizes, Kandinsky Library, Centre Georges Pompidou.

48 Anne Dangar, letter to Albert Gleizes, 31 August 1940, Fonds Albert Gleizes, Kandinsky Library, Centre Georges Pompidou.

49 Anne Dangar, letter to Albert Gleizes, 11 Sept 1940, Fonds Albert Gleizes, Kandinsky Library, Centre Georges Pompidou.

50 Adams, 2004, p 154.

51 Anne Dangar, letter to Albert Gleizes, 17 January 1942, Fonds Albert Gleizes, Kandinsky Library, Centre Georges Pompidou.

52 Anne Dangar, letter to Grace Crowley, 12 November 1944, Grace Crowley papers, SLNSW. For further discussion of Dangar's time at Maĉon, see Adams, 2004, pp 158–61.

53 Anne Dangar, letter to Otho Orde Hastings Dangar, quoted in 'Australian woman in occupied France', *Narrandera Argus and Riverina Advertiser*, 13 March 1945, p 3. According to Dangar, the Swiss Consul in charge of British subjects arranged their release. Dom Angelico Surchamp later attributed her liberation to the intervention of the Australian consul. Dom Angelico Surchamp, in Dangar, *Lettres à la Pierre-qui-Vire*, Zodiaque, Saint-Léger-Vauban, 1972, p 15.

54 Anne Dangar, letter to Albert Gleizes, 16 October 1943, Fonds Albert Gleizes, Kandinsky Library, Centre Georges Pompidou.

55 Adams, 2004, p 165.

56 Adams, 2004, pp 165–66.

57 Adams, 2004, p 166.

58 Anne Dangar, letter to Albert Gleizes, 9 April 1944, Fonds Albert Gleizes, Kandinsky Library, Centre Georges Pompidou.

59 Anne Dangar, letter to Jacqueline Lerat, 11 July 1945, artist files, Musée des beaux-arts de Lyon. My thanks to Salima Halal for giving me access to these files. Jacqueline Lerat, *Jacqueline Lerat: une oeuvre en mouvement*, La Revue de la Céramique et du Verre, Vendin-le-Vieil, 2010; *Jacqueline Lerat, Anne Dangar: une rencontre 1942–1951*, Argile Editions, Banon, 1999. Like Dangar, Lerat was interested in combining tradition with modernity, adapting the salt-fired stoneware long-connected to the Bourges region to innovative sculptural forms.

60 Anne Dangar, letter to Jacqueline Lerat, 13 May 1942, artist files, Musée des beaux-arts de Lyon.

61 'Il est un jour qui ne commence pas avec la fin d'hier pour le comme toujours de demain mais qui est cessent aujourd'hui.' This phrase loosely translates to 'your today does not yield with tomorrow, for neither does it follow yesterday' from Saint Augustine's *Confessions*, book XI, chapter 13.

62 Anne Dangar, letter to Albert Gleizes, 7 June 1945, Fonds Albert Gleizes, Kandinsky Library, Centre Georges Pompidou.

63 Anne Dangar, letter to Albert Gleizes and Juliette Roche, 31 March 1946, Fonds Albert Gleizes, Kandinsky Library, Centre Georges Pompidou.

64 Anne Dangar, letter to Albert Gleizes and Juliette Roche, 11 November 1945, Fonds Albert Gleizes, Kandinsky Library, Centre Georges Pompidou; Anne Dangar, letter to Albert Gleizes and Juliette Roche, 26 December 1945, Fonds Albert Gleizes, Kandinsky Library, Centre Georges Pompidou.

65 Adams, 2004, pp 165–66. See exhibition invitation to 'Les colonies françaises', 29 September – 7 October 1945, Papers of Anne Dangar, National Gallery Research Library and Archives.

66 Anne Dangar, letter to Albert Gleizes and Juliette Roche, 3 August 1946, Fonds Albert Gleizes, Kandinsky Library, Centre Georges Pompidou.

67 Anne Dangar, letter to Albert Gleizes and Juliette Roche, 7 April 1947, Fonds Albert Gleizes, Kandinsky Library, Centre Georges Pompidou.

68 Marie de Segue, 'In France 15 years, artist to return', *The Sun* (Sydney), 18 March 1945, p 12.

69 Anne Dangar, letter to Albert Gleizes and Juliette Roche, 8 February 1947; Anne Dangar, letter to Albert Gleizes and Juliette Roche, 26 April 1946; Dangar, letter to Gleizes and Roche, 31 March 1946, all in Fonds Albert Gleizes, Kandinsky Library, Centre Georges Pompidou.

70 Anne Dangar, letter to Albert Gleizes and Juliette Roche, 26 August 1947, Fonds Albert Gleizes, Kandinsky Library, Centre Georges Pompidou.

71 Anne Dangar, letter to Albert Gleizes, 17 July 1948, Fonds Albert Gleizes, Kandinsky Library, Centre Georges Pompidou.

72 Cédric Lesac, 'Humiles et quieti et operantes: Anne Dangar et Angelico Surchamp une amitié au nom de Dieu', in David Butcher, *Anne Dangar, céramiste: le cubisme au quotidien*, exh cat, Musée de Valence art et archéologie, Valence, 2016, p 127.

73 As she outlines to Michaud, the commission takes 21 months to complete. Anne Dangar, letter to Marcel Michaud, 23 February 1951, Archives Marcel Michaud, Musée des beaux-arts de Lyon. Surchamp later founded a magazine, *Zodiaque*, which featured Dangar as the focus in 1952 and 1972. See 'Le renouveau de la poterie: Anne G Dangar potière', *Zodiaque*, no 8, April 1952; 'Anne Dangar, 20 ans après', *Zodiaque*, no 91, January 1972.

74 Anne Dangar, letter to Grace Crowley, 20 Sept 1948, Grace Crowley papers, SLNSW.

75 *Albert Gleizes*, Galerie des Garets, 38 rue de Courcelles, Paris, 20 April – 11 May 1948. Anne Dangar, letter to Albert Gleizes, 2 January 1948, Fonds Albert Gleizes, Kandinsky Library, Centre Georges Pompidou.

76 Anne Dangar, letter to Albert Gleizes, 17 June 1949, Fonds Albert Gleizes, Kandinsky Library, Centre Georges Pompidou.

77 Anne Dangar, letter to Albert Gleizes and Juliette Roche, 8 August 1949, Fonds Albert Gleizes, Kandinsky Library, Centre Georges Pompidou. De Cissey later developed her own cubist pottery practice after Dangar's model and, for a period, lived and worked at Moly-Sabata. For more on De Cissey/Dalban, Dangar and Moly-Sabata, see Peter Brooke, 'La succession de Moly-Sabata' in Butcher, pp 149–59, as well as his contribution to this publication, 'After Anne Dangar', pp 184–93.

78 Anne Dangar, letter to Albert Gleizes, 15 August 1950, Fonds Albert Gleizes, Kandinsky Library, Centre Georges Pompidou.

79 Anne Dangar, letter to Albert Gleizes and Juliette Roche, 12 January 1951, Fonds Albert Gleizes, Kandinsky Library, Centre Georges Pompidou.

80 For an in-depth analysis of the significance of Catholicism to French folklore and Cubism, see Adams, 2004.

81 Adams, 2004, p 217. As she recalled, she was originally baptised Methodist, then Presbyterian and confirmed Anglican. See Anne Dangar, letter to Ruby Singleton, 23 March 1951, Grace Crowley papers, SLNSW.

82 Anne Dangar, letter to Grace Crowley, 22 September 1949, Grace Crowley papers, SLNSW.

83 Dangar, letter to Gleizes and Roche, 12 January 1951.

84 As Adams notes, due to the short notice of the baptism ceremony, Gleizes was not able to attend the event. Adams, 2004, p 217.

85 Anne Dangar, letter to Grace Crowley, 12 January 1950, Grace Crowley papers, SLNSW; Adams, 2004, p 204.

86 Dangar, letter to Crowley, 22 September 1949.

87 Frederick D McCarthy, *Australian Aboriginal decorative art*, Trustees of the Australian Museum, Sydney, 1948.

88 See Anne Dangar, letter to Dom Angelico Surchamp, 11 October 1950, in Dangar, 1972, p 121.

89 Anne Dangar, letter to Albert Gleizes and Juliette Roche, 10 October 1950, Fonds Albert Gleizes, Kandinsky Library, Centre Georges Pompidou.

90 Dangar, letter to Michaud, 23 February 1951.

91 Dangar, letter to Michaud, 23 February 1951.

92 Lucie Deveyle, letters to Grace Crowley, 15 August 1951, 7 September 1951, Grace Crowley papers, SLNSW.

93 Albert Gleizes, letter to Grace Crowley, 18 September 1951, Grace Crowley papers, SLNSW. She was joined by Gleizes in 1953, Deveyle in 1956 and Roche in 1980.

94 Grace Crowley, interviewed by Gleeson, 25 August 1978, James Gleeson Oral History Collection, MS 23, National Gallery Research Library and Archives. Deveyle remained at Moly-Sabata until her death in 1956. Dangar's position in the pottery was filled by Jean-Claude Libert from 1952 to 1955, and then Geneviève de Cissey until she established her own pottery in Ampuis with her husband Charles Dalban in 1960. Moly-Sabata remained unoccupied for several decades until the Fondation Albert Gleizes, established by Juliette Roche, renovated the building. It reopened as a regional art centre in 1989 with the assistance of Gilka Béclu, the daughter of César Geoffray, and Aguilberte Dalban, the daughter of Geneviève de Cissey, also a potter. Today Moly-Sabata is a vibrant contemporary artists' residence administered by enthusiastic staff, with four light-filled artist studios that host creative practitioners from around the world. See Adams, 2004, pp 223–29; 'Moly-Sabata résidence d'artistes', website for Moly-Sabata artist residence, 2024, viewed 16 February 2024, https://www.moly-sabata.com.

95 *Du cubisme aux arts traditionnels: Paris, Aix-en-Provence, Saint-Rémy-de-Provence, Toulon, Lyon*, exh cat, Papeteries Condat, Paris, 1953.

96 Two exhibitions of Dangar's work have been held in Australia, *Anne Dangar at Moly-Sabata: tradition and innovation*, 2001, curated by Helen Topliss at the National Gallery of Australia, Kamberri/Canberra, and *Anne Dangar: ceramics from Moly-Sabata*, 2018, curated by Leanne Santoro at the Art Gallery of New South Wales, Gadigal Nura/Sydney.

After Anne Dangar: Geneviève Dalban and the amis d'Albert Gleizes

1 There is a good account of the traditional method accessible online (in French) at https://www.lafabriquedecliou.com/notre-histoire/les-techniques/, website of the pottery at Cliousclat. Anne Dangar visited and consulted with Cliousclat, which was near the village of Mirmande, restored and used as a centre by her old teacher André Lhote. Unless otherwise noted, all translations from the French in this essay are by the author.

2 Peter Brooke, *Albert Gleizes: for and against the twentieth century*, Yale University Press, New Haven, CT, 2001, p 128. The footnote reference in my book mistakenly attributes this to 'J.R.Gleizes: *Souvenirs—1926–33*, p.3'. It should have read Gleizes: *Souvenirs—1926–33*, p.3. 'J.R.Gleizes' is Madame [Juliette Roche] Gleizes.

3 Bruce Adams, *Rustic Cubism: Anne Dangar and the art colony at Moly-Sabata*, University of Chicago Press, Chicago, 2004, pp 201–03. *L'homme devenu peintre*, never published during Gleizes's life, has now been published by the Fondation Albert Gleizes. An English translation is available on my website at http://www.peterbrooke.org/form-and-history/texts/painter. *La peinture et ses lois: ce qui devait sortir du cubisme* has long been out of print but an English translation has been published by Francis Boutle publishers.

4 Taken from 'Témoignages de moments vécus à la poterie des Chals recueillis lors du décès de Jean-Marie Paquaud en 1988' in *Petites histoires des poteries et tuileries du pays roussillonnais*, Réalisation collective, Association Figlinae, Terres de potiers, Roussillon, 2001, pp 42–43.

5 See https://www.poteriedeschals.fr. A comparison might be made with the fate of Moly-Sabata itself.

6 Dom Angelico Surchamp, 'Introduction' in Anne Dangar, *Lettres à la Pierre-qui-Vire*, Zodiaque, Saint-Léger-Vauban, 1972, pp 14–15. Surchamp felt that the Guénonians had tried to prejudice Gleizes against him. I discuss the quarrel over Guénon at some length in my book and have an essay on the relations between Gleizes, Guénon and Ananda Coomaraswamy on my website at http://www.peterbrooke.org/form-and-history/coomaraswamy.

7 Henri Giriat, *D'une ligne de transmission—Geneviève de Cissey Dalban (1926–2002)*, Association des amis d'Albert Gleizes, Brecon, Wales, 2003, pp 1–2.

'The beautiful day is over ...': on the afterlife of Anne Dangar

1 Albert Gleizes, letter to Grace Crowley, 18 September 1951, Grace Crowley papers, 1927–1974, MLMSS 3252/vols 2–7, MLMSS 3252/vol 1X, State Library of New South Wales, Gadigal Nura/Sydney.

2 Daniel Robbins, 'Albert Gleizes: reason and faith in modern painting', *Albert Gleizes 1881–1953: a retrospective exhibition*, exh cat, The Solomon R Guggenheim Museum, New York, in collaboration with Musée national d'art moderne, Paris, & Museum am Ostwall, Dortmund, 1964, p 24.

3 Albert Gleizes, 'La belle journée est passée …' (The beautiful day is over), *Zodiaque*, no 25, April 1955, unpag.

4 Topliss's book was, in fact, the second edited selection of Dangar's letters, Crowley having done the first in the late 1970s at the time she divided them to give to the Mitchell Library in Sydney and the National Art Archive, Art Gallery of New South Wales.

5 Grace Crowley, letter to Albert Gleizes, 16 September 1951, Fonds Albert Gleizes, MV 698–699, Kandinsky Library, Musée national d'art moderne, Centre Georges Pompidou, Paris.

6 Crowley, letter to Gleizes, 16 September 1951.

7 Mary Webb, letter to Grace Crowley, 16 February 1954, Grace Crowley archive, MS1980.1, National Art Archive, Art Gallery of New South Wales, Gadigal Nura/Sydney.

8 Mary Webb, letter to Grace Crowley, 21 October 1952, Grace Crowley papers, SLNSW.

9 Mary Webb, aerogram to Grace Crowley, 11 September 1953, Grace Crowley papers, SLNSW.

10 Mary Webb, letter to Grace Crowley, 31 December 1953, Grace Crowley archive, National Art Archive, AGNSW.

11 Mary Webb, aerogram to Grace Crowley, 31 January 1954, Grace Crowley archive, National Art Archive, AGNSW.

12 Webb, letter to Crowley, 16 February 1954.

13 Webb, letter to Crowley, 16 February 1954.

14 Mary Webb, aerogram to Grace Crowley, 15 March 1954, Grace Crowley archive, National Art Archive, AGNSW.

15 Hal Missingham, letter to Grace Crowley, 3 March 1954, Grace Crowley archive, National Art Archive, AGNSW.

16 Webb, aerogram to Crowley, 15 March 1954.

17 *Zodiaque*, no 25, April 1955, features a photo of Dangar's studio on the cover. Dangar had already been the subject of an article in *Zodiaque*, no 8, April 1952, unpag.

18 Mary Webb, aerogram to Grace Crowley, 5 July 1954, Grace Crowley archive, National Art Archive, AGNSW.

19 Mary Webb, aerogram to Grace Crowley, 12 March 1955, Grace Crowley archive, National Art Archive, AGNSW.

20 Mary Webb, aerogram to Grace Crowley, 18 May 1957, Grace Crowley archive, National Art Archive, AGNSW.

21 Grace Crowley, letter to Jim Alexander, 19 December 1976, Grace Crowley file, Jim Alexander Gallery records, MS 13705, State Library Victoria, Naarm/Narrm/Melbourne.

22 After Paris, *Du cubisme aux arts traditionnels* toured to Aix-en-Provence, Saint-Rémy-de-Provence, Toulon and Lyon.

23 Mary Webb, letter to Grace Crowley, 18 February 1955, Grace Crowley archive, National Art Archive, AGNSW.

24 In December 1958 it fell to Michel Seuphor to write to Crowley advising her of the passing of Mary Webb, the third death in eight years to reach out from France and touch Crowley. In his letter he expressed his hope, as he had in earlier letters about Dangar, that some of Webb's work would now enter the collections of museums in Australia. Dangar's work eventually did so in 1969, and Webb's in 1976—although a work by Webb was only exhibited in an Australian museum for the first time in 2011.

25 See Crowley's undated notes headed 'Some dates' regarding her 1960 trip to France, written for Daniel Thomas, the curator of her 1975 retrospective at the Art Gallery of New South Wales, Grace Crowley archive, National Art Archive, AGNSW.

26 For a complete list of exhibitions see 'Exhibition history' in this volume, p 222.

Exhibition history

This list includes all exhibitions known to feature Dangar's work during her lifetime and until the publication of this present volume. Exhibitions listed are derived from Anne Dangar's letters held across numerous archives worldwide, from the French press and journals as well as contemporaneous exhibition catalogues, Bruce Adams's PhD thesis and book *Rustic Cubism* 2004, and David Butcher's exhibition catalogue *Anne Dangar, céramiste: le cubisme au quotidien* 2016.

Solo exhibitions are marked with an asterisk [*].

1912

Exhibition of Anne Dangar's and pupils' work at Good Templars Hall, Thunggutti/Dunghutti Country/Kempsey, NSW, June

1915

Exhibition of Anne Dangar's and pupils' work at the Dangar family home 'Shaweetah', Thunggutti/Dunghutti Country/Kempsey, NSW, December

1919

Sydney Art School exhibition, galleries at Victoria Markets, Gadigal Nura/Sydney, October–December

1920

The Julian Ashton exhibition, Education Department's Art Gallery, Gadigal Nura/Sydney, 13–28 February

Exhibition of Australian art arranged with Gayfield Shaw, Marcus Clark and Co. department store, Mulubinba/Newcastle, NSW, 7–15 October

1921

Paintings in oil and water colours and drawings in black and white by eleven Australian women, Anthony Horderns' Fine Art Gallery, Gadigal Nura/Sydney, 1–14 June

1924

First annual exhibition of work by the Younger Group of Australian Artists, Anthony Horderns' Fine Art Gallery, Gadigal Nura/Sydney, July

1925

Second annual exhibition of the Younger Group of Australian Painters, Anthony Horderns' Fine Art Gallery, Gadigal Nura/Sydney, October

1929

Group still-life exhibition, Grosvenor Galleries, Gadigal Nura/Sydney, October

1931

* Exhibition of pottery, Moly-Sabata, Sablons, October–November

1932

First annual group exhibition of Moly-Sabata, Moly-Sabata, Sablons, spring

Exposition de poteries d'art rural, Musée d'Annonay, Annonay, November

Exposition régionale artisanale de Tournon, Tournon-sur-Rhône, December

1933

Exhibition of pottery and children's work, Moly-Sabata, Sablons, 2–16 July

Fête d'Annonay, Annonay, 14 July

Group exhibition, Le Pigeonnier, Saint-Félicien, August–September

1934

Group exhibition featuring Moly-Sabata, Le Pigeonnier, Saint-Félicien, August

Annual exhibition of Moly-Sabata, Moly-Sabata, Sablons, 7–31 October

Exhibition of Anglo-American painters, Association Florence Blumenthal, Paris, November

1935

Group exhibition, Musée d'Annonay, January

Association des artistes modernes américains et anglais, Galeries de Paris, Paris, July

Annual exhibition of Moly-Sabata, quai Jules-Roche, Serrières, 15–25 August

Group exhibition, Musée d'Annonay, September

Moly-Sabata exhibition, Stylclair, Lyon, November–December

1936

Annual exhibition of Moly-Sabata, Moly-Sabata, Sablons, 7–21 June

Group exhibition, gallery/shop of Jacques Martin, Grenoble, October–November

1937

Exhibition organised by Les amis d'Annonay, Hôtel de Ville, Annonay, February

* Solo exhibition, studio of Grace Crowley, Gadigal Nura/Sydney, April

Group display of Moly-Sabata, Pavillon du Forez-Vivarais, Exposition internationale des arts et techniques dans la vie moderne, Paris, 25 May – 25 November

Group exhibition of popular pottery, pavilion of the Union des artistes modernes, Exposition internationale des arts et techniques dans la vie moderne, Paris, 25 May – 25 November

Les maîtres de l'art indépendant, 1895–1937, Petit Palais, Paris, June–October

Group exhibition, gallery/shop of Jacques Martin, Grenoble, September–December

Group exhibition, Musée des arts décoratifs, Paris, December

1938

Exhibition of rural crafts, L'hôtel des syndicats du Sud-Est, Lyon, January

Group exhibition, Folklore, Lyon, February

Témoignage group exhibition, Galerie Matières et Formes, Paris, 10 May – 3 June

Groupe des indépendants d'Avignon, Avignon, May–June

32e groupe des artistes de ce temps, Petit Palais, Paris, June

Moly-Sabata, Galerie Sambon, Paris, June

Annual exhibition of Moly-Sabata, Moly-Sabata, Sablons, September

Group exhibition, Salon d'automne de Lyon, Lyon, 8 October – 17 November

Aspect actuel du cubisme chez quelques aînés et quelques jeunes, Salon d'automne, Paris, 11 November – 18 December

L'art sacré moderne, Musée des arts décoratif, Paris, December

1940

Artisans de France, Galerie Révillon, Paris, 10 April – 10 May

1941

Moly-Sabata exhibition, Annonay, May
Group exhibition, Musée d'Avignon, Avignon, May
Group exhibition curated by Jean Chevalier, Vienne, June

1942

Group exhibition of ceramics, Galerie Solution, Lyon, May
Annual exhibition of Moly-Sabata, Moly-Sabata, Sablons, 26 September – 4 October

1944

Spring collective exhibition of the Association des amis du musée, Musée de Valence, Valence, April

1945

Annual exhibition of Moly-Sabata, Moly-Sabata, Sablons, September
Les colonies françaises, Moly-Sabata, Sablons, 29 September – 7 October
Group exhibition, Folklore, Lyon, 8 December 1945 – 8 January 1946

1946

Group exhibition, Galerie M.A.I., Paris, April
Foreign art by artists living in the neighbourhood of Lyon, Galerie Annette Richard, Lyon, December

1947

Art sacré contemporain [with Albert Gleizes], Chapelle du lycée, Ampère, 13 September – 20 October
Artisanat français et exotique—poteries et tissages de Moly-Sabata—meubles Stylclair, Folklore, Lyon, 2–31 December

1948

Artisans de France, Galerie Révillon, Paris, April
Albert Gleizes [gouaches by Gleizes, ceramics after Gleizes by Dangar], Galerie des Garets, Paris, 20 April – 11 May
Group exhibition, 'La Bastie' gallery, Avignon, June
Exposition d'art sacré, Palais des Papes, Avignon, 20 July – 30 October
Salon d'automne, Lyon, autumn
Group exhibition, Galerie Style, Saint-Étienne, November

1949

Premier salon international du groupe Contraste, Palais municipal, Lyon, 15 January – 6 February
Exhibition of sacred art, Grenoble, May
Group exhibition, Sorgues, May
Exposition du Dauphiné, Moly-Sabata, Sablons, 16 July
Salon d'automne, Lyon, October
Group exhibition, Folklore, Lyon, December

1950

Exhibition of sacred art, Vézelay, March–April
Group exhibition, Sorgues, May
Group exhibition, Folklore, Lyon, December
Group exhibition, Galerie Style, Saint-Étienne, December

1951

Group exhibition of pottery, Aix-en-Provence, February–March

1953

Du cubisme aux arts traditionnels, École des beaux-arts, Paris, March–April; touring to Aix-en-Provence, Saint-Rémy-de-Provence, Toulon and Lyon [unknown dates]

1960

École de Paris: art décoratif, National Museum of Western Art, Tokyo, 15 October 1960 – 11 December 1961

1971

L'art de la poterie en France de Rodin à Dufy, Musée national de céramique, Sèvres, 9 June – 25 October

1975

Project 4: Grace Crowley, Art Gallery of New South Wales, Gadigal Nura/Sydney, 10 May – 8 June

1978

Australian pottery, 1900 to 1950, Shepparton Arts Centre, Vic, 5 September – 5 Oct; touring to Art Gallery of New South Wales, Gadigal Nura/Sydney, 7 December 1978 – 9 January 1979; National Gallery of Victoria, Naarm/Narrm/Melbourne, 18 January – 8 February 1979; and Art Gallery of South Australia, Tarntanya/Adelaide, 24 February – 25 March 1979

1981

Paris-Paris: créations en France, 1937–1957, Centre Georges Pompidou, Paris, 28 May 1981 – 2 November 1982
Céramique française contemporaine: sources et courants, Musée des arts décoratifs, Paris, 16 October 1981 – 4 January 1982

1984

Autour d'Albert Gleizes, Town Hall, Étretat, 28 July – 16 August

1987

Survey of drawings, Woolloomooloo Gallery, Gadigal Nura/Sydney, 18 March – 5 April

1989

Marcel Michaud: Stylclair-groupe Témoignage, Espace lyonnais d'art contemporain, Lyon, 29 April – 4 June

1991

* *Anne Dangar*, Fondation Albert Gleizes, Moly-Sabata, Sablons, 6–21 April

1995

Women hold up half the sky, National Gallery of Australia, Kamberri/Canberra, 8 March – 25 April
Delinquent angel: Australian historical, Aboriginal and contemporary ceramics, Museo internazionale delle ceramiche, Faenza, Italy, 16 September – 22 October

1997

Un combat pour l'art moderne, hommage à René Deroudille, Musée des beaux-arts, Lyon, 26 May – 26 August

1999

L'art de la terre vernissée: du moyen âge à l'an 2000, Musée des beaux-arts, Arras, 4 February – 30 April; touring to Musée national de la céramique, Sèvres, 1 October 1999 – 10 January 2000

2000

Céramiques de peintres, Musée de la faïence, Marseille, 22 June – 17 September

Modern Australian women: paintings and prints 1925–1945, Art Gallery of South Australia, Tarntanya/Adelaide, 24 November 2000 – 25 February 2001; National Gallery of Australia, Kamberri/Canberra, 13 July – 26 August 2001

2001

**Anne Dangar at Moly-Sabata: tradition and innovation*, National Gallery of Australia, Kamberri/Canberra, 13 July – 28 October

2002

De la couleur et du feu, céramiques d'artistes de 1885 à nos jours, Musée de la faïence, Château Pastré, Marseille, 23 June – 3 September

2003

Patrimoine en Isère: pays de Roussillon, Town Hall, Roussillon, 21 September – 30 November

2006

* *'Miss Dangar', potière: 1885–1951*, La fabrique du pont d'Aleyrac, Saint-Pierreville, 16 September – 12 November

2009

Albert Gleizes & Moly-Sabata—Anne Dangar, Jean-Claude Libert, Robert Pouyaud, Maison des arts, Antony, 12 May – 25 July

Anne Dangar et les Sablonnais, Moly-Sabata, Sablons, 18–19 September

Cubism and Australian art, Heide Museum of Modern Art, Naarm/Narrm/Melbourne, 24 November 2009 – 8 April 2010

2011

Le poids du monde: Marcel Michaud (1898–1958), Musée des beaux-arts de Lyon, 22 October 2011 – 23 January 2012

2012

Transmission: trois potières 1931–2012: Anne Dangar—Geneviève de Cissey—Aguilberte Dalban, Fondation Albert Gleizes, Moly-Sabata, Sablons, 15–16 September

Dessins des enfants de Sablons dirigés par Anne Dangar en 1944, Moly-Sabata, Sablons, 15–16 September

Lyon et l'art moderne 1920–1941, de Bonnard à Signac, Musée municipal Paul-Dini, Villefrance-sur-Saône, 14 October 2012 – 10 February 2013

2013

Sydney moderns: art for a new world, Art Gallery of New South Wales, Gadigal Nura/Sydney, 6 July – 7 October

2014

Albert Gleizes et ses disciples: René-Maria Burlet, Jean Chevalier, Anne Dangar, Daniel Gloria, Andrée Le Coultre, Robert Pouyaud, Paul Règny, Masion Ravier, Morestel, 30 March – 22 June

2015

Los modernos, Museo Nacional de Arte, Mexico City, 11 November 2015 – 3 April 2016; touring to Museo de las Artes Universidad de Guadalajara, Guadalajara, 21 April – 10 July 2016

2016

**Anne Dangar, céramiste: le cubisme au quotidien*, Musée de Valence, Valence, 16 June 2016 – 26 February 2017

2017

Abstraction: celebrating Australian women abstract artists, National Gallery of Australia touring exhibition: Geelong Art Gallery, Vic, 25 February – 7 May 2017; Newcastle Art Gallery, NSW, 21 May – 23 July 2017; Cairns Art Gallery, Qld, 15 September – 24 November 2017; Tweed Regional Gallery, Murwillumbah, NSW, 2 March – 20 May 2018; QUT Art Museum, Meeanjin/Brisbane, 1 June – 26 August 2018

2018

**Anne Dangar: ceramics from Moly-Sabata*, Art Gallery of New South Wales, Gadigal Nura/Sydney, 11 August – 21 October

2020

Know My Name: Australian women artists 1900 to now, part 1, National Gallery of Australia, Kamberri/Canberra, 14 November 2020 – 4 July 2021

2022

Vivre le cubisme à Moly-Sabata, Musée de l'ancien évêché, Grenoble, 25 May – 9 October

Catalogue of exhibited works

All works are from the collection of the National Gallery of Australia unless otherwise stated.

Works by Anne Dangar are ordered first by media then chronologically. They are followed by collaborative works, then works by associated artists listed alphabetically by name then chronologically. Works created by Dangar's students are listed at the end.

Measurements are height × width × depth or height × diameter at the widest point. Image measurements refer to the edge of painted surfaces and sheet measurements to the whole page. Sight measurements refer to the visible area of a work that may be obscured by a frame or matte.

Dangar rarely titled or dated her ceramics. Most have been designated curatorially derived titles and dates. These titles are listed in roman, with artist-given titles in italics. Collaborations with and after Albert Gleizes are recorded in italics and correspond with his original titles. Brackets around a date-span indicates the work is known to have been made in that period, though the work itself is undated. These dates have been established through archival and provenance research, stylistic analysis and the use of Dangar's monogram. Prior to 1930 she signed her ceramics 'AD'. From 1933 she signed her ceramics 'MSD' or a variation of 'MSGD'.

From 1930 Dangar worked in several potteries in different departments of the Auvergne-Rhône-Alpes region of France, including Saint-Désirat in the Ardèche; Roussillon in Isère; and Saint-Vallier, Saint-Uze and Cliousclat in the Drôme. From 1947 she also worked out of her own pottery at Moly-Sabata, Sablons, in Isère. Though the identity of the pottery cannot always be confirmed, Dangar's ceramics were produced in one of these locations and the place of creation is listed as Auvergne-Rhône-Alpes, France. Exhibitions held in Dangar's lifetime are included where known or likely.

ANNE DANGAR
Australia 1885 – France 1951

CERAMICS

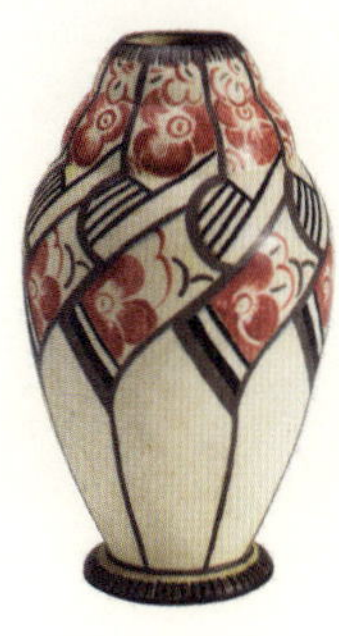

cat 1 p 43
Vase (1926–29)
Paris or Gadigal Nura/Sydney
glazed handpainted earthenware
21.5 × 12 (diam) cm
monogram on base, 'AD'
private collection

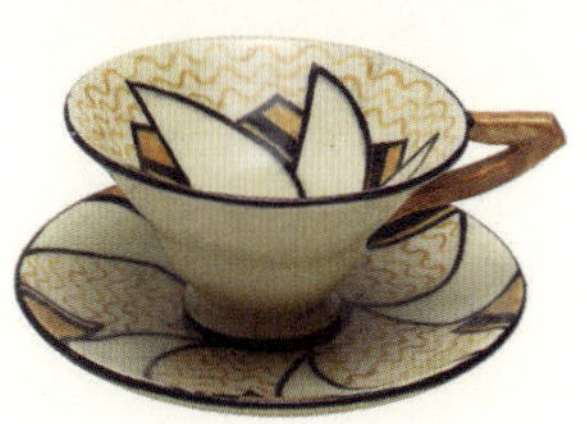

cat 2
Teacup and saucer (1926–29)
Paris or Gadigal Nura/Sydney
glazed handpainted earthenware
7 × 13 (diam) cm (overall)
monogram on base, 'AD'
collection of Mary Ralston,
great-great-niece of Anne Dangar

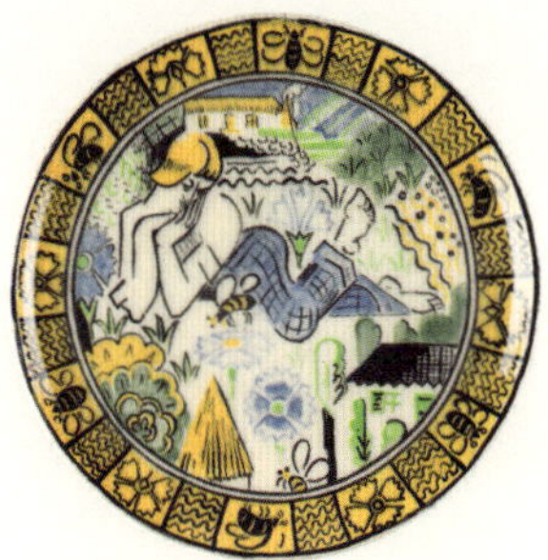

cat 3 p 37
Illustration to a poem by James Stephens plate
(1926–29)
Paris or Gadigal Nura/Sydney
glazed handpainted earthenware
3.7 × 32.5 (diam) cm
monogram and inscription on base, 'AD /
Illustration to a poem / by James Stephens.'
Powerhouse Museum, Gadigal Nura/Sydney
Daphne Mayo Bequest 1981
A8174

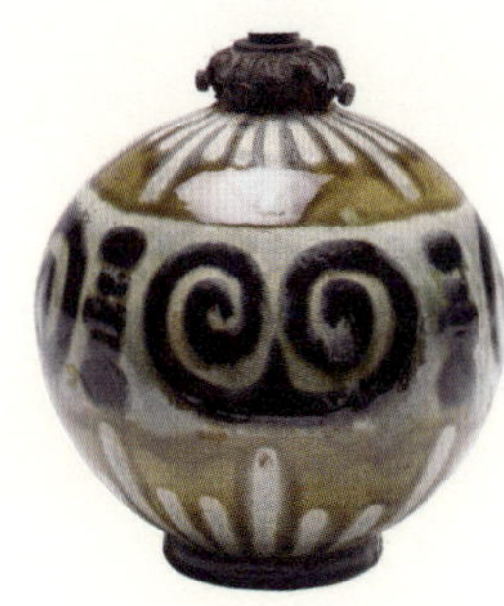

cat 4
Lamp base 1929
Gadigal Nura/Sydney
glazed earthenware
16 × 13.5 (diam) cm
monogram on base, 'AD'
collection of Margaret Cargill,
great-niece of Anne Dangar

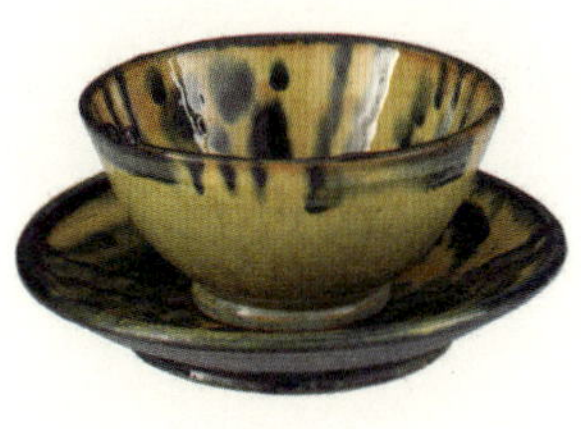

cat 5 p 72
Bowl and saucer (1930–32)
Auvergne-Rhône-Alpes, France
wheel-thrown glazed earthenware
with slip decoration
8.5 × 18.4 (diam) cm (overall)
monogram on base, 'A'
National Gallery of Victoria, Naarm/Narrm/
Melbourne
Gwynneth White Adamson Bequest 1997
1997.113.A-B

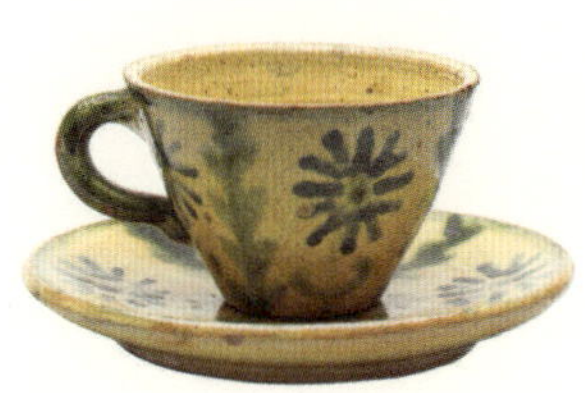

cat 6 p 73
Cup and saucer (1930–32)
Auvergne-Rhône-Alpes, France
wheel-thrown glazed earthenware
with slip decoration
8.5 × 18.5 (diam) cm (overall)
no inscriptions
Art Gallery of South Australia, Tarntanya/
Adelaide
South Australian Government Grant 1997
973C18A(A&B)

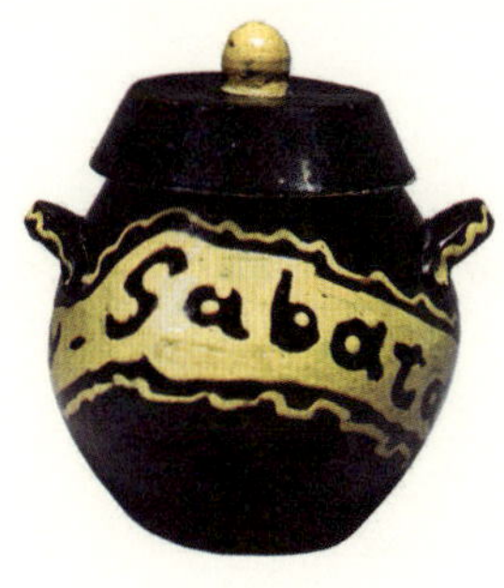

cat 7 p 79
Moly-Sabata honey pot with lid (1931–33)
Auvergne-Rhône-Alpes, France
wheel-thrown glazed earthenware
with slip decoration
28.5 × 20.5 (irreg diam) cm (overall)
no inscriptions
purchased 2002
2002.50.A-B

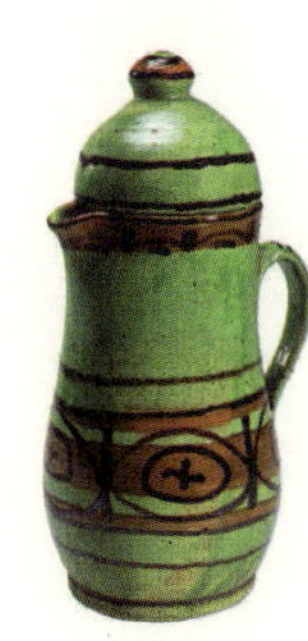

cat 8 p 77
Coffee pot with lid (1931–33)
Auvergne-Rhône-Alpes, France
wheel-thrown glazed earthenware
with slip decoration
29 × 12 (irreg diam) cm (overall)
no inscriptions
purchased 2002
2002.47.A-B

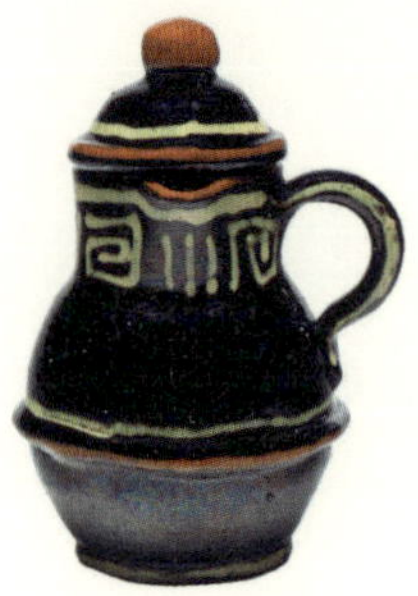

cat 9
Hot-water jug with lid (1931–32)
Auvergne-Rhône-Alpes, France
wheel-thrown glazed earthenware
with slip decoration
18.5 × 14.5 (irreg diam) cm (overall)
no inscriptions
Art Gallery of New South Wales, Gadigal
Nura/Sydney
purchased with funds provided by
the Mollie Douglas Bequest 2017
17.2017.A-B

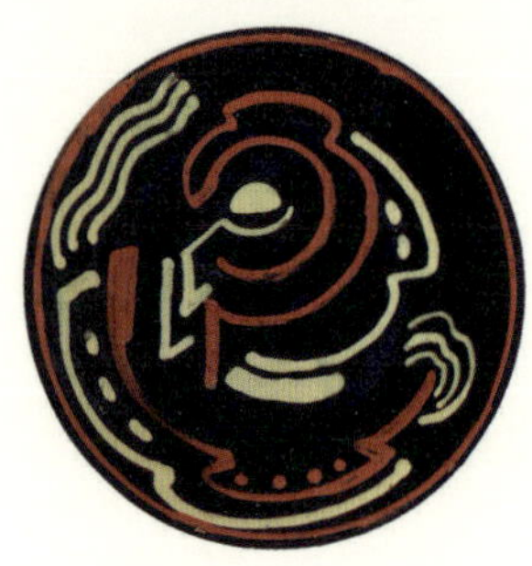

cat 10
Plate with cubist design (1931–33)
Auvergne-Rhône-Alpes, France
wheel-thrown glazed earthenware
with slip decoration
3 × 25 (diam) cm
no inscriptions
Art Gallery of New South Wales, Gadigal
Nura/Sydney
purchased with funds provided by
the Mollie Douglas Bequest 2017
18.2017

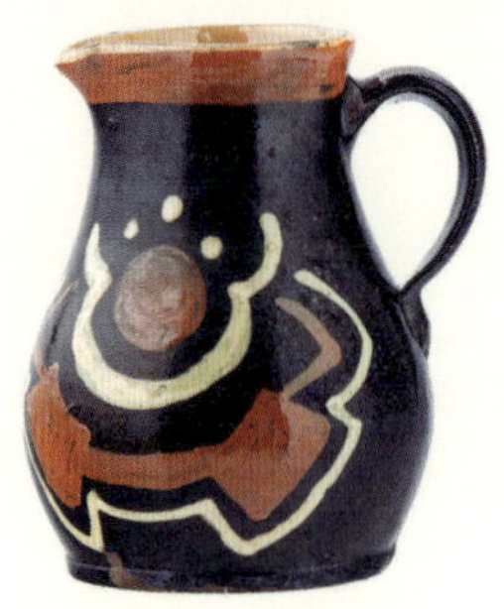

cat 11 p 100
Jug (1931–33)
Auvergne-Rhône-Alpes, France
wheel-thrown glazed earthenware
with slip decoration
16.5 × 14 (irreg diam) cm
no inscriptions
Art Gallery of South Australia, Tarntanya/
Adelaide
gift of Joan Beer, Frank Choate, Elizabeth
H Finnegan OAM, Theo S Maras AM OLJ,
David McKee, Pam McKee, Diana McLaurin,
Tom Pearce and John Phillips through the
Art Gallery of South Australia Foundation
Collectors Club 2013
20138C147A

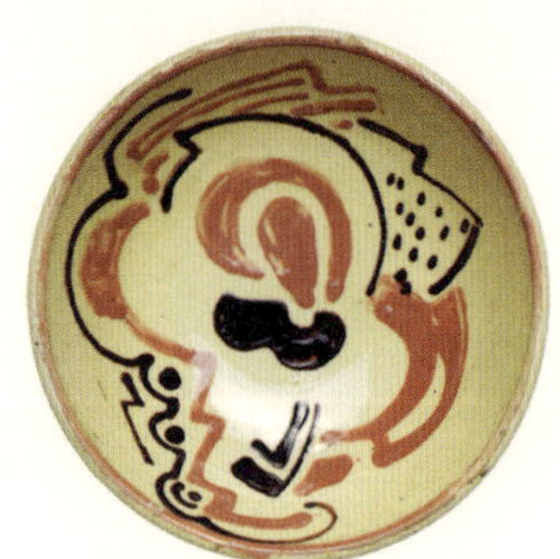

cat 12 p 123
Bowl (1931–33)
Auvergne-Rhône-Alpes, France
wheel-thrown glazed earthenware
with slip decoration
5 × 18 (diam) cm
no inscriptions
collection of Colin Beutel and Conal Coad

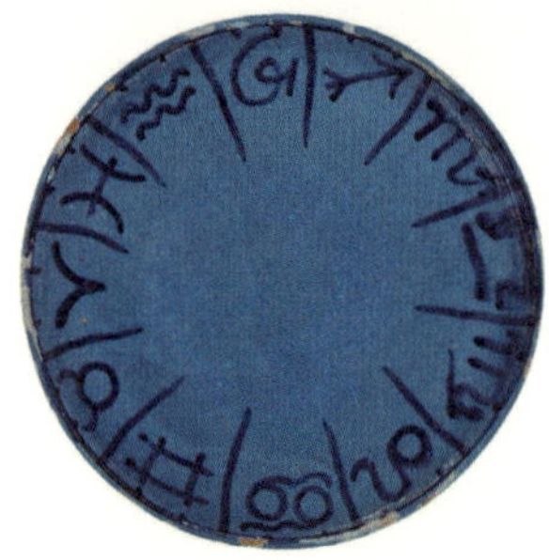

cat 13
Plate decorated with signs of the zodiac
(1932–33)
Auvergne-Rhône-Alpes, France
wheel-thrown glazed earthenware
with slip decoration
3.5 × 38.5 (diam) cm
no inscriptions
Art Gallery of New South Wales, Gadigal
Nura/Sydney
gift of Grace Crowley 1969
C6.1969

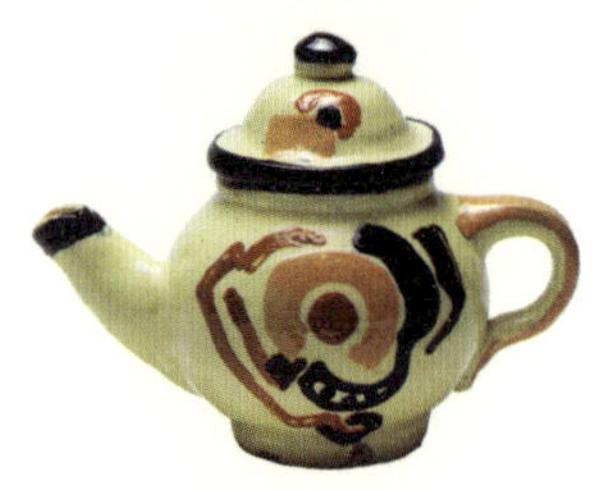

cat 14 p 74
Teapot (1932–33)
Auvergne-Rhône-Alpes, France
wheel-thrown glazed earthenware
with slip decoration
15.7 × 21.1 × 12.8 cm (overall)
no inscriptions
purchased 1977
77.275.A-B

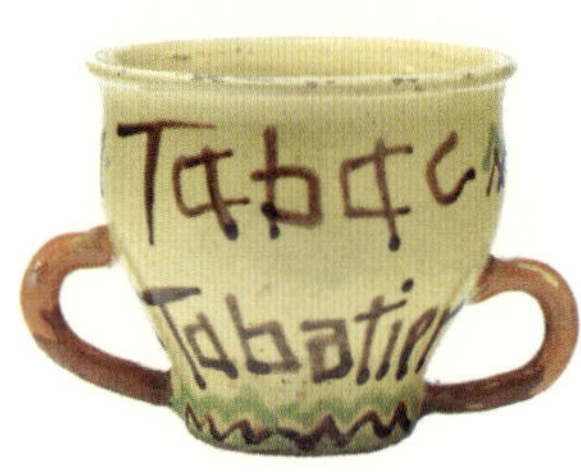

cat 15 p 75
Tobacco jar (1932–33)
Auvergne-Rhône-Alpes, France
wheel-thrown glazed earthenware
with slip decoration
13.2 × 20.4 × 15.5 cm (irreg)
no inscriptions
Art Gallery of New South Wales, Gadigal
Nura/Sydney
gift of Mrs Fizelle 1970
C1.1970

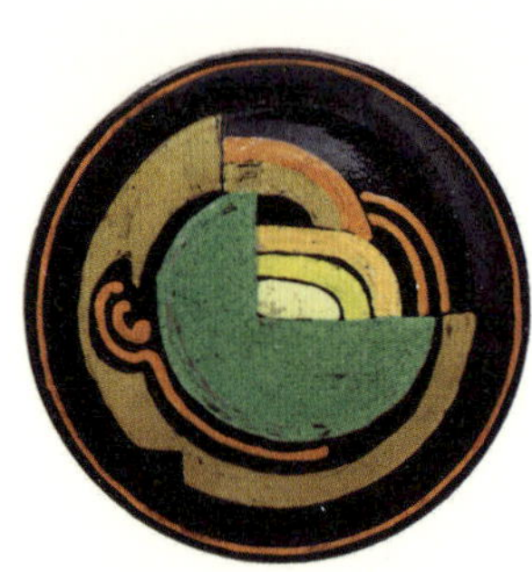

cat 16 p 82
Plate with cubist design (1932–33)
Auvergne-Rhône-Alpes, France
wheel-thrown glazed earthenware
with slip decoration
3 × 36 (diam) cm
no inscriptions
bequest of Michael Fizelle 1985
85.562

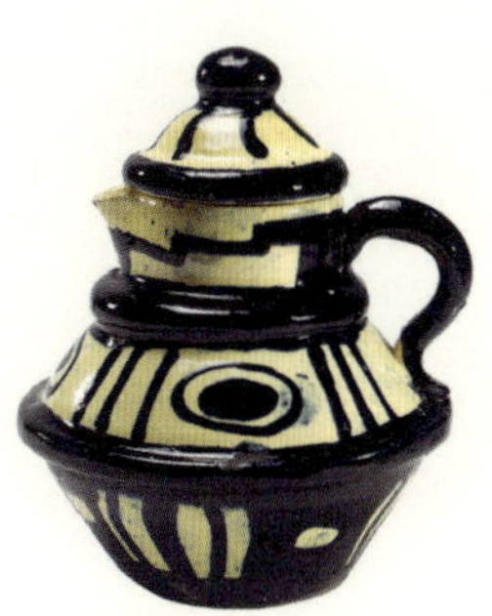

cat 17 p 76
Coffee pot with lid (1932–33)
Auvergne-Rhône-Alpes, France
wheel-thrown glazed earthenware
with slip decoration
18 × 15 × 15.5 cm (overall)
no inscriptions
gift of Grace Buckley in memory
of Grace Crowley 1982
82.239.A-B

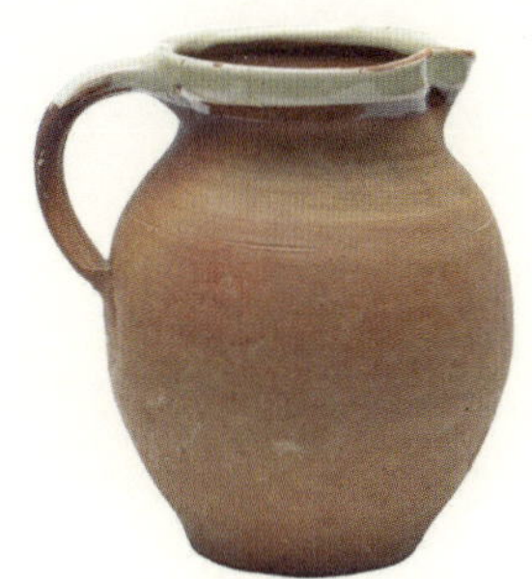

cat 18
Jug (1933–35)
Auvergne-Rhône-Alpes, France
wheel-thrown earthenware, partially-glazed
17 × 16 (irreg diam) cm
no inscriptions
Art Gallery of South Australia, Tarntanya/
Adelaide
gift of the Michelmore family in recognition
of Tracey Lock curating the exhibition *Dorrit
Black: unseen forces*, Art Gallery of South
Australia 2014
20146C24

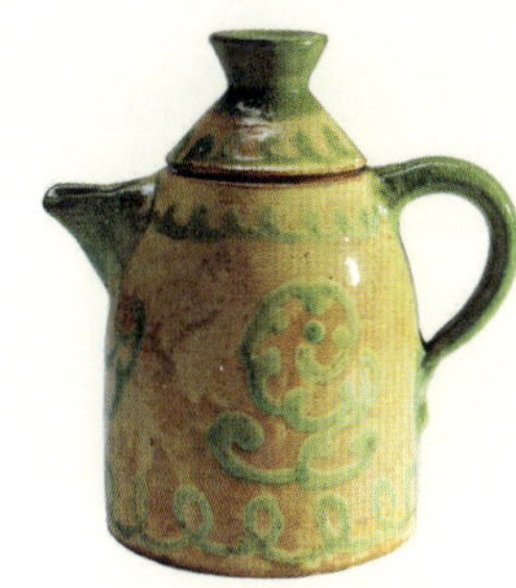

cat 19
Teapot (1933–35)
Auvergne-Rhône-Alpes, France
wheel-thrown glazed earthenware
with slip decoration
19.5 × 19 (irreg diam) cm (overall)
monogram below handle, 'MSD'
collection of Mary Ralston,
great-great-niece of Anne Dangar

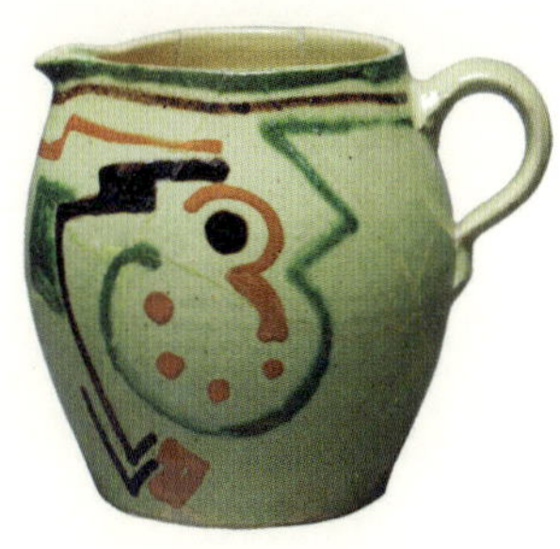

cat 20 p 120
Jug (1933–38)
Auvergne-Rhône-Alpes, France
wheel-thrown glazed earthenware
with slip decoration
15.2 × 17.8 × 14.7 cm
monogram near base, 'MSD'
bequest of Eileen Berndt 1991
92.139

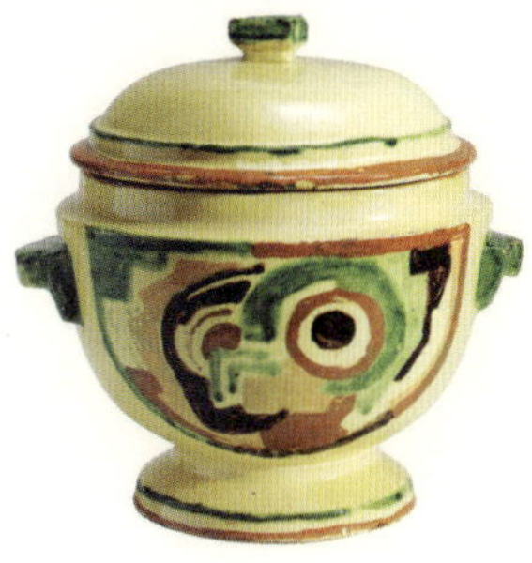

cat 21 p 121
Soup tureen with cubist design (1933–38)
Auvergne-Rhône-Alpes, France
wheel-thrown glazed earthenware
with slip decoration
27.5 × 29 × 25 cm (overall)
monogram near base, 'MSD'
bequest of Eileen Berndt 1991
92.140.A-B

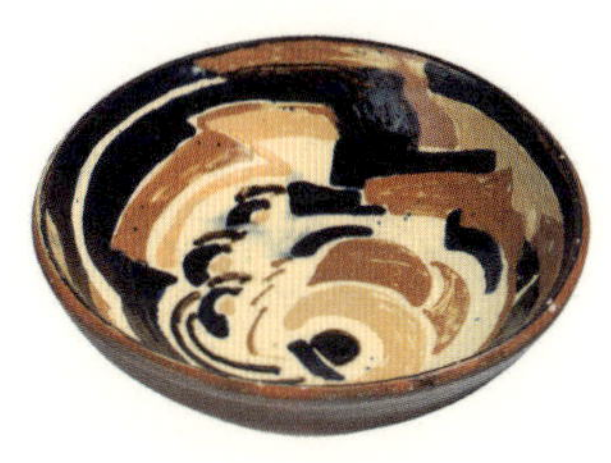

cat 22 p 129
Bowl with cubist design (1933–38)
Auvergne-Rhône-Alpes, France
wheel-thrown glazed earthenware
with slip decoration
8.1 × 28.4 (diam) cm
monogram on side, 'MSD'
gift of Grace Crowley 1979
79.1308

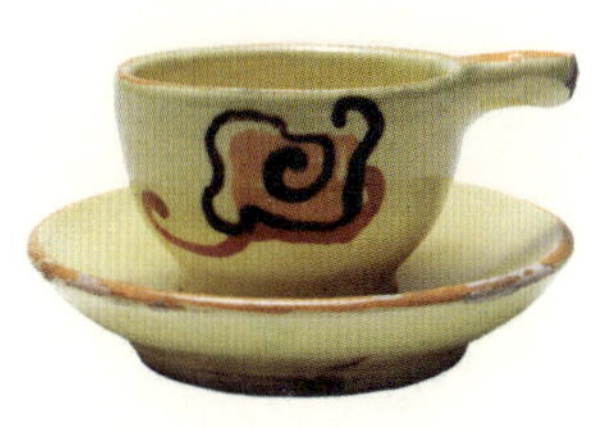

cat 23
Cup and saucer (1933–38)
Auvergne-Rhône-Alpes, France
wheel-thrown glazed earthenware
with slip decoration
8.5 × 13.9 (diam) cm (overall)
monogram on verso of saucer, 'MSD'
purchased 1978
78.1156.A-B

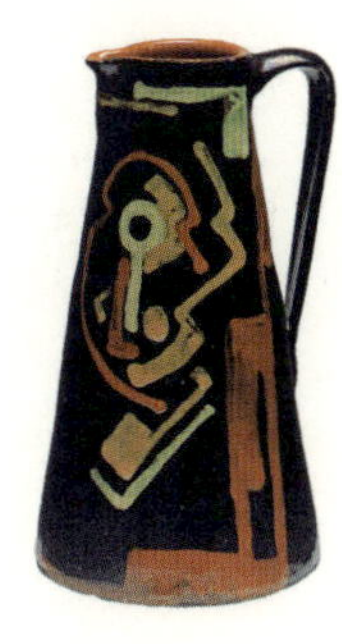

cat 24 p 124
Jug (1933–38)
Auvergne-Rhône-Alpes, France
wheel-thrown glazed earthenware
with slip decoration
23.9 × 13.7 (irreg diam) cm
monogram on side, 'MSD'
gift of Grace Crowley 1979
79.1307

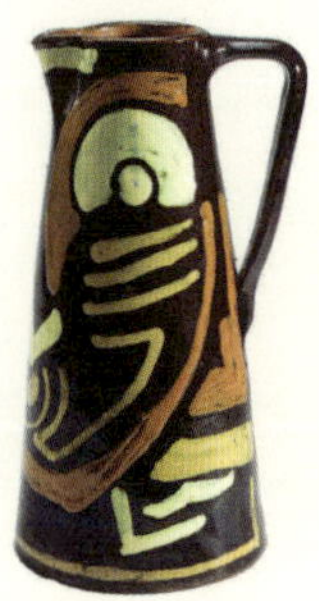

cat 25 p 125
Jug (1933–38)
Auvergne-Rhône-Alpes, France
wheel-thrown glazed earthenware
with slip decoration
26.6 × 13.2 (irreg diam) cm
monogram at base below handle, 'MSD'
bequest of Michael Fizelle 1985
85.561

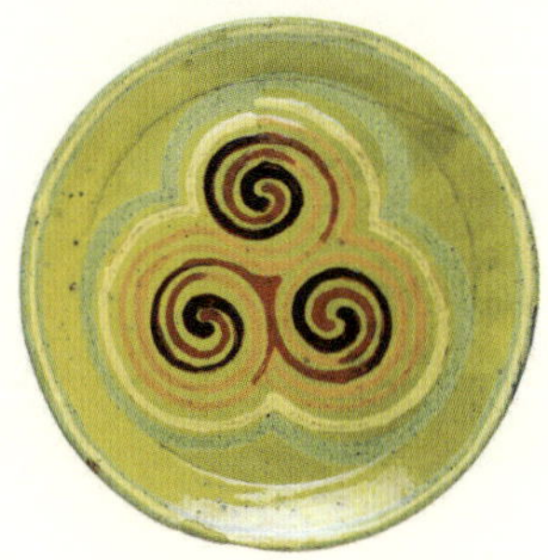

cat 26 p 201
Plate (1933–38)
Auvergne-Rhône-Alpes, France
wheel-thrown glazed earthenware
with slip decoration
3 × 37.4 (diam) cm
monogram on base, 'MSD'
gift of Grace Buckley in memory
of Grace Crowley 1982
82.236

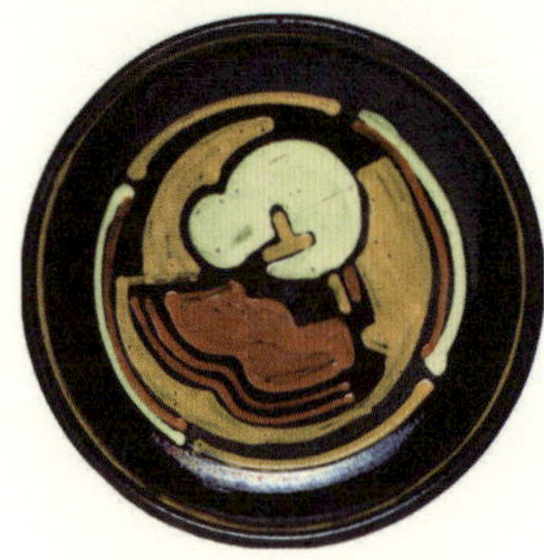

cat 27 p 128
Plate with cubist design (1933–38)
Auvergne-Rhône-Alpes, France
wheel-thrown glazed earthenware
with slip decoration
3.8 × 25.5 (diam) cm
monogram on side, 'MSD'
purchased 1978
78.1155

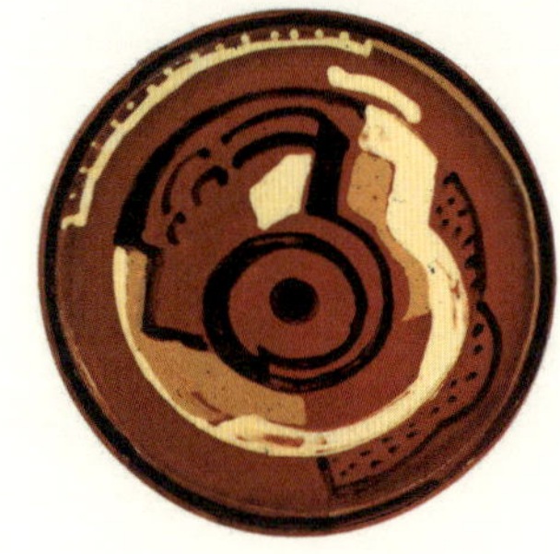

cat 28
Plate with cubist design (1933–38)
Auvergne-Rhône-Alpes, France
wheel-thrown glazed earthenware
with slip decoration
3 × 26.3 (diam) cm
monogram on verso, 'MSD'
Art Gallery of New South Wales, Gadigal
Nura/Sydney
gift of Mrs Michael Fizelle 1969
C4.1969

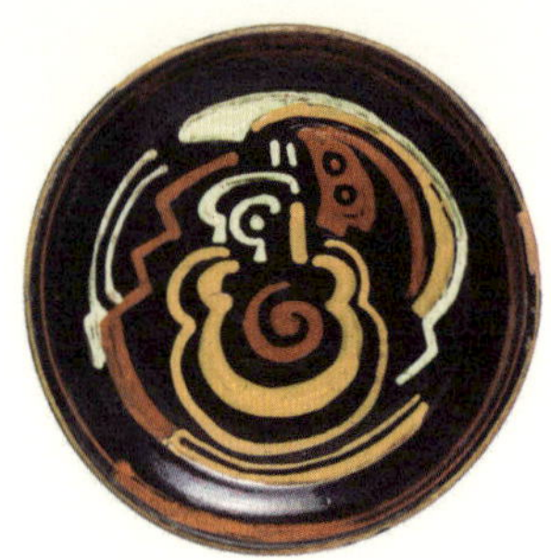

cat 29
Plate (1933–38)
Auvergne-Rhône-Alpes, France
wheel-thrown glazed earthenware
with slip decoration
4.5 × 33 (diam) cm
monogram on verso, 'MSD'
collection of Colin Beutel and Conal Coad

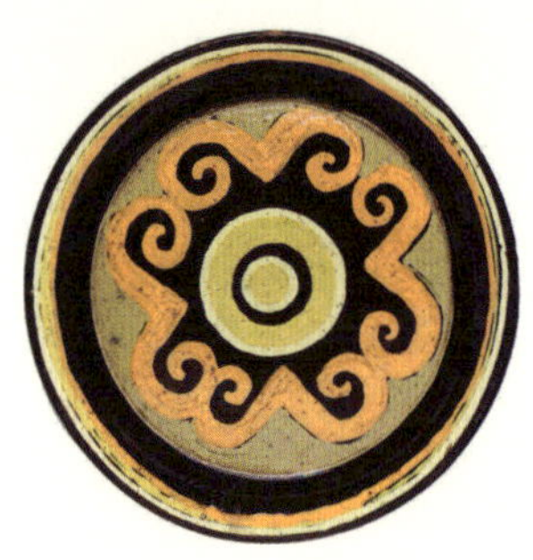

cat 30 p 126
Plate (1933–38)
Auvergne-Rhône-Alpes, France
wheel-thrown glazed earthenware
with slip decoration
2.5 × 40 (diam) cm
monogram on rim of base, 'MSD'
collection of Colin Beutel and Conal Coad

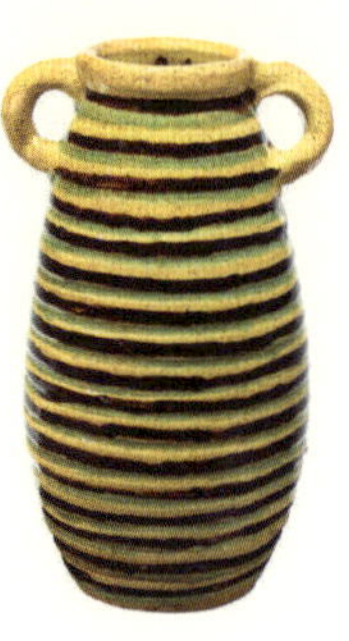

cat 31 p 78
Vase (1933–46)
Auvergne-Rhône-Alpes, France
wheel-thrown glazed earthenware
with slip decoration
30 × 18 (irreg diam) cm
monogram inside lip, 'MSD'
Art Gallery of New South Wales, Gadigal
Nura/Sydney
purchased with funds provided by the
Mollie Douglas Bequest 2017
27.2017

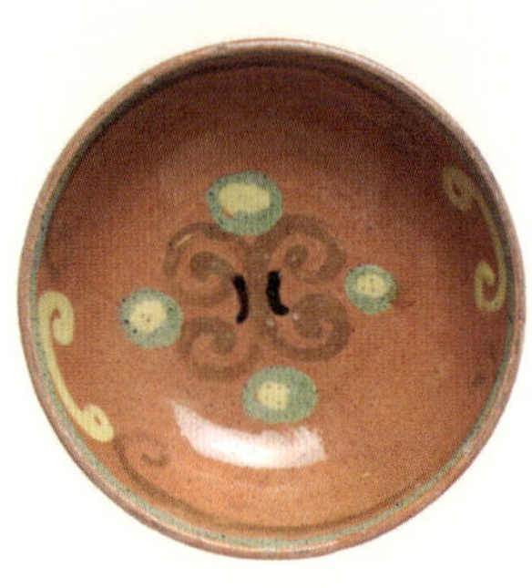

cat 32
Bowl (1933–50)
Auvergne-Rhône-Alpes, France
wheel-thrown glazed earthenware
with slip decoration
5 × 18.6 (diam) cm
monogram on side, 'MSD'
collection of Colin Beutel and Conal Coad

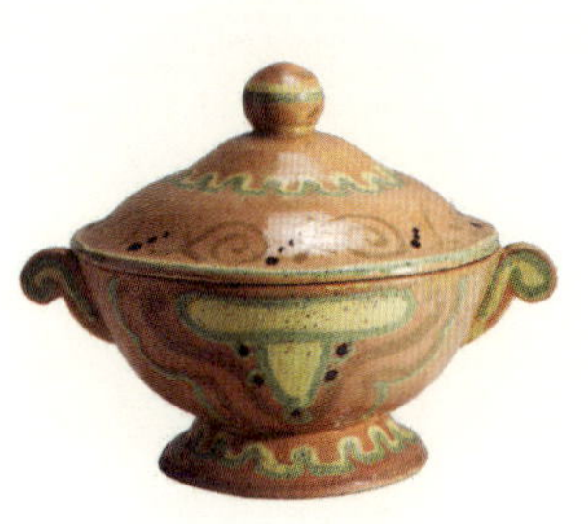

cat 33
Soup tureen (1933–50)
Auvergne-Rhône-Alpes, France
wheel-thrown glazed earthenware
with slip decoration
25 × 33.5 × 26 cm (overall)
monogram on base, 'MSD'
collection of Colin Beutel and Conal Coad

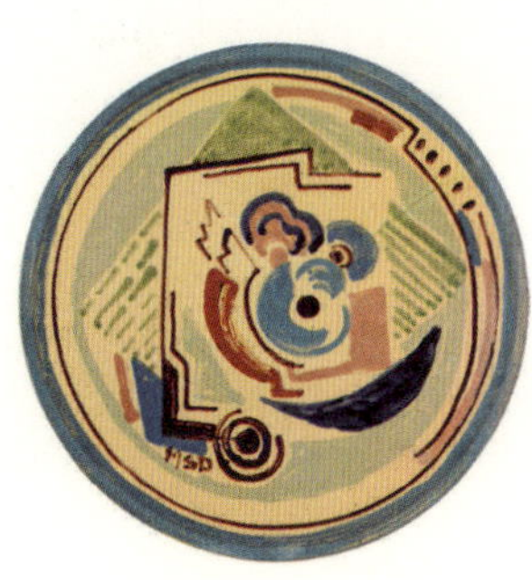

cat 34 p 89
Cubist plaque (1933–50)
Auvergne-Rhône-Alpes, France
wheel-thrown glazed earthenware
with slip decoration
3 × 38.5 (diam) cm
monogram lower left, 'MSD'
Art Gallery of New South Wales, Gadigal Nura/Sydney
purchased with funds provided by the Mollie Douglas Bequest 2017
85.2017

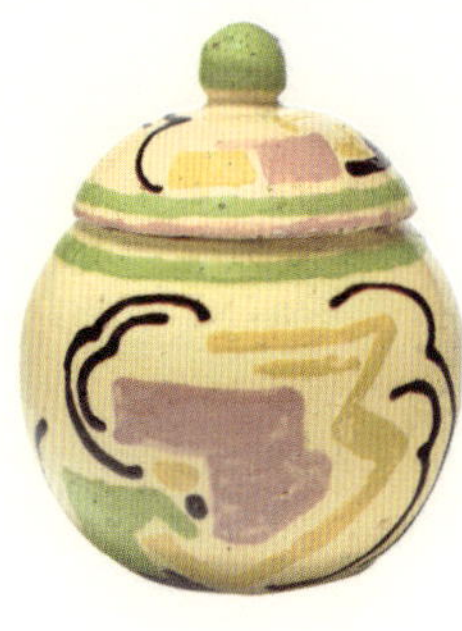

cat 35 p 122
Jar with cubist design (1933–50)
Auvergne-Rhône-Alpes, France
wheel-thrown glazed earthenware
with slip decoration
17 × 14 (diam) cm (overall)
monogram inside lid, 'M.S.D.'
Art Gallery of New South Wales, Gadigal Nura/Sydney
purchased with funds provided by the Mollie Douglas Bequest 2017
19.2017.A-B

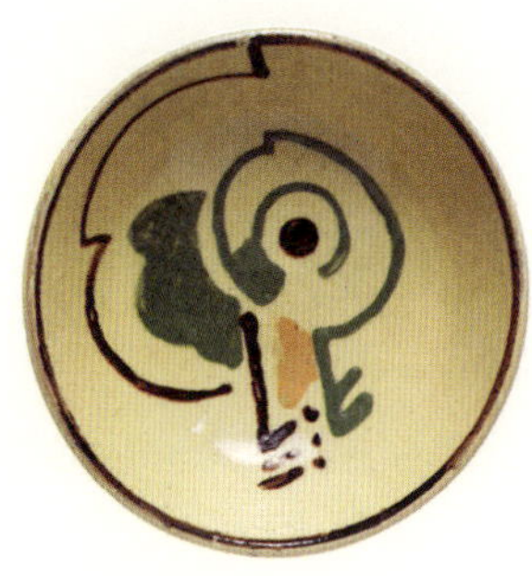

cat 36
Bowl (1933–50)
Auvergne-Rhône-Alpes, France
wheel-thrown glazed earthenware
with slip decoration
5 × 18.5 (diam) cm
monogram on side, 'MSD'
collection of Colin Beutel and Conal Coad

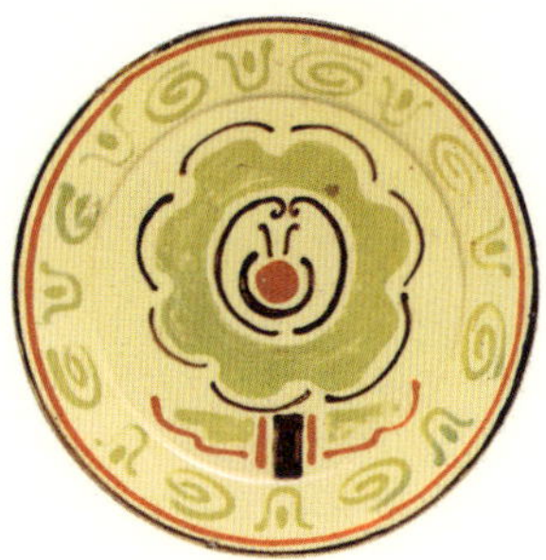

cat 37
Plate (1933–50)
Auvergne-Rhône-Alpes, France
wheel-thrown glazed earthenware
with slip decoration
2.5 × 33 (diam) cm
monogram on verso, 'MSD'
collection of Colin Beutel and Conal Coad

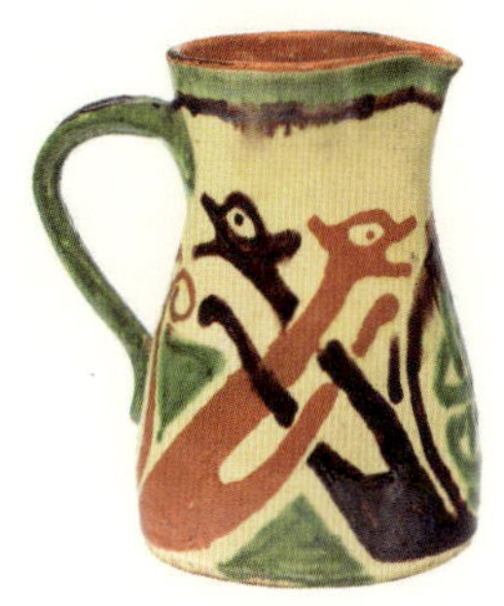

cat 38 p 118
Jug with Celtic serpent design (1933–50)
Auvergne-Rhône-Alpes, France
wheel-thrown glazed earthenware
with slip decoration
23.5 × 21.5 (irreg diam) cm
monogram below handle, 'MSD'
Art Gallery of New South Wales, Gadigal Nura/Sydney
purchased with funds provided by the Mollie Douglas Bequest 2017
83.2017

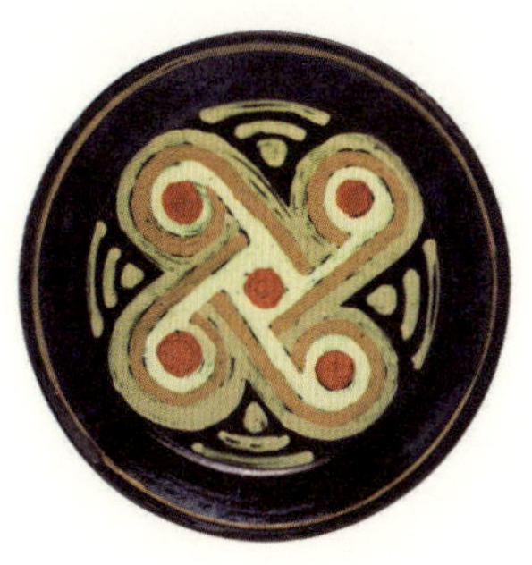

cat 39
Plate with Celtic-style decoration (1933–50)
Auvergne-Rhône-Alpes, France
wheel-thrown glazed earthenware
with slip decoration
2 × 35.7 (diam) cm
monogram on base of edge, 'MSD'
purchased 2002
2002.44

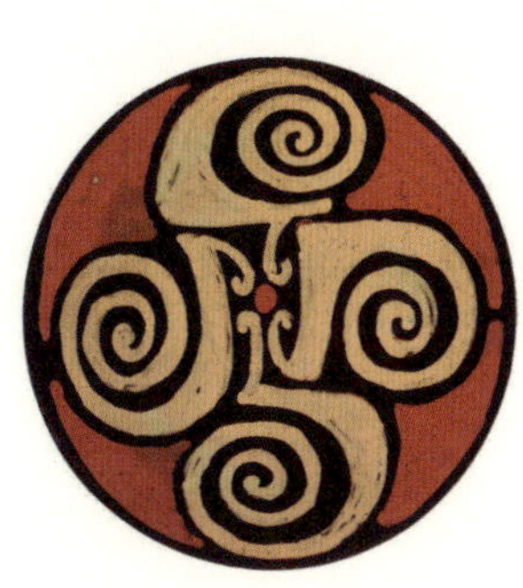

cat 40 p 127
Plate with spiral design (1933–50)
Auvergne-Rhône-Alpes, France
wheel-thrown glazed earthenware
with slip decoration
7.5 × 34 (diam) cm
monogram on verso, 'MSD'
Art Gallery of New South Wales, Gadigal Nura/Sydney
purchased with funds provided by the Mollie Douglas Bequest 2017
21.2017

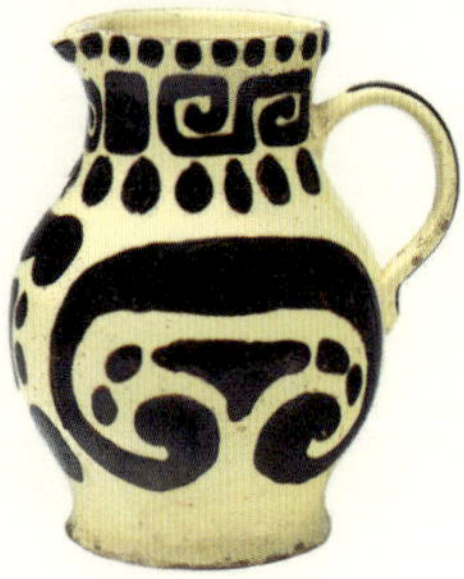

cat 41 p 156
Water jug (1933–50)
Auvergne-Rhône-Alpes, France
wheel-thrown glazed earthenware
with slip decoration
22 × 20 (irreg diam) cm
monogram below handle, 'M.S.D.'
Art Gallery of New South Wales, Gadigal Nura/Sydney
purchased with funds provided by the Mollie Douglas Bequest 2017
16.2017

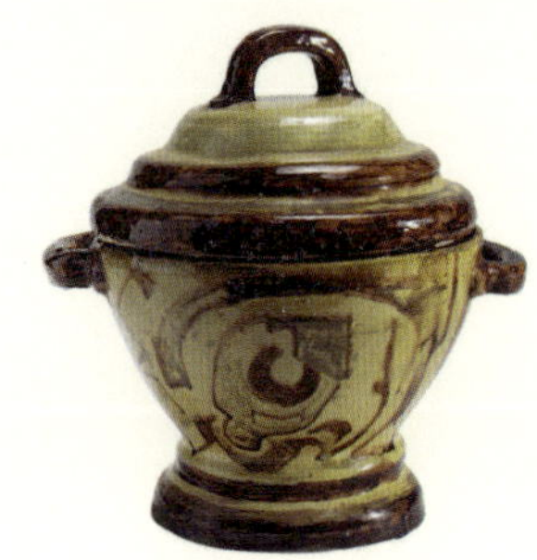

cat 42
Soup tureen with cubist design (1933–50)
Auvergne-Rhône-Alpes, France
wheel-thrown glazed earthenware
with slip decoration
28 × 32 × 34 cm (overall)
monogram on base, 'MSD'
collection of Colin Beutel and Conal Coad

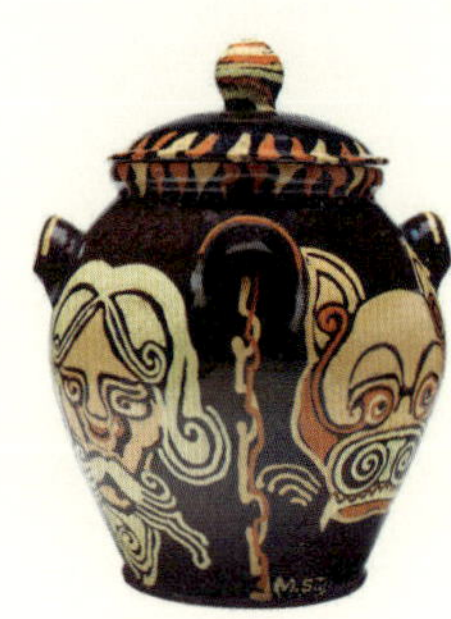

cat 43
Jar with gargoyle design with lid 1934
likely Anjaleras Pottery, Cliousclat, France
wheel-thrown glazed earthenware
with slip decoration
51 × 40 (diam) cm (overall)
monogram at base, 'M.S.D.'
Art Gallery of New South Wales, Gadigal Nura/Sydney
gift of the Albert Gleizes Foundation 2017
134.2017.a-b

EXHIBITED: Annual exhibition of Moly-Sabata, Moly-Sabata, Sablons, 7–31 October 1934

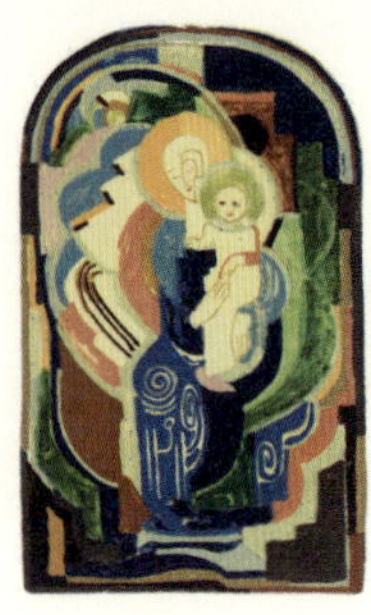

cat 44 p 92
La Vierge et l'enfant Jésu (*Virgin and Child*) 1934
Anjaleras Pottery, Cliousclat, France
glazed and incised earthenware
with slip decoration
56.8 × 35 × 1.5 cm
monogram on lower right edge, 'M.S.D.'
Queensland Art Gallery | Gallery of Modern Art, Meeanjin/Brisbane
purchased 2007
Queensland Art Gallery Foundation Grant
2007.191

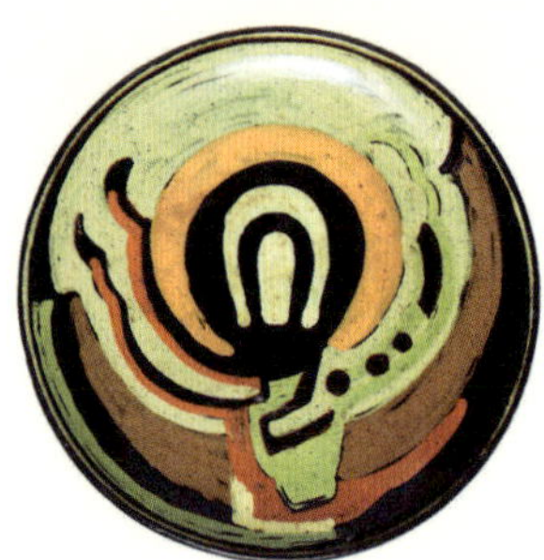

cat 45 p 119
Plate (1934–35)
Auvergne-Rhône-Alpes, France
wheel-thrown glazed earthenware
with slip decoration
3.5 × 36 (diam) cm
monogram verso on edge, 'MSD'
gift of Ruth Ainsworth 1998
98.191

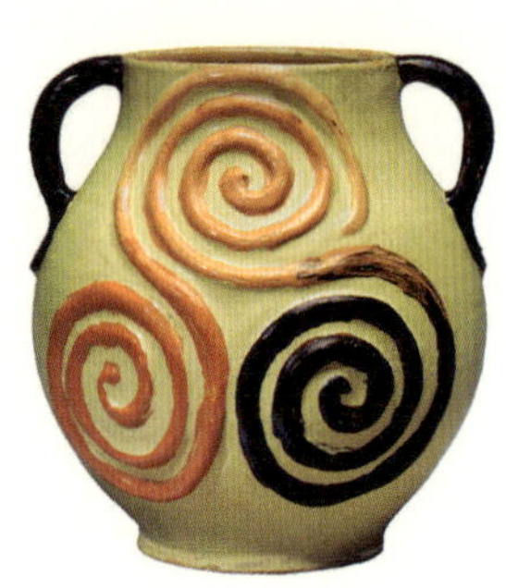

cat 46 p 90
Pot with spiral decoration (1934–50)
Anjaleras Pottery, Cliousclat, France
wheel-thrown glazed earthenware
with slip decoration
36 × 32.4 (irreg diam) cm
monogram on inner neck rim, 'MSD'
purchased 2002
2002.51

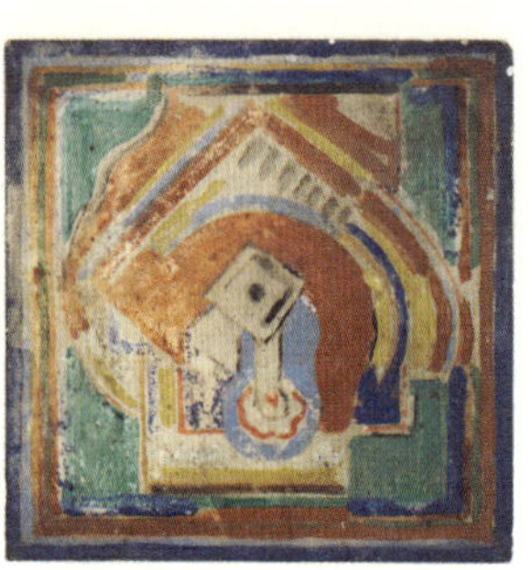

cat 47
Tile with cubist design (1935–39)
Auvergne-Rhône-Alpes, France
painted cement tile
19.8 × 19.8 × 1.7 cm
no inscriptions
purchased 2002
2002.41

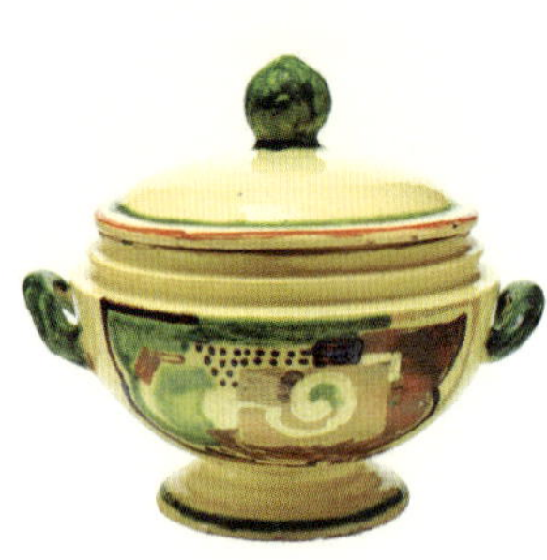

cat 48 p 150
Soup tureen with cubist design (1936–37)
Auvergne-Rhône-Alpes, France
wheel-thrown glazed earthenware
with slip decoration
29 × 33.6 × 27.1 cm (overall)
monogram on base, 'MSD'
Art Gallery of New South Wales, Gadigal Nura/Sydney
purchased with funds provided by the Mollie Douglas Bequest 2017
87.2017.A-B

LIKELY EXHIBITED: Group exhibition of popular pottery, pavilion of the Union des artistes modernes, Exposition internationale des arts et techniques dans la vie moderne, Paris, 25 May – 25 November 1937, or *Les maîtres de l'art indépendant, 1895–1937*, Petit Palais, Paris, June–October 1937

EXHIBITED: *32e groupe des artistes de ce temps*, Petit Palais, Paris, June 1938

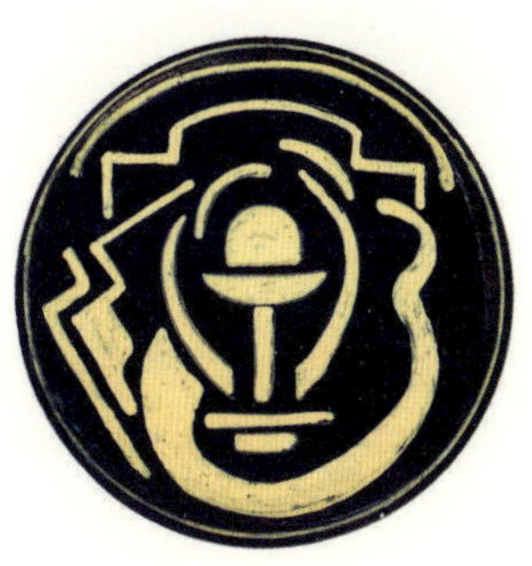

cat 49 p 154
Plate with cubist design (1936–38)
Auvergne-Rhône-Alpes, France
wheel-thrown glazed earthenware
with slip decoration
3.8 × 34.7 (diam) cm
monogram on verso, 'MSD'
Art Gallery of New South Wales, Gadigal
Nura/Sydney
purchased with funds provided by the
Mollie Douglas Bequest 2017
84.2017

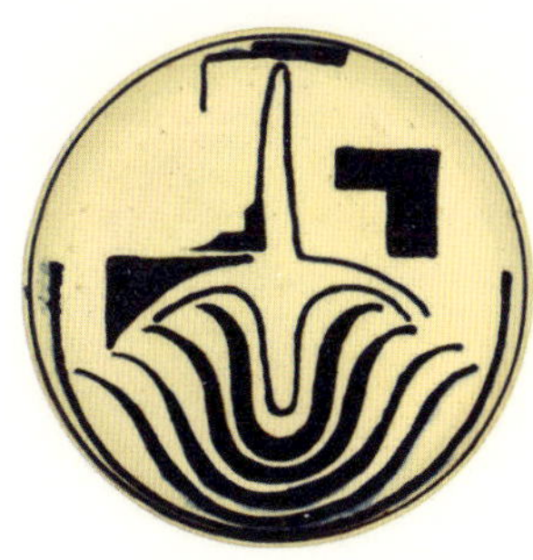

cat 50 p 155
Plate with cruciform design (1936–38)
Auvergne-Rhône-Alpes, France
wheel-thrown glazed earthenware
with slip decoration
3.6 × 37.5 (diam) cm
monogram on verso, 'MSD'
Art Gallery of New South Wales, Gadigal
Nura/Sydney
purchased with funds provided by the
Mollie Douglas Bequest 2017
23.2017

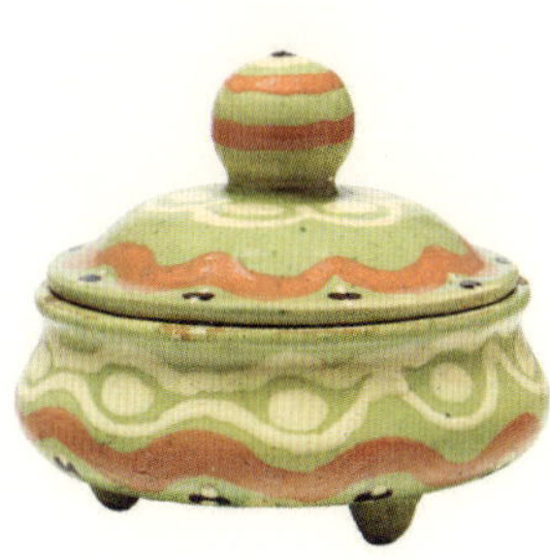

cat 51
Vegetable dish with lid (1936–38)
Auvergne-Rhône-Alpes, France
wheel-thrown glazed earthenware
with slip decoration
17 × 20.2 (diam) cm (overall)
monogram on base and inside of lid, 'MSD'
Art Gallery of New South Wales, Gadigal
Nura/Sydney
purchased with funds provided by the
Mollie Douglas Bequest 2021
7.2021.A-B

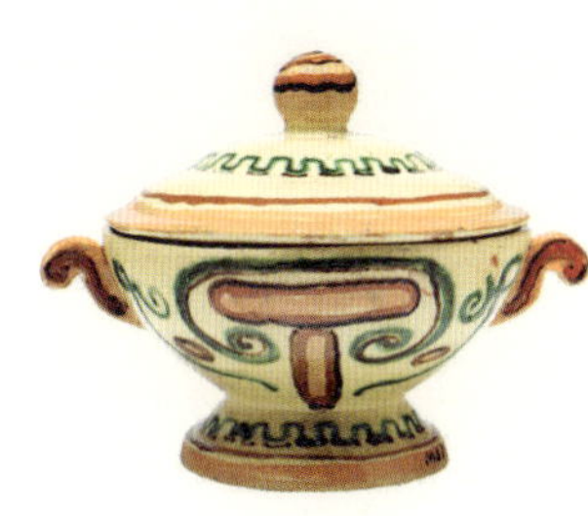

cat 52 p 151
Soup tureen with geometric designs (1936–38)
Auvergne-Rhône-Alpes, France
wheel-thrown glazed earthenware
with slip decoration
35 × 25.5 (irreg diam) cm (overall)
monogram on base, 'MSD'
Art Gallery of New South Wales, Gadigal
Nura/Sydney
purchased with funds provided by the
Mollie Douglas Bequest 2021
6.2021.A-B
EXHIBITED: *Moly-Sabata*, Galerie Sambon, Paris, June 1938

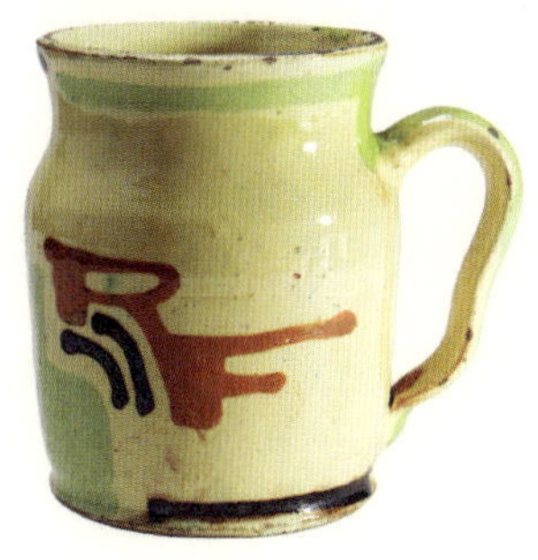

cat 53 p 197
Beer mug for Rah Fizelle 1937
Auvergne-Rhône-Alpes, France
wheel-thrown glazed earthenware
with slip decoration
12.2 × 13.4 × 10.2 cm
no inscriptions
gift of Grace Buckley in memory
of Grace Crowley 1982
82.238

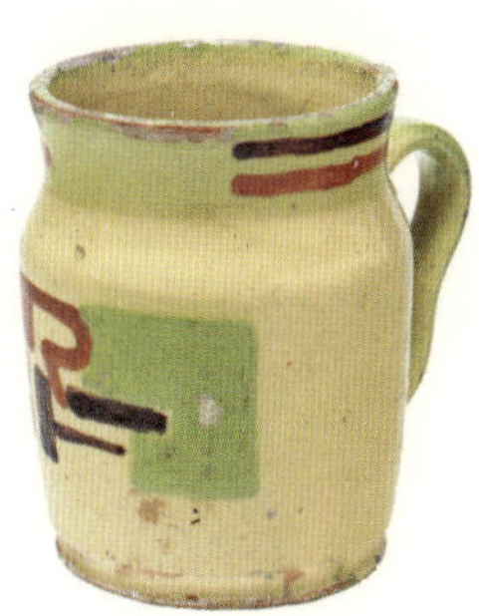

cat 54
Beer mug for Rah Fizelle 1937
Auvergne-Rhône-Alpes, France
wheel-thrown glazed earthenware
with slip decoration
12.5 × 13.7 × 10.2 cm
no inscriptions
Art Gallery of New South Wales, Gadigal
Nura/Sydney
gift of Mrs Michael Fizelle 1969
C5.1969

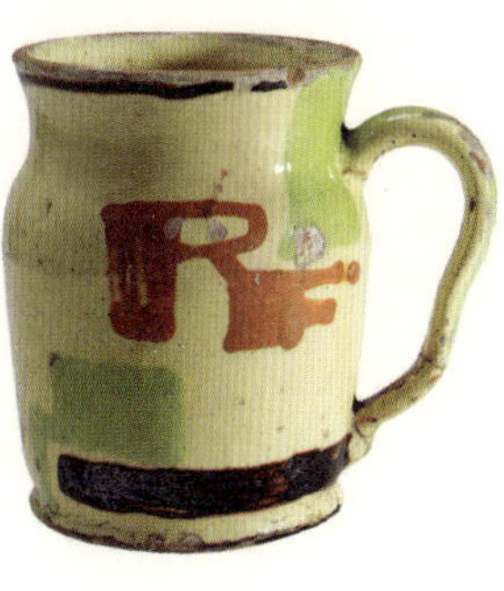

cat 55
Beer mug for Rah Fizelle 1937
Auvergne-Rhône-Alpes, France
wheel-thrown glazed earthenware
with slip decoration
12.3 × 13.6 × 10.2 cm
no inscriptions
gift of Grace Buckley in memory of
Grace Crowley 1982
82.237

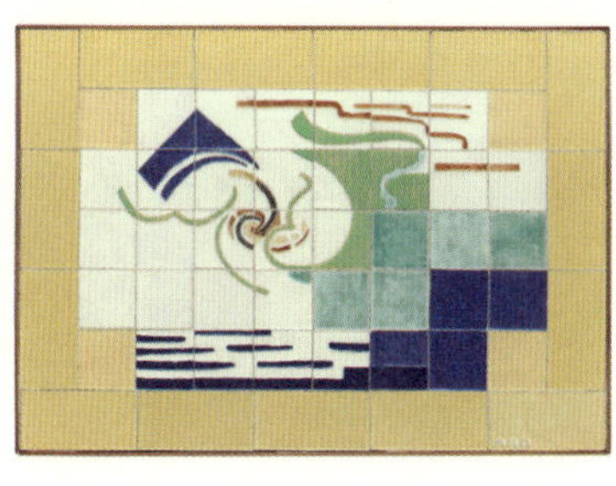

cat 56
Cubist tabletop 1937
Saint-Vallier, France
enamel glazed industrial ceramic tiles, wood
34.5 × 102.1 × 71.5 cm
monogram lower right, 'MSD'
private collection, Dangar family

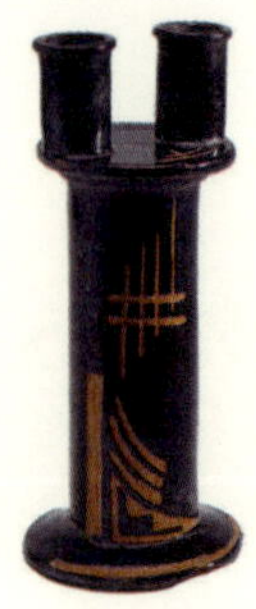

cat 57
Candlestick 1938
Auvergne-Rhône-Alpes, France
wheel-thrown incised and glazed earthenware
with slip decoration
33 × 13 (irreg diam) cm
no inscriptions
private collection, Dangar family

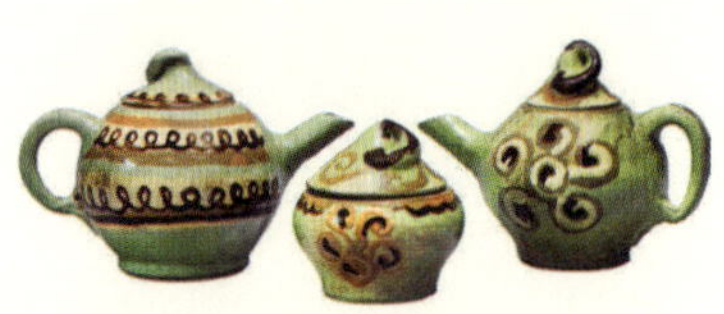

cat 58 p 152
Moroccan-style tea set (1940–48)
Auvergne-Rhône-Alpes, France
wheel-thrown glazed earthenware
with slip decoration
teapot and lid 1: 19 × 15.5 × 28 cm (overall)
teapot and lid 2: 19 × 15 × 25.5 cm (overall)
sugar bowl and lid: 14 × 13.2 (diam) cm (overall)
monogram on bases of teapot 1 and sugar bowl, 'MSD'
purchased 2002
2002.45.1-3.A-B

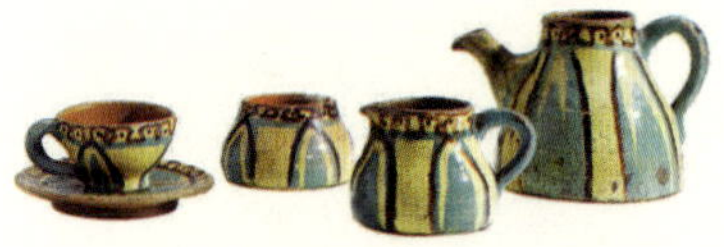

cat 59 p 8
Moroccan-style tea set (1940–48)
Auvergne-Rhône-Alpes, France
wheel-thrown glazed earthenware
with slip decoration
teapot: 13.3 × 15 × 21 cm
teacup and saucer: 6 × 15 (diam) cm (overall)
milk jug: 8.5 × 12.5 (irreg diam) cm
sugar bowl: 6.8 × 10.6 (irreg diam) cm
monogram on bases of teacup, sugar bowl and saucer, and on handle of teapot, 'MSD'
purchased 2002
2002.40.1-4.A-B

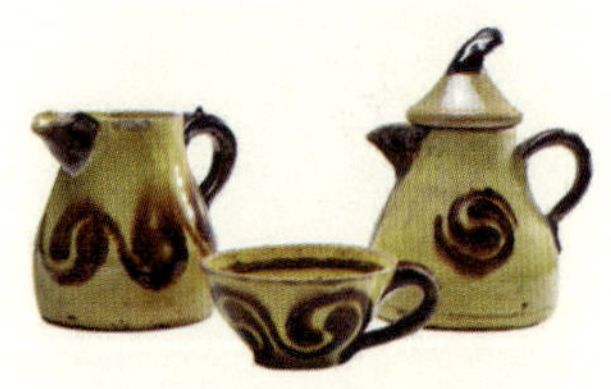

cat 60
Moroccan-style tea set (1940–48)
Auvergne-Rhône-Alpes, France
wheel-thrown glazed earthenware
with slip decoration
teapot: 21 × 13.5 (irreg diam) cm (overall)
milk jug: 15 × 13 (irreg diam) cm
teacup: 6.5 × 12.5 (irreg diam) cm
monogram on bases of jug, teapot and teacup, 'MSD'
purchased 2002
2002.43.1-3

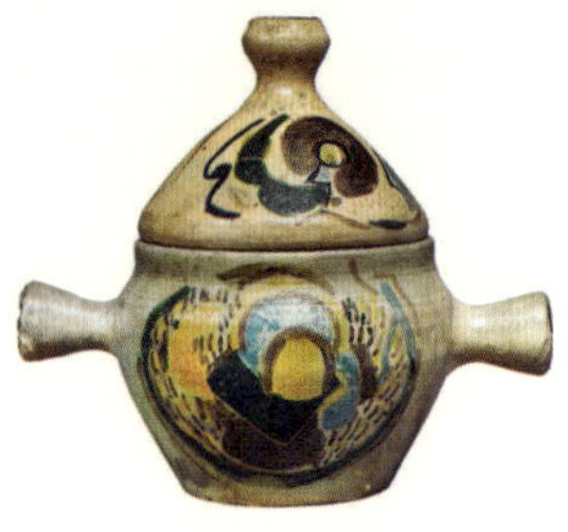

cat 61 p 168
Couscoussier (1940–48)
Auvergne-Rhône-Alpes, France
wheel-thrown glazed earthenware
with slip decoration
29 × 33 × 21 cm (overall)
monogram on base of bowl, 'MSD'
purchased 2002
2002.42.A-B

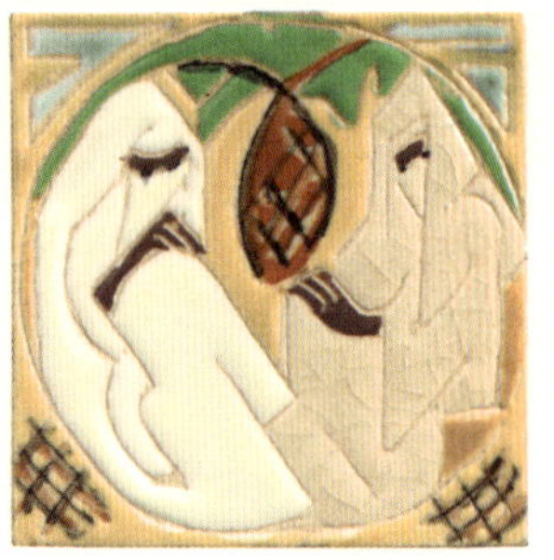

cat 62 p 158
Two Moroccans (1943–45)
Saint-Vallier, France
enamel glazed industrial ceramic tile
10 × 10 × 1 cm
monogram on edge, 'AGD'
gift of David Herbert 2024
2024.11

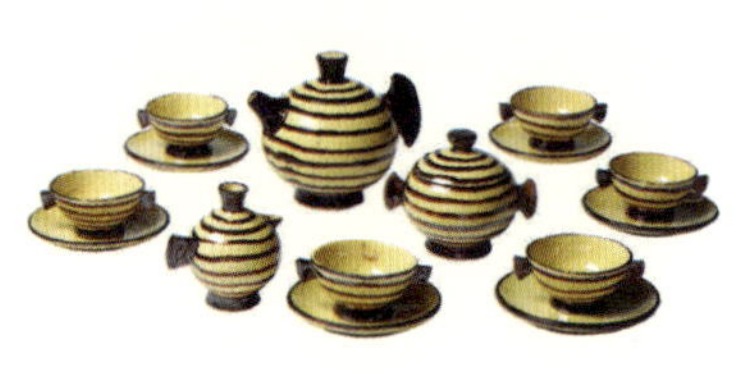

cat 63 p 157
Tea service (1945–50)
Auvergne-Rhône-Alpes, France
wheel-thrown glazed earthenware
with slip decoration
teapot with lid: 16 × 14 (irreg diam) cm
milk pot with lid: 12 × 9 (irreg diam) cm
sugar bowl with lid: 13 × 12 (irreg diam) cm
teacup: 5.5 × 10 (irreg diam) cm (each)
saucer: 2 × 15 (irreg diam) cm (each)
monogram on bases and undersides of lids of 11 pieces, 'M.S.D'
Queensland Art Gallery | Gallery of Modern Art, Meeanjin/Brisbane
purchased 2011 with funds from Margaret Mittelheuser AM and Cathryn Mittelheuser AM through the Queensland Art Gallery Foundation
2011.091.001-015

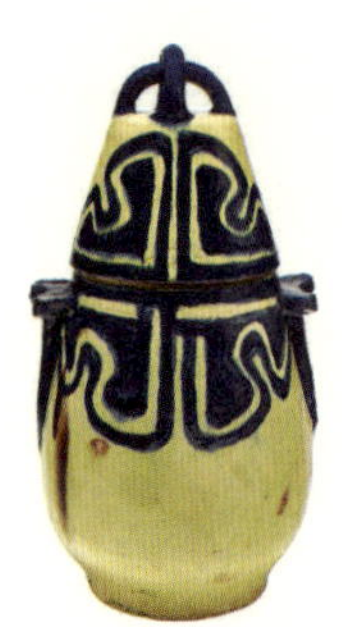

cat 64 p 210
Conical pot with lid (1947–49)
Auvergne-Rhône-Alpes, France
wheel-thrown glazed earthenware
with slip decoration
53.5 × 28 (irreg diam) cm (overall)
monogram on base, 'MSD'
Art Gallery of New South Wales, Gadigal Nura/Sydney
purchased with funds provided by the Mollie Douglas Bequest 2017
82.2017.A-B

cat 65 p 211
Jar with lid (1947–49)
Auvergne-Rhône-Alpes, France
wheel-thrown glazed earthenware
with slip decoration
42.2 × 39.6 (irreg diam) cm (overall)
monogram near base, 'M.S.D.'
Art Gallery of New South Wales, Gadigal Nura/Sydney
gift of the Albert Gleizes Foundation 2017
135.2017.A-B

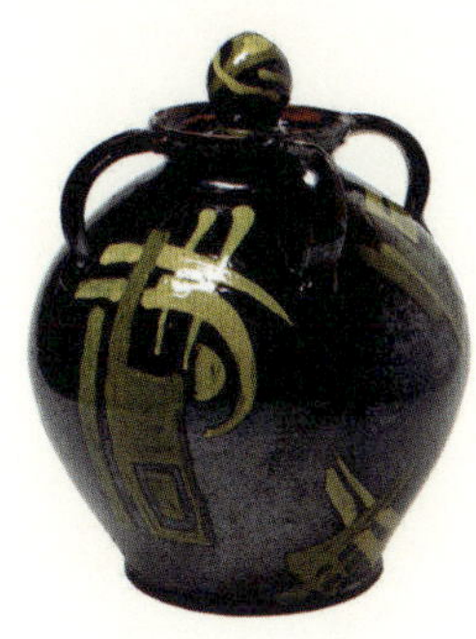

cat 66
Urn with Chinese-inspired characters (1948–49)
Auvergne-Rhône-Alpes, France
wheel-thrown glazed earthenware
with slip decoration
40 × 32.5 (irreg diam) cm (overall)
monogram on base, 'MSD'
Queensland Art Gallery | Gallery of Modern Art, Meeanjin/Brisbane
purchased 2004
Queensland Art Gallery Foundation
2004.308A-B

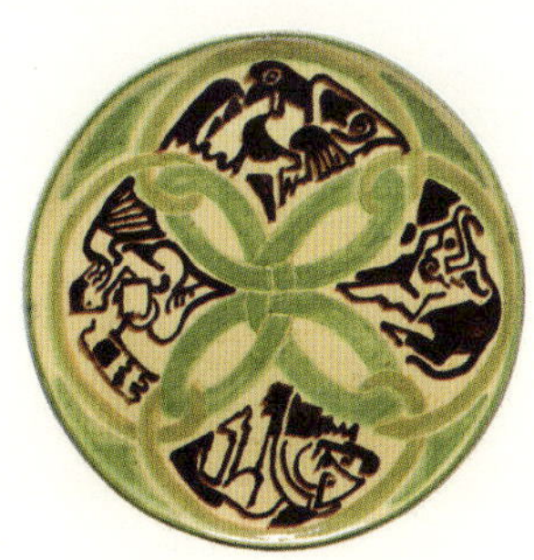

cat 67 p 153
Plate with Celtic motifs and figures representing the four beasts from Revelation 4 (1948–49)
Auvergne-Rhône-Alpes, France
wheel-thrown incised and glazed earthenware
with slip decoration
3 × 44.3 (diam) cm
monogram on verso, 'M.S.D.'
Queensland Art Gallery | Gallery of Modern Art, Meeanjin/Brisbane
purchased 2004
Queensland Art Gallery Foundation
2004.307

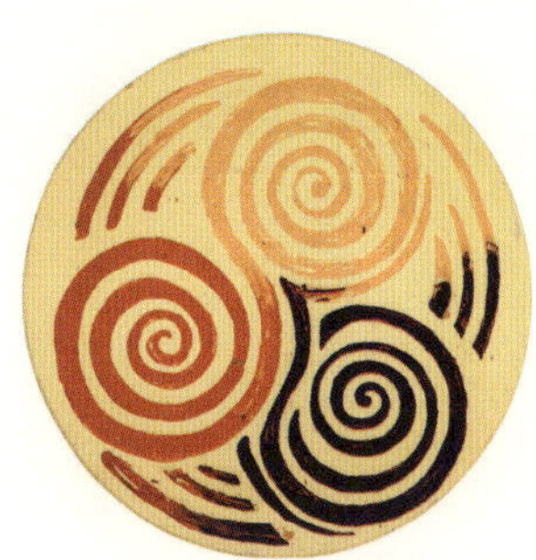

cat 68 p 4
Plate with spirals (1948–50)
Auvergne-Rhône-Alpes, France
wheel-thrown glazed earthenware
with slip decoration
1.8 × 46.5 (diam) cm
monogram on verso, 'MSD'
Art Gallery of New South Wales, Gadigal Nura/Sydney
purchased with funds provided by the Mollie Douglas Bequest 2017
22.2017

PAINTINGS

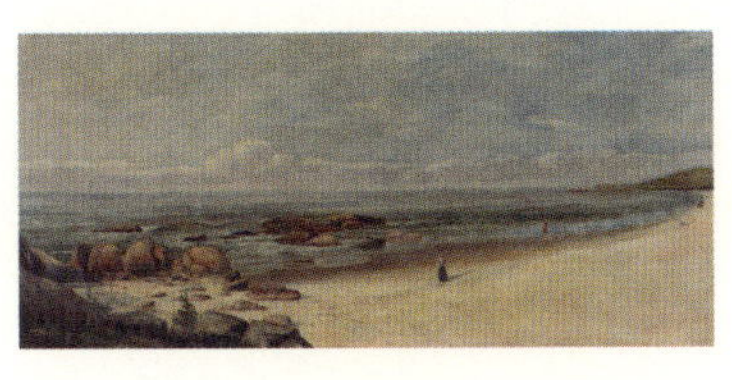

cat 69 p 29
Trial Bay landscape (1912–15)
Thunggutti/Dunghutti Country/Kempsey NSW
oil on canvas
68 × 135 cm
Macleay River Historical Society, Thunggutti/Dunghutti Country/Kempsey, NSW
LIKELY EXHIBITED: Exhibition of Anne Dangar's and pupils' work at Good Templars Hall, Kempsey, June 1912; Exhibition of Anne Dangar's and pupils' work at the Dangar family home 'Shaweetah', Kempsey, December 1915

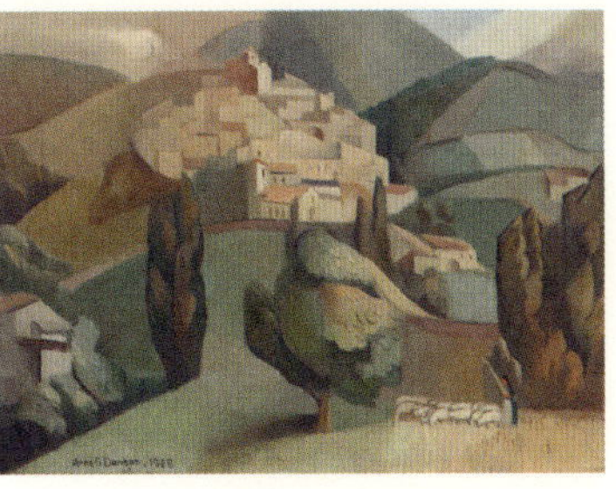

cat 70 p 46
Mirmande, La Drôme 1928
Mirmande, France
oil on canvas mounted on board
55.5 × 72.5 cm
signed lower left, 'Anne. G. Dangar - 1928'
private collection

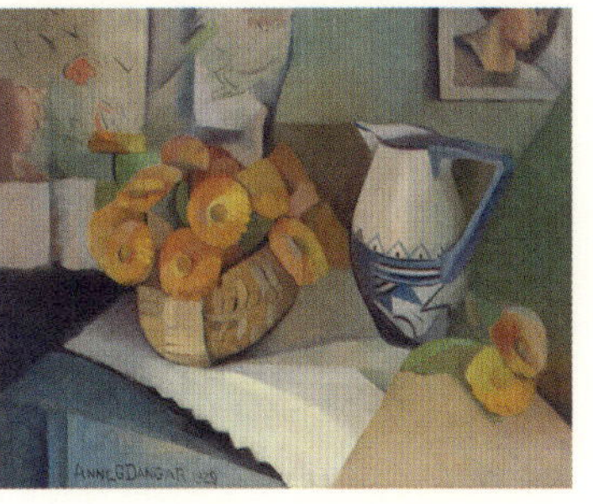

cat 71 p 41
Still life 1929
Gadigal Nura/Sydney
oil on canvas
63 × 78.5 cm
signed lower left, 'Anne G Dangar. 1929'
collection of Mary Ralston, great-great-niece of Anne Dangar

WORKS ON PAPER

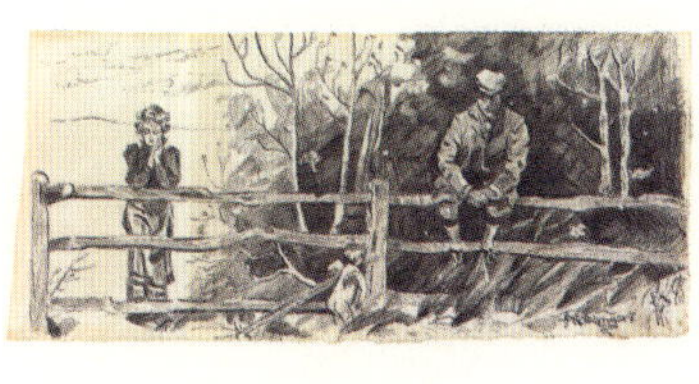

cat 72 p 25
Golf is not the only game on earth after an illustration by Charles Dana Gibson (1911–12)
Thunggutti/Dunghutti Country/Kempsey, NSW, or Gadigal Nura/Sydney
ink on paper
18 × 42 cm (sight)
signed lower right, 'A. G. Dangar'
private collection

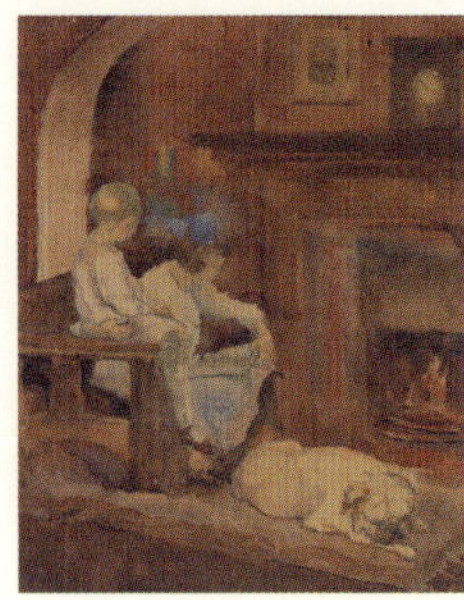

cat 73
Mary Joyce and Judy Singleton reading at Henley (1923–25)
Wallumedegal Country/Henley, Sydney
watercolour on paper
30 × 23 cm (sight)
private collection, Dangar family

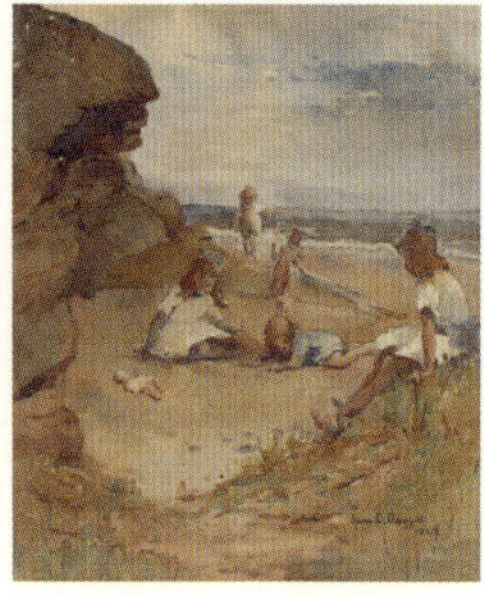

cat 74 p 30
Beach at Henley 1923
Wallumedegal Country/Henley, Sydney
watercolour on paper
39 × 33 cm (sight)
signed and dated lower right, 'Anne. G. Dangar. / 1923'
collection of Pamela Collins,
great-niece of Anne Dangar

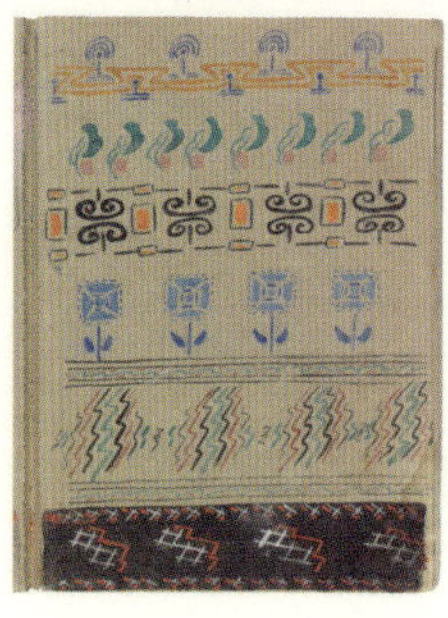

cat 75 p 36
Repeat designs for porcelain painting (1926–28)
Paris
in Sketchbook 1926–32
Paris, Gadigal Nura/Sydney and Moly-Sabata, Sablons, France
gouache on paper
sheet 35.2 × 26 cm
purchased 2012
2012.2191.2.A-AM

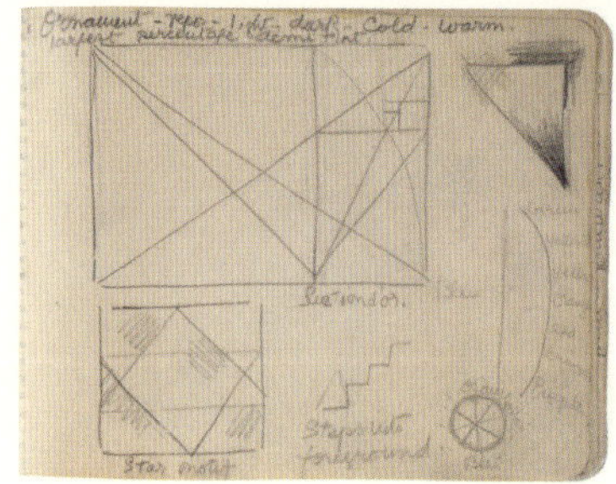

cat 76 p 56
Compositional diagrams using the *section d'or* (golden mean)
in Notebook 1927–29
Paris
pencil on paper
sheet 13.8 cm × 18 cm
Grace Crowley archive
National Art Archive, Art Gallery of New South Wales, Gadigal Nura/Sydney
bequest of Grace Crowley 1979
ARC106.11.1

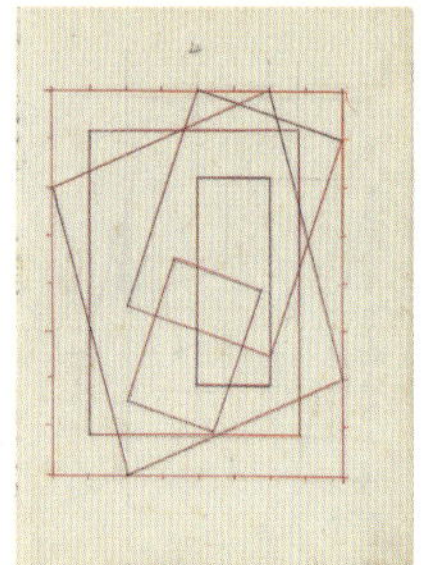

cat 77
Exercise in rotation with five rectangles
in Sketchbook 1930s
Moly-Sabata, Sablons, France
pencil and ink on paper
sheet 31 × 22 cm
purchased 2012
2012.2378

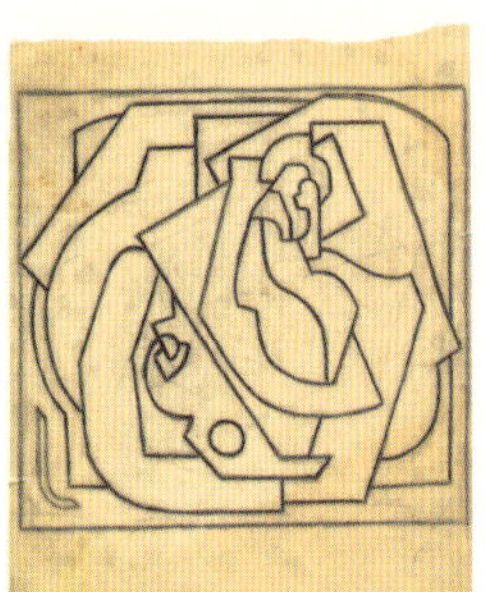

cat 78
Design for cubist composition 1930s
Moly-Sabata, Sablons, France
pencil on tracing paper
sheet 31.9 × 27.4 cm
purchased 2012
2012.2196

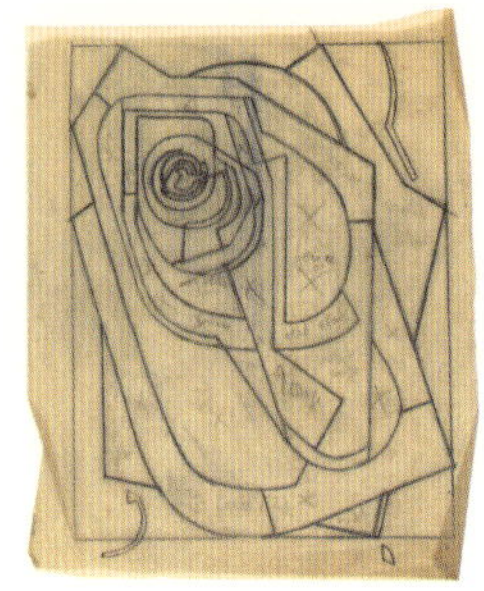

cat 79 p 80
Design for cubist composition with colour notes 1930s
Moly-Sabata, Sablons, France
pencil on tracing paper
sheet 28.6 × 25.1 cm
purchased 2012
2012.2327

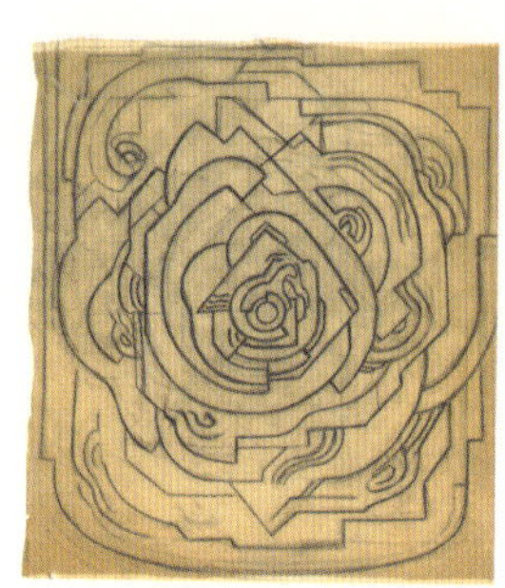

cat 80
Design for cubist composition 1930s
Moly-Sabata, Sablons, France
pencil on tracing paper
sheet 36.2 × 32.3 cm
purchased 2012
2012.2228

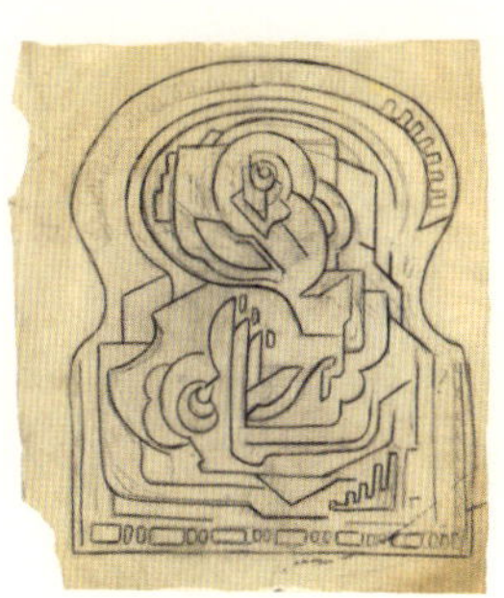

cat 81
Design for curved cubist composition 1930s
Moly-Sabata, Sablons, France
pencil on tracing paper
sheet 39.4 × 34.3 cm
purchased 2012
2012.2231

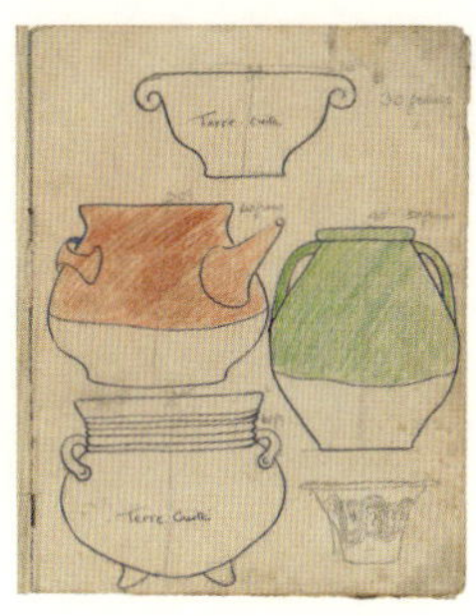

cat 82
Five ceramic forms with simple glaze decoration in Sketchbook 1930s
Moly-Sabata, Sablons, France
ink, pencil and coloured pencil on paper
sheet 31 × 24.1 cm
purchased 2012
2012.2191.6.A-S

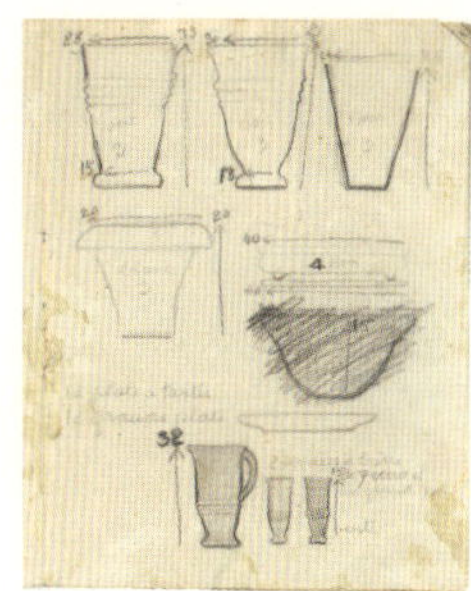

cat 83
Ten ceramic forms with dimensions in Sketchbook 1930s
Moly-Sabata, Sablons, France
pencil on paper
sheet 30.9 × 23.8 cm
purchased 2012
2012.2191.4.A-J

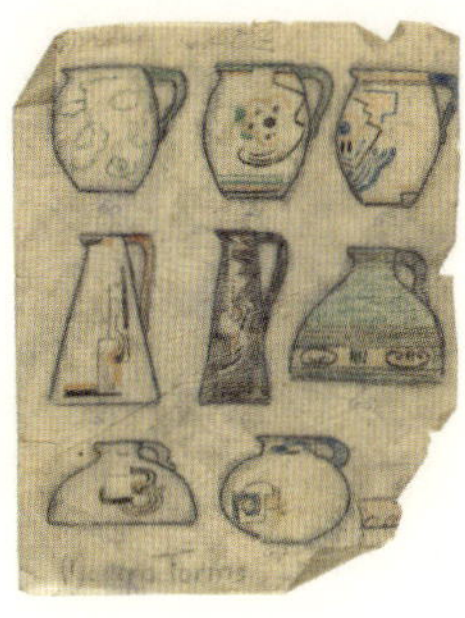

cat 84
Modern forms 1930s
Moly-Sabata, Sablons, France
pencil, coloured pencil and ink on tracing paper
sheet 26.5 × 20.9 cm
purchased 2012
2012.2191.8.D

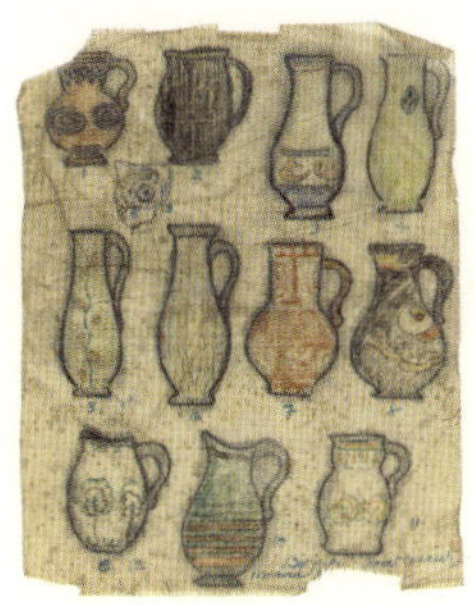

cat 85
Designs for jugs with modern decoration 1930s
Moly-Sabata, Sablons, France
pencil, coloured pencil and ink on tracing paper
sheet 26.6 × 21.1 cm
purchased 2012
2012.2191.8.F

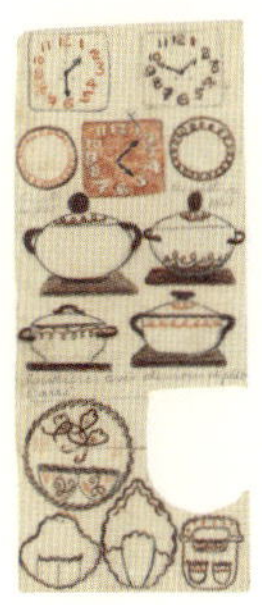

cat 86
Designs for clocks, tureens and wall vases 1930s
Moly-Sabata, Sablons, France
pencil and coloured pencil on paper
sheet 37.2 × 15.4 cm (irreg)
purchased 2012
2012.2191.8.B.AB

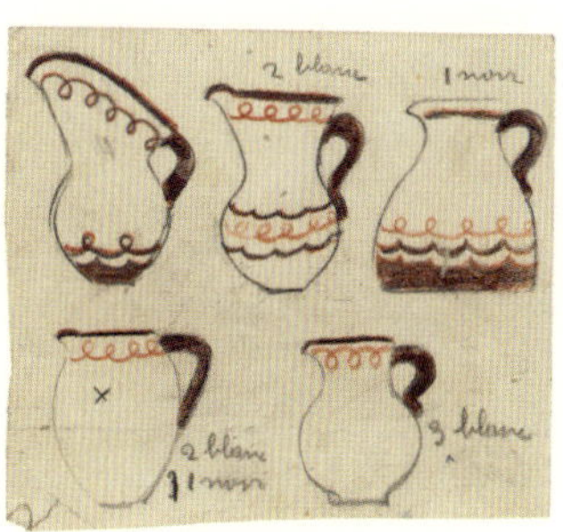

cat 87
Five jugs with decorative designs 1930s
Moly-Sabata, Sablons, France
pencil and coloured pencil on paper
sheet 13.4 × 15.2 cm
purchased 2012
2012.2191.8.H

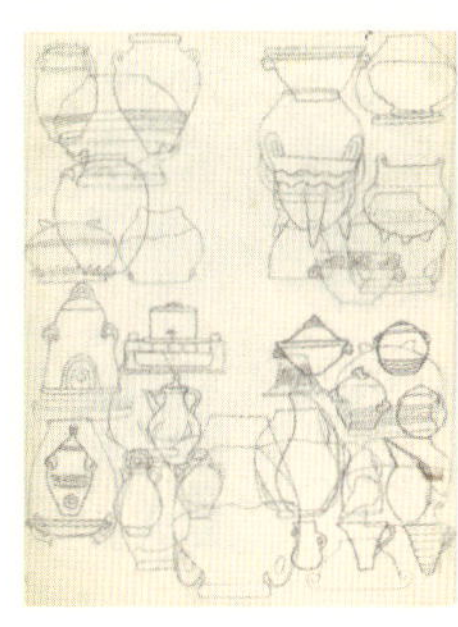

cat 88 p 71
Designs of ceramic forms 1930s
Moly-Sabata, Sablons, France
pencil on paper
sheet 65.3 × 50 cm
purchased 2012
2012.2258

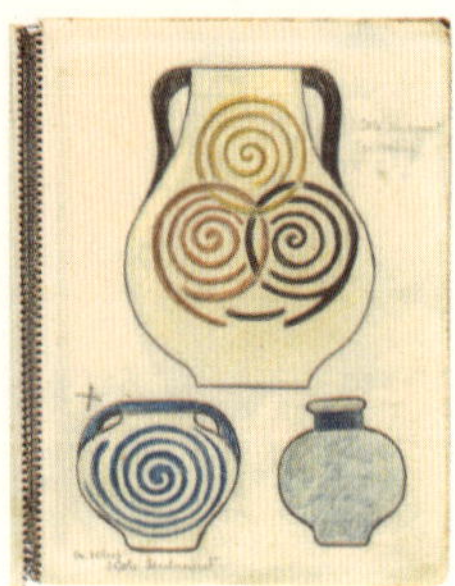

cat 89
Spiral pot with handles, spiral pot and blue pot in Stock book 1930s
Moly-Sabata, Sablons, France
pencil and coloured pencil on paper
sheet 32.1 × 24 cm
purchased 2012
2012.2191.1.A-AU

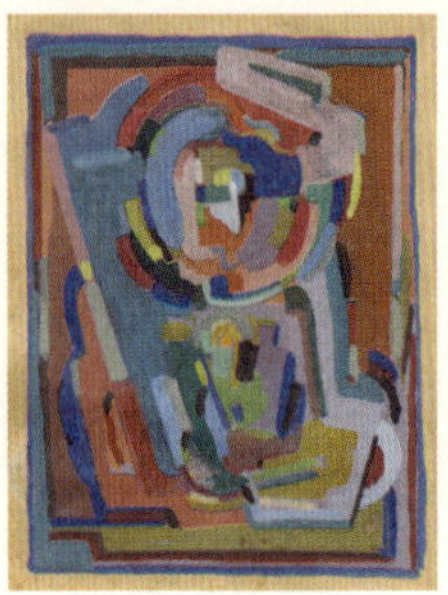

cat 90 **p 81**
Cubist composition (1931–33)
Moly-Sabata, Sablons, France
gouache on paper
image 28.3 × 15
sheet 32.4 × 31.1 cm
purchased 2012
2012.2191.17.3

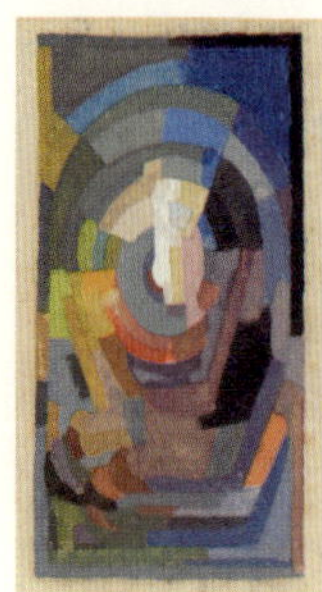

cat 91
Cubist composition (1931–33)
Moly-Sabata, Sablons, France
gouache on paper
image 28.6 × 14.4 cm
sheet 31 × 21 cm
purchased 2012
2012.2191.17.2

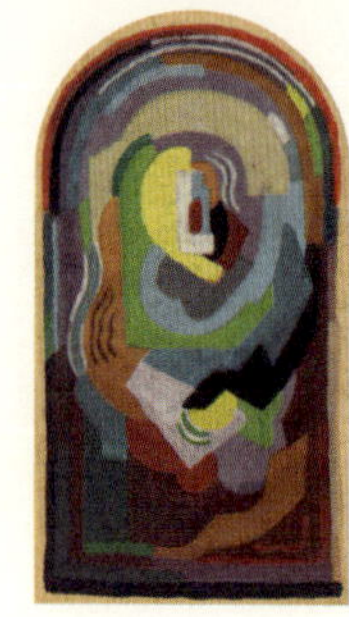

cat 92 **p 93**
Cubist composition (1931–33)
Moly-Sabata, Sablons, France
gouache on paper
image 25.2 × 18.7 cm
sheet 43 × 22.5 cm
purchased 2012
2012.2191.17.1

cat 93
Design for plate with cubist decoration (1934–48)
Moly-Sabata, Sablons, France
pencil on tracing paper
sheet 36.9 × 36.6 cm
purchased 2012
2012.2229

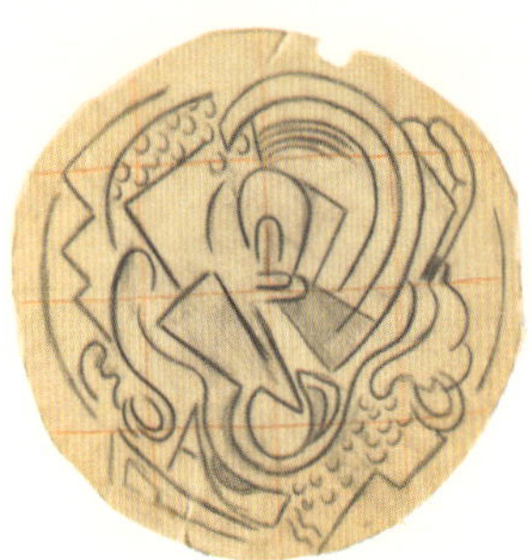

cat 94
Design for plate with cubist decoration (1934–48)
Moly-Sabata, Sablons, France
pencil and conté crayon on tracing paper
sheet 38.5 × 35.7 cm
purchased 2012
2012.2259

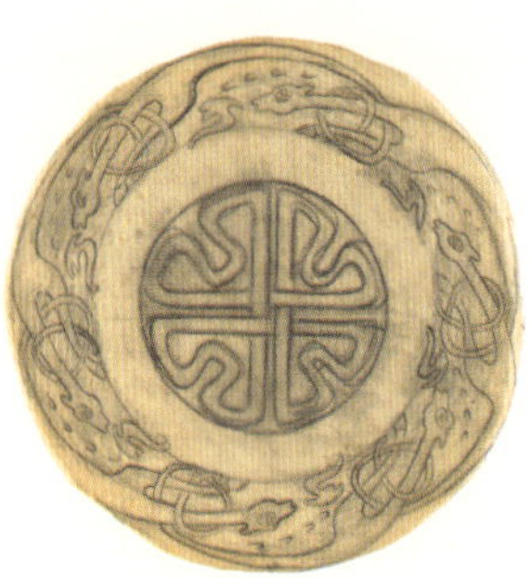

cat 95
Design for plate with Celtic dragons and interlaced linear decoration (1934–48)
Moly-Sabata, Sablons, France
pencil on tracing paper
sheet 39.2 × 39.4 cm
purchased 2012
2012.2191.81

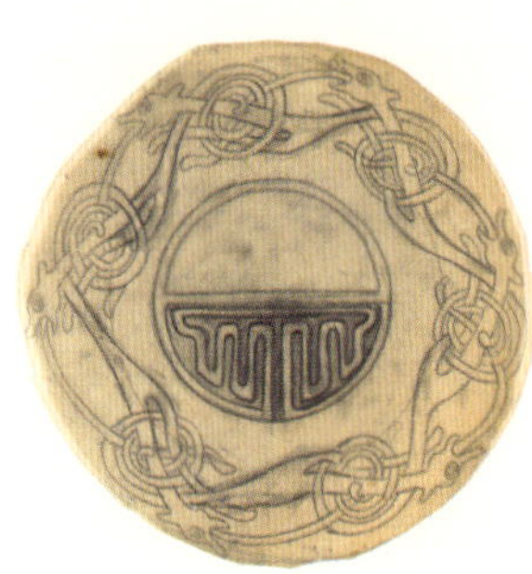

cat 96
Design for plate with Celtic dragons and coiled linear decoration (1934–48)
Moly-Sabata, Sablons, France
pencil on tracing paper
sheet 40.8 × 40.3 cm
purchased 2012
2012.2191.75

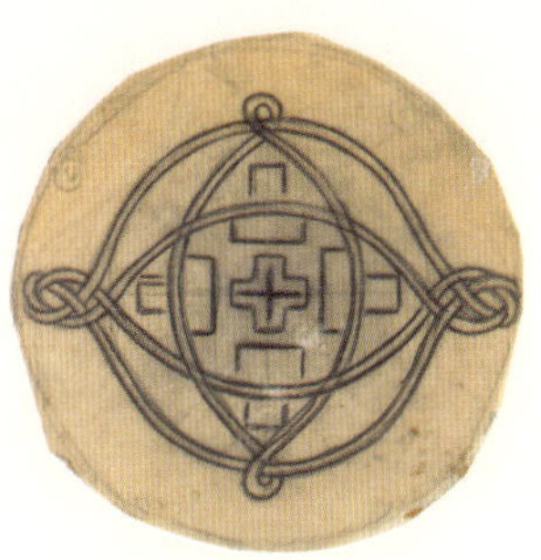

cat 97
Design for plate with Celtic-inspired interlocking cord and cruciform decoration (1934–48)
Moly-Sabata, Sablons, France
pencil on tracing paper
sheet 24.3 × 23.8 cm
purchased 2012
2012.2191.98

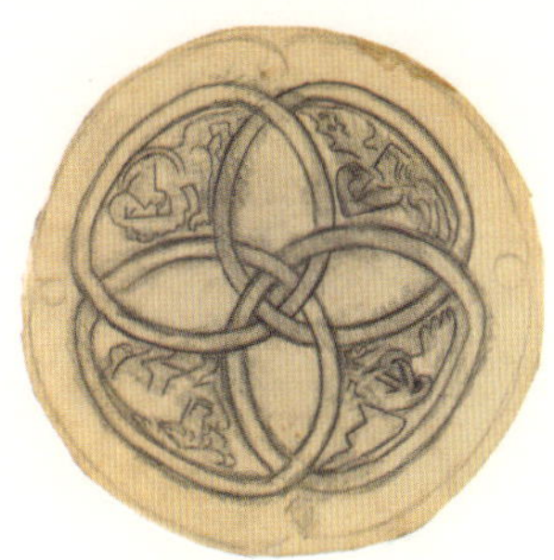

cat 98
Design for plate with Celtic interlocking decoration and symbols of the four Evangelists (ox, eagle, lion and man) (1934–48)
Moly-Sabata, Sablons, France
pencil on tracing paper
sheet 41.1 × 40.9 cm
purchased 2012
2012.2191.78

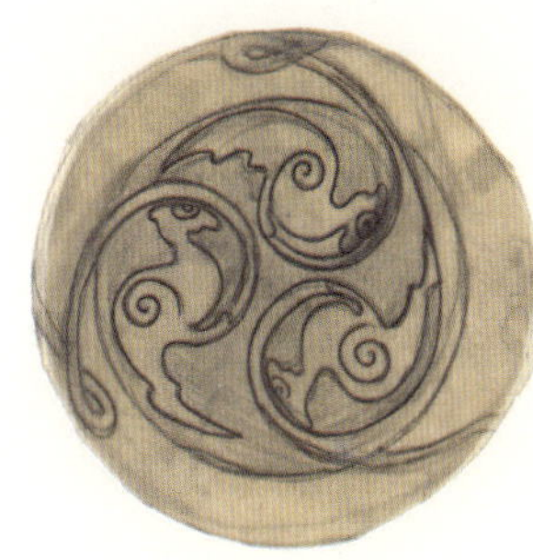

cat 99
Design for plate with Celtic-inspired interlocking decoration (1934–48)
Moly-Sabata, Sablons, France
pencil on tracing paper
sheet 21.1 × 20.6 cm
purchased 2012
2012.2191.77

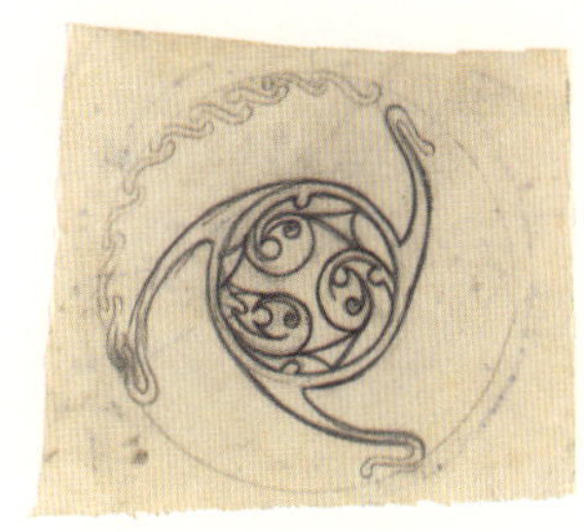

cat 100
Design for plate with Celtic-inspired interlocking decoration (1934–48)
Moly-Sabata, Sablons, France
pencil on tracing paper
sheet 25.4 × 28.5 cm
purchased 2012
2012.2191.11

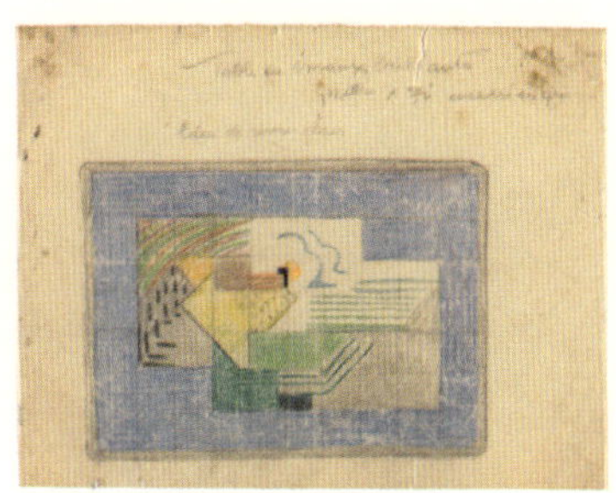

cat 101
Design for ceramic tiled tabletop (1935–39)
Moly-Sabata, Sablons, France
pencil and coloured pencil on tracing paper
sheet 23.7 × 30.4 cm
purchased 2012
2012.2264

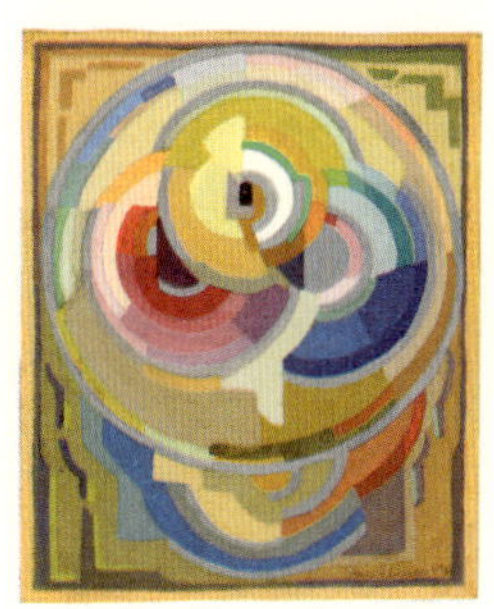

cat 102 p 165
Gouache 1936
Moly-Sabata, Sablons, France
gouache on paper
image 33 × 27 cm
sheet 35 × 28.9 cm
signed and dated lower right, 'Anne G. Dangar 1936'
purchased 2002
2002.52

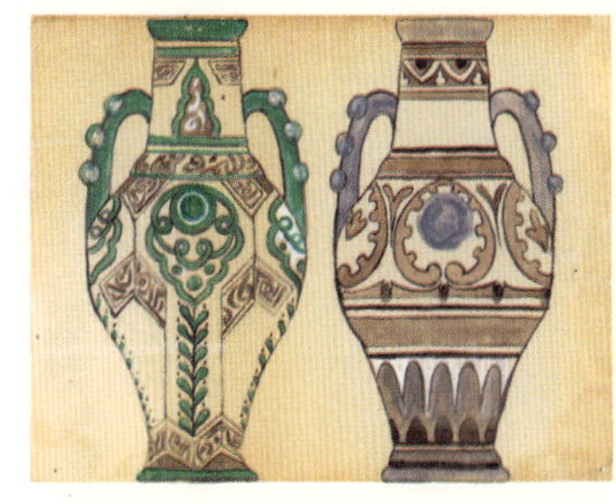

cat 103 p 166
Drawings of Moroccan vases 1939
Fez
watercolour and gouache on paper
sheet 50.3 × 65 cm
purchased 2012
2012.2266

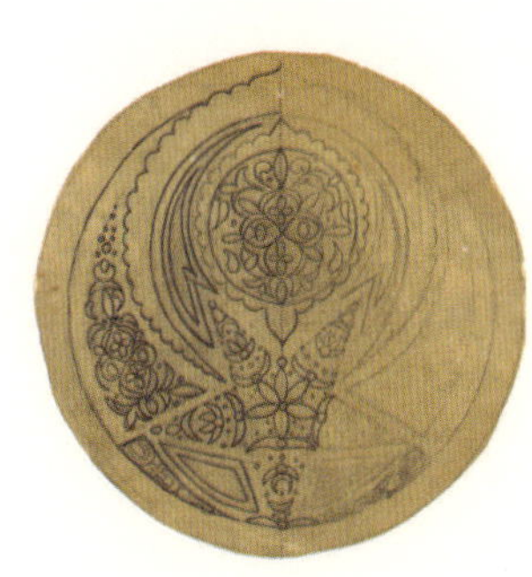

cat 104 p 149
Design for plate with Moroccan-inspired design (1940–48)
Moly-Sabata, Sablons, France
pencil on tracing paper
sheet 36 × 37 cm
purchased 2012
2012.2191.66

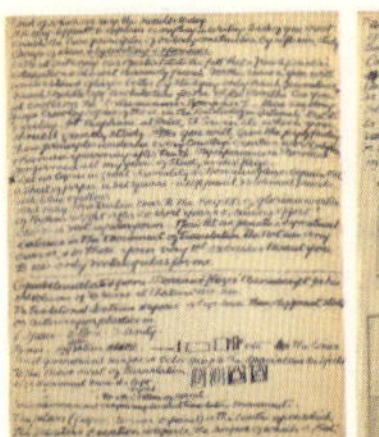
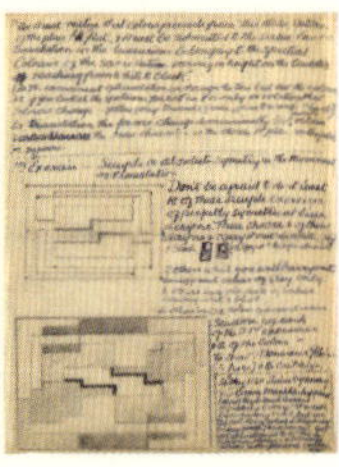

cat 105 p 103
Drawing and translation of *La forme et l'histoire* by Albert Gleizes 1940
Moly-Sabata, Sablons, France
ink on paper
sheet 27.9 × 20.9 cm (each)
Grace Crowley archive
National Art Archive, Art Gallery of New South Wales, Gadigal Nura/Sydney
bequest of Grace Crowley 1979
ARC106.11.17.A-B

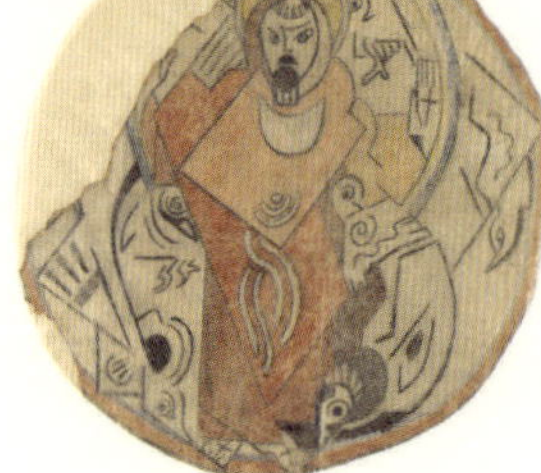

cat 106 p 170
Preparatory drawing for plate depicting Robert Pouyaud as Saint Francis of Assisi 1940
Moly-Sabata, Sablons, France
pencil and coloured chalk pencil on tracing paper
sheet 50.5 × 48.4 cm (irreg)
purchased 2012
2012.2269

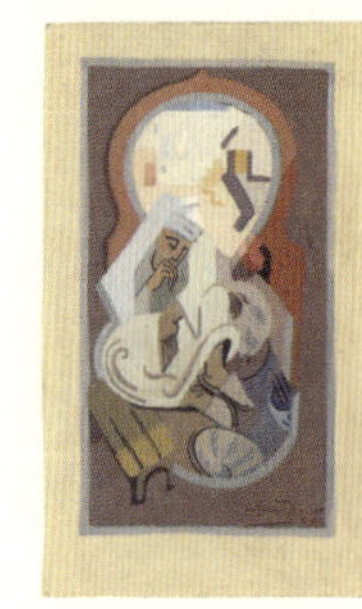

cat 107 p 159
Moroccan figure in doorway 1943
Moly-Sabata, Sablons, France
gouache on paper
image 35.5 × 25.2 cm
sheet 42.6 × 29.5 cm
signed and dated lower right, 'Anne Dangar / '43'
purchased 2012
2012.2191.17.4

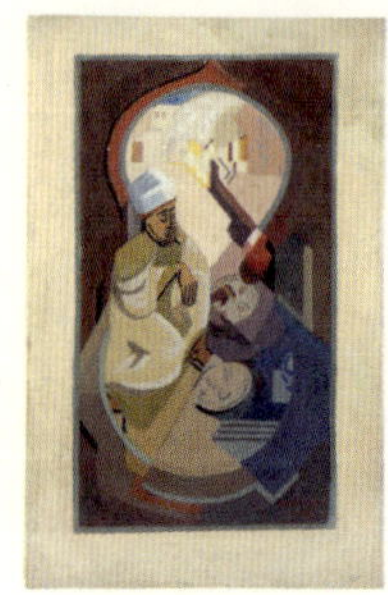

cat 108
Two Moroccan figures 1943
Moly-Sabata, Sablons, France
gouache on cardboard
cardboard 68 × 44 cm
Art Gallery of South Australia, Tarntanya/Adelaide
purchased 2015
20151P1

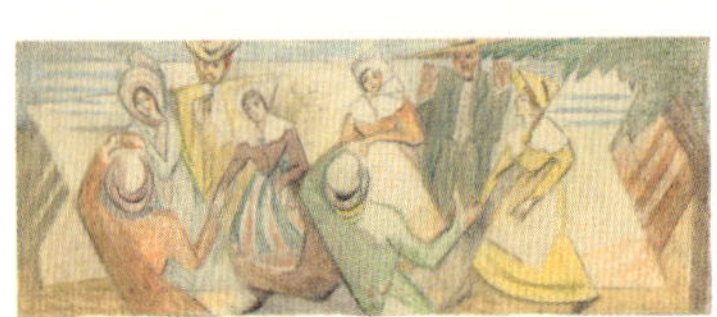

cat 109
Le quadrille de la Mascotte (*The Mascot quadrille*)
preliminary drawing for mural painting in the *salle des fêtes*, Hôtel Schaeffer (1946–47)
Moly-Sabata, Sablons, France
coloured pencil on paper
sheet 25 × 64.6 cm
purchased 2012
2012.2273

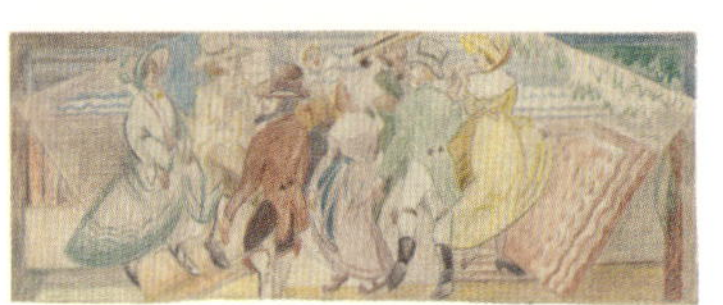

cat 110
Première figure du quadrille (*First step of the quadrille*) preliminary drawing for mural painting in the *salle des fêtes*, Hôtel Schaeffer (1946–47)
Moly-Sabata, Sablons, France
coloured pencil on paper
sheet 24.9 × 65.3 cm
purchased 2012
2012.2191.41

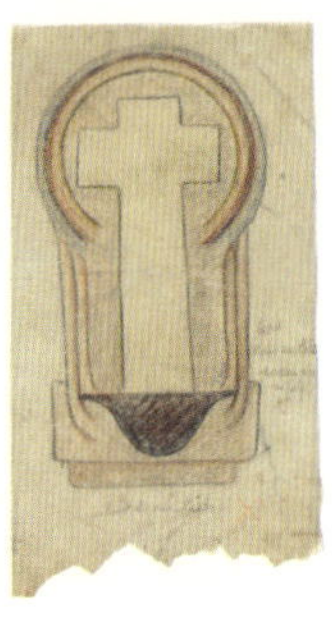

cat 111
Design for a holy water stoup for the chapel of the abbey La Pierre-qui-Vire 1948
Moly-Sabata, Sablons, France
pencil and coloured pencil on paper
sheet 33.4 × 17.8 cm (irreg)
purchased 2012
2012.2397

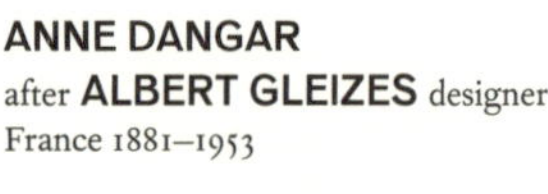

ANNE DANGAR
after **ALBERT GLEIZES** designer
France 1881–1953

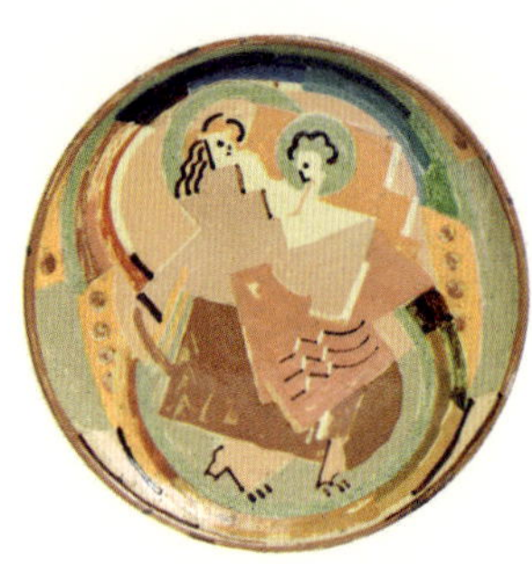

cat 112 p 160
Mère et enfant (*Mother and child*) (1935–37)
Anjaleras Pottery, Cliousclat, France
wheel-thrown glazed earthenware with slip decoration
3 × 46 (diam) cm
monogram and inscription on verso, 'M.S.D. après un tableau / de Albert Gleizes 1935'
collection of Colin Beutel and Conal Coad

LIKELY EXHIBITED: Group exhibition of popular pottery, pavilion of the Union des artistes modernes, Exposition internationale des arts et techniques dans la vie moderne, Paris, 25 May – 25 November 1937; *Les maîtres de l'art indépendant, 1895–1937*, Petit Palais, Paris, June–October 1937

EXHIBITED: *32e groupe des artistes de ce temps*, Petit Palais, Paris, June 1938

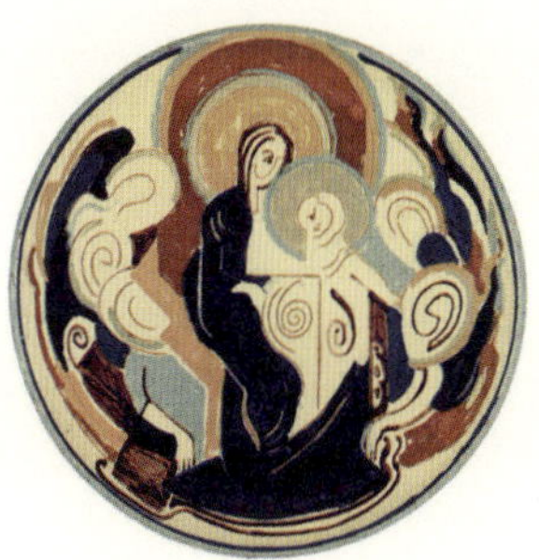

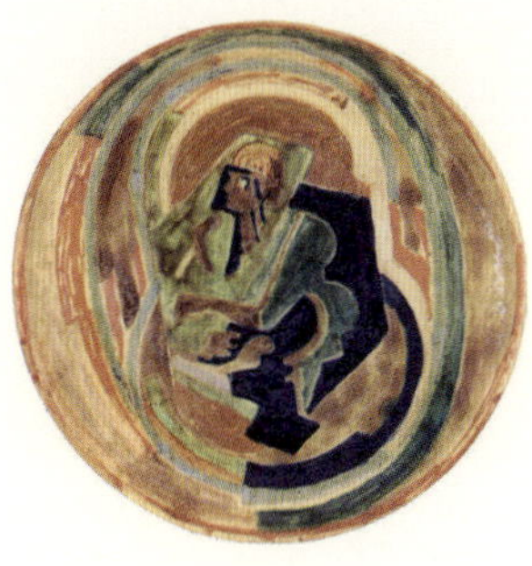

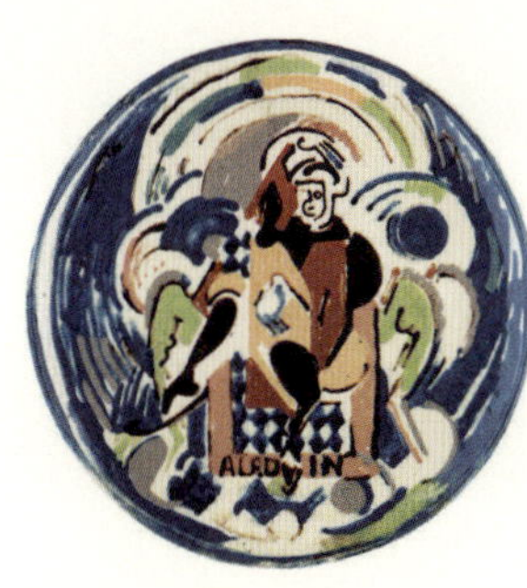

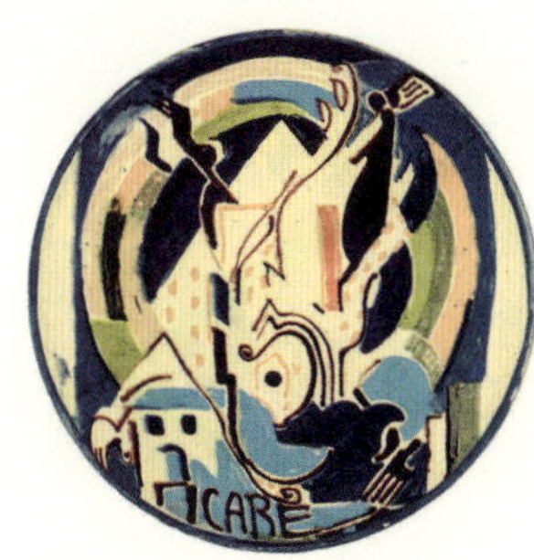

cat 113 p 94
La Vierge et l'Enfant en majesté entourés de six anges (*Virgin and Child in majesty surrounded by six angels*) after Cimabue (1936–37)
Anjaleras Pottery, Cliousclat, France
wheel-thrown glazed earthenware
with slip decoration
4 × 44 (diam) cm
monogram on verso, 'MSD'
Art Gallery of New South Wales, Gadigal Nura/Sydney
purchased with funds provided by the Mervyn Horton Bequest 2017
4.2017

LIKELY EXHIBITED: Group exhibition of popular pottery, pavilion of the Union des artistes moderne, Exposition internationale des arts et techniques dans la vie moderne, Paris, 25 May – 25 November 1937; *Les maîtres de l'art indépendant, 1895–1937*, Petit Palais, Paris, June–October 1937

cat 114
Femme au gant (*Woman with glove*) (1936–38)
likely Anjaleras Pottery, Cliousclat, France
wheel-thrown glazed earthenware
with slip decoration
2.8 × 49.5 (diam) cm
no inscriptions
Art Gallery of New South Wales, Gadigal Nura/Sydney
purchased with funds provided by the Mollie Douglas Bequest 2021
5.2021

cat 115 p 206
Aladin (*Aladdin*) (1938–48)
likely Anjaleras Pottery, Cliousclat, France
wheel-thrown glazed earthenware
with slip decoration
2.5 × 37.5 (diam) cm
monogram on verso, 'M.S./GD'
Art Gallery of South Australia, Tarntanya/Adelaide
gift of the Art Gallery of South Australia Foundation 2012
20121C1A

cat 116 p 205
Icare (*Icarus*) 1939
likely Anjaleras Pottery, Cliousclat, France
wheel-thrown glazed earthenware
with slip decoration
2.7 × 48.6 (diam) cm
monogram on verso, 'M.S.D Gleizes 1939'
Art Gallery of New South Wales, Gadigal Nura/Sydney
purchased with funds provided by the Mollie Douglas Bequest 2017
86.2017

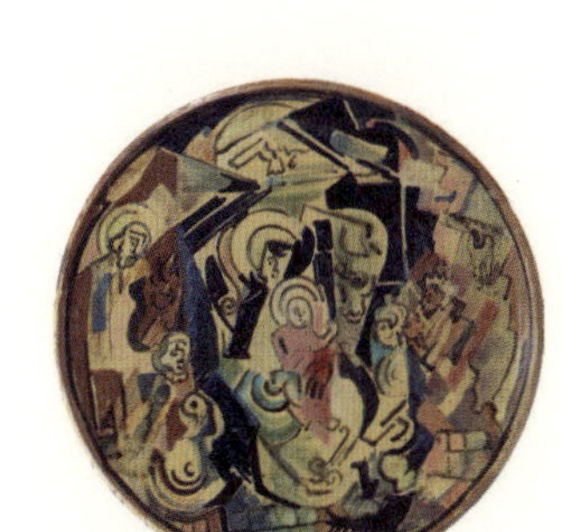

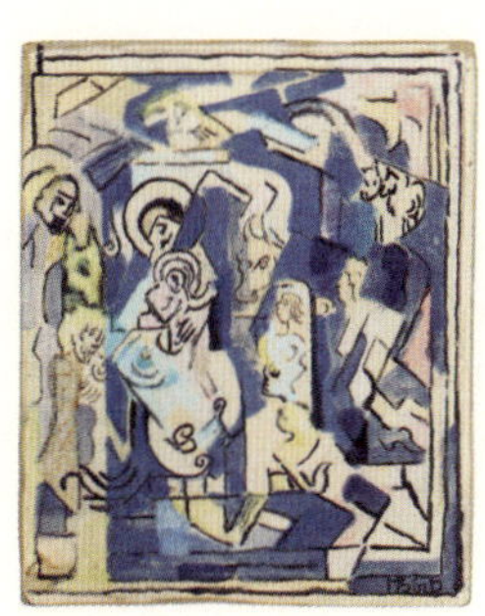

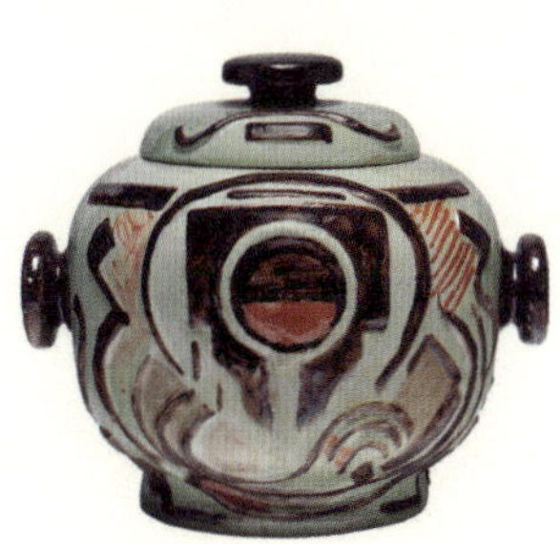

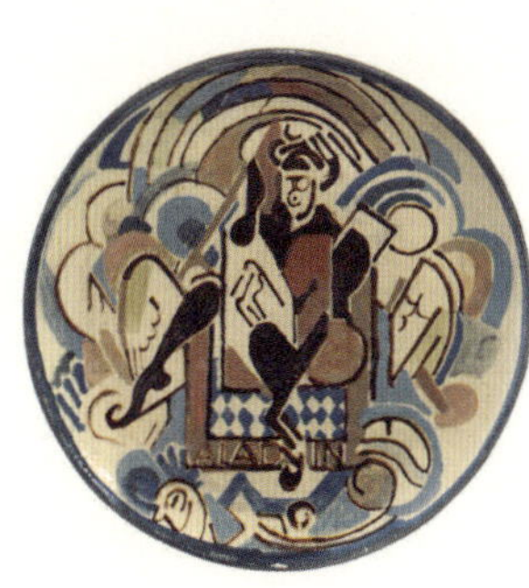

cat 117 p 209
L'Adoration des Mages (*Adoration of the Magi*) (1945–46)
likely Anjaleras Pottery, Cliousclat, France
wheel-thrown glazed earthenware
with slip decoration
2 × 52 (diam) cm
monogram on base, 'MSGD'
purchased 2002
2002.49

cat 118 p 177
L'Adoration des Mages (*Adoration of the Magi*) (1945–46)
Auvergne-Rhône-Alpes, France
glazed earthenware with slip decoration
41.7 × 34.2 × 1.8 cm
monogram lower right, 'MSGD'
Art Gallery of New South Wales, Gadigal Nura/Sydney
purchased with funds provided by the Mollie Douglas Bequest 2017
20.2017

cat 119 p 212
Pot with lid and handles (1946–49)
Auvergne-Rhône-Alpes, France
wheel-thrown glazed earthenware
with slip decoration
31 × 36 (irreg diam) cm (overall)
monogram on side below handle and verso of lid, 'MSGD'
purchased 2002
2002.46.A-B

cat 120 p 207
Aladin (*Aladdin*) 1948
likely Anjaleras Pottery, Cliousclat, France
wheel-thrown glazed earthenware
with slip decoration
2 × 45 (diam) cm
monogram on base, 'MSGD'
purchased 2002
2002.48

LIKELY EXHIBITED: *Albert Gleizes* [Gouaches by Gleizes, ceramics after Gleizes by Dangar], Galerie des Garets, Paris, 20 April – 11 May 1948

ANNE DANGAR
after **ALBERT GLEIZES** designer
Continued

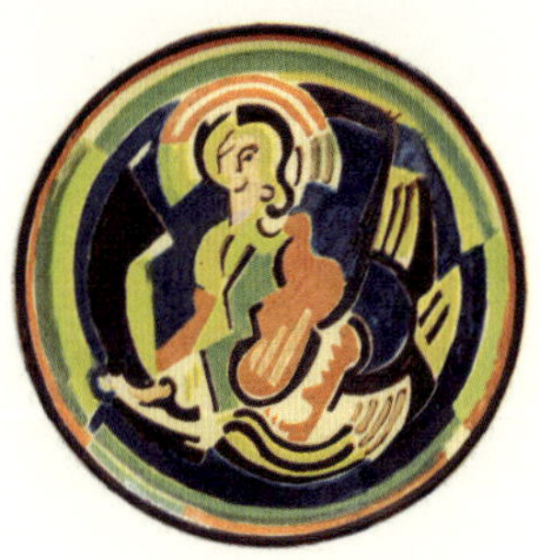

cat 121 p 204
Figure en gloire (*Figure in glory*) 1948
likely Anjaleras Pottery, Cliousclat, France
wheel-thrown glazed earthenware
with slip decoration
2.5 × 48.7 (diam) cm
monogram on verso, 'M.S.G.D'
Art Gallery of South Australia, Tarntanya/Adelaide
gift of the Art Gallery of South Australia Foundation 2012
20129C8A
LIKELY EXHIBITED: *Albert Gleizes* [Gouaches by Gleizes, ceramics after Gleizes by Dangar], Galerie des Garets, Paris, 20 April – 11 May 1948

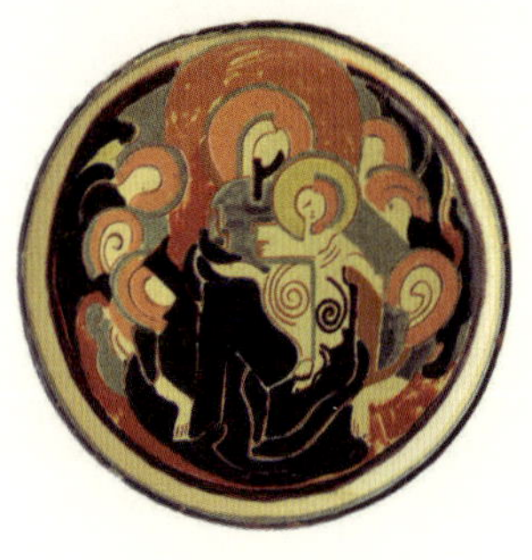

cat 122 p 208
La Vierge et l'Enfant en majesté entourés de six anges (*Virgin and Child in majesty surrounded by six angels*) after Cimabue 1948
likely Anjaleras Pottery, Cliousclat, France
wheel-thrown glazed earthenware
with slip decoration
4.8 × 45.6 (diam) cm
monogram on rim of base, 'M.S.D.'
National Gallery of Victoria, Naarm/Narrm/Melbourne
presented through the NGV Foundation by the Albert Gleizes Foundation, Member, 2005
2005.57
LIKELY EXHIBITED: *Albert Gleizes* [Gouaches by Gleizes, ceramics after Gleizes by Dangar], Galerie des Garets, Paris, 20 April – 11 May 1948

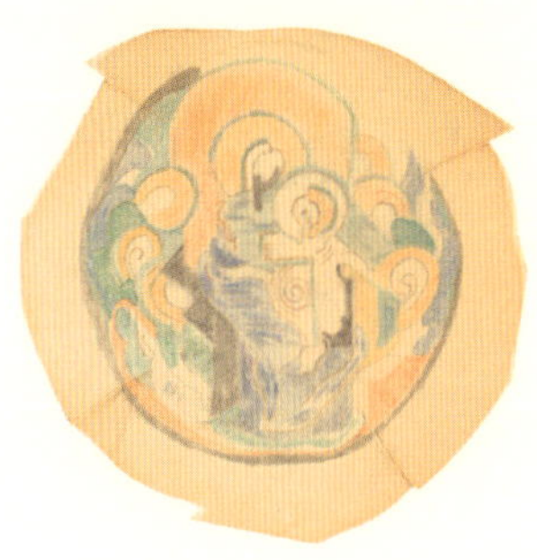

cat 123
La Vierge et l'Enfant en majesté entourés de six anges (*Virgin and Child in majesty surrounded by six angels*) design for plate after Cimabue c 1937
Moly-Sabata, Sablons, France
coloured pencil on tracing paper
sheet 53.9 × 54.5 cm (irreg)
purchased 2012
2012.2265

ANNE DANGAR
UNIDENTIFIED FRENCH CHILD
active France 1930s

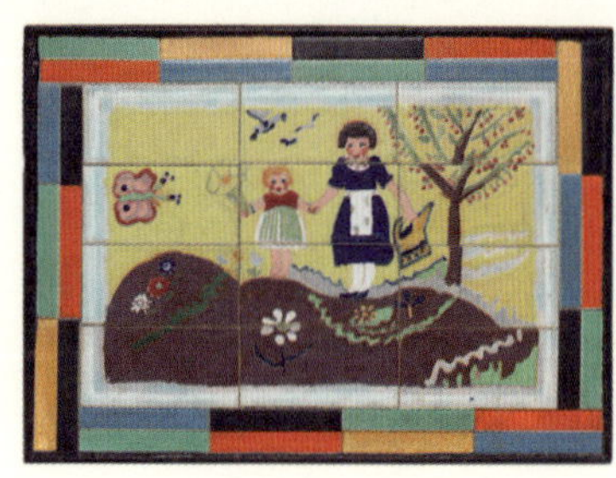

cat 124
Tabletop based on child's drawing 1937
Saint-Vallier, France
enamel glazed industrial ceramic tiles, cast iron
49 × 69.5 × 50.5 cm
no inscriptions
private collection

ANNE DANGAR
JACQUELINE LERAT
France 1920–2009

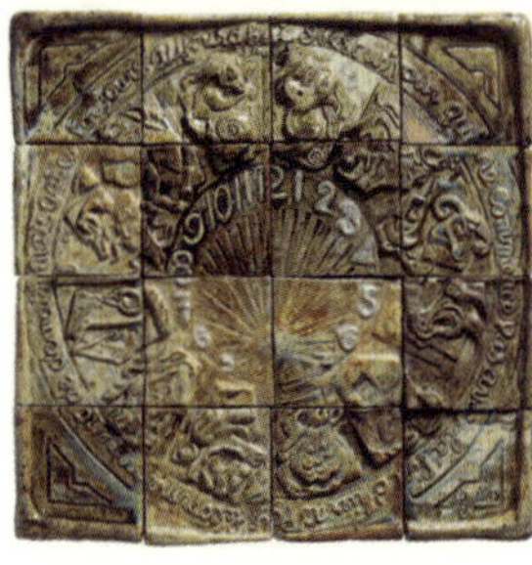

cat 125 p 174
Sundial 1945
La Borne pottery, Bourges, Centre-Val de Loire, France
16 hand-built salt-fired stoneware panels with relief decoration
4.6 × 73.5 × 73.5 cm (overall)
4.6 × 18 × 18 cm (each)
monogram lower right, 'MSD'
purchased 2023
2023.134.A-P
EXHIBITED: Group exhibition, Folklore, Lyon, 8 December 1945 – 8 January 1946

ANNE DANGAR
LUCIE DEVEYLE
France 1908–1956
JEAN-MARIE PAQUAUD
France 1909–1988

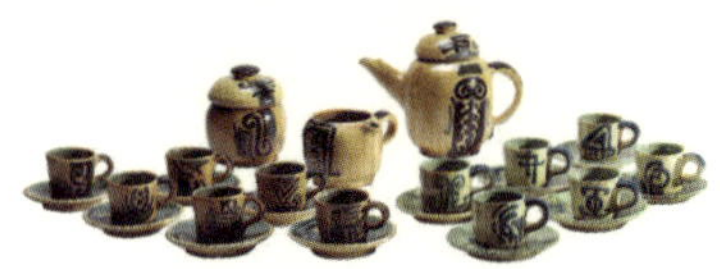
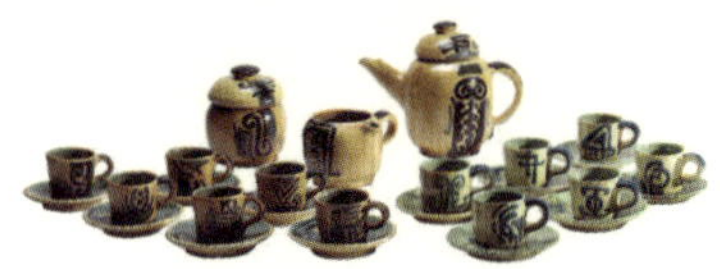

cat 126 p 213
Tea service 1949–51
Poterie Bert, Roussillon, France
wheel-thrown glazed earthenware
with slip decoration
teapot: 19.5 × 26 (irreg) cm (overall)
sugar bowl: 14.5 × 11.8 (irreg) cm (overall)
milk jug: 9.8 × 15.3 (irreg) cm
teacup and saucer: 8 × 13.4 (diam) cm (overall, each)
monogram on base of all pieces except one teacup and saucer, 'MSD'
purchased 2024
2024.84.A-O

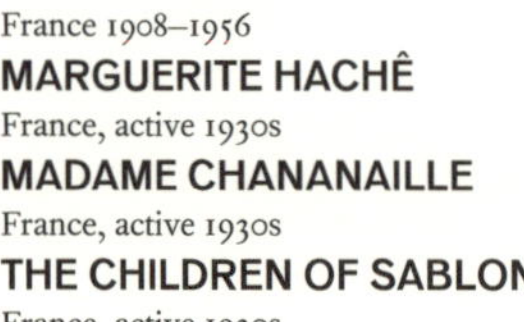

ANNE DANGAR
LUCIE DEVEYLE
France 1908–1956
MARGUERITE HACHÊ
France, active 1930s
MADAME CHANANAILLE
France, active 1930s
THE CHILDREN OF SABLONS
France, active 1930s

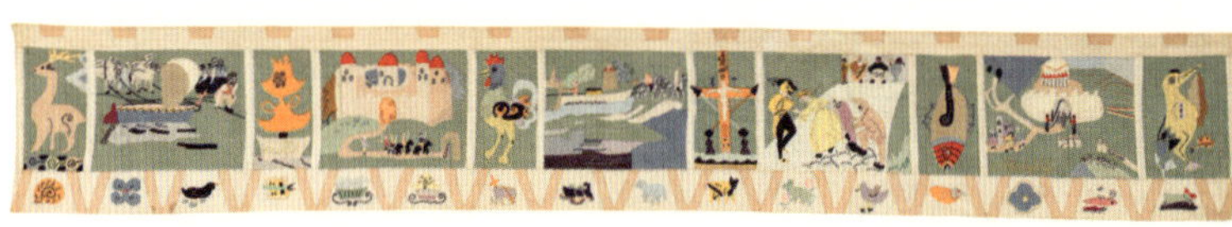

cat 127 pp 162–63
History of the Rhône wall hanging 1936–37
Moly-Sabata, Sablons, France
embroidered and appliquéd cotton and linen
77.5 × 515 cm
Musée des beaux-arts de Lyon, France
EXHIBITED: Group display of Moly-Sabata, Pavillon du Forez-Vivarais, Exposition internationale des arts et techniques dans la vie moderne, Paris, 25 May – 25 November 1937

RALPH BALSON
England 1890 – Australia 1964

cat 128
Painting 1941
Gadigal Nura/Sydney
oil on cardboard on composition board
47.2 × 78.7 cm
purchased 2010
2010.321

cat 129 p 102
Constructive painting 1951
Gadigal Nura/Sydney
oil on cardboard
63 × 78.8 cm
bequest of Grace Crowley 1979
80.1086

DORRIT BLACK
Australia 1891–1951

cat 130
Study with two figures 1929
Paris
gouache on paper on card
image 17.5 × 13.3 cm
sheet 27.5 × 17.8 cm
Art Gallery of South Australia, Tarntanya/Adelaide
South Australian Government Grant 1972
728P7

cat 131 p 101
Still life with jug and ladle c 1935
Tarntanya/Adelaide
oil on canvas on composition board
50.5 × 40.5 cm
Art Gallery of South Australia, Tarntanya/Adelaide
gift of Joan Beer, Frank Choate, Elizabeth H. Finnegan OAM, Theo S Maras AM OLJ, David McKee, Pam McKee, Diana McLaurin, Tom Pearce and John Phillips through the Art Gallery of South Australia Foundation Collectors Club 2013
20138P29

cat 132 p 198
The posy 1945
Tarntanya/Adelaide
oil on canvas
63 × 55 cm
collection of Colin Beutel and Conal Coad

ESTELLE CREED
Australia 1904–1997

cat 133 p 42
Designs for ceramics and decoration 1929
Gadigal Nura/Sydney
pencil and watercolour on paper
sheet 38 × 57 cm
collection of JJ Glassock and family

cat 134 p 40
Still life with jug 1929
Gadigal Nura/Sydney
oil on canvas
36.6 × 46.6 cm
purchased 2024
2024.63

cat 135
Study in translation and rotation (1930–31)
Moly-Sabata, Sablons, France
black and red pencil on paper
sheet 24.2 × 27 cm
purchased 2024
2024.64

cat 136 p 110
Cubist exercise using Gleizes's principles (1930–31)
Moly-Sabata, Sablons, France
gouache on paper
image 29.4 × 10.3 cm
sheet 32.2 × 15.6 cm
collection of JJ Glassock and family

cat 137
Cubist exercise using Gleizes's principles (1930–31)
Moly-Sabata, Sablons, France
gouache on paper
image 30.5 × 12.2 cm
sheet 32.2 × 15.6 cm
collection of JJ Glassock and family

GRACE CROWLEY
Australia 1890–1979

cat 138 p 34
Study for *Sailors and models* (1928–29)
Paris
pencil on paper
sheet 56.8 × 88.6 cm
gift of Grace Buckley in memory of Grace Crowley 1980
80.1333

cat 139 p 35
Sailors and models (1928–29)
Paris
oil on canvas
54.6 × 81.6 cm
gift of Grace Buckley in memory of Grace Crowley 1980
80.1334

cat 140
Cubist exercise using Gleizes's principles 1929
Paris
gouache, pen and colour inks and black pencil on paper
image 14.2 × 11.2 cm
sheet 18 × 15.6 cm
gift of Grace Buckley in memory of Grace Crowley 1980
80.1337.A

cat 141
Cubist exercise using Gleizes's principles 1929
Paris
gouache, pen and colour inks and black pencil on paper
image 13.7 × 10.5 cm
sheet 18 × 15.6 cm
gift of Grace Buckley in memory of Grace Crowley 1980
80.1337.B

cat 142
Cubist exercise using Gleizes's principles 1929
Paris
gouache, pen and colour inks and black pencil on paper
image 12.7 × 10.8 cm
sheet 14.2 × 12.4 cm
gift of Grace Buckley in memory of Grace Crowley 1980
80.1339.A

cat 143
Cubist exercise using Gleizes's principles 1929
Paris
gouache, pen and colour inks and black pencil on paper
image 13 × 10.8 cm
sheet 14.2 × 12.4 cm
gift of Grace Buckley in memory of Grace Crowley 1980
80.1339.B

cat 144 p 54
Cubist composition, study for a mural decoration by Albert Gleizes 1929
Moly-Sabata, Sablons, France
drawing in black pencil on paper
sheet 20.7 × 26.8 cm
gift of Grace Buckley in memory of Grace Crowley 1980
80.1346

cat 145
Cubist composition, study for a mural decoration by Albert Gleizes 1929
Moly-Sabata, Sablons, France
black pencil on paper
sheet 20.8 × 26.8 cm
gift of Grace Buckley in memory of Grace Crowley 1980
80.1347A

cat 146 p 104
Painting 1951
Gadigal Nura/Sydney
oil on composition board
58.4 × 70.6 cm
purchased 1969
69.194

RAH FIZELLE
Australia 1891–1964

cat 147
Construction II c 1939
Gadigal Nura/Sydney
oil on board
91 × 65 cm
Queensland Art Gallery | Gallery of Modern Art
purchased 2012 with funds from Philip Bacon AM
through the Queensland Art Gallery Foundation
2012.300

ALBERT GLEIZES
France 1881–1953

cat 148 p 84
Femme au gant noir (*Woman with black glove*)
1920
France
oil on canvas
126 × 100 cm
private international collection

cat 149
La Vierge et l'Enfant en majesté entourés de six anges (*Virgin and Child in majesty surrounded by six angels*) design for plate after Cimabue c 1937
France
gouache over pen and ink on tracing paper
on cardboard
image 48.2 (diam) cm
cardboard 48.2 × 52.1 cm (irreg)
National Gallery of Victoria, Naarm/Narrm/
Melbourne
purchased NGV Foundation, 2012
2012.291

DORE HAWTHORNE
Australia 1895–1977

cat 150 p 39
Some of Grace Crowley's Port Macquarie class 1930
Gadigal Nura/Sydney
oil on canvas
34 × 52 cm
private collection

EVIE HONE
Ireland 1894–1955

cat 151
Seated figure 1929
Moly-Sabata, Sablons, France
pochoir on paper
image 41.8 × 25.3 cm
sheet 45.6 × 29.6 cm (irreg)
Art Gallery of New South Wales, Gadigal
Nura/Sydney
purchased with funds provided by the
Florence Turner Blake Bequest 1959
DB39.1959

ROBERT POUYAUD
France 1901–1970

cat 152 p 99
Diagrams illustrating pochoir technique and Gleizes's principles of translation and rotation 1930
gouache on card
France
sheet 27 × 21.2 cm
Grace Crowley archive
National Art Archive, Art Gallery of New South Wales, Gadigal Nura/Sydney
bequest of Grace Crowley 1979
ARC106.11.12.1.A-E11.12

cat 153
Cubist composition 1931
in Robert Pouyaud and César Geoffray, *Suite de sons et de couleurs pour piano*, Moly-Sabata, Éditions Sablons, France, 1931
pochoir on paper
image 25.5 × 18 cm
sheet 41.3 × 32 cm
collection of Colin Beutel and Conal Coad

ROBERT POUYAUD
after **ALBERT GLEIZES** designer

cat 154
Peinture à trois éléments (*Painting in three elements*) (1927–29)
France
pochoir in 13 colours on paper
image 37.9 × 28.8 cm
sheet 53.6 × 43 cm
Art Gallery of New South Wales, Gadigal Nura/Sydney
bequest of Grace Crowley 1980
187.198

NINETTE DOZ
France, active 1930s

cat 155 p 96
Exercises in translation
in Student workbook 1940s
Moly-Sabata, Sablons, France
pencil and coloured pencil on paper
sheet 31.5 × 24.3 cm
National Gallery of Australia Research Library and Archives, Kamberri/Canberra

LOUIS PEGERON
active 1940s

cat 156
Cubist composition 1941
Moly-Sabata, Sablons, France
pencil, coloured pencil on paper
sheet 25.1 × 30 cm
National Gallery of Australia Research Library and Archives, Kamberri/Canberra

UNIDENTIFIED STUDENT OF ANNE DANGAR
active 1940s

cat 157
Château in landscape 1940s
Moly-Sabata, Sablons, France
pencil, coloured pencil and crayon on paper
sheet 23.9 × 30.9 cm
National Gallery of Australia Research Library and Archives, Kamberri/Canberra

cat 158
Jug, horse and notes on colour theory
in Student workbook 1940s
Moly-Sabata, Sablons, France
pencil and coloured pencil on paper
sheet 31.3 × 24.3 cm
National Gallery of Australia Research Library and Archives, Kamberri/Canberra

cat 159
Moly-Sabata and two ducks 1940s
Moly-Sabata, Sablons, France
pencil, coloured pencil and crayon on paper
sheet 24.2 × 31.3 cm
National Gallery of Australia Research Library and Archives, Kamberri/Canberra

cat 160
Notes on colour theory
in Student workbook 1940s
Moly-Sabata, Sablons, France
pencil and coloured pencil on paper
sheet 31.1 × 24.2 cm
National Gallery of Australia Research Library and Archives, Kamberri/Canberra

cat 161
Man fishing 1943
Moly-Sabata, Sablons, France
pencil, coloured pencil and crayon on paper
sheet 31.4 × 24.2 cm
National Gallery of Australia Research Library and Archives, Kamberri/Canberra

cat 162
Market scene 1943
Moly-Sabata, Sablons, France
pencil, coloured pencil and crayon on paper
sheet 23.7 × 30.9 cm
National Gallery of Australia Research Library and Archives, Kamberri/Canberra

cat 163
Seated woman
in Student workbook 1940s
Moly-Sabata, Sablons, France
pencil and coloured pencil on paper
sheet 31.3 × 24.3 cm
National Gallery of Australia Research Library and Archives, Kamberri/Canberra

cat 164
Woman weaving and child 1943
Moly-Sabata, Sablons, France
pencil, coloured pencil and crayon on paper
sheet 23.7 × 30.9 cm
National Gallery of Australia Research Library and Archives, Kamberri/Canberra

List of figures

fig 1 p 10
Anne Dangar at the Clovis Nicolas pottery
in Saint-Désirat, the Ardèche
France
June 1931
gelatin silver photograph
unknown photographer
Fonds Albert Gleizes, Kandinsky Library,
Musée national d'art moderne,
Centre Georges Pompidou, Paris

fig 2 p 18
Farewell to Mr and Mrs John Bryson,
in Elizabeth Dangar's garden
Thunggutti/Dunghutti Country/Kempsey,
NSW
1912
gelatin silver photograph
unknown photographer
Macleay River Historical Society collection,
Thunggutti/Dunghutti Country/Kempsey

fig 3 p 19
Portrait of Anne Dangar
in *The Home: An Australian Quarterly*, vol 2,
no 4, 1 December 1921, p 108

fig 4 p 20
Otho Orde and Elizabeth Dangar's golden
wedding anniversary
NSW
1918
gelatin silver photograph
unknown photographer
Macleay River Historical Society collection,
Thunggutti/Dunghutti Country/Kempsey

fig 5 p 20
The Singleton family at Mondrook
Biripi Country/Mondrook, NSW
1917
gelatin silver photograph
unknown photographer
private collection

fig 6 p 20
Anne Dangar
NSW
c 1925
gelatin silver photograph
unknown photographer
Grace Crowley archive
National Art Archive, Art Gallery of
New South Wales, Gadigal Nura/Sydney
bequest of Grace Crowley 1979
ARC106.23.27

fig 7 p 21
Passport photograph of Anne Dangar
Gadigal Nura/Sydney
1926
gelatin silver photograph
unknown photographer
Grace Crowley archive
National Art Archive, Art Gallery of
New South Wales, Gadigal Nura/Sydney
bequest of Grace Crowley 1979
ARC106.23.3

fig 8 p 21
Académie Lhote
Paris
1927–28
gelatin silver photograph
unknown photographer
Archives André Lhote, private collection, Paris

fig 9 p 23
Postcard of Mirmande (the Drôme)
France
date unknown
private collection

fig 10 p 23
Alexandre Mercereau, *Quelques peintres: André Lhote*, Chez Jacques Povolozky, Paris,
1921
Grace Crowley archive
National Art Archive, Art Gallery of
New South Wales, Gadigal Nura/Sydney
bequest of Grace Crowley 1979

fig 11 p 24
Advertisement for Anne Dangar's art instruction
in *Undergrowth: A Magazine of Youth and Ideals*,
July–August 1929

fig 12 p 26
Presbyterian church members at a picnic
Thunggutti/Dunghutti Country/Kempsey,
NSW
early 1900s
gelatin silver photograph
unknown photographer
Macleay River Historical Society collection,
Thunggutti/Dunghutti Country/Kempsey

fig 13 p 31
Julian Ashton
England 1951 – Australia 1942
View of the North Head, Sydney Harbour 1888
Eora Country/Sydney
watercolour on paper
image 34.9 × 23.9 cm
sheet 35.2 × 24.1 cm
National Gallery of Victoria, Naarm/
Narrm/Melbourne
purchased 1965
1523-5

fig 14 p 52
Albert Gleizes
La Crucifixion (*The Crucifixion*) 1927
France
distemper on canvas
213 × 175 cm
Musée national d'art moderne,
Centre Georges Pompidou, Paris
gift of Mme Juliette Roche-Gleizes 1964
AM 4222 P

fig 15 p 55
Albert Gleizes
France 1881–1953
Le Couronnement de la Vierge
(*Coronation of the Virgin*) 1927
France
oil on canvas
229 × 229 cm
Musée national d'art moderne,
Centre Georges Pompidou, Paris
gift of Mme Juliette Roche-Gleizes 1964
AM 4245 P

fig 16 p 61
Cécile Pouyaud, Anne Dangar and
Robert Pouyaud at Moly-Sabata
Sablons, France
1930
gelatin silver photograph
unknown photographer
Grace Crowley archive
National Art Archive, Art Gallery of
New South Wales, Gadigal Nura/Sydney
bequest of Grace Crowley 1979
ARC106.23.1

fig 17 p 61
Anne Dangar creating pochoirs at Moly-Sabata
Sablons, France
c 1931
gelatin silver photograph
unknown photographer
Fonds Albert Gleizes, Kandinsky Library, Musée
national d'art moderne,
Centre Georges Pompidou, Paris

fig 18 p 62
Anne Dangar's business card
1930s–40s
Papers of Anne Dangar
National Gallery of Australia Research Library
and Archives, Kamberri/Canberra

fig 19 p 63
Anne Dangar and students at Moly-Sabata
Sablons, France
c 1931
gelatin silver photograph
unknown photographer
Fonds Albert Gleizes, Kandinsky Library,
Musée national d'art moderne,
Centre Georges Pompidou, Paris

fig 20 p 64
Lucie Deveyle, Anne Dangar, Mido and
Gilka Geoffray at Moly-Sabata
Sablons, France
1930s
gelatin silver photograph
unknown photographer
Fonds Albert Gleizes, Kandinsky Library,
Musée national d'art moderne,
Centre Georges Pompidou, Paris

fig 21 p 64
César Geoffray, René Corniot, Mido Geoffray,
Anne Dangar, Gilka Geoffray and Madame
Geoffray-Mandy in the gardens at Moly-Sabata
Sablons, France
1931
gelatin silver photograph
unknown photographer
Grace Crowley archive
National Art Archive, Art Gallery of
New South Wales, Gadigal Nura/Sydney
bequest of Grace Crowley 1979
ARC106.23.17

fig 22 p 64
Anne Dangar, Gilka and Mido Geoffray
at Moly-Sabata
Sablons, France
1931
gelatin silver photograph
unknown photographer
Fonds Albert Gleizes, Kandinsky Library,
Musée national d'art moderne,
Centre Georges Pompidou, Paris

fig 23 p 65
Gilka Geoffray, René Corniot, Mido and
César Geoffray, Anne Dangar and Madame
Geoffray-Mandy, on the stairs at Moly-Sabata
Sablons, France
1931
gelatin silver photograph
unknown photographer
Grace Crowley archive
National Art Archive, Art Gallery of
New South Wales, Gadigal Nura/Sydney
bequest of Grace Crowley 1979
ARC106.23.2

fig 24 p 66
Juliette Roche, Albert Gleizes and Anne Dangar
France
1930s–40s
gelatin silver photograph
unknown photographer
Fonds Albert Gleizes, Kandinsky Library,
Musée national d'art moderne,
Centre Georges Pompidou, Paris

fig 25 p 67
Albert Gleizes in his studio
France
c 1934
gelatin silver photograph
unknown photographer
Grace Crowley archive
National Art Archive, Art Gallery of
New South Wales, Gadigal Nura/Sydney
bequest of Grace Crowley 1979
ARC106.23.3

fig 26 p 68
Installation view featuring ceramics by
Anne Dangar, textiles by Juliette Roche and
paintings by the Moly-Sabata community,
annual exhibition at Moly-Sabata
Sablons, France
1934
gelatin silver photograph
unknown photographer
Grace Crowley archive
National Art Archive, Art Gallery of
New South Wales, Gadigal Nura/Sydney
bequest of Grace Crowley 1979
ARC106.23.35

fig 27 p 68
Paintings by Anne Dangar's students on
display at the annual Moly-Sabata exhibition
Moly-Sabata, Sablons, France
c 1934
gelatin silver photograph
unknown photographer
Fonds Albert Gleizes, Kandinsky Library,
Musée national d'art moderne,
Centre Georges Pompidou, Paris

fig 28 p 69
Installation view featuring ceramics by
Anne Dangar and paintings by Albert Gleizes,
annual exhibition at Moly-Sabata
Sablons, France
1934
gelatin silver photograph
unknown photographer
Grace Crowley archive
National Art Archive, Art Gallery of
New South Wales, Gadigal Nura/Sydney
bequest of Grace Crowley 1979
ARC106.23.5

fig 29 p 69
Installation view featuring ceramics by
Anne Dangar, textiles by Juliette Roche and
paintings by Albert Gleizes, annual exhibition
at Moly-Sabata
Sablons, France
1934
gelatin silver photograph
unknown photographer
Grace Crowley archive
National Art Archive, Art Gallery of
New South Wales, Gadigal Nura/Sydney
bequest of Grace Crowley 1979
ARC106.23.15

fig 30 p 70
Annual exhibition of Moly-Sabata,
quai Jules-Roche, Serrières, 15–25 August
France
1935
gelatin silver photograph
unknown photographer
Fonds Albert Gleizes, Kandinsky Library,
Musée national d'art moderne,
Centre Georges Pompidou, Paris

fig 31 p 70
Postcard of Serrières sent to Dorrit Black
inscribed by Anne Dangar
France
c 1930
Papers of Dorrit Black
National Gallery of Australia Research Library
and Archives, Kamberri/Canberra

fig 32 p 70
Francine Bensa
France 1893–1975
Ateliers Moly Sabata Sablons Isère 1937
France
woodcut, printed in black ink, from one block
sheet 8.9 × 14 cm
Papers of Anne Dangar
National Gallery of Australia Research Library
and Archives, Kamberri/Canberra

fig 33 p 87
Anne Dangar
Australia 1885 – France 1951
Plate depicting Serrières bridge 1930–34
Auvergne-Rhône-Alpes, France
wheel-thrown glazed earthenware
with slip decoration
3 × 33.5 (diam) cm
private collection

fig 34 p 91
Robert Pouyaud
France 1901–1970
Poteries d'Etrurie
in Albert Gleizes, *La forme et l'histoire*,
Chez Jacques Povolozky, Paris, 1932, p 82

fig 35 p 95
Cimabue (Cenni di Pepe)
Florence 1240 – (likely) Pisa 1302
La Vierge et l'Enfant en majesté entourés de six anges (maestà) (*Virgin and Child in majesty surrounded by six angels*) (1275–1300)
Italy
tempera on gold on wood
427 × 280 cm
Musée du Louvre, Paris
INV254

fig 36 p 106
Estelle Creed
Australia 1904–1997
Sydney Harbour Bridge under construction 1929
Gadigal Nura/Sydney
oil on canvas adhered to board
38.5 × 44 cm (sight)
private collection

fig 37 p 109
Estelle Creed
Reclining nude 1929
Paris
oil on canvas
36.3 × 53.4 cm
private collection

fig 38 p 112
Grace Crowley with Rah Fizelle and friends in Crowley's roof garden, 227 George St, Sydney
Gadigal Nura/Sydney
c 1935
gelatin silver photograph
unknown photographer
Grace Crowley archive
National Art Archive, Art Gallery of New South Wales, Gadigal Nura/Sydney
bequest of Grace Crowley 1979
ARC106.21.3

fig 39 p 116
Portrait of Grace Crowley
Paris
c 1927
gelatin silver photograph
photograph: P Deibo
Grace Crowley archive
National Art Archive, Art Gallery of New South Wales, Gadigal Nura/Sydney
bequest of Grace Crowley 1979
ARC106.21.1

fig 40 p 133
Les maîtres de l'art indépendant, 1895–1937, catalogue for exhibition in which Anne Dangar's work was displayed
Éditions arts et métiers graphiques, Paris, 1937

fig 41 p 134
Aspect actuel du cubisme chez quelques aînés et quelques jeunes, Salon d'automne, 1938, featuring ceramics and gouaches by Anne Dangar, and paintings by Robert Delaunay and Albert Gleizes
Paris
1938
gelatin silver photograph
photograph: Marc Vaux
Fonds Albert Gleizes, Kandinsky Library, Musée national d'art moderne, Centre Georges Pompidou, Paris

fig 42 p 134
Anne Dangar's ceramics, including *Mère et enfant* (*Mother and child*) 1935–37
in Maximilien Gauthier, 'Moly-Sabata', *Art et Décoration*, September–October 1938, p 299
collection of Colin Beutel and Conal Coad

fig 43 p 134
Anne Dangar's ceramics
in Maximilien Gauthier, 'Moly-Sabata', *Art et Décoration*, September–October 1938, p 297
collection of Colin Beutel and Conal Coad

fig 44 p 135
Photograph of Anne Dangar's tiled panel 'after Albert Gleizes' displayed in the Exposition internationale des arts et techniques dans la vie moderne, Paris
France
1937
gelatin silver photograph
photograph: J Roseman
Grace Crowley archive
National Art Archive, Art Gallery of New South Wales, Gadigal Nura/Sydney
bequest of Grace Crowley 1979
ARC106.24.1

fig 45 p 135
The Forez-Vivarais pavilion in the Centre Regional at the Exposition international, Paris
France
1937
photograph: Cliché Samand
private collection

fig 46 p 136
Anne Dangar on the balcony at Moly-Sabata
Sablons, France
1940s
gelatin silver photograph
unknown photographer
Grace Crowley archive
National Art Archive, Art Gallery of New South Wales, Gadigal Nura/Sydney
bequest of Grace Crowley 1979
ARC106.23.6

fig 47 p 137
Anne Dangar and baby at Moly-Sabata
Sablons, France
1940s
gelatin silver photograph
unknown photographer
Grace Crowley archive
National Art Archive, Art Gallery of New South Wales, Sydney/Gadigal Nura
bequest of Grace Crowley 1979
ARC106.23.26

fig 48 p 138
Arts indigènes Marrakech
Morocco
1939
gelatin silver photograph
unknown photographer
Fonds Albert Gleizes, Kandinsky Library, Musée national d'art moderne, Centre Georges Pompidou, Paris

fig 49 p 138
Sidi Hassan Ben-Cherif and Anne Dangar, Fez
Morocco
1939
gelatin silver photograph
unknown photographer
Fonds Albert Gleizes, Kandinsky Library, Musée national d'art moderne, Centre Georges Pompidou, Paris

fig 50 p 138
Anne Dangar and potter, Fez
Morocco
1939
gelatin silver photograph
unknown photographer
Fonds Albert Gleizes, Kandinsky Library, Musée national d'art moderne, Centre Georges Pompidou, Paris

fig 51 p 139
Anne Dangar in Fez
Morocco
1939
gelatin silver photograph
unknown photographer
Fonds Albert Gleizes, Kandinsky Library, Musée national d'art moderne, Centre Georges Pompidou, Paris

fig 52 p 139
Anne Dangar and potters, Fez
Morrocco
1939
gelatin silver photograph
unknown photographer
Fonds Albert Gleizes, Kandinsky Library, Musée national d'art moderne, Centre Georges Pompidou, Paris

fig 53 p 140
Anne Dangar with pottery apprentices at the Centre artisanal de poterie et arts plastiques de Mâcon
Mâcon, France
1942
gelatin silver photograph
unknown photographer
Fonds Albert Gleizes, Kandinsky Library, Musée national d'art moderne, Centre Georges Pompidou, Paris

fig 54 p 140
Anne Dangar and students at Moly-Sabata
Sablons, France
c 1942
gelatin silver photograph
photograph: Marius Cochard
Fonds Albert Gleizes, Kandinsky Library, Musée national d'art moderne, Centre Georges Pompidou, Paris

fig 55 p 141
Anne Dangar and students at Moly-Sabata
Sablons, France
c 1942
gelatin silver photograph
photograph: Marius Cochard
Fonds Albert Gleizes, Kandinsky Library, Musée national d'art moderne, Centre Georges Pompidou, Paris

fig 56 p 142
Unidentified man, Lucie Deveyle, Anne Dangar and Geoffrey Dangar at Moly-Sabata
Sablons, France
23 February 1945
gelatin silver photograph
unknown photographer
private collection

fig 57 p 144
Anne Dangar at work in the pottery, Roussillon
France
1940s
gelatin silver photograph
unknown photographer
Grace Crowley archive
National Art Archive, Art Gallery of New South Wales, Gadigal Nura/Sydney
bequest of Grace Crowley 1979
ARC106.23.7

fig 58 p 145
First firing in the kiln at Moly-Sabata
Sablons, France
August 1947
gelatin silver photograph
unknown photographer
Fonds Albert Gleizes, Kandinsky Library, Musée national d'art moderne, Centre Georges Pompidou, Paris

fig 59 p 145
Jean-Marie Paquaud, Anne Dangar and unknown potter at Moly-Sabata
Sablons, France
August 1947
gelatin silver photograph
unknown photographer
Fonds Albert Gleizes, Kandinsky Library, Musée national d'art moderne, Centre Georges Pompidou, Paris

fig 60 p 145
Jacqueline Bouvet (later Lerat), Anne Dangar and pottery apprentices at the Centre artisanal de poterie et arts plastiques de Mâcon
Mâcon, France
1942
gelatin silver photograph
unknown photographer
National Gallery of Australia Research Library and Archives, Kamberri/Canberra

fig 61 p 146
Anne Dangar at wedding in Saulce-sur-Rhône
France
July 1950
gelatin silver photograph
unknown photographer
Fonds Albert Gleizes, Kandinsky Library, Musée national d'art moderne, Centre Georges Pompidou, Paris

fig 62 p 147
Anne Dangar at her pottery wheel in her studio at Moly-Sabata
Sablons, France
July 1950
gelatin silver photograph
unknown photographer
Grace Crowley archive
National Art Archive, Art Gallery of New South Wales, Gadigal Nura/Sydney
bequest of Grace Crowley 1979
ARC106.23.9

fig 63 p 147
Anne Dangar wedging clay in her studio at Moly-Sabata
Sablons, France
July 1950
gelatin silver photograph
unknown photographer
Grace Crowley archive
National Art Archive, Art Gallery of New South Wales, Gadigal Nura/Sydney
bequest of Grace Crowley 1979
ARC106.23.10

fig 64 p 148
Anne Dangar and her godson Daniel Steinbach at Moly-Sabata
Sablons, France
March 1951
gelatin silver photograph
unknown photographer
Fonds Albert Gleizes, Kandinsky Library, Musée national d'art moderne, Centre Georges Pompidou, Paris

fig 65 p 169
Anne Dangar
Button 1943–45
Auvergne-Rhône-Alpes, France
hand-built glazed earthenware
3 × 1 × 1 cm (irreg)
private collection

fig 66 p 169
Anne Dangar
Button 1943–45
Auvergne-Rhône-Alpes, France
hand-built glazed earthenware
3 × 1 × 1 cm (irreg)
private collection

fig 67 p 169
Anne Dangar
Button 1943–45
Auvergne-Rhône-Alpes, France
hand-built glazed earthenware
3 × 1 × 1 cm (irreg)
private collection

fig 68 p 171
Anne Dangar
Saint Francis of Assisi 1940
Auvergne-Rhône-Alpes, France
wheel-thrown glazed earthenware with slip decoration
2.5 × 44.5 (diam) cm
private collection

fig 69 p 173
Anne Dangar
The landing 1944
Auvergne-Rhône-Alpes, France
wheel-thrown glazed earthenware
with slip decoration
2.2 × 32.3 (diam) cm
private collection

fig 70 p 176
Georges Rouault
France 1871–1958
Tête de jeune fille 1939
lithograph
in *Verve*, vol 2, nos 5–6, July–October 1939
transferred to collection from Research Library
and Archives 1981
National Gallery of Australia, Kamberri/
Canberra
81.705

fig 71 p 178
Anne Dangar
Mural in the *salle des fêtes* 1947, Hôtel Schaeffer
Serrières, France
photographed 2022

fig 72 p 180
Carved trees
in Frederick D McCarthy, *Australian Aboriginal decorative art*, Australian Museum, Sydney,
1948, p 24
National Gallery of Australia Research Library
and Archives, Kamberri/Canberra

fig 73 p 181
Anne Dangar
First Nations scar tree designs copied from
Australian Aboriginal decorative art 1950
Moly-Sabata, Sablons, France
pencil on paper
sheet 42.2 × 20.5 cm (irreg)
purchased 2012
2012.2254

fig 74 p 182
Anne Dangar
Pot 1950–51
Auvergne-Rhône-Alpes, France
wheel-thrown glazed earthenware
with slip decoration
49 × 41 × 35 cm
Musée des beaux-arts de Lyon
purchased 2008
2008-31

fig 75 p 184
Geneviève de Cissey-Dalban in Anne Dangar's
pottery at Moly-Sabata
Sablons, France
c 1956
gelatin silver photograph
unknown photographer
private collection

fig 76 p 187
Geneviève de Cissey-Dalban crossing the
courtyard of Moly-Sabata during a flood
of the Rhône
Sablons, France
1955 or 1957
gelatin silver photograph
unknown photographer
private collection

fig 77 p 187
Geneviève de Cissey-Dalban in the garden
of Moly-Sabata
Sablons, France
c 1955
gelatin silver photograph
unknown photographer
private collection

fig 78 p 188
Geneviève de Cissey-Dalban in her pottery
at Ampuis
France
1978
chromogenic photograph
unknown photographer
private collection

fig 79 p 188
Geneviève de Cissey-Dalban in her pottery
at Ampuis
France
1978
chromogenic photograph
unknown photographer
private collection

fig 80 p 188
Geneviève de Cissey-Dalban in her pottery
at Ampuis
France
1978
chromogenic photograph
unknown photographer
private collection

fig 81 p 190
Geneviève de Cissey-Dalban
France 1926–2002
Aguilberte Dalban
born France 1965
Pot with cubist designs (recto) (1995–98)
Ampuis, France
wheel-thrown glazed earthenware
with slip decoration
43 × 34 (diam) cm
private collection

fig 82 p 191
Geneviève de Cissey-Dalban
France 1926–2002
Aguilberte Dalban
born France 1965
Pot with cubist designs (verso) (1995–98)
Ampuis, France
wheel-thrown glazed earthenware
with slip decoration
43 × 34 (diam) cm
private collection

fig 83 p 194
The interior of Grace Crowley's flat in Manly
Eora Country/Sydney
1979
transparency
unknown photographer
Helen Maxwell Archive
National Gallery of Australia Research Library
and Archives, Kamberri/Canberra

Selected bibliography

Writings by Anne Dangar

'Reminiscences', *Undergrowth: A Magazine of Youth and Ideals*, first issue, May 1925, unpag.

'At Wagstaff Point', *Undergrowth: A Magazine of Youth and Ideals*, March–April 1926, unpag.

'Letters from France', *Undergrowth: A Magazine of Youth and Ideals*, May–June 1926, unpag.

'The house with blue shutters', *Undergrowth: A Magazine of Youth and Ideals*, July–August 1926, unpag.

'Letters from abroad: learning in Paris', *Undergrowth: A Magazine of Youth and Ideals*, May–June 1927, unpag.

'By way of reply', *Undergrowth: A Magazine of Youth and Ideals*, September–October 1928, unpag.

'To-day', *Undergrowth: A Magazine of Youth and Ideals*, January–February 1929, unpag.

'La poterie', *L'Atelier de la Rose*, no 1, nd [1950], pp 22–24.

Lettres à la Pierre-qui-Vire, Zodiaque, Saint-Léger-Vauban, 1972, unpag.

Archival material

Archives André Lhote, private collection, Paris.

Archives Marcel Michaud, Musée des beaux-arts de Lyon, Lyon.

Estelle Creed family archive, private collection.

Fonds Albert Gleizes, MV 698–699, Kandinsky Library, Musée national d'art moderne, Centre Georges Pompidou, Paris.

Grace Crowley archive, MS1980.1, National Art Archive, Art Gallery of New South Wales, Gadigal Nura/Sydney.

Grace Crowley papers, 1927–1974, MLMSS 3252/vols 2–7, MLMSS 3252/vol 1X, State Library of New South Wales, Gadigal Nura/Sydney.

Hazel de Berg, Grace Crowley speaks about Ralph Balson, in the Hazel de Berg collection, sound recording, 1966, DeB 173, National Library of Australia, Kamberri/Canberra.

Hazel de Berg notes on Grace Crowley interview, unpublished transcript, National Gallery of Australia Research Library and Archives, Kamberri/Canberra.

Helen Maxwell Archive, MS 66, National Gallery of Australia Research Library and Archives, Kamberri/Canberra.

Jacqueline Lerat artist files, Musée des beaux-arts de Lyon, Lyon.

James Gleeson Oral History Collection, MS 23, National Gallery of Australia Research Library and Archives, Kamberri/Canberra.

Jean Chevalier papers, Musée des beaux-arts de Lyon, Lyon.

Jim Alexander Gallery records, MS 13705, State Library Victoria, Naarm/Narrm/Melbourne.

Macleay River Historical Society collection, Thunggutti/Dunghutti Country/Kempsey.

Papers of Anne Dangar, MS 158, National Gallery of Australia Research Library and Archives, Kamberri/Canberra.

Papers of Dorrit Black, Art Gallery of South Australia Research Library, Tarntanya/Adelaide.

Papers of Dorrit Black, MS 74, National Gallery of Australia Research Library and Archives, Kamberri/Canberra.

Books, chapters, articles and other sources

Adams, Bruce. 'The promise of the rainbow: Anne Dangar at Moly-Sabata 1930–1951', PhD thesis, University of Sydney, 1998.

———. *Rustic Cubism: Anne Dangar and the art colony at Moly-Sabata*, University of Chicago Press, Chicago, 2004.

'Anne Dangar, 20 ans après', *Zodiaque*, no 91, January 1972.

Berthon, Laurence. 'Céramiques d'Anne Dangar au musée des beaux-arts de Lyon', *Bulletin des Musées et Monuments Lyonnais*, no 1, 1998.

———. *Miss Dangar potière (1885–1951)*, exhibition catalogue, La Fabrique du Pont d'Aleyrac, Saint-Pierreville, 2006.

Brooke, Peter. *Albert Gleizes: for and against the twentieth century*, Yale University Press, New Haven, CT, 2001.

Butcher, David. *Anne Dangar, céramiste: le cubisme au quotidien*, exhibition catalogue, Musée de Valence art et archéologie, Valence, 2016.

Crowley, Grace. 'Grace Crowley's student years', in Janine Burke, *Australian women artists, 1840–1940*, Greenhouse Publications, Collingwood, Vic, 1980.

Dubois, André. *Anne Dangar et Moly-Sabata, les sources chez Albert Gleizes*, Les amis d'Albert Gleizes, Ampuis, 1997.

Geoffray, César. 'Dix ans de présence à Moly-Sabata', in *Mémoires de l'Académie des sciences, belles-lettres et arts de Lyon*, JB Ballière, Paris, 1975.

'Le renouveau de la poterie: Anne G. Dangar potière', *Zodiaque*, no 8, April 1952.

Lee, Phil. 'Anne Garvin Dangar and the Dangar family of Kempsey', *Macleay River Historical Society Journal*, no 234, November 2023.

Lock-Weir, Tracey. *Dorrit Black: unseen forces*, exhibition catalogue, Art Gallery of South Australia, Adelaide, 2014.

Louvet, Suzy, and Sylvie Vincent. *Vivre le cubisme à Moly-Sabata*, exhibition catalogue, Musée de l'ancien évêché, Grenoble, 2022.

Maxwell, Helen. 'Profile of Anne Dangar', *Art and Australia*, vol 26, no 3, Autumn 1989, pp 419–23.

Taylor, Elena. *Grace Crowley: being modern*, exhibition catalogue, National Gallery of Australia, Canberra, 2006.

Topliss, Helen (ed). *Earth, fire, water, air: Anne Dangar's letters to Grace Crowley, 1930–1951*, Allen & Unwin, St Leonards, NSW, 2000.

Topliss, Helen. *Modernism and feminism: Australian women artists 1900–1940*, Craftsman House, Roseville, NSW, 1996.

Contributors

Dr Peter Brooke

Peter Brooke was a painter and writer, and a specialist on cubist artist Albert Gleizes, who was the subject of his book *Albert Gleizes: for and against the twentieth century* (Yale University Press, New Haven, 2001), the artist's first major biography. Brooke also translated several of Gleizes's most important essays. He spent over ten years in France, studying painting with Gleizes's follower Geneviève Dalban, working with the Association des amis d'Albert Gleizes in Ampuis, and researching and cataloguing Gleizes's unpublished writings. He was awarded a doctorate from Cambridge University in 1980 for his dissertation 'Controversies in Ulster Presbyterianism, 1790–1836'. He passed away during the preparation of this publication in early 2024.

ADS Donaldson

ADS Donaldson is an artist, art historian and curator. He studied at Sydney College of the Arts; the Kunstakademie Düsseldorf; the Royal Danish Academy of Fine Arts, Copenhagen; the École des beaux-arts, Paris; and the University of Sydney. Donaldson's work is held in the collections of the National Gallery of Australia, Museum of Contemporary Art Australia, and Art Gallery of New South Wales, as well as in various state and university art galleries and museums. He is co-author with Rex Butler of *UnAustralian art: ten essays on a transnational art history* (Power Publications, Sydney, 2023), as well as co-author and co-curator with Ann Stephen of *JW Power: Abstraction-Création: Paris 1934* (Power Publications, Sydney, 2012). He is an Honorary Associate of the Power Institute, the University of Sydney.

Dr Rebecca Edwards

Rebecca Edwards is Curator, Australian Art, at the National Gallery of Australia, Kamberri/Canberra. She began her career at the National Gallery in 2012, cataloguing the newly acquired Anne Dangar archive in the Australian Prints and Drawings collection. Since then she has held curatorial roles at the National Gallery of Victoria (NGV) and written, presented and curated exhibitions on various aspects of Australian art. Major projects include co-curating *Colony: Australia 1770–1861* (NGV, 2015) and *Jeffrey Smart* (National Gallery, 2021) and contributing to *Know My Name: Australian women artists: 1900 to now* (National Gallery, 2020 and 2021). She was awarded a doctorate in art history from the University of Melbourne in 2019.

Angela Goddard

Angela Goddard is a curator, writer, Director of the Griffith University Art Museum (GUAM), Meeanjin/Brisbane. She is also chair of University Art Museums Australia, and a board member of Sheila: A Foundation for Women in Visual Art. Recent publications include *Richard Bell reader: Tate Modern* and *Richard Bell reader: documenta fifteen*, co-edited with Megan Tamati-Quennell (both GUAM, 2022), and *Gordon Bennett: selected writings*, co-edited with Tim Riley Walsh (GUAM with Power Publications, Sydney, 2022). Recent exhibitions include *Taring padi: tanah tumpah darah*, co-curated with Alexander Supartono (GUAM, 2024), *Round about or inside*, co-curated with Wouter Davidts (GUAM, 2021, and Vandenhove, Ghent, 2022), and *Rebecca Belmore: turbulent water*, co-curated with Wanda Nanibush (GUAM, 2021, and Buxton Contemporary, Naarm/Narrm/Melbourne, 2021–22).

Anne O'Hehir

Anne O'Hehir is Curator, Photography, at the National Gallery of Australia, Kamberri/Canberra. She has curated a large number of exhibitions for the National Gallery, including *Nan Goldin: The ballad of sexual dependency* (2023–24), *Light moves: contemporary Australian video art* (2016) and *Diane Arbus: American portraits* (2016), as well as co-curating *The body electric*, part of the Know My Name initiative focusing on women's practice (2020–21), *Colour my world: handcoloured Australian photography* (2015) and *Carol Jerrems: photographic artist* (2012). She speaks and writes widely on photography and has contributed to a number of recent publications on women in photography.

Elena Taylor

Elena Taylor has curated major exhibitions and written extensively in the areas of Australian modernism, expatriatism and women artists. She curated the retrospective *Grace Crowley: being modern* (National Gallery, 2006) and authored the first book on this artist. Other publications and exhibitions include *Australian impressionists in France: 1885–1915* (NGV, 2013) and *Brave new world: Australia 1930s* (NGV, 2017). Taylor is currently Senior Curator of the University of New South Wales Art Collection, Gadigal Nura/Sydney, and was previously curator of Australian art at the National Gallery of Victoria and curator of Australian painting and sculpture at the National Gallery of Australia.

Index

Page numbers in *italics* indicate illustrations.

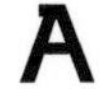

B

C

D

H

K

L

M

N

O

P

Q

R

S

T

U

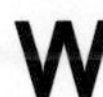

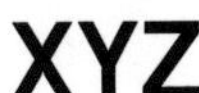

Acknowledgements

Curator's acknowledgements

I wish to thank Nick Mitzevich, Director of the National Gallery of Australia, for the opportunity to delve into Anne Dangar's life and art through this publication and the exhibition it accompanies. My thanks also to Adam Lindsay, Deputy Director; Natasha Bullock, former Assistant Director, Artistic Programs; Deborah Hart, Head Curator, Australian Art; and Debbie Ward, Head of Conservation and Registration for their support.

This project would have been impossible without the Sid and Fiona Myer Foundation, which funded this publication and enabled me to undertake important field research in Dangar's adopted home, France. My sincere thanks also to the Gordon Darling Foundation for allowing me to retrace Dangar's steps in Australia through a domestic travel grant.

One of the great pleasures of this project has been meeting the individuals who have safeguarded Dangar's practice and legacy over many years and there would not be a catalogue nor an exhibition without their generosity. In Australia, I am indebted to members of Dangar's family: Margaret Cargill, Pamela Collins, Brett Davis, Jane Hathaway, Stephen Mills, Andrew Moncrieff and Mary Ralston. My thanks also to the descendants of Estelle Creed, Dangar's student, for sharing her story with me, and to Angela Goddard for bringing her work to my attention. In France, I am hugely grateful to the staff at Moly-Sabata: Pierre David, Virginie Retornaz, Joël Riff and David de Jong Garboud, for hosting me during my visit; and to members of the wider community: Pierre and Nicole Alexandre, Gérard Boissonnet, Aguilberte Dalban, Jean-Jacques Dubernard, Suzanne Sondermeyer, Charles and Daniel Steinbach, and the Mayor of Sablons, Laurent Teil, for sharing their collections, stories and memories of Dangar with me. I am grateful for the support of the Fondation Albert Gleizes (now Association Albert Gleizes), especially Alain Huriez, President, as well as my colleagues at institutions in France for granting access to their collections and archives, including Dominique Bermann Martin, Archives André Lhote, Paris; Christian Briend and Anne Delebarre, Musée national d'art moderne, Centre Georges Pompidou, Paris; Salima Hellal and library staff, Musée des beaux-arts de Lyon; Dominique Dendraël, Musée du Hiéron, Paray-le-Monial; and Sylvie Vincent, Musée de l'ancien evêché, Grenoble.

This exhibition and publication build on the foundational research on Dangar undertaken by Bruce Adams, David Butcher and Helen Topliss, as well as the scholarship on Albert Gleizes by Peter Brooke, who passed away during work on this publication. I would like to acknowledge Bruce, David and Peter for their generosity in the early stages of this project. My thanks also to former National Gallery of Australia curators Roger Butler, Robert Bell, John McPhee and Daniel Thomas for their insight, advice and stewardship of Dangar's work into the collection, and Helen Maxwell for her important early research.

I am grateful to all directors and staff at state and regional galleries who have assisted me in my research and loaned key works to the exhibition. These include Michael Brand, Wayne Tunnicliffe, Denise Mimmocchi, Claire Eggleston and former staff Leanne Santoro and Steven Miller, Art Gallery of New South Wales; Rhana Devenport, Tracey Lock, Elle Freak and Rebecca Evans, Art Gallery of South Australia; Tony Ellwood, Beckett Rozentals, Cathy Leahy and Amanda Dunsmore, National Gallery of Victoria; Sylvie Ramond and Salima Hellal, Musée des beaux-arts de Lyon; Lisa Havilah and Eva Czernis-Ryl, Museum of Applied Arts and Sciences; Chris Saines and Samantha Littley, Queensland Art Gallery | Gallery of Modern Art; Sean Bridgeman at the National Film and Sound Archive; and Phil Lee and the volunteer staff at the Kempsey Museum and Macleay River Historical Society. My special thanks to the numerous private collectors who have enthusiastically loaned treasured works from their collection and shared their knowledge of Dangar and her work, including Colin Beutel and Conal Coad, Julian Glassock and family, members of the Dangar family and other private collectors who wish to remain anonymous. I would also like to acknowledge the support of David Herbert and Jacqueline Gloria.

I am fortunate to work alongside an exceptional team of people at the National Gallery and thank them all for their dedication to this project. Thank you to the hardworking publications team Penny Sanderson, Meagan Down and Emma Round; imaging team Sam Cooper, Eleni Kypridis and Brooke Shannon; editor Linda Michael and proofreaders Helen Curran and Clare Williamson; and designers David Pidgeon and Alex Ward of Pidgeon Ward for their attention to detail in bringing this catalogue together. My thanks also to the contributors to this catalogue, ADS Donaldson, Angela Goddard, Anne O'Hehir, Elena Taylor and the late Peter Brooke, for their expertise and erudition. Special thanks to Tina Baum for her generous insight and advice on the inclusion of First Nations placenames throughout this publication. I am grateful to my inimitable exhibition team, exhibitions manager Dominique Nagy, loan registrar Kate Buckingham, exhibition designers Emma Doy and Aislinn King, as well as conservators Kim Goldsmith (objects), Fiona Kemp, James Ward, Kassandra Coghlan, Andrea Wise (paper), Jocelyn Evans, Emily Vearing (paintings), Micheline Ford, Carmella Mollica, Michelle Hunter (textiles), and Masahiro Asaka, Surya Bajracharya and Scott Franks (mount cutting) for their consideration and care. My thanks also to the Research Library and Archives staff: Elizabeth Little, Jack Ennis and Simon Underschultz for assisting in my research; Ellen Newton for enthusiastically documenting the Anne Dangar Papers; and Gordon Darling Australian Prints and Drawings interns past and present for their work on the immense archive of works on paper: Massimo Martelli, Johanna McMahon, and especially Amelia Brown. Very special thanks to Alice Rezende for her invaluable administrative support.

Just as Dangar relied on her close friends and community, this project would not have been possible without my own. Many colleagues and friends have offered support, guidance and mentorship and have acted as a sounding board over many years. My heartfelt thanks to Laurie Benson, Alisa Bunbury, Carol Cains, Deirdre Cannon, Kelli Cole, Deborah Hart, Anthony Hopkins, Cathy Leahy, Simeran Maxwell, Keren Nicholson, Sarina Noordhuis-Fairfax, Anne O'Hehir, Leanne Santoro, Susan van Wyk, my parents Robin and Megan Edwards, and especially Alison Inglis and Shaune Lakin. I am particularly grateful to Andrew Donaldson and Elena Taylor for their encouragement and generosity.

My final thanks go to Anne Dangar herself. Immersing myself in your art and life will undoubtedly be among the highlights of my curatorial career. I am privileged to have been entrusted with your story.

REBECCA EDWARDS

National Gallery acknowledgements

The Hon Anthony Albanese MP, Prime Minister of Australia

GOVERNING MINISTERS

The Hon Tony Burke MP, Minister for the Arts
Susan Templeman MP, Special Envoy for the Arts

NATIONAL GALLERY COUNCIL

Ryan Stokes AO, Chair
Abdul-Rahman Abdullah
The Hon Richard Alston AO
Esther Anatolitis
Ilana Atlas AO, Deputy Chair
Stephen Brady AO CVO
Helen Cook
Sam Edwards
Dr Nick Mitzevich, Director
Sally Scales
Prof Sally Smart

NATIONAL GALLERY FOUNDATION

Stephen Brady AO CVO, Chair
Philip Bacon AO, Deputy Chair
Julian Beaumont OAM
Anthony Berg AM
Julian Burt
Terrence Campbell AO
Sue Cato AM
The Hon Ashley Dawson-Damer AM
James Erskine
Tim Fairfax AC
Andrew Gwinnett
Hiroko Gwinnett
John Hindmarsh AM
Wayne Kratzmann AM
The Hon Dr Andrew Lu AM
Dr Peter Lundy RFD, Secretary
Michael Maher
Dr Michael Martin
Dr Nick Mitzevich, Director
Roslyn Packer AC
Penelope Seidler AM
Ezekiel Solomon AM
Kerry Stokes AC
Ryan Stokes AO
Ray Wilson OAM

NATIONAL GALLERY EXECUTIVE

Dr Nick Mitzevich, Director
Adam Lindsay, Deputy Director
Susie Barr, Assistant Director, Marketing, Communications and Visitor Experience
Sophie Gray, Project Director, Capital Works Taskforce
Alison Halpin, Chief Operating Officer
Felicity McGinnes, Chief Finance Officer
Helen Gee, Sophie Hunter, Elizabeth Smith, Lillee Keating and Wellin Pan, Directorate

CURATOR

Dr Rebecca Edwards, Curator, Australian Art

NATIONAL GALLERY MANAGEMENT TEAM

Samantha Braniff, Head of Partnerships, and staff
Jade Carson, Chief Information Officer, and staff
Georgia Close, Head of National Learning, and staff
Tracy Cooper-Lavery, Head of Art Across Australia, and staff
Terri Dwyer, Head of Human Resources, and staff
Mary Fisher, Head of Financial Accounting, and staff
Tayla French, A/Head of Financial Planning and Analysis, and staff
Stefan Giammarco, Head of Visitor Experience, and staff
Deborah Hart, Head Curator, Australian Art, and staff
Greg Ible, Head of Estate Management, and staff
Magda Keaney, Head Curator, International Art, and staff
Elizabeth Little, Manager, Research Library and Archives, and staff
Marika Lucas-Edwards, Principal Content Strategist and Head of Digital, and staff
Elizabeth Malone, Head of Commercial Operations, and staff
Fiona McQueenie, Head of Communications, and staff
Dominique Nagy, Head of Exhibitions, and staff
Kanesan Nathan, Head of Marketing, and staff
Chris Reid, Head of Governance and Strategic Planning, and staff
Maryanne Voyazis, Head of Development and Executive Director, National Gallery Foundation, and staff
Debbie Ward, Head of Conservation and Registration, and staff
Daryl West-Moore, Head of Creative Studio, and staff

Supporters

STRATEGIC PARTNERS

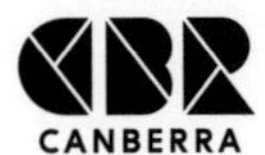

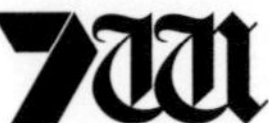

MAJOR PARTNER

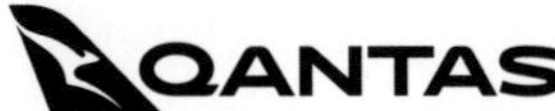

PUBLICATION PARTNERS

Gordon Darling Foundation
Sid and Fiona Myer Family Foundation

MAJOR LENDER

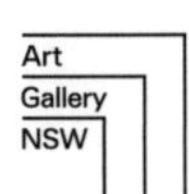

PUBLICATION SUPPORTERS

Geoff Hassall OAM and Virginia Milson

PROMOTIONAL PARTNER

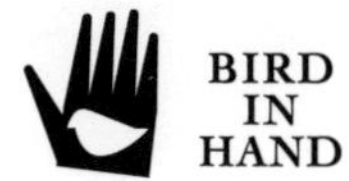

PHOTOGRAPH CREDITS

All reproductions are courtesy the National Gallery's digital team, unless otherwise stated.

© Archives André Lhote: p 21 (fig 8); image © Art Gallery of New South Wales: pp 4 and 235 (cat 68), 20 (fig 6), 21 (fig 7), 23 (fig 10), 56 and 236 (cat 76), 61 (fig 16), 64 (fig 21), 65 (fig 23), 67 (fig 25), 68 (fig 26), 69 (figs 28 and 29), 75 and 228 (cat 15), 78 and 230 (cat 31), 89 and 231 (cat 34), 94 and 239 (cat 113), 99 (cat 152), 103 and 240 (cat 105), 116 (fig 39), 118 and 231 (cat 38), 112 (fig 38), 122 and 231 (cat 35), 127 and 231 (cat 40), 135 (fig 44), 136 (fig 46), 137 (fig 47), 144 (fig 57), 147 (figs 62 and 63), 150 and 232 (cat 48), 151 and 233 (cat 52), 154 and 233 (cat 49), 155 and 233 (cat 50), 156 and 232 (cat 41), 177 and 239 (cat 118), 205 and 241 (cat 116), 210 and 234 (cat 64), 211 and 235 (cat 65), 228 (cats 9, 10 and 13), 230 (cat 28), 232 (cat 43), 233 (cats 51 and 54), 239 (cat 114); image courtesy Art Gallery of South Australia: pp 73 and 227 (cat 6), 100 and 228 (cat 11), 101 (cat 131), 204 and 242 (cat 121), 206 and 241 (cat 115), 229 (cat 18), 240 (cat 108); image courtesy Margaret Cargill: p 20 (fig 5); photo Jenni Carter: p 39 (cat 150); © Centre Pompidou, MNAM-CCI Bibliothèque Kandinsky, Dist. GrandPalaisRmn/Fonds Gleizes: pp 10 (fig 1), 61 (fig 17), 62 (fig 19), 64 (figs 20 and 22), 66 (fig 24), 68 (fig 27), 70 (fig 30), 134 (fig 41), 138 (figs 48, 49 and 50), 139 (figs 51 and 52), 140 (figs 53 and 54), 141 (fig 55), 145 (figs 58 and 59), 146 (fig 61), 148 (fig 64); © Centre Pompidou, MNAM-CCI, Dist. GrandPalaisRmn/ image Centre Pompidou, MNAM-CCI: pp 52 (fig 14), 55 (fig 15); photo Martial Couderette: pp 87 (fig 33), 169 (figs 65, 66 and 67), 171 (fig 68), 173 (fig 69), 190 (fig 81), 191 (fig 82); image courtesy Aguilberte Dalban: pp 184 (fig 75), 187 (figs 76 and 77), 188 (figs 78, 79 and 80); photo Ryan Hernandez: pp 37 and 227 (cat 3); image © Lyon MBA, photo Alain Basset: p 182 (fig 74); image © Lyon MBA, photo Martial Couderette: pp 162–63 and 242 (cat 127); image courtesy Macleay River Historical Society: pp 18 (fig 2), 20 (fig 4), 26 (fig 12); © Musée du Louvre, Dist. GrandPalaisRmn/Angèle Dequier: p 95 (fig 35); image courtesy National Gallery of Victoria: pp 31 (fig 13), 72 and 227 (cat 5), 208 and 242 (cat 122); photo QAGOMA: pp 92 and 232 (cat 44), 153 and 235 (cat 67), 157 and 234 (cat 63), 235 (cat 66); photo Joe Ruckli: p 109 (fig 37).

COPYRIGHT

We thank those who wish to remain anonymous, and the following:

© the artist: pp 70 (fig 32), 96 (cat 155), 99 (cat 152), 184 (fig 75), 187 (figs 76 and 77), 188 (figs 78, 79 and 80); © Ralph Balson Estate: p 102 (cat 129); © Estate of Estelle Creed: pp 40 (cat 134), 42 (cat 133), 106 (fig 36), 109 (fig 37), 110 (cat 136); © Estate of Grace Crowley: pp 34 (cat 138), 35 (cat 139), 54 (cat 144), 104 (cat 146); © Estate of Geneviève de Cissey Dalban: pp 190 and 191 (figs 81 and 82); © Estate of Dore Hawthorne: p 39 (cat 150); © André Lhote. ADAGP/Copyright Agency, 2024: p 23 (fig 10); © Georges Rouault. ADAGP/Copyright Agency, 2024: p 176 (fig 70).

Published on the occasion of the exhibition
Anne Dangar
7 December 2024 – 27 April 2025
National Gallery of Australia
Ngunnawal Country
Parkes Place East, Parkes
ACT 2600

The National Gallery of Australia is an Australian Government Agency.

A catalogue record for this work is available from the National Library of Australia.

TITLE: Anne Dangar
EDITOR: Rebecca Edwards*
ISBN: 9780642335098
FIRST PUBLISHED: December 2024

DESIGN: Pidgeon Ward
MANAGING EDITOR: Meagan Down*
PUBLISHING MANAGER: Penny Sanderson*
TEXT EDITOR: Linda Michael
PROOFREADER: Clare Williamson
FRENCH-LANGUAGE PROOFREADER: Helen Curran
INDEXER: Sherrey Quinn, Libraries Alive!
IMAGING: Sam Cooper, Eleni Kypridis and Brooke Shannon*
RIGHTS AND PERMISSIONS: Emma Round*
PRE-PRESS: Splitting Image, Melbourne
PRINTED BY: Australian Book Connection, China

COVER ART

All works by Anne Dangar. All works from the collection of the National Gallery of Australia. Front cover (clockwise from top): **cat 16** Plate with cubist design 1932–33 (detail); **cat 27** Plate with cubist design 1933–38 (detail); **cat 21** Soup tureen with cubist design 1933–38. Back cover (clockwise from top): **cat 17** Coffee pot with lid 1932–33 (detail); **cat 20** Jug 1933–38 (detail); **cat 25** Jug 1933–38.

* National Gallery of Australia